Y0-AUY-968

Consequences of Growing Up Poor

Consequences of Growing Up Poor

Greg J. Duncan
Jeanne Brooks-Gunn
Editors

Russell Sage Foundation ◆ New York

The Russell Sage Foundation

The Russell Sage Foundation, one of the oldest of America's general purpose foundations, was established in 1907 by Mrs. Margaret Olivia Sage for "the improvement of social and living conditions in the United States." The Foundation seeks to fulfill this mandate by fostering the development and dissemination of knowledge about the country's political, social, and economic problems. While the Foundation endeavors to assure the accuracy and objectivity of each book it publishes, the conclusions and interpretations in Russell Sage Foundation publications are those of the authors and not of the Foundation, its Trustees, or its staff. Publication by Russell Sage, therefore, does not imply Foundation endorsement.

Library of Congress Cataloging-in-Publication Data

Consequences of growing up poor / Greg Duncan and Jeanne Brooks-Gunn, editors.
p. cm.
Includes bibliographical references and index.
ISBN 0-87154-143-2 (alk. paper)
1. Poor children—United States. 2. Poverty—United States.
I. Duncan, Greg J. II. Brooks-Gunn, Jeanne.
HV741.C623 1997 96-53161
305.23′086′9420793—dc21 CIP

The paper used in this publication meets the minimum requirements of American National Standard for Information Sciences—Permanence of Paper for Printed Library Materials. ANSI Z39.48-1992.

Text design by Suzanne Nichols.

RUSSELL SAGE FOUNDATION
112 East 64th Street, New York, New York 10021
10 9 8 7 6 5 4 3 2

For Bob, Remy, Dorothy, Ellen, Mitch, and Paul

Contents

Contributors

Jeanne Brooks-Gunn is Virginia and Leonard Marx Professor of Child Development at Teachers College, Columbia University. She is also director of the Center for Young Children and Families and co-directs the Adolescent Study Program at Teachers College.

Greg J. Duncan is professor of education and social policy and a faculty associate in the Institute for Policy Research at Northwestern University.

Terry Adams is research associate at the Institute for Social Research, University of Michigan.

William Axinn is associate professor of sociology and senior research associate of the Population Research Institute, Pennsylvania State University.

Bernard Boulerice is statistical consultant for the Research Unit on Children's Psycho-Social Maladjustment.

Karen P. Carver is postdoctoral research associate at the Carolina Population Center, University of North Carolina.

Katherine Jewsbury Conger is research scientist at the Center for Family Research, Iowa State University.

Rand D. Conger is professor of sociology and psychology and director of the Center for Family Research, Iowa State University.

Mary Corcoran is professor of political science in the Department of Public Policy and Social Work, University of Michigan.

Randal D. Day is professor of human development at Washington State University.

Glen H. Elder, Jr. is professor of sociology at the University of North Carolina.

Thomas L. Hanson is assistant professor of child and family studies at Syracuse University.

Robert M. Hauser is the Vilas Research Professor of Sociology at the University of Wisconsin, Madison. He also directs the Wisconsin Longitudinal Study.

Robert Haveman is John Bascom Professor of Economics and Public Affairs at the University of Wisconsin, Madison.

Donald J. Hernandez is study director of the Board on Children, Youth, and Families of the National Academy of Sciences and Institute of Medicine. He is also senior subject matter expert, Survey of Program Dynamics of the U.S. Bureau of the Census.

Pamela K. Klebanov is research scientist at Teachers College, Columbia University.

Sanders Korenman is associate professor in the school of public affairs at Baruch College and a member of the doctoral faculty in economics at the City University of New York Graduate Center. He is also a member of the National Bureau of Economic Research.

Ellen L. Lipman is a child psychiatrist and member of the Centre for Studies of Children at Risk. She is also assistant professor in the department of psychiatry, McMaster University, Hamilton, Ontario.

Nancy Maritato was a research associate at the National Research Council who worked on the Behavioral and Social Science and Education Commission.

Susan E. Mayer is associate professor of sociology in the Harris Graduate School of Public Policy Studies, University of Chicago.

Sara S. McLanahan is professor of sociology and public affairs at Princeton University. She is also a member of the Board on Children, Youth, and Families of the National Academy of Sciences and Institute of Medicine.

Jane E. Miller is assistant research professor at Institute for Health, Health Care Policy, and Aging Research. She is also assistant professor in the Department of Urban Studies and Community Health at Rutgers University.

Natalie C. Mullis received her bachelor of arts in economics from University of Colorado, Boulder.

The National Institute of Child Health and Development (NICHD) is a collaborative group conducting a longitudinal study of the effects of early child care.

David R. Offord is a child psychiatrist and director of the Centre for Studies of Children at Risk. He is also professor of psychiatry, McMaster University, Hamilton, Ontario.

Linda Pagani is assistant professor of psycho-education at the University of Montreal.

Kathleen M. Paasch is associate in research in the Department of Human Development at Washington State University.

H. Elizabeth Peters is associate professor in the Department of Policy Analysis and Management at Cornell University.

Judith R. Smith is associate professor at Fordham University Graduate School of Social Services. She is also research associate at the Center for Young Children and Families at Teachers College, Columbia University.

Megan M. Sweeney is doctoral candidate in sociology at the University of Wisconsin-Madison.

Jay D. Teachman is professor and chair of human development at Washington State University.

Elizabeth Thomson is professor of sociology at the University of Wisconsin-Madison.

Arland Thornton is professor of sociology, research scientist of the Institute for Social Research, and associate director of the Population Studies Center, University of Michigan.

Richard E. Tremblay is both professor of psychology and psychiatry and director of the Research Unit on Children's Psycho-Social Maladjustment.

Kathryn Wilson is assistant professor of economics at Kent State University.

Barbara Wolfe is professor of economics and preventive medicine and director of the Institute for Research on Poverty at the University of Wisconsin, Madison.

Chapter 1

Poor Families, Poor Outcomes: The Well-Being of Children and Youth

Jeanne Brooks-Gunn, Greg J. Duncan, and Nancy Maritato

In any given year from 1987 to 1996, about one in five of all American children—some twelve to fourteen million—lived in families in which total income failed to exceed even the spartan thresholds used to define poverty. That so many of the youngest citizens of the wealthiest nation in the world are living poor is cause for concern. Indeed, the United States has a higher rate of poverty than most other Western industrialized nations (Smeeding and Rainwater 1995). And that child poverty has increased since the 1970s is also troubling (Hernandez 1993; see chapter 2). This volume explores the consequences and correlates of growing up poor as well as the mechanisms through which poverty influences children. The volume is organized around three key topics, with a primary focus on the research findings and a secondary concern with their policy implications.

First, we examine the consequences of income poverty for children and youth and show that children raised in low-income families score lower than children from more affluent families do on assessments of health, cognitive development, school achievement, and emotional well-being. We examine both the effects of longer- and shorter-term poverty upon children and the effects of the timing of poverty bouts upon well-being in the first two decades of life. The last two themes have implications for public policy vis-à-vis the timing of income supports to families.

A second key topic is whether or not links between income poverty and child well-being are due to income per se or to the other family conditions that often occur with poverty. For example, poor families are also more likely to be headed by a single parent, a parent with low educational attainment, an unemployed parent, a parent in the low-wage market, a divorced parent, or a young parent. These familial conditions might account in large measure for the association between low income and less favorable outcomes for children. Specifically, we ask whether or not the effects of income poverty are due to household structure, parents' age, or parents' education. If, for example, family income does not matter much (in a statistical sense, with controls for other family conditions), then policies aimed at altering those family conditions might alleviate poverty. For example, if mothers' education turns out to be the most important predictor of children's well-being and if income plays a very minor role, then enhancing parents' education, rather than raising the minimum wage, increasing the earned-income tax credit, or providing unemployment insurance, might become a primary policy objective.

A third consideration is the pathways through which income, or lack thereof, might influence children's outcomes. Families who are poor may not be able to purchase goods for children, such as food, housing, stimulating toys, books, and so forth. Income poverty may affect more than purchasing power in a family, however. Poor parents might exhibit less adequate emotional health; they may be more depressed, more irritable, or more labile in their emotions. These emotional moods might result in less consistent parenting, more punitive behavior, or less firm behavior. The struggle to make ends meet might also leave parents with little time to spend with their children or leave them feeling too drained to interact with their children when they are with them. When poor parents do work, they may not be able to obtain high-quality or consistent child care, resulting in less verbal interaction, more chaotic and less regular routines, and so on. The point is that income poverty may have much to do with what goes on within the family, which then affects the child (Brooks-Gunn and Duncan 1997; Chase-Lansdale and Brooks-Gunn 1995; Wilson, Ellwood, and Brooks-Gunn 1995). In chapters 5–17, research teams examine possible "mediators" of links between child and youth outcomes and family income.

The determination of mechanisms or pathways through which poverty influences children may provide insight into the types of interventions that might lessen that influence. That is, if parenting skills are critical for the well-being of young children, then home visiting programs such as Parents as Educators, Healthy Families America, and Home Instruction for Young Preschool and Primary School Youngsters might be expanded (Brooks-Gunn, Denner, and Klebanov 1995; Smith 1995).

A topic not covered in this volume is the way poverty may influence children not through intrafamilial life but through extrafamilial experiences. Poor families are more likely to live in neighborhoods with other poor families, and their children are more likely to attend schools with fewer resources and more poor classmates than more affluent families are. Poor children may not fare very well in large part because of their communities of residence, not just because of their family situations (Brooks-Gunn, Duncan, and Aber forthcoming; Brooks-Gunn, Duncan, and Klebanov 1996; Brooks-Gunn, Duncan, Klebanov, and Sealand 1993; Crane 1991; Jencks and Petersen 1991; Wilson 1991). However, an examination of the effects of neighborhood income on families is beyond our scope.

Another topic not addressed in this volume is whether or not income is an adequate measure of impoverishment. Income, while important, is surely not the only determinant of well-being. Many other dimensions of impoverishment can exist, from anxiety and fear about one's personal safety when living in a high-crime neighborhood or with abusive family members to suffering from inadequate medical care, and from homelessness to loneliness or helplessness.

In this introductory chapter, we first review trends in poverty in the United States. Then we briefly discuss the developmental frameworks that have guided inquiry into how lives unfold and change outcomes. The next section reviews the effects of poverty for four age groups—prenatal-infancy, early childhood, late childhood, and adolescence.[1] We end by describing the way in which the volume is organized.

POVERTY TRENDS

Measuring Income Poverty

As discussed in detail in chapter 2, one in five of all children in the United States reside below the poverty threshold. In 1993 this figure was a little under $12,000 for a family of three people. Poverty thresholds take household size into account and are adjusted each year for cost of living using the consumer price index. Families whose incomes are above the threshold are considered "not poor," and families below the threshold are classified as "poor," for any given year. Income-to-needs ratios are often calculated (needs being based on family size); when translated into a ratio based on the poverty threshold, poverty is defined as 1.0 (see chapter 2).

Children from families whose yearly incomes place them above the poverty threshold but not very much above it are classified as "near poor." For example, some federal programs provide services for families whose income is up to 1.85 times the poverty threshold. About another 20 percent of all children are living in families whose incomes are above the poverty line (1.0) but not above 1.85 (for a family of three, an income of between $12,000 and $22,000). Thus, two in every five children live in poor or near-poor families.

Rates of Poverty for Children

In 1959, the first year for which official poverty rates are available, 27 percent of children were living in poverty (see table 1.1). The poverty rate for children was substantially higher than that for adults aged eighteen to sixty-four but lower than that for the elderly. Over the subsequent thirty years, the proportion of each age group in poverty declined. After 1989, however, as the rate of poverty rose overall, the proportion of children in poverty climbed more rapidly and in the 1990s was about twice as high as that of adults aged 18–64 and 70 percent higher than that of the elderly. This change was principally a result of the more generous social security benefits for the elderly, which lifted many out of poverty since the mid-1970s (see Hernandez 1993; chapter 2).

TABLE 1.1 / Poor Children and Adults in the United States, 1959–89 (Percent)

Year	Children (<18 years)	Adults (18–64 years)	Elders (>65 years)
1959	27.3	17.0	35.2
1969	14.0	8.7	25.3
1979	16.4	8.9	15.2
1989	19.6	10.2	11.4

Source: Current Population Survey, 1996.

The demographic trends in family patterns and in individual behavior—changes in marriage and divorce rates, nonmarital fertility rates, and unemployment rates (especially for less educated and younger adults)—help explain the relative increase in the proportion of children in poverty. The increase in the number of single parents, both those who have children outside of marriage and those who experience a divorce, is one of the important causes of the rise in the number of poor children (see chapter 3). The number of unmarried women having children has risen dramatically, and childbirth outside of marriage is not confined to teenagers. In 1990, two-thirds of black women and almost one-fifth of white women (19 percent) had children outside of marriage (Ventura 1995). Rates were highest for teenagers but were also high for women in their early twenties. Poverty rates are high for children in families with one adult, particularly because employment rates are low among single mothers, many of whom are young and have not completed high school. (For descriptions of these trends, see Cherlin 1992; Hernandez 1993; chapter 2; for a discussion of unmarried mothers and their children, see Garfinkel and McLanahan 1986 and Furstenberg, Brooks-Gunn, and Morgan 1987; for a discussion of single parenthood, see McLanahan and Sandefur 1994; and for an analysis of the family, see Becker 1991.) Marital disruptions also have increased since 1970. Since the remarriage rate is lower than the divorce rate, the number of formerly-married, single mothers has increased. Poverty rates for children in families in which a divorce has occurred are high, especially since incomes for custodial mothers drop precipitously after a divorce (McLanahan and Sandefur 1994; Duncan 1991; chapter 3).

Family demographic changes are only part of the story of children in poverty. Hernandez (1993) has estimated that 28 percent of children whose families were poor following a marital separation were poor before their parents separated. If fathers rejoined their children in families, it has been estimated, about 40 percent of children would move from below to above the official poverty line.

Persistent Poverty

The aforementioned estimates are for single years only. Poverty often continues for years. Both single-year and multiple-year estimates of poverty indicate that

TABLE 1.2 / Six-Year Family and Neighborhood Poverty Levels for White and Black Children, Ages 0–3, 1980

	Average % of Individuals in Neighborhood Who Were Poor over Six Years					
Years Family Was Poor	0–10	10–20	20–30	30–40	40+	Total
White (*n* = 796)						
None	50.6	19.5	3.1	1.0	.0	74.2
1–4 years	8.6	9.2	1.8	.4	.3	20.2
5–6 years	1.6	3.0	.9	.1	.0	5.6
Total	60.8	31.7	5.8	1.4	.3	100.0
Black (*n*= 568)						
None	4.6	12.4	12.5	2.5	1.5	33.6
1–4 years	1.7	7.0	10.9	5.4	2.4	27.4
5–6 years	3.7	13.4	13.8	3.5	4.5	39.0
Total	10.1	32.8	37.2	11.5	8.4	100.0

Source: Panel Study of Income Dynamics; Duncan, Brooks-Gunn, and Klebanov 1994.

black and Hispanic children are much more likely to be poor, and for longer periods of time, than white children are. Among black and white children who were under three years of age in 1980 and were part of the Panel Study of Income Dynamics (PSID), a nationally representative sample of families, black children were more likely to be poor in any given year, and were much more likely to be poor for multiple years (table 1.2). For example, about three-quarters of white children were never poor in the six-year period, compared with only one-third of black children (Duncan, Brooks-Gunn, and Klebanov 1994). Such differences account for over one-half of the black-white differences in children's IQ scores (Brooks-Gunn et al. 1996).[2]

CHILDREN IN FAMILIES IN COMMUNITIES

The study of children generally and particularly of those in poverty has taken a variety of approaches involving demography, developmental and social psychology, economics, ethnography, and sociology—all looking at the causes and consequences of poverty for children. The disciplines naturally highlight different aspects of children's lives and yield perspectives and insights that are sometimes difficult to integrate (Brooks-Gunn et al. 1991; Cherlin 1992; Duncan 1991). Consequently, the collective "pictures" of poor children and of the diversity in their individual and family lives are somewhat fragmented. We cannot do justice to this range of inquiry here; we refer the reader to several excellent volumes on the current state of knowledge about children in poverty: Chase-Lansdale and Brooks-Gunn (1995), Huston (1991a), Huston, McLoyd, and Garcia-Coll (1994), and Fitzgerald et al. (1995). For more general treatments of the economics of children in families, see Browning (1992) and Haveman and Wolfe (1994).

Three of the more prominent frameworks used to study how the family and the community and its social institutions influence children are theories of individual risk and resilience, theories that feature resource allocation decisions within families, and ecological theory. Three levels of analysis of children and their development illustrate the variety of approaches found in the various literatures on children, in particular on children in poverty: the individual, the family, and extrafamilial contexts.

The Child as Individual

One framework focusing on individuals and their own developmental process is that of risk and resiliency, developed to explain why children are likely to show lower well-being in the face of certain biological and environmental conditions (Garmezy and Rutter 1983; Werner and Smith 1982). Biological factors typically are early indicators of physical health (such as illness at birth, low birth weight, and physical disability). Environmental factors include a variety of family conditions and parental characteristics as well as neighborhood and school conditions.

Neighborhood, family, and school poverty are sometimes studied as environmental threats to children's well-being. They are said to increase a child's risk for less-than-optimal outcomes. However, not all children react the same to biological or environmental risks. Some children from poor families do well, while some children from more affluent families have difficulties. In the view of Garmezy and Rutter (1983), some children are resilient to the untoward consequences of negative conditions. Risk and resilience models have been used to study poor children and their families and to assess the impact of impoverishment on children (see, for example, Elder 1974; Furstenberg, Brooks-Gunn, and Morgan 1987; Sameroff et al. 1993).

A related line of inquiry, also focused on the individual, considers continuities and discontinuities in the development process. Here the biological notion of critical periods in normal development, as noted in certain nonhuman species, arises as possibly applicable to the development of poor children. If in certain periods of development deprivation cannot (or cannot easily) be overcome by subsequent intervention, being in poverty during those periods may be particularly detrimental. (See Rutter 1994 and Carnegie Corporation of New York 1994 for contributions to this important debate.)

The Child's Family

One important framework for looking at the role of the family in children's well-being is that of decisions regarding the allocation of the family's resources. Families make decisions about the number of children they have, the expenditure of various resources—of time and money—on each child, and a variety of family circumstances, processes, and activities that influence their children. In part the children partake of the economic condition of the family, and this is the rationale for defining poverty at the level of the family unit. The children share the resources with their adult family members but do not necessarily share them equally, and generally children do not have a major say in decisions about the allocation of the family's limited economic resources.

The literature on the family includes explorations of altruism, incentives to support children after divorce, and sometimes implicit and subtle contracting among family members. For example, an overlapping intergenerational implicit contracts model hypothesizes that family members agree that in exchange for nurturance, care, and economic support during times of dependency (as during childhood and old age), family members will fulfill their incurred obligation to work and produce sufficiently during their middle years and will share their income with their dependent family members; in this manner the family offers one solution to the problem of caring for dependents, including children.

Investments in children—human capital investments—by the family are an important focus of research. Families expend resources on their children's health, education, and nurturance as investments that pay off later in the child's well-being as an adult. Wealth levels; farsightedness (that is, low discount rates); the structure and stability of the family; tax structures and their implicit incentives; the yield on investments in formal schooling, training programs, or social networks; and the extent of altruism in the family have all been suggested as affecting the levels of these investments. Families that have limited economic resources or are dysfunctional are much less capable of making substantial investments in their children, thus offering the rationale for collective intervention on behalf of the child's well-being and future capabilities. (As representative of this broad literature of family resource allocation to children, see Espenshade 1984; Ellwood 1988; Lazear and Michael 1987; Betson 1990; Haveman and Wolfe 1994; Becker 1991; Browning 1992; Weiss and Willis 1985).

The Child in Larger Contexts

A third level of analysis emphasizes that children grow up in a number of contexts or ecologies. The first two decades of life are almost always spent in families, and while early development takes place primarily in the family context, the family itself resides in multiple contexts (for example, occupation, neighborhood, kin networks, friendship networks). Each of these contexts has an influence on family systems as well as on the individuals within families. Even an examination of the effects on children of a social institution such as schools, for instance, must consider the family; without parents' cooperation and a consistency of indications to the child about what is important and expected, it is difficult to teach children

(Brooks-Gunn, Denner, and Klebanov 1995). The most effective school experiences are thought to be based on partnerships among parents, teachers, and children. These partnerships are more difficult to achieve in conditions of poverty, and frequently economic poverty in the family accompanies impaired health in the child and poor-quality schools, illustrating the interconnections among the institutions of family, school, and neighborhood as influences on children.

Perhaps the most influential theory of this broader context in the child development literature is the ecological system model closely associated with the writing of Bronfenbrenner (1979, 1989). Bronfenbrenner and his colleagues identify family, kin, peers, schools, neighborhood, community, region, and country as the relevant contexts or ecological systems in which children learn. The division of these contexts into various levels emphasizes the importance of sustained, consistent interactions, and the insistence on looking at the ways in which various levels interact with one another to produce personal development has had a major impact on the study of children and youth (Moen, Elder, and Luscher 1995).

Best known in Bronfenbrenner's work is the division of contexts into five systems—microsystems, mesosystems, ecosystems, macrosystems, and chronosystems. Microsystems are those in which face-to-face interactions occur (family, school, peer group, workplace). Most work on interchanges at this level focuses on the family. Mesosystems are the linkages between two or more settings containing the individual (that is, processes involving school and family). Ecosystems also involve linkages between settings, but in this case those in which the person is not present (for example, the association between the parent's workplace and the parent's home or marital relationship influences the child even though the child is not present in either system). Macrosystems consist of the culture in which the first three systems operate, referring to belief systems, knowledge, customs, and lifestyles, for instance. Changes in the individual and in the environment over time are the domain of chronosystems.

These contextual systems focus on the interchanges among individuals, among systems, and among individuals and systems. Children whose families are poor are thought to live in different ecological systems than children whose families are not poor. Of particular importance is the fact that differences are probably present in the ecosystems larger than the family and that the interactions among systems probably differ for poor and not-poor families. However, little work has directly tested these premises (see Garcia-Coll et al. 1997; Gottfried 1984; Wachs and Gruen 1982).

THREE POVERTY ISSUES

In this section we briefly review the literature on the consequences of childhood poverty, the links between family characteristics and poverty, and the pathways through which poverty operates.

Consequences of Poverty during Childhood

Our review of transitional periods over the life course is organized into four age groupings: the prenatal-infancy period, the young childhood period, the middle-childhood period, and the adolescent period (Brooks-Gunn, Guo, and Furstenberg 1993). Each covers one or two major transitions in the child's life that involve role changes; school entrances, moves, and exits; biological maturation; possible cognitive reorganizations; or some combination. Borrowing from Rutter's turning points framework (1994), Graber and Brooks-Gunn (1996) have suggested that many turning points are linked to transitions. Transition-linked turning points involve events that might alter behaviors or contexts in which children operate. The premise underlying this framework is that "transitional periods are characterized by developmental challenges that are relatively universal; that most individuals navigate transitional periods; and [that] these periods require new models of adaptation to biological, psychological, or social changes" (Graber and Brooks-Gunn 1996, p. 769).

What is relevant here is that each of these periods (1) is characterized by somewhat different indicators of well-being, (2) may be affected by income poverty in various ways, and (3) might have a unique constellation of pathways through which income poverty affects development. For example, nutrition is expected to be a more important pathway in the prenatal-infancy period than in the middle-childhood, adolescent, and young adulthood periods. Indeed, the Women, Infants, and Children (WIC) program targets the prenatal-infancy period for exactly this reason.

We review results from either large multisite studies or national studies, such as the PSID, the National Longitudinal Study of Youth (NLSY), the National Health Insurance Study (NHIS), and High School and Beyond (HSB; see Brooks-Gunn, Brown, et al. 1995 for a review of national data sets containing measures of child and adolescent developmental outcomes). We review only smaller-scale studies that are longitudinal and have data on family income and household size available. Additionally, almost all the studies cited here provide estimates of income poverty in regression equations that control for other family conditions, such as ethnicity, maternal education, maternal age at the child's birth, and marital status. Other family characteristics that are not measured and not included in the regression equations may account for the family income effects reported here. The more family characteristics controlled, the more likely that estimates of family income effects are not due to selectivity.

PRENATAL-INFANCY PERIOD The literature on the effects of income poverty upon the pregnant woman, the neonate, and the infant in the first year of life includes a variety of outcomes. The most frequently studied are the perinatal outcomes—timely receipt of prenatal care, smoking during pregnancy, low birth weight, and perinatal complications. In the first year of life, growth, receipt of recommended well-baby visits, and up-to-date immunizations are the typical measures of well-being studied.

Receipt of timely prenatal care (in the first trimester of pregnancy), smoking during pregnancy, and low birth weight (2,500 g or less) are all related to low income (Egbuonu and Starfield 1982; Kleinman and Kessel 1987; Klerman 1991; McGauhey and Starfield 1993). The first two are themselves associated with low birth weight and intrauterine growth retardation (the latter defined as *small for gestational age*). Relatively long-term effects of low birth weight, found through middle childhood and adolescence, include grade failure, receipt of special education, lower school achievement, behavior problems, and the like (Klebanov, Brooks-Gunn, and McCormick 1994a, 1994b; McCormick 1989; McCormick et al. 1992; McCarton et al. 1997). These negative effects are most pronounced in children with a very low birth weight (under 1,500 g), although children who weigh 1,500–2,500 g at birth are also, as a group, at risk for less positive outcomes than are children weighing over 2,500 g at birth. Such effects persist into the childhood years, even controlling for current parental income, education, and age, as reported in large multisite samples of children followed from birth through age eight or nine. At the same time, postpartum income affects low-birth-weight children's intelligence test scores and school achievement scores (Brooks-Gunn, Klebanov, and Duncan 1996; Klebanov, Brooks-Gunn, and McCormick 1994a). Children who suffer from perinatal complications, such as low birth weight, as well as family income poverty have been termed at double risk (Liaw and Brooks-Gunn 1994; Parker, Greer, and Zuckerman 1988; McCormick and Brooks-Gunn 1989; Sameroff and Chandler 1975).

Infants from poor families are less likely to have immunizations that are up-to-date and to follow the recommended pediatric guidelines for well-baby care (Cunningham and Hahn 1994; Brooks-Gunn et al. forthcoming; Monheit and Cunningham 1992). However, poor children who are covered by Medicaid (that is, public insurance) are more likely to meet health visit guidelines than are both poor children without public insurance and near-poor children without any insurance. That is, in some analyses, receipt of insurance predicts early health care more strongly than income poverty does.

EARLY CHILDHOOD YEARS A few studies of the young childhood period have examined income poverty's association with intelligence test scores and behavior problem scores when children are five years of age (Duncan, Brooks-Gunn, and Klebanov 1994; Korenman, Miller, and Sjaastad 1995). Research on two data sets, the NLSY—Child Supplement and the Infant Health and Development Program (IHDP), has found that, controlling for other family characteristics, income's effects on intelligence and verbal test scores at ages two, three, and five years are quite large—about one-third of a standard deviation (Chase-Lansdale et al. 1991; IHDP 1990; Brooks-Gunn et al. 1994).[3] In addition, the literature on behavior problems during the early childhood years is based on mothers' reports of children's behavior problems, including aggression, tantrums, anxiety, and moodiness. Income-to-needs ratios are associated with behavior problems for five-year-olds (Smith et al. 1996).

Both well-baby health care and nonmaternal child care during this age period have been examined vis-à-vis income poverty. Well-baby health care continues to lag for poor young children; again, the links with income poverty are primarily found for those poor and near-poor children without health insurance (Cunningham and Hahn 1994). The type of child care used is associated with income poverty, as poor mothers are more likely to use relative care than nonrelative care, presumably because of its lower cost (Baydar and Brooks-Gunn 1991; Cattan 1991; Hofferth and Phillips 1991). Additionally, more affluent families seem to use center-based care most frequently, followed by poor families. Near-poor families are least likely to use center-based care (NICHD Child Care Research Network in this volume). This last finding is thought to be due to the availability and cost of center-based child care for poor versus near-poor families; the most notable example is that poor families are eligible for Head Start (Currie and Thomas 1995; Lee et al. 1990; Phillips et al. 1994; Volling and Belsky 1993). In addition, the availability of child care is restricted in poor communities (Collins and Hofferth 1996). This brief summary of health care and child care in the young childhood years does not take into account the quality of the services provided to families of different income levels. Chapter 6 reports the results of a study incorporating a measure of quality by the National Institute of Child Health and Human Development Early Child Care Research Network.

LATE CHILDHOOD YEARS Measures of child well-being after entrance into school include school achievement test scores, behavior problems as reported by teachers and parents, grade failure, and learning and attention problems. Current work involves other domains of well-being, such as children's reports of school disengagement, of self-efficacy and self-esteem, and of depressive and aggressive behavior (Harter 1990; Cairns and Cairns 1986; Nolen-Hoeksma 1994; Connell et al. 1994). However, almost nothing is known about links between these domains and income poverty. Chapters 5, 7, 8, 9 and 11 report on studies of the late childhood years.

ADOLESCENT YEARS The adolescent period is often divided into two epochs. The early adolescent period covers the transition from elementary school to junior or middle school as well as pubertal and family transitions (Brooks-Gunn and Reiter 1990; Eccles, Lord, and Buchanan 1996; Eccles et al. 1993; Flanagan and Eccles 1993; Paikoff and Brooks-Gunn 1991). Outcomes that have been studied include school engagement, peer relationships, juvenile delinquency, self-esteem, grades in school, and, to a much lesser extent, achievement test scores. Almost no national studies on young adolescent outcomes have included both income and other family characteristics in the analyses.

The late adolescent period focuses on the transition to high school and, for some youth, the transition to sexual intercourse, drug and alcohol use, and smoking. Outcomes include those listed for the young adolescent period as well as pregnancy, childbirth, school dropout, and high school graduation. Many studies have examined the effects of income on teenage childbearing in girls and on high school dropout or completion for boys and girls (Brooks-Gunn, Guo, and Furstenberg 1993; Graham, Beller, and Hernandez 1993; Haveman and Wolfe 1995; Haveman,

Wolfe, and Spaulding 1991). In this volume, chapters 10, 12, 13, 14, and 17 report on studies of schooling outcomes.

PERSISTENCE AND TIMING OF POVERTY Thus far, we have only considered the effects of family income upon child and youth outcomes. We next examine poverty per se, beyond the income-to-needs ratio, and review the literature on the persistence and timing of poverty.

The fact that income-to-needs ratio is associated with children's outcomes does not reveal whether there are differences between children just above and those just below the poverty line. From a policy perspective, the question is whether or not increasing the income of poor and near-poor children might make a difference in their lives. Chapters 5–17 report on studies of this issue.

Some children live in poverty for a short time while others spend a significant portion of their childhoods in poverty. The number of years in poverty is significantly associated with negative outcomes for children. For example, based on IHDP data on five-year-olds, children who lived in poverty for four or five years had IQ scores 9 points lower than children who had never lived below the poverty line in their first five years. In contrast, children who had been poor for some but not all of the years had IQ scores that were, on average, 4 points lower than those of nonpoor children (Duncan, Brooks-Gunn, and Klebanov 1994). In this volume, chapters 5–7 and 9–16 look at the effects of persistent versus short-term poverty.

Developmental theory postulates that the timing of events is critical to an understanding of their effects on children. That is, various events or environmental conditions might influence the cognitive and social skills and competencies children have acquired as well as the contexts in which they reside. Prior environmental conditions also may influence children's experience of current environmental conditions. Family income or poverty is just one of a series of environmental conditions of interest (Brooks-Gunn 1995; Bronfenbrenner 1979). Given that family and neighborhood resource theories now include developmental perspectives, more attention is being paid to possible timing effects (Brooks-Gunn et al. 1995; Haveman and Wolfe 1994). For example, Haveman, Wolfe, and Spaulding (1991) and Brooks-Gunn, Guo, and Furstenberg (1993) have built models for predicting high school completion and dropout based on events that occurred in various periods of childhood. In the Baltimore Study of Teenage Parenthood, for example, welfare receipt and income in the early childhood years were associated with high school dropout more strongly than were similar measures of family economic well-being from the late childhood and early adolescent years. Welfare receipt in the early years was highly associated with school readiness scores, which in turn predicted grade failure, school completion, and literacy (Baydar, Brooks-Gunn, and Furstenberg 1993; Guo, Brooks-Gunn, and Harris forthcoming). In a similar approach using the PSID (which has income data for each year of the child's life, unlike the small Baltimore study), Duncan et al. (in press) constructed age-specific estimates of income effects for early childhood, late childhood, and early adolescence. The study also looked at the effects of income by age for children in lower- and higher-income families. Income as measured in early childhood affected the completed schooling of children from lower-income families. In chapter 18 we examine the findings from the eleven longitudinal studies in this volume based on the timing of the income measure.

Income, Education, and Family Structure

Poverty, low levels of parental education, and single parenthood often go hand-in-hand, and it has been difficult to tease apart the effects of each upon children. However, large data sets include enough children who are poor and live in two-parent households and children who are not poor and live in single-parent households to allow for statistical controls of variables such as family structure and parents' education. All of the studies described here looked at income, education, and family structure in sets of regressions and coded these variables the same way.

The most recent literature on parents' education has focused mainly on mothers' education because so many children live in single-mother households, making the father's education perhaps less salient (at least on a day-to-day basis). More practically, often data on the father's education are missing. In any case, mothers' education is a strong and consistent predictor of children's outcomes—from IQ test scores at age five through school completion rates at ages nineteen and twenty (Duncan, Brooks-Gunn, and Klebanov 1994; Haveman and Wolfe 1995). It is unclear whether the effects of mothers' education are larger or smaller than those of family income. This issue is a facet of each of the studies in chapters 5–17.

Turning to family structure, research has demonstrated that being reared in a single-parent family is associated with less positive child and youth outcomes than is being reared in a two-parent family (McLanahan and Sandefur 1994; chapter 3). Chapters 5–17 look at family structure effects even with controls for income effects.

Pathways through Which Poverty Operates

How does income influence children's outcomes? A number of pathways might exist, but little research has investigated most of these possible mechanisms. Most work has focused on the provision of learning experiences, parents' emotional and physical health, and parenting behavior (Brooks-Gunn 1995; Conger et al. 1993, 1994; McLoyd et al. 1994). In this volume, chapters 5–17 examine possible mediators of income-outcome links.

ORGANIZATION OF THIS VOLUME

As we have just reviewed, many studies have shown that children raised in low-income families score lower than children from more affluent families do on assessments of health, cognitive development, and positive behavior. In general, the better the measure of family income and the longer the period over which it is measured, the stronger the association between the family's economic well-being and children's outcomes. Understanding why and when these associations exist is the goal of the research presented in this book.

The distinction between correlation and causation is crucial for understanding our motivations. That children from poor families fare worse than others is consistent with a variety of causal explanations. An obvious one is that income itself matters for the well-being of children. Income allows parents to provide their children with safer, more stimulating home environments; to live in communities with better schools, parks, and libraries and more challenging peers; to afford tuition and other expenses associated with higher education; to purchase or otherwise gain access to higher-quality health care; and in many other ways to buy the things that promote the health and development of their children.

Alternative explanations abound. Low-income families differ from their higher-income counterparts in many ways other than their level of economic resources. Families with low incomes are less likely to contain the child's two biological parents or include adults holding either college degrees or high-status occupations, and they are more likely to live in poor neighborhoods, receive income from welfare, contain adults with mental or physical problems, and so on. Perhaps it is these other, less readily quantifiable, characteristics of low-income households that matter more than income itself.

Informed public policy depends critically on sorting out which of these many possible explanations is correct. If it is literally true that money "buys" better children, then the distribution of family income and the proportion of U.S. children living in families with inadequate financial resources are the key indications of children's future well-being. And, in assessing the costs and benefits of a given policy, the likely effects of that policy on low-income families' ability to provide their children with an adequate standard of living become central considerations.

If, on the other hand, less optimal child development is caused not by a lack of income itself but by the correlated characteristics of poor families, then policy should be concerned less with reducing income-based poverty than with addressing parenting skills, neighborhood conditions, or similar causes directly.

THE STUDIES IN THIS BOOK

The chapters in this book constitute a coordinated effort to understand both correlation and causation with respect to family economic well-being and child development.

To provide a context for the analyses presented in chapters 5 through 17, the volume includes chapters by Mayer (chapter 4), McLanahan (chapter 3), and Hernandez (chapter 2). Hernandez presents a picture of poor children and families in the United States today, as well as, a historical analysis of changes in the rates and consequences of poverty over the past forty years. Mayer considers changes in standards of living as measured by the quality of housing and the presence of various appliances in the home. She makes the argument that the relatively high rates of poverty do not reflect, in part, the relative rise in living standards. McLanahan provides detail on the demographic condition most clearly linked to poverty status—single parenthood.

Chapters 5–17 are based on analyses of data from a diverse set of child development studies, all of which contain high-quality and, if possible, longitudinal measures of family income. Regrettably, the requirement of income data eliminated a number of otherwise excellent studies of child development. The studies cover many important domains of child well-being and span all developmental stages—from early childhood through adolescence and even into middle age.

Through these studies we attempt to provide some consistency in measuring family income across studies and to fill in the gaps in our knowledge about income effects across different age periods. For example, very few studies have examined outcomes in the early childhood, late childhood, and early adolescent years, and few have examined school achievement, instead relying on measures of school completion. Emotional behavior and school-related behavior have not been examined in any detail, even though the adult literature on gradients of socioeconomic status and health includes emotional health outcomes (Adler et al. 1993). Finally, studies have not considered the same set of covariates, making it difficult to estimate effect sizes of income, family structure, and parental education upon child and youth outcomes.

The chapters in this volume address the following questions:

- Does income matter?
- When does income matter?
- For what outcomes does income matter?
- Why does income matter?

To calibrate each of the data sets against the others, the authors of chapters 5–17 were asked to perform a series of replication analyses that related children's outcomes to the same set of measures of family income, demographic structure, and other aspects of the socioeconomic status of the parental family. These analyses provide a set of a baseline associations between family income and children's outcomes that reveal at what points in child- and adulthood and for what developmental domains the poverty-outcome associations are the strongest. If anything, these simple descriptive associations are likely to overstate the true causal role of income. Thus, insignificant associations are of particular interest, since they suggest combinations of domain and developmental stage that are unaffected by the economic circumstances of the families in which the children are raised.

In each chapter, the authors exploit the unique strengths of their data to isolate the causal role of income in the process of children's and adults' development. Here the multidisciplinary nature of the authors' backgrounds becomes apparent, as they take very different approaches to modeling causal connections between economic status and development.

A life of poverty is statistically associated with higher rates of activities detrimental to individuals and to society, such as crime, violence, underemployment, unemployment, and isolation from the larger community. The costs of poverty are borne not only by the children reared in such circumstances but by society at large. In addition to direct government expenditures, these costs include a smaller number of educated citizens, an increase in neighborhoods characterized by danger, less social cohesion, and lower rates of social and political participation.

Children depend on others for their well-being. Because of their developmental status, children enter or avoid poverty by virtue of their family's economic circumstances. They typically cannot alter their status by themselves, at least until they approach the late adolescent years. Federal policies ensure that children whose families are earning less than the poverty threshold receive some of the basic necessities of life—food, shelter, and clothing. In addition, health care is provided to many poor children, and early childhood education to a subset of poor children. Even so, one in five children lives below the poverty threshold in the 1990s, and, as this volume documents, these children do not fare as well as those living above that threshold.

We thank the National Institute of Child Health and Human Development Research Network on Child and Family Well-Being for supporting the writing of this chapter as well as for sponsoring the 1995 conference Growing Up Poor: Consequences for Children and Youth. Russell Sage Foundation's contribution is appreciated, as is that of the Board on Children, Youth, and Families, National Academy of Sciences, and Institute of Medicine. We are also grateful for feedback by members of the National Academy of Science's Committee on Defining Poverty, especially Connie Citro, Robert Michael, Robert Hauser, Rebecca Black, and Sheldon Danziger. We also thank Dorothy Duncan and Phyllis Gyamfi for editorial assistance and the Canadian Institute for Advanced Research.

NOTES

1. In addition, the source of the family's income has been shown to have an independent effect on children's well-being. Studies have investigated the effects on children of welfare receipt as a source of income, for example. (See Duncan, Hill, and Hoffman 1988; Furstenberg, Brooks-Gunn, and Morgan 1987; Haveman, Wolfe, and Spaulding 1991; and Zill et al. 1991; and more generally, Ellwood 1988; Wilson 1987; and Zaslow et al. 1995). Others have looked at child support payments (see Baydar and Brooks-Gunn 1994; Beller and Graham 1991; Garfinkel et al. 1994; Sonenstein and Calhoun 1990; Teachman 1992; Maccoby and Mnookin 1992; and Weiss and Willis 1993). These topics are beyond the scope of this volume.
2. Black children are also more likely than white children to live in poor neighborhoods. For example, in the same sample of children who were three years of age or younger in 1980, about two-fifths of the white children lived in neighborhoods (defined by census tracts) where 10 percent or fewer of the households had incomes of less than $10,000, whereas only one in ten black children lived in such neighborhoods (Duncan,

Brooks-Gunn, and Klebanov 1994: 304). Just under 2 percent of the white children and over 20 percent of the black children lived in neighborhoods where 30 percent or more of the neighbors were poor (see table 1.2). These striking, and disturbing, statistics reflect that black and white children's experiences of neighborhood poverty barely overlap.

3. Since intelligence and verbal ability tests are normed to have a mean of 100 and a standard deviation of 15 or 16, a hypothetical child whose family's income was at the poverty threshold (1.0) would have an IQ score 5 to 6 points lower than a hypothetical child whose family's income was twice the poverty threshold (these hypothetical children being reared by mothers with the same marital status, education, and race and being the same sex, birth weight, and age).

Chapter 2

Poverty Trends

Donald J. Hernandez

This chapter addresses three questions: How have children's poverty rates changed since the Great Depression, especially from 1973 to 1993? To what extent can changes in income from fathers, mothers, other relatives, and the government and the rise in mother-only families account for these poverty trends? What are the explanations for the historic changes in fathers' and mothers' income and the rise in mother-only families?

CHANGES IN POVERTY RATES

Childhood poverty rates have changed enormously since the Great Depression. Childhood poverty as measured by U.S. Bureau of the Census official poverty rates fell sharply during the 1960s (see figure 2.1). Since then, but especially since 1979, official poverty has increased substantially. By 1993, 22.7 percent of children were officially classified as poor, the highest poverty rate experienced by children since the mid-1960s.

For studies of long-term change, however, increasing numbers of scholars are calling into question the official measure. One major limitation of the current official measure is that it fails to take into account changing social perceptions about income levels. For example, during the twenty six years from 1947 to 1973, median family income more than doubled (see figure 2.2). In light of this enormous increase, a corresponding change most likely occurred in social perceptions regarding the amount of income needed to maintain a ''normal'' or ''adequate'' level of living.

That such judgments are relative has been noted for at least 200 years. Adam Smith emphasized in the *Wealth of Nations*, for example, that poverty must be defined in comparison to contemporary standards of living. He defined economic hardship as the experience of being unable to consume commodities that ''the custom of the country renders it indecent for creditable people, even of the lowest order, to be without'' (cited in U.S. Congress 1989, 10). More recently, Galbraith

FIGURE 2.1 / Official Poverty Rate for Children under 18, 1959–93

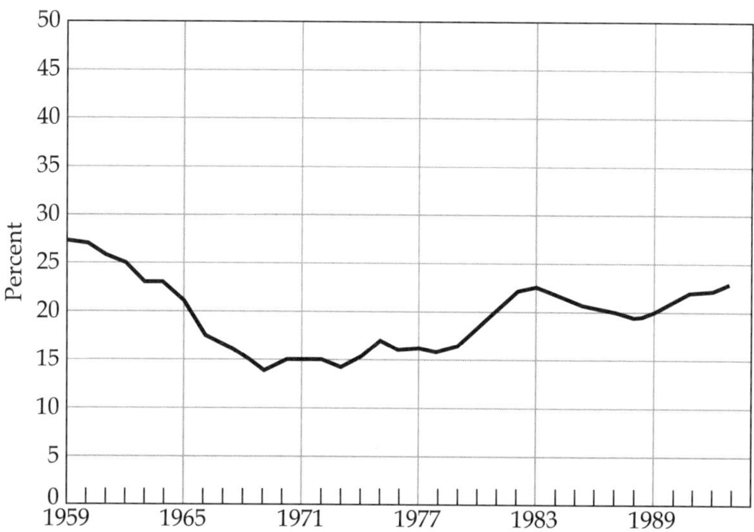

Source: U.S. Department of Commerce (1995).

FIGURE 2.2 / Median Family Income by Type of Family, 1947–90

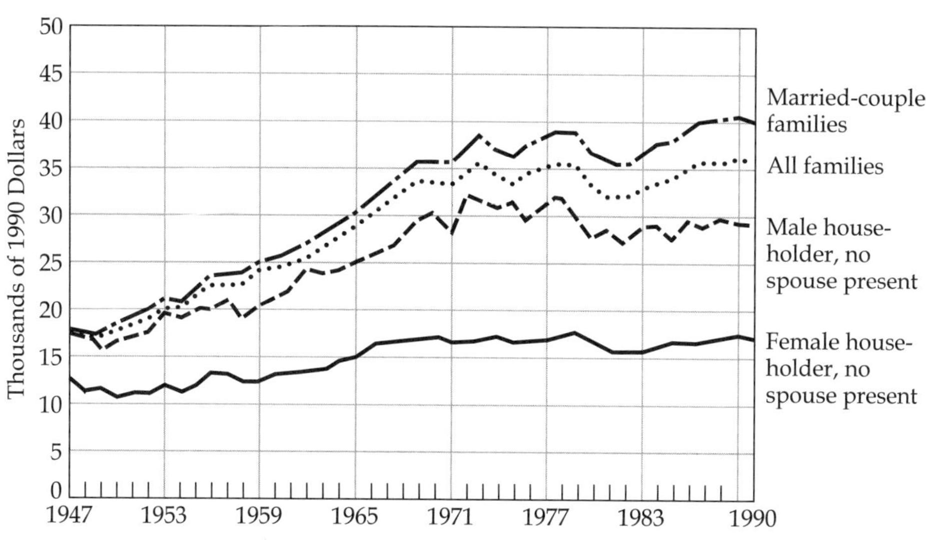

Source: U.S. Department of Commerce (1995).

argued that "people are poverty-stricken when their income, even if adequate for survival, falls markedly behind that of the community. Then they cannot have what the larger community regards as the minimum necessary for decency; and they cannot wholly escape, therefore, the judgment of the larger community that they are indecent. They are degraded, for, in a literal sense, they live outside the grades or categories which the community regards as respectable" (1958: 323–24).

Based on these insights, additional literature, and Rainwater's (1974) comprehensive review of existing U.S. studies and original research, in earlier work I developed a measure of relative poverty using poverty thresholds set at 50 percent of median family income in specific years and adjusted for family size (Fuchs 1965; Expert Committee on Budget Revisions 1980; Hernandez 1993).

Relative Poverty and Family Income

What are the historic and recent trends in relative poverty? After the Great Depression, the relative poverty rate among children dropped sharply, from 38 percent in 1939 to 27 percent in 1949 (figure 2.3). The 1950s and 1960s each brought much smaller declines. After 1969, and especially after 1979, childhood relative poverty increased, reaching 29 percent in 1993. By 1993, then, nearly three in ten children lived in relative poverty.[1]

Children experienced increasing inequality in their family incomes after 1969, as increases occurred in the proportions both at the top and at the bottom of the income distribution. Meanwhile, the proportion living in middle-class comfort or near-poor frugality declined from 52 percent in 1969 to 47 percent in 1993.[2]

Relative Poverty by Age, Family Situation, and Race

Historic trends in relative poverty are broadly similar for children at various ages, but preschoolers were substantially more likely than adolescents to be living in relative poverty in 1979–93 (Hernandez 1993). Throughout the era, children in two-parent families experienced much lower relative poverty rates than children in mother-only families, while black children have been much more likely than white children to be poor (Hernandez 1993). As of 1988, 22 percent of white children and 53 percent of black children lived in relative poverty, and by 1993 these figures had increased to 24 percent for whites and 54 percent for blacks.

ACCOUNTING FOR POVERTY TRENDS

To what extent can changes in the rate of relative poverty during childhood be accounted for by changes in income provided by fathers, mothers, and other family members or received from government welfare programs? Figure 2.4 shows

FIGURE 2.3 / Relative Income Levels of Children, 1939–88

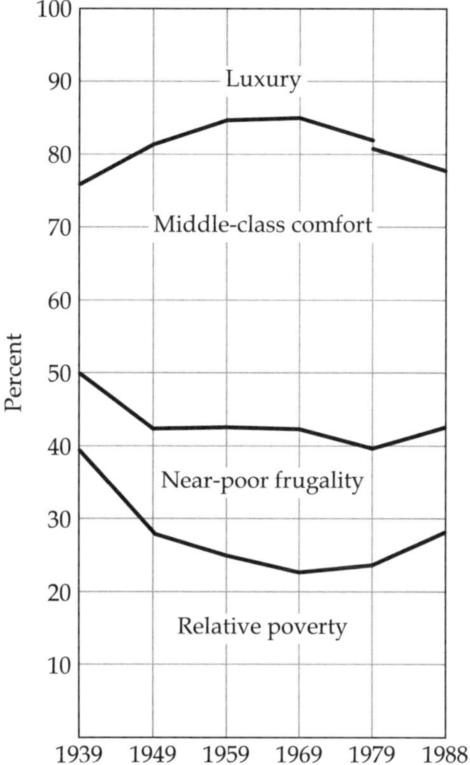

Source: Hernandez (1993) fig. 7.1, p. 245.

several hypothetical trends in relative poverty based on the availability of different sources of income for children overall and for children in two-parent families. If, for example, only the income of fathers in the home had been available (shown by the top line in both graphs), the relative poverty rate for children would have fallen sharply during the 1940s, fallen much more slowly or not at all during the 1950s and 1960s, and risen substantially during the 1980s.

The addition of mothers' income to that of fathers over the same period (shown in both graphs in figure 2.4 by the second line from the top) acted to speed the decline in children's relative poverty during the 1940s, 1950s, and 1960s and to slow the subsequent increase in relative poverty during the 1970s and 1980s. In fact, by 1988 14 percent of all children and 11 percent of children in two-parent families depended on their mother's income to lift them out of relative poverty. Next, except for the 1940s, additional income from relatives other than parents in the home (shown by the third line) served to reduce the relative poverty rate

FIGURE 2.4 / Relative Poverty Rates and Effects of Parents' Income and Government Welfare: 1939–88

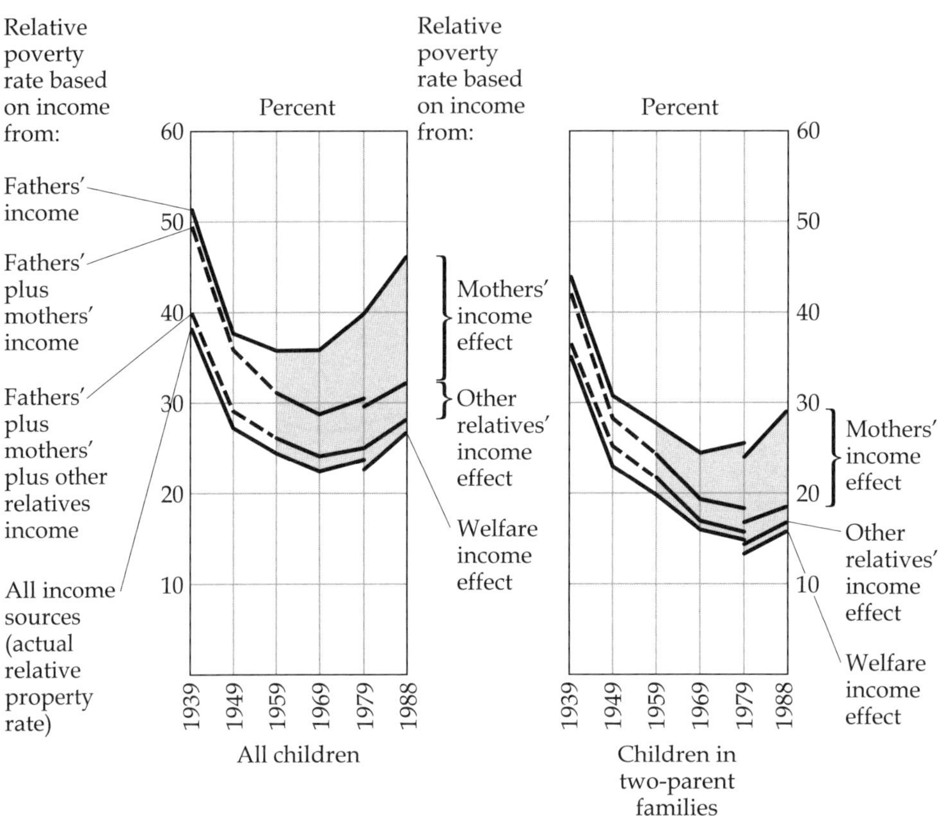

Source: Hernandez (1993) fig. 9.1, p. 339.

Note: Separate estimates of income from mothers and government welfare not available for 1949.

by a nearly constant and comparatively small 4–5 percentage points for children overall and by a nearly constant and even smaller 1–2 percentage points for children in two-parent families.

Finally, both for children overall and for children in two-parent families, Aid to Families with Dependent Children (AFDC) and Social Security acted to reduce the relative poverty rate by a stable and small 1–2 percentage points in any given year (shown by the bottom lines in figure 2.4). Hence, the role of these welfare programs in reducing children's relative poverty has been quite limited throughout the era since the Great Depression, although additional noncash food and housing programs introduced since the 1960s have had important additional effects of 2–3 percentage points.[3]

FIGURE 2.5 / Family Types for Children through Age Seventeen, 1790–1989[a]

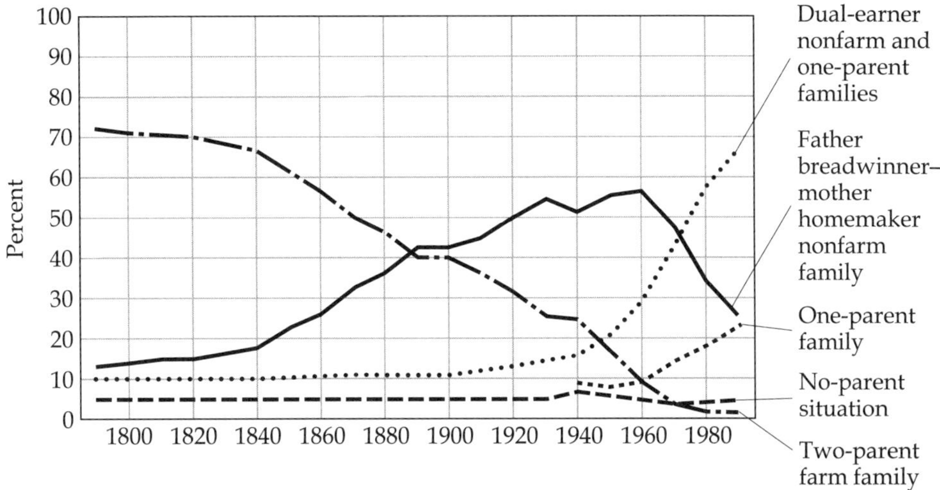

Source: Hernandez (1993) fig. 4.1, p. 103.

a. Estimates for ten-year intervals to 1980 and for 1989.

SOURCE OF CHANGE IN RELATIVE POVERTY

These trends suggest that an explanation of historic poverty trends requires an understanding of the reasons for (1) the increases in mothers' labor force participation and hence mothers' income, (2) the rise in mother-only families, which has reduced many children's access to their fathers' income, and (3) the changes in fathers' income. It is useful to begin by looking at historic sources of the rise in family income.

The Rise in Fathers' Nonfarm Work

For hundreds of years, agriculture and the two-parent farm family represented the primary forms of economic production and family organization in Western countries. However, the shift away from farming to the nonfarm father-as-breadwinner, mother-as-homemaker system of family organization was very rapid. In the one hundred years between 1830 and 1930, the proportion of children living in nonfarm families with breadwinner fathers and homemaker mothers expanded from only 15 percent to a majority of 55 percent (see figure 2.5).

This change represented a historically unprecedented transformation in the nature of childhood. In two-parent farm families, family members worked side by

FIGURE 2.6 / Actual Expected Sibsizes for Adolescents Born 1865–1994

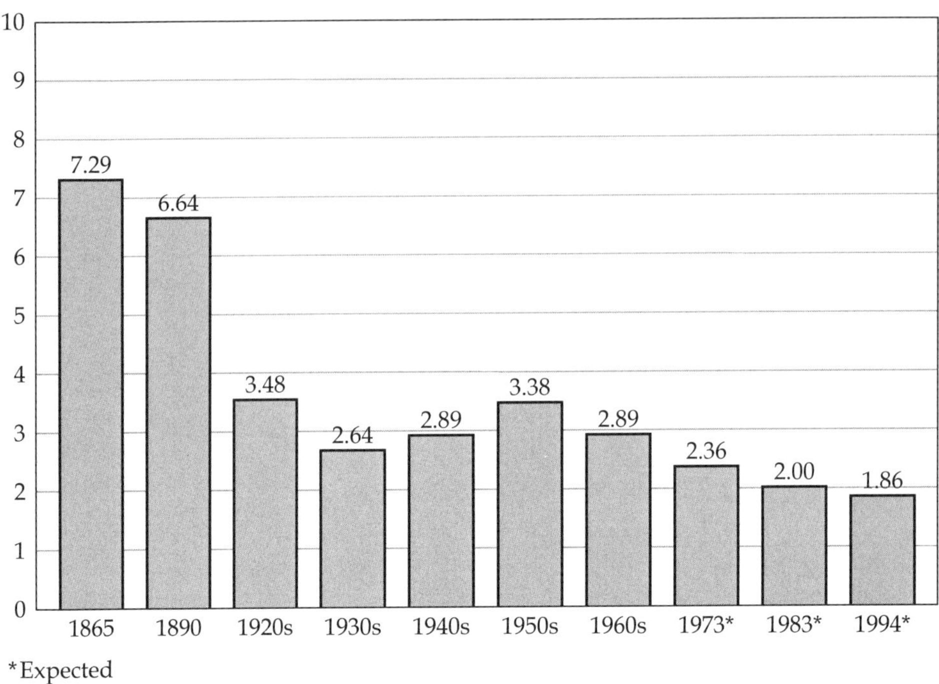

*Expected

Source: Hernandez (1993) table 2.2, p. 29.

side to sustain themselves in small communities. In contrast, two-parent urban families consisted of fathers who spent their workday away from home earning the income required to support the family and mothers who remained in the home to care for their children and perform domestic functions. Although one hundred years may seem like a long time, the life expectancy of a newborn today is nearly seventy-six years (Kochanek and Hudson 1995). Hence, the transformation of the family economy required little more than one human lifetime by today's standards.

The Decline in Large Families

The enormous shift in the family economy was accompanied by a dramatic decline in large families. The median number of siblings in the families of adolescents dropped from 7.3 to only 2.6 between 1865 and 1930 (figure 2.6). This change required only sixty-five years—less than a human lifetime.

The Rise in Educational Attainment

A third revolutionary change in children's lives occurred during the same era. School enrollment rates nearly doubled to 80–95 percent, depending on the age group, and the number of days students spent in school doubled. By 1940, then, school days accounted for 59 percent of all the nonweekend days in the year. Since the children of one era are the parents of the next, this enormous increase in schooling also led, in due course, to large increases in parents' education (Hernandez 1993).

EXPLAINING THE CHANGES

Why did these revolutions in fathers' work, family size, and schooling occur between the mid- to late 1800s and the 1940s? The shift from farming to urban occupations was typically necessary to improve the family's relative economic status or to keep families from losing ground compared with others. The incomes provided by urban jobs were higher than the incomes that many people could earn through farming. And in some cases, the economic situation of families in rural areas was extremely precarious; in such situations even poorly paid or dangerous jobs in urban areas appeared attractive. In short, a fundamental cause of the massive migration from farms to urban areas was the comparatively favorable economic opportunities in urban areas.

The reasons for the drop in family size grow partly out of the shift away from farming. The shift from agriculture to urban work meant that families had to purchase housing, food, clothing, and other necessities with cash, making the costs of supporting each additional child more obvious. At the same time, the passage of laws restricting child labor and mandating universal child education sharply reduced children's potential economic contribution to their parents and families. In addition, economic growth led to increases in expected standards of consumption. Hence, the costs of supporting each additional child at a "normal" level increased over time. As a result, more and more parents limited their family size to a comparatively small number of children so that the available income could be spread less thinly.

As farming gave way to the industrial economy and family size shrank, school enrollment increased as labor unions sought to ensure jobs for adults (mainly fathers) by limiting child labor. In addition, as time passed, higher educational attainments became increasingly necessary to obtain jobs that offered higher incomes and greater prestige. Hence, parents encouraged and fostered higher educational attainments among their children as a path to occupational and economic success in adulthood. Once again, their motivation was to improve their children's relative social and economic standing.

FIGURE 2.7 / Children with Mothers in the Labor Force, 1940–90

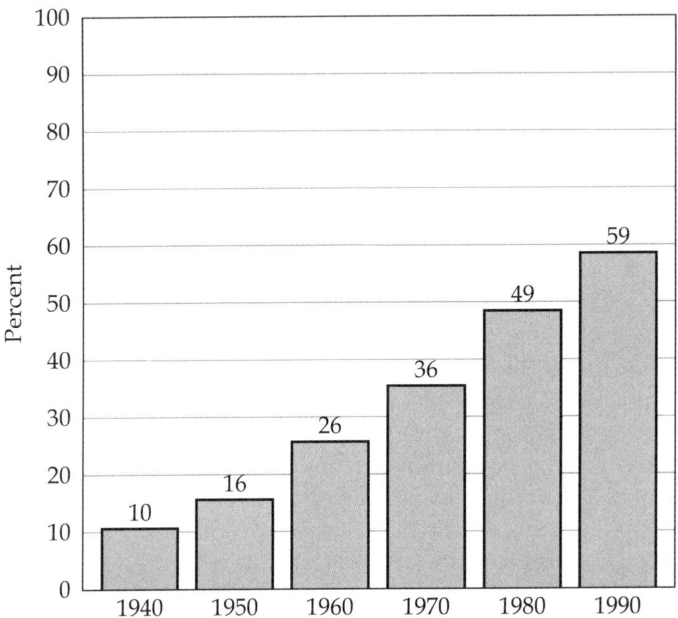

Source: Hernandez (1993) table 4.1, p. 109.

The Rise in Mothers' Labor Force Participation

After 1940, two additional revolutions in children's families began. First was the explosion in mothers' employment outside the home. In 1940 only 10 percent of children lived with a mother who was in the labor force (figure 2.7) By 1990 nearly 60 percent of children had a mother working outside the home, a sixfold increase in fifty years.

What caused this revolutionary rise? Much of the answer lies in the historic changes in the family and economy. As suggested, between the early days of the Industrial Revolution and about 1940, many parents had three major avenues for maintaining, improving, or regaining their economic standing relative to other families. First, they could move off the farm and the husband could work in a comparatively well-paid job in the growing urban-industrial economy. Second, they could limit themselves to a smaller number of children than other families had and thus divide family resources among fewer people. Third, they could acquire more education.

By 1940, however, only 23 percent of Americans lived on farms, and 70 percent of parents had only one or two dependent children in the home. Consequently, for many parents the first two avenues to altering their relative economic standing had run their course (Elder 1974). Furthermore, since most persons complete their education by age twenty-five, obtaining additional schooling beyond that age is often difficult or impractical.

With the closing of these avenues, a fourth major avenue to increasing family income emerged between 1940 and 1960, namely, paid work by wives and mothers. The supply of workers from traditional sources of female nonfarm labor, that is, unmarried women, was either stagnant or declining, while the demand for female workers was increasing (Oppenheimer 1970). Meanwhile, wives and mothers were becoming increasingly available and well qualified for work outside the home. By 1940 the unprecedented increases in children's school enrollment had effectively released mothers from personal child care responsibilities for a period equivalent to about two-thirds of an adult full-time workday for about two-thirds of an adult full-time work year, except for the few years before children entered elementary school.

Paid work outside the home for mothers was becoming increasingly attractive in the U.S. competitive, consumption-oriented society for another reason. Families in which the father's income was comparatively low could, by virtue of the mother's work, move economically ahead of families in which the father had the same occupational status but the mother did not work outside the home. Families with comparatively well-paid fathers were thus at a disadvantage, making the prospect of mothers' work more attractive (Oppenheimer 1982). In addition, with the historic rise in the divorce rate paid work became increasingly attractive to mothers as a hedge against the possible economic disaster of losing most or all of the father's income through divorce.

Immediate economic insecurity and need, associated with fathers' lack of access to full-time employment, also made mothers' work attractive. In the Great Depression year of 1940, 40 percent of children lived with fathers who did not work year round, full time (figure 2.8). This proportion declined after the Great Depression but continued at high levels. Even with the post-1960 expansion in mother-only families, the proportion of all children living with fathers who did not work year round, full time was 22–25 percent from 1973 to 1993. This has been a powerful incentive for many mothers to work for pay.

The desire to alter their family's relative social and economic status is not the only reason that wives and mothers enter the labor force. Additional reasons to work include the personal, nonfinancial rewards of the job itself, the opportunity to be productively involved with other adults, and the satisfactions associated with having a career in a high-prestige occupation. Nonetheless, for many mothers economic insecurity and need provide a powerful incentive to work for pay.

The importance of sheer economic necessity in fostering growth in mothers' employment is reflected in the following. In 1988 one of every eight American children in a two-parent family (12 percent) either was living in official poverty despite the mother's paid employment or would have been living in official poverty if the mother had not been working. Even more striking, in 1988 one of every five American children in a two-parent family (20 percent) either was living in

FIGURE 2.8 / Children Living with a Father Working Less Than Full Time, Year Round, 1940–90

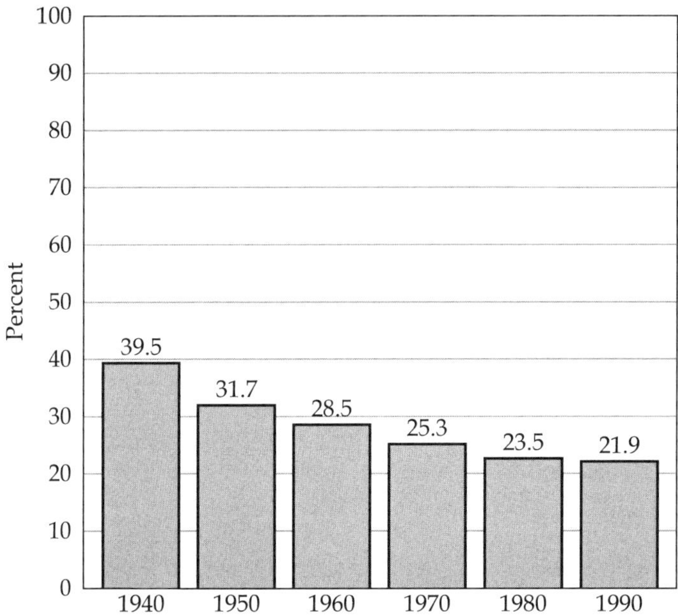

Source: Hernandez (1993) fig. 4.4, p. 110.

relative poverty despite the mother's work or would have been living in relative poverty without the mother's work. Based on the official poverty measure, this suggests that the mothers of 20–25 percent of children in two-parent families with working mothers are working out of economic necessity. Based on the relative poverty measure, this figure rises to 35–40 percent.

At middle income levels, too, the work of wives and mothers is important for the economic standing of many families. This is reflected in the increasing difference between the median incomes of married-couple families with and without the wife in the paid labor force. Among married-couple families in 1949 and 1959, the median income of families with the wife in the paid labor force was 26 percent greater than that of families with the wife not working for pay. The advantage for families with a working wife increased to 31 percent in 1969, 40 percent in 1979, 57 percent in 1989, and an extraordinary 69 percent in 1993. The increasingly large economic advantage enjoyed by families with wives working for pay and the continuing desire of families to maintain, improve, or regain their relative economic status have no doubt contributed substantially to the enormous increase

FIGURE 2.9 / Divorce, 1860–1988[a]

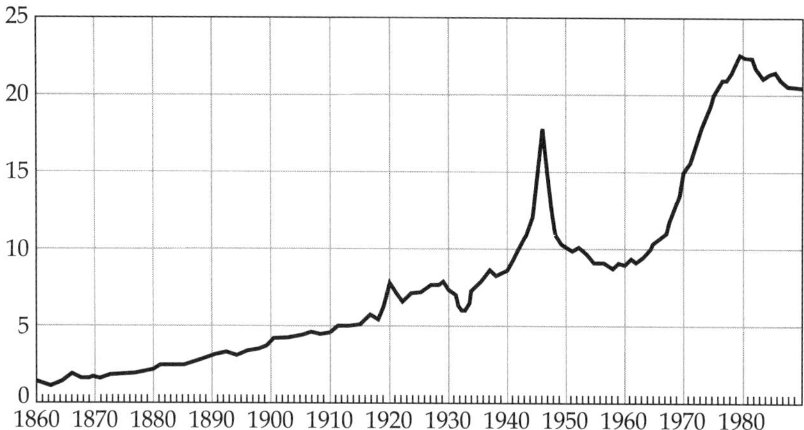

Source: U.S. Department of Health and Human Services (1991); Jacobson (1950).
a. Divorces per 1,000 married women fourteen to forty-four years old.

in the proportion of married-couple families with a working wife, from only 23 percent in 1949, to 34 percent in 1969, 49 percent in 1979, 58 percent in 1989, and 61 percent in 1993.

The Rise in Mother-Only Families

Twenty years after the beginning of the sharp increase in mothers' work outside the home, yet another enormous change in family life began, namely, an unprecedented increase in mother-only families. Between the 1860s and the 1960s, except for three temporary spikes associated with the world wars and the Great Depression, there was a remarkably steady eightfold increase in divorce (see figure 2.9).

Why did this sustained increase occur? Preindustrial farm life compelled the economic interdependence of husbands and wives. Fathers and mothers had to work together to maintain the family. But a father with a nonfarm job could, if he desired, depend on his own work alone for his income. At the same time, in moving to urban areas husbands and wives left behind the rural, small-town social controls that once censured divorce. Later, similar to the independence that nonfarm work gave men, the post-1940 increase in mothers' labor force participation meant that a mother with a job could separate or divorce and keep her own income.

In addition, the economic insecurity and need associated with erratic or limited employment prospects for many men contributed to the increasing divorce rate and to out-of-wedlock childbearing. Recent studies of divorce have shown that instability in husbands' work, declines in family income, and a low ratio of family income to needs lead to heightened hostility between husbands and wives, lower marital quality, and increased risk of divorce (Conger et al. 1990; Conger and Elder 1994; Elder et al. 1992; Liker and Elder 1983).

In fact, each of the three economic recessions between 1970 and 1982 led to intensified increases in mother-only families compared with each preceding nonrecessionary period. Rough estimates of the size of this recession effect on children have assumed that without each recession the average annual increase in mother-only families would have been the same during recession years as it was during the immediately preceding nonrecessionary period (Hernandez 1993). The results suggest that recessions accounted for about 30 percent of the overall increase in mother-only families between 1968 and 1988 or about 50 percent of the increase in mother-only families with separated or divorced mothers.

Seventy percent of the increase in mother-only families for white children between 1960 and 1988 can be accounted for by the rise in separation and divorce. In the case of black children, the explanation is more complicated. Between 1940 and 1960, the proportion of children living in a mother-only family with a divorced or separated mother increased much more for black children than for white children. But, especially since 1970, the proportion of black children living in mother-only families with a never-married mother has also increased.

Most likely, the factors that led to increased separation and divorce among whites also apply to blacks. As a further explanation, however, the proportion of blacks living on farms between 1940 and 1960 dropped much more dramatically than did the proportion of whites. In 1940, 44 percent of black children lived on farms; by 1960 this figure had plummeted to only 11 percent. This startling drop and the extraordinary economic pressures and hardships faced by black families may largely explain why more black children than white children lived in mother-only families by 1960.

Subsequently, the joblessness of young black men aged sixteen to twenty-four exceeded joblessness among young white men (see figure 2.10; Wilson 1987). This gap expanded from an almost negligible difference in 1955 to a 15–25 percentage point difference between 1975 and 1989. Faced with this large and rapid reduction in the availability of black men of family-building age who might provide significant support to a family, many young black women appear to have decided to forgo a temporary and unrewarding marriage—a marriage, in some cases, in which a jobless or poorly paid husband might act as a financial drain. Thus, the increasing racial gap in joblessness may well be the major cause of the increasing racial gap in the proportion of all children living in mother-only families with never-married mothers.

As a result of the sharp rise in divorce and out-of-wedlock childbearing, the proportion of children living with their mother and with no father in the home approximately tripled from 6–8 percent between 1940 and 1960, to 20 percent by 1990, and to 23 percent by 1993.

FIGURE 2.10 / The Gap between White Male and Black Male Employment, by Age, 1955–88

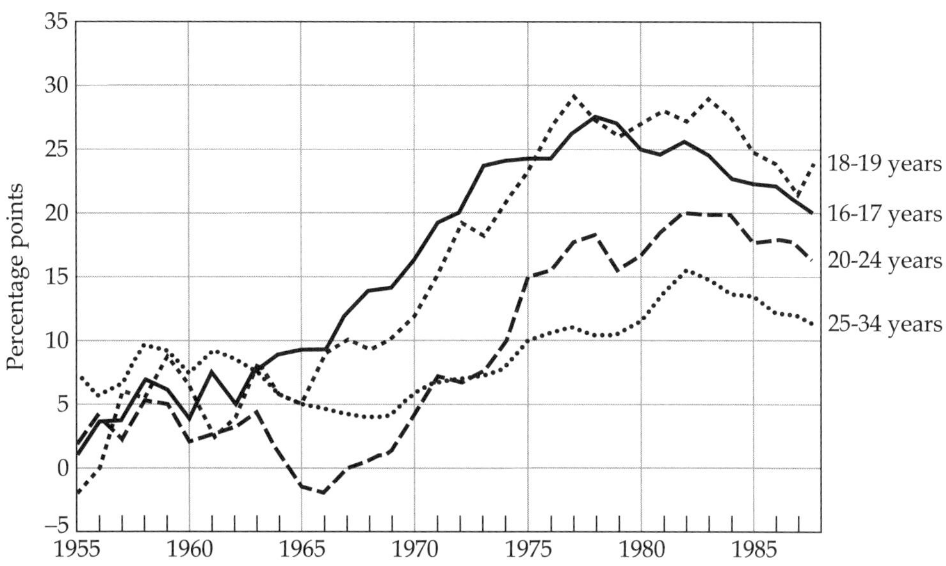

Source: Hernandez (1993) fig. 10.1, p. 403.

Changes in Fathers' Income

The substantial increases in the relative and official poverty rates for children between the late 1970s and the mid-1990s have been associated with similar declines in the income of working men, especially those in the prime ages for fathering and rearing children. In addition, after the early 1970s, especially after 1979, the proportion of men with "low earnings," that is, annual earnings less than the official poverty level for a four-person family, increased sharply (McNeil 1992). Especially striking is the deterioration after 1979 of the earnings of male year-round, full-time workers of the usual ages when children are in the home (figure 2.11). The proportion of men aged eighteen to twenty-four with low earnings dropped from 35 percent to 17 percent between 1964 and 1974 but jumped to 40 percent by 1990. Similarly, the proportion of men aged twenty-five to thirty-four with low earnings fell from 12 percent to only 5 percent but then rose to 15 percent, and the proportion for men aged thirty-five to fifty-four with low earnings decreased from 13 to 5 percent but then increased to 9 percent.

The trends were similar for white and black males with year-round, full-time work, but a much higher proportion of blacks than whites had low earnings. Of such workers who were white, the proportion dropped from 15 percent to 7 per-

FIGURE 2.11 / Year-Round Full-time Male Workers with Low Annual Earnings, 1964, 1969, 1974, 1979, 1984, 1989, and 1990

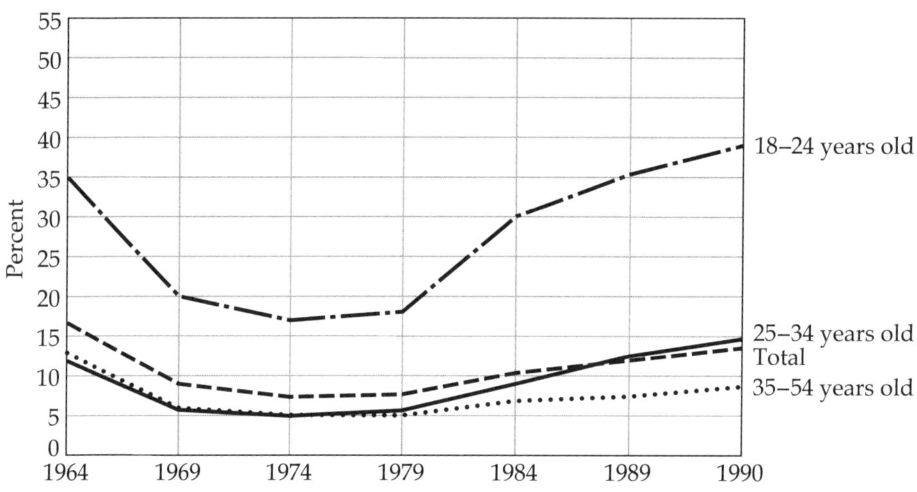

Source: McNeil (1992).

cent between 1964 and 1974 but rose to 13 percent by 1990. Among black male year-round, full-time workers, the proportion with low earnings decreased from a very high 38 percent to 14 percent between 1964 and 1974 but jumped to 22 percent by 1990. Among male year-round, full-time workers of Hispanic origin, the proportion with low earnings also increased sharply between 1974 and 1990, from 12 percent to 28 percent. Finally, among husbands in married-couple families who were year-round, full-time workers, the proportion with low earnings plummeted from 13 percent to 5 percent between 1964 and 1974 but jumped to 9 percent by 1990.

In light of the steep declines during the late 1960s in the proportion of working men and husbands whose incomes could not lift a family of four out of official poverty and the similarly steep increases after 1974 and especially after 1979, it is not surprising that trends in relative and official poverty rates followed a similar pattern from 1969 to 1993. Children experienced large increases in relative and official poverty after 1969 and especially after 1979.

Of course, children living in mother-only families have substantially less income available from their fathers than do children living with both parents. According to one recent and prominent upper-bound estimate, for example, changes in family structure account for nearly one-half of the 4.5 percentage point increase in official child poverty rates between 1980 and 1988 (Eggebeen and Lichter 1991). Unfortunately, this statistic is an overestimate of the effect in the context of demographic accounting resulting from a substantial improvement during the early

1980s in the identification of mother-only families in the Current Population Survey, which provides the basis for the estimate. As a result, the actual increase is substantially less than the measured estimate, and the 2.3 percentage point estimate of the effect of mother-only families on poverty is more accurately 1.5 percentage points or a bit less. Hence, while about one-third of the increase in child poverty during the 1980s can be accounted for by the rise in mother-only families, about two-thirds of the increase is unrelated and is directly accounted for by declining income.[4]

In other words, aside from the rise in mother-only families, childhood poverty rates and trends were affected directly by historic trends in the proportion of children living with fathers who work full-time but have low incomes and of those living with fathers who have only part-time work or are jobless in any given year. Both of these features of fathers' work also indirectly but importantly affect childhood poverty through their influence on divorce and out-of-wedlock childbearing. That is, the role of fathers' low income in fostering the rise in mother-only families and its influence on mothers' labor force participation have influenced historic trends both in the amount of income in the home and in divorce (Eggebeen and Lichter 1991; Hernandez 1993).

The importance of low incomes among absent fathers can be seen in estimates by Sorensen (1995). With a perfect child support system, according to Sorensen, access to absent fathers' income would have reduced the number of children officially classified as poor in 1989 by one million or less, that is, by less than 10 percent.[5] The official poverty rate for all children in 1989 would have been reduced by 1–2 percentage points, from 19.6 percent to about 18 percent. With a perfect child support system in 1993, then, the official poverty rate for children might have been reduced from about 23 percent to about 21 percent.

CONCLUSIONS

In the 1940s, even in the 1960s, childhood poverty probably was viewed as resulting mainly from the fathers' unemployment, unstable employment, lack of full-time employment, and low earnings. Today, poverty is often seen as resulting from the rise of mother-only families.

While the rise of mother-only families is without doubt increasingly important as a proximate cause of childhood poverty, the historical analysis presented here strongly suggests that employment insecurity and low earnings for fathers continue to be prime determinants of the levels of and the trends in childhood poverty, both because of their direct effect on family income and because of their indirect contribution to the rise in mother-only families. This analysis also strongly suggests that mothers' employment has become increasingly important in determining childhood poverty levels and trends, both directly because of the income mothers bring into the home and indirectly by facilitating separation and divorce.

In short, today, as was the case in the 1940s, childhood poverty trends do not mainly follow trends in mother-only families that are independent of economic factors; instead those trends mainly respond to the economic and employment experiences of fathers and mothers.

NOTES

1. In 1993 median family income was $36,857, and the relative poverty threshold for a family of four was $18,428.50, while the official poverty threshold for a family of four with two adults and two children was $14,654. The median income figure used here was estimated directly from microdata files based on specific dollar income values, while the figure of $36,959 published by the U.S. Bureau of the Census is obtained by interpolating within broader income categories.
2. With family size adjustments based on the equivalence scales implicit in the official poverty measure, "near-poor" is defined as above the relative poverty level but less than 75 percent of the median, "middle-class comfort" is defined as above the near-poor level but less than 50 percent of the median, and "luxury" is defined as 150 percent or more of the median.
3. For a discussion of the additional effects of noncash benefits, health, insurance, and taxes, see Hernandez (1993: 253–59).
4. See Saluter (1986: 8) for a discussion of the improved measurement procedures. Perhaps as much as 1.0 percentage point of the 2.3 percentage point increase in official poverty attributed to family structure change may be an artifact of improved measurement.
5. Sorensen (1995) estimates that 1.4 million people would be lifted out of poverty by a perfect child support system. Sorensen (personal communication, February 1995) estimated that these people live in 0.4 million families. If there were one adult in each of these families, that is, 0.4 million adults, the number of children in these families would be 1.0 million. Since some of these families have additional adults, typically because the mother has (re)married and a stepfather is in the home, the estimate of 1.0 million children lifted out of poverty is somewhat high.

Chapter 3

Parent Absence or Poverty: Which Matters More?

Sara S. McLanahan

Poverty and economic insecurity, though important determinants of successful child development, are not the only factors affecting children's well-being. Parents' education, the number of siblings, and the presence or absence of both parents in the household also govern the quality and quantity of parental resources and ultimately children's development. In this chapter I focus on one of these factors: whether both parents live in the household. Whereas two of the parental resources above have been changing in ways that favor child development—more parental education, fewer siblings—the proportion of children growing up with both biological parents declined dramatically from the 1960s to the 1990s. In 1960, approximately 12 percent of all children were living apart from one of their parents. In 1995 the number approached 40 percent. Demographers estimate that over half of all children born in the early 1980s will live apart from a parent before reaching age eighteen (Bumpass 1984). The increase in family instability and single parenthood has stimulated considerable concern among policy makers and the public more generally. Part of this concern is over the fact that children in one-parent families, especially those in mother-only families, have extraordinarily high poverty rates. About half of mother-only families in the United States are poor during any given year. Another part of the concern arises from fears about welfare costs and long-term dependency. About 50 percent of mother-only families receive welfare during the course of a year, and a nontrivial proportion are on welfare for long periods of time. The latter raises questions about whether welfare does more harm than good and whether it leads to intergenerational dependence. Finally, many people are concerned over what they see as a decline in "family values." They view the increase in divorce and nonmarital childbearing as indicators of a flight from parental responsibility and a rise in individualism, and they worry about the loss of community and social capital. Underlying all of these concerns—poverty, welfare dependence, and social values—is a shared concern for children and for what changes in family structure mean for the next generation of Americans.

Below I address several questions about the effects of family structure on children's well-being and development. Next, I examine the papers in this volume to see whether children who grow up with only one of their parents are less successful, on average, than children who grow up with both parents. I also look at whether differences are consistent across different indicators of children's well-being and whether they persist into adulthood. I then examine the variation among different types of nonintact families: growing up with a never-married mother versus growing up with a divorced mother, recent family disruptions versus early disruptions, and the effect of remarriage. These variations are important insofar as policy makers often treat different types of single-parent families differently. Many welfare reform proposals, for example, impose harsh penalties on unwed mothers; others provide incentives to encourage remarriage. A final set of questions deals with the size and persistence of family structure effects relative to the effects of income.

Chapters 5 and 7–17 in this volume serve as my database. Although the primary purpose of each paper was to examine how income is related to children's well-being, the authors also examined how particular types of family structures are related to children's well-being before and after controlling for differences in income. Thus, their findings, reported in the tables labeled "Replication Analysis" in each chapter, can be used to answer the questions posed above.

Before discussing the results, three caveats are in order. First, the family structure "effects" discussed in this chapter are based on correlational evidence, not experimental data. Therefore, some unobserved variable, such as alcoholism or lack of parental commitment, might be responsible for the correlation between family structure and children's well-being. This qualification applies to poverty effects as well. A second caveat has to do with the inability to sort out the causal relationships between family structure and income. Research has established that divorce and single parenthood increase poverty, and that poverty and economic instability increase divorce and out-of-wedlock childbearing. But none of the studies in the database distinguishes between these two effects. I discuss this limitation later. Finally, in all of these studies income is more likely than family structure to be measured with error, which means that the poverty coefficients are likely to be biased downward relative to the family structure coefficients.

BACKGROUND

The social science perspective on the importance of family structure in determining children's well-being has undergone several changes since the 1960s. The prevailing wisdom prior to 1970 was that divorce and single parenthood had large, negative consequences for children's intellectual achievement and social adjustment. In the early 1970s researchers critical of the previous work on methodological grounds challenged this view, arguing that the negative outcomes associated with single parenthood were due primarily to poverty and racial discrimination

(Herzog and Sudia 1973). During the 1970s, a number of ethnographic studies lent support to this alternative hypothesis by highlighting the strengths of single-parent families and by documenting the extended-family networks upon which poor single mothers relied for emotional and economic support (Stack 1974). These ethnographic studies made it clear that single mothers were not raising their children alone.

But just as the early view of single parenthood painted an overly negative picture, the revisionist perspective was overly positive. And as new data became available during the late 1970s, the pendulum began to swing back toward a more skeptical assessment of the consequences of family dissolution. Inspired by the findings of two small, longitudinal studies of middle-class families undergoing divorce, researchers began to mine the large national data sets for more conclusive evidence (Wallerstein and Kelly 1980; Hetherington et al. 1983; Furstenberg et al. 1987). After a decade of research, a new consensus has emerged with regard to the effects of family structure on children: children who grow up with only one biological parent are less successful, on average, than children who grow up with both parents. These differences extend to a broad range of outcomes, and they persist into adulthood (McLanahan and Sandefur 1994; Haveman and Wolfe 1991; Cherlin and Furstenberg 1991; Amato and Keith 1991; Seltzer 1994). The size of the family structure effect ranges from small to moderate depending on the outcome being examined. Measures of cognitive achievement, such as test scores, grade point average (GPA), and years of school, show rather modest effects. In contrast, indicators of behavioral problems, such as skipping school and early childbearing, show more substantial effects.

The cause of the parent's absence is less important than the absence itself. Children raised by never-married mothers do nearly as well as children raised by divorced and separated mothers (once mothers' education and race are taken into account), and both do worse than children raised by both biological parents. Children raised by widowed mothers are the exception: by most accounts they do as well as children from intact families. The timing of family disruption is not very important. Disruptions in adolescence are often just as harmful as disruptions in early childhood. Nor is the length of time spent in a single-parent family a significant determinant of children's well-being.

Perhaps the most surprising finding to emerge from the recent research is that remarriage does not mitigate the negative consequences of single parenthood. Children raised in stepparent families do just about as well (or as poorly) as children raised in single-parent families do. This finding suggests that income is not the only factor accounting for the negative effects of a parent's absence. However, income is clearly the most important factor. It explains about 50 percent of the difference in the educational achievement of children raised in one- and two-parent families. Aside from economic hardship, children raised by only one parent are disadvantaged in two other areas: they receive less parental supervision (especially from their fathers), and they have less social capital (because their families move more often). These two factors account for the remaining differences in children's well-being.

DOES FAMILY STRUCTURE MATTER?

The first question I ask in regard to the twelve studies is simply, does family structure matter?[1] Does living apart from a biological parent, usually the father, reduce a child's chances of success? Are certain areas of children's well-being more vulnerable to a parent's absence than others? Are negative consequences more likely to appear in childhood than in adulthood? Table 3.1 summarizes the information on these questions from chapters 5 and 7–17.

The child well-being indicators are grouped into six domains: test scores, educational attainment, behavioral problems, psychological problems, jobs and income, and physical health. These domains were selected both because they represent important and distinct areas of children's well-being and because the authors chose to focus on them. Each domain incorporates evidence from at least three data sets.

Test scores include IQ tests (Stanford-Binet and the Wechsler Preschool and Primary Scale of Intelligence) and cognitive ability tests (the Peabody Picture Vocabulary Test, the Peabody Individual Achievement Test, and the Armed Forces Qualifying Test). Measures of *educational attainment* include grade retention, GPA, high school graduation, college attendance, and college graduation. *Behavioral problems* include school behavior problems, hyperactivity, and fighting. Teen out-of-wedlock childbearing is also in this domain. *Psychological problems* include externalizing behavior (that is, "acting"), internalizing behavior such as anxiety and depression, and low self-esteem. *Jobs and income* include hourly wages, work experience, occupational status, and poverty status, and *health* includes measures of wasting and stunting, chronic health, and early mortality. Grouping the outcome measures according to domain will show whether the answer to the question (Does family structure matter?) is more consistent in some domains than in others. Organizing the studies by the age of the respondents will show whether the effects of a parent's absence are concentrated in childhood or adolescence or occur throughout the life course.

To determine whether family structure matters for children's well-being, I examined the coefficients from the models that do not control for family income. Most of the authors treated family structure as a set of dummy variables based on what the marital status of the mother was (divorced or separated, never married, remarried, widowed) and whether the disruption was recent or not. If any of the family structure coefficients in a particular domain was statistically significant, I recorded a *yes* in the relevant column in table 3.1. I took this rather liberal approach for several reasons. First, none of the authors tested the statistical significance of the differences among family structure categories. Second, splitting nonintact families into multiple categories reduces the number of cases in each group, which makes it more difficult to find statistically significant effects. Third, not all family structures are mutually exclusive. Most children in stepfamilies, for example, have also lived in single-parent families. Thus, learning that living in a stepfamily reduces children's well-being reveals something about living

TABLE 3.1 / Does Family Structure Matter for Children's Well-Being?

	Domain						
Chapter and Research Team	Age of Respondents (Years)	Test Scores	Educational Attainment	Behavioral Problems	Psychological Problems	Jobs and Income	Health
7. Smith, Brooks-Gunn, and Klebanov							
Infant Health and Development Program	2–8	yes[a]					
National Longitudinal Survey of Youth	2–8	mix[b]					
5. Korenman and Miller	5						no[c]
8. Hanson, McLanahan, and Thomson	5–18		yes	yes	yes		
9. Lipman and Offord	8–16		mix	yes	yes		yes
10. Pagani-Kurtz, Boulerice, and Tremblay	12		yes	yes	yes		
11. Conger, Conger, and Elder	14–17		yes				
14. Haveman, Wolfe, and Wilson	21–27		yes	yes			
16. Axinn, Duncan, and Thornton	23		yes		no		
12. Peters and Mullis	24–25	yes	yes			mix	
13. Teachman, Paasch, Day, and Carver	25		no				
15. Corcoran and Adams	24–31					yes	
17. Hauser and Sweeney	34, 54		yes		no	mix	mix

Source: Data from chapters 5 and 7–17.

a. Evidence of a positive effect.

b. Contradictory evidence.

c. Evidence of a negative effect.

in a single-parent family as well. In the next section I discuss whether certain types of single parenthood appear to affect children more negatively than others do.

A *no* in table 3.1 means that a study found no evidence of a negative effect, and *mix* means the evidence was contradictory. The latter can occur because some researchers looked at more than one outcome within a particular domain. Hauser and Sweeney (chapter 17), for example, found that family structure was related to job status but not to poverty. Lipman and Offord (chapter 9) found that it was related to school performance but not to school failure.

Most of the entries in the table are *yes*. Only two research teams found no evidence that family structure matters—Korenman and Miller (chapter 5), who looked at stunting and wasting, and Teachman, Paasch, Day, and Carver (chapter 13), who looked at college attendance, college graduation, and years of schooling. Several other research teams found that family structure mattered in some domains but not in others. Axinn, Duncan, and Thornton (chapter 16), for example, found that a parent's absence reduced educational attainment but not self-esteem. Hauser and Sweeney found that it affected educational and occupational attainment but not depression or poverty.

Perhaps the most surprising findings were those reported by Smith, Brooks-Gunn, and Klebanov (chapter 7). In their analysis of the children in the National Longitudinal Survey of Youth (NLSY), they found very little evidence that a parent's absence was related to children's test scores. Indeed, living with a divorced single mother increased the reading scores of NLSY children, and living with a recently divorced mother increased math scores. These results are something of an anomaly and may be due to the fact that the children in the NLSY were born to younger-than-average mothers. Whatever the reason, these results invite future investigation on whether NLSY children in divorced families continue to do better than their peers as they grow older.

Across domains, family structure appears to be more important in some areas of children's well-being than in others. *Behavioral problems* show the most consistent negative effects. All four of the studies that examined children's outcomes in this domain found that a parent's absence was associated with more behavioral problems. Hanson, McLanahan, and Thomson (chapter 8) found that family disruption increased school behavior problems. Pagani, Boulerice, and Tremblay (chapter 11) found more fighting and hyperactivity among children from nonintact families, and Lipman and Offord found evidence of social impairment. In addition, Haveman, Wolfe, and Wilson (chapter 14) found that girls from nonintact families were more likely to become unwed teen mothers than were girls from intact families.

The indicators of *psychological problems* also show a consistent pattern, although the negative effects appear to decline with age. Studies of school-aged children found that parent absence increased psychological problems, whereas studies of adults found no differences between children raised in intact and nonintact families. Axinn, Duncan, and Thornton, for example, found no differences in self-esteem at age twenty-three, and Hauser and Sweeney found no differences in depression. These studies suggest that some of the psychological problems associated with family disruption may be limited to the period shortly before and after divorce or at least to the time the child is living at home.

Educational attainment received the most attention of all the domains. With one exception (Teachman et al.) all of the research teams that examined this set of indicators found at least some evidence that a parent's absence had negative consequences for children's school achievement. Hanson, McLanahan, and Thomson; Conger, Conger, and Elder (chapter 10), Lipman and Offord; and Pagani, Boulerice, and Tremblay found negative effects on school performance; Peters and Mullis (chapter 12) and Haveman, Wolfe, and Wilson found that children from nonintact families were less likely to graduate from high school, and Peters and Mullis and Hauser and Sweeney reported lower rates of college attendance and graduation.

The fact that family disruption has stronger and more consistent effects on educational attainment than on test scores suggests that something besides cognitive ability is responsible for the poorer school performance of children from nonintact families. Problem behavior may be the culprit here. Although some of the "acting out" that accompanies family instability may be short-lived, it can have lasting consequences if it occurs at a critical time in the child's life. Irregular school attendance and risky sexual behavior in adolescence, for example, can lead to early childbearing, premature exits from school, or both, which often have irreversible consequences.

The evidence for the *jobs and income* domain was more mixed. Peters and Mullis found that family structure was not related to hourly wages. They did report, however, that father's absence reduced work experience, especially men's experience. The latter finding is consistent with recent studies showing that young men from nonintact families are more likely to be "idle"—neither at work nor in school—in their early twenties than are young men from intact families (McLanahan and Sandefur 1994; Haveman and Wolfe 1994). Hauser and Sweeney also found that fathers' absence was negatively related to occupational attainment. With respect to income, the studies were mixed. Corcoran and Adams (chapter 15) found that living in a nonintact family increased the risk of poverty in young adulthood, whereas Hauser and Sweeney found no effects on either poverty or income in midlife.

The evidence for physical *health* was also mixed. Korenman and Miller found no evidence that family disruption was related to stunting or wasting among preschool children; Lipman and Offord found more chronic health problems among slightly older children. Hauser and Sweeney found no differences in the physical health of people in their fifties, yet respondents raised in nonintact families were more likely to die prematurely. The people in Hauser and Sweeney's sample were born in the early 1940s, which means that death was a more important reason for the absence of a parent for this population. Thus, the correlation between family structure and premature death may be due to a genetic vulnerability that caused higher mortality among both parents and offspring. (The other studies were based on respondents born in the 1960s and later.)

DOES TYPE OF FAMILY STRUCTURE MATTER?

The next question is whether the type of nonintact family matters. Is growing up with a divorced mother better than growing up with a never-married mother? Are early disruptions worse than later disruptions? Is it better to live with a single father than a single mother? Does remarriage help? Most of the thirteen studies distinguished among different types of nonintact families, and many used the same categories. Thus, the estimates reported in the replication analysis tables shed at least some light on the questions posed above. The answers, however, must be viewed as very tentative since, as noted, none of the authors tested the statistical significance of differences between family structure coefficients.

Table 3.2 reports the evidence on different types of nonintact families from nine studies. Two—Korenman and Miller and Teachman et al.—found no evidence of family structure effects, and Conger, Conger, and Elder as well as Corcoran and Adams used single indicators of nonintact family structure. Thus only nine of the thirteen studies contain information on variation within different types of nonintact families.

The authors looked at several types of nonintact families, including stepfamilies and families headed by divorced, never married, and widowed mothers. Some researchers combined divorced and never-married parents into one category, and several distinguished between recent and long-term disruptions.

The information on types of nonintact families is more difficult to summarize than that on family structure in general. Not all of the authors used the same categories, so simply counting the number of times a particular category appears is not possible. Instead, I adjusted the counts by the number of times a category *might* have appeared. All nine studies contained information on stepfamilies; six, on families headed by divorced parents; four, on never-married mothers; three, on divorced and never-married mothers combined; two, on widowed parents; Three studies identified recent disruptions (see column two in table 3.2).

If all of the family structure categories in a particular study were statistically significant (about one-third of the time), I wrote *all* in the table. Families headed by divorced parents were the most consistent in terms of their effect on children. The divorce coefficient was negative and significant in eleven out of twelve possible times (entries with either *all* or *div* in the table).[2] This includes studies that found either the recent divorce or longterm divorce coefficient statistically significant. The only exception is the study by Smith, Brooks-Gunn, and Klebanov, which found that divorce increased the test scores of the children in the NLSY.

Eight studies looked at the combined effects of living with a divorced mother or never-married mother. Seven show that growing up with a divorced or never-married mother reduces children's well-being. The only exception is the study by Peters and Mullis, which found that single parenthood was not related to test scores. Notably, both studies that found the divorce (or single-parent) coefficient not statistically significant used children's test scores as the outcome.

TABLE 3.2 / Does Type of Family Structure Matter for Children's Well-Being?

	Domain						
Chapter and Research Team	Types of Nonintact Families Studied	Test Scores	Educational Attainment	Behavioral Problems	Psychological Problems	Jobs and Income	Health
7. Smith, Brooks-Gunn, and Klebanov							
Infant Health and Development Program	div, nm, rec, stp	all, rec					
National Longitudinal Survey of Youth	div, nm, rec, stp	stp, rec					
8. Hanson, McLanahan, and Thomson	div, nm, stp		div, nm	all	all		
9. Lipman and Offord	div, nm, rec, stp		div, rec	div, rec	div, nm, rec		div
10. Pagani, Boulerice, and Tremblay	rec, sig, stp		rec, sig	all, rec	all, rec		
14. Haveman, Wolfe, and Wilson	sig, stp		all	sig			
16. Axinn, Duncan, and Thornton	div, stp, wid		div, stp				
12. Peters and Mullis	sig, stp	stp	all			sig	
17. Hauser and Sweeney	div, stp, wid		div, stp			div, stp	

Source: Data from chapters 5 and 7–17.

nm = never married; div = divorced; wid = widowed; stp = stepfamily; rec = recent disruption; sig = single parent (divorced, widowed, or never married); all = types of nonintact family studies.

Four studies looked at never-married mothers, for a total of nine estimates; five showed statistically significant effects. That children raised by never-married mothers do no worse than children raised by divorced mothers may surprise some readers, but the results are quite robust, and they are consistent with those reported in other studies. In contrast, living with a widowed parent appears to be much less harmful than living with a divorced or never-married mother. Both Axinn, Duncan, and Thornton and Hauser and Sweeney found that children who grow up with widowed parents do just about as well as children who grow up with both biological parents.

All of the studies provided information on stepfamilies, and over half found that remarriage reduced children's well-being. In the recent literature on family disruption and children's well-being, numerous researchers have found that remarriage is no panacea for single parenthood, despite the fact that it increases family income. Notably, the stepfamily coefficient is less likely to be statistically significant when the outcome is educational attainment (as opposed to behavioral problems or psychological adjustment). All of the researchers who looked at educational outcomes among school-aged children (Hanson, McLanahan, and Thomson, Lipman and Offord, and Pagani, Boulerice, and Tremblay) found that children in stepfamilies were doing about as well as children in original two-parent families.[3] However, those who looked at high school graduation and college attainment found that growing up in a stepfamily was associated with lowered educational attainment.

Recent disruptions appear to be especially harmful. Nearly all of the studies that looked at recent disruptions found negative and statistically significant effects. This suggests that some of the negative consequences associated with divorce and remarriage may be short lived. Three studies looked at whether family disruption had different effects on girls and boys. Two found that a parent's absence was worse for girls—Lipman and Offord on school performance and Corcoran and Adams on poverty—and one found that it was worse for boys—Peters and Mullis on work experience (not shown).

WHICH MATTERS MORE: INCOME OR FAMILY STRUCTURE?

A final set of questions deals with the relationship between family structure and income. Do family structure effects persist after income is taken into account? Which has a greater effect, a parent's absence or poverty? As noted, other researchers have found that income accounts for as much as half of the lower achievement among children from nonintact families (McLanahan and Sandefur 1994; Hanson et al. 1995). The twelve studies in the database permit a test of the robustness of this finding across other data sets and other child outcomes.

The question of whether income "accounts for" the negative consequences associated with single parenthood is part of a larger debate over whether the absence of a father itself reduces children's well-being, or whether it is just a proxy for economic disadvantage. For some people, saying that income accounts for the family structure effect is equivalent to saying that family structure does not matter, but the truth is not so simple. Even a finding that the family structure coefficient was not statistically significant once income was taken into account would not necessarily mean that the absence of a parent had no negative consequences for children. The proverbial "chicken or egg" problem would persist: was low income a cause or consequence of family disruption? If poverty or economic instability caused the family to break up, then it would make sense to say that family structure itself had no harmful effects on children's well-being. Alternatively, if family disruption pushed the family into poverty, the conclusion would have to be that family structure mattered. These two interpretations have important implications for policy makers who want to minimize the negative consequences associated with single parenthood.

None of the studies distinguished between pre- and postdivorce income, so the issue of whether poverty or family structure came first cannot be resolved. However, it is possible to look at whether the effects of family structure persisted after income was taken into account. If they did, something other than poverty was responsible for the lower school performance and higher incidence of problem behavior among children in nonintact families. In addition to examining the extent to which income might "account for" the effects of family structure, I also look at which of the two effects is larger (more negative)—coming from a nonintact family or coming from a poor family. Here I simply compare the two coefficients for family structure and poverty.

Table 3.3 summarizes the findings for this set of questions. Here I used the coefficients for divorced, unmarried, or single mother (whichever was larger). I did not include the coefficients for stepfamilies since they did not change very much when income was taken into account. Thus the entries in the table show whether the effects of living with an unmarried mother persisted, did not persist, or were inconsistent after income was taken into account.

The researchers measured poverty differently. Some distinguished between long- and short-term poverty, others distinguished between early and late poverty, and still others compared families below the poverty line with families at different points above the poverty line. Two studies (Hanson, McLanahan, and Thomson and Hauser and Sweeney) did not measure poverty per se but compared families at different points above and below the poverty line. To measure the effects of poverty in these studies, I used the coefficients that contrasted poor families with families earning one to two times the poverty line.

Several aspects of the data on the effects of family structure and poverty are noteworthy. First, there are many more *yes* than *no* entries in table 3.3. In the majority of studies, family structure effects persisted even after differences in poverty status were taken into account. This does not mean that income explained none of the family structure effect in these studies. With few exceptions, nearly all of the single-parent coefficients became smaller once the poverty variables

TABLE 3.3 / Does Family Structure Matter More Than Poverty for Children's Well-Being?

Chapter and Research Team	Domain: Test Scores	Educational Attainment	Behavioral Problems	Psychological Problems	Jobs and Income	Health
7. Smith, Brooks-Gunn, and Klebanov						
Infant Health and Development Program	yes[a] <[b]					
National Longitudinal Survey of Youth	no[c] <					
8. Hanson, McLanahan, and Thomson		yes =[d]	yes >[e]	yes >		
9. Lipman and Offord		yes =	yes >	yes >		yes >
10. Pagani-Kurtz, Boulerice, and Tremblay		no <	yes >	yes >		
11. Conger, Conger, and Elder		yes <				
14. Haveman, Wolfe, and Wilson		yes <	yes >			
16. Axinn, Duncan, and Thornton		yes =				
12. Peters and Mullis	no <	no <			yes >	
13. Teachman, Paasch, Day, and Carver						
15. Corcoran and Adams					yes <	
17. Hauser and Sweeney		yes/no >, <			yes >	yes >

Source: See table 3.1.

a. Family structure effect persisted after income was added to the model.

b. Family structure effect is smaller than poverty effect.

c. Family structure effect did not persist after income was added to the model.

d. Family structure effect equals poverty effect.

e. Family structure effect is larger than poverty effect.

were added to the models. Rather, the results indicate that poverty and low income are not the only factors that account for differences in the well-being of children in intact and nonintact families.

The data also show whether the net effects of family structure on child well-being were smaller (or larger) than the net effects of poverty. Of the twenty-four entries, twelve indicate that the parent absence coefficient was larger (more negative) than the poverty coefficient. Nine entries show more negative effects for poverty, and three show equal effects. Notice that eight of the nine entries showing more negative effects of poverty appear in the domains of test scores and educational achievement, as do all three of the entries showing equal effects. These findings suggest the net effects of poverty on cognitive ability and school achievement are equal to or larger than the net effects of family disruption. In contrast, for three other outcomes—behavioral problems, psychological problems, and health—the findings suggest that parent absence is more important than income.[4]

SUMMARY AND CONCLUSION

Does family structure affect children's well-being? The answer is overwhelmingly yes. All but two of the studies in chapters 5 and 7–17 found that growing up in a nonintact family had negative consequences for children's well-being across a broad range of outcomes.

This result does not mean that all types of nonintact families have similar consequences. Indeed, the answer to the second question—does the type of family structure matter?—is also yes. Although this conclusion must be tentative, it is fair to say that living in some types of nonintact families is more difficult for children than living in others. Growing up with a divorced or never-married mother is almost always associated with lower educational attainment and more behavioral and psychological problems. In contrast, growing up with a widowed parent is almost never associated with poorer outcomes for children. The timing of the parent's absence matters as well. Recent disruptions, including both divorce and remarriage, are especially difficult for children.

The evidence is inconclusive with respect to sex differences. For some outcomes, family disruption appears to have more negative effects on girls; for others, on boys. But there is no clear pattern in these results.

Does remarriage help? The twelve studies demonstrate quite clearly that remarriage is not a panacea for divorce or out-of-wedlock childbearing. Although children in stepfamilies fare somewhat better than children in single-parent families in educational attainment, they do somewhat worse based on measures of behavioral and psychological problems. Thus, the answer to the question depends on the outcome.

Does family structure matter more than income? The answer is also ambiguous. The twelve studies show that although family structure is related to poverty, the two are not proxies for one another. In most instances, coming from a nonintact family reduces a child's chances of success, even after low income is taken into account. In some instances, the net effect of family structure is larger than the net effect of poverty: on others, it is smaller. Based on these studies, I suspect that family structure is more important than poverty in determining behavioral and psychological problems, whereas poverty is more important than family structure in determining educational attainment.

The fact that parent absence still matters after taking income into account does not imply that policy makers should not try to minimize the economic distress of single mothers. Indeed, based on what is known to date, reducing the economic insecurity of families headed by single mothers is probably the most effective tool for protecting children from the negative consequences of family disruption. Reducing poverty might also mitigate some of the negative effects of living in a stepfamily. If single mothers were more economically secure, they might take more time in selecting a new partner, which, in turn, might make remarriage more beneficial for children.

NOTES

1. The paper by Smith et al. (chapter 7) contains two sets of analyses that we treat as two separate studies.
2. The six studies that look at *divorced* parents yield twelve different estimates.
3. The exception was the math scores for seven- and eight-year-olds. Children in stepfamilies did worse on this measure than children in original two-parent families.
4. Hauser and Sweeney found that the divorce coefficient was larger than the income coefficient in one instance—college attendance. They also found that the poverty coefficient was larger for college graduation.

Chapter 4

Trends in the Economic Well-Being and Life Chances of America's Children

Susan E. Mayer

Children raised in poor families are more likely than affluent children to drop out of high school and to have a baby as a teenager. When poor children grow up, they get less education, are less likely to work, earn lower wages when they do, and are more likely to become single parents than affluent children. A common view is that the economic well-being of children's families began to deteriorate in the 1970s, and that, as a consequence, children's chances for success also deteriorated.

The first section of this chapter describes the theories that try to explain why parents' income influences children's outcomes. The second section describes trends in parents' economic well-being since 1959. In the third section I assess trends in dropping out of high school, teenage childbearing, single motherhood among young women, years of schooling completed among young adults, young men's wages and earnings, and what I call male "idleness"—the chance that a twenty-four-year-old male who is not in school did no paid work in the previous year. I find that trends in neither the level nor the distribution of these outcomes follow trends in parents' income. The last section explores plausible explanations for the divergence in these trends.

PARENTS' INCOME AND CHILDREN'S OUTCOMES

Two theories of the way parents' income affects children's life chances—what I call the *investment* theory and the *good-parent* theory—dominate social science. These theories differ about whether the absolute level of parents' income or parents' income relative to the income of other families is important to children's outcomes. This distinction is important because, as the next section shows, parents' income increased rapidly in the 1960s, but inequality hardly changed. Then, in the 1970s and 1980s, parents' income grew slowly, but inequality increased.

According to the investment theory, the relationship between parents' and children's economic success is the result of endowments that parents pass on to their children combined with what parents invest in their children (Becker 1991; Becker and Tomes 1986). Endowments include both biological traits, such as a child's sex and race, and cultural traits, such as placing a high value on education. Parents invest both time and money in their children's "human capital," especially by investing in their education but also by purchasing health, food, housing, and other goods and services that improve children's future well-being. How much parents invest in their children is determined by their own values and norms, their ability to finance investments (which is influenced by their income and their access to capital), and by the availability of alternative sources of investment, such as government programs.

The investment theory holds that children raised in affluent families succeed more often than those raised in poor families because rich parents both pass on superior endowments and can invest more in their children. Investment models imply that parents' absolute purchasing power influences children's life chances, because the importance of income derives from what it buys. Thus if parents' income increases, children's outcomes will improve, at least if other major influences stay more or less the same. If the income of rich parents increases faster than the income of poor parents, the outcomes of both rich and poor children will improve but at different rates. In principle, growth in inequality could affect some behaviors if higher demand among the rich increases the price of some goods. If, for example, the demand for post-secondary education increases as a result of higher incomes among the rich, poor children will be less likely to attend college even if their families' real income remains the same.

In contrast to the investment theory, the good-parent theory holds that low income hurts children, not because poor parents have less money to invest in their children but because low income decreases the quality of parents' nonmonetary investments, such as their interactions with their children. This in turn hurts children's chances for success.

There are at least two versions of the good-parent theory: the *parental stress* version and the *role-model* version. The parental stress version holds that poverty is stressful and that stress diminishes parents' ability to be supportive, consistent, and involved with their children (McLoyd 1990; Pearlin et al. 1981; Huston et al. 1994; Elder 1974; Elder, Liker, and Cross 1984; Elder, Van Nguyen, and Caspi 1985; Conger et al. 1992). Poor parenting, in turn, hurts the social and emotional development of children, which limits their educational and social opportunities.[1]

This model implies that parents' relative economic standing, as well as their absolute level of economic resources, may be important to children's well-being. If parental stress mostly depends on how much parents provide for their family, parents will experience less stress as their income rises. As a result, their parenting practices will improve. If, on the other hand, parents' stress mostly depends on how they evaluate their living standard relative to the living standards of other families, parents will experience stress even when their own income grows if it does not grow as fast as the income of others.

The role-model version of this theory holds that, because of their position at the bottom of the social hierarchy, low-income parents develop values, norms, and behaviors that cause them to be "bad" role models for their children. Role-model hypotheses sometimes also hold that this behavior, which is dysfunctional for the middle class, is a rational response to poverty. This hypothesis is likely to describe families experiencing long-term poverty who have adapted to their economic conditions. In families experiencing short-term poverty, stress may have a greater effect on parental behavior.

According to the role-model hypothesis, neither increasing parents' income nor providing parents with the means to invest in their children's human capital is likely to improve children's life chances, at least in the short run, but it could help in the long run by changing parents' values and behavior. A stronger version of the role model hypothesis holds that among families living in a "culture of poverty," values and behavior will not change at all in response to income changes. In either case, short-term trends in parents' income would not predict trends in children's chances for success.

Both the investment and the good-parent theories try to explain why children's chances for success depend on their parents' income. But the fact that poor children fare worse than rich children does not necessarily mean that low parental income per se hurts children. Poor parents differ from rich parents in many ways besides income. For instance, low-income parents usually have less education and are less likely to marry, which could also explain disparities in rich and poor children's life chances. Comparing trends in parents' income to trends in children's outcomes also cannot prove that parental income does or does not affect children's outcomes. Nor can assessing these trends suggest whether the investment or good-parent theory is more likely to be correct, since both imply that the trends should parallel one another and neither makes strong claims about the role of income inequality. Nonetheless, if trends in parental income do parallel trends in children's outcomes, this would strongly suggest that parental income affects children's outcomes. If the trends are not parallel, the conclusion is more ambiguous; it might mean that parents' income does not affect children's outcomes, that factors with a greater effect on children's outcomes changed at the same time as parents' income, or that trends in either children's outcomes or parents' income are mismeasured.

TRENDS IN PARENTS' INCOME

To support the claim that the economic conditions of children have deteriorated, social scientists and policy makers often cite the increase in the poverty rate among children. The official poverty line has been severely criticized on many grounds (Citro and Michael 1995; Mayer and Jencks 1989; Ruggles 1990). For example both the poverty rate in any one year and the trend in the poverty rate are influenced by how poverty thresholds are adjusted for changes in prices, whether families or households are the unit of analysis, and by what data are used (Jencks and Mayer 1996). Here I do not compare trends in the official poverty rate to trends in children's outcomes partly because of the arbitrariness of the official measure and partly because a poverty rate, however accurate, describes only what happened to children at the bottom of the income distribution. It does not describe what happened to average or to affluent children. Those who worry about children's life chances usually do not worry much about what happens at the top of the income distribution, but if relative economic standing rather than absolute economic standing influences children, trends at the top of the income distribution may affect children at the bottom.

Income of the Median Child

Table 4.1 shows trends in the real household income of children between 1959 and 1989 using census data and between 1969 and 1989 using the Current Population Survey (CPS).[2] Trends in economic indicators can be highly sensitive to what years one chooses to discuss, since economic indicators are influenced by the business cycle. Business cycle peaks (assessed as peak years of growth in gross domestic product) occurred in about 1969, 1973, 1979, and 1989, so the table shows years after a peak.

The mean of the third quintile is approximately the median income, so both the census and the CPS data show that the income of the median child's household increased during the 1970s and hardly changed during the 1980s. In the census, household income for the median child increased very rapidly during the 1960s.

These estimates make no adjustment for differences in household size. This strategy makes the unlikely assumption that from a child's viewpoint the benefits of additional siblings (or additional adults) exactly equal the costs. Children's households declined from 4.25 to 3.39 individuals between 1969 and 1989. Table 4.1 also shows estimates of the per capita income of children's households. This adjustment assumes that when household size doubles, household income must also double for the household to maintain the same living standard. It thus assumes that there are no economies of scale in larger households. These two alternative adjustments for household size presumably bracket the "true" equivalence scale.

Census data show that median per capita income increased very rapidly in the 1960s. Both census and CPS data show that median per capita income increased sharply in the 1970s and less in the 1980s. In both data sets the increase in per capita median income was much greater than the increase in unadjusted median income in both the 1970s and 1980s. Much of the improvement in real per capita income is thus traceable to declining household size rather than to rising income.

Regardless of the adjustment for family size or the data set, the real household income of the median child grew during the 1970s, then grew at a slower rate during the 1980s.

TABLE 4.1 / Mean Income for Children's Households, by Income Decile or Quintile and Year, 1959–89 (in 1992 Dollars)

Year	Decile		Quintile[a]			
	First	Second	Second	Third	Fourth	Fifth
Household income						
Census data						
1959	3,844	10,752	17,995	25,071	33,112	58,608
1969	6,021	15,662	24,939	34,696	45,834	77,087
1979	5,330	14,527	25,244	37,812	51,155	85,535
1989	4,619	13,467	24,367	37,902	53,826	93,912
Change (%)						
1959–69	56.6	45.7	38.6	38.4	38.4	31.5
1969–79	−11.5	−7.3	1.2	9.0	11.6	11.0
1979–89	−13.3	−7.3	−3.5	0.2	5.2	9.8
1969–89	−23.3	−14.0	−2.3	9.2	17.4	21.8
CPS[b] data						
1969	8,085	16,871	25,338	34,668	45,262	74,449
1979	6,321	14,800	24,941	37,252	50,286	81,047
1989	5,217	13,049	23,490	37,320	53,414	91,292
Change (%)						
1969–79	−21.8	−12.3	−1.6	7.5	11.1	8.9
1979–89	−17.5	−11.8	−5.8	0.2	6.2	12.6
1969–89	−35.5	−22.7	−7.3	7.6	18.0	22.6
Per capita income						
Census data						
1959	781	2,166	3,689	5,215	6,860	11,869
1969	1,353	3,326	5,268	7,217	9,408	15,365
1979	1,402	3,606	6,043	8,718	11,571	18,596
1989	1,247	3,428	5,961	8,988	12,664	21,468
Change (%)						
1959–69	73.2	53.6	42.8	38.4	37.1	29.5
1969–79	3.6	8.4	14.7	20.8	23.0	21.0
1979–89	−11.1	−4.9	−1.4	3.1	9.4	15.4
1969–89	−7.9	3.1	13.2	24.5	34.6	39.7
CPS data						
1969	1,864	3,648	5,354	7,392	9,402	16,238
1979	1,663	3,679	6,026	8,711	11,491	17,399
1989	1,433	3,335	5,778	9,062	12,666	21,006
Change (%)						
1969–79	−10.8	0.9	12.6	17.8	22.2	7.2
1979–89	−13.8	−9.3	−4.1	4.0	10.2	20.7
1969–89	−23.1	−8.6	7.9	22.6	34.7	29.4

Source: Tabulations by David Knutson from census and Current Population Survey data.

a. Means for the top quintile are biased downward due to top-coding.

b. Current Population Survey.

Trends in the median child's household income are sensitive to the way income is adjusted for changes in prices. Most government publications on family income use the consumer price index for urban families (CPI-U). Economists agree that the CPI-U overstated the annual rate of inflation during the 1970s because of the way it computed housing costs. This problem was especially severe during the late 1970s when the cost of buying a new house increased rapidly. In 1983 the error was corrected with the introduction of the CPI-U-X1. It clearly yields a better measure of changes in household income over time than the CPI-U, and I used it in table 4.1 When census data are adjusted for prices using the CPI-U, the median child's real income hardly changed between 1969 and 1989. The same data adjusted using the CPI-U-X1 yields a 9.2 percent increase in real household income between 1969 and 1989.

Many economists prefer to measure price changes using the implicit price deflator for personal consumption expenditures (PCE) in the National Income and Product Accounts. It implies that the real income of the median household with children rose 6.7 percent between 1969 and 1989. The implicit price deflator is difficult to interpret, however, because it does not describe the price of a fixed market basket of goods. The fixed-weight PCE index for the market basket that consumers bought in 1987 rose more slowly than the implicit price deflator. With this index the median income of households with children increased 15.3 percent between 1969 and 1989.

Most economists who study these matters also believe that standard price adjustments underestimate the value of qualitative improvements in the goods and services that consumers buy. If this bias means that the true rate of inflation was 1 point less than the fixed-weight PCE index implies, the purchasing power of the median households with children would have risen by 42 percent between 1969 and 1989. (See Jencks and Mayer 1996 for a discussion of the effect of various measures of price changes on the child poverty rate.)

Although different adjustments for prices yield different conclusions about the extent of the increase in median income between 1969 and 1989, only the discredited CPI-U yields no change.

Income Inequality

According to the census data in table 4.1, during the 1960s income grew faster for low-income than for high-income children, so income inequality declined. However, both CPS and census data show that in the 1970s and the 1980s income unadjusted for household size fell for children in the poorest fifth of the income distribution and grew for children whose households were in the top half of the income distribution. Income inequality thus increased during these decades.

Census and CPS data yield different trends in per capita income during the 1970s. In the census data income increased for children in the poorest 20 percent of families between 1969 and 1979, while CPS data show that income declined over the same period. In both data sets, per capita income fell during the 1980s for children in the poorest fifth of the income distribution, and income increased during both decades for children in the top half of the income distribution.

Regardless of the data set or the adjustment for family size between 1969 and 1989, income grew much more rapidly in the top half of the income distribution than in the bottom half—resulting in an increase in income inequality. However, in the census data the growth in per capita income inequality is almost all attributable to growth in income at the top of the income distribution, and very little to a decline at the bottom of the distribution. Because income grew more at the top of the distribution than in the middle, the relative position of those in the middle deteriorated even though their absolute position improved. Whether the net result is to make children in the middle better or worse off depends on whether relative or absolute economic well-being affects children more.

Annual Versus Permanent Income

All the estimates so far rely on household income measured in only one year. Annual income has two components: a relatively stable, or *permanent*, component which ensures that income in one year is fairly highly correlated with income in other years, and an unstable, or *transitory*, component that keeps the interannual correlation below 1.00. Most economists believe that the transitory component of income has little effect on a family's living standard, because when income is low, parents borrow against future income or use savings from past income in order to consume at the level of their permanent income. As an indicator of children's true economic well-being, most economists would probably measure families' permanent incomes. Studies show that using several years of parents' income increases the intergenerational correlation of income (Solon 1992; Zimmerman 1992). Other studies show that using only one year of income can seriously underestimate the relationship between parents' income and high school graduation (An, Haveman, and Wolfe 1992; Mayer 1997), children's cognitive test scores, teenage childbearing, and educational attainment (Mayer 1997). This implies that trends in families' permanent income more reliably reflect trends in children's well-being.

Unfortunately, no data set actually measures permanent income. But longitudinal data sets can reveal whether inequality in income averaged over several years increased at the same rate as inequality of income measured in a single year. I used the 1989 wave of the Panel Study of Income Dynamics (PSID) to calculate measures of income averaged over 1968–72, 1973–77, 1978–82, and 1983–87. Table 4.2 compares trends in the distribution of these five-year income averages with trends in the distribution of income measured in the year in the middle of the interval. As is well known, there is less inequality in the five-year averages than in a single year.[3]

Inequality grew more for income measured in a single year (the decline in both

TABLE 4.2 / Inequality in Children's Household Income, Measured in One Year and Averaged over Five Years, 1970–87 (1992 Dollars)

	Quintile			Ratio	
Period and Year	First	Third	Fifth	20/50	20/80
One year					
1970	14,171	37,643	80,739	0.376	0.175
1975	13,777	37,998	87,165	0.363	0.158
1980	12,628	39,955	91,616	0.316	0.138
1985	9,446	40,333	93,578	0.234	0.101
Change, 1970–80	−33.3	7.2	15.9	−0.142	−0.074
Five-year average					
1968–72	16,663	38,099	78,687	0.437	0.212
1973–77	16,309	40,003	86,554	0.408	0.188
1978–82	14,798	40,168	88,184	0.368	0.168
1983–87	12,524	40,379	90,247	0.309	0.139
Change, 1970–80	−24.8	6.0	14.7	−0.128	−0.073

Source: Tabulations by Tim Veenstra using the 1989 wave of the Panel Study of Income Dynamics (PSID). Sample includes all children.

the ratio of the 20th to the 50th and of the 20th to the 80th percentile was greater) than for income averaged over five years. But the difference in the trend is too small to be of much interest. For this time period, trends in annual income appear to parallel trends in longer-term income. This finding implies, and other research also shows (Duncan, Smeeding, and Rodgers 1992), that income volatility did not increase much over this period, though it may have increased more in earlier periods.

Income measures produce a relatively consistent story about the economic well-being of the average child: it increased in the 1970s and 1980s. However, the degree of improvement is sensitive to the method used to adjust for prices, the adjustment for household size, and the data set used for the estimates. Income inequality during the 1970s and 1980s grew, but different adjustments for household size and different data sets produce different conclusions about the decline in income at the bottom of the distribution.

TRENDS IN CHILDREN'S OUTCOMES

In this section, I consider the relationship between trends in parents' income and trends in seven outcomes among teenagers and young adults: dropping out of high school, educational attainment, teenage childbearing, single motherhood,

TABLE 4.3 / Children's Outcomes, 1970–90

Children's Outcomes	Year Outcome Measured 1970	1976	1980	1985	1990	Change 1970–80	1980–90
Births per 1,000 women aged 15–19	68.3	53.5	53.0	51.0	59.6	−15.3	6.1
14- to 24-year-olds not graduated from high school and not enrolled (%)	12.2	11.8	12.0	10.6	10.6	−0.2	−1.4
24-year-olds							
Mean years of education	12.4	12.9	12.8	12.8	12.9	0.4	0.1
Hours worked by males last week	41.5	40.8	41.7	41.4	41.0	0.2	−0.7
Males' hourly wage ($1992)	12.58	11.51	11.62	10.35	10.26	−0.96	−1.36
Males idle (%)	6.5	13.4	11.4	13.7	11.6	4.9	0.2
Women who were single mothers (%)	[a]	11.2	10.2	14.1	16.5	[a]	6.3

Sources: Information about births to teenage girls from U.S. Department of Commerce (1993c, table 93). All other estimates by David Knutson using CPS data.

a. Data not available on single mothers in 1970.

men's wages, and hours worked, and the chances that a twenty-four-year-old male who is not in school or the military has not worked for a full year.

Most outcomes are measured at a particular age. An assessment of trends in teenage childbearing, for instance, must compare cohorts of twenty-year-olds, since one cannot tell whether a woman will become a teenage mother until she has had her twentieth birthday. Women who reach the age of twenty in a given year will not necessarily have had the same average family income as children who were under twenty in earlier years. Thus repeated cross-sections of parental income, such as those shown in table 4.1, might not represent the experiences of cohorts of children. Nonetheless, because median income increased over the entire 1959–89 period, it is safe to assume that successive cohorts of children have had higher cumulative incomes over their childhood than earlier cohorts.

If parents' income has a large effect on children's outcomes relative to other factors, children's outcomes ought to have improved as well since then. High school dropout rates and years of education did improve between 1970 and 1990 (table 4.3). Births to teenage girls declined between 1970 and 1980 but increased by 1990, even though the parental income of teenagers born in 1970 was higher than that of teenagers born in 1960. The number of hours worked by young men hardly changed, but since it was already close to forty hours per week, we would

TABLE 4.4 / Trends in the Distribution of Parental Income (1992 Dollars)

Year Income is Measured	Year Children Turned Twenty	Cohort		
Income[a]		All	Poorest 20%	Richest 40%
Median				
1968–71	1974–77	41,956	16,390	72,641
1972–75	1978–81	46,434	18,587	77,646
1976–79	1982–85	47,912	16,322	84,396
1980–83	1986–89	43,029	14,653	80,405
Change (%)				
1968–83		2.6	10.6	10.7
1972–83		−7.3	−21.2	3.6
As % of Median				
1968–71	1974–77	100	0.391	1.731
1972–75	1978–81	100	0.400	1.672
1976–79	1982–85	100	0.341	1.761
1980–83	1986–89	100	0.341	1.869

Source: Calculations by Tim Veenstra using the 1989 wave of the PSID.

a. Measured when children were fourteen years old.

not expect much change. The percentage of twenty-four-year-old men who were idle increased, young men's wages declined, and the percentage of twenty-four-year-old women who were single mothers increased. Thus the overall pattern is mixed: some outcomes improved as parental income rose, but others did not.

The income of children in the bottom of the income distribution was lower in both absolute and relative terms during the 1970s and 1980s than during the 1950s and 1960s. Thus if income affects children's life chances, children who were poor in the 1970s ought to have fared better than children who were poor in the 1980s. Conversely, the outcomes of affluent children ought to have improved over this period.

We cannot use the census or CPS to estimate the distribution of children's outcomes over their parents' income groups. For this we need longitudinal data. I use the PSID for this task. Children's outcomes are described in appendix 4A.

For comparison with the CPS and census data, table 4.4 shows trends in median income and income for the poorest 20 percent of fourteen-year-olds in the PSID. Because the PSID oversamples low-income households, the number of unweighted cases in the richest 20 percent of the sample is sometimes too small to provide reliable estimates. Consequently, I show income trends for the richest 40 percent of children. Because there are too few cases in the PSID to assess trends year by year, I aggregated over four-year periods. Children who were twenty years old between 1974 and 1977 were fourteen in 1968–71, the first four years of the PSID. Children who were twenty-four years old between 1978 and 1981 were fourteen in 1968–71.

As noted, one year of parents' income is not as highly correlated with children's outcomes as several years. In addition, if income when children are younger has a greater effect than income during adolescence on their outcomes, the correlation between trends in outcomes and trends in parents' income at age fourteen will be biased downward. Evidence on the importance of parents' income at different ages is equivocal. However, for these outcomes, income at younger ages appears to have no greater effect than income at age fourteen (Mayer 1997).

Among the poorest 20 percent of fourteen-year-olds, parental income fell from 40 percent of median income in 1972–75 to 34.1 percent in 1980–83. As in the census and CPS data, the growth in inequality in the PSID resulted from both a decline in income near the bottom and an increase near the top. None of these children was born after 1973, when inequality began to increase, but after 1975 each successive cohort of fourteen-year-olds experienced more inequality. Thus if income during adolescence affects children's well-being, success should have been redistributed from poor to rich children over these years. The extent to which children's outcomes change depends on how much parents' income changes and how much parental income affects children's outcomes. Thus, instead of comparing trends in parents' income to trends in children's outcomes, a better strategy might be to compare the magnitude of observed changes in children's outcomes to the magnitude expected based on the changes in their parents' income.

I estimated the effect of a 10 percent change in parents' income on each outcome. The first column in table 4.5 shows this estimate. The second column shows the expected change in each outcome based on the change in income that occurred between 1972–75 to 1980–83 in the poorest 20 percent of the income distribution, a decline of 21.2 percent. I used the change over this period rather than the change since 1968–71 because it is bigger. The third column shows the expected change for the richest 40 percent of children based on their 3.6 percent increase in income between 1972 and 1983. Columns 4 and 5 show the observed changes in each outcome over the same period.

Two points are obvious from this table. First, the expected changes in these outcomes are relatively small. This is because the effect of income is modest and the change in income, though historically large, is also modest. Second, the expected changes in the outcomes are largely unrelated to the observed changes. Taken together, the results imply that neither the trends in the overall level of children's outcomes nor the trends in their distribution parallel trends in parents' income.

EXPLAINING THE TRENDS

Children's outcomes might not follow the same trend as their parents' income if income has a weak effect on children's outcomes, or if other factors that have a greater effect on children's outcomes changed at the same time as parents' income.

TABLE 4.5 / Change in Children's Outcomes, 1972–83

Outcome	Predicted Change for 10% Income Increase	Expected Change		Observed Change	
		Poorest[a] 20%	Richest[b] 40%	Poorest 20%	Richest 40%
At age 20					
Gave birth as teen (%)	−1.70	3.60	−.060	−1.10	−9.60
Dropped out of school (%)	−1.30	2.80	−0.50	−5.60	−2.80
At age 24					
Years of education	0.111	−0.235	0.040	−0.002	0.003
Hours worked, male workers	10.9	−23.1	0.382	216	159
Wages, male workers ($1992)	0.13	−0.28	0.05	−0.10	−2.36
Males idle (%)	−0.28	0.60	−0.10	−4.20	−8.60
Single mothers (%)	−2.20	4.70	−0.79	4.70	−0.20

Source: See table 4.4. Estimates of the effect of income are from equations in which each outcome is regressed on (log) income when children were fourteen years old.

Effect of 10 percent increase in parents' income.

a. Based on actual 21.2 percent decrease in parents' income between 1972–75 and 1980–83.

b. Based on actual 3.6 percent increases in parents' income between 1972–75 and 1980–83.

Many of the chapters in this book, and a considerable amount of other research, try to estimate how much parents' income affects children's outcomes. But researchers still disagree about the size of these effects, so the estimates in column 1 of table 4.5 are sometimes larger and sometimes smaller than those obtained by other researchers. The effect of parental income shown in table 4.5 is downwardly biased because it is based on only one year of income. But it is upwardly biased because it does not control all the factors that both increase parental income and improve children's outcomes. Estimates that try to take into account unobserved parental characteristics usually produce estimates of the effect of several years of income on these outcomes that are modest (Mayer 1997).

Even if income has an important effect on children's outcomes relative to other factors, the trends might not appear to parallel one another if either trend is poorly measured. In this section, I assess the accuracy of income trends. The wide range of uncertainty about the true rate of inflation and the possibility that taxes, saving, borrowing, noncash benefits, noncash assets, consumer efficiency, and need may have changed substantially over time mean that parents' command over resources might not track trends in household income very closely. In addition, much of the increase in parents' income in the middle and at the top of the income distribution was the result of mothers working more in the labor market and less at home production. The decline in home production presumably offset some of these gains in income (Gottschalk and Mayer 1995; Michael 1994). Many of these same factors influence children's well-being.

Trends in children's material living conditions demonstrate that trends in income do not necessarily follow trends in families' command over resources. No single data set collects information on all the living conditions that might be important to children, but a combination of data sets provides information on trends on housing conditions, access to medical care, and ownership of some common consumer durables.

Housing

Table 4.6 uses data from the census and the American Housing Survey to show trends in the percentage of children living in homes with various problems by household income. The mean for the third quintile represents the likelihood that the median child experienced the condition. The first part of the table shows that most design inadequacies declined slightly for the median child. The likelihood that the median child lacked central heat increased.

Maintenance problems were also fairly constant between 1973 and 1989 for the median child. The likelihood of living in a crowded home declined for the median child, as did the likelihood that their parents reported that crime was a problem in their neighborhood.

The slight improvement in most of these housing conditions for the median child is not surprising since median parental income increased a bit over this period. It is also not surprising that low-income children are more likely than the average child to experience all these housing problems. But among children whose household income is very low (the bottom decile), almost all these problems improved between the early 1970s and the late 1980s, even though their real household income declined. The exception is cracks in the wall or ceiling, which increased for middle-class children as well. Low-income children were also more likely to live in rented housing than in earlier periods, but so were middle-class children.

The last column of table 4.6 shows whether the percentage point difference between children in the bottom decile and children in the middle quintile widened, narrowed, or stayed the same in the 1970s and 1980s.[4] The gap between the middle and the bottom narrowed for almost all maintenance problems and design inadequacies. But neighborhood crime increased for low-income children relative to middle-class children, and the gap in home ownership widened between children at the bottom and children in the middle. From 1970–1990 as a whole, therefore, inequality in housing conditions between the bottom and the middle seems to have declined somewhat, even though income inequality between the bottom and the middle increased.

TABLE 4.6 / Percent of Children Living in Homes with Selected Problems, by Parents' Income, 1973–89[a]

Measure and Year	Income Decile		Income Quintile		Change in Gap, 1970–89
	First	Second	Third	Fifth	
Design inadequacies					
Incomplete bathroom[b]					
1973–75	11.4	7.5	0.9	0.3	
1981–83	6.1	4.1	1.0	0.2	
1985–89	2.5	2.2	0.7	0.6	
Change, 1973–89	−8.9	−5.3	−0.2	0.3	–[c]
No sewer or septic system					
1973–75	8.1	5.1	0.6	0.1	
1981–83	2.7	1.9	0.3	0.0	
1985–89	1.7	0.9	0.1	0.0	
Change, 1973–89	−6.4	−4.2	−0.5	−0.1	–
No central heat					
1973–75	46.2	42.9	8.7	6.8	
1981–83	35.7	38.1	22.2	9.1	
1985–89	32.3	34.7	21.4	9.6	
Change, 1973–89	−13.9	−8.2	12.7	2.8	–
No electric outlets in one or more rooms					
1973–75	12.1	10.0	3.5	1.9	
1981–83	9.3	6.6	3.1	1.6	
1985–89	6.0	6.0	2.4	1.1	
Change, 1973–89	−6.1	−4.0	−1.1	−0.8	–
Maintenance problems					
Holes in floor					
1973–75	8.2	5.6	1.8	0.6	
1981–83	8.9	7.3	1.6	0.6	
1985–89	7.0	5.8	1.4	0.6	
Change, 1973–89	−1.2	0.2	−0.4	0.0	0[d]
Open cracks in wall or ceiling					
1973–75	17.9	14.3	5.6	2.8	
1981–83	19.2	16.2	5.4	2.6	
1985–89	19.9	15.9	6.3	3.2	
Change, 1973–89	2.0	1.6	0.7	0.4	0

TABLE 4.6 / (*continued*)

Measure and Year	Income Decile		Income Quintile		Change in Gap, 1970–89
	First	Second	Third	Fifth	
Maintenance problems					
Leaky roof					
1973–75	16.5	14.2	7.2	5.3	
1981–83	14.9	12.8	7.0	4.9	
1985–89	11.9	12.5	8.5	7.3	
Change, 1973–89	−4.6	−1.7	1.3	2.0	−
Other housing conditions					
Crime problem in neighborhood					
1973–75	18.9	19.1	16.5	16.6	
1981–83	19.1	18.7	14.4	14.5	
1985[e]	26.3	19.6	14.1	11.8	
Change, 1973–85	7.4	.5	−2.4	−4.8	+[f]
More than one person per room					
1973–75	31.6	34.7	19.0	11.6	
1981–83	22.7	26.7	13.5	5.9	
1985–89[g]	19.2	23.4	10.9	5.3	
Change, 1973–89	−12.4	−11.3	−8.1	−6.3	−
Tenant					
1973–75	62.5	54.5	23.9	9.1	
1981–83	67.8	62.2	24.8	7.6	
1985–89	78.2	68.9	31.0	8.1	
Change, 1973–89	13.7	14.4	17.1	−1.0	−

Sources: Tabulations of the American Housing Survey (AHS) data by Tim Veenstra.

a. Unweighted sample sizes for bottom decile are 7,638 in 1973–75, 5,033 in 1977–79, 4,424 in 1981–83, and 4,027 in 1985–89. Data are for families, not households.

b. Complete plumbing located in a single room within the unit.

c. − Decrease of 2 or more percentage points.

d. 0 Change of less than 2 percentage points.

e. Respondent's judgment.

f. + Increase of 2 or more percentage points.

g. Room count increased slightly in 1985 due to questionnaire change.

TABLE 4.7 / Children's Annual Doctor Visits, by Parents' Income, 1970–89

	Income Decile		Income Quintile				
Age and Year	First	Second	Second	Third	Fourth	Fifth	*M*
No Doctor Visit Last Year (%)							
Under 7							
1970	27.0	25.9	19.2	15.9	11.4	9.4	16.4
1980	12.1	11.7	11.8	10.2	10.4	7.2	10.3
1982	15.1	13.7	16.0	11.8	9.9	8.4	12.1
1989	13.7	14.9	13.8	10.4	7.7	5.3	10.3
7–17							
1970	45.1	45.0	41.5	36.9	32.4	25.7	36.3
1980	31.1	34.3	33.3	30.8	26.3	26.0	29.8
1982	31.2	33.9	35.3	32.3	27.1	23.0	30.1
1989	31.2	32.0	31.4	27.3	23.9	17.5	26.4
Doctor Visits in a Year							
Under 7							
1970	3.4	3.4	3.5	4.2	4.4	4.4	4.0
1980	3.7	4.1	4.2	4.2	4.3	4.3	4.2
1982	3.4	3.5	3.2	3.7	3.8	4.2	3.7
1989	3.6	3.7	3.6	4.0	4.0	4.7	4.0
7–17							
1970	2.0	1.9	1.9	2.1	2.4	2.6	2.2
1980	2.6	2.1	2.1	2.3	2.5	2.5	2.3
1982	2.6	2.1	2.1	2.2	2.6	2.5	2.3
1989	2.6	2.6	2.1	2.3	2.5	3.1	2.6

Source: Tabulations by David Knutson from public-use data tapes from the National Health Interview Survey. Unweighted cell sizes range from 987 to 8,072.

Medical Care

In table 4.7 I extend this analysis to a different domain, medical care, by estimating the percentage of children who had not visited a doctor in the previous year and the number of doctor visits for children with at least one visit. I estimated these separately for children under seven years old and for children seven to seventeen years old, since the medical needs of the two age groups may be different. The Health Interview Survey (HIS) was changed in 1982 in ways that affect these estimates, so the estimates for 1970 and 1980 are comparable to one another but not to the estimates for 1982 and 1989.

Like most other resources available to children, doctor visits increased during both the 1970s and 1980s. Among children less than seven years old the likelihood of visiting a doctor increased much more for low-income children than for children in general between 1970 and 1980. But from 1982 to 1989 the increase for

TABLE 4.8 / Percent of Children with Selected Consumer Durables and Telephone Service, by Parents' Income, 1970–90

	Income Decile		Income Quintile			
Measure and Year	First	Second	Second	Third	Fourth	Fifth
Motor vehicle						
1970	59.8	76.4	90.4	95.6	97.6	98.8
1980	58.6	78.1	89.7	95.7	97.7	98.4
1990	57.3	82.1	91.7	97.0	98.0	99.0
Change, 1970–90	−2.5	5.7	1.3	1.4	0.4	0.2
Two or more motor vehicles						
1970	13.2	20.0	32.3	44.4	57.6	74.8
1980	14.2	21.0	35.3	50.7	64.7	76.6
1990	17.3	34.3	56.4	75.3	86.6	92.9
Change, 1970–90	4.1	14.3	24.1	30.9	29.0	18.1
Air conditioning						
1973–75	27.5	31.8	41.1	48.9	55.2	62.2
1981–83	36.6	39.6	49.1	57.3	63.7	69.2
1985–89	41.5	47.4	57.9	64.9	69.7	72.8
Change, 1970–90	14.0	15.6	16.8	16.0	14.5	10.6
Telephone						
1970	60.8	66.9	83.0	91.7	95.0	98.5
1980	72.1	80.2	88.7	95.8	98.3	99.0
1990	68.7	79.7	90.8	96.5	98.3	99.5
Change, 1970–90	7.9	12.8	7.8	4.8	3.3	1.1

Sources: Tabulations for 1970, 1980, and 1990 are from census data; others are from the AHS.

low-income children was about the same as for the average child. The trends are similar for the number of doctor visits. Among children aged seven to seventeen, low-income children were more likely than the average child to have visited a physician in the previous year by 1980 and remained more likely to do so in 1989. They also visited the doctor at least as often as more affluent children. Children's access to physicians did not deteriorate, as one might have expected given the reduction in both their parents' overall purchasing power and in insurance coverage.[5]

Consumer Durables and Telephone Service

Table 4.8 shows several additional measures of material well-being. Some, such as having at least two cars and air conditioning, might be considered luxuries, but others, like having a telephone, might be considered necessities. Because parents' tastes vary, some will choose to forgo air conditioning in favor of a telephone, and others will have the opposite preference. But if parents purchase goods and services in the order of their importance, families that have two cars are also likely to have other more basic material resources.

Children's households became more likely to have all of these items between the early 1970s and the late 1980s. Poor children's households became less likely to have at least one motor vehicle. However, their likelihood of having two or more vehicles increased, implying that the bottom income decile includes more very poor households but also more "mistakes." The improvement for low-income children was greater than for children in general. On these items, poor children apparently became more like middle-class children.[6]

The evidence on children's living conditions suggests that from the 1970s to the 1990s trends in parents' income are not a reliable guide to trends in children's living conditions. Therefore, trends in parents' income may not reflect trends in parents' command over resources.

Theories of the effect of parental income on children's outcomes contend that income is important because it is synonymous with command over resources. They therefore hold that parents' command over resources helps children either by increasing the quality and quantity of the goods and services that parents purchase for their children, or by reducing parental stress. Therefore, the fact that trends in measured parental income are weakly associated with trends in command over resources at least partly accounts for the weak relationship between trends in parental income and children's outcomes.

Regardless of the explanation, trends in parents' income are not a reliable gauge of trends in children's outcomes. Although children from poor families fare much worse than children from rich families in all years, one cannot conclude that when parents' income declines over time, children's life chances also decline.

APPENDIX

DESCRIPTION OF THE VARIABLES

Income

I convert all income variables to 1992 dollars using the CPI-U-X1 price adjustment. Total family income includes all taxable and transfer income of the family head, the wife, and others. I count the face value of the food stamps as income. All data sets top-code income. In the PSID the maximum value for income in survey years 1968–80 is $99,999. After that, the top-code is $9.9 million. For consistency, I top-code all income to the 1992 equivalent of $99,999 ($189,172). I follow a similar procedure in other data sets.

Teenage Childbearing

To calculate the mother's age when a child was born, I compare the date of birth of each girl to the date of birth of her oldest child. If this age is less than twenty, the mother is counted as a teenage mother and the variable is coded as 1. If there is no birth or the mother was twenty or older, teenage childbearing is coded as 0. If data on either birth history or mother's birth date are missing, this variable is coded as missing.

Dropout

If a child completed fewer than twelve years of schooling and was not enrolled in school by age twenty, he or she is counted as having dropped out of high school. When information on education or student status at age twenty is not available, I use information from when the child was twenty-one or up to age twenty-five. If information on education is still missing, dropout is counted as missing.

Years of Education

Years of education is the highest number of years of completed schooling in the year a child turned twenty-four years old. It is top-coded at seventeen years, because that is the top-code in earlier years of the PSID.

Male Hours of Work

Male hours of work is the average annual number of hours a male who was not a student and who was at least twenty years old reported working in 1983 and 1984. This variable is calculated for males who report at least one hour of work.

Male Hourly Wage

Male hourly wage is total earnings divided by total number of hours worked averaged over 1983 and 1984 for male workers who were not students and who were at least twenty years old. The top 1 percent and bottom 1 percent of wages were trimmed.

Male Idleness

A male who was not in school, not in the military, and who reported working fewer than one hundred hours for the entire year that he was twenty-four years old is counted as idle.

Single Motherhood

A woman is counted as having been a single mother if she ever had a baby and was not married before turning twenty-four years old. If a woman did not have a baby or was always married after she had a baby, she is counted as not having been a single mother.

The section of this chapter on income and material well-being is part of a long-term collaboration with Christopher Jencks. Many of the ideas and much of the analysis are the result of this joint work. However, any errors are mine alone. This work would not have been possible without the research assistance of David Knutson and Tim Veenstra.

NOTES

1. The transactional model of child development is a closely related elaboration of the stress model (Sameroff and Chandler 1975; Scarr and McCartney 1983; Parker, Greer, and Zuckerman 1988). Transactional models hold that children's characteristics, such as their cognitive ability, temperament, and health, shape their responses to the environment and that these responses in turn transform the environment.
2. I use household income rather than family income. The Census Bureau defines a family as everyone living in a single housing unit who is related by blood, marriage, or adoption. Thus, if a woman lives in her home (and is what the Census Bureau refers to as the "reference" person) with a boyfriend and their child, the mother and child are counted as one family and the father is counted as a separate unrelated individual. This distinction does not seem reasonable, and as rates of cohabitation increase it may increasingly distort the true economic well-being of children. A household is all the people who live in a single housing unit, regardless of their relationship to one another.
3. The poorest 20 percent of children's families reported incomes averaging $10,867 in 1969 in the CPS but $16,390 between 1967 and 1971 in the PSID (both in 1992 dollars). Income is higher for the PSID cohorts partly because the income of parents of fourteen-year-olds tends to be higher than the income of all parents, partly because the PSID sample excludes Hispanics, partly because the PSID might be better than the CPS or census at getting low-income respondents to report their income, and perhaps partly because attrition in the PSID at the bottom of the income distribution is not fully offset by reweighting. In all data sets income at the bottom of the distribution declined after the early 1970s.

4. An alternative strategy for comparing the relative well-being of different kinds of households is to divide the decile mean by the grand mean rather than subtracting one from the other. But when the outcome is dichotomous, this approach often yields different answers when one measures the presence of a resource than when one measure its absence. Because of this problem, most analysts prefer to examine differences in dichotomous outcomes by dividing the odds of one group's having a given outcome by the odds of the other group's having it. Like the arithmetic difference between proportions, odds ratios yield the same results regardless of whether one counts people with or without an attribute. But when the base rate is very high or very low, a small absolute difference between two groups can translate into a very large difference in odds ratios. Changes in odds ratios are therefore unlikely to have a linear relationship to any plausible utility function. That problem is not always solved by using arithmetic differences, but it is usually lessened.
5. Even when health status is taken into account, the association between income and doctor visits increased for children between 1982 and 1989. For a more detailed analysis of doctor visits that controls self-reported health status, the presence of acute and chronic conditions, and bed days in the past year, see Mayer (1992).
6. Although not shown in this chapter, the conclusions about material well-being are qualitatively the same regardless of the adjustment for household size.

Chapter 5

Effects of Long-Term Poverty on Physical Health of Children in the National Longitudinal Survey of Youth

Sanders Korenman and Jane E. Miller

An important step in understanding the disadvantages associated with poverty in the United States is a recognition of the dynamic nature of poverty for individuals and families and the implications of poverty dynamics for assessing its effects (Bane and Ellwood 1986; Duncan and Rodgers 1991; Duncan 1994a). In their analysis of data from the Panel Study of Income Dynamics, Ashworth, Hill, and Walker (1994) found that 38 percent of children born between 1969 and 1973 experienced poverty in at least one year before reaching age fifteen. Poverty patterns were heterogeneous: of the children who had been poor, 25 percent had been poor for only one short spell whereas 5 percent were poor during their entire childhood. Because children's poverty histories are dynamic and heterogeneous, it may be inappropriate to characterize a child's poverty history with a measure of poverty status based on a short-term observation of income. Nonetheless, studies of the effects of poverty on children's health in the United States have relied on measures of poverty based on family income in the year a child is observed.

Researchers have begun to study the effects of persistent poverty or poverty at different ages on children's health (see Duncan 1994a for a review). For example, in our previous work, we found poor nutritional status (as measured by low height-for-age and low weight-for-height) to be more prevalent among children in persistently poor families. Moreover, differences in nutritional status appeared to be greater when measured with an indicator of long-term poverty based on a ten-year average of income-to-needs ratio than one based on poverty status at the time of assessment (Miller and Korenman 1994a). On the other hand, in comparing the experiences of siblings, Currie and Thomas (1993a, 1995) find little relation between a three-year average of income centered at age three and height at age five.

One reason deficits in nutritional status in early childhood might be greater based on long-term rather than single-year (current) poverty measures is that poverty during the prenatal period or early childhood is particularly detrimental to health and development (see, for example, Carnegie Corporation 1994). These periods of heightened vulnerability may be captured by a long-term, but not a single-year, measure of income. Another explanation is that bias from measurement error in income is less severe for estimates based on a long-term income measure than for those based on a short-term measure because a long-term measure will reduce the influence of fluctuations resulting from random errors in measurement (see the Discussion section).

Long-term poverty has also been linked to adverse health outcomes for infants. For example, Starfield et al. (1991) report larger differentials in the incidence of low birth weight (LBW)—a widely used indicator of child health—based on long-term poverty measures than based on poverty status in the year of pregnancy. Gould and LeRoy (1988), who analyzed patterns of low birth weight by race and socioeconomic status using data from a large cohort of births from Los Angeles County, California, found a strong inverse relation between median family income (at the census tract level) and the incidence of LBW among both black and white infants.

In addition to prenatal deficits, poor children may not receive postnatal nutrition that is adequate to support normal growth. Poor prenatal and postnatal growth together may cause severe nutritional deprivation for low-income children. With the exception of the studies discussed above, we know of no other national, longitudinal studies that examine the effects of poverty on physical growth for American children. Although several studies have examined children's growth in developing countries, the findings may be of limited applicability to the United States because of differences in the severity and duration of poverty and nutritional deprivation, in disease patterns, and in health care systems (see Martorell and Habicht 1986 for a summary).

In this chapter, we use data from the National Longitudinal Survey of Youth (NLSY), 1979–91, that provide background information on socioeconomic characteristics and annual data on income and family structure for a nationally representative sample of women selected in 1979. In combination with assessments of the health and development of the children born to this cohort of women, these data provide an excellent opportunity to investigate the effect of poverty dynamics on children's physical health and development in the United States (for example, Chase-Landsdale et al. 1991). We investigate the relations between income and timing or duration of poverty on the one hand and indicators of nutritional status and motor and social development (MSD) on the other. (The MSD index provides a measure of how a child's physical, language, and motor skills compare to standards for children of the same age.) Better estimates of the relationships between poverty history and child health may aid in the formulation of health and social policies. For example, identifying ages at which children are most vulnerable to the effects of poverty may allow resources to be targeted effectively, as demonstrated by the age range of children, youth, and young adults studied in this volume (Children's Defense Fund 1994).

The chapter is organized as follows: in the next two sections, we describe the NLSY data and measures used for the analysis. We then present the replication analysis in which we estimate a series of models that is common to the studies in chapters 5–17. In these models, we compare the prevalence of "stunting" and "wasting" for children with different experiences in the depth, duration, and timing of poverty, with and without controls for a variety of socioeconomic variables and measures of family structure. The following section contains a series of extension models intended to bolster causal inference, taking advantage of several features of the NLSY data. For example, in some analyses we relate differences among first cousins (the children of mothers who are sisters) in nutritional status to differences in their family incomes as a way to control for unmeasured characteristics that may be common to sisters and therefore to isolate better effects of income on child health. We conclude with a summary and discussion of our results relative to those of previous studies and some suggestions for future research.

DATA AND SAMPLE

We used data from the NLSY, which has gathered information in annual interviews from a cohort of approximately 6,000 women aged fourteen to twenty-one in 1979 (at baseline). Since 1986 the NLSY has also collected information in a series of biennial Child Supplements (CS) about the children of women in the sample. More than 90 percent of the women eligible to be interviewed remained in the sample as of 1988 (Baker et al. 1993).

The NLSY by design oversampled black, Hispanic, and disadvantaged white women to provide the large samples needed for a study of potential health disadvantages associated with poverty.[1] When weighted with sampling weights, the children of the NLSY represent a cross-section of children born to a nationally representative sample of women aged fourteen to twenty in January 1979 (twenty-five to thirty-one in January 1990), which is estimated to include more than two-thirds of the eventual childbearing to that cohort. Since births to older women are not represented, the sample further overrepresents children born to low-income, minority, and less-educated women, particularly among the oldest children in the sample (Baker et al. 1993). Race and the child's age at the time of assessment were controlled in all models.

We used information on children's nutritional status from the 1988 and 1990 CS, and on motor and social development, from the 1986 and 1988 CS. We did not include information on nutritional status from the 1986 CS. Weight and height data were collected for children of all ages. Our sample included children born between 1979 and the time of the 1988 CS.[2] For the nutritional status analysis, we studied children aged five to seven years (sixty to ninety-five months in the year they were assessed), and for the motor and social development analysis, we studied children aged zero to two years (zero to thirty-five months at assessment). In other work, we have studied children at all ages represented in the sample (Miller and Korenman 1994a; Korenman, Miller, and Sjaastad 1995).

MEASURES

Child Health

We analyzed two anthropometric indicators of nutritional status, low height-for-age (stunting) and low weight-for-height (wasting), that are considered to be risk factors for poor health in adults and children (Elo and Preston 1992; Martorell and Ho 1984; Miller, Fine, and Adams-Taylor 1989). These measures are widely used indicators of nutritional status for populations but are not specific enough to identify malnourished individuals. We classified a child as having low height-for-age if his or her height was below the 10th percentile for children of the same age and sex, and as having low weight-for-height if his or her weight was below the 10th percentile for children of the same height and sex based on standards recommended by the National Center for Health Statistics (NCHS) and the World Health Organization (Sullivan and Gorstein 1990; World Health Organization Working Group 1986). These standards were derived from measurements of healthy, middle-class children in the United States (Waterlow et al. 1977). Cases in which height-for-age or weight-for-height were more than six standard deviations from the mean (fewer than 2 percent of cases) were set to missing (Waterlow et al. 1977).

In the extensions section, we include analyses of the prevalence of overweight, a continuous measure of height-for-age, and an index of MSD. "Overweight" was defined as weight-for-height in excess of the 90th percentile according to the NCHS standards. The height-for-age *z*-score was our continuous measure of height (that is, the number of standard deviations a child's height is above or below the mean for children of the same age and sex). We studied a continuous measure of height mainly because fixed-effects analyses (differences among children who are first cousins) are more straightforward to conduct and interpret for continuous outcomes than for dichotomous outcomes such as stunting.

The MSD index was constructed from fifteen questions asked of mothers regarding the physical and social development of their children aged zero to three years.[3] MSD items were derived from the Bayley, Gesell, and Denver scales of child development, which have been shown to have high reliability and validity. NLSY children's scores on the MSD index accorded with the expected patterns with regard to age, sex, and birth weight of the child (Baker et al. 1993). The questions were specific to the age of the child in narrow age ranges (for example, three to twelve months), reflecting rapid development at young ages. For example, the mother of a three-month-old was asked whether her child could roll over without assistance, whereas the mother of a nine-month-old was asked whether her child could crawl. The MSD percentile score was computed by comparing responses to national standards for children of the same age and sex based on the 1981 National Health Interview Survey (Baker et al. 1993).

Age and Assessment Year

The analysis sample consisted of children who were between five and seven years of age at assessment (between sixty and ninety-five months, inclusive). We selected these age groups to match as closely as possible the ages of children in the study by Duncan, Brooks-Gunn, and Klebanov (1994) as well as to ensure a sample large enough (and old enough) to construct measures of the duration and timing of poverty.[4] In our analysis we used the first available genuine measure (as opposed to maternal report) of height and weight for each child at age five to seven years. For example, if the child was aged five in 1988 and genuine measures of height and weight were available, we used those data. If the child was not measured in 1988 or if the data were not genuine measures, we used the 1990 measures, if available. We excluded data collected in 1986 because it is not known whether the interviewers collected information on height and weight using measuring tapes and scales. Of the roughly 5,300 children of all ages for whom the 1988 CS contains height and weight data, 80 percent were measured using a measuring tape and scale, while the remaining 20 percent of heights and weights were reported by the mother. In 1990, tape and scale measures were available for about half the sample. Therefore, we dropped about 32 percent of children aged five to seven from our analysis sample because their height and weight were reported by their mother rather than measured.[5]

About 60 percent of the cases used for the replication analyses come from the 1990 CS (the remainder come from 1988), in which the mean age of the children at assessment was 5.9 years (70.0 months; standard deviation = 8.4 months). In all models we controlled for the child's age in months at assessment.

Income

At the time of this analysis, income data were available for calendar years 1978–90. The income-to-needs ratio in any year was calculated by dividing family income by the census poverty line, which varies according to the size of the family and its age composition (for example, U.S. Department of Commerce 1993). For the nutritional status analyses, our measure of long-term income was an average of up to eight years of family income (relative to needs) for children aged five or six and up to nine years for children aged seven. For six- and seven-year-olds, this period included the prenatal year through the year of assessment. (Before deletion for other reasons, we dropped fifteen cases from the analysis sample because they lacked information needed for the calculation of the long-term income-to-needs.) For five-year-olds, this period included the prenatal year through the year following the child's assessment. In analyses of the MSD index, our long-term income measure was the average of the income-to-needs ratios for all available years up to the year of assessment (up to ten years). We also explored possible nonlinearities in effects of income-to-needs by entering four categories: less than 1 (poor), 1–2, 2–3, 3–4, and 4 or above (the reference category).

Duration and Timing of Poverty

Following Duncan, Brooks-Gunn and Klebanov (1994), we defined four categories of poverty duration: never poor, always poor, poor in some years, and missing duration status. Duration was considered missing if there were fewer than five income observations (11 percent of cases). Among those with five or more years of income information, the always-poor category consisted of children who were poor in all years for which income information is available (eight or nine is the maximum possible), the never poor were those who were not poor in any year for which income information is available, and the remaining children were classified as sometimes poor.

We based the timing of poverty on the average of the income-to-needs ratio in the first and second halves of a child's life: early and late poverty, respectively. The early and late income averages for each child were based on family income in four years (for children aged seven, the late average could include up to five years). If either the early or late income-to-needs ratio was missing (3 percent of cases), timing was considered missing. The not-poor category consisted of children whose average income-to-needs ratio was greater than 1 in both periods. The other timing categories were poor early, not late; poor late, not early; and poor both periods.

Family Structure

The family structure variables were defined as in Sandefur, McLanahan, and Wojkiewicz (1992). The categories corresponded to the mother's marital status at the time of the child's birth and in the assessment year (table 5.1). The average number of siblings of the child living in the household (number in household) was calculated for the period over which we take the average of income.

Other Variables

The mother's race/ethnicity was classified as Hispanic, non-Hispanic black, and other non-Hispanic (predominantly white). The sex and birthweight of the child were also included as controls. Missing values for birthweight were assigned the mean for their race and long-term poverty category. The highest grade completed by the mother was measured at the time of the last available interview. In some analyses we also included controls for the mother's age at first birth and score on the Armed Forces Qualifications Test (AFQT, a measure of academic ability and achievement administered in 1980) and indicator variables for premature birth (less than 37 weeks gestation) and short length at birth (less than 19 inches).

Siblings

The baseline NLSY sample design is household based, so that all youths aged fourteen to twenty who resided in sampled households in 1979 were eligible for inclusion in the sample (Center for Human Resource Research 1993). Furthermore, the children of women in the sample were eligible for inclusion in the CS if they resided with their mother. Statistical procedures that assume the data are derived from a simple random sample are likely to understate standard errors of estimates, so in all the results presented below we have corrected the standard errors for correlation among siblings using Huber's method, where the clustering variable is the mother's identification code (Huber 1967; Stata Corporation 1993).

An obvious problem with interpreting cross-sectional estimates of the effects of poverty on children's well-being is heterogeneity bias: poor families may differ in unmeasured ways from families that are not poor, and these differences may be related to children's health. We took two analytical approaches to addressing this problem. The first was to explore the sensitivity of cross-sectional estimates to the addition of more detailed controls to the models. For example, we estimated models in which we added controls for the mother's AFQT score, height and weight (body mass index: weight in kilograms divided by the square of height in meters), and indicators of infant health (birth weight and short length at birth). Second, we related differences between (or among) first cousins (whose mothers are sisters) in our measures of the children's health and development to differences in their family incomes. These fixed-effects estimates allowed us to control for unobserved characteristics common to sisters that could have led to bias in cross-sectional estimates. Although none of these methods can establish causal relationships, they can serve to build or undermine confidence in causal inferences.[6] In fixed-effects estimates we entered an effect for each mother's household of origin (in the cousins subsample) and present standard error estimates that account for correlation among siblings.

Although these fixed-effects methods provide controls for unobserved factors that are common to first cousins, they do not account for unobserved differences between cousins (for example, father's height) that might have been correlated with income and with anthropometric measures of nutritional status based on height and weight. Nor do these methods correct for biases that might result from the endogenous or simultaneous determination of children's health and income (for example, children's health problems may reduce the family's labor supply and therefore family income). However, we suspect that the reverse causal effects of children's health on family income are unlikely to have been an important source of bias. Indeed, this is one advantage of using a sample of children to estimate the health effects of poverty, since bias from reverse causation should be much less important than in a sample of adults. While endogeneity problems may be important and may, in principle, be remediable through the use of instrumental variables techniques, we know of no good candidates for instruments in the NLSY (Bound, Jaeger, and Baker 1995).

REPLICATION ANALYSIS

For the replication analysis we studied the prevalence of low height-for-age and low weight-for-height for children five to seven years old at the time of assessment. Although height and weight information was collected at each assessment, as noted, we selected one measure per child. The sample used in the analyses of low height-for-age consisted of 1,698 children for whom height information was known to be measured (as opposed to reported by the mother). For analyses of low weight-for-height, the sample consisted of 1,468 children for whom both height and weight were measured. About one-third of the children in the sample had non-Hispanic black mothers, and one-fifth had Hispanic mothers. Sample means and proportions are presented in table 5.1 separately for non-Hispanic black, and nonblack children. Eight and one-half percent of children in the sample were below the 10th percentile of national standards for height-for-age, and about 12.2 percent were below the 10th percentile of weight-for-height. Black children appeared less likely to be either stunted or wasted and were more likely to be overweight than nonblack children (figures not shown).[7]

Estimated coefficients and associated standard errors from a series of logistic regression models of stunting and wasting are presented in tables 5.2 and 5.3, respectively, for the replication analysis. The models included different measures of income or poverty status. The first model contained no income controls; the remaining models included controls for income or income-to-needs ratio (continuous or categorical); some models included interactions of income-to-needs ratio with race or sex variables. With the exception of model 2, all models included controls for the child's sex, birth weight, and age in months at assessment as well as the mother's race, years of schooling, and marital status.

Stunting

In the model summarized in column 2 of table 5.2, the coefficient of the long-term average income-to-needs measure was −0.26 with a standard error of 0.09, suggesting that the risks of having a low height-for-age declined with increasing

TABLE 5.1 / Characteristics of Children in the Sample, by Race[a]

Measure	Full Sample	Nonblack	Black
Outcomes (%)			
Low weight-for-height[b]	12.2	12.4	12.0
Low height-for-age[c]	8.5	9.1	7.4
Explanatory variables			
Child's characteristics			
Boy (%)	51.0	52.0	49.3
Birth weight (100 g)	32.4	32.9	31.4
	(5.7)	(5.7)	(5.5)
Height (inches)	46.7	46.6	47.0
	(3.0)	(2.9)	(3.0)
Age at assessment (years)	5.9	5.9	5.9
	(0.8)	(0.8)	(0.8)
Mother's characteristics			
Black (%)	35.0	0.0	100.0
Hispanic (nonblack) (%)	24.5	37.7	0.0
Completed schooling, 1990 (years)	12.0	11.9	12.2
	(2.0)	(2.2)	(1.7)
Marital status (%)			
Married at birth and assessment	45.4	60.3	17.7
Never married at assessment	18.6	7.2	39.6
Not married at birth, married at assessment	13.5	11.2	17.8
Married at birth, not married at assessment	12.7	14.0	10.1
Divorced, separated, or widowed at birth and assessment	3.9	3.7	4.4
Other or missing	5.9	3.4	10.4
Family income variables[d]			
Income-to-needs ratio	1.8	2.1	1.3
	(1.3)	(1.3)	(1.0)
Income $\times$ 10^{-3} ($1990)	2.6	3.0	1.9
	(1.8)	(1.8)	(1.5)
Number in family	1.9	1.8	1.9
	(0.9)	(0.9)	(1.0)

TABLE 5.1 / (*continued*)

Measure	Full Sample	Nonblack	Black
Income-to-needs category			
<1	32.2	22.3	50.7
1–2	31.4	32.1	30.3
2–3	19.4	23.5	12.0
3–4	10.8	14.0	2.2
>4	6.1	8.2	4.9
Duration of poverty			
Never poor	38.6	48.3	19.8
Poor some years	42.5	39.7	47.8
Poor all years	13.0	7.6	22.9
Missing[e]	9.7	8.5	11.8
Timing of poverty[f]			
Poor early, not late	10.4	8.2	14.5
Poor late, not early	6.1	6.3	5.9
Poor early and late	24.1	15.9	39.6
Not poor	56.6	67.6	35.6
Missing	2.8	2.0	4.4
N	1,698	1,104	594

Source: Data from the National Longitudinal Survey of Youth (NLSY) Child Supplements (CS) on children aged sixty to ninety-five months at assessment (1988 or 1990) with tape and scale measurements of height and weight available.

a. Values are sample means. Standard deviations in parentheses.

b. Below 10th percentile of the National Center for Health Statistics (NCHS) standard for age and sex.

c. Below 10th percentile of NCHS standard for age and sex.

d. Averages from prenatal year through the year of or following assessment. See text for details.

e. Fewer than five observations (years) of family income available for the child.

f. Based on average income-to-needs ratio in roughly two halves of a child's lifetime: "early" (prenatal year through age two) and "late" (age three through assessment year). See text for details.

income. The income coefficient fell by about 20 percent when controls for marital status and schooling were added (column 3).

In column 4, income and family size variables are entered separately rather than as an income-to-needs ratio. Low income appeared to be responsible for a relatively large share of the effect of low income-to-needs on stunting, while the effect of average family size over the period was smaller and not statistically significant.

(Text continued on p. 86.)

TABLE 5.2 / Replication Analysis: Estimated Effects of Average Income-to-Needs Ratio on Low Height-for-Age under Different Model Specifications, Full Sample[a]

	Model								
Variable	1	2	3	4	5	6	7	8	9
Child's characteristics									
Boy	0.10	0.10	0.08	0.08	0.08	0.10	0.10	0.08	0.14
	(0.18)	(0.18)	(0.18)	(0.18)	(0.18)	(0.18)	(0.18)	(0.18)	(0.31)
Birth weight (100 g)	−0.08	−0.07	−0.07	−0.07	−0.07	−0.08	−0.07	−0.07	−0.07
	(0.01)	(0.02)	(0.02)	(0.02)	(0.02)	(0.02)	(0.02)	(0.02)	(0.02)
Age at assessment (months/12)	−0.10	−0.10	−0.11	−0.10	−0.10	−0.09	−0.10	−0.11	−0.10
	(0.12)	(0.12)	(0.12)	(0.12)	(0.12)	(0.12)	(0.12)	(0.12)	(0.12)
Mother's characteristics									
Black	−0.21	−0.51	−0.30	−0.29	−0.29	−0.23	−0.29	−0.46	−0.30
	(0.25)	(0.24)	(0.26)	(0.26)	(0.26)	(0.26)	(0.26)	(0.43)	(0.26)
Hispanic (nonblack)	−0.01	−0.01	−0.05	−0.05	−0.05	−0.01	−0.04	−0.35	−0.05
	(0.23)	(0.23)	(0.23)	(0.23)	(0.24)	(0.23)	(0.24)	(0.41)	(0.23)
Schooling completed, 1990 (years)	−0.13		−0.09	−0.10	−0.10	−0.12	−0.10	−0.10	−0.09
	(0.04)		(0.05)	(0.05)	(0.05)	(0.04)	(0.04)	(0.05)	(0.05)
Marital history									
Never married at assessment	−0.21		−0.43	−0.50	−0.41	−0.30	−0.40	−0.43	−0.43
	(0.30)		(0.32)	(0.32)	(0.32)	(0.33)	(0.33)	(0.33)	(0.32)
Not married at birth, married at assessment	−0.26		−0.37	−0.40	−0.37	−0.24	−0.39	−0.38	−0.37
	(0.30)		(0.30)	(0.30)	(0.30)	(0.30)	(0.32)	(0.30)	(0.30)
Married at birth, not married at assessment	0.25		0.11	0.05	0.13	0.24	0.19	0.10	0.11
	(0.26)		(0.26)	(0.27)	(0.26)	(0.27)	(0.26)	(0.26)	(0.26)
Divorced, separated, or widowed at birth and assessment	0.48		0.26	0.19	0.29	0.44	0.24	0.25	0.25
	(0.43)		(0.43)	(0.44)	(0.44)	(0.43)	(0.44)	(0.43)	(0.44)
Other or missing	0.09		−0.11	−0.19	−0.09	0.05	−0.08	−0.11	−0.11
	(0.38)		(0.40)	(0.40)	(0.40)	(0.40)	(0.40)	(0.40)	(0.40)

Family income variables								
Average income-to-needs ratio	−0.26	−0.21					−0.28	−0.20
	(0.09)	(0.10)					(0.15)	(0.12)
Black by average income-to-needs ratio							0.09	
							(0.22)	
Hispanic by average income-to-needs ratio							0.18	
							(0.20)	
Boy by average income-to-needs ratio								−0.04
								(0.16)
Income × 10^{-3} ($1990)			−0.18					
			(0.08)					
Number in family			−0.05					
			(0.09)					
Average income-to-needs category								
<1				0.99				
				(0.58)				
1–2				0.80				
				(0.54)				
2–3				0.56				
				(0.56)				
3–4				0.52				
				(0.59)				
Duration of poverty								
Some years					−0.09			
					(0.24)			
All years					0.27			
					(0.34)			
Missing					0.05			
					(0.33)			

(*Table continued on p. 82.*)

TABLE 5.2 / *(continued)*

Variable	Model								
	1	2	3	4	5	6	7	8	9
Timing of poverty									
Early, not late							0.49		
							(0.33)		
Late, not early							0.18		
							(0.39)		
Early and late							0.47		
							(0.27)		
Missing							−0.26		
							(0.54)		
Constant	2.16	0.92	2.12	2.39	1.41	1.97	1.68	2.29	2.08
	(0.97)	(0.85)	(0.97)	(1.01)	(1.08)	(1.05)	(1.02)	(0.98)	(1.01)

Source: Authors' calculations from logit models using data from the NLSY CS on children aged sixty to ninety-five months at assessment (1988 or 1990).

a. $N = 1{,}698$. Mean of dependent variable = 0.097. Standard errors in parentheses.

TABLE 5.3 / Replication Analysis: Effect of Average Income-to-Needs Ratio on Low Weight-for-Height under Different Model Specifications, Full Sample[a]

	Model								
Variable	1	2	3	4	5	6	7	8	9
Child's characteristics									
Boy	0.04	0.04	0.04	0.04	0.05	0.04	0.04	0.04	0.21
	(0.16)	(0.16)	(0.16)	(0.16)	(0.16)	(0.16)	(0.16)	(0.16)	(0.27)
Birth weight (100 g)	−0.05	−0.05	−0.05	−0.05	−0.05	−0.05	−0.05	−0.05	−0.05
	(0.01)	(0.01)	(0.01)	(0.01)	(0.01)	(0.01)	(0.01)	(0.01)	(0.01)
Age at assessment (months/12)	−0.31	−0.34	−0.31	−0.32	−0.30	−0.31	−0.32	−0.31	−0.31
	(0.14)	(0.14)	(0.14)	(0.14)	(0.14)	(0.14)	(0.14)	(0.14)	(0.14)
Height (inches)	0.14	0.14	0.13	0.14	0.13	0.14	0.13	0.14	0.13
	(0.04)	(0.04)	(0.04)	(0.04)	(0.04)	(0.04)	(0.04)	(0.04)	(0.04)
Mother's characteristics									
Black	−0.08	−0.07	−0.08	−0.08	−0.06	−0.05	−0.07	−0.08	−0.08
	(0.21)	(0.20)	(0.22)	(0.21)	(0.21)	(0.21)	(0.22)	(0.37)	(0.22)
Hispanic (nonblack)	0.38	0.32	0.38	0.37	0.39	0.42	0.31	0.60	0.38
	(0.21)	(0.20)	(0.20)	(0.20)	(0.21)	(0.21)	(0.21)	(0.37)	(0.20)
Schooling completed, 1990 (years)	0.09		0.09	0.09	0.08	0.09	0.10	0.09	0.09
	(0.04)		(0.04)	(0.04)	(0.04)	(0.04)	(0.04)	(0.04)	(0.04)
Marital history									
Never married at assessment	−0.08		−0.10	−0.13	−0.04	−0.06	−0.18	−0.13	−0.10
	(0.25)		(0.27)	(0.27)	(0.28)	(0.28)	(0.27)	(0.27)	(0.27)
Not married at birth, married at assessment	−0.29		−0.30	−0.32	−0.27	−0.21	−0.24	−0.29	−0.30
	(0.26)		(0.27)	(0.26)	(0.27)	(0.27)	(0.27)	(0.27)	(0.27)
Married at birth, not married at assessment	−0.21		−0.23	−0.25	−0.17	−0.15	−0.38	−0.22	−0.23
	(0.27)		(0.27)	(0.27)	(0.27)	(0.27)	(0.27)	(0.27)	(0.27)

(Table continued on p. 84.)

TABLE 5.3 / *(continued)*

Variable	Model 1	2	3	4	5	6	7	8	9
Divorced, separated, or widowed at birth and assessment	−0.40		−0.42	−0.43	−0.36	−0.36	−0.57	−0.43	−0.43
	(0.47)		(0.48)	(0.48)	(0.49)	(0.48)	(0.50)	(0.49)	(0.48)
Other or missing	0.06		0.04	0.02	0.09	0.12	−0.16	0.03	0.04
	(0.33)		(0.34)	(0.34)	(0.35)	(0.34)	(0.35)	(0.34)	(0.34)
Family income variables									
Average income-to-needs ratio		0.06	−0.02					0.03	0.03
		(0.06)	(0.08)					(0.10)	(0.09)
Black by average income-to-needs ratio								−0.08	
								(0.16)	
Hispanic by average income-to-needs ratio								−0.11	
								(0.16)	
Boy by average income-to-needs ratio									−0.09
									(0.12)
Income $\times 10^{-3}$ ($1990)				−0.02					
				(0.06)					
Number in family				−0.05					
				(0.10)					
Average income-to-needs category									
<1					−0.15				
					(0.41)				
1–2					−0.24				
					(0.38)				
2–3					0.10				
					(0.38)				
3–4					−0.17				
					(0.41)				

Duration of poverty									
Some years						−0.30			
						(0.20)			
All years						0.05			
						(0.33)			
Missing						−0.26			
						(0.33)			
Timing of poverty									
Early, not late							−0.15		
							(0.30)		
Late, not early							0.94		
							(0.29)		
Early and late							0.20		
							(0.24)		
Missing							−0.61		
							(0.62)		
Constant	−5.93	−5.13	−5.96	−5.75	−5.76	−5.85	−6.41	−6.08	−6.07
	(1.49)	(1.39)	(1.50)	(1.53)	(1.04)	(1.03)	(1.03)	(1.52)	(1.49)

Source: Authors' calculations from logit models using data from the NLSY CS on children aged sixty to ninety-five months at assessment (1988 or 1990).

a. $N = 1{,}489$. Mean of dependent variable = 0.122. Coefficients from logit models with standard errors in parentheses.

FIGURE 5.1 / Relative Odds of Low Height-for-Age, by Income-to-Needs Category[a]

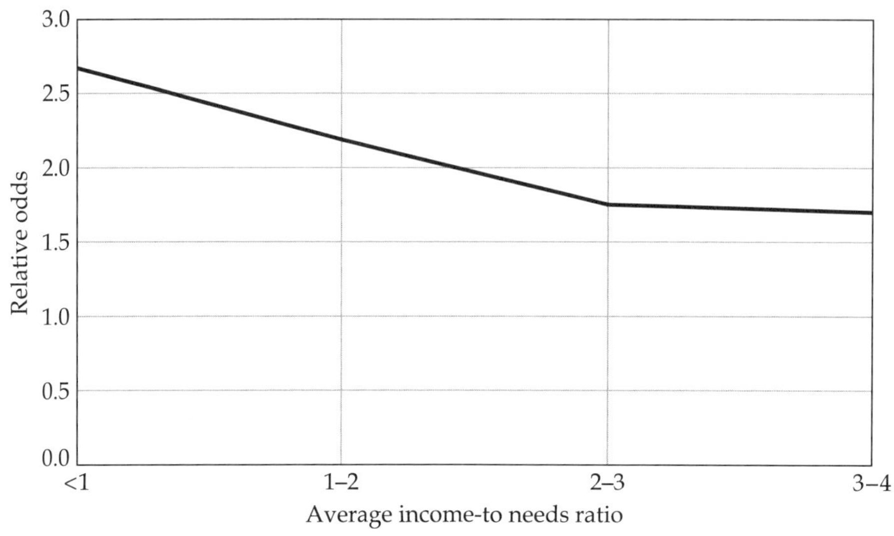

Source: Authors' calculations. See endnote 8.

a. Reference category is average income-to-needs (1978–90) > 4.0.

The model in column 5 included categories of long-term income-to-needs rather than the continuous measure in order to determine whether the relation between the income-to-needs ratio and stunting was nonlinear and, more specifically, to identify effects associated with long-term poverty. The coefficient of the poverty indicator was 0.99 ($p < .10$), corresponding to a relative odds of stunting of 2.7 among poor children compared with their higher-income counterparts (income-to-needs ratio greater than 4.0). Put differently, the prevalence of stunting among poor children was roughly 7.7 percentage points higher than among children with an average family income in excess of four times the poverty line (controlling for race, age, and other characteristics included in the model). There was also evidence of more stunting among near-poor children (income-to-needs ratio between 1 and 2, relative odds, 2.2), although this effect is not statistically significant. The relative odds from these models are presented graphically in figure 5.1.

Figure 5.2 shows the relationship between stunting and more detailed long-term categories of income-to-needs ratio.[8] The risk of stunting dropped fairly sharply between the very poor (average income-to-needs ratio < 0.5) and the less poor (average income-needs ratio 0.5–1.0); the risk declined more gradually as the income-to-needs ratio increased above the poverty line.

The estimated effects of the duration of poverty (table 5.2, column 6) suggest

FIGURE 5.2 / Relative Odds of Low Height-for-Age, by Detailed Income-to-Needs Category[a]

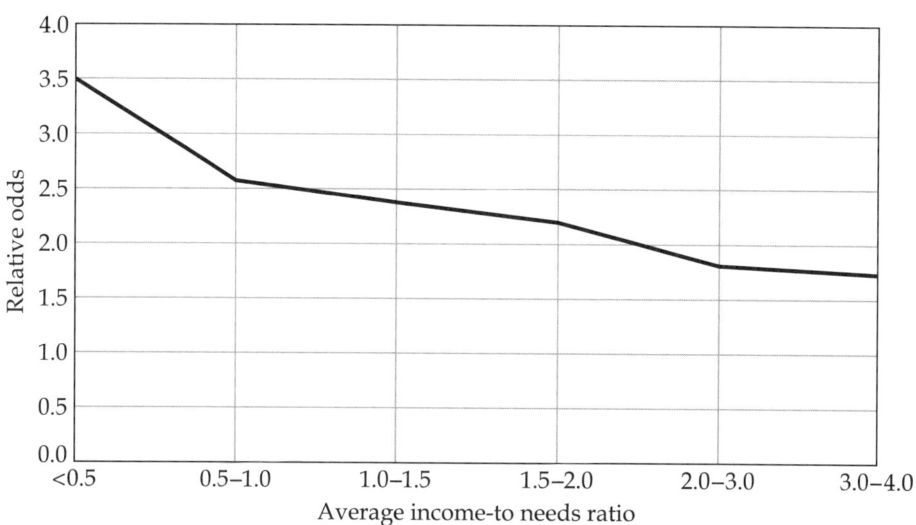

Source: Authors' calculations. See endnote 8.

a. Reference category is average income-to-needs (1978–90) > 4.0.

that children who were chronically poor exhibited an elevated prevalence of stunting, although the effect was not significant. However, the estimates in column 7 suggest that what appears to be an effect of poverty duration in column 6 may instead reflect poverty timing. The estimates in column 7 indicate that children who were poor both early and late experienced essentially the same risk of stunting as children who were poor in their early years only (relative odds of 1.63 and 1.60; $p < .10$ in the former case).[9]

Finally, models in which the average income-needs variable interacted with race or gender controls are presented in columns 8 and 9, respectively. The association between income and stunting appeared greater for whites. Although the interaction terms were fairly large, they were not precisely estimated. In all models, lower birth weight children were more likely to have a low-height-for-age. Higher maternal schooling was associated with a lower prevalence of stunting.

Wasting

In table 5.3 and figure 5.3, we present results from an analogous series of models for low weight-for-age. In contrast to the results for stunting, we found little evidence that income or poverty affected the prevalence of low weight-for-age. An

FIGURE 5.3 / Relative Odds of Low Weight-for-Height, by Income-to-Needs Category[a]

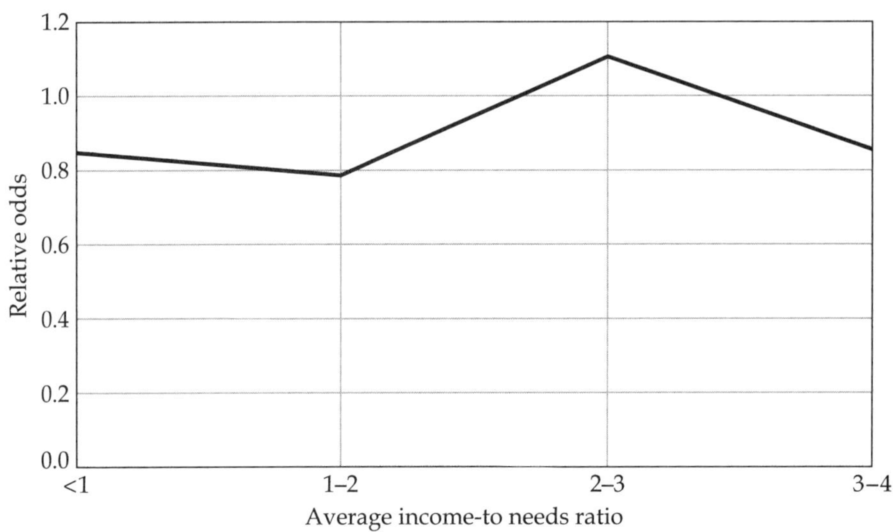

Source: Authors' calculations. See endnote 8.

a. Reference category is average income-to-needs (1978–90) > 4.0.

exception is the significant and very large effect of recent (that is, late) poverty on wasting (column 7; relative odds = 2.6; $p < .001$). A more detailed breakdown of income-to-needs categories revealed a slight excess risk of wasting among the very poor (figure 5.4), although the risk was not statistically significantly different from that in the reference group (the very poor category contains 10.6 percent of the sample).

EXTENSIONS

Stunting, Wasting, and Overweight

In table 5.4 we present estimated coefficients of the long-term average income-to-needs variable from logit models corresponding to the specification presented in column 3 of tables 5.2 and 5.3 for various subsamples, defined on the basis of sex and race/ethnicity. We also include results from an analysis of a binary variable that indicates the child was overweight (above the 90th percentile of weight-for-height). Each cell of the table represents the estimated effect of the long-term average income-to-needs variable from a logit model for the specified subsample. As in the previous models for stunting, we found some evidence that boys bene-

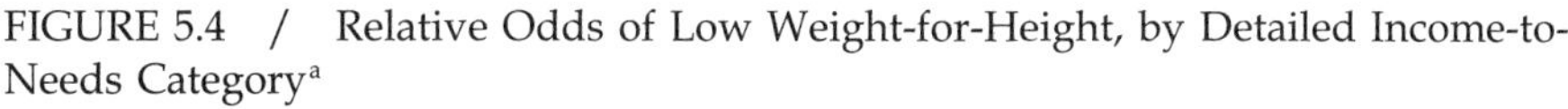

FIGURE 5.4 / Relative Odds of Low Weight-for-Height, by Detailed Income-to-Needs Category[a]

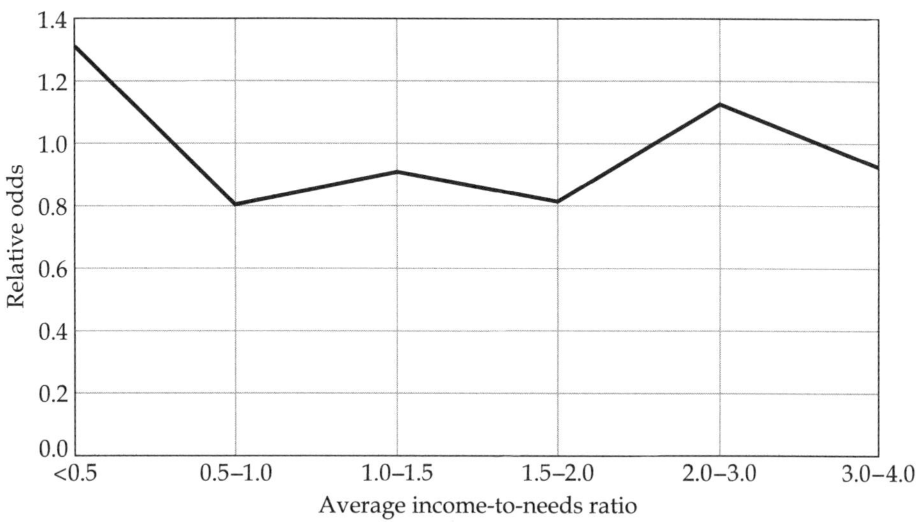

Source: Authors' calculations. See endnote 8.

a. Reference category is average income-to-needs (1978–90) > 4.0.

fited more than girls from increased income and that blacks benefited less than whites.[10] There was little evidence that poverty affected a child's odds of being overweight.

Table 5.5 presents ordinary least squares (OLS) and fixed-effects models of stunting and *z*-scores of height-for-age. By comparing first cousins (whose mothers are sisters), we controlled for unmeasured factors common to sisters that may have led to bias in our estimated effects of income or poverty. Two possible sources of measurement error bias in the first set of models (binary stunting outcome) are likely to have caused downward bias (attenuation bias) in the fixed-effects estimates relative to the cross-sectional estimates. The first source of bias is well known: bias from measurement error in the income variable is exacerbated in fixed-effects estimates. However, unlike the case of a continuous outcome, measurement error in the binary outcome for stunting also leads to attenuation bias, as long as there is a within-family correlation in reporting behavior (Angrist and Lavy 1994, 9–13).

For each outcome and sample, we present estimates from two specifications. The first includes controls for the child's age, sex, and birth order (first or other) and the mother's race, schooling, AFQT score, and age at first birth. The second model added controls for mother's height, weight (body mass index), and indicators of the child's health as an infant (birth weight and short length at birth).

TABLE 5.4 / Estimated Effects of Average Income-to-Needs Ratio on Low Height-for-Age and Low and High Weight-for-Height, Various Subsamples[a]

Sample and Model[b]	Height-for-Age[c] Low	Weight-for-Height[d] Low	Weight-for-Height High	N[e]	
				Height-for-Age	Weight-for-Height
1. Full sample	−0.21	−0.02	−0.01	1,698	1,489
	(0.10)	(0.08)	(0.05)		
2. Girls	−0.12	0.05	−0.04	831	722
	(0.12)	(0.11)	(0.10)		
3. Boys	−0.32	−0.09	0.02	867	767
	(0.16)	(0.11)	(0.10)		
4. Black, non-Hispanic	−0.11	0.14	0.04	594	531
	(0.20)	(0.15)	(0.14)		
5. Non-black	−0.23	−0.07	−0.03	1,104	958
	(0.12)	(0.09)	(0.10)		
Nonblack					
6. Girl	−0.11	−0.02	−0.00	530	441
	(0.14)	(0.12)	(0.11)		
7. Boy	−0.33	−0.12	−0.09	574	505
	(0.18)	(0.13)	(0.15)		
Black, non-Hispanic					
8. Girl	−0.16	0.35	−0.14	301	269
	(0.21)	(0.19)	(0.18)		
9. Boy	0.15	−0.06	0.35	293	262
	(0.33)	(0.23)	(0.24)		

Source: Authors' calculations from logit models using data from the NLSY CS on children aged sixty to ninety-five months at assessment (1988 or 1990).

a. Coefficients from logit models with standard errors in parentheses.

b. In addition to lifetime average income-to-needs ratio for child, controls are, where appropriate for the subsample, the child's sex, age, and birth weight and the mother's race, marital history, and completed schooling.

c. Below 10th percentile of NCHS standard for age and sex.

d. Below 10th percentile of the National Center for Health Statistics (NCHS) standard for age and sex.

e. Tape measurement available for height-for-age; tape and scale measurement available for weight-for-height.

The first two models (rows 1 and 2) are analyses of the binary outcome for stunted. Figures in these rows are OLS (linear probability model) estimates and heteroskedasticity-consistent standard errors (for example, Angrist and Lavy 1994). In general, these estimates are similar to those presented in table 5.2.[11] In the remaining rows of table 5.5 we present estimates from analyses of height-for-age (*z*-score). In rows 3 and 4 we entered the income-to-needs ratio in a linear form. In rows 5–8 we entered a quadratic of the income-needs ratio to allow for

TABLE 5.5 / Estimated Effects of Average Income-to-Needs Ratio on Low Height-for-Age and Height-for-Age, Full Sample and Cousins Subsample[a]

Outcome Variable and Specification	Full Sample XSEC[c]	Cousins Subsample[b]	
		XSEC[c]	Fixed-Effects[d]
Low height-for-age			
1. Socioeconomic status + demographic controls[e]	−0.014	0.010	−0.028
	(.006)	(.017)	(.019)
2. Socioeconomic status + demographic controls + maternal and infant size[f]	−0.008	0.015	−0.012
	(.006)	(.017)	(.016)
Height-for-age (z-score)			
Linear specifications			
1. Socioeconomic status + demographic controls[e]	0.072	0.038	0.091
	(.028)	(.100)	(.075)
2. Socioeconomic status + demographic controls + maternal and infant size[f]	0.035	0.003	0.035
	(.026)	(.090)	(.087)
Quadratic specifications			
1. Socioeconomic status + demographic controls[e]			
Average income-to-needs ratio	0.200	0.125	0.124
	(.061)	(.265)	(.223)
(Average income-to-needs ratio)^2	−0.019	−0.016	−0.006
	(.007)	(.042)	(.036)
2. Socioeconomic status + demographic controls + maternal and infant size[f]			
Average income-to-needs ratio	0.129	0.027	0.026
	(.058)	(.247)	(.261)
(Average income-to-needs ratio)^2	−0.014	−0.005	−0.000
	(.007)	(.039)	(.043)
N	1,698	210	210

Source: Authors' calculations from ordinary least squares (OLS) and fixed-effects models using data from the NLSY CS on children aged sixty to ninety-five months at assessment (1988 or 1990).

a. Heteroskedasticity-consistent standard errors in parentheses.

b. Sample children who have a first cousin (a child of the sister of the sample child's mother) in the sample.

c. Cross-sectional estimates.

d. Computed by entering a dummy variable for the baseline (origin) household of the mother of each child in the cousins subsample.

e. Controls include (where appropriate) child's age (years), sex, and birth order (first vs. higher); mother's race, schooling, marital history, Armed Forces Qualifying Test score, age at birth of first child, and the average income-to-needs ratio of the family over the child's lifetime.

f. Controls include, in addition to those listed in note e, child's short length at birth (<19 inches) and birth weight (100 g); and mother's body mass index (k/m^2) and height (inches).

the possibility that the contribution of increased income to improvements in child health diminished as income increased.

In brief, results from the cross-sectional models support the addition of a quadratic income term. The effect of income on height was fairly large (and statistically significant) for poor households. (The cross-sectional estimates suggest that height-for-age reached a maximum at about four to five times the poverty threshold.) The fixed-effects estimates, however, were much smaller, suggesting that heterogeneity bias may be important. However, error in income measurement was also responsible for the attenuation of estimated effects.

Motor and Social Development

Table 5.6 presents coefficients (and standard errors) from OLS and fixed-effects models in which the dependent variable was the percentile score of the index of MSD. Poverty or low income was generally associated with a lower index of development, although the estimated effects were sensitive to the specification. In particular, estimates for the full sample were much smaller than corresponding estimates for the "cousins" subsample; in the full sample, differences in the MSD index shrank and became statistically insignificant when more detailed controls were added to the models, whereas no such pattern appeared in the subsample of first cousins. Finally, family fixed-effects estimates suggested larger effects of income and poverty status than either set of cross-section estimates did.

DISCUSSION

On balance, our analyses provide evidence that poverty has an adverse effect on health and development in early childhood for a national sample of children followed prospectively to ages five to seven years. The estimates vary too widely

TABLE 5.6 / Estimated Effects of Average Income-to-Needs Ratio on Motor and Social Development[a]

Independent Variable	Full sample XSEC[c]	Cousins Subsample[b] XSEC[c]	Cousins Subsample[b] Fixed-Effects[d]
1. Basic controls[e]			
Average income-to-needs category			
<1	−4.7	−8.7	−12.3
	(1.9)	(5.1)	(5.9)
1–2	−1.5	−5.7	−15.7
	(1.9)	(4.6)	(5.0)
2–3	−0.4	−6.7	0.3
	(1.7)	(4.7)	(4.9)

TABLE 5.6 / *(continued)*

Independent Variable	Full sample XSEC[c]	Cousins Subsample[b] XSEC[c]	Fixed-Effects[d]
2. Basic controls + infant health[f]			
Average income-to-needs category			
<1	−5.9	−7.8	−12.3
	(1.9)	(5.0)	(5.7)
1–2	−2.2	−4.5	−15.7
	(1.7)	(4.4)	(5.0)
2–3	−1.0	−7.7	−2.0
	(1.7)	(4.6)	(4.9)
3. Basic controls + infant health + maternal characteristics			
Average income-to-needs category			
<1	−4.2	−11.1	−11.4
	(2.5)	(6.1)	(6.4)
1–2	−1.3	−7.7	−15.7
	(2.0)	(4.9)	(4.8)
2–3	−0.5	−9.7	−2.0
	(1.8)	(4.7)	(4.9)
Average income-to-needs ratio			
1. Basic controls[e]	0.9	1.6	3.9
	(0.5)	(1.3)	(1.6)
2. Basic controls + infant health[f]	1.2	1.2	3.9
	(0.5)	(1.3)	(1.5)
3. Basic controls + infant health + maternal characteristics[g]	0.6	1.9	3.8
	(0.6)	(1.7)	(1.6)

Source: Authors' calculations from OLS and fixed-effects models of motor and social development using data from the NLSY CS on children aged zero to thirty-five months at assessment (1986 or 1988).

a. NLSY Children aged zero to thirty-five months in 1986 or 1988. Number of observations: full sample: 2344; cousins subsample: 400.

b. The cousins subsample are sample children who have a first cousin who is also in the sample (that is, their mothers are sisters).

c. XSEC: cross-section. Fixed-effects estimates are computed by entering a dummy variable for the baseline (origin) household of the mother of each child in the cousins subsample.

d. Basic controls are long-term poverty category, sex, and age (in years) of child (two dummy variables), and race of mother.

e. Controls include those listed in note d and birth weight, premature birth (< 37 weeks gestation), and short length (< 19 inches) of child.

f. Controls include those listed in note e and mother's age at first birth, AFQT score, and marital history (five dummy variables).

across outcomes, subsamples, and specifications, however, to make precise quantitative statements about the relationship between poverty and the physical health of children in the NLSY. The largest and most robust estimates relate to stunting. Long durations of poverty appear to be associated with elevated risks of stunting. Poverty had no significant effect on stunting among black children in the sample; although the effect was in the expected direction, it was not precisely estimated (see table 5.4).

The absence of a strong association between poverty and nutritional status among black children is consistent with other cross-sectional evidence. According to Allen (1990, 926),

> Black children are heavier than white children and taller after 2 years of age. This results in a substantially higher proportion of White children than Black being classified in the small group of "malnourished" as defined by their smaller weight, length, and growth percentiles. For example, in the NHANES[National Health and Nutrition Examination Survey]1 about four times more White children than Black fell below 90% of the NCHS median value for weight (2.5% of white children below the poverty level compared to 0.6% for similar black children).

The weaker relationship between poverty and nutritional status found among black as compared to white children in previous studies may have resulted from greater error in measuring income among black children. Because our estimates are based on multiple observations of income, they should be less influenced by bias from random errors in the measurement of income than those derived from a single cross-sectional sample such as the NHANES1. We did find some evidence that poverty has a smaller effect on blacks than on whites, although the race-poverty interaction term is not statistically significant. The effect of poverty on height for blacks had the expected sign and was not trivial in size but was not statistically significant.

The relationship between lifetime poverty and stunting may reflect the ability of a long-term income measure to capture the effects of poverty in the prenatal year and at ages zero to three rather than the effect of long duration per se. In particular, children in the sample who were poor in the first and second "halves" of early childhood were no more likely to be stunted than those who were poor in the early period only. Other studies have shown a similar responsiveness of weight to short-term deprivation, while more sustained deprivation results in compromised growth in height that may not be subsequently "caught up" in more favorable times (Tanner 1986; Martorell and Ho 1984; World Health Organization Working Group 1986).

We found relatively little evidence of a relationship between long-term poverty and under- or overweight-for-height.[12] Evidence that height but not weight deficits are associated with poverty is not an unusual finding. Peterson and Chen (1990, 937) report that "the proportion of children with low weight-for-height in community-based surveys is less than expected in the reference population. . . . Excess prevalence of stunting has, however, been documented among low income children."

On the other hand, we found that recent (late) poverty was associated with substantially higher odds of low weight-for-height. This finding is consistent with evidence from several countries that short-term deprivation results in adjustments in body weight (Martorell and Ho 1984; World Health Organization Working Group 1986).[13] For example, in a study of Kenyan children, McDonald et al. (1994) found that, during a food shortage, school-age children's weight-for-height decreased significantly but subsequently recovered when the shortage ended. In contrast, early poverty and even sustained poverty were not associated with low weight-for-height in our sample. In conjunction with our findings regarding effects of early or longer-term poverty on height, children who are poor early (and possibly early and late) may be more likely to be of short stature but to have adequate weight for height.

Since children born into poverty are more likely than other children to be small at birth, their higher risks of stunting and being underweight in the first few years of life may in part reflect these initial deficits. Gayle et al. (1987) estimate that 20–40 percent of the prevalence of short stature among children in the Pediatric Nutrition Surveillance System (PedNSS) was attributable to small size at birth (for example, LBW). The prevalence of low height-for-age differs greatly between LBW and normal-birth-weight (NBW) infants, particularly in the first six to nine months of life. For example, nearly 70 percent of infants reported to be LBW were stunted at age three months, compared to approximately 10 percent of NBW infants. By one year of age, the gap had narrowed considerably, with 30 and 10 percent of LBW and NBW infants stunted; the pattern remained essentially the same up to age two years (the upper end of the age range studied). The persistence of this gap shows the importance of size at birth for predicting size at older ages. Cruise (1973) and Martell et al. (1978) also found appreciable differences in the size of NBW versus LBW children through at least the age of three years.

Consistent with these studies, we found that birth weight was significantly and inversely correlated with the risks of both low height-for-age and low weight-for-height among five- to seven-year-old children. However, significant differences in stunting by long-term income category remained after controls for birth weight were included in the models. Given the importance of the relations between poverty, size at birth, and subsequent size, the role of prenatal income merits separate consideration in future research on poverty and physical growth.

Studies of several large national data sets have demonstrated that income in the year of measurement is positively associated with children's height, weight, hemoglobin, and fat stores (as assessed by triceps skinfold measurements) (Jones, Nesheim, and Habicht 1985; Hamill, Johnston and Lemeshow 1972; Owen et al. 1974; U.S. Department of Health, Education, and Welfare 1972). Others have found excessive rates of stunting and wasting among children in the PedNSS (U.S. Department of Health and Human Services 1987; Trowbridge 1983).[14]

Our earlier results suggested that the differentials described in previous studies of nutritional status (such as those just discussed), which were based on current income, may substantially understate the differentials in nutritional status between persistently poor and nonpoor children (Miller and Korenman 1994a). In interpreting our findings that long-term poverty was associated with larger deficits in children's nutritional status, we noted that measurement error bias would be more severe for estimates based on a short-term income classification than for those based on a long-term classification because longer-term measures smooth annual fluctuations, including those due to random measurement error (Solon 1992). Since the NLSY prospectively collects annual information on individual income sources and amounts for each family member, the income information in the NLSY is of higher quality than that collected in many health surveys. Nonetheless, random errors in the measurement of income will lead to some misclassification of poverty status, which will cause downward bias in the estimated effects of poverty.[15]

Although there is no entirely satisfactory way to determine the importance of measurement error, the effects of late (or recent) income appear relatively larger in models of wasting than in models of stunting, while the effects of early or longer-term income appear most important in the stunting models. These differences in the responsiveness of height and weight to deprivation are consistent with patterns observed in other countries and suggest that at least part of the difference between the effects of long-term versus short-term poverty is real: that is, it is unlikely that measurement error alone could account for the effects related to the timing of poverty.

Analyses that attempted to estimate causal relationships between income and height yielded mixed results. The estimated effects of poverty on stunting in early childhood appear related to the height of the child's mother and the child's weight and length at birth, both plausible pathways through which poverty can influence nutritional status in early childhood. The mother's height may be thought of as a control for the child's genetic height potential or as a pathway through which material disadvantage affects the child's health. Because of high intergenerational correlation in economic status (for example, Solon 1992), one might not want to interpret results from models that include these more detailed controls as estimates of the "total" effect of poverty on children's health; rather, because of high intergenerational correlation in economic status, the effects of the mother's height and the child's length and weight in infancy on stunting clearly include some "indirect" effects of family poverty on the child's health.

Poverty appeared to affect stunting in comparisons of first cousins, at least in the model that excluded controls for maternal height and weight. The estimated effect of income on a continuous measure of height-for-age was fairly strong at low levels of income but essentially disappeared in models that included fixed effects for maternal household of origin. This finding is consistent with those of Currie and Thomas (1995), who found little evidence for an effect of income on height in fixed-effect analyses of siblings. However, both Currie and Thomas's and our family fixed-effects estimates are likely to suffer from attenuation bias, which is known to increase with the level of intrafamily correlation in the explanatory variable (that is, income).

Finally, we found evidence that poverty inhibits motor and social development in the first three years of life. However, adding controls for maternal characteristics associated with poverty sometimes had little effect on the income coefficients or caused them to move in an unexpected direction.

CONCLUSION

Why is poverty associated with substandard nutritional status among U.S. children? In answering this question, it is important to keep in mind that anthropometric measures such as those we studied are not proxies for dietary intake but are indicators of health for populations (Pollitt 1988; Miller, Fine, and Adams-Taylor 1989), since they may be influenced by frequency and severity of illness as well as other environmental stressors. The question then becomes, do poor children present evidence of malnutrition mainly because their families lack the financial resources to purchase a nutritionally adequate diet (that is, because of food shortage) or are other factors such as dietary practices and knowledge, accessibility of nutritious food (for example, location of supermarkets), neighborhood characteristics that increase health risks (for example, lead exposure), or health care availability and utilization more important in determining nutritional status and health (Allen 1990; Peterson and Chen 1990)?

Correlational evidence alone cannot establish a convincing case for a causal relationship between poverty and health. Nonetheless, further research that explores hypotheses regarding specific mechanisms that may mediate relations between poverty and nutritional status could refine and bolster specific interpretations and aid in the formulation of appropriate policies (Marini and Singer 1988). In our view, the most promising avenue for investigation, therefore, is to document mechanisms such as diet, availability or utilization of health services, illnesses, or "social" factors such as abuse, neglect, or violence.

Although the great strength of the NLSY is the detailed socioeconomic information it collects in a longitudinal design, it contains limited information on illness and health status and none on diet. Better documentation of causal processes will therefore most likely require the creative use of existing health information sources, possibly in conjunction with longitudinal social surveys. Unfortunately, existing national surveys of health and nutritional status in the United States typically include information on income or poverty status in the year of measurement only. For example, the latest NHANES survey (round III, 1988–94) can be used to relate differences in illness history and diet across income groups to observed patterns of nutritional status but does not contain the longitudinal income information needed to construct a poverty history. Future research would benefit from the collection of data that would include assessments of children's health status, their illness histories, information on their dietary and health practices, and their access to and use of health services. Our research also suggests that consideration should be given to designing health surveys to capture the dynamic nature of individual and family poverty in the United States.

NOTES

1. Because of financial limitations the NLSY dropped the children of women in the disadvantaged white oversample after the 1988 survey round (Baker et al. 1993).
2. The exclusion of children born after 1988 did not affect the analysis sample for height and weight since the sample was restricted to children aged five to seven years at assessment. However, the exclusion of children born between the 1988 and 1990 CSs did reduce the sample used for analysis of the MSD index. In addition, we excluded a few children who were born by the time of the 1988 CS, who were under age thirty-six months as of 1990, and who had not been given the MSD assessment prior to 1990.
3. The MSD index is available for children through age four years. However, there is little variation in the index for children above age three so we have included only children through age thirty-five months in our analyses.
4. We expanded the ages studied beyond five years to increase the sample size and the precision of estimates. We did not include children younger than five because we wished to construct a long-term income measure that corresponded to a child's lifetime and that would allow us to explore the importance of the timing of poverty. In particular, we wanted early and late poverty measures each to be based on information on income for at least three years.
5. In an earlier version of this chapter, our sample included children for whom weight and height information was collected by maternal reports in addition to those for whom that information was collected using a measuring tape and scale. Overall, the principal results was not sensitive to the inclusion of children with maternal reports of height and weight. However, the results were sensitive for some subsamples (for example, black children). Currie and Thomas (1995), who include maternal reports of height in their sample, report little evidence of heaping, suggesting the data are of good quality (p. 347, fn. 14; see also Currie and Thomas 1993b; cited in Currie and Thomas 1993a). However, the existing validation evidence regarding the accuracy of caretakers' reports of children's heights and weights is mixed (Allen 1990, 926). Moreover, the discussant of an earlier version of the present paper, Duncan Thomas, suggested that we exclude maternal reports of height and weight. Therefore, we have done so.
6. For a discussion of the circumstances under which fixed-effects estimates strengthen the case for a causal interpretation, see Currie and Thomas (1993a, 5–9). They estimate mother fixed-effects estimates (sibling differences) for height at age five using a three-year average of income centered at age three for children in the NLSY. We did not estimate mother fixed effects because our measure of lifetime income was correlated very highly among siblings (greater than 0.9), whereas the correlation among first cousins was about 0.5.
7. For weight-for-height, 17.0 percent were above the ninetieth percentile (15.7 and 19.4 percent for nonblack and black children, respectively).

8. The estimated coefficients (*coef*), standard errors (*SE*), and relative odds (*RO*) from models with the more detailed income categories follow:

Long-term income-to-needs	Stunting			Wasting		
	coef	SE	RO	coef	SE	RO
<0.5	1.25	.64	3.5	0.26	.51	1.3
0.5–1.0	0.94	.58	2.6	−0.25	.41	0.8
1.0–1.5	0.86	.57	2.4	−0.15	.42	0.9
1.5–2.0	0.80	.56	2.2	−0.24	.40	0.8
2.0–3.0	0.57	.56	1.8	0.13	.38	1.1
3.0–4.0	0.53	.59	1.7	−0.15	.41	0.9
>4.0 (reference)						

9. In our analyses of the larger sample that included heights collected by maternal reports (not shown), the coefficients of the poor early and poor both early and late variables were 0.55 and 0.52 respectively, each with p-values less than .01.

10. We also estimated multinomial logit models (not shown) of low or high weight in which the reference category consisted of children with weight-for-height between the 10th and 90th percentiles of the NCHS standards. The results were very similar to the corresponding results reported in table 5.4.

11. The sample sizes were too small to permit separate fixed-effect estimation for the subsamples of black, Hispanic, and nonblack, non-Hispanic children.

12. Although more than 10 percent of the sample was above the ninetieth percentile of the NCHS standard of weight-for-height, in general the prevalence of overweight was not significantly related to low income.

13. Portions of this discussion are drawn from Miller and Korenman (1994).

14. The PedNSS monitors children in the Women, Infants and Children (WIC) program, the Early Periodic Screening, Diagnosis and Treatment Program, and publicly funded maternal and children's health clinics. It is important to consider that the PedNSS population will not be representative of all poor children if the participants differ from poor nonparticipants in health behaviors or access to health care, if the programs improve nutritional status, or if, like WIC, the programs give priority to children with clinical evidence of malnutrition or health problems.

15. Random error in the measurement of income in the NLSY and other longitudinal surveys can be of fundamental importance; this type of measurement error led early studies to overstate the extent of economic mobility across generations (Solon 1992; Zimmerman 1992).

Chapter 6

Poverty and Patterns of Child Care

The NICHD Early Child Care Research Network

Child care has moved to center stage in federal and state policies designed to address the problems of poor families. In the past, child care was linked to federal policies designed to reduce poverty, either as a support for parents as they work or as a vehicle for preventing poverty in the next generation through early intervention. In the late 1990s infant child care for families in poverty is of acute interest in light of proposed reforms in welfare policy that would require parents to participate in the work force as early as thirteen weeks after an infant is born. Child care is an essential service if policies designed to move families from welfare into the paid labor force are to succeed. Moreover, the extent and quality of child care experiences are important determinants of whether programs promoting economic self-sufficiency for parents have positive or harmful consequences for the development of their young children.

The central purpose of this chapter is to show how poverty affects the child care experiences of infants. Much of the research on the relations between poverty or income and child care has confounded ethnic group, family structure, and parents' education with economic indicators of socioeconomic status or has relied exclusively on demographic proxies of income and poverty status (Baydar and Brooks-Gunn 1991; Howes and Stewart 1987; Phillips, McCartney, and Scarr 1987; Phillips et al. 1994).

Public policy debates, in contrast, revolve around the importance of income in comparison with other aspects of socioeconomic status. There is considerable practical importance in discerning whether income supplements or child care subsidies alone would improve the child care that very young children receive or whether other characteristics of families with high or low incomes are the more powerful determinants of the amount and quality of the child care they use. These issues are under particular scrutiny for families in long-term poverty and those receiving public assistance because they are the target of poverty policies. Moreover, children in persistent poverty are more at risk for developmental deficits than are those in transitory poverty, and children in families that are poor and on welfare show higher rates of behavior problems and worse cognitive outcomes than children in families who are poor but not on welfare (Duncan, Brooks-Gunn, and Klebanov 1994; Bolger et al. 1995; Brooks-Gunn 1995; Moore et al. 1995; Phillips and Bridgman 1995).

In this chapter we describe infants' child care experiences by the age at which the infants entered nonmaternal care, the number of hours in care, the type of care (who provided care in what setting), and the observed quality of the social and physical environment. We address the following questions: What are the effects of family characteristics on the child care received during the first fifteen months of life? What are the effects of family income and poverty status independent of associated family characteristics? Does duration of poverty or receipt of public assistance predict patterns of child care?

EARLIER RESEARCH ON PATTERNS OF CHILD CARE

Family Characteristics

Earlier work has demonstrated links between patterns of child care and several family characteristics associated with poverty. A variety of these characteristics, including membership in a minority ethnic group, small family size, high levels of maternal education, and single-parent status, predict mothers' early return to work after childbirth and therefore influence children's age of entry into nonmaternal care and the amount of such care they receive (Baydar and Brooks-Gunn 1991; Garrett, Lubeck, and Wenk 1991; Leibowitz, Klerman, and Waite 1992).

According to representative national surveys, African American children enter care earlier and for longer hours, on average, than European American children do. Small families and high levels of maternal education are also associated with the extensive use of nonmaternal care (see, for example, Becerra and Chi 1992; Caughy, Di Pietro, and Strobino 1994; Hayes, Palmer, and Zaslow 1990; Brayfield, Deich, and Hofferth 1993). Single parents use more care, different types of child care, poorer-quality care, and care with which they are less satisfied than two-parent families do (Brayfield, Deitch, and Hofferth 1993).

In contrast, the influence of other adults in the household on families' child care choices has been largely unexplored. A common assumption in welfare debates is that informal care by relatives will meet a sizable share of the demand for child care among mothers engaged in welfare-to-work activities. But some evidence indicates that comparatively few families can arrange for care by relatives (Waite, Leibowitz, and Witsberger 1991).

Income

Income per se, rather than its demographic correlates, might be an especially important determinant of child care use. Care for infants and toddlers is particularly expensive and is often in short supply (Culkin, Morris, and Helburn 1991). Among families who pay for child care those of different income levels spend strikingly disparate percentages of their family income on it. Very low income families spend between one-quarter and one-third of their income on child care, compared to 6 percent for families whose income is above the U.S. median (Phillips and Bridgman 1995; U.S. Department of Commerce 1995).

Earlier studies show that families with high incomes generally use more child care than low-income families do (Baydar and Brooks-Gunn 1991; Garrett, Lubeck, and Wenk 1991; Leibowitz, Klerman, and Waite 1992). Maternal income and other sources of income, however, probably have different effects on the age at which children enter care and on the amount of care. Maternal employment contributes to both family income and the amount of nonmaternal care needed, whereas other sources of income (for example, paternal earnings) may reduce the need for nonmaternal care by supporting the family while the mother cares for an infant at home (Leibowitz, Klerman, and Waite 1992).

By contrast, both parents' earnings are likely to contribute to the type and quality of care because a family's overall resources determine its ability to purchase care. In a recent study of family-based child care, the quality of care and the family's income were positively and linearly related: the lower the family's income, the lower the quality of the family's care arrangements (Galinsky et al. 1994). Earlier studies show that socioeconomically deprived families tend to rely on poorer-quality child care arrangements than more advantaged families do (Howes and Stewart 1987; Howes and Olenick 1986; Phillips, McCartney, and Scarr 1987; Vandell and Corasaniti 1990). Moreover, many low-income parents are not fully satisfied with their care arrangements and would change them if they could (Kisker and Silverberg 1991; Meyers and van Leuwen 1992; Sonenstein and Wolf 1991).

For children in child care centers, however, the relation between family income and quality may not be linear. In a large multisite study, centers serving high- or low-income families provided higher-quality care for preschool-age children than did those serving middle-income families (Phillips et al. 1994). One reason may be the relatively high-quality early intervention programs that are available to some of the poorest U.S. families. Families with earned incomes below the poverty threshold are also most likely to be eligible for direct public subsidies, which expand the range of child care options available to low-income families (Helburn 1995; Layzer, Goodsen, and Moss 1993; Long and Clark 1995; Siegel and Loman 1991; U.S. Department of Health and Human Services 1995). Affluent families are most likely to benefit from tax credits, while near-poor and lower-middle-income families are less likely to receive public subsidies of any kind than either the poor or the affluent are (Hofferth 1995a).

THE CURRENT STUDY

Collectively, these several strands of research document consistent links between family economic factors and patterns of child care, but the studies share several limitations. Many used samples of children in a restricted socioeconomic range, included children of a wide age range in the same analyses, and focused on a particular type of care. It is therefore difficult to decipher the issues that only or more powerfully affect families living in poverty relative to near-poor and more affluent families, that are specific to infants and toddlers (as contrasted with older children), or that apply across the range of naturally occurring child care arrangements used by families. These issues lie at the heart of the poverty debates in the 1990s.

The indices of child care have also been limited. Because samples have typically been drawn from child care settings, little information is available about the wide range of care settings and types used by parents or about children who are not in child care. Age of entry has rarely been studied, though some developmental psychologists consider entry within the first three months of life as potentially most disruptive to the parent-child relationship. Others stress the six- to twelve-month period as a critical time for the formation of attachment to the parents (Clarke-Stewart, Gruber, Fitzgerald 1994). Finally, only a handful of available studies have included careful, on-site assessments of child care quality, thus limiting conclusions to issues of cost, access, and timing and extent of child care.

In contrast, the study on which this chapter is based—the National Institute of Child Health and Human Development (NICHD) Study of Early Child Care—is a prospective study of families that span the range of economic circumstances from poor to affluent. It captures naturally occurring patterns of child care, ranging from relative and family care to child care centers. A complete child care history obtained from birth provides information about the timing of entry and types of care used. Extensive observations of the quality of children's primary care arrangements conducted at six and fifteen months of age enable us to supplement results about the timing of entry and the amount and type of child care for infants and toddlers living in poverty with detailed information about the quality of care that they experience.

METHOD

Participants

The participants in this study were the sample drawn for the NICHD Study of Early Child Care (NICHD Early Child Care Research Network, in press). They were recruited from thirty-one hospitals at the following sites throughout 1991: Little Rock, Arkansas; Orange County, California; Lawrence and Topeka, Kansas; Boston, Massachusetts; Philadelphia, Pennsylvania; Pittsburgh, Pennsylvania; Charlottesville, Virginia; Morgantown and Hickory, North Carolina; Seattle Washington; and Madison, Wisconsin.[1] During selected twenty-four-hour sampling periods, 8,986 women giving birth were visited in the hospital.[2] Of these, 5,416 met the eligibility criteria for the study. A subset of this group was selected in accordance with a conditionally random sampling plan designed to ensure that the recruited families included mothers who planned to work full time (60 percent) or part time (20 percent) in the child's first year as well as some who planned to stay at home with the child (20 percent). A total of 1,364 families with healthy newborns were enrolled when the infants were one month of age (58 percent of those who were invited to participate). The sample reflected the demographic diversity (economic, educational, and ethnic) of the eligible families.

The data for the analyses presented here are based on the 1,281 children who participated in the study at least through age fifteen months. Table 6.1 shows the demographic characteristics of the families in the sample.

Data Collection

Mothers and the target children were visited in their homes when the children were one, six, and fifteen months old. At each visit, mothers responded to a standardized interview containing questions about the household composition, the family's health, and the family members' education and employment history and status, and to a set of questionnaires. Families were telephoned at three-month intervals to update information about child care and family characteristics.

When the children were six and fifteen months old, children who were in ten or more hours a week of nonmaternal care were observed in the primary child care setting (the one in which they spent the most time). At fifteen months of age, 920 infants had some regular nonmaternal care; 825 were in child care for ten or more hours per week; 658 (80 percent of those eligible) were observed. The remaining 20 percent were not observed because the caregivers refused to allow the observation or because a visit could not be scheduled within the required age bracket.

FAMILY CHARACTERISTICS The family and child characteristics examined were ethnic group, sex, family size, mother's education, family structure (single mother or two parents), and presence of adult relatives in the home.

The child's ethnicity was determined by the mother's report using the U.S. Census categories (1) American Indian, Eskimo, or Aleut; (2) Asian or Pacific Islander; (3) black or African American; (4) white; or (5) Other. In response to a second question, she indicated whether the child was Hispanic or non-Hispanic. The child's sex was included in the analyses for purposes of control, but there were no hypotheses about the effects of gender.

We defined family size as the number of children in the family when the target child was fifteen months (not one month) old so that the measure would include siblings born after the target child. We scored mother's education when the child was one month old as a five-level variable in which 1 equaled less than a high school education; 2, high school graduation; 3, some post–high school education; 4, college graduation; and 5, some postcollege school.

A partner's presence in or absence from the home was determined at each contact (one, three, six, nine, twelve, and fifteen months). We included both the mother's initial status (whether a partner was present or absent at one month) and the ratio of occasions on which a partner was present in the home over the first fifteen months of the child's life because both were considered important. We also noted whether one or more adult relatives lived in the home when the target child was one month old.

ECONOMIC PREDICTORS The measure of total income from each of three different sources was based on the mother's report: the mother's current earnings, her partner's current earnings, and the value of all other income. To assess income other than earnings, we asked the mothers two questions. The first was whether they received any income from each of the following: food stamps; Aid to Families with Dependent Children (AFDC); the supplemental food program for Women, Infants, and Children (WIC); Social Security; disability benefits; child support or alimony; unemployment benefits; savings; rental properties; other investments; and other. The second question asked for the total monthly amount received from all of these sources. Therefore, we could not distinguish income from means-tested programs from other sources of unearned income. Because of this, when mothers reported receiving food stamps, AFDC benefits, or WIC benefits, we did not include unearned income in total family income. The rationale for this decision was that eligibility for means-tested programs is usually based on income thresholds that do not include means-tested transfer payments (and child care subsidies).

Two measures of family income were calculated for measurement at one, six, and fifteen months): the income-to-needs ratio (the total annual family income divided by the poverty threshold for that family's size in that year) and the proportion of total family income contributed by maternal earnings.[3] Temporal stability was high for the income-to-needs ratio. The correlations across time periods ranged from .72 to .84. Therefore, we used the average for the three time periods in most analyses to avoid the atypical nature of family work patterns around the time of childbirth. Duration of poverty was defined as the number of assessments of three (at ages one, six, and fifteen months) in which the family income was below the poverty threshold.

Public assistance was coded as the number of assessment periods in which the family reported receiving AFDC benefits, WIC benefits, or food stamps. Child care subsidies were coded based on parents' responses to a question about whether they received direct financial help with the costs of child care or subsidized care from any of four possible sources: the government (AFDC-related payments, block grants), their employer, tax credits, or private persons (for example, free or reduced-cost care from a friend or relative).

We assessed maternal work hours when the infants were fifteen months old based on mothers' reports of the number of weekly hours they worked for pay at all jobs. Because the distributions were multimodal and somewhat skewed, we grouped the hours into seven levels (see table 6.1).

CHARACTERISTICS OF CHILD CARE We examine four characteristics of child care for this study: (1) the child's age at entry into care, (2) the quantity of care, (3) the type of care, and (4) the quality of care.

TABLE 6.1 / Demographic Characteristics of Families in the Sample

Characteristic	*N*	%
Ethnicity of child		
European American	985	76.9
African American	158	12.3
Hispanic	51	4.0
Other	87	6.8
Number of children in family		
1	522	40.7
2	473	36.9
3	204	15.9
4	54	4.2
5	15	1.2
6+	13	1.0
Mother's education		
Less than 12th grade	122	9.5
High school/general equivalency diploma	267	20.8
Some college	430	33.6
Bachelor's-level work	272	21.2
Postgraduate work	190	14.8
Partner at home		
Yes	1,100	85.9
No	181	14.1
Other adults in family		
Yes	176	13.7
No	1,105	86.3
Income-to-needs ratio		
<1.0	206	16.7
1.0–1.99	227	18.4
2.0–2.99	213	17.3
3.0–3.99	190	15.4
4.0+	398	32.3
Mother's work hours		
0	435	35.0
1–9	51	4.1
10–19	73	5.9
20–29	117	9.4
30–39	134	10.0
40–49	352	28.3
50+	80	6.4

Source: National Institute of Child Health and Human Development (NICHD) Study of Early Child Care. Sample included families of 1,281 children who participated in the study from 1991 at least through age fifteen months.

AGE OF ENTRY Age of entry was the child's age (in months) at the time she or he first experienced ten or more hours a week of nonmaternal care. We analyzed these ages categorically rather than as a continuous variable because of the possibility of nonlinear relations between the predictors and age at entry. We created five categories designed to capture important developmental epochs: (1) zero to two months, (2) three to five months, (3) six to eleven months, (4) twelve to fifteen months, and (5) no care by fifteen months.

QUANTITY OF CARE Quantity was defined as the average number of hours per week spent in child care at age fifteen months. At each assessment period, mothers reported the number of hours per week that their children were cared for on a regular basis by someone other than themselves.

TYPE OF CARE We classified children's primary child care arrangements when they entered ten or more hours per week of care into one of five categories: father (the father was regularly responsible for child when the mother was not home), grandparent (in the child's or the grandparent's home), in-home (care in the child's own home by anyone other than a parent or grandparent), child care home (care in someone else's home by someone other than a parent or grandparent), or child care center. For children in multiple child care settings, the type of care in which the child spent the most time was considered primary. We selected the first type of care experienced by the child for analysis because it may be an especially important indicator of the parent's choice of care in conjunction with entering or reentering the labor force.

QUALITY OF CARE When the children were aged fifteen months, we observed the child care settings on two half-days scheduled within a two-week interval. The three quality measures were designed to assess both the individual child's experience within the setting and the physical, social, and developmentally appropriate characteristics of the child care setting.[4]

The first measure, the Observational Record of the Caregiving Environment (ORCE), was designed for this study to assess the quality of caregiving for an individual child rather than at the level of caregivers or classrooms. The system reflects what is usually considered high quality in infant care—that is, care that is attentive and appropriately responsive, expresses positive affect and affection, is not excessively restrictive or intrusive, and offers activities that promote the infant's cognitive and social development.

We observed each child for four cycles of forty-four minutes over two days and recorded the frequencies of caregiving behaviors each minute for thirty minutes of a cycle. A composite variable, positive caregiving frequency, was the sum of standardized scores for eight categories (shared positive affect, positive physical contact, responds to vocalization, asks question, other talk, stimulates cognitive development, stimulates social development, and facilitates infant behavior).

At the end of each cycle, the observers rated the caregiver on a set of 4-point scales including sensitivity/responsiveness to nondistressed communication, positive regard, stimulation of cognitive development, detachment (reflected), and flat affect (reflected). Summing those ratings yielded a second composite, positive caregiving rating.

For both, we tested observer reliability by having observers at all sites code videotapes and comparing their ratings with master codes on three occasions. In addition, pairs of observers conducted within-site live observations in home and center settings. Reliabilities (Pearson correlations) for the composite positive caregiving frequency were .98 (videotapes) and .86 (live); for the composite, positive caregiving ratings they were .94 (videotapes) and .90 (live).

The second measure of the quality of care was Caldwell and Bradley's 1984 Home Observation for Measurement of the Environment (HOME) Inventory (with the wording of some items modified by Caldwell and Bradley to make them more appropriate for home-based child care situations), which was completed in all home care arrangements. The inventory includes subscales measuring the emotional and verbal responsivity of the caregiver, the acceptance of the child, the organization of the environment, the provision of appropriate play materials, the caregiver's involvement with the child, and variety in daily stimulation.

Third, an abbreviated form of the Assessment Profile for Early Childhood Programs was collected in child care homes and centers (Abbott-Shim and Sibley 1987). For child care homes, the Profile consisted of items selected from two scales: Safety and Health, and Learning Environment (play materials and spaces). In child care centers, the profile included these scales plus Individualizing (having spaces and plans for each child), Adult Needs (providing opportunities for staff development and communication with parents), and Physical Environment (organization and adequacy of space). Three items were added to assess quiet, crowding, and clutter in the environment (from Wachs 1991).

Analyses

Two types of analyses were conducted: generalized logit models for categorical dependent variables (age of entry and type of care) and ordinary least squares (OLS) regressions for continuous dependent variables (hours in care and quality measures). We tested family predictors with and without income in each as well as in additional models specific to particular dependent variables.

All family predictors except ethnic group were either continuous or dichotomous. Ethnic group was coded as one of four categories in the logit analyses: African American, European American, Hispanic American, and all others. In the regressions, we used dummy coding to contrast the ethnic groups; European American (non-Hispanic) was the uncoded category to which others were compared. The child's sex was included for purposes of control.

In the OLS regressions, the income-to-needs ratio was dummy coded into five levels (less than 1.0, poor; 1.0–1.99, near poor; 2.0–2.99; 3.0–3.99; and greater than 4.0) in order to test nonlinear effects and to make specific comparisons between families in poverty and those in other income groups. In conformity with the other analyses in this volume, we omitted the near-poor group. For the generalized logit analysis, however, dummy codes would have used a large number of degrees of freedom, so we treated income-to-needs ratio as a continuous variable.

In the analyses of age of entry, hours in care, and type of care, we included a second income variable, the percentage contributed by mother's earnings, because maternal earnings are likely to have different effects than other income does. For these dependent variables, we conducted additional analyses to examine the effects of the duration of poverty and the effects of receiving public assistance.

RESULTS

Age of Entry

In the logit analyses (table 6.2), both family characteristics (model 1) and income (model 2) predicted the age at which children entered child care. Table 6.3 shows the means for significant predictors.

FAMILY PREDICTORS Family size and mother's education were the only significant family characteristics predicting children's age at entry into care. Children who entered care between the ages of three and five months came from the smallest families and had mothers with the highest levels of education. Children who were not in child care by age fifteen months were from the largest families and had mothers with the lowest levels of education.

INCOME Both the income-to-needs ratio and the proportion of income contributed by the mother's earnings significantly predicted children's age at entry into care. Children who entered care between three and five months of age had families with the highest income levels. Children who entered care very early, before the age of three months, were in families with the highest percentage of income from the mother's earnings. These income patterns remained even when the family and child variables were included in the model.

DURATION OF POVERTY AND ASSISTANCE Duration of poverty was significant when added to the effects of family characteristics. We tested the effects of receiving public assistance with income controlled in order to distinguish the effects of assistance from those of poverty (see tables 6.2 and 6.3). Both duration of poverty and the number of occasions on which the family had received assistance were significant. Families who had experienced poverty once during the child's life and those who had received assistance once were most likely to have children who entered care early (age zero to two months) and least likely to have children who had never been in care. Families who were continuously poor, continuously receiving assistance, or both were least likely to have children who entered care early and most likely to have children who had not entered care at all.

TABLE 6.2 / Predictors of Children's Age of Entry into Ten or More Hours of Care under Different Model Specifications[a]

	Model			
Independent Variable	1	2	3	4
Intercept	47.46***	18.28*	54.53**	30.23***
Ethnicity	12.07	7.72	13.18	7.22
Sex	1.57	1.03	0.63	1.16
Family characteristics				
Children in family at fifteen months	53.41***	10.46*	50.26***	9.94
Mother's education	21.96***	11.16*	17.28***	14.68**
Partner at home (at one month)	3.27	1.60	9.46	4.36
Other adults in family	1.41	1.58	1.51	1.94
Income				
Average income-to-needs ratio		25.67***	—	20.12***
Income from mother's earnings (%)		173.18***	—	170.42***
Duration of poverty			15.96**	—
Public assistance				27.08***

* $p < .05$. ** $p < .01$. *** $p < .001$.

Source: Authors' calculations from logit models using data from the NICHD Study of Early Child Care on 1,281 children born in 1991 who participated in the study at least until age fifteen months.

a. Values are chi-squares. $df = 4$ for all variables except ethnicity, for which $df = 12$.

Hours in Child Care

The second dependent variable was the average number of hours per week spent in child care (table 6.4). Only children who were in some child care at age fifteen months were included in the analyses. The number of hours spent in care was related to the child's age at entry; children who entered care early were likely to experience more hours of care at age fifteen months than those who entered late ($r = -.61$). Some of the predictors followed similar patterns for the two variables.

FAMILY CHARACTERISTICS Models 1 and 3 in table 6.4 show the effects of family characteristics without and with income variables included. Overall, children from ethnic minority families tended to have more hours of child care than children in European American, non-Hispanic families, but the difference was significant only for "other" ethnic groups. Children from small families also received

TABLE 6.3 / Mean Levels of Independent Variables Predicting Age of Entry into Child Care

Independent Variable	Age of Entry (Months) 0–2	3–5	6–11	12–15	No Care by Fifteen Months
Family characteristics					
Children in family at fifteen months	1.84	1.68	1.94	2.11	2.32
Mother's education	2.10	2.39	1.98	2.17	1.92
Average income-to-needs ratio	3.26	4.01	3.10	2.60	2.66
Income from mother's earnings (%)	51	45	38	37	18
Duration of poverty (%)					
Never	41	22	11	3	22
Once	54	19	8	2	16
Twice	35	21	22	3	19
Three times	26	19	12	8	35
Public assistance (%)					
Never	43	22	10	3	21
Once	50	16	17	3	14
Twice	43	18	15	2	23
Three times	26	19	17	9	29

Source: Authors' calculations from logit models using data from the NICHD Study of Early Child Care on 1,281 children born in 1991 who participated in the study at least until age fifteen months.

more hours of care than those from larger families. Neither the presence of a partner at one month nor the proportion of occasions that a partner was present in the fifteen months of the child's life contributed significantly to predicting hours in child care.

INCOME Models 2 and 3 show income effects without and with family characteristics. In general, children in the high-income families spent the most hours in child care, but the effects of income were not linear. The number of hours in child care predicted for children in poor families was higher than for those in near-poor families (model 2), although this pattern was not significant with family variables controlled (model 3). The means for the five income-to-needs groups clarify the meaning of these findings (table 6.5). Lower-income families were less likely to have children in *any* child care than higher-income families were, but those children in care in all income groups averaged more than thirty hours a week.

TABLE 6.4 / Predictors of Children's Hours in Care at Age Fifteen Months[a]

Independent Variable	Model[b] 1	2	3	4	5	6	7	8	9
df	875	876	799	807	865	807	798	807	798
Ethnicity[c]									
African American	4.09		3.77		1.28		4.87		2.29
	(2.27)		(2.18)		(1.86)		(2.49)		(2.31)
Hispanic	3.61		5.96		2.40		5.93		5.39
	(3.19)		(2.91)*		(2.57)		(3.37)*		(2.90)
Other nonwhite	7.56		6.46		4.79		8.51		5.72
	(2.45)**		(2.26)**		(2.00)*		(2.62)**		(2.27)*
Family characteristics									
Sex	0.01		−0.24		0.87		0.23		0.29
	(1.18)		(1.07)		(0.96)		(1.23)		(1.07)
Children in family	−1.71		−0.39		−0.64		−1.55		−0.37
	(0.61)**		(0.58)		(0.50)		(0.66)*		(0.58)
Mother's education	−0.54		−3.08		−1.31		−1.38		−2.76
	(0.57)		(0.59)***		(0.55)*		(0.63)*		(0.59)***
Partner at home	0.77		5.49		−2.60		−.092		4.64
	(3.86)		(3.16)		(3.14)		(4.36)		(3.16)
Partner at home (frequency)	−3.99		−6.44		−0.78		−7.59		−3.77
	(5.69)		(4.45)		(4.71)		(6.20)		(4.54)
Other adult relative in home	3.03		3.70		3.87		3.45		4.08
	(1.99)		(1.95)*		(1.66)*		(2.17)		(1.94)*
Income-to-needs ratio[d,e]									
<1.00		4.77	0.86	8.20	4.48			−4.20	−1.09
		(2.03)*	(2.69)	(2.11)***	(2.16)*			(2.67)	(2.77)
2.00–2.99		0.99	1.67	−1.28	−0.12			1.55	3.50
		(1.78)	(1.83)	(1.69)	(1.65)			(1.98)	(1.94)
3.00–3.99		4.03	6.83	0.44	2.69			4.10	8.61
		(1.85)*	(1.98)**	(1.78)	(1.80)			(2.11)	(2.07)***
4.00+		6.16	11.13	1.66	4.66			9.27	12.98
		(1.60)***	(1.89)***	(1.56)	(1.78)**			(1.96)***	(2.00)***

Income from mother's earnings (%)[d]		31.51 (1.95)***	33.40 (2.22)***	7.20 (2.86)*	6.92 (2.75)*			31.86 (2.31)***	33.98 (2.21)***
Amount time mother employed				5.00 (0.39)***	4.69 (0.39)***				
Duration of poverty						0.43 (1.21)	−2.88 (1.10)**		
Public assistance								2.69 (0.96)**	2.41 (0.86)**
Adjusted R^2	0.0318***	.2375***	.2806***	.3681***	.3766***	.007	.0382***	.2024***	.2868***

$^{*} p < .05$. $^{**} p < .01$. $^{***} p < .001$.

Source: Author's calculations from ordinary least squares regressions using data from the NICHD Study of Early Child Care on children born in 1991 who participated in the study until at least fifteen months.

a. Values are unstandardized regression weights. Standard errors of betas in parentheses.

b. All models include site differences.

c. European American, non-Hispanic is the omitted group.

d. Based only on fifteen-month assessment for comparability with time at which mother's work hours were assessed.

e. Income-to-needs ratio 1.00–1.99 is the omitted group.

TABLE 6.5 / Child's Mean Hours in Child Care, Percentage of Family Income from Mother's Earnings, and Mother's Weekly Hours at Work and in School, by Economic Variables[a]

Economic Variable	*N*	Children in Child Care (%)	Hours in Care (per Week)	Income from Mother (%)	Mother's Work Hours (per Week)	Mothers Hours in School (per Week)
Income-to-needs ratio						
<1.00	206	48.5	33.14	29.7	15.75	8.83
1.00–1.99	227	67.8	33.19	43.2	28.43	1.49
2.00–2.99	213	74.6	32.61	38.2	29.21	0.79
3.00–3.99	190	73.7	36.10	40.1	32.08	1.76
4.00+	398	84.9	36.00	34.5	30.45	0.98
Duration of poverty						
Three times	104	49.0	32.09	22.9	13.08	11.27
Twice	68	64.7	40.26	44.4	30.43	4.09
Once	123	71.5	35.80	49.9	33.40	1.82
Never	847	75.7	34.04	34.5	29.14	1.05
Public assistance						
Three times	131	55.0	36.03	25.2	19.93	9.90
Twice	128	61.7	34.76	41.4	29.10	4.00
Once	70	64.3	35.00	37.1	29.30	2.71
Never	895	77.1	34.35	37.1	29.30	1.00

Source: National Institute of Child Health and Human Development (NICHD) Study of Early Child Care. Sample included families of 1,281 children who participated in the study from 1991 at least through age fifteen months.

a. Except percentage of children in child care, all values based on the 891 children who received any nonmaternal care.

FAMILY CHARACTERISTICS AND INCOME With income controlled, mother's education had a strong negative effect on hours of care. These analyses suggest that children in long hours of care had mothers with relatively little education compared with others in their income bracket. At the same time, children in long hours of care came from families with higher incomes (though not necessarily high incomes) than did others whose mothers had similar levels of education. Mothers with relatively little education may have worked longer hours to supply a given level of income to their families; their children were most likely to be in long hours of child care. Not surprisingly, the percentage of family income derived from the mother's earnings also predicted hours in care. Those families to which the mother contributed high percentages of income had children with long hours in child care.

Because an infant's time in child care is likely to be heavily dependent on the mother's employment, we analyzed two additional models (4 and 5) with the mother's work hours included. The patterns of income and education effects were similar to those found in the models without work hours (see table 6.5 for mean work hours and hours in school for each income group). Although poor families used as much child care as other families did, the mothers worked considerably less and spent more time in school.

Duration of poverty (models 6 and 7) predicted hours in care (see table 6.5 for relevant means). Families living in poverty throughout their infants' lives were less apt to use any child care than never-poor or sometimes-poor families. When children were in child care, the differences in the amount of care were relatively small, but chronically poor mothers spent less time working and more time in school than nonpoor mothers did. They also contributed a lower percentage of their family incomes than did mothers who were not chronically poor. Mothers who had experienced some poverty, by contrast, worked slightly more hours and contributed a higher percentage of their family incomes than never-poor mothers did.

Duration of receipt of public assistance (models 8 and 9), with overall income controlled, was positively related to hours in child care. The means indicate that mothers receiving public assistance had children in slightly more care but worked fewer hours and spent more hours in school than did those who did not receive assistance (table 6.5).

Type of Care

Family variables and income might be especially important influences on parents' selection of an initial care experience for their children. The results of the generalized logit analyses testing family characteristics without income (model 1) and with income (model 2) (table 6.6) show that family size, mother's education, a partner at home, and an adult relative in the home all predicted the type of care children entered as infants. The effects of maternal education, however, were accounted for by income. Both family income and percentage of income contributed by the mother's earnings significantly predicted the type of infant care.

As the means for the five types of care show (table 6.7), the most distinctive group was children receiving "in-home" care by someone other than a parent or grandparent. Children in that group were in relatively large families with highly educated mothers and high incomes. Families with incomes in the moderate range and, in particular, those with more than half of the family income contributed by the mother were more likely to rely on out-of-home care by nonrelatives (in other homes and centers) than were lower-income families and families in which mothers contributed a lower percentage of the total income.

The other findings are trivial: children in their father's care were most likely to have two parents, and children in their grandparents' care were most likely to have an adult relative at home. Duration of poverty also predicted the type of care (model 3), but receiving public assistance did not (model 4; see table 6.7).

TABLE 6.6 / Predictors of Children's Type of Care at Entry into Ten or More Hours of Child Care[a]

	Model		
Independent Variable	1	2	3
Intercept	22.02***	51.38***	19.69**
Ethnicity	6.98	13.02	18.07
Sex	5.06	7.31	5.05
Family characteristics			
Children in family at fifteen months	20.83***	27.25***	46.01***
Mother's education	26.48***	6.00	30.97***
Partner at home (at one month)	23.27***	26.69***	19.61***
Other adults in family	10.63*	13.24*	10.42
Income			
Average income-to-needs ratio		72.13***	
Income from mother's earnings (%)		90.93***	
Duration of poverty			12.16*

* $p < .05$. ** $p < .01$. *** $p < .001$.

Source: Authors' calculations from logit models using data from the NICHD Study of Early Child Care on 1,281 children born in 1991 who participated in the study at least until age fifteen months.

a. Values are chi-squares. $df = 4$ for all variables except ethnicity for which $df = 12$.

Predictors of Child Care Quality

We expected demographic characteristics and income to have different relationships to quality in different types of care. Therefore, we performed the quality analyses within each of the five types of care.[5] Because the numbers of cases were low, a reduced set of predictors was selected on the basis of initial analyses and conceptual rationales. The demographic predictors were ethnicity (white non-Hispanic versus all other groups), sex, family size, and mother's education. Income-to-needs ratio in five dummy-coded categories was the income predictor. The number of cases was insufficient to test the relationship between quality of care and duration of poverty or public assistance. All analyses included sites as controls (see table 6.8).

ETHNICITY There were few differences in the caregiving observed for minority and nonminority children. In all home-based settings, minority children's care was rated lower on the HOME Inventory than was care received by nonminority children, but those differences decreased when income was taken into account. In child care centers, ethnic group was not related to quality measures.

TABLE 6.7 / Mean Levels of Independent Variables Predicting Type of Child Care at Entry

	Type of Care				
Independent Variable	Father	Grandparent	In-home	Child Care Home	Child Care Center
N	198	140	133	251	106
Family characteristics					
Children in family at fifteen months	1.89	1.68	2.10	1.70	1.65
Mother's education	2.09	1.95	2.58	2.21	2.34
Partner at home (proportion)	0.96	0.81	0.83	0.82	0.86
Other adults in family (proportion)	0.09	0.26	0.13	0.14	0.09
Income					
Average income-to-needs ratio	3.01	2.91	5.25	3.46	3.78
Income from mother's earnings (%)	0.42	0.47	0.41	0.51	0.52
Duration of poverty					
Never (proportion)	0.23	0.16	0.17	0.30	0.14
Once	0.36	0.20	0.05	0.32	0.06
Twice	0.23	0.16	0.16	0.36	0.09
Three times	0.24	0.24	0.18	0.22	0.11

Source: National Institute of Child Health and Human Development (NICHD) Study of Early Child Care. Sample included families of 1,281 children who participated in the study from 1991 at least through age fifteen months.

CHILD'S SEX In both child care homes and centers, care given to girls scored higher than care received by boys. The sex-related difference appeared on the observed frequencies and ratings of caregiving and on the other quality measures in child care homes.

FAMILY SIZE In settings that were most homelike (father, grandparent, and in-home care), family size was negatively related to the frequency and rating of positive caregiving as well as to other quality measures. Children in larger families had care that received lower scores than did care for those in smaller families.

MOTHER'S EDUCATION In some homelike settings, mother's education predicted some quality measures, but income differences accounted for the effects

(Text continued on p. 123.)

TABLE 6.8 / Predictors of Quality of Care at Age Fifteen Months, by Type of Care[a]

	Positive Caregiving Frequency	Positive Caregiving Rating	HOME Inventory	Profile
	Father Care			
df	92	92	89	
Ethnicity	−1.23	−1.16	−3.50	—
	(0.72)	(0.68)	(1.15)**	
Sex	0.67	0.24	0.37	—
	(0.60)	(0.56)	(0.96)	
Children in family	−1.62	−1.01	−1.39	—
	(0.40)***	(0.38)**	(0.65)*	
Mother's education	0.23	0.18	0.99	—
	(0.30)	(0.28)	(0.49)*	
R^2	.2024***	.0758	.2588***	—
df	92	92	89	—
Income-to-needs ratio				
<1.00	−1.54	−1.80	−6.63	—
	(1.07)	(0.96)	(1.67)***	
2.00–2.99	0.02	0	−0.58	—
	(0.82)	(0.74)	(1.28)	
3.00–3.99	0.76	−0.49	0.57	—
	(0.92)	(0.84)	(1.44)	
4.00+	2.95	1.95	2.56	—
	(0.95)**	(0.86)*	(1.53)	
Adjusted R^2	.1153*	.0542	.2161*	
df	88	88	85	—
Ethnicity	−0.94	−0.99	−2.95	
	(0.78)	(0.74)	(1.24)*	
Sex	0.64	0.20	0.30	—
	(0.59)	(0.56)	(0.95)	
Children in family	−1.51	−0.88	−1.14	—
	(0.41)*	(0.38)*	(0.64)	
Mother's education	0	0.06	0.68	—
	(0.32)	(0.31)	(0.52)	
Income-to-needs ratio				
<1.00	−0.49	−0.95	−4.38	—
	(1.09)	(1.03)	(1.72)*	
2.00–2.99	−0.28	−0.27	−1.49	—
	(0.79)	(0.75)	(1.27)	
3.00–3.99	0.41	−0.88	−0.94	—
	(0.93)	(0.88)	(1.48)	

TABLE 6.8 / (*continued*)

	Positive Caregiving Frequency	Positive Caregiving Rating	HOME Inventory	Profile
Income-to-needs ratio				
4.00+	2.07	1.19	0.33	—
	(1.00)*	(0.94)	(1.62)	
Adjusted R^2	.2191*	.0919	.2855*	—
	Grandparent Care			
df	63	63	62	—
Ethnicity	0.31	0.10	−2.24	—
	(0.86)	(0.83)	(1.46)	
Sex	0.26	0.67	1.41	—
	(0.65)	(0.63)	(1.12)	
Children in family	−1.20	−0.83	−1.62	—
	(0.33)***	(0.32)*	(0.55)**	
Mother's education	0.09	0.41	1.69	—
	(0.35)	(0.34)	(0.59)**	
R^2	.2016**	.1459*	.2608***	—
df	63	62	62	—
Income-to-needs ratio				
<1.00	−0.06	−1.56	−1.42	—
	(1.16)	(1.04)	(2.08)	
2.00–2.00	2.37	2.11	4.48	—
	(1.25)	(1.11)	(2.21)*	
3.00–3.99	2.08	1.15	4.14	—
	(1.10)	(0.98)	(1.96)*	
4.00+	2.90	2.24	4.69	—
	(1.14)*	(1.02)*	(2.01)*	
Adjusted R^2	.1580*	.2385*	.1734*	—
df	59	58	58	—
Ethnicity	1.15	0.94	−1.33	—
	(0.87)	(0.81)	(1.53)	
Sex	0.23	0.48	1.43	—
	(0.64)	(0.60)	(1.14)	
Children in family	−1.13	−0.65	−1.49	—
	(0.33)**	(0.31)*	(0.58)*	
Mother's education	−0.49	−0.35	1.00	—
	(0.40)	(0.37)	(0.70)	

(Table continued on p. 120.)

TABLE 6.8 / (*continued*)

	Positive Caregiving Frequency	Positive Caregiving Rating	HOME Inventory	Profile
Income-to-needs ratio				
<1.00	0.71	−1.15	0.82	—
	(1.15)	(1.08)	(2.07)	
2.00–2.99	2.98	2.49	4.14	—
	(1.19)*	(1.12)*	(2.12)	
3.00–3.99	2.26	1.49	3.22	—
	(1.08)*	(1.01)	(1.97)	
4.00 +	3.48	2.78	3.58	—
	(1.14)**	(1.07)*	(2.05)	
Adjusted R^2	.2825*	.2766*	.2768*	—
	In-home Care			
df	84	83	84	—
Ethnicity	−1.33	−1.31	−4.35	—
	(0.65)*	(0.62)*	(1.28)**	
Sex	0.39	0.71	0.94	—
	(0.48)	(0.44)	(0.94)	
Children in family	−0.64	−0.41	−1.18	—
	(0.26)*	(0.24)	(0.51)*	
Mother's education	0.55	0.61	1.21	—
	(0.25)*	(0.23)**	(0.49)*	
R^2	.2888***	.3881*	.2739***	—
df	84	83	84	—
Income-to-needs ratio				
<1.00	−3.84	−2.07	−5.00	—
	(1.22)**	(1.18)	(2.39)*	—
2.00–2.99	−1.43	−1.13	0.02	—
	(1.17)	(1.14)	(2.30)	
3.00–3.99	0.29	0.56	3.78	—
	(1.01)	(0.98)	(1.98)	
4.00+	0.66	1.13	4.92	—
	(0.87)	(0.84)	(1.70)**	
Adjusted R^2	.3251*	.3596*	.3095*	—
df	80	79	80	—
Ethnicity	−0.58	−1.04	−2.47	
	(0.69)	(0.67)	(1.35)	
Sex	0.33	0.73	0.86	—
	(0.46)	(0.44)	(0.90)	

	Positive Caregiving Frequency	Positive Caregiving Rating	HOME Inventory	Profile
Children in family	−0.67	−0.27	−1.01	—
	(0.27)*	(0.26)	(0.53)	
Mother's education	0.43	0.67	0.56	—
	(0.29)	(0.27)*	(0.56)	
Income-to-needs ratio				
<1.00	−4.10	−1.86	−4.91	—
	(1.21)**	(1.16)	(2.39)*	
2.00–2.99	−2.06	−2.68	−1.31	—
	(1.30)	(1.24)*	(2.56)	
3.00–3.99	−0.53	−0.63	2.15	—
	(1.07)	(1.04)	(2.11)	
4.00+	−0.77	−0.63	2.25	—
	(1.02)	(0.98)	(2.01)	
Adjusted R^2	.3721*	.4185*	.3535*	—
	Child Care Homes			
df	186	186	186	185
Ethnicity	−0.32	−0.67	−3.58	−1.92
	(0.50)	(0.51)	(0.93)***	(0.82)*
Sex	0.88	1.32	3.13	1.45
	(.40)*	(0.40)**	(0.74)***	(0.65)*
Children in family	−0.05	−0.04	−0.44	0.22
	(0.24)	(0.25)	(0.45)	(0.40)
Mother's education	0.24	0.24	0.63	0.85
	(0.18)	(0.18)	(0.34)	(0.38)**
R^2	.1178***	.0563*	.2475***	.1661***
df	186	186	186	185
Income-to-needs ratio				
<1.00	−0.80	−0.59	−4.84	−5.19
	(0.79)	(0.82)	(1.54)**	(1.26)***
2.00–2.99	−0.11	0.03	−0.43	−0.18
	(0.65)	(0.67)	(1.26)	(1.04)
3.00–3.99	0.17	0.42	1.11	0.48
	(0.68)	(0.69)	(1.31)	(1.07)
4.00+	0.68	1.21	1.86	1.48
	(0.62)	(0.63)	(1.20)	(0.98)
Adjusted R^2	.0994**	.0099	.1578***	.2018***

(Table continued on p. 122.)

TABLE 6.8 / (*continued*)

	Positive Caregiving Frequency	Positive Caregiving Rating	HOME Inventory	Profile
df	182	182	182	181
Ethnicity	−0.22	−0.51	−3.15	−1.28
	(0.52)	(0.53)	(0.95)**	(0.81)
Sex	0.85	1.28	3.00	1.26
	(0.40)*	(0.41)*	(0.73)***	(0.63)*
Children in family	0.01	0.03	−0.14	0.60
	(0.25)	(0.25)	(0.46)	(0.39)
Mother's education	0.13	0.08	0.30	0.32
	(0.22)	(0.22)	(0.40)	(0.34)
Income-to-needs ratio				
<1.00	−0.63	−0.40	−3.98	−5.05
	(0.82)	(0.82)	(1.49)**	(1.28)***
2.00–2.99	−0.29	−0.20	−1.31	−0.73
	(0.67)	(0.67)	(1.21)	(1.04)
3.00–3.99	−0.05	0.11	−0.14	−0.02
	(0.69)	(0.70)	(1.26)	(1.08)
4.00+	0.28	0.72	−0.05	0.52
	(0.70)	(0.71)	(1.28)	(1.10)
Adjusted R^2	.1056**	.0496	.2666***	.2305***
	Child Care Center			
df	111	111	—	102
Ethnicity	0.07	0.35	—	−2.09
	(0.44)	(0.71)	—	(1.46)
Sex	0.63	1.07	—	0.47
	(0.30)*	(0.49)*	—	(1.03)
Children in family	0.02	−0.24	—	−0.36
	(0.14)	(0.22)	—	(0.46)
Mother's education	−0.04	0.04	—	0.92
	(0.15)	(0.24)	—	(0.51)
R^2	.2011***	.0599	—	.3017***
df	111	111	—	102
Income-to-needs ratio				
<1.00	0.94	2.04	—	1.13
	(0.63)	(1.01)*	—	(1.99)
2.00–2.99	−0.08	1.05	—	2.41
	(0.55)	(0.88)	—	(1.77)
3.00–3.99	0.29	1.52	—	4.91
	(0.56)	(0.90)	—	(1.79)**

	Positive Caregiving Frequency	Positive Caregiving Rating	HOME Inventory	Profile
Income-to-needs ratio				
4.00+	0.46	0.92	—	5.06
	(0.48)	(0.78)	—	(1.55)**
Adjusted R^2	.1951***	.0535	—	.3289***
df	107	107	—	98
Ethnicity	0.04	0.56	—	−1.31
	(0.46)	(0.72)	—	(1.42)
Sex	0.59	1.11	—	0.20
	(0.32)	(0.50)*	—	(1.00)
Children in family	0.03	−0.42	—	−0.47
	(0.15)	(0.23)	—	(0.46)
Mother's education	−0.08	0.27	—	0.61
	(0.18)	(0.29)	—	(0.58)
Income-to-needs ratio				
<1.00	0.66	2.45	—	2.20
	(0.67)	(1.06)*	—	(2.13)
2.00–2.99	−0.16	1.22	—	2.26
	(0.58)	(0.89)	—	(1.84)
3.00–3.99	0.41	1.72	—	4.31
	(0.57)	(0.91)	—	(1.85)*
4.00+	0.49	0.38	—	3.67
	(0.55)	(0.86)	—	(1.74)*
Adjusted R^2	.1955***	.0903*	—	.3325***

* $p < .05$. ** $p < .01$. *** $p < .001$.

Source: Author's calculations from ordinary least squares regressions using data from the NICHD Study of Early Child Care on children born in 1991 who participated in the study until at least fifteen months.

a. Values are unstandardized regression weights. Standard deviations in parentheses. All regressions include site.

of education. With income in the model, education was not significant in virtually all tests.

INCOME We expected income to have different effects on the quality of care that is usually free (fathers' and grandparents' care) than of care that is paid for. For those in the father's care, income added little to the variance predicted by family characteristics. For those in grandparents' care, there was an apparent threshold, with children from families falling above 200 percent of the poverty line getting better care than those below that level.

In both in-home care and child care homes, children living in poverty received care that was scored significantly lower on most quality measures than did children in families with incomes above poverty. For in-home care, the differences appeared in two measures: frequency of positive caregiving and the HOME Inventory. For child care homes, this pattern occurred on the measures that included the total environment (the HOME Inventory and the Profile) but not on observed frequency of caregiving or ratings.

The pattern in centers differed from that in all other types of child care. Instead of a linear relation between income and quality, the pattern was slightly curvilinear, with children from poor families receiving care that scored higher than that received by children from near-poor families. The difference was significant only for positive caregiving ratings, but the pattern was apparent for all three measures.

Child Care Subsidies

One reason for a curvilinear relation of income to quality of care could be the availability of subsidies. The majority of poor families whose child was in center care reported receiving government subsidies (table 6.9); only about one-quarter of poor families using child care homes received government subsidies. Poor families using any kind of care were considerably less likely than other families to report receiving tax credits. Employer-subsidized care was relatively rare for all income groups.

The percentage of poor families receiving private subsidies in the form of financial help or free child care ranged from 9 percent to 83 percent depending on the type of care. When poor and near-poor families used in-home care by nonrelatives or relatives other than grandparents, they typically received it free or at reduced cost, but such "subsidies" from grandparents were slightly less likely for poor families than for more affluent families. Moreover, poor families were somewhat less likely than more affluent families to receive privately provided free or reduced-cost care in child care homes or centers.

DISCUSSION

Family Characteristics

The first question we addressed was whether family and child characteristics were related to patterns of infant child care. Our analyses replicated some earlier findings for these very young children, but differences in family income at least partially accounted for many of the effects of family demographic and structural variables. In particular, family characteristics that tend to be associated with poverty—membership in a minority ethnic group, low levels of maternal education, and single-mother status—had relatively few effects on the quantity and quality of child care when income was taken into account.

TABLE 6.9 / Percentage of Families Receiving Child Care Subsidies at Child's Age Fifteen Months, by Type of Care and Income-to-Needs Ratio[a]

Source of Subsidy	Income-to-Needs Ratio <1.00	1.00–1.99	2.00–2.99	3.00–3.99	4.00+
		Father Care			
Government	10.0	8.8	0.0	0.0	0.0
Private	80.0	88.2	88.5	89.5	83.3
Employer	0.0	0.0	0.0	0.0	5.6
Tax credit	0.0	5.9	7.7	5.3	16.7
N	10	34	26	19	18
		Grandparent Care			
Government	22.2	0.0	0.0	0.0	0.0
Private	55.6	75.0	75.0	62.5	85.0
Employer	0.0	0.0	0.0	0.0	0.0
Tax credit	0.0	16.7	37.5	6.3	10.0
N	9	12	16	16	20
		In-Home Care			
Government	0.0	0.0	0.0	0.0	0.0
Private	83.3	33.3	25.0	18.8	15.8
Employer	0.0	0.0	0.0	0.0	1.8
Tax credit	0.0	44.4	25.0	37.5	38.6
N	6	9	8	16	57
		Child Care Home			
Government	26.3	2.9	0.0	0.0	5.7
Private	21.1	11.8	36.6	26.3	25.7
Employer	10.5	2.9	0.0	0.0	2.9
Tax credit	31.6	55.9	61.0	55.3	61.4
N	19	34	41	38	70
		Child Care Center			
Government	63.6	17.6	4.5	0.0	0.0
Private	9.1	5.9	22.7	15.0	12.7
Employer	18.2	11.8	13.6	0.0	10.9
Tax credit	36.4	70.6	68.2	90.0	81.8
N	11	17	22	20	55

Source: National Institute of Child Health and Human Development (NICHD) Study of Early Child Care. Sample included families of 1,281 children who participated in the study from 1991 at least through age fifteen months.

a. Each child is entered only for the primary type of care, but the subsidy information applies to all types of care received by the child.

Although European American infants tended to receive somewhat fewer hours of nonmaternal care than those who were African American, Hispanic American, and from other ethnic groups, there were no differences by ethnic group in age at entry into care and few associations between ethnic group and quality of care. Unlike earlier studies, we found almost no differences in quality or quantity of care between single-mother and two-parent families. Differences based on ethnicity or single-mother status may have declined over the mid-1990s as women from all segments of the U.S. population entered the work force in large numbers during the first year of their children's lives, or previously reported differences may have been largely a function of income.

Similarly, infants in small families entered child care earlier and for more hours than did those in larger families. When cared for by fathers, grandparents, and in-home caregivers, infants in small families (often with one child) also received more frequent positive interactions and more highly rated care than did those in larger families. In most instances these arrangements were limited to children from only one family, so that family size was a proxy for the adult-child ratio in that care setting. Adult-child ratios are known to affect quality in most child care settings; they seem to have a similar effect within families.

Extended families might also be expected to provide help with child care. In this study, when an adult relative lived in the home, children experienced slightly more hours of nonmaternal child care than in families without other adults present in the home.

Income and Poverty

Our second major question was whether income and poverty status predicted patterns of child care with or without taking family characteristics into account. The relation between income and the age at entry into nonmaternal care was not linear. Children entering care at different developmental epochs (or not entering at all) lived in families that occupied different ecological niches defined by patterns of family resources, maternal employment, and reliance on maternal earnings.

Infants who entered care very early (before age three months) and were in long hours of child care at fifteen months came from families whose current incomes were moderately high but that had often experienced transitory poverty and received public assistance earlier in the infant's life, probably because the family depended heavily on the mother's earnings.

Infants who entered care a little later—between three and five months of age—came from families with the highest total incomes. Mothers' incomes made a large contribution to these families' affluence, but nonmaternal income was high as well. Therefore, the family had sufficient income to get along for a few months without the mother's earnings. Because these mothers were typically well educated, they may have had professional and managerial jobs that provided the paid leave and flexibility to allow them to spend a few months caring for the infant full time before relying on nonmaternal child care.

Some infants who were not in care by fifteen months came from families with relatively low incomes. Mothers in this group had relatively little education and probably low earning power. Persistently poor families and families receiving assistance continuously over the child's life were most likely to be in this group.

Children who had entered care early spent longer hours in care at age fifteen months than did those who entered later. The higher the family income, the more hours children spent in nonmaternal care. By fifteen months, therefore, the infants in affluent families were spending long hours in care, suggesting that the parents had returned to full-time employment and that the mothers' incomes were an important contribution to the family's affluence.

Within income brackets, mothers with relatively low levels of education placed their infants in care for long hours. In poor families in which mothers had relatively little education, the mothers may have had to work longer hours at lower wages than better educated women did to provide a given level of income for their families. In many cases, this work effort appears to have been accountable for lifting the family out of poverty. This was possible, however, only if infants entered care very early for long hours, making issues of quality particularly salient for these families.

Interestingly, long hours of infant care for families in chronic poverty were less closely tied to hours of maternal employment or percentage of family income contributed by the mother than was the case for families living just above the poverty threshold and for those for whom poverty was sporadic rather than persistent. One reason is that chronically poor mothers were attending school (which could include job-training programs). The availability of child care may have enabled these mothers to acquire training that would eventually allow them to move out of poverty.

Families using types of care that are usually paid for (that is, child care homes, centers, and in-home care) had higher incomes than those using parent and grandparent care. Although a higher income may have enabled families to purchase care, the causal direction is not clear. Mothers whose children were cared for regularly by fathers or grandparents used fewer hours of child care and contributed a lower proportion of the family income than did those who used other forms of care (NICHD Early Child Care Research Network in press). Whether such mothers living in poverty could obtain free care if they worked full time is not at all clear.

Whatever the type of care, its quality is the important determinant of children's well-being. Our findings, which replicated earlier studies with older children, showed that poor infants received relatively poor-quality care in home-based settings (Galinsky et al. 1994). Income appears to play a more important role in this pattern than family structure or demographic characteristics associated with poverty.

Of the two types of quality measures examined (caregiving directed to the study child and more general evaluations of the quality of the social and physical environment) family income generally predicted the overall quality of the social and physical environment better than it predicted the quality of the adult-child interactions. The care of poor infants in their own homes, either by fathers or other in-home caregivers, received HOME Inventory scores that were particularly low. This finding is consistent with a large body of literature showing that the quality of the maternal home environment as measured by the HOME Inventory is associated with socioeconomic status (Bradley, Caldwell, and Rock 1988). It suggests continuity of the child's home environmental quality whether the mother, the father, or other caregivers are in that setting.

When fathers provided care, poor children were as likely as more affluent ones to experience positive adult-child interactions. Hence, poor children in their fathers' care were receiving affectionate and positive attention even though the physical and intellectual environment was somewhat less adequate than that of children in nonpoor families. When others cared for children at home in poor families, however, they were less likely to be attentive and positive toward the child, suggesting that in-home care by people other than parents and grandparents may put poor children particularly at risk.

The environments in child care homes where poor infants were cared for were rated low in quality on both the HOME Inventory and the Profile. That is, they provided relatively few social and environmental supports for the children's development. Families in poverty may have a limited choice of child care homes because of cost or proximity and may select child care homes that are similar to their own home environments. An extensive literature shows that low-quality home environments are associated with relatively poor intellectual and academic skills (Bradley et al. 1989). This relationship raises concerns about the impact of poor-quality child care environments on children's cognitive and social development, particularly when children are exposed to these environments in the first year of life. Notably, however, the caregiving observed in child care homes did not differ by family income; poor infants were as likely as affluent ones to receive attentive, positive care. Later analyses of the cognitive and social development of the children in this study will help to determine whether the differences in quality associated with income have an influence on children's overall development.

In center-based care, our findings were consistent with earlier results for older children showing that children from poor and affluent families tended to receive better-quality care than those with incomes slightly above poverty (Phillips et al. 1994). One reason may have been the availability of subsidies for low-income families. Although the number was small, poor families using center-based care were considerably more likely to receive government subsidies for care than were poor families using other forms of care or nonpoor families. Parents most likely underreport the subsidies because they probably did not know about or consider subsidies given directly to the child care setting rather than to the parents. This pattern of findings suggests that government subsidies can provide access to high-quality care for poor children.

In addition, public subsidies can provide critical support for mothers' work efforts. Economic modeling has shown associations among the price of child care, potential economic returns on maternal employment, and work effort. For low-income families, the higher the price of child care, the lower the employment rate (Fronstin and Wissoker 1994). Providing a full subsidy to poor and near-poor mothers who pay for child care has sizable effects on the proportion of mothers who work that are not found when these models are applied to nonpoor families (U.S. General Accounting Office 1994).

For mothers receiving welfare, child care subsidies play an important role in the parents' choice of and satisfaction with child care and, relatedly, in their efforts to move from welfare reliance into jobs. Mothers are significantly more likely to complete welfare-to-work programs when they have high levels of trust in their child care providers and perceive that their child care arrangements are safe than when they are concerned about those arrangements (Meyers 1993). Public subsidies, by expanding the range of affordable child care options, appear to facilitate parents' efforts to reconcile their child care needs, which are determined largely by their work demands, and their preferences regarding the care they provide for their children (Phillips 1995; Siegel and Loman 1991).

The final question we addressed was whether the duration of poverty or the receipt of public assistance was related to patterns of care. Notably, two-thirds of the families who were poor throughout the measurement period used some nonparental care by the time the child was fifteen months old. Similarly, over 70 percent of the families who received public assistance throughout the period used some nonparental care. Although not all of this care can be assumed to facilitate mothers' employment, much of it probably resulted from mothers' pursuit of education or activity in the work force.

Perhaps the most telling finding, however, is that people who were temporarily poor sometime in the young child's life were most likely to put their children in care very early. Mothers' employment may have helped to lift these families out of poverty. This pattern underscores the importance of child care for young infants as an essential support system enabling mothers to provide an income for their families.

CONCLUSION

Children's experiences with child care during the first year of life are considerably influenced by the income levels of their families. Infants whose families were consistently poor, receiving public assistance, or both over the child's first fifteen months of life were least likely to enter care early or to be in any care at age fifteen months. When family poverty was transitory and when families were subsisting in near-poverty, children entered care early and for long hours, suggesting that extensive maternal employment was important in lifting the family out of poverty.

The quality of care that poor children received in the home-based settings used by most parents was relatively low. Only in child care centers did poor children receive care that was comparable in quality to that provided to their more affluent peers. The cost of most center care for infants is well beyond the means of poor parents; this higher-quality option is probably available to them only if they receive public or private subsidies.

The Study of Early Child Care is directed by a Steering Committee and supported by the National Institute of Child Health and Human Development (NICHD) through cooperative agreement U10, which calls for a scientific collaboration between the grantees and the NICHD staff. The participating investigators are Mark Appelbaum, Vanderbilt University; Dee Ann Batten, Vanderbilt University; Jay Belsky, Pennsylvania State University; Cathryn Booth, University of Washington; Robert Bradley, University of Arkansas at Little Rock; Celia Brownell, University of Pittsburgh; Bettye Caldwell, University of Arkansas for Medical Sciences; Susan Campbell, University of Pittsburgh; Alison Clarke-Stewart, University of California, Irvine; Jeffrey Cohn, University of Pittsburgh; Martha Cox, University of North Carolina–Chapel Hill; Kaye Fendt, National Institute of Child Health and Human Development; Sarah Friedman, National Institute of Child Health and Human Development; Kathryn Hirsh-Pasek, Temple University; Aletha Huston, University of Kansas; Nancy Marshall, Wellesley College; Kathleen McCartney, University of New Hampshire; Marion O'Brien, University of Kansas; Margaret Tresch Owen, University of Texas–Dallas; Deborah Phillips, University of Virginia; Henry Ricciuti, National Institute of Child Health and Human Development; Susan Spieker, University of Washington; Deborah Lowe Vandell, University of Wisconsin–Madison; and Marsha Weinraub, Temple University. We wish to express our appreciation to the study coordinators at each site who supervised the data collection, to the research assistants who collected the data, and especially to the families and child care providers who cooperated willingly with our repeated requests for information. We are grateful to Greg Duncan, Suzanne Randolph, and Duncan Thomas for reading and commenting upon earlier versions of the chapter.

NOTES

1. In a multisite study, site differences can contribute to patterns of association among independent and dependent variables. In the ordinary least squares regressions, site differences were controlled. Inclusion of sites in the logit analyses would have reduced the degrees of freedom greatly. Therefore, interactions of site *x* age of entry and site *x* type of care were tested initially. For age of entry, these interactions were negligible, but they were large and significant for type of care. Therefore, some of the reported differences among types of care may reflect characteristics on which sites differed.
2. In selecting participants, we used the following criteria to exclude atypical cases from the pool of potential subjects: (1) mothers younger than eighteen years of age at the time of the child's birth (3.8 percent of potential subjects); (2) families who did not anticipate remaining in the catchment area of the study for at least the next year (4.4 percent); (3) infants of multiple births, those with obvious disabilities, or those who remained in the hospital more than seven days postpartum (6.2 percent); (4) mothers

who had medical problems or acknowledged substance abuse or were placing their infants for adoption (4.3 percent); (5) mothers who did not speak English (4.4 percent); (6) mothers who lived more than an hour's travel time from the lab site or who were enrolled in another study (9.0 percent); and (7) mothers who lived in neighborhoods deemed by police to be too unsafe for visitation (1.5 percent). Of the mothers who were eligible, 1.5 percent refused to be interviewed in the hospital, and 3.4 percent asked not to be called when they returned home.

3. Family size affects the income-to-needs ratio because the needs are estimated based partly on the number of people supported by the income. Therefore, the effects of family size may be underestimated in the models that include the income-to-needs ratio.
4. Detailed descriptions of these quality measures, their reliabilities, and their relationships with other measures of child care are reported in NICHD Early Child Care Research Network (1996).
5. Analyses were calculated for all types of care combined, but little variance was accounted for. This procedure obscured the variation in patterns of predictors across types of care.

Chapter 7

Consequences of Living in Poverty for Young Children's Cognitive and Verbal Ability and Early School Achievement

Judith R. Smith, Jeanne Brooks-Gunn, and Pamela K. Klebanov

Although living in poverty has adverse consequences for children, how it actually influences children's outcomes is not well understood. Does a family's income poverty affect children's ability to learn or to achieve in school? Does the extent or timing of a family's poverty have ramifications for children's cognitive development? How does living in a single-parent family already stressed by poverty influence a child's learning capacity? Can a parent provide an enriched home environment that compensates for a low family income?

Most work comparing outcomes such as cognition, language, school achievement, and behavior problems in the poor and nonpoor has focused on older children and adolescents rather than on young children, in part because most longitudinal data sets target adolescents and young adults, not young children (Brooks-Gunn, Klebanov, and Liaw 1995; Chase-Lansdale et al. 1991). Notable exceptions are the Children of the National Longitudinal Survey of Youth (NLSY) and the Infant Health and Development Project (IHDP), the two data sets highlighted in this chapter. We expect that young children, typically defined as children from birth through age eight, may be vulnerable to the negative effects of growing up in an income-impoverished household, just as older children and adolescents are. In fact, we predict that the effects of poverty may be more negative for younger children than for older children and youths. Research has documented the importance of prenatal care on the health and well-being of young children as well as the positive effect of growing up in a stable, stimulating environment. The first three years of life have been shown to be a critical time for the development of both brain cells and the capacity to form trusting human relationships (Bornstein and Sigman 1986; Carnegie Corporation 1994; Chugani, Phelps, and Mazziotta 1987; Institute of Medicine 1985; Kolb 1989; McCormick et al. 1992; McEwen and Stellar 1993; Rutter 1990; Sroufe 1979).

THE CURRENT STUDY

This chapter focuses on four issues concerning the consequences for children of growing up poor: income poverty, the effect of family structure, the influence of human capital, and the child's home environment. We present findings on the effects of income poverty by analyzing the two longitudinal data sets that include outcomes for young children: the Children of the NLSY and the IHDP. Each allows for the study of the links between poverty and young children's cognitive ability and early school achievement. Conducting parallel analyses on both data sets allowed us to test the generalizability of the findings and compare effects across different assessment batteries. The Children of the NLSY includes children born to the women in the NLSY, who were first studied when they were teenagers. Their children were first studied in 1986 and have been seen every other year since then. New children enter the samples as they are born (Baker and Mott 1989; Chase-Lansdale et al. 1991). The IHDP follows almost 1,000 children born in eight medical centers across the country in 1985. All were low birth weight and premature, making them a select sample (IHDP 1990; Brooks-Gunn et al. 1993; Brooks-Gunn, Klebanov, and Liaw 1995). Unlike the Children of the NLSY, the IHDP children have been assessed every year over the first five years of life. The IHDP includes standardized assessments that are not available in the NLSY: full-scale intelligence (IQ) tests, intensive clinical home visits, and videotaped observations. Together, the samples provide a window on the effects of poverty on young children's cognitive ability and achievement.

Income Poverty

In our examination of income poverty, we considered the relative size of poverty effects in four age groups, in the two samples, and for three different measurements of cognitive ability and early scholastic achievement. We explored five questions. First, are the effects of income poverty of a similar size over all the young childhood years? In the NLSY we examined the same children at three different ages and compared them with a group of children from the IHDP. The IHDP data also include information from the second year of life, which allowed us to look at whether or not poverty effects are evident as early as intelligence may be reliably measured. Second, do the effects of income poverty differ as a function of the type of assessment conducted? Using the two samples, we looked at three different measures of cognitive ability: IQ, verbal ability, and school achievement. Although the IHDP conducted full-scale IQ tests, the Children of the NLSY (and many other large field surveys) used only a short verbal ability test, the Peabody Picture Vocabulary Test–Revised (PPVT-R, Dunn and Dunn 1981).[1] We tested whether the effects of poverty differed when measured by performance on the verbal ability test and on a full-scale IQ test. The Children of the NLSY administered the Peabody Individual Achievement Test (PIAT). Therefore, we also investigated whether achievement and verbal comprehension tests are similarly linked to poverty. Each of these tests measures different things and has built-in limitations. The PPVT-R test has been shown to be less reliable for non-English-speaking students as well as for black children, as it measures a child's receptive vocabulary for standard American English, which black children may not be learning at the same rates as white children (Korenman, Miller, and Sjaastad 1995). The PIAT, which measures achievement in school, shows the child's ability to learn but not the child's aptitude to learn (Angoff 1988).

Third, within our examination of income poverty we focused on the persistence of poverty, the timing of poverty, and potential nonlinear income effects. While poverty is often short term, or transient, many children remain poor for a significant period of time. Few studies have addressed the question of the effects of persistent poverty on young children's outcomes. In our earlier work with the IHDP, the IQ test scores of five-year-old children whose families were persistently poor (over a four-year age span) were on average 9 points lower (on an IQ scale with a standard deviation of 16) than the scores of children whose families were never poor, controlling for a number of demographic characteristics. The IQ scores of the five-year-old children who had lived in poverty for some of their early years were on average 4 points lower than the scores of children who were never poor (Duncan, Brooks-Gunn, and Klebanov 1994). In this study, we examined the effects of transient and persistent poverty in the three age groups in the Children of the NLSY. Additionally, we expanded the findings from the IHDP sample to include the effects of persistent poverty on two- and three-year-olds and to report on parallel analyses done with data on five-year-olds (Duncan, Brooks-Gunn, and Klebanov 1994).

Fourth, we looked at the timing of family poverty, a topic that has received little attention, even though developmental approaches postulate that various experiences have different effects on skills, competencies, and expectancies across the life span. Developmental theorists have long believed in the primacy of early experience: experiences occurring during infancy and the preschool years were thought to affect children more than experiences later on did (Bloom 1961; Hunt 1961). Indeed, evidence from studies of children in foster care, in institutionalized care, and in high-quality early intervention programs was used as part of the rationale for programs such as Head Start (Brooks-Gunn and Hearn 1982; Zigler 1979). The belief in the primacy of early experience has been modified as evidence has mounted about the possibility for change across the life span (Lerner and Foch 1987).

Using our samples, which contained children from two to eight years of age, we compared the timing of poverty within the early childhood years. Early poverty is defined as occurring during infancy, and late poverty, during preschool. Therefore, we did not expect to find timing effects within this limited comparison. Studies that have reported timing effects have compared early childhood with later development and typically have divided their data into larger epochs—preschool, elementary school, junior high school, and high school years (Baydar, Brooks-Gunn, and Furstenberg 1993; Brooks-Gunn, Guo, and Furstenberg 1993; Haveman, Wolfe, and Spalding 1991).

Finally, we studied whether or not the effects of income poverty are linear.

That is, do children living below the poverty line have substantially worse outcomes than those above the poverty line, or are the effects similar across the income distribution? Because children living in families with incomes near the poverty line (although they are not officially poor) often live in difficult circumstances and are likely to move in and out of poverty, they may respond similarly to those living below the poverty line on achievement or verbal ability assessments. Data on whether living in a family with a total income slightly above the poverty level affects a child's well-being are important, as tax and income support policies are likely to affect children both just below and just above the poverty line. If outcomes differ significantly for children living, for example, at 50 percent, 100 percent, and 150 percent of the official poverty line, then the Earned Income Tax Credit, which keeps many families above the poverty line, could be targeted for expansion or at least not for reduction. In summary, we analyzed income poverty for two samples of young children, for several age groups, for three measures of cognitive ability, and with several measures of family poverty.

Family Structure

Being income poor has been found to be highly associated with family structure. Poverty rates are two to three times higher for children whose mothers have never married or have divorced. We charted the separate effects of family structure and income poverty, following the research of Garfinkel and McLanahan (1986), McLanahan (1985), and McLanahan and Sandefur (1994). At the same time, because many families who experience divorce were poor prior to the separation (see chapter 2) and because household transitions themselves may be linked to disruptions and reorganizations of family life that have effects beyond those of income poverty, our analyses capture transitional effects. We examined changes in family structure over time, controlling for income effects. We expected to find that family structure, particularly instability in marital status (divorce or remarriage) and living in a single-parent family would affect children's outcomes. However, following past literature, we hypothesized that income accounts for a substantial portion of the family structure effects.

The Influence of Human Capital

The third issue involves the influence of human capital upon children's outcomes and the link between family income and mothers' education. Are the effects of mothers' education primarily exerted through income, or are they relatively independent? We expected mothers' education to contribute to child outcomes even after we controlled for family income (in contrast to what is expected for family structure). Mothers' education is sometimes considered a proxy for the amount of learning provided to the child, the literacy environment of the home, the parental engagement in the school, and the belief in the importance of schooling and learning (that is, aspects of human capital). However, we tested this premise across ages, on two different types of assessments, and in two samples.

Home Environment

The last issue is whether or not the young child's home environment mediates the effects of the mother's education and family income upon cognitive abilities. We expected these effects both to be mediated by the mother's provision of learning experiences in the home (Brooks-Gunn, Klebanov, and Liaw 1995; Klebanov, Brooks-Gunn, Chase-Lansdale, and Gordon forthcoming; Wachs and Gruen 1982).

METHOD

Sample

The data reported for this study were drawn from the Children of the NLSY, a panel study of 12,000 young men and women begun in 1979, and the IHDP. The Children of the NLSY includes detailed longitudinal demographic information on the families as well as cognitive and socioemotional assessments of the young children administered biannually. The original NLSY study oversampled poor and minority youths, providing samples of disadvantaged families large enough for analyses.

Our sample from the Children of the NLSY consisted of 966 children who were three and four years of age in 1986. We examined the links between poverty and children's outcomes at three ages: (1) at three and four years (1986), (2) two years later at five and six years (1988), and (3) at seven and eight years (1990).[2] We included all children who were between thirty-six months and fifty-nine months of age in 1986. We excluded Hispanic children from our analyses, as two assessments that became key outcome variables (the PPVT-R and the PIAT) were not administered in Spanish, resulting in missing data in some cases and English assessments for bilingual but primarily Spanish-speaking children in other cases (Baydar and Brooks-Gunn 1991). Of the 966 children, 38 percent were African American. The mean years of education for the mothers of all the children was 11.7 years. The mothers' average age at the child's birth was twenty-one.[3] About one-half (49 percent) of the children lived in families whose mothers were married continuously from birth until the 1986 assessment. About one-fifth (22 percent) lived in families headed by females that experienced no marriage or remarriage during the early years of the study period; 12 percent experienced a change from a two-parent to a one-parent family, and 15 percent experienced a change from a one-parent to a two-parent family. The average family income for the children when they were three to four years old was $21,851. Thirty-eight percent of the children had lived in families with an average income-to-needs ratio below the official poverty line. Eleven percent were poor during each of the first three or four years of their lives, while 45 percent experienced poverty for some of these years. Table 7.1 presents the means and standard deviations for the outcome and explanatory variables.

TABLE 7.1 / Characteristics of Children in the NLSY Sample, by Race[a]

Variables	Full Sample	White	Black
Outcomes			
PPVT-R (1986)[b]	86.8	94.2	74.4
	(20.4)	(18.4)	(17.4)
PIAT Reading[c]	103.3	103.9	102.3
Recognition (1988, ages 5–6 years)	(12.1)	(12.1)	(10.9)
PIAT Mathematics (1988, ages 5–6 years)	98.6	100.9	94.9
	(12.6)	(12.4)	(12.1)
PIAT Reading	103.6	106.5	100.5
Recognition (1990, ages 7–8 years)	(13.5)	(13.5)	(12.8)
PIAT Mathematics (1990, ages 7–8 years)	99.2	102.5	95.6
	(12.2)	(11.7)	(11.7)
Independent variables			
Child's characteristics			
Male	0.48	0.50	0.46
	(0.50)	(0.50)	(0.50)
Black	0.38	0.00	1.00
	(0.48)	(0.00)	(0.00)
Low birth weight (<2,500 g)	0.09	0.08	0.12
	(0.29)	(0.27)	(0.32)
Family characteristics			
Mother's education (years)	11.7	11.7	11.9
	(3.3)	(3.9)	(1.8)
Married, continuously	0.49	0.63	0.22
	(0.50)	(0.48)	(0.42)
Divorced or separated, continuously	0.04	0.04	0.04
	(0.19)	(0.19)	(0.19)
Female head of household, continuously	0.22	0.06	0.50
	(0.42)	(0.23)	(0.50)
Change to one-parent family	0.12	0.15	0.09
	(0.33)	(0.35)	(0.28)
Change to two-parent family	0.15	0.14	0.16
	(0.36)	(0.35)	(0.37)
HOME cognitive (1986, ages 5–6 years)[d]	97.4	100.3	91.9
	(15.9)	(14.8)	(16.5)
HOME emotional support (1986, ages	97.6	100.0	912.9
3–4 years)	(15.4)	(14.9)	(14.6)
HOME cognitive (1988, ages 5–6 years)	97.7	100.3	93.4
	(14.9)	(14.1)	(15.2)

(Table continued on p. 138.)

TABLE 7.1 / *(continued)*

Variables	Full Sample	White	Black
HOME emotional support (1988, ages 5–6 years)	97.8 (14.4)	100.1 (13.4)	93.2 (14.7)
Family income variables			
Average income-to-needs ratio			
Birth to ages 3–4 years	1.7 (1.1)	1.9 (1.2)	1.1 (0.78)
Birth to ages 5–6 years	1.7 (1.1)	2.0 (1.1)	1.2 (0.79)
Average yearly income ($1992)			
Ages 3–4 years	21,851.1 (14,494.9)	25,079.8 (14,667.1)	16,427.3 (12,457.5)
Ages 5–6 years	22,678.8 (14,035.8)	26,194.2 (14,276.5)	16,845.8 (11,469.6)
Ages 7–8 years	23,433.5 (14,240.7)	27,054.5 (14,651.9)	17,438.5 (11,218.7)
Average number in family, birth to ages 3–4 years	4.3 (1.7)	3.8 (1.0)	5.0 (2.2)
Average income-to-needs ratio, first three years			
< 1	0.38 (0.49)	0.25 (0.43)	0.60 (0.49)
1–2	0.33 (0.47)	0.35 (0.48)	0.29 (0.46)
2–3	0.18 (0.39)	0.24 (0.43)	0.08 (0.27)
> 3	0.10 (0.31)	0.15 (0.36)	0.03 (0.17)
Duration of poverty			
First three years			
Never	0.34 (0.47)	0.46 (0.50)	0.14 (0.35)
Some years	0.45 (0.50)	0.39 (0.49)	0.57 (0.50)
All years	0.18 (0.38)	0.09 (0.29)	0.37 (0.48)
First five years			
Never	0.26 (0.44)	0.36 (0.48)	0.10 (0.30)

TABLE 7.1 / (*continued*)

Variables	Full Sample	White	Black
Some years	0.40	0.38	0.41
	(0.49)	(0.49)	(0.49)
All years	0.04	0.01	0.10
	(0.20)	(0.12)	(0.30)

Source: Data on 966 children drawn from the Children of the National Longitudinal Survey of Youth (NLSY) who were three to four years old in 1986.

a. Values are means. Standard deviations in parentheses. Not all children took each child assessment. Missing data on variables also limited the people in the regression analyses. PPVT-R analyses were conducted on 784 children between three and four years of age. PIAT Reading analyses were conducted on 852 children between five and six years of age and 621 children between seven and eight years of age. PIAT Math analyses were conducted on 862 children between five and six years of age and 613 children between seven and eight years of age.

b. Peabody Picture Vocabulary Test—Revised.

c. Peabody Individual Achievement Test.

d. Home Observation of Measurement of the Environment.

The sample from the IHDP consisted of 895 children from an eight-site randomized clinical trial designed to test the efficacy of educational and family-support services in reducing the incidence of developmental delays in low-birth-weight, preterm infants (Brooks-Gunn, Klebanov, and Liaw 1995; IHDP 1990; McCormick et al. 1991). Infants weighing 2,500 grams or less at birth were screened for eligibility if their postconceptional age between January 7, 1985, and October 9, 1985, was thirty-seven weeks or less and if they were born in one of the eight participating medical institutions (University of Arkansas for Medical Sciences at Little Rock, Albert Einstein Medical Center, Harvard Medical School, University of Miami School of Medicine, University of Pennsylvania School of Medicine, University of Texas Health Science Center at Dallas, University of Washington School of Medicine, and Yale University School of Medicine). Of the 1,302 infants who met enrollment criteria, 274 (21 percent) were eliminated because consent was refused, and forty-three were withdrawn before entry into their assigned group, leaving a birth cohort of 985 infants. One-third of the sample was assigned to an intervention group (N = 377), and two-thirds to the follow-up group (N = 608) immediately after discharge from the nursery (IHDP 1990). The children in the study reported here were those in the intervention and follow-up groups only. In all analyses, we controlled for participation in the treatment group. The intervention included (1) home visits to families for the first three years of life, (2) a preschool program in the second and third years of life, and (3) a series of group meetings for parents every other month in the second and third years of life. Children were assessed when they were one, two, three, and five years of age. At the three-year assessment, 92 percent of the sample was seen, and at five years of age, 82 percent of the original birth cohort sample was given the cognitive assessment. (At the three-year assessment point, funds were available to test children throughout the country, whereas such funds were not available at the five-year assessment; Brooks-Gunn, Klebanov, and Liaw 1995). The sample used for these studies was limited to those children who had address data available for geocoding (using the same sample as in Duncan, Brooks-Gunn, and Klebanov 1994, $N = 895$).

Of the 895 children in the IHDP sample, 55 percent were African American, 11 percent were Hispanic, and 34 percent were non-Hispanic white.[4] Mean years of education for the mothers of all children was 11.8. About one-half (48 percent) of the children lived in families whose mothers were married continuously from birth until assessment at age three. One-third (36 percent) lived in families that were headed by a female and experienced no marriage or remarriage during the early years of the study period, while 14 percent were in a household headed by a female for part of the three years. The average income for the families when the children were one to three years of age was $21,458. Forty-four percent of the children had lived in families with an average income-to-needs ratio below the official poverty line. About one-quarter (27 percent) were poor during each of the first three years of their lives, and 19 percent experienced transient poverty. Table 7.2 presents the means and standard deviations for the outcome and independent variables.

Measures

CHILDREN'S OUTCOMES In the Children of the NLSY, the PPVT-R was given to the children at ages three to four years. This assessment requires the child to comprehend verbal labels (shown a card with four pictures on it, the child points to the one representing a word pronounced by the assessor). Although the PPVT-R provides an estimate of the child's receptive vocabulary, verbal ability, and scholastic aptitude, it is not an intelligence test but a measure of the child's receptive English vocabulary and verbal ability (Dunn and Dunn 1981). While the PPVT-R is considered a good predictor of school performance and literacy (Brooks-Gunn, Guo, and Furstenberg 1993), the child's score on this and other standardized tests is also associated with several family and environmental variables. We used the standardized score, with a mean of 100 and a standard deviation of 15.[5]

When the children were five to six and seven to eight years of age, they took the PIAT, a wide-range measure of academic achievement for children aged five and over that is among the most widely used brief assessments of academic achievement (Dunn and Markwardt 1970). It has high test-retest reliability and concurrent validity. Of the three scores derived for this achievement test, two are presented in this chapter: those for Mathematics and Reading Recognition. The PIAT Mathematics assessment consists of eighty-four multiple-choice items of increasing difficulty. It begins with early skills (recognizing numerals) and progresses to measuring advanced concepts in geometry and trigonometry. The child

(Text continued on p. 144.)

TABLE 7.2 / Characteristics of the Children in the IHDP Sample, by Race[a]

Variables	Full Sample	White	Black
Outcomes			
Bayley IQ[b]			
Age 1 year	107.54	109.28	106.11
	(17.79)	(18.22)	(17.30)
Age 2 years	96.20	101.09	92.12
	(19.64)	(21.45)	(16.96)
Stanford-Binet IQ, age 3 years	87.35	94.05	81.86
	(19.98)	(22.58)	(15.58)
PPVT-R[c]			
Age three years	86.69	93.88	80.58
	(17.49)	(18.07)	(14.42)
Age 5 years	80.44	90.25	72.79
	(21.72)	(22.56)	(17.61)
WPPSI,[d] age 5 years			
Full-scale IQ	90.74	98.44	84.79
	(17.55)	(18.43)	(14.21)
Independent variables			
Child's characteristics			
Male	0.49	0.51	0.47
	(0.50)	(0.50)	(0.50)
Black	0.55	0.00	1.00
	(0.50)	(0.00)	(0.00)
Birth weight (g)	1,788.02	1,843.93	1,741.70
	(459.32)	(441.08)	(469.33)
Family characteristics			
Mother's education (years)	11.81	12.36	11.35
	(2.47)	(2.74)	(2.12)
Female head of household			
None of the time, age 2 years	0.45	0.25	0.61
	(0.50)	(0.43)	(0.49)
None of the time, age 3 years	0.48	0.68	0.31
	(0.50)	(0.47)	(0.46)
Some of the time, age 3 years	0.14	0.14	0.15
	(0.35)	(0.34)	(0.35)
All of the time, age 3 years	0.36	0.18	0.52
	(0.48)	(0.38)	(0.50)
None of the time, age 5 years	0.35	0.56	0.18
	(0.48)	(0.50)	(0.38)
All of the time, age 5 years	0.21	0.06	0.33
	(0.40)	(0.24)	(0.47)

(Table continued on p. 142.)

Variables	Full Sample	White	Black
Some of the time			
Multiple changes, age 5 years	0.07	0.05	0.08
	(0.25)	(0.23)	(0.28)
Some of the time			
Marital change to 2 parents, age 5 years	0.05	0.05	0.06
	(0.23)	(0.22)	(0.23)
Some of the time			
Marital change to 1 parent, age 5 years	0.16	0.14	0.18
	(0.37)	(0.34)	(0.39)
Other, age 5 years	0.11	0.10	0.11
	(0.31)	(0.30)	(0.32)
HOME learning environment, age 3 years	21.05	23.60	18.99
	(5.95)	(5.43)	(5.54)
HOME physical environment, age 3 years	5.30	5.91	4.80
	(1.83)	(1.62)	(1.84)
HOME warmth, age 3 years	5.12	5.62	4.72
	(1.66)	(1.31)	(1.80)
Family income variables			
Income-to-needs ratio, age 1 year	1.74	2.53	1.07
	(1.75)	(2.10)	(0.98)
Average, income-to-needs ratio			
Ages 1 and 2 years	1.76	2.51	1.12
	(1.67)	(1.99)	(0.96)
Ages 1–3 years	1.77	2.53	1.13
	(1.63)	(1.92)	(0.95)
Ages 1–4 years	1.77	2.52	1.16
	(1.57)	(1.84)	(0.93)
Average yearly income ($1992)			
Ages 1 and 2 years	20,916.87	27,963.77	14,958.88
	(16,937.20)	(19,083.46)	(12,021.32)
Ages 1–3 years	21,458.63	28,925.67	15,238.79
	(16,904.12)	(18,986.33)	(11,782.74)
Ages 1–4 years	22,001.82	29,649.66	15,679.46
	(16,877.97)	(18,910.50)	(11,664.03)
Average size of household			
Ages 1 and 2 years	4.97	4.49	5.36
	(2.35)	(2.10)	(2.46)
Ages 1–3 years	4.87	4.44	5.22
	(2.19)	(1.97)	(2.29)
Ages 1–4 years	4.85	4.46	5.18
	(2.09)	(1.91)	(2.18)

TABLE 7.2 / (*continued*)

Variables	Full Sample	White	Black
Average income-to-needs category			
Age 3 years			
< 1	0.44	0.25	0.60
	(0.50)	(0.44)	(0.49)
1–2	0.26	0.27	0.26
	(0.44)	(0.44)	(0.44)
2–3	0.12	0.16	0.08
	(0.32)	(0.37)	(0.26)
> 3	0.18	0.32	0.06
	(0.38)	(0.47)	(0.24)
Duration of poverty			
First 3 years			
Never	0.38	0.60	0.20
	(0.49)	(0.49)	(0.40)
Some years	0.19	0.13	0.24
	(0.46)	(0.42)	(0.48)
All years	0.27	0.13	0.40
	(0.45)	(0.33)	(0.49)
First 4 years			
Never	0.33	0.54	0.16
	(0.47)	(0.50)	(0.36)
Some years	0.42	0.33	0.50
	(0.49)	(0.47)	(0.50)
All years	0.20	0.08	0.31
	(0.40)	(0.27)	(0.46)

Source: Data on 966 children drawn from the Infant Health and Development Program (IHDP) born between January 7 and October 5, 1985.

a. Values are means. Standard deviations in parentheses. Not all children took each child assessment. Missing data on variables also limited the people in the regression analyses. PPVT-R analyses were conducted on 784 children between three and four years of age. PIAT Reading analyses were conducted on 852 children between five and six years of age and 621 children between seven and eight years of age. PIAT Math analyses were conducted on 862 children between five and six years of age and 613 children between seven and eight years of age. N for analyses for each child outcome variable varies due to missing data (Bayley age two, N = 786; PPVT-R age three, N = 713; Stanford-Binet, age three, N = 799; PPVT-R age five, N = 721; WPPSI age five, N = 720).

b. Bayley Scales of Infant Development.

c. Peabody Picture Vocabulary Test—Revised.

d. Wechsler Preschool and Primary Scale of Intelligence.

looks at each problem and then chooses an answer by pointing to or naming one of four options. The Reading Recognition assessment, which measures word recognition and pronunciation ability, considered essential components of reading achievement, contains eighty-four items that increase in difficulty. The skills assessed include matching letters, naming names, and reading single words aloud (Baker et al. 1993). We used the standardized score on both assessments, each of which has a mean of 100 and a standard deviation of 15.[6]

The IHDP administers three full-scale intelligence tests. The Bayley Scales of Infant Development, which measure the child's overall intelligence at age two, are the most commonly used measure of the cognitive ability of children under the age of three (Bayley 1969). The test, which is individually administered, assesses the developmental functioning of infants and young children. It has three parts that are considered complementary: a Mental Scale to assess sensory-perceptual abilities and early acquisition of "object constancy"; a Motor Scale to measure motor coordination and skills; and an Infant Behavior Record to assess the child's social and objective orientations toward the environment. The Mental Scale is reported here. The Stanford-Binet Intelligence Scale, which measures general mental adaptability, was used at age three (Terman and Merrill 1973). The Wechsler Preschool and Primary Scale of Intelligence (WPPSI) was given to the IHDP children when they were five years of age (Wechsler 1967). The WPPSI is also an individually administered clinical instrument that includes three measures of IQ: verbal, performance, and full scale. The full-scale measure is reported here. The reliability of the three measures ranges from .93 to .96 (Sattler 1982). Evidence of the instrument's construct validity is its high correlation with the Stanford-Binet. Additionally, the PPVT-R was given at ages three and five years.

Family-Level Poverty

We calculated a family's income-to-needs ratio by dividing the family's total income for each year of the child's life by the official U.S. poverty threshold for the child's family based on the number of people in the household for each year of the child's life up to and including the income data for the year of the assessment. To compensate for the fluctuations in the consumer price index over the years (used to adjust the poverty threshold each year), all income was translated into 1992 dollars. Based on the work of Duncan, Brooks-Gunn, and Klebanov (1994), we used several different measures of family income. The first three were the average income-to-needs ratio for the first three years of the child's life; the average family income up to the assessment year, along with the average family size over this period; and four categories of income-to-needs ratio: less than 1 (poor), 1–2 (near poor, the omitted reference category), 2–3 (middle income), and 3 or above (affluent, to examine possible nonlinear effects). Fourth, following Duncan, Brooks-Gunn, and Klebanov (1994), we created two measures of the timing and duration of poverty. We assessed the timing of poverty in the NLSY sample by calculating three dummy variables: whether the child experienced poverty

(1) early in life (the first or second year of life) and not during the third or fourth year of life; (2) later in early childhood—only during the third year or fourth year but not during the first two years of life; and (3) at all assessment points. Fifth, for duration of poverty, we calculated a variable representing transient poverty over the four assessment points (at one, two, or three points) versus consistent poverty over the three or four data points. For the NLSY children's outcomes at ages three to four, we measured the family income in each year of the child's life up to and including the assessment year. Early poverty was defined as occurring during the first or second year of life. At ages five to six and seven to eight, we also measured family poverty in each of the years up to and including the fifth or sixth year. Early poverty was defined for these analyses as occurring during the first three years of life, and later poverty, during year four or five.[7]

In the IHDP sample, we constructed income-to-needs variables as described above, with some variation because of the data available. In constructing family poverty variables for children at age two, we averaged the income-to-needs ratio at one and two years, and for three years of age, we averaged the income-to-needs ratio over one, two, and three years. For the age five analyses, we averaged the income-to-needs ratio over the four calendar years prior to the five-year assessment. For the five-year analyses, we defined transient poverty as poverty in one, two, or three of the four calendar years. Persistent poverty was defined as being poor for all of the four years. For the age five analyses, early poverty was defined as poverty at either one or two years of age; late poverty, as poverty at three or four years of age.

Family-Level Variables

CHILD CHARACTERISTICS The child's sex, ethnicity, age in months at assessment, and birth weight were included in all NLSY analyses. Low birth weight was calculated as weight under 2,500 grams. In the IHDP, the child's sex, ethnicity, and birth weight (a continuous measure) are included.

FAMILY CHARACTERISTICS In the NLSY, the mother's education was the highest grade she achieved up to the year of the child's assessment. Following Sandefur, McLanahan, and Wojtiewicz (1992), family structure was the stability and instability in the family composition over time. We coded family structure into five categories: (1) consistently married over the four measurement points (omitted reference group), (2) female headship at each of the four measurement times, (3) consistently divorced or separated at each of the four measurement times, (4) change in family structure from a two-parent to a one-parent family, and (5) change in family from a one-parent to a two-parent family.

In the IHDP analyses, family structure is coded somewhat differently at each age. Family structure is assessed at age two by a dummy variable (female head, yes or no). At age three, family structure is assessed in terms of whether the family had a female head some, none, or all of the time the child was between two and three years of age. At age five, six categories of family structure are used: (1) the families who never had a female head of household between two to five years (omitted group in regressions), (2) families who had a female head at two to five years and in which the mother had never married by the five year assessment, (3) families who had a female head when the child was two to five years old and mother was divorced, widowed, or separated by five years, (4) families with a female head when the child was two years, but not at five years old (remarried or late first marriage), (5) families who had two parents at two years, but female head when the child was five years (divorced group), and (6) other.

HOME ENVIRONMENT To examine the effects of poverty on the family learning environment, the Home Observation of Measurement of the Environment (HOME) Inventory assesses the learning materials in the home, the experiences offered by the mother, and the amount of warmth expressed toward the child (Caldwell and Bradley 1984; Bradley et al. 1989; Gottfried 1984; Wachs and Gruen 1982). The HOME Inventory is highly associated with a variety of child outcome, often being a stronger predictor of cognitive and school academic readiness than maternal education is (in regressions entering both variables; Bradley et al. 1989). In the IHDP the full HOME scale was used, while the Children of the NLSY used a short form of the HOME (Baker and Mott 1989). The full assessment consists of fifty-five items that include both maternal reports and interviewer ratings designed to capture the cognitive stimulation and emotional support available in the home. Often eight subscales are used (Bradley et al. 1989, 1994). Three composite scales are used in the chapter—Home Learning, Physical Environment and Maternal Warmth (Brooks-Gunn, Klebanov and Liaw 1995; Klebanov, Brooks-Gunn and Duncan 1994; Sugland, et al. 1995). The HOME short form used in the Children of the NLSY consists of twenty-six items—fifteen are based on maternal report and eleven are completed by the interviewer (based on observations of the home environment and mother-child interactions). Two global subscales are used—a cognitive stimulation subscale and an emotional support subscale (Baker and Mott 1989).[8]

RESULTS

We conducted a series of parallel ordinary least square (OLS) multiple linear regressions to examine the effects of income, family structure, human capital, and the home environment on young children's cognitive outcomes (tables 7.3–7.8; see the appendix for complete regression tables).

Effects of Income on Young Children's Cognition and Achievement

We examined four measures of income effects: family income, duration of poverty, timing of poverty, and nonlinear effects of income.

TABLE 7.3 / Average Effect of Income-to-Needs Ratio on Children's Assessment Scores[a]

Sample and Assessment	Effect
NLSY[b]	
PPVT, age 3–4 years (1986)	3.68*
	(0.64)
	[0.20]
PIAT Mathematics, age 5–6 years (1988)	3.08*
	(0.45)
	[0.25]
PIAT Reading Recognition, age 5–6 years (1988)	3.35*
	(0.43)
	[0.29]
PIAT Mathematics, age 7–8 years (1990)	2.97*
	(0.52)
	[0.27]
PIAT Reading Recognition, age 7–8 (1990)	2.93*
	(0.58)
	[0.24]
IHDP[c]	
Bayley,[c] age 2 years	3.71*
	(0.46)
	[0.32]
PPVT, age 3 years	3.04*
	(0.42)
	[0.28]
Stanford-Binet, age 3 years	4.00*
	(0.47)
	[0.33]
PPVT, age 5 years	4.54*
	(0.57)
	[0.33]
WPPSI, age 5 years	3.57*
	(0.47)
	[0.32]

* $p < .05$.

Sources: Authors' calculations from ordinary least squares (OLS) multiple linear regressions using data on children from the NLSY and IHDP. Data on 966 children drawn from the Children of the National Longitudinal Survey of Youth (NLSY) who were three to four years old in 1986.

a. Values are unstandardized regression coefficients. Standard errors in parentheses; standardized coefficients in brackets.

b. Regression models include child's race, birth weight, and sex; mother's education; and family structure variables.

c. Regression models as in note b, plus site and treatment group.

INCOME-TO-NEEDS RATIO We estimated the average effect of the income-to-needs ratio on each of the cognitive assessments in the Children of the NLSY and IHDP samples at the three points in time, controlling for family structure, ethnicity, mother's education, child's age, and birth weight (table 7.3). The effects were quite comparable in the Children of the NLSY for the three- to four-year-olds, the five- to six-year-olds, and the seven- to eight-year-olds: a change in one unit of the income-to-needs ratio (that is, increasing the average family income from 1.0 point to 2.0 points above the poverty line) was associated with a 3.0- to 3.7-point increase in the child's score on the PPVT-R or PIAT.

In the IHDP data, the effect of income on the child's PPVT-R score increased slightly over time. When the child was three years of age, the effect of a 1.0-point increase in the average income-to-needs ratio is 3.0 points, and at five years of age it is 4.5 points. The effects on the PPVT-R at age three were somewhat smaller than those found for the full-scale Stanford-Binet IQ test (3.0 versus 4.0 points). Income was also associated with scores at two years of age: an increment in the income-to-needs ratio of one unit is associated with a 3.7-point increase in the child's score on the Bayley assessment, which is similar to the effect found at age three on the Stanford-Binet and at age five on the WPPSI. In summary, the effects of income appeared fairly consistent over the early childhood years and across assessments.

Using the age five data, we also tested through hierarchical regression whether IQ at age three was a significant contributor to verbal ability scores at age five, controlling for family background, including average income-to-needs ratio. When the PPVT-R score at age five was the dependent variable, adding the child's PPVT-R score at age three added .12 to adjusted R^2 ($p < .001$). Controlling for the PPVT-R score at age three and the income-to-needs ratio in the first three years of life, the income-to-needs ratio at age four was still a significant contributor to IQ at age five, and the change in R^2 was significant ($p < .01$). Thus the effects of the income-to-needs ratio were associated with PPVT-R scores at ages three and five as well as with a change in IQ scores.

Using the child's IQ score on the WPPSI test at age five, we replicated the above hierarchical analyses and got parallel results. Controlling for the child's age three IQ score (Stanford-Binet) led to a .3 addition in the adjusted R^2, and the change was statistically significant. Controlling again for the average income-to-needs ratio at age four added .006, and the change was statistically significant.

We ran parallel hierarchical analyses on the Children of the NLSY data, with the PIAT Mathematics and Reading Recognition tests as the dependent variable, to see if controlling for the child's PPVT-R score at ages three to four still resulted in income's having effects on children's scores at ages five to six. As expected, the PPVT-R was positively associated with the PIAT Reading Recognition score at ages five to six, as was the income-to-needs ratio in the early years. Adding the family's average income-to-needs ratio during the child's fourth year of life resulted in a R^2 change of .004 ($p < .10$), and the beta was still significant for income.[9]

TABLE 7.4 / Effects of Duration of Poverty on Assessment Scores[a]

Sample and Duration of Poverty[b]	Assessment				
		PIAT			
	PPVT-R, Ages 3–4 Years (1986)	Math, Ages 5–6 Years (1988)	Reading Recognition, Ages 5–6 Years (1988)	Math, Ages 7–8 Years (1990)	Reading Recognition, Ages 7–8 Years (1990)
NLSY[c]					
Transient poverty	−2.43	−5.3*	−5.9*	−2.75*	−3.35*
	(1.83)	(1.14)	(1.10)	(1.24)	(1.37)
	[−0.04]	[−0.17]	[−0.20]	[−0.10]	[−0.11]
Continuous poverty	−7.06*	−5.7*	−9.2*	−6.75*	−8.47*
	(2.53)	(2.18)	(2.73)	(1.86)	(2.06)
	[−0.10]	[−0.07]	[−0.12]	[−0.17]	[−0.20]
	Bayley, Age 2 Years	PPVT-R, Age 3 Years	Stanford-Binet, Age 3 Years	PPVT-R, Age 5 Years	WPPSI, Age 5 Years
IHDP[d]					
Transient poverty	−3.36	−4.48*	−6.05*	−4.51*	−4.02*
	(1.88)	(1.52)	(1.72)	(1.99)	(1.62)
	[−0.07]	[−0.12]	[−0.14]	[−0.10]	[−0.11]
Continuous poverty	−6.99*	−7.33*	−8.63*	−9.58*	9.06*
	(1.76)	(1.69)	(1.90)	(2.57)	(2.10)
	[−0.17]	[−0.19]	[−0.19]	[−0.18]	[−0.21]

* $p < .05$.

Sources: Authors' calculations from ordinary least squares (OLS) multiple linear regressions using data on children from the NLSY and IHDP. Data on 966 children drawn from the Children of the National Longitudinal Survey of Youth (NLSY) who were three to four years old in 1986.

a. Values are unstandardized regression coefficients. Standard errors in parentheses; standardized coefficients in brackets.

b. Children from families that were never poor were the omitted group.

c. Regression models include child's race, birth weight, and sex; mother's education; and family structure variables.

d. Regression models as in note c, plus site and treatment group.

DURATION OF POVERTY At all four ages from two through eight years, for each assessment and across both data sets, children who lived in families that experienced persistent poverty had scores 6–9 points lower than those children who never lived in poverty (table 7.4). In the Children of the NLSY sample, three- and four-year-old children who lived in continuous poverty had PPVT-R scores 7.1 points lower than children who were never poor. Continuous poverty had a stronger effect on the child's Reading Recognition score than on the Mathematics score at both ages (−9.2 points on the Reading test at ages five to six compared with −5.7 points on the Mathematics test; −8.5 points compared with −6.8 points at ages seven to eight). In the IHDP sample, the effect of continuous poverty on the child's Bayley score at age two was −7.0 points; on the PPVT-R at age three, a 7.0 point decrease compared with the never-poor group; and on the Stanford-Binet IQ test in the same year, an 8.6 point decrease. The negative effect on the PPVT-R score of living in consistent poverty increased as the child got older (−7.3 points at age three compared with −9.6 points at age five). The effect on the WPPSI at age five was −9.1 points.

We also examined the effect on children's scores of living in poverty for only part of the early years. Living in transient poverty had a negative effect on most of the children's assessments in both data sets, although the effect was less harmful than that of living in continuous poverty. In the Children of the NLSY sample, three- and four-year-old children who were poor only some of their first three years of life had scores on average 2.4 points lower than those who were never poor, but the effect did not achieve statistical significance. The effect of transient poverty on the child's PIAT achievement score measured at ages five to six and seven to eight was, however, significantly different than for those children who were never poor. Children who were poor for some of the first five years of their lives had Mathematics scores 5.3 points lower and Reading Recognition scores 5.9 points lower than those who were never poor. At seven to eight years of age, income affected the PIAT scores of those who lived in poverty only some of the five or six years somewhat less than at ages five to six (−2.7 points on Mathematics and −3.3 points on Reading Recognition). In the IHDP sample, the effect of transient poverty was 4–6 points on the test scores at two, three, and five years of age.

TIMING OF POVERTY The effect of the timing of poverty was not significant in either data set. At ages three to four (NLSY) or age three (IHDP), the effect of early poverty was not significantly different than that of never living in poverty or of living in poverty in the third year of life. No timing effects were found at the other ages across assessments. We expect that the truncated division of time periods explains this finding.[10]

NONLINEAR EFFECTS OF INCOME We tested nonlinear effects in two stages: first with the four income-to-needs categories described above and, second, with the low end of the income sample divided as a way of studying the effects of being very poor (see table 7.5). A significant difference was found between the effects of income-to-needs ratio on the poor (income-to-needs ratio less than 1) and on the near-poor group of families (income-to-needs ratio 1–2) in both data sets. In the Children of the NLSY sample, children living below the poverty level at ages three to four had PPVT-R scores on average 6.3 points lower than the children in the near-poor group. This effect persisted at ages five to six and seven to eight on the achievement tests but diminished somewhat with age (−5.2 points on the PIAT Mathematics and Reading Recognition at ages five to six, −4.7 points on Mathematics and −4.2 points on Reading Recognition at ages seven to eight). In the IHDP sample, a child's Bayley IQ score already showed the negative effects of living below the poverty line compared with living just above the poverty line by two years of age (a 5-point difference between the groups). These effects were fairly constant on the IQ assessments at ages three and five. When assessing the differential effects of income on a child's PPVT-R score, we found that, on average, living below the poverty line affected a five-year-old child's PPVT-R score twice as much as it did a three-year-old's score compared with those in the near-poor group.

In comparing the effects of income on children's scores in the near-poor and the middle-income groups (income-to-needs ratio 2–3), we found no differences in either data set on the three- or four-year-old children's PPVT-R scores. There were, however, significant differences on the achievement tests. Children living in middle-income groups had higher achievement scores than did those living in families with incomes in the near-poor range. At ages five to six, there was on average a 4.2-point difference in the scores on the PIAT Reading Recognition test but no significant difference on the PIAT Mathematics test. When the children were seven to eight years of age, their scores differed by 4.4 points on the Reading test and 3.1 points on the Mathematics test. In the IHDP sample, at age five those in the middle-income group had WPPSI scores on average 4.7 points higher than the near-poor group did. No significant differences were found on the PPVT-R given at age five.

As for the near-poor group compared with the affluent group (income-to-needs greater than 3), children in the affluent group in the Children of the NLSY sample had scores approximately 4–6 points higher than the near-poor group on all assessments. In the IHDP, the difference between the affluent group and the near-poor group at ages two through five was 9–10 points.

Both samples contain a heavy concentration of children living in families with very low incomes. We therefore examined the nonlinear breakpoints of those living deep in poverty and those living near poverty using the near-poor group, defined as 150 percent to 200 percent of the poverty level, as the contrast group (table 7.6). Children aged three to four living in families with incomes below 50 percent of the official poverty line in the NLSY had PPVT-R scores 10.0 points lower than those of the near-poor group. The PIAT achievement scores at ages five to six were also 10.0 points lower than those of the near-poor group. At ages seven to eight, the effect diminished slightly, and there was approximately a 7.0- to 9.0-point difference between the groups. In the IHDP, the scores also differed significantly between these groups, and the negative effect increased between ages two and five. Children's Bayley scores at age two in the very poor group were on average 6.0 points lower than those of children living in the near-poor group. At age three, there was a 9.7 point difference, and at age 5 children's scores are

(Text continued on p. 156.)

TABLE 7.5 / Nonlinear Effects of Income-to-Needs Ratio on Children's Assessment Scores[a]

	Assessment				
		PIAT			
Sample and Income-to-Needs Ratio[b]	PPVT-R, Ages 3–4 Years (1986)	Math, Ages 5–6 Years (1988)	Reading Recognition, Ages 5–6 Years (1988)	Math, Ages 7–8 Years (1990)	Reading Recognition, Ages 7–8 Years (1990)
NLSY[c]					
< 1	−6.28*	−5.2*	−5.21*	−4.67*	−4.20*
	(1.8)	(1.00)	(1.04)	(1.20)	(1.42)
	[−0.15]	[−0.19]	[−0.20]	[−0.18]	[−0.15]
2–3	2.16	2.16	4.23*	3.08*	4.36*
	(1.82)	(1.82)	(1.10)	(1.25)	(1.39)
	[0.04]	[0.04]	[0.14]	[0.11]	[0.14]
> 3	5.58*	3.70*	4.09*	6.18*	4.45*
	(2.23)	(1.43)	(1.38)	(1.62)	(1.83)
	[0.09]	[0.07]	[0.11]	[0.16]	[0.11]

	Bayley, Age 2 Years	PPVT-R, Age 3 Years	Stanford-Binet, Age 3 Years	PPVT-R, Age 5 Years	WPPSI, Age 5 Years
IHDP[d]					
< 1	5.13*	−2.54	−4.74*	−6.67*	−5.76*
	(1.56)	(1.33)	(1.48)	(1.68)	(1.37)
	[−0.13]	[−0.07]	[−0.12]	[0.15]	[−0.16]
2–3	−0.32	2.95*	3.91	4.15	4.65*
	(2.12)	(1.85)	(2.06)	(2.34)	(1.91)
	[−0.01]	[0.05]	[0.06]	[0.06]	[0.09]
> 3	9.96*	9.20*	10.75*	10.65*	9.02*
	(2.08)	(1.78)	(1.99)	(2.34)	(1.92)
	[0.20]	[0.20]	[0.21]	[0.19]	[0.20]

* $p < .05$.

Sources: Authors' calculations from ordinary least squares (OLS) multiple linear regressions using data on children from the NLSY and IHDP. Data on 966 children drawn from the Children of the National Longitudinal Survey of Youth (NLSY) who were three to four years old in 1986.

a. Values are unstandardized regression coefficients. Standard errors in parentheses; standardized coefficients in brackets.

b. Children from families with income-to-needs ratios of 1–2 were the omitted group.

c. Regression models include child's race, birth weight, and sex; mother's education; and family structure variables.

d. Regression models as in note c, plus site and treatment group.

TABLE 7.6 / Nonlinear Effects of Being Very Poor on Assessment Scores[a]

Sample and Income-to-Needs Ratio[b]	Assessment				
		PIAT			
	PPVT-R, Ages 3–4 Years (1986)	Math, Ages 5–6 Years (1988)	Reading Recognition, Ages 5–6 Years (1988)	Math, Ages 7–8 Years (1990)	Reading Recognition, Ages 7–8 Years (1990)
NLSY[c]					
< 0.5	−10.06*	−10.5*	−10.08*	−8.74*	−6.82*
	(2.64)	(1.79)	(1.72)	(2.04)	(2.30)
	[−0.15]	[−0.24]	[−0.24]	[−0.21]	[−0.15]
0.5–1.0	−6.96*	−5.02*	−4.42*	−4.77*	−4.24*
	(2.11)	(1.36)	(1.30)	(1.58)	(1.78)
	[−0.15]	[−0.17]	[−0.16]	[−0.17]	[−0.13]
1.0–1.5	1.53	−2.41*	−1.33	−2.69*	−1.35
	(2.23)	(1.41)	(1.35)	(1.59)	(1.78)
	[−0.03]	[−0.07]	[−0.04]	[0.08]	[0.04]
2.0–3.0	1.42	1.04	4.47*	1.81	3.5*
	(2.18)	(1.33)	(1.28)	(1.50)	(1.68)
	[0.02]	[0.03]	[0.15]	[0.06]	[0.11]
> 3.0	4.89*	2.12	4.41*	3.39*	3.5*
	(2.54)	(1.68)	(1.62)	(1.89)	(2.12)
	[0.07]	[0.05]	[0.10]	[0.08]	[0.07]
Adjusted R^2	0.28	0.14	0.15	0.16	0.16
Constant	111.38	89.56	106.75	98.28	81.08
N	734	858	847	611	603

	Bayley, Age 2 Years	PPVT-R, Age 3 Years	Stanford-Binet, Age 3 Years	PPVT-R, Age 5 Years	WPPSI, Age 5 Years
IHDP[d]					
< 0.5	−6.04*	−7.45*	−9.69*	−12.32*	−9.14*
	(2.58)	(2.06)	(2.31)	(2.79)	(2.29)
	[−0.12]	[−0.16]	[−0.18]	[−0.21]	[−0.19]
0.5–1.0	−3.71*	−6.37*	−6.94*	−11.79*	−7.38*
	(2.36)	(1.86)	(2.08)	(2.51)	(2.06)
	[−0.08]	[−0.16]	[−0.15]	[−0.24]	[−0.19]
1.0–1.5	1.00	−6.30*	−5.24*	−7.77*	−3.21
	(2.52)	(1.99)	(2.23)	(2.59)	(2.13)
	[0.02]	[−0.13]	[−0.09]	[−0.14]	[−0.07]
2.0–3.0	−0.11	−0.65	1.11	−0.63	2.73
	(2.66)	(2.14)	(2.39)	(2.82)	(2.32)
	[−0.002]	[−0.01]	[0.02]	[−0.01]	[0.05]
> 3.0	10.54*	5.78*	8.11*	6.18*	7.27*
	(2.60)	(2.06)	(2.30)	(2.77)	(2.28)
	[0.21]	[0.13]	[0.16]	[0.11]	[0.16]
Adjusted R^2	0.3	0.42	0.38	0.38	0.36
Constant	78.55	80.26	73.55	73.72	71.43
N	772	718	799	721	781

$^* p < .05$.

Sources: Authors' calculations from ordinary least squares (OLS) multiple linear regressions using data on children from the NLSY and IHDP. Data on 966 children drawn from the Children of the National Longitudinal Survey of Youth (NLSY) who were three to four years old in 1986.

a. Values are unstandardized regression coefficients. Standard errors in parentheses; standardized coefficients in brackets.

b. Children from families with income-to-needs ratios of 1.5–2.0 were the omitted group.

c. Regression models include child's race, birth weight, and sex; mother's education; and family structure variables.

d. Regression models as in note c, plus site and treatment group.

on average 9.1 points lower on the WPPSI and 12.3 points lower on the PPVT-R than those for the near-poor group.

In the Children of the NLSY sample, we also found a significant difference between the scores of the children with an average family income-to-needs ratio between 50 percent and 100 percent of the poverty level and those with an average family income-to-needs ratio between 150 percent and 200 percent of the poverty level on all assessments. The strongest difference was at age three to four on the PPVT-R (a 7.0-point difference). The effect on the achievement tests was a 4.2- to 5.0-point difference. In the IHDP sample, the difference between these groups did not show up at age two but was significant on all other assessments: the PPVT-R at age three exhibited a 6.0-point difference; the Stanford-Binet at age three and the WPPSI at age five, a 7.0-point difference; and the PPVT-R at age five, a 12.3-point difference.

Within the NSLY sample, the differences between the scores of children with a family income-to-needs ratio of 1.0–1.5 and those with family income-to-needs ratios of 1.5–2.0 were not statistically significant at the .05 level. Within the IHDP sample, the differences were significant on the Stanford-Binet at age three, the PPVT-R at age three, and the PPVT-R at age five (a 5.2–7.7 point difference).

Family Structure

We estimated the separate effects of family structure and income poverty on assessment scores (table 7.7). First we examined the effects of family structure and then added income-to-needs ratios to the regression equation. We found family structure effects in both data sets when the analyses did not control for income; however, these effects disappeared when we controlled for income. For example, in the Children of the NLSY sample, children aged three to four who lived continuously in a female-headed household had PPVT-R scores 4.4 points lower than those who lived in two-parent families. Also, children who lived in a family in which the single mother married had PPVT-R scores 5.4 points lower than those in two-parent families. Yet, with income in the model, these effects were no longer statistically significant. On the PIAT achievement scores, without controlling for income, children aged seven to eight whose mothers remarried had scores 3.2 points lower than did the children in the contrasting two-parent families. With income in the model, this effect also disappeared.

In the IHDP sample, the negative effects of living in a family headed by a female became stronger as the child got older. For example, growing up in a family where the mother was continuously never married lowered scores on the Stanford-Binet test by 3.6 points at age three and on the PPVT-R by −8.4 points at age five. Yet, when we controlled for family income, these effects were no longer significant.

Human Capital

We also investigated whether the effects of income and mother's education have independent effects on young children's outcomes (table 7.8). Although the effects of a mother's education on her young child's cognitive scores were reduced by adding the family's income to the regression, they remained significant in most of the analyses.[11] In the Children of the NLSY sample, the unstandardized coefficient for mother's education was reduced by 26 percent with income in the model, but the mother's education remained statistically significant in predicting PPVT-R scores at ages three to four. Adding income to the model on the regression for the PIAT Math at ages five to six reduced the unstandardized coefficient for the mother's education by 35 percent, but the effect of the mother's education again remained significant. On the Reading test at age five and six, mother's education was not significant with income in the model. At ages seven to eight on the Reading test, the unstandardized coefficient for mother's education was reduced by 33 percent with controls for average family income, but the mother's education was still a significant explanatory variable. On the Mathematics test, the mother's education lost statistical significance with income in the model.

We found similar results for the IHDP sample. Once income was entered into the model, the variance explained by the mother's education decreased on average 50 percent, but effects of the mother's education remained statistically significant. The standardized coefficients for mother's education were larger in the IHDP sample than in the NLSY sample up to ages five to six. By seven to eight years of age, however, the standardized coefficients for mother's education in the NLSY on the PIAT Reading Recognition were as high as those seen at earlier ages for the IHDP. In both data sets, the standardized coefficient for mother's education increased as the child got older. Overall, the results suggest that mother's education and family income have independent effects on young children's cognitive outcomes.

Home Learning Environment

The final set of analyses look at whether the mother's education and family income are mediated by the child's home environment. We estimated (1) the effects of the income-to-needs ratio averaged over the child's lifetime on scores on the various cognitive/achievement assessments, with and without controls for the cognitive stimulation and emotional support available as measured by the HOME Inventory; and (2) the effects of the mother's education, without income, with and without controls for the cognitive and emotional stimulation in the home, as measured by the HOME Inventory (table 7.9).

In both data sets, variations in the provision of cognitive and emotional stimulation in the home reduced the effects of the income-to-needs ratio on all of the child's cognitive measures at each developmental period, but income continued to be a significant explanatory variable. In the Children of the NLSY sample, the HOME Inventory was taken at ages three to four and five to six. We controlled for both assessments in separate regressions. Each reduced the income effects, but

(Text continued on p. 160.)

TABLE 7.7 / Effects of Family Structure and Income Poverty on Children's Assessment Scores[a]

	Assessment									
			PIAT							
	PPVT-R, Ages 3–4 Years (1986)		Math, Ages 5–6 Years (1988)		Reading Recognition, Ages 5–6 Years (1988)		Math, Ages 7–8 Years (1990)		Reading Recognition, Ages 7–8 Years (1990)	
Sample and Structure[b]	Without Income	With Income	Without Income	With Income	Without Income	With Income	Without Income	With Income	Without Income	With Income
NLSY[c]										
Female head continuously	−4.43*	1.43	−1.31	1.22	−1.65	1.13	0.65	1.2	−1.85	−0.04
	(1.92)	(1.96)	(1.27)	(1.24)	(1.24)	(1.25)	(1.34)	(1.35)	(1.51)	(1.52)
	[−0.09]	[0.03]	[−0.04]	[0.04]	[−0.06]	[0.04]	[0.02]	[0.04]	[0.06]	[−0.01]
Divorced or separated continuously	2.1	4.93	−0.81	1.05	−1.2	0.77	1.8	2.99	5.44	6.53*
	(3.22)	(3.22)	(2.15)	(2.11)	(2.11)	(2.06)	(2.5)	(2.45)	(2.9)	(2.85)
	[0.02]	[0.05]	[−0.01]	[0.02]	[−0.10]	[0.01]	[0.03]	[0.05]	[0.07]	[0.09]
Change to one parent	2.06	2.64	1.07	2.13	−0.06	1.11	2.9	3.68*	0.93	1.66
	(2.02)	(1.97)	(1.3)	(1.30)	(1.28)	(1.25)	(1.57)	(1.54)	(1.74)	(1.71)
	[0.03]	[0.04]	[0.03]	[0.05]	[−0.01]	[0.03]	[0.07]	[0.09]	[−0.02]	[0.04]
Change to two parents	−5.43*	−2.32	−2.45*	−0.69	−1.79	0.15	−3.18*	−1.99	−0.61	0.55
	(1.88)	(1.9)	(1.26)	(1.25)	(1.22)	(1.2)	(1.42)	(1.4)	(1.58)	(1.56)
	[−0.10]	[−0.04]	[−0.07]	[−0.02]	[−0.05]	[0.01]	[−0.09]	[−0.06]	[−0.01]	[−0.01]
	Bayley, Age 2 Years		PPVT-R, Age 3 Years		Stanford-Binet, Age 3 Years		WPPSI, Age 5 Years			
IHDP[d]										
Female head at 24 months	−3.79*	−1.42								
	(1.35)	(1.33)								
	[−0.10]	[−0.04]								

Female head continuously	−0.79	1.47	−3.64*	−0.67		
	(1.26)	(1.26)	(1.42)	(1.40)		
	[−0.02]	[0.04]	[−0.09]	[−0.02]		
Female head some years	−3.83*	−1.34	−6.02*	−2.74		
	(1.59)	(1.58)	(1.79)	(1.75)		
	[−0.08]	[−0.03]	[−0.11]	[−0.05]		
Female head at 2–5 years					−6.63*	−2.94
					(2.06)	(2.03)
					[−0.12]	[−0.05]
Female head at 2–5 years, ever married					−8.38*	−3.86
					(2.83)	(2.78)
					[−0.10]	[−0.05]
Female head at 2–5 years, not at age 5					−7.12*	−2.63
					(3.16)	(3.08)
					[−0.07]	[−0.03]
Not female head at 2 years, female head age 5					−6.73*	−3.37
					(2.06)	(2.02)
					[−0.11]	[−0.06]
Other					−6.06*	−2.19
					(2.41)	(2.36)
					[−0.09]	[−0.03]

* $p < .05$.

Sources: Authors' calculations from ordinary least squares (OLS) multiple linear regressions using data on children from the NLSY and IHDP. Data on 966 children drawn from the Children of the National Longitudinal Survey of Youth (NLSY) who were three to four years old in 1986.

a. Values are unstandardized regression coefficients. Standard errors in parentheses; standardized coefficients in brackets.

b. Children living in continuous two-parent families were the omitted group.

c. Regression models include child's race, birth weight, and sex; mother's education; and family structure variables.

d. Regression models as in note c, plus site and treatment group.

income remained significant. On the PPVT-R assessment in the NLSY sample, controlling for the learning in the HOME when the children are three to four reduced the income effect by 42 percent (1.6 points). On the PIAT Math, at ages five to six, controlling for the home learning when the children were three to four reduced the income effect by 44 percent (1.1 points); controlling for the home environment at ages five to six reduced the income effect further by 35 percent, but income continued to be statistically significant in explaining the child's PIAT Mathematics score. On the PIAT Reading Recognition at ages five to six, controlling for home environment at ages three to four reduced the income effect by 25 percent, controlling for the home environment at ages five to six further reduced the income effect by 20 percent. On the PIAT Mathematics at ages seven to eight, controlling for home environment at ages three to four reduced the income effect by 18 percent (.5 points); controlling for the home environment again at ages five to six reduced the unstandardized coefficient for income by 11 percent. Controlling for the home environment at ages three to four on the child's PIAT Reading Recognition score at ages seven to eight reduced the income effect by 26 percent, while controlling for the home environment at ages five to six reduced the standardized income effect by 25 percent.

In the IHDP sample, the HOME Inventory is an important mediator; yet income effects continued to be significant even after controlling for the child's home environment. Controlling for the home environment at age three on the various assessments reduced the income effect by 33–40 percent.

We conducted similar analyses for the effect of the mother's education, controlling for family income and the home environment. In both data sets, the HOME Inventory was an important mediator: the unstandardized coefficient for mother's education decreased approximately 50 percent in the IHDP analyses that used the full HOME Inventory and somewhat less in the Children of the NLSY sample (from 13 to 29 percent), which used the short form of the HOME Inventory. Yet the mother's education remains significant in predicting most of the outcomes for children in both data sets, with the exception of the child's score on the Stanford-Binet at age three, the PPVT-R at age five in the IHDP, and the PIAT Math in the NLSY at ages seven and eight.

DISCUSSION

Living in poverty affects even very young children negatively. While previous work supports our general finding, little work to date has documented the consequences of family income during infancy and the preschool years separately from other demographic characteristics of the family, most notably parents' education and occupation. That is, the developmentally oriented studies of children under age five typically have not included income measures, and the national longitudinal studies prior to the Children of the NLSY did not assess verbal ability or early school achievement.

TABLE 7.8 / Effects of Mother's Education Control for Income[a]

Sample and Assessment	Effect: Without Income	Effect: With Income
NLSY[b]		
PPVT-R, ages 3–4 years (1986)	0.57*	0.42*
	(0.18)	(0.18)
	[0.10]	[0.07]
PIAT		
Math, ages 5–6 years (1988)	0.45*	0.29*
	(0.12)	(0.12)
	[0.12]	[0.08]
Reading, ages 5–6 years (1988)	0.18	0.13
	(0.10)	(0.10)
	[0.07]	[0.05]
Math, ages 7–8 years (1990)	0.96*	0.41
	(0.27)	(0.29)
	[0.14]	[0.05]
Reading, ages 7–8 years (1990)	1.8*	1.2*
	(0.30)	(0.32)
	[0.23]	[0.16]
IHDP[c]		
Bayley, age 2 years	1.50*	0.56*
	(0.27)	(0.28)
	[0.19]	[0.07]
Stanford-Binet, age 3 years	2.02*	1.06*
	(0.26)	(0.27)
	[0.25]	[0.13]
PPVT-R		
Age 3 years	1.79*	1.06*
	(0.23)	(0.24)
	[0.25]	[0.15]
Age 5 years	2.28*	1.25*
	(0.30)	(0.32)
	[0.26]	[0.14]
WPSSI, age 5 years	2.08*	1.27*
	(0.25)	(0.26)
	[0.29]	[0.18]

Sources: Authors' calculations from ordinary least squares (OLS) multiple linear regressions using data on children from the NLSY and IHDP. Data on 966 children drawn from the Children of the National Longitudinal Survey of Youth (NLSY) who were three to four years old in 1986.

a. Values are unstandardized regression coefficients. Standard errors in parentheses; standardized coefficients in brackets.

b. Regression models include child's race, birth weight, and sex; mother's education; and family structure variables.

c. Regression models as in note b, plus site and treatment group.

TABLE 7.9 / The Home Environment as a Mediator of Income Effects[a]

	Assessment				
		PIAT			
Sample and Control	PPVT-R, Ages 3–4 Years (1986)	Math, Ages 5–6 Years (1988)	Reading Recognition, Ages 5–6 Years (1988)	Math, Ages 7–8 Years (1990)	Reading Recognition, Ages 7–8 Years (1990)
NLSY[b]					
Income coefficient	3.68*	2.51*	3.2*	2.97*	2.93*
	(0.62)	(0.44)	(0.43)	(0.52)	(0.58)
	[0.21]	[0.21]	[0.29]	[0.27]	[0.24]
Controlling for home environment					
1986	2.05*	1.42*	2.44*	2.24*	2.15*
	(0.63)	(0.44)	(0.43)	(0.53)	(0.29)
	[0.12]	[0.12]	[0.29]	[0.20]	[0.17]
1986 and 1988		0.92*	1.95*	1.9*	1.59*
		(0.45)	(0.43)	(0.54)	(0.59)
		[0.08]	[0.17]	[0.17]	[0.13]
Mother's education					
Without income	0.57*	0.45*	0.61*	0.96*	1.84*
	(0.18)	(0.13)	(0.12)	(0.27)	(0.29)
	[0.10]	[0.12]	[0.17]	[0.14]	[0.23]
Controlling for income	0.42*	0.32*	0.45*	0.37	1.2*
	(0.18)	(0.12)	(0.12)	(0.29)	(0.32)
	[0.07]	[0.08]	[0.12]	[0.05]	[0.16]

Controlling for income and home, 1986	0.30* (0.17) [0.05]	0.24* (0.12) [0.06]	0.39* (0.12) [0.11]	0.07* (0.29) [0.01]	0.89* (0.32) [0.12]

	PPVT-R, Age 3 Years	Stanford-Binet, Age 3 Years	PPVT-R, Age 5 Years	WPPSI, Age 5 Years
IHDP[c]				
Income coefficient	3.04*	4.00*	4.54*	3.57*
	(0.42)	(0.47)	(0.57)	(0.47)
	[0.28]	[0.33]	[0.33]	[0.32]
Controlling for home environment, age 3	1.97*	2.72*	2.89*	2.15*
	(0.43)	(0.47)	(0.58)	(0.47)
	[0.18]	[0.22]	[0.21]	[0.19]
Mother's education				
Without income	1.79*	2.02*	2.28*	2.08*
	(0.23)	(0.21)	(0.30)	(0.25)
	[0.25]	[0.25]	[0.26]	[0.29]
Controlling for income	1.06*	1.06*	1.25*	1.27*
	(0.27)	(0.27)	(0.32)	(0.26)
	[0.15]	[0.13]	[0.14]	[0.18]
Controlling for income and home environment, 1986	0.53*	0.42	0.58	0.70*
	(0.25)	(0.27)	(0.31)	(0.26)
	[0.08]	[0.05]	[0.07]	[0.10]

Sources: Authors' calculations from ordinary least squares (OLS) multiple linear regressions using data on children from the NLSY and IHDP. Data on 966 children drawn from the Children of the National Longitudinal Survey of Youth (NLSY) who were three to four years old in 1986.

a. Values are unstandardized regression coefficients. Standard errors in parentheses; standardized coefficients in brackets.

b. Regression models include child's race, birth weight, and sex; mother's education; and family structure variables.

c. Regression models as in note b, plus site and treatment group.

Poverty and Cognitive Ability

Evidence from this study shows that family poverty affected the cognitive abilities of children in two very different samples, as measured at separate ages. Three types of assessment were used: IQ, verbal ability, and achievement tests. Effects of income were found at each age from two to eight years. Average income-to-needs ratios were fairly consistent over time and assessments: a change in one unit of the family income-to-needs ratio was associated with a 3.0- to 3.7-point increase in the child's score on the various cognitive assessments. In the IHDP sample, for which we compared the effects of income on the scores of the same children on the same assessment over time, the income-to-needs ratio tended to affect verbal ability test scores more strongly with age. We await the availability of the age eight IHDP data to see if this trend holds. In contrast, in the Children of the NLSY sample, the effects of income on the child's PIAT achievement test scores decreased at ages seven to eight possibly because of the positive effects of school attendance. Income affected the IHDP children's IQ tests scores more than their verbal ability test scores at age three. In the NLSY sample, income effects were slightly stronger on the PIAT Reading Recognition test than on the PIAT Mathematics test at ages five to six.

Duration of poverty has very negative effects on children's IQ, verbal ability, and achievement scores. Children who lived in persistently poor families scored 6–9 points lower on the various assessments than children who were never poor. In addition, the negative effects of persistent poverty seem to get stronger as the child gets older, as shown by the PPVT-R scores for the IHDP sample. Transient poverty also affected the scores, but the effects were generally 4–5 points lower than the effects of living in continuous poverty.

In this study, we did not find that timing of poverty made a difference in children's outcomes, in part because the comparisons of early and late poverty were based on very short time periods (that is, the first two and second two or the first three and second three years of life). We had expected such trends to appear at ages seven to eight, at which time comparisons between earlier and later poverty periods would be based on lengths of time comparable to those used in the Panel Study of Income Dynamics and in the Baltimore Study of Teenage Motherhood (Baydar, Brooks-Gunn, and Furstenberg 1993; Brooks-Gunn, Guo, and Furstenberg 1993; Wolfe 1991).[12] However, such trends did not emerge in the data on the NLSY children of this age.

The effects of family poverty varied dramatically depending on whether a family was very poor (family income below 50 percent of the poverty level), poor, or near poor. Children in the very poor group had scores 7–12 points lower than did children in the near-poor group. Children whose families had incomes slightly higher (between 50 percent and 100 percent of the poverty level) scored somewhat closer to the near-poor contrast group (4–7 points lower but 12 points lower on the PPVT-R at age five in the IHDP sample). These results, if not accounted for by unmeasured familial differences, suggest that increasing family income from very poor to near-poor will dramatically improve the cognitive well-being of young children.

Family income affected the IHDP children as early as age two, based on an infant intelligence test. And the effect of income at age two was quite similar to that found at ages three and five. Exploratory analyses on the age one infant intelligence test scores from the IHDP suggest that the income effect is not seen, or is very small, at this earlier age. This pattern of findings suggests that standardized intelligence tests evidence the effects of income as soon as they begin to tap verbal, quantitative, and reasoning abilities. The test items given in the first year of life are primarily visual-motor and social in nature, although some rudimentary concept formation items also appear (Brooks-Gunn, Liaw, and Klebanov 1992; Brooks-Gunn and Weinraub 1983; McCall, 1983). Yet the predictive validity of tests given in the first eighteen months of life is quite low. By two to three years, however, intelligence test scores are relatively predictive of scores in the later preschool years (Lewis 1983).

The results from the two very different data sets are quite comparable. The effect of income on the PPVT-R scores, the one assessment that is included in both data sets, was somewhat smaller for the NLSY children than for the IHDP children (for example, for an income-to-needs ratio at ages three to four the standardized coefficient is 0.20 in the NLSY and 0.28 in the IHDP). Any differences may be due to variations in sample composition. Of particular interest is whether the IHDP findings are stronger because children in the sample were low birth weight. We cannot address this question adequately, but we found no income–birth weight interactions in either sample, suggesting that the income effects were quite comparable across the birth weight distribution. Also, the effects did not change for the IHDP when the very light babies—those weighing 1,000 g and under at birth—were excluded. Other aspects of the sample composition might be important. For example, in analyses of the NLSY children who were three to four years of age in 1988 (and who were born to mothers less likely to be teen mothers), the coefficient for the income-to-needs ratio for the PPVT-R was smaller than that found for the children who were three to four years of age in 1986 (2.1 and 3.6, respectively). The same was true of this cohort's PIAT scores in 1990 (when they were five and six years of age). More work is needed to understand such variation.

As in previous work, we eliminated family structure effects in both samples and across ages by controlling for income. These data are somewhat different from those reported by Garfinkel and McLanahan (1986), McLanahan (1991), and McLanahan and Sandefur (1994) in that household structure had almost no effect when income was entered into the equation. We suspect that the family household factors may become more salient with age, in that they influence the outcomes of youths even with controls for income. Possible reasons include the particularly detrimental effects of moving to new schools (often accompanying a family change) during junior and senior high school and perhaps the increased salience of supervision and monitoring during the adolescent years (see chapter 3 this volume). Interestingly, without controls for income at age three, family structure affected the NLSY children's verbal ability scores more strongly than they did their school achievement scores (PIAT). Both living in a female-headed household continuously and having a second parent entering the family affected the scores. Previous work on stepfamilies suggests that remarriage (and possibly a first marriage for a never-married mother) is often a stressful event for children, even though it often brings additional financial resources (Booth and Dunn 1994). The IHDP data also illustrate the effects of living continuously in a female-headed household as well as one headed by a female adjusting to the entrance of a male into the household (via remarriage or first marriage) and the exit of a male from the household (via divorce and separation) at age five, the one age for which these combinations could be calculated. At the younger ages, living in a family continuously or transiently headed by a female also contributed to lower test scores, although these effects disappeared when the income variable was entered.

Mother's Education and Cognitive Ability

The effect of human capital (mother's education) on a child's cognitive ability was of interest. Developmentalists have examined the effects of parents' education on young children's outcomes rather than the effects of family income. In part, this emphasis is due to the conceptual interest in human capital and the ways in which education may influence interactions and the literacy environment of the home. Indeed, parents' education is always linked to young children's outcomes. Our analyses complement earlier work, as expected. However, we also looked at whether or not the effects of income and parents' education (here, mother's education) have independent effects on young children's outcomes. The addition of income into equations with mother's education resulted in a decrease in the standardized coefficient for mother's education of about 33–40 percent in the Children of the NLSY cohort. The drops were larger for the IHDP sample—approximately 50 percent for the same two age periods. However, in both cases the coefficients for mother's education remained significant across ages on most measures. The results suggest that mother's education and family income have independent effects on children's cognitive outcomes.

Finally, we examined how the provision of learning experiences in the home mediates the effects of both income and mother's education. The drop in the standardized coefficient for the family income-to-needs ratio, once we controlled for the home environment, was about 10 points on the PPVT-R and the PIAT Mathematics for the NLSY children and about 10–12 points on the PPVT-R and the various IQ tests for the IHDP children. The drop in the beta for mother's education with controls for income was 3–4 points on the PPVT-R and the PIAT Mathematics in the NLSY sample and about 10 points on the PPVT-R and various IQ tests in the IHDP sample. Yet, when we also controlled for the HOME environment and income, the beta for mother's education dropped about 5 points on the assessments in the NLSY and about 17 points in the IHDP analyses.[13] This suggests that in these analyses the home experience mediated the effects of the mother's education more strongly than family income did. This finding fits with the belief that education is linked to specific ways of talking, playing, interacting, and reading with young children (Bradley et al. 1989; Sugland et al. 1995). It also suggests that working on increasing the educational levels of mothers will affect children via their home experiences, a tenet upon which many early childhood intervention programs are based (Chase-Lansdale and Brooks-Gunn 1995; Clarke-Stewart and Fein 1983).

These findings have implications for policies directed at improving the well-being of young children. Increases in the income of poor families are likely to raise the performance of young children. The effects could be seen as early as age two. Income-transfer policies that raised a family's income to the near-poor level would improve the cognitive ability and performance of young children. In addition, raising the educational level of parents could have similar effects on young children, and doing both might even have an even greater effect. Other fruitful strategies might be more indirect programmatic ones, such as helping mothers read more to their children (as well as read more themselves) and teaching mothers about intellectually stimulating learning activities that they can do at home with their children (Brooks-Gunn, Denner, and Klebanov 1995; Snow 1986). In sum, income and tax benefits aimed at increasing the family income of poor families, as well as early intervention programs aimed at improving the home learning environment, for parents and children, would improve the school readiness and cognitive ability of the nation's youngest citizens.

APPENDIX: REPLICATION ANALYSIS

The six models in appendix tables 7A.1–7A.10 all control for child's race, age, sex, and birth weight and mother's education, as well as site and treatment group in the IHDP analyses. The models control additionally for the following: model 1, family structure but not average income-to-needs ratio; model 2, average income-to-needs ratio but not family structure; model 3, family structure and average income-to-needs ratio; model 4, family structure, average income, and number of people in the household; model 5, family structure and nonlinear income categories; and model 6, family structure and duration of poverty.

TABLE 7A.1 / NLSY Replication Analysis Effects of Family Characteristics and Income on Children's Verbal Ability (PPVT-R) at Ages Three and Four[a]

	Model					
Variable	1	2	3	4	5	6
Black	−17.77***	−17.05***	−16.13***	−15.4***	−16.49***	−17.12***
	(1.58)	(1.37)	(1.59)	(1.6)	(1.59)	(1.58)
Child's age	−0.3***	−0.3***	−0.26***	−0.26***	−0.26**	−0.29***
	(0.09)	(0.09)	(0.09)	(0.09)	(0.09)	(0.09)
Male	−2.22~	−1.94~	−1.88~	−1.72	−1.81	−2.25~
	(1.27)	(1.22)	(1.24)	(1.24)	(1.25)	(1.27)
Mother's education	0.57***	0.42*	0.42*	0.36*	0.42*	0.53**
	(0.18)	(0.18)	(0.18)	(0.18)	(0.18)	(0.18)
Low birth weight	−2.55	−2.75	−2.17	−1.13	−2.31	−2.33
	(2.27)	(2.17)	(2.23)	(2.24)	(2.24)	(2.26)
Family structure[b]						
Female head of household	−4.43*		−1.43	−0.55	−0.57	−2.47
	(1.92)		(1.96)	(1.96)	(2.03)	(2.01)
Divorced or separated	2.1		4.93~	4.08	5.4~	4.88
	(3.23)		(3.22)	(3.21)	(3.25)	(3.35)
Change to one parent	2.06		2.64	2.37	2.63	2.89
	(2.02)		(1.97)	(1.96)	(1.98)	(2.02)
Change to two parents	−5.43***		−2.32	−3.16~	−1.83	−4.51~
	(1.89)		(1.91)	(1.9)	(1.94)	(1.92)

Family income						
Average income-to-needs ratio		3.74***	3.68***			
		(0.6)	(0.64)			
Average income ($10,000)				2.5***		
				(4.8)		
Number in household				−1.9***		
				(0.42)		
Income-to-needs ratio[c]						
< 1					−6.28***	
					(1.62)	
> 2 < 3					2.16	
					(1.82)	
> 3					5.58*	
					(2.23)	
Duration of poverty						
Transient						−2.43***
						(1.83)
Continuous						−7.06***
						(2.54)
Adjusted R^2	0.25	0.28	0.28	0.29	0.28	0.26
N	784	787	766	768	766	784
Constant	103.56	97.69	95.91	104.53	103.08	105.9

$\sim p < .1$. $^{*} p < .05$. $^{**} p < .01$. $^{***} p < .001$.

Source: Authors' calculations using data from the Children of the NLSY, 1986 cohort. See text for description of models.

a. Values are OLS unstandardized coefficients based on unweighted data. Standard errors in parentheses.

b. Children who lived in continuous two-parent families were the omitted group.

c. Children from families with income-to-needs ratios of 1–2 were the omitted group.

TABLE 7A.2 / NLSY Replication Analysis Effects of Family Characteristics and Income on Children's PIAT Achievement Reading Recognition Score at Ages Five and Six [a]

	Model					
Variable	1	2	3	4	5	6
Black	−0.96	0.95	0.40	0.84	0.65	−0.34
	(1.02)	(0.85)	(1.00)	(1.01)	(1.00)	(1.01)
Child's age	−0.09~	−0.09~	−0.08~	−0.08	−0.09~	−0.07
	(0.05)	(0.05)	(0.05)	(0.05)	(0.05)	(0.05)
Male	−3.37***	−3.38***	−3.34***	−3.29***	−3.21***	−3.65***
	(0.81)	(0.77)	(0.78)	(0.78)	(0.78)	(0.80)
Mother's education	0.61***	0.44***	0.45***	0.41***	0.47***	0.55***
	(0.12)	(0.12)	(0.12)	(0.12)	(1.2)	(0.12)
Low birth weight	−4.71***	−3.66**	−3.83**	−3.49**	−3.90**	−4.59**
	(1.50)	(1.39)	(1.45)	(1.45)	(1.45)	(1.47)
Family structure[b]						
Female head of household	−1.65		1.13	1.42	1.7	0.21
	(1.24)		(1.25)	(1.26)	(1.27)	(1.26)
Divorced or separated	−1.2		0.77	0.15	1.6	0.75
	(2.11)		(2.06)	(2.06)	(2.07)	(2.11)
Change to one parent	−0.06		1.11	0.82	1.15	0.90
	(1.29)		(1.25)	(1.26)	(1.24)	(1.27)
Change to two parents	−1.79~		0.15	−0.13	0.08	−0.23
	(1.22)		(1.21)	(1.21)	(1.20)	(1.23)

Family income						
Average income-to-needs ratio		3.22***	3.35***			
		(0.40)	(0.43)			
Average income ($10,000)				2.3***		
				(0.32)		
Number in household				−1.41***		
				(0.30)		
Income-to-needs ratio[c]						
< 1					−5.21***	
					(1.04)	
> 2 < 3					4.23***	
					(1.10)	
> 3					4.09***	
					(1.38)	
Duration of poverty						
Transient						−5.94***
						(1.10)
Continuous						−9.17***
						(2.73)
Adjusted R^2	0.07	0.13	0.12	0.13	0.13	0.09
N	852	873	852	852	852	852
Constant	106.04	101.34	100.07	106.4	105.65	109

~ $p < .1$. * $p < .05$. ** $p < .01$. *** $p < .001$.

Source: Authors' calculations using data from the Children of the NLSY, 1988 cohort. See text for description of models.

a. Values are OLS unstandardized coefficients based on unweighted data. Standard errors in parentheses.

b. Children who lived in continuous two-parent families were the omitted group.

c. Children from families with income-to-needs ratios of 1–2 were the omitted group.

TABLE 7A.3 / NLSY Replication Analysis Effects of Family Characteristics and Income on Children's PIAT Math Achievement Test Score at Ages Five and Six[a]

	Model					
Variable	1	2	3	4	5	6
Black	−5.61***	−3.84***	−4.35***	−3.97***	−4.22***	−5.07***
	(1.04)	(0.88)	(1.03)	(1.04)	(1.04)	(1.04)
Child's age	0.14**	0.14**	0.15**	0.15**	0.14**	0.14**
	(0.06)	(0.05)	(0.05)	(0.05)	(0.05)	(0.06)
Male	−2.36***	−2.47***	−2.3**	−2.31**	−2.21**	−2.6**
	(0.83)	(0.80)	(0.81)	(0.81)	(0.81)	(0.82)
Mother's education	0.45***	0.28**	0.29**	0.26*	0.32***	0.39***
	(0.13)	(0.12)	(0.12)	(0.12)	(0.12)	(0.12)
Low birth weight	−3.7*	−2.24~	−2.8*	−2.52~	−2.85*	−3.6*
	(1.54)	(1.45)	(1.51)	(1.5)	(1.51)	(1.53)
Family structure[b]						
Female head of household	−1.31		1.22	1.80	1.69	0.25
	(1.27)		(1.30)	(1.30)	(1.32)	(1.31)
Divorced or separated	−0.81		1.05	0.91	1.76	0.77
	(2.15)		(2.12)	(2.12)	(2.13)	(2.16)
Change to one parent	1.07		2.13	2.15	2.09	1.9
	(1.32)		(1.30)	(1.30)	(1.30)	(1.32)
Change to two parents	−2.45		−0.69	−0.68	−0.90	−1.08
	(1.26)		(1.25)	(1.25)	(1.25)	(1.27)

	(1)	(2)	(3)	(4)	(5)	(6)
Family income						
Average income-to-needs ratio		2.9***	3.08***			
		(0.42)	(0.45)			
Average income ($10,000)				2.4***		
				(0.33)		
Number in household				−1.05***		
				(0.31)		
Income-to-needs ratio[c]						
< 1					−5.19***	
					(1.08)	
> 2 < 3					2.5*	
					(1.15)	
> 3					3.7**	
					(1.43)	
Duration of poverty						
Transient						−5.3***
						(1.14)
Continuous						−5.7*
						(2.83)
Adjusted R^2	0.09	0.13	0.13	0.15	0.13	0.11
N	862	884	862	862	862	862
Constant	86.9	83.53	81.41	86.16	87.0	91.8

~ $p < .1$. * $p < .05$. ** $p < .01$. *** $p < .001$.

Source: Authors' calculations using data from the Children of the NLSY, 1988 cohort. See text for description of models.

a. Values are OLS unstandardized coefficients based on unweighted data. Standard errors in parentheses.

b. Children who lived in continuous two-parent families were the omitted group.

c. Children from families with income-to-needs ratios of 1–2 were the omitted group.

TABLE 7A.4 / NLSY Replication Analysis Effects of Family Characteristics on Children's PIAT Reading Recognition Test at Ages Seven and Eight[a]

	Model					
Variable	1	2	3	4	5	6
Black	−5.56***	−3.09**	−3.57**	−3.02*	−3.35**	−4.65***
	(1.26)	(1.38)	(1.3)	(1.3)	(1.3)	(1.3)
Child's age	0.16*	0.15*	0.16*	0.15*	0.15*	0.15*
	(0.16)	(0.15)	(0.07)	(0.07)	(0.07)	(0.07)
Male	−2.83**	−2.9***	−2.99***	−2.89***	−2.99***	−2.96***
	(1.02)	(0.99)	(1.00)	(1.00)	(1.00)	(1.01)
Mother's education	1.84***	1.15***	1.23***	1.07***	1.23***	1.54***
	(0.29)	(0.31)	(0.32)	(0.32)	(0.32)	(0.30)
Low birth weight	−1.39	−0.73	−0.87	−0.59	−0.7	−0.8
	(1.91)	(1.84)	(1.88)	(1.87)	(1.87)	(1.89)
Family structure[b]						
Female head of household	−1.85		−0.04	0.42	0.5	−0.02
	(1.50)		(1.52)	(1.54)	(1.56)	(1.56)
Divorced or separated	5.44		6.53*	6.14*	6.93*	7.9**
	(2.9)		(2.85)	(2.88)	(2.85)	(2.92)
Change to one parent	0.93		1.66	1.43	1.34	1.37
	(1.74)		(1.71)	(1.72)	(1.71)	(1.72)
Change to two parents	−0.61		0.55	0.5	0.8	0.28
	(1.57)		(1.56)	(1.57)	(1.57)	(1.58)

Family income						
Average income-to-needs ratio		2.99***	2.93***			
		(0.56)	(0.58)			
Average income ($10,000)				2.2***		
				(0.43)		
Number in household				−1.27***		
				(0.38)		
Income-to-needs ratio[c]						
< 1					−4.2***	
					(1.42)	
> 2 < 3					4.36***	
					(1.39)	
> 3					4.45*	
					(1.83)	
Duration of poverty						
Transient						−3.35**
						(1.37)
Continuous						−8.47***
						(2.07)
Adjusted R^2	0.13	0.15	0.16	0.17	0.16	0.15
N	613	613	613	613	613	613
Constant	70.43***	72.77***	71.3***	78.51***	76.10***	76.03***

* $p < .05$. ** $p < .01$. *** $p < .001$.

Source: Authors' calculations using data from the Children of the NLSY, 1990 cohort. See text for description of models.

a. Values are OLS unstandardized coefficients based on unweighted data. Standard errors in parentheses.

b. Children who lived in continuous two-parent families were the omitted group.

TABLE 7A.5 / NLSY Replication Analysis Effects of Family Characteristics on Children's PIAT Math Test Scores at Ages Seven and Eight[a]

Variable	Model					
	1	2	3	4	5	6
Black	−6.51***	−4.12***	−4.52***	−4.74***	−4.21***	−5.77***
	(1.13)	(1.02)	(1.16)	(1.17)	(1.16)	(1.15)
Child's age	0.01	0.01	0.01	0.01	0.01	0.01
	(0.06)	(0.06)	(0.06)	(0.06)	(0.06)	(0.06)
Male	−0.54	−0.68	−0.67	−0.67	−0.71	−0.65
	(0.92)	(0.90)	(0.90)	(0.89)	(0.89)	(0.91)
Mother's education	0.99***	0.36	0.35	0.41	0.29	0.76
	(0.27)	(0.28)	(0.29)	(0.29)	(0.29)	(0.28)
Low birth weight	−4.09*	−2.96~	−3.54*	−3.7*	−3.37*	−3.55*
	(1.71)	(1.66)	(1.67)	(1.67)	(1.67)	(1.71)
Family structure[b]						
Female head of household	−0.65		1.2	1.73~	1.96	0.83
	(1.35)		(1.35)	(1.37)	(1.39)	(1.40)
Divorced or separated	1.8		3.0	4.0~	3.48	3.66
	(2.51)		(2.46)	(2.49)	(2.46)	(2.54)
Change to one parent	2.94~		3.68*	4.05**	3.58*	3.24*
	(1.57)		(1.54)	(1.55)	(1.54)	(1.56)
Change to two parents	−3.18*		−1.99	−1.55	−1.77	−2.44~
	(1.42)		(1.40)	(1.41)	(1.41)	(1.44)

Family income						
Average income-to-needs ratio		2.79***	2.97***			
		(0.50)	(0.52)			
Average income ($10,000)				2.3***		
				(0.38)		
Number in household				−0.1		
				(0.34)		
Income-to-needs ratio[c]						
< 1					−4.67***	
					(1.26)	
> 2 < 3					3.08**	
					(1.25)	
> 3					6.18***	
					(1.62)	
Duration of poverty						
Transient						−2.75*
						(1.24)
Continuous						−6.75***
						(1.86)
Adjusted R^2	0.12	0.15	0.16	0.18	0.19	0.15
N	621	639	621	621	621	621
Constant	90.84***	92.84***	91.71***	90.71***	97.14***	95.44***

* $p < .05$. ** $p < .01$. *** $p < .001$.

Source: Authors' calculations using data from the Children of the NLSY, 1990 cohort. See text for description of models.

a. Values are OLS unstandardized coefficients based on unweighted data. Standard errors in parentheses.

b. Children who lived in continuous two-parent families were the omitted group.

TABLE 7A.6 / IHDP Replication Analysis Effects of Family Characteristics and Income on Bayley IQ Test at Age Two[a]

	Model					
Variable	1	2	3	4	5	6
Black	−5.80***	−3.49**	−3.14*	−3.83***	−3.54**	−4.72**
	(1.41)	(1.36)	(1.40)	(1.39)	(1.41)	(1.49)
Male	−3.96***	−4.28***	−4.26***	−4.24***	−4.12***	−4.06***
	(1.21)	(1.16)	(1.16)	(1.17)	(1.18)	(1.24)
Low birth weight	5.30***	4.98***	5.00***	5.00***	5.08***	5.16***
	(1.33)	(1.28)	(1.28)	(1.28)	(1.29)	(1.37)
Mother's education	1.50***	0.59*	0.56*	0.67*	0.73**	1.15***
	(0.27)	(0.28)	(0.28)	(0.28)	(0.29)	(0.29)
Female head	−3.79**		−1.42	−1.19	−1.85	−2.14
	(1.35)		(1.33)	(1.35)	(1.37)	(1.45)
Income-to-needs ratio		3.82***	3.71***			
		(1.45)	(0.46)			
Average income ($10,000)				2.92***		
				(0.44)		
Number in household				−0.92***		
				(0.26)		

Income-to-needs ratio[b]						
< 1					−5.13***	
					(1.56)	
2–3					−0.32	
					(2.12)	
> 3					9.96***	
					(2.08)	
Duration of poverty						
Transient						−3.36~
						(1.88)
Continuous						−6.99***
						(1.76)
Adjusted R^2	0.26	0.32	0.32	0.31	0.31	0.28
N	786	786	786	786	786	720
Constant	72.48	72.72	73.68	77.44	79.25	77.89

~ $p < .1$. * $p < .05$. ** $p < .01$. *** $p < .001$.

Source: Authors' calculations using data from the IHDP. See text for description of models.

a. Values are OLS unstandardized coefficients. Standard errors in parentheses. Table values based on unweighted data.

b. Children from families with income-to-needs ratio of 1–2 are the omitted group.

TABLE 7A.7 / IHDP Replication Analysis Effects of Family Characteristics and Income on Verbal Ability at Age Three (PPVT-R)[a]

	Model					
Variable	1	2	3	4	5	6
Black	−11.00***	−8.56***	−8.91***	−9.35***	−9.37***	−9.78***
	(1.20)	(1.16)	(1.20)	(1.17)	(1.20)	(1.27)
Male	−0.83	0.55	0.62	0.69	0.68	0.58
	(1.03)	(0.99)	(0.99)	(0.98)	(1.01)	(1.06)
Low birth weight	0.61	0.32	0.39	0.42	0.47	0.58
	(1.13)	(1.09)	(1.09)	(1.08)	(1.11)	(1.16)
Mother's education	1.78***	1.04***	1.06***	1.01***	1.17***	1.44***
	(0.23)	(0.24)	(0.24)	(0.24)	(0.25)	(0.25)
Female head[b]						
Some of time	−3.83*		−1.34	−1.12	−1.88	−2.32
	(1.59)		(1.58)	(1.56)	(1.60)	(1.69)
All of time	−0.79		1.47	2.38~	1.26	1.20
	(1.26)		(1.26)	(1.26)	(1.31)	(1.37)
Income-to-needs ratio		2.99***	3.04***			
		(0.40)	(0.42)			
Average income ($10,000)				2.44***		
				(0.39)		
Number in household				−1.43***		
				(0.24)		

Income-to-needs ratio[c]						
< 1					−2.54~	
					(1.33)	
2–3					2.95	
					(1.85)	
> 3					9.20***	
					(1.78)	
Duration of poverty						
Transient						−4.48**
						(1.52)
Continuous						−7.33***
						(1.68)
Adjusted R^2	0.38	0.43	0.43	0.44	0.41	0.40
N	718	718	718	718	718	667
Constant	72.78	73.48	72.94	79.84	76.45	77.96

~ $p < .1$. * $p < .05$. ** $p < .01$. *** $p < .001$.

Source: Authors' calculations using data from the IHDP. See text for description of models.

a. Values are OLS unstandardized coefficients. Standard errors in parentheses. Table values based on unweighted data.

b. Children from families never headed by a female are the omitted group.

c. Children from families with income-to-needs ratio of 1–2 are the omitted group.

TABLE 7A.8 / IHDP Replication Analysis Effects of Family Characteristics and Income on Stanford-Binet IQ at Age Three[a]

	Model					
Variable	1	2	3	4	5	6
Black	−7.51***	−4.87***	−4.77***	−5.28***	−5.37***	−6.01***
	(1.35)	(1.29)	(1.33)	(1.32)	(1.34)	(1.43)
Male	−3.21***	−3.57***	−3.49***	−3.50**	−3.40**	−3.54**
	(1.16)	(1.09)	(1.11)	(1.10)	(1.12)	(1.19)
Low birth weight	4.00**	3.62**	3.71**	3.73**	3.78**	3.96**
	(1.07)	(1.20)	(1.22)	(1.21)	(1.22)	(1.30)
Mother's education	2.02***	1.08***	1.06***	1.08***	1.20***	1.59***
	(0.26)	(0.27)	(0.27)	(0.27)	(0.28)	(0.28)
Female head[b]						
Some of time	−6.02***		−2.74	−2.53	−3.41~	−4.05*
	(1.79)		(1.75)	(1.75)	(1.78)	(1.90)
All of time	−3.64**		−0.66	0.16	−0.61	−1.24
	(1.42)		(1.40)	(1.42)	(1.46)	(1.54)
Income-to-needs ratio		4.14***	4.00***			
		(0.44)	(0.47)			
Average income ($10,000)				3.42***		
				(0.44)		
Number in household				−1.14***		
				(0.27)		

Income-to-needs ratio[c]						
< 1					−4.74**	
					(1.48)	
2–3					3.91	
					(2.06)	
> 3					10.75***	
					(1.99)	
Duration of poverty						
Transient						−6.05***
						(1.72)
Continuous						−8.63***
						(1.90)
Adjusted R^2	0.34	0.39	0.40	0.40	0.38	0.36
N	799	815	799	799	799	728
Constant	65.18	64.40	65.39	69.92	70.89	71.75

$\sim p < .1$. * $p < .05$. ** $p < .01$. *** $p < .001$.

Source: Authors' calculations using data from the IHDP. See text for description of models.

a. Values are OLS unstandardized coefficients. Standard errors in parentheses. Table values based on unweighted data.

b. Children from families never headed by a female are the omitted group.

c. Children from families with income-to-needs ratio of 1–2 are the omitted group.

TABLE 7A.9 / IHDP Replication Analysis Effects of Family Characteristics and Income on Children's Verbal Ability at Age Five (PPVT-R)[a]

	Model					
	1	2	3	4	5	6
Black	−10.72***	−8.35***	−7.74***	−8.39***	−8.41***	−9.34***
	(1.58)	(1.498)	(1.56)	(1.55)	(1.57)	(1.68)
Male	−0.82	−0.95	−0.97	−0.99	−0.89	−1.04
	(1.33)	(1.26)	(1.28)	(1.27)	(1.29)	(1.38)
Birth weight	1.62	1.63	1.53	1.60	1.47	1.74
	(1.47)	(1.39)	(1.41)	(1.40)	(1.43)	(1.52)
Mother's education	2.28***	1.31***	1.25***	1.28***	1.42***	1.94***
	(0.30)	(0.31)	(0.32)	(0.31)	(0.32)	(0.33)
Female head, 24–60 months[b]						
Never married at 60 months	−6.64**		−2.94	−2.10	−2.66	−4.12
	(2.06)		(2.03)	(2.04)	(2.09)	(2.25)
Divorced, separated, or widowed	−8.38**		−3.86	−2.28	−3.25	−4.97
	(2.83)		(2.78)	(2.80)	(2.85)	(3.08)
Female head at 24 months, but not at 60 months	−7.12**		−2.63	−1.98	−2.96	−4.10
	(3.16)		(3.08)	(3.08)	(3.13)	(3.38)
Not female head at 24 months but female head at 60 months	−6.73**		−3.37	−2.82	−4.04	−5.14*
	(2.06)		(2.02)	(2.02)	(2.05)	(2.20)
Other family structure	−6.06**		−2.19	−1.57	−2.77	−4.18
	(2.41)		(2.36)	(2.36)	(2.39)	(2.56)
Income-to-needs ratio		4.87***	4.54***			
		(0.54)	(0.57)			

Average income ($10,000)				3.63		
				(5.17)		
Number in household				−1.49***		
				(0.32)		
Income-to-needs ratio[c]						
< 1					−6.67***	
					(1.68)	
2–3					4.15	
					(2.34)	
> 3					10.65***	
					(2.34)	
Duration of poverty						
Transient						−4.51*
						(1.99)
Continuous						−9.58***
						(2.57)
Adjusted R^2	0.33	0.39	0.39	0.39	0.37	0.34
N	721	721	721	721	721	667
Constant	62.72	58.44	61.46	67.73	69.38	67.34

$\sim p < .1$. * $p < .05$. ** $p < .01$. *** $p < .001$.

Source: Authors' calculations using data from the IHDP. See text for description of models.

a. Values are OLS unstandardized coefficients. Standard errors in parentheses. Table values based on unweighted data.

b. Children from families never headed by a female from ages twenty-four to sixty months are the omitted group.

c. Children from families with income-to-needs ratio of 1–2 are the omitted group.

TABLE 7A.10 / IHDP Replication Analysis Effects of Family Characteristics and Income on Full-Scale IQ (WPPSI) at Age Five[a]

	Model					
	1	2	3	4	5	6
Black	−7.79***	−5.97***	−5.44***	−5.90***	−5.82***	−6.49***
	(1.30)	(1.23)	(1.29)	(1.28)	(1.29)	(1.38)
Male	−1.44	−1.55	−1.56	−1.60	−1.50	−1.64
	(1.09)	(1.04)	(1.05)	(1.05)	(1.06)	(1.13)
Birth weight	4.84***	4.72***	4.77***	4.81***	4.74***	4.96***
	(1.21)	(1.14)	(1.17)	(1.16)	(1.17)	(1.28)
Mother's education	2.08***	1.31***	1.27***	1.30***	1.33***	1.77***
	(0.25)	(0.26)	(0.26)	(0.26)	(0.26)	(0.27)
Female head, 24–60 months[b]						
Never married at 60 months	−5.37**		−2.46	−1.82	−1.82	−3.02~
	(1.69)		(1.68)	(1.69)	(1.71)	(1.84)
Divorced, separated, or widowed	−4.69*		−1.13	0.04	−0.18	−1.48
	(2.33)		(2.29)	(2.32)	(2.33)	(2.52)
Female head at 24 months, but not at 60 months	−3.82		−0.28	0.20	−0.07	−1.01
	(2.60)		(2.54)	(2.54)	(2.56)	(2.77)
Not female head at 24 months but female head at 60 months	−3.48*		−0.83	−0.45	−1.12	−2.01
	(1.70)		(1.67)	(1.67)	(1.68)	(1.80)
Other family structure	−4.87**		−1.82	−1.36	−2.02	−3.13
	(1.98)		(1.95)	(1.95)	(1.96)	(2.10)
Income-to-needs ratio		3.73***	3.57***			
		(0.45)	(0.47)			

Average income ($10,000)				2.95***		
				(0.43)		
Number in household				−1.01***		
				(0.27)		
Income-to-needs ratio[c]						
< 1					−5.76***	
					(1.37)	
2–3					4.65	
					(1.91)	
> 3					9.02***	
					(1.92)	
Duration of poverty						
Transient						−4.02**
						(1.62)
Continuous						−9.06***
						(2.10)
Adjusted R^2	0.31	0.36	0.36	0.36	0.36	0.33
N	720	720	720	720	720	662
Constant	64.54	62.17	63.54	67.55	69.29	68.72

~ $p < .1$. * $p < .05$. ** $p < .01$. *** $p < .001$.

Source: Authors' calculations using data from the IHDP. See text for description of models.

a. Values are OLS unstandardized coefficients. Standard errors in parentheses. Table values based on unweighted data.

b. Children from families never headed by a female from ages twenty-four to sixty months are the omitted group.

c. Children from families with income-to-needs ratio of 1–2 are the omitted group.

We want to thank the Child and Family Well-Being Network of the National Institute for Child Health and Human Development Family for their support of the writing of this paper. In addition, we want to thank the Robert Wood Johnson Foundation, Pew Charitable Trusts, March of Dimes Foundation, the Bureau of Maternal anf Child Health and Resources Development, HRSA, PHS, DHHS, and NICHD for their support of the Infant Health and Development Program and T.R. Gross, the Director of the National Study Office and C. Ramey, the Director of the Program Development Office of the Infant Health and Development Program. The participating universities and site directors were Patrick H. Casey, M.D., University of Arkansas for Medical Sciences (Little Rock, AR); Marie McCormick, M.D., Harvard Medical School (Boston); Cecelia McCarton, M.D., Albert Einstein Medical Center (New York); Charles R. Bauer, M.D., University of Miami School of Medicine (Miami); Judy Berhbaum, M.D., University of Pennsylvania School of Medicine (Philadelphia); Jon E. Tyson, MD., and Mark Swanson, M.D., University of Texas Health Science Center at Dallas; Clifford J. Sells, M.D., and Forrest C. Bennett, M.D., University of Washington School of Medicine (Seattle); and David T. Scott, Ph.D., Yale University School of Medicine (New Haven, CT). The Longitudinal Study Office is directed by Cecelia McCarton and Jeanne Brooks-Gunn. Steve McClaskie, Frank Mott and Paula Baker of the Center for Human Resource Research at Ohio State University provided technical assistance with the National Longitudinal Survey of Youth data. Special thanks go to Greg Duncan and the Canadian Institute for Applied Research, as well as the staff of the Center for Young Children and Families, including Tama Leventhal and Phyllis Gyamfi for their assistance in manuscript preparation.

NOTES

1. IQ tests must be administered by a trained psychologist and therefore are too expensive to be included in large national field studies.
2. We conducted preliminary parallel analyses for children of the same age from the 1988 NLSY cohort, whose mothers were older (twenty-three at the child's birth) and had stayed in school longer (12.2 compared to 11.7 years). Results were parallel, although the effects of income were less in the sample of children with older mothers (the 1988 vs. the 1986 cohort).
3. The children who were born by 1986 were more likely to have young mothers than were children born between 1986 and 1994. The NLSY children are becoming more representative as the older women in the NLSY become mothers.
4. Consistent with previous analyses that examined the effect of poverty on children and their families, the IHDP analyses included the subsample of Hispanics, although they were excluded in the NLSY analyses (Brooks-Gunn, Duncan et al. 1993; Duncan, Brooks-Gunn, and Klebanov 1994; Klebanov, Brooks-Gunn, and Duncan 1994). However, recent IHDP analyses of the effect of poverty in concert with familial risks on young children and their families were done with and without Hispanic families in both the IHDP and NLSY data sets (Klebanov and Brooks-Gunn 1994; Klebanov et al.

forthcoming; Chase-Lansdale et al. forthcoming). The exclusion of the Hispanic subsample did not alter the significance of the earlier findings that included Hispanics. These results are available from the authors.

5. Children who took the PPVT prior to 1990 and received standardized scores below 40 were given a score of 40 (N = 6; Baker and Mott 1989). These scores were used in our analyses. Analyses without these cases had parallel findings.
6. There is some evidence that the NLSY sample scored above average on the PIAT Mathematics score, compared with the standardized scores for a sample of children in the late 1960s, yet below average in coping with more complex mathematics concepts and operations. This result may be due to external influences such as television, which may raise minimal mathematics knowledge without necessarily enhancing advanced mathematics capabilities (Baker et al. 1993).
7. Family income data were missing in the NLSY on the following percentages: 21 percent in the first year of life, 16 percent in years two and three, 14 percent in year four, 16 percent in year five, and 18 percent in year six. Mean substitution performed on the timing and duration variables maintained the full number of cases.
8. In some analyses, we also examined the mother's total raw score on the Armed Forces Qualifying Test (AFQT), administered to the NLSY mothers in 1980.
9. Parallel analyses with PIAT Mathematics score as the dependent variable revealed that adding the child's PPVT-R score led to a R^2 change of .08, and the income-to-needs variable becomes only marginally significant. If the family income for year four is added, income-to-needs is no longer significant.
10. Results available from the authors.
11. We also examined the effects of the mother's education controlling for her cognitive ability. Because the mother's cognitive score was so highly correlated with her education, these results were not significant.
12. These studies looked at high school, not elementary school, outcomes.
13. The effect of the HOME Inventory is stronger in the IHDP analyses. This may be because the full version of the HOME Inventory was used in the IHDP analyses, whereas the NLSY uses the short form.

Chapter 8

Economic Resources, Parental Practices, and Children's Well-Being

Thomas L. Hanson, Sara McLanahan, and Elizabeth Thomson

Research has shown that poverty has harmful consequences for children. Children from economically disadvantaged families exhibit lower levels of physical development, cognitive functioning, academic achievement, self-esteem, social development, and self-control than do children from more advantaged families (see, for example, Duncan, Brooks-Gunn, and Klebanov 1994; Elder, Nguyen, and Caspi 1985; Huston 1991a; McLoyd 1990; Miller and Korenman 1993). Many of these disadvantages are precursors to economic and emotional problems in young adulthood (McLanahan and Sandefur 1994; Haveman and Wolfe 1994). Persistent economic disadvantage has been found to be particularly harmful to children's development (Duncan, Brooks-Gunn, and Klebanov 1994; Miller and Korenman, 1993).

Economic hardship may influence child well-being in a number of ways. It may reduce parents' ability to supply adequate food and materials necessary for a child's healthy development; reduce a family's access to important community resources such as safe neighborhoods, good schools, adequate recreational facilities, and health services; and undermine effective socialization practices that foster cognitive and social development in children.

The analysis in this chapter uses data from the National Survey of Families and Households (NSFH) to examine the relationship between economic deprivation and children's well-being. We pay special attention to the relationship between family income and parental socialization and ask whether differences in parental practices can "account for" the lower achievement and poorer adjustment of children in economically disadvantaged households. We first discuss previous research on the relationships between family income and both parenting practices and children's well-being. We then describe the data and variables used in the analyses. The following three sections report the results, and the last section discusses our conclusions and why they might differ from those based on other data.

BACKGROUND

A substantial body of research has shown that parental warmth, involvement, and moderate control facilitate children's adjustment and achievement (Baumrind 1966; Maccoby and Martin 1983). Children appear to benefit when they are raised in homes where parents are warm, responsive, and highly involved with their children; where parents monitor and direct children's behavior and punish misdeeds in a consistent and nonhostile manner; and where parents have high and clearly stated expectations (Loeber and Stouthamer-Loeber 1986; Patterson 1982; Maccoby and Martin 1983). Warm, responsive parenting is thought to provide children with a sense of security and trust (Bradley et al. 1994). Consistent parental supervision and discipline are thought to effectively deter undesirable behavior. High and clearly stated parental expectations can provide a sense of direction and motivation to children.

There is evidence that poverty and economic hardship diminish parents' ability to provide these resources to children. Economic hardship, income loss, and unemployment have been found to reduce parental responsiveness, warmth, and supervision and to increase inconsistent discipline practices and the use of harsh punishments (for example, Sampson and Laub 1994; Conger et al. 1992; McLoyd et al. 1994; McLeod and Shanahan 1993; Lempers, Clarke-Lempers, and Simons 1989). These differences in parental practices have been found to "account for" much of the association between economic resources and children's well-being (Elder 1974; Elder et al. 1992; Patterson 1992; McLeod and Shanahan 1993; Sampson and Laub 1994; Conger et al. 1992; McLoyd et al. 1994; McLeod and Shanahan 1993; Lempers, Clark-Lempers, and Simons 1989). There is also evidence that warm, supportive, noncoercive parental practices and supervision buffer children from some of the negative consequences of economic deprivation and other forms of family stress (Mosley and Thomson 1994; Bradley et al. 1994).

Although the notion that parental practices mediate the effect of economic hardship on children's well-being has empirical support, much of the work in this area has been based on small or community-based samples. Evidence derived from national samples is less consistent. Using data from the National Longitudinal Survey of Youth (NLSY), McLeod and Shanahan (1993) found mixed support for the parental practices explanation. Mothers' responsiveness and punitive behavior mediated much of the effect of *current* poverty on children's well-being (internalizing and externalizing behavior) but actually suppressed the effect of *persistent* poverty on these outcomes. The authors speculate that immediate financial difficulties have more deleterious consequences for parenting than past economic difficulties because the former are more stressful than the latter. As poverty persists, families appear to adapt, and punitive parental practices decline.

Miller and Korenman (1993), also using NLSY data, report that persistent poverty has more negative consequences for children's health and cognitive development than short-term economic stress does. In addition, low income was related to low scores on the Home Observation for Measurement of the Environment

(HOME) Inventory, which accounts for 18–43 percent of the effects of persistent economic deprivation on children's welfare. Unfortunately, the items on the HOME Inventory measure household resources, such as reading materials and physical appearance, as well as parental practices, such as discipline methods, so it is difficult to know whether parenting practices or material resources per se are responsible for the results.

Studies based on the NSFH also raise questions about whether the "parenting deficit" hypothesis can account for the association between low income and poor outcomes for children. In a study examining whether differences in income and parental socialization can account for the effects of family structure on children's well-being. Thomson, McLanahan, and Hanson (1994) show that these two determinants of children's well-being are not closely related. Likewise, in a study of two-parent families Mosley and Thomson (1994) report similar findings for the association between income and parenting. Neither of these two studies used the full range of parenting variables, and neither focused specifically on the relationship between income and parenting. Nevertheless, the findings raise questions about the relationship between economic resources and parental practices.

Our study used the NSFH data to examine in more detail the association between income and parenting. We use a broader range of economic resource measures than used in past studies and include a larger set of indicators of parenting and children's well-being. We examine children in two-parent and one-parent households and test for interactions between income and parental practices in models predicting children's outcomes.

DATA AND MEASURES

Data

The data for the analysis come from the first wave of the NSFH, a national probability sample of adults residing in the United States. The sample includes 13,017 individuals—a main sample of 9,643 individuals and a double sample of minority households, single parent households, households with stepchildren, cohabiting couples, and recently married persons numbering 3,374 individuals. The interview response rate of the NSFH is 0.743. (For details on the NSFH see Sweet, Bumpass, and Call 1988.)

Interviews were conducted with a randomly selected adult in the household, referred to as the primary respondent. For households with children under age nineteen, the NSFH includes information gathered from primary respondents about a randomly selected child in the household (the focal child) with regard to such areas as parental practices and child behavior. These parental reports are used to construct measures of children's well-being.

The sample used in the analyses presented below contained households in which the focal child was between the ages of five and eighteen. We excluded cases with missing values on the parenting measures (913 cases) and each relevant measure of child well-being when it was used as a dependent variable.[1] These restrictions limited the potential sample size to 2,778 households.

Variables

CHILDREN'S WELFARE We examined eight children's outcome variables: two measures of academic achievement, one of behavior problems at school, four reflecting various psychological dimensions of child welfare, and one global measure of children's well-being (table 8.1). Academic performance was measured with single indicators. If the focal child was between the ages of five and eleven we measured academic performance by the parent's report of the child's relative class rank (school performance), ranging from near the bottom of the class (1) to one of the best in the class (5). If the focal child was between the ages of twelve and eighteen the parent's report of the child's usual grades, grade point average, was used as a measure of academic performance. This variable ranges from 0 to 4, where mostly As was coded 4, As and Bs as 3.5, and mostly Fs as 0. Because the two academic performance items applied to children in different age groups, we examined children between the ages of five and eleven separately from those older than eleven in the academic performance models.

No school behavior problems is a dichotomous variable with the value 0 if the parent had been asked to meet with a teacher or principal because of the child's behavior problems during the past year, the child had been suspended or expelled from school during the past year, or the child had dropped out of school. Otherwise, the variable was coded as 1. The majority of children coded 0 had parents who were asked to meet with a teacher or principal because of behavior problems.

We measured the children's psychological well-being by parents' reports of how often the child exhibited four behaviors during the three months prior to the survey: low externalizing behavior, low internalizing behavior, sociability, and initiative. Each measure had three response categories (not true, sometimes true, and often true). A series of confirmatory factor analysis models treated each of these items as an ordinal manifestation of an underlying continuous indicator (Muthén 1984). Externalizing behavior was measured by reports of how often the children lost their temper easily and bullied or were cruel or mean to others. The frequency of being fearful or anxious and unhappy, sad, or depressed measured internalizing behavior. Parents' reports of how often the focal children got along with other children, carried out responsibilities, and did what they were asked measured sociability, and reports of how often the children were willing to try new things, kept themselves busy, and were cheerful and happy measured the initiative dimension of their adjustment. Using the results from the confirmatory factor analysis models, we constructed factor scores to represent these four dimensions of child psychological well-being and standardized them to have a mean of 0 and a standard deviation of 1. The global measure of child welfare was parents'

TABLE 8.1 / Descriptive Statistics and Correlations of Measures of Children's Well-Being and Parenting Practices

Variable	1	2	3	4	5	6	7	8	9	10	11	12	13	Mean	*SD*
Children's well-being															
1. School performance														2.94	0.96
2. Grade point average														2.87	0.82
3. No school behavior problems	0.19	0.35												0.84	0.37
4. Low externalizing behavior	0.20	0.29	0.28											0.00	1.00
5. Low internalizing behavior	0.17	0.25	0.22	0.78										0.00	1.00
6. Sociability	0.26	0.34	0.26	0.70	0.55									0.00	1.00
7. Initiative	0.24	0.27	0.19	0.50	0.65	0.75								0.00	1.00
8. Quality of life	0.26	0.31	0.25	0.36	0.43	0.39	0.44							3.53	0.59
Parenting practices															
9. Parental control	0.09	0.07	0.07	0.00	0.06	0.02	0.10	0.14						0.00	1.00
10. Mother's activities	0.10	0.12	0.08	0.09	0.10	0.15	0.17	0.15	0.38					0.00	1.00
11. Father's activities	0.10	0.12	0.10	0.10	0.12	0.11	0.15	0.17	0.33	0.33				0.00	1.00
12. Positive responses	0.05	0.04	0.04	0.04	0.04	0.06	0.08	0.09	0.16	0.16	0.16			0.00	1.00
13. Negative responses	−0.05	−0.06	−0.03	−0.15	−0.09	−0.10	−0.05	−0.00	0.26	0.19	0.16	−0.17		0.00	1.00
14. Aspirations	0.01	0.08	−0.01	0.12	0.11	0.14	0.12	0.13	0.14	0.12	0.14	0.03	0.08	0.00	1.00

Source: Authors' calculations based on data on 2,778 households from the National Survey of Families and Households (NSFH), Wave I.

a. Values in columns 1–13 are pairwise Pearson correlation coefficients.

reports of how well the child's life was going (quality of life). Responses ranged from not well at all (1) to very well (4).

We coded all of the children's well-being measures so that high values indicated high levels of well-being. The correlations in the top panel of table 8.1 indicate that the children's well-being measures were moderately to strongly associated with each other. The correlations among the psychological well-being measures (externalizing, internalizing, sociability, and initiative) were particularly high.

PARENTING PRACTICES Six measures of parenting practices were used in the analysis: parental control, mother's activities, father's activities, positive responses, negative responses, and parents' aspirations. Parental control is a summary measure based on when the child was allowed to be left at home alone (0, alone overnight; 1, at night but not overnight; 2, in afternoon but not overnight or at night; 3, none of these times), television restrictions (0, no restrictions; 1, restrictions on the amount or type of program; 2, restrictions on the amount and type of program), and rules concerning notifying the parents of the child's whereabouts when the child was away from home (1, all of the time; 0, other responses). We constructed a standardized factor score to represent parental control based on the results of a confirmatory factor analysis of these three items.[2]

We assigned the mother's (father's) activities a standardized factor score based on the frequency of time they reported spending with children on the following activities: weekly breakfasts, weekly dinners (0–7), leisure activities away from home, work on a project or play together at home, private talks, help with reading or homework (ranging from never or rarely to almost every day, 1–6), and organized youth activities (school, religious, community, or athletic activities). The last item was a dichotomous variable indicating whether the parent participated in any organized activities during an average week.

Positive responses were measured by how often parents praised and hugged the child, and negative responses, by how often parents yelled at and spanked the child. These four items ranged from never (1) to very often (4). We constructed standardized factor scores for positive and negative responses using the results from a two-factor confirmatory factor analysis model.

Parents were asked to rate as not at all important (1) to extremely important (7) their children's performance in twelve areas (for example, do well in school, be independent, do well in athletics). We averaged these items to create a global measure of parents' aspirations for children.

ECONOMIC RESOURCES We used two measures of household economic resources: income-to-needs ratio, which measures the family's standard of living, and debt from bills. Household income, which we used to construct the income-to-needs ratio, included the annual income of all household members obtained from (1) wages and salaries; (2) self-employment; (3) Social Security or Supplemental Security Income; (4) other pensions, annuities, and survivors' benefits; (5) public assistance; (6) other government programs; (7) child support and alimony; and

(8) other sources of cash income. In addition, household income included primary respondents' and their spouses' or partners' income from interest, dividends, and other investments. After converting the household income into 1992 dollars, we computed the income-to-needs ratio dividing gross household income by the poverty thresholds established by the U.S. Bureau of the Census.[3] An income-to-needs ratio at or below 1 indicated that the household was officially poor, while an income-to-needs ratio above 1 indicated that the household was nonpoor. We used the income-to-needs ratio rather than family income as our measure of a family's economic resources because the former adjusts for differences in household size, taking into account economies of scale. We believe it is a better measure of the family's standard of living than income per se. Household income and income relative to needs were top-coded at $100,000 and ten, respectively. This top-coding resulted in better fitting models and more pronounced income coefficients.[4]

Debt from bills was a dichotomous variable indicating whether or not the family had owed money for bills for more than two months. This item, which we used as an indicator of economic stress, did not take into account debt from credit card and charge accounts, installment loans, personal loans from banks and other businesses, personal loans from friends or relatives, mortgage loans, or auto loans. These forms of debt are not likely to be good indicators of stress from economic hardship because most are contingent on having a low credit risk.

FAMILY STRUCTURE Our measure of family structure was based on the relationship of each parent to children in the household. We included ten family types: (1) original two-parent, (2) mother-stepfather, (3) father-stepmother, (4) two stepparents, (5) cohabitation intact, (6) mother-partner, (7) father-partner, (8) two partners, (9) divorced mother, and (10) never-married mother. Original two-parent families were married-couple families in which all of the children were born to or adopted together by the couple in the household. Mother-stepfather families were married-couple families in which at least one child had a biological (adopted) mother and a stepfather in the household. Father-stepmother families had at least one child with a biological (adopted) father and a stepmother in the household. Families with two stepparents were married-couple families in which at least one child had a stepmother in the household *and* another child had a stepfather in the household. Note that all three stepparent family types could contain biological children of both parents. Cohabitation intact, mother-partner, father-partner, and two-partner families were analogous to original two-parent families and the three types of stepparent families, except that the parents in the household were not married. Divorced-mother families were households with children that contained biological, ever-divorced mothers without partners. Never-married-mother families contained never-married mothers and children.

CONTROL VARIABLES In the analyses, we controlled for parental age (age of randomly selected parent in household), race/ethnicity (European American, African American, Mexican American, other), parents' education (less than high school, high school, some college, and college degree or more), region, and metropolitan status. We also controlled for the presence of a child under age six (dummy) in the household, the presence of a child between the ages of twelve and eighteen (dummy) in the household, and the age and sex of the focal child. A dummy variable indicating the presence of missing values on household income was included as a covariate in the regression analyses.

REPLICATION ANALYSIS: THE EFFECTS OF INCOME TO NEEDS ON CHILD WELL-BEING

We first examine the effects of household income on each measure of child welfare using a variety of specifications (table 8.2). The estimates for school performances and quality of life were based on ordered logit models; the estimates for no school behavior problems, on binary logit models; and the remaining estimates, on ordinary least squares regression models. With the exception of the coefficients from model 1, all the coefficients in table 8.2 come from models that control for the effects of the variables described in the previous section. Model 1 does not include controls for parents' education and family structure. (See appendix tables 8A.1–8A.8 for the entire set of coefficients from the models.)

Overall, the results suggest that economic status is positively associated with children's well-being in all of the areas considered. Absent controls for parents' education and family structure (model 1), income relative to needs increased well-being in the areas of school performance, GPA, school behavior problems, externalizing behavior, internalizing behavior, sociability, initiative, and quality of life. However, when we controlled for the effects of parents' education and family structure (model 2), the effect of income-to-needs was reduced by between 40 and 65 percent for school performance, GPA, and school behavior problems and by between 15 and 27 percent for low externalizing, low internalizing, sociability, initiative and quality of life. The linear effects of income-to-needs on school behavior problems were not statistically significant at conventional levels with controls for parents' education and family structure. With some exceptions, the effects of the other measures of economic status on child well-being tell a similar story. With the exception of school behavior problems, household income had positive effects on every measure of children's well-being considered (model 3). However, the effects of household income appear to be quite small. For example, a $10,000 increase in household income was only associated with an increase in sociability of about 2.5 percent of a standard deviation. The effects are even less strong for some of the other measures of child well-being. We suspect that these weak effects are due to the fact that household income was assessed at only one time-period—which results in a low level of reliability.

We found only one significant interaction effect between race/ethnicity and income-to-needs ratio (model 6): the positive effect of income-to-needs ratio on

(Text continued on p. 206.)

TABLE 8.2 / Replication Analysis: Effects of Economic Resources on Children's Well-Being

	Model[a]						
	1	2	3	4	5	6	7
School Performance[b]							
Income-to-needs ratio	0.167*	0.099*				0.090*	0.130*
Household income ($10,000)			0.085*				
Number of children			−0.021				
Income-to-needs ratio							
<0.5							
0.5–1.0					0.045		
1.0–2.0				0.152	0.179		
2.0–3.0				0.379*	0.406#		
3.0–4.0				0.361*	0.388#		
4.0+				0.574*	0.602*		
by African American						−0.016	
by Mexican American						0.164	
by other						0.035	
by female							−0.062
χ^2	135.34	181.56	181.89	180.41	180.45	181.70	183.57
df	14	26	27	29	30	29	27

Grade point average[c]							
Income-to-needs ratio	0.056*	0.023				0.019#	0.033*
Household income ($10,000)			0.019*				
Number of children			−0.010				
Income-to-needs ratio							
<0.5							
0.5–1.0					0.079		
1.0–2.0				0.164*	0.206*		
2.0–3.0				0.116	0.160#		
3.0–4.0				0.205#	0.249*		
4.0+				0.148*	0.191*		
by African American						0.034	
by Mexican American						0.003	
by other						−0.010	
by female							−0.019
R^2	0.073	0.105	0.104	0.106	0.106	0.106	0.105

(Table continued on p. 200.)

TABLE 8.2 / *(continued)*

	Model[a]						
	1	2	3	4	5	6	7
No school behavior problems[d]							
Income-to-needs ratio	0.103*	0.036*				0.042	0.023
Household income ($10,000)			0.032				
Number of children			0.047				
Income-to-needs ratio							
<0.5							
0.5–1.0					0.125		
1.0–2.0				0.093	0.162		
2.0–3.0				0.014	0.084		
3.0–4.0				0.255	0.324		
4.0+				0.238	0.308		
by African American						−0.047	
by Mexican American						0.081	
by other						−0.139	
by female							0.042
χ^2	213.60	267.54	268.19	269.12	269.42	269.51	268.28
df	14	26	27	29	30	29	27

Low externalizing behavior[c]							
Income-to-needs ratio	0.043*	0.032*				0.036*	0.045*
Household income ($10,000)			0.015#				
Number of children			−0.098*				
Income-to-needs ratio							
<0.5							
0.5–1.0					−0.089		
1.0–2.0				0.046	−0.004		
2.0–3.0				0.097	0.045		
3.0–4.0				0.164*	0.113		
4.0+				0.178*	0.126		
by African American						0.000	
by Mexican American						−0.015	
by other						−0.091	
by female							−0.026#
R^2	0.045	0.053	0.060	0.053	0.053	0.054	0.054

(Table continued on p. 202.)

TABLE 8.2 / *(continued)*

	Model[a]						
	1	2	3	4	5	6	7
Low internalizing behavior[c]							
Income-to-needs ratio	0.041*	0.030*				0.015*	0.023*
Household income ($10,000)			0.016[#]				
Number of children			−0.052*				
Income-to-needs ratio							
<0.5							
0.5–1.0					0.009		
1.0–2.0				0.039	0.044		
2.0–3.0				0.123*	0.129		
3.0–4.0				0.162*	0.167*		
4.0+				0.158*	0.163*		
by African American						0.005	
by Mexican American						−0.050	
by other						−0.059	
by female							−0.037*
R^2	0.042	0.051	0.052	0.051	0.051	0.052	0.052

Sociability[c]							
Income-to-needs ratio	0.039*	0.031*				0.032*	0.028*
Household income ($10,000)			0.025*				
Number of children			−0.039*				
Income-to-needs ratio							
<0.5							
0.5–1.0					−0.001		
1.0–2.0				0.177*	0.176*		
2.0–3.0				0.257*	0.256*		
3.0–4.0				0.295*	0.294*		
4.0+				0.267*	0.266*		
by African American						0.003	
by Mexican American						0.040	
by other						−0.082[#]	
by female							0.005
R^2	0.026	0.041	0.042	0.045	0.045	0.043	0.041

(Table continued on p. 204.)

TABLE 8.2 / *(continued)*

	Model[a]						
	1	2	3	4	5	6	7
Initiative[c]							
Income-to-needs ratio	0.037*	0.031*				0.028*	0.034*
Household income ($10,000)			0.024*				
Number of children			−0.022				
Income-to-needs ratio							
<0.5							
0.5–1.0					0.188*		
1.0–2.0				0.208*	0.315*		
2.0–3.0				0.241*	0.349*		
3.0–4.0				0.309*	0.417*		
4.0+				0.251*	0.359*		
by African American						0.014	
by Mexican American						0.046	
by other						−0.054	
by female							−0.007
R^2	0.035	0.047	0.046	0.050	0.052	0.048	0.047
Quality of life[b]							
Income-to-needs ratio	0.112*	0.095*				0.101*	0.106*

Household income ($10,000)			0.085*				
Number of children			−0.086*				
Income-to-needs ratio							
<0.5							
0.5–1.0					0.318[#]		
1.0–2.0				0.111	0.290[#]		
2.0–3.0				0.323*	0.504*		
3.0–4.0				0.532*	0.713*		
4.0+				0.574*	0.755*		
by African American						−0.014	
by Mexican American						−0.025	
by other						−0.079	
by female							−0.021
χ^2	249.84	337.16	344.21	339.51	342.96	337.94	337.60
df	14	26	27	29	30	29	27

* $p < .05$. [#] $p < .10$.

Source: Authors' calculations based on data on 2,778 households from the National Survey of Families and Households (NSFH), Wave I.

a. Models 2–7 include controls for race/ethnicity, parents' age, the presence of a child under age six in the household (dummy), the presence of a child between the ages of twelve and eighteen in the household (dummy), metropolitan status, region, parents' education, the child's age, the child's sex, and family structure. Model 1 includes all the controls in models 2–7 except for parents' education and family structure. See tables 8A.1–8A.8 for complete coefficients.

b. Based on ordered logit models.

c. Based on ordinary least squares (OLS) models.

d. Based on binary logit models.

school performance was significantly less pronounced for those classified as "other" on race/ethnicity than for whites. In addition, income relative to needs was more weakly associated with externalizing behavior ($p \leq .10$) and internalizing behavior for girls than was the case for boys (model 7).

THE EFFECTS OF ECONOMIC RESOURCES AND PARENTAL PRACTICES ON CHILDREN'S WELL-BEING

Two-Parent Households

Here we ask whether parental practices mediate the effects of economic resources on children in two-parent households (table 8.3). Model 1 estimated the effects of income-to-needs ratio and household debt on child welfare, excluding the parenting variables, and model 2 estimated the same effects including the latter. Both models included the set of background variables described in the Data and Measures section. For all of the outcomes except for quality of life, we chose a linear specification of the relationship between income-to-needs ratio and child welfare. The substantive results remained the same when we used dummy variables to capture nonlinear effects of income relative to needs.

In general, income-to-needs ratio had a positive effect on children in two-parent households (model 1), although the coefficients were not statistically significant (for GPA and no school behavior problems). The household debt coefficient was negative and statistically significant for three outcomes: no school behavior problems, low internalizing behavior ($p < .10$), and quality of life.

Does low income reduce children's well-being by reducing parental involvement and effectiveness? For the most part, the results from model 2 suggest that it does not. The income coefficients changed very little when the parenting variables were added to the model. Parenting practices accounted for less than 7 percent of the effects of income-to-needs ratio on school performance and quality of life and between 13 and 31 percent of its effects on internalizing, sociability, and initiative. In the case of externalizing and internalizing behavior, however, parenting practices mediated a nontrivial proportion of the effect of income on children—accounting for approximately 30 percent. The results were also mixed for household debt. Parenting practices accounted for small proportions of the effects of debt on school behavior problems (5 percent) and quality of life (10 percent) and a moderate proportion of the effect of debt on low internalizing behavior (23 percent).

Although the results from model 2 generally show that parenting practices do not account for much of the association between income and children's well-being in two-parent families, they do indicate that parental practices are related to children's welfare. Parental involvement (from fathers as well as mothers) positively affected children's well-being, as did high parental aspirations. Likewise, negative responses (yelling and spanking) were inversely associated with children's welfare. Positive responses (hugging and praising) had beneficial effects on three ar-

TABLE 8.3 / Effects of Economic Resources and Parenting Practices on Children's Well-Being in Two-Parent Families

	Outcome and Model															
	School Performance		Grade Point Average		No School Behavior Problems		Low Externalizing Behavior		Low Internalizing Behavior		Sociability		Initiative		Quality of Life	
Independent Variable	1	2	1	2	1	2	1	2	1	2	1	2	1	2	1	2
Economic resources																
Income-to-needs ratio	0.141*	0.044*	0.011	0.008	−0.012	0.029	0.029*	0.020#	0.020#	0.014	0.029*	0.023*	0.031*	0.027*	0.060*	0.056*
Debt	0.135	0.148	−0.138	−0.122	−0.401*	−0.378#	−0.089	−0.056	−0.118#	−0.091	−0.009	0.024	−0.009	0.022	−0.336*	−0.301*
Parenting																
Parental control		0.017		−0.055		−0.038		−0.026		−0.040		−0.071*		−0.061#		−0.087
Mother's activities		0.125#		0.083*		−0.004		0.041		0.047#		0.095*		0.097*		0.116*
Father's activities		0.082		0.066*		0.267*		0.109*		0.091*		0.110*		0.105*		0.231*
Positive responses		0.150#		−0.011		0.048		0.015		0.015		0.036		0.040#		0.127*
Negative responses		0.022		−0.064#		−0.257*		−0.129*		−0.088*		−0.079*		−0.062*		−0.072
Aspirations		0.137#		0.107*		0.124		0.128*		0.120*		0.121*		0.104*		0.236*
R^2			0.10	0.13			0.07	0.10	0.06	0.09	0.05	0.09	0.05	0.09		
χ^2	106.26	119.50			137.16	159.69									177.28	233.30
df	25	31			24	30									26	32
N	907		824		1,716		1,783		1,783		1,783		1,783		1,820	

* $p < .05$. # $p < .10$.

Source: Authors' calculations based on data on 2,778 households from the National Survey of Families and Households (NSFH), Wave I.

eas of children's well-being: school performance ($p < .10$), initiative ($p < .10$), and quality of life.

Surprisingly, parental control appeared to reduce children's well-being. The coefficients for this variable were negative in all of the models except for school performance, and they were statistically significant for sociability and initiative ($p < .10$). This seemingly perverse effect may be due to reverse causality. Parents may monitor children with behavior problems more closely than they do children without these problems.

One-Parent Households

The results reported here (table 8.4) were consistent with those for two-parent households, although in general income-to-needs ratio appeared to have a more pronounced effect on the well-being of children in one-parent households than on that of children in two-parent households.

Income-to-needs ratio significantly related to all of the indicators of children's well-being except school performance (model 1). In the areas of GPA and internalizing behavior, the effects of income were less positive at higher levels. Household debt reduced children's well-being in the areas of school performance ($p < .10$), school behavior problems, externalizing behavior, internalizing behavior, sociability ($p < .10$), and quality of life. Differences in parenting practices do not explain the differences in the well-being of children in low- and high-income households. The income coefficients changed very little when the parenting variables were included in the model. Similarly, the effects of debt on children's well-being did not change when parenting practices were added to the model.

Although parenting practices did not account for the association between economic resources and child well-being in one-parent households, parental practices were associated with child well-being. Mother's activities, negative responses, and parental aspirations significantly affected many of the indicators of children's well-being, while parental control and positive responses did not.

Overall, our results thus far provide little support for the notion that low income reduces children's well-being by undermining parenting practices, with two exceptions. In two-parent households, parenting practices accounted for about one-third of the effect of the income-to-needs ratio on externalizing behavior and about 23 percent of the effect of household debt on internalizing behavior. The fact that our measures of parenting practices did not account for much of the effect of economic resources on the children's welfare does not mean that those practices did not play an important role in determining the children's well-being; clearly they did, as shown in tables 8.3 and 8.4. Parenting practices, however, may have failed to account for the effects of economic resources on the children's wellbeing either because they were only weakly related to economic resources or because their effects differed by economic status. We turn to these issues below.

TABLE 8.4 / Effects of Economic Resources and Parenting Practices on Children's Well-Being in One-Parent Families

	Outcome and Model															
	School Performance		Grade Point Average		No School Behavior Problems		Low Externalizing Behavior		Low Internalizing Behavior		Sociability		Initiative		Quality of Life	
Independent Variable	1[b]	2[c]	1	2	1	2	1	2	1	2	1	2	1	2	1	2
Economic resources																
Income-to-needs ratio	0.098	0.111	0.169*	0.176*	0.178*	0.179*	0.100*	0.099*	0.088*	0.090*	0.068*	0.074*	0.159*	0.178*	0.135*	0.141*
Income-to-needs ratio^2			−0.017*	−0.018*									−0.016*	−0.017		
Debt	−0.435#	−0.386#	−0.084	−0.093	−0.575*	−0.599*	−0.207*	−0.215*	−0.189*	−0.191*	−0.159*	−0.159#	−0.133	−0.136#	−0.471*	−0.494*
Parenting																
Parental control		0.106		0.041		−0.015		−0.048		−0.012		0.008		−0.044		−0.011
Mother's activities		0.046		0.062		0.233*		0.184*		0.184*		0.223*		0.236*		0.395*
Positive responses		0.122		0.012		−0.151		−0.047		−0.066#		0.002		−0.006		0.034
Negative responses		−0.161		−0.075#		−0.250*		−0.217*		−0.188*		−0.167*		−0.131*		−0.311*
Aspirations		0.168#		0.072*		0.022		0.041		0.070*		0.115*		0.126*		0.232*
R^2			0.13	0.15			0.06	0.12	0.06	0.11	0.05	0.12	0.04	0.11		
χ^2	54.84	63.44			62.12	74.70									72.54	132.98
df	19	24			19	24									19	24
N	427		488		915		941		941		941		941		956	

$^* p < .05$. $^\# p < .10$.

Source: Authors' calculations based on data on 2,778 households from the National Survey of Families and Households (NSFH), Wave I.

EFFECTS OF ECONOMIC RESOURCES ON PARENTAL PRACTICES

Table 8.5 shows the net effects of income and household debt on parenting practices in two-parent and one-parent households. All of the coefficients were based on models that controlled for the effects of background variables and all are based on OLS regression models. For the most part, income was not significantly related to most of the measures of parenting practices we examined. However, in two-parent households, the results for yelling and spanking provide some support for the notion that low income is associated with more punitive parenting practices: income-to-needs ratio was negatively related to negative responses. Results not shown in table 8.5 showed that parents in poor two-parent households actually expressed higher aspirations for their children than did parents in nonpoor households and that poverty status was negatively associated with positive responses in one-parent households.[5] Overall, however, the results suggest that income-to-needs ratio is not strongly related to effective parenting practices, at least not as measured by the questions used in the NSFH survey.

Our other measure of economic resources, household debt, was related to some of the parenting measures in expected ways in two-parent households. Debt reduced mother's activities ($p < .10$) and father's activities ($p < .10$) and increased negative responses ($p < .10$), suggesting that economic stress is associated with less parental involvement and harsher punishments in two-parent households. Debt was not related to parenting practices in one-parent households.

The results in table 8.5 suggest that economic resources do not have particularly strong or consistently negative effects on parenting. This explains why differences in parenting practices did not account for much of the differences in well-being between children in low- and high-income families. Even so, differences in the *effects* of parenting might account for some of the differences in children's outcomes. Poor children are exposed to more environmental stressors than nonpoor children, live in more dangerous communities, and by definition face a higher degree of material hardship. Exposure to multiple stressors may reduce a child's capacity to respond positively to good parenting practices. Moreover, parental authority and respect may be partly a consequence of economic success. Parents who are perceived as poor providers may receive less admiration and respect from their children than parents perceived as being good providers, which may reduce the effectiveness of parenting practices. Of course, the reverse may also be true; high levels of parental control, warmth, and expectations may do more to protect poor children than nonpoor children because the former are exposed to more risks. Parents' resources may matter more for children when other resources are lacking. We examined these issues by allowing parenting practices to have different effects on the well-being of poor and nonpoor children.

Two-Parent versus One-Parent Households

We first focus on the effects for two-parent households (table 8-6) of parenting practices on children's well-being separately by poverty status for two-parent and

(Text continued on p. 213.)

TABLE 8.5 / Effects of Economic Resources on Parenting Practices in Families[a]

Independent Variable	Outcome					
	Parental Control	Mother's Activities	Father's Activities	Positive Responses	Negative Responses	Aspirations
Two-parent families (*N* = 1,821)						
Income-to-needs ratio	0.012	−0.005	−0.010	0.002	−0.065*	−0.013
Debt	−0.013	−0.113#	−0.104#	−0.001	0.108#	−0.017
R^2	0.52	0.16	0.17	0.05	0.22	0.15
One-parent families (*N* = 957)						
Income-to-needs ratio	−0.018	−0.033		−0.005	−0.035	−0.018
Debt	−0.076	0.061		0.027	0.007	−0.085
R^2	0.48	0.19		0.05	0.20	0.09

* $p < .05$. # $p < .10$.

Source: Authors' calculations based on data on 2,778 households from the National Survey of Families and Households (NSFH), Wave I.

a. Based on OLS models with controls for background variables.

TABLE 8.6 / Effects of Economic Resources and Parental Practices on Children's Well-Being in Two-Parent Families, by Poverty Status

	Outcome							
Independent Variable	School Performance	GPA	No School Behavior Problems	No Externalizing Behavior	No Internalizing Behavior	Sociability	Initiative	Quality of Life
Economic resources								
Poverty	−0.440	0.056	−0.341	−0.154	−0.111	−0.377*	−0.462*	−0.485*
Debt	0.136	−0.127	−0.376#	−0.065	−0.099	0.013	0.012	−0.338*
Parenting								
Nonpoor families								
Parental control	0.032	−0.084*	−0.094	−0.034	−0.044	−0.083*	−0.078*	−0.136#
Mother's activities	0.169*	0.091*	0.009	0.046#	0.045#	0.093*	0.094*	0.169*
Father's activities	0.073	0.058#	0.306*	0.121*	0.113*	0.126*	0.128*	0.244*
Positive responses	0.147#	−0.020	0.024	0.002	0.003	0.032	0.047#	0.113*
Negative responses	−0.022	−0.062#	−0.286*	−0.144*	−0.099*	−0.097*	−0.080*	−0.119#
Aspirations	0.104	0.105*	0.097	0.102*	0.096*	0.121*	0.107*	0.208*
Poor families								
Parental control	0.172	0.234#^	0.461~	0.009	−0.031	0.012	0.097~	0.199
Mother's activities	−0.034	0.088	0.101	0.072	0.114	0.161#	0.163#	−0.273^
Father's activities	0.287	0.086	−0.005	0.012	−0.099	−0.025~	−0.071^	0.215
Positive responses	0.030	0.122	0.355	0.190*^	0.195*^	0.125	−0.013	0.255
Negative responses	0.020	−0.034	0.228	−0.018	−0.023	0.068~	0.059	0.314^
Aspirations	0.238	0.181	0.436	0.347*^	0.326*^	0.175*	0.131	0.467*
R^2		0.15		0.11	0.11	0.10	0.10	
χ^2	107.75		169.72					244.25
df	37		36					37
N	907	824	1,716	1,783	1,783	1,783	1,783	1,820

* Significantly different from 0 ($p < .05$). # Significantly different from 0 ($p < .10$). ^ Significantly different from nonpoor coefficient ($p < .05$). ~ Significantly different from nonpoor coefficient ($p < .10$).

Source: Authors' calculations based on data on 2,778 households from the National Survey of Families and Households (NSFH), Wave I.

one-parent households. A comparison of the effects of parenting across poor and nonpoor households reveals several interesting differences. First, parental control appears to have had a more positive effect on children's well-being in poor than in nonpoor households. The difference was statistically significant for three indicators of children's well-being: GPA, school behavior problems ($p < .10$), and initiative ($p < .10$). These results suggest that strict parenting may have had more beneficial effects on economically deprived children, who probably encountered more risks than other children.

In some areas, children in poor families were less negatively affected by yelling and spanking and more positively affected by hugging and praising and by living with parents who have high aspirations for them. In only three instances did any evidence show that children in poor households benefited less from good parenting than did children in nonpoor households: mother's activities had a less positive effect on children's quality of life, and father's activities had a less positive effect on sociability and initiative. In addition, as noted above, poor children appear to have been less severely affected by spanking and yelling than other children were. Otherwise, the effects of parenting practices were either no different for children or they favored those in poor households.

The results for one-parent households (table 8.7) were more mixed than those for two-parent households. Parental control had more positive effects on five of the eight indicators of children's well-being. Negative responses had less deleterious consequences for children from poor households than for those from nonpoor households in the areas of GPA, school behavior problems, sociability ($p < .10$), and initiative ($p < .10$), again suggesting that more authoritarian parenting may have some benefits for poor children. There was some evidence that children in poor households benefit less from parents' activities than children in nonpoor households, possibly because poor parents are under more stress. Finally, the effects of parental aspirations on children's well-being were less positive in poor households than in nonpoor households in the areas of externalizing ($p < .10$) and sociability ($p < .10$). Recall that for two-parent households parental aspirations had more beneficial effects on the well-being of children in poor households than for those in nonpoor households. Thus, only in the area of parental control is there clear evidence that children in poor households benefit more from good parenting than children in nonpoor households do. For most of the other areas considered, the effects of parenting practices were either similar or less beneficial for children in poor households.

To illustrate the interaction effects of parenting and income on children's well-being, we plotted predicted values for each measure of children's well-being by income level and parenting based on the results of the models in tables 8.6 and 8.7 (figure 8.1). For children in poor and nonpoor households, we plotted the predicted value of children's well-being for households with mean values on *all* of the parenting measures, those with values one standard deviation below the mean, and those with values one standard deviation above the mean.[6]

The figures for two-parent households indicate that poor children benefit more from effective parenting practices than nonpoor children do in GPA, school be

(Text continued on p. 219.)

TABLE 8.7 / Effects of Economic Resources and Parenting Practices on Child Well-Being in One-Parent Families, by Poverty Status

	Outcome							
Independent Variable	School Performance	GPA	No School Behavior Problems	No Externalizing Behavior	No Internalizing Behavior	Sociability	Initiative	Quality of Life
Economic resources								
Poverty	−0.503	−0.251*	−0.591*	−0.212*	−0.213*	−0.277*	−0.269*	−0.318#
Debt	−0.344	−0.103	−0.644*	−0.250*	−0.210*	−0.181*	−0.147#	−0.526*
Parenting								
Nonpoor families								
Parental control	0.017	0.052	−0.171	−0.134*	−0.084	−0.059	−0.101#	−0.095
Mother's activities	0.072	0.048	0.522*	0.249*	0.248*	0.286*	0.293*	0.382*
Positive responses	0.283	−0.032	−0.252*	−0.108*	−0.144*	−0.018	−0.010	−0.004
Negative responses	−0.114	−0.149*	−0.523*	−0.220*	−0.221*	−0.223*	−0.192*	−0.330*
Aspirations	0.063	0.103*	0.074	0.090*	0.098*	0.165*	0.145*	0.238*
Poor families								
Parental control	0.320	0.010	0.272^	0.111^	0.111^	0.147*^	0.087^	0.177
Mother's activities	0.008	0.094	−0.217^	0.077^	0.069^	0.141*~	0.155*~	0.442*
Positive responses	−0.119	0.069	−0.053	−0.001	0.025^	−0.016	−0.032	0.033
Negative responses	−0.159	0.079^	0.132^	−0.242*	−0.151*	−0.100#~	−0.050~	−0.288*
Aspirations	0.300*	0.030	0.031	−0.031~	0.043	0.046~	0.094#	0.212*
R^2		0.18		0.13	0.12	0.14	0.12	
χ^2	70.10		101.93					133.24
df	29		29					29
N	427	488	915	941	941	941	941	956

Source: Authors' calculations based on data on 2,778 households from the National Survey of Families and Households (NSFH), Wave I.

FIGURE 8.1 / Effects of Parental Practices and Income on Child Welfare: Two-Parent Households

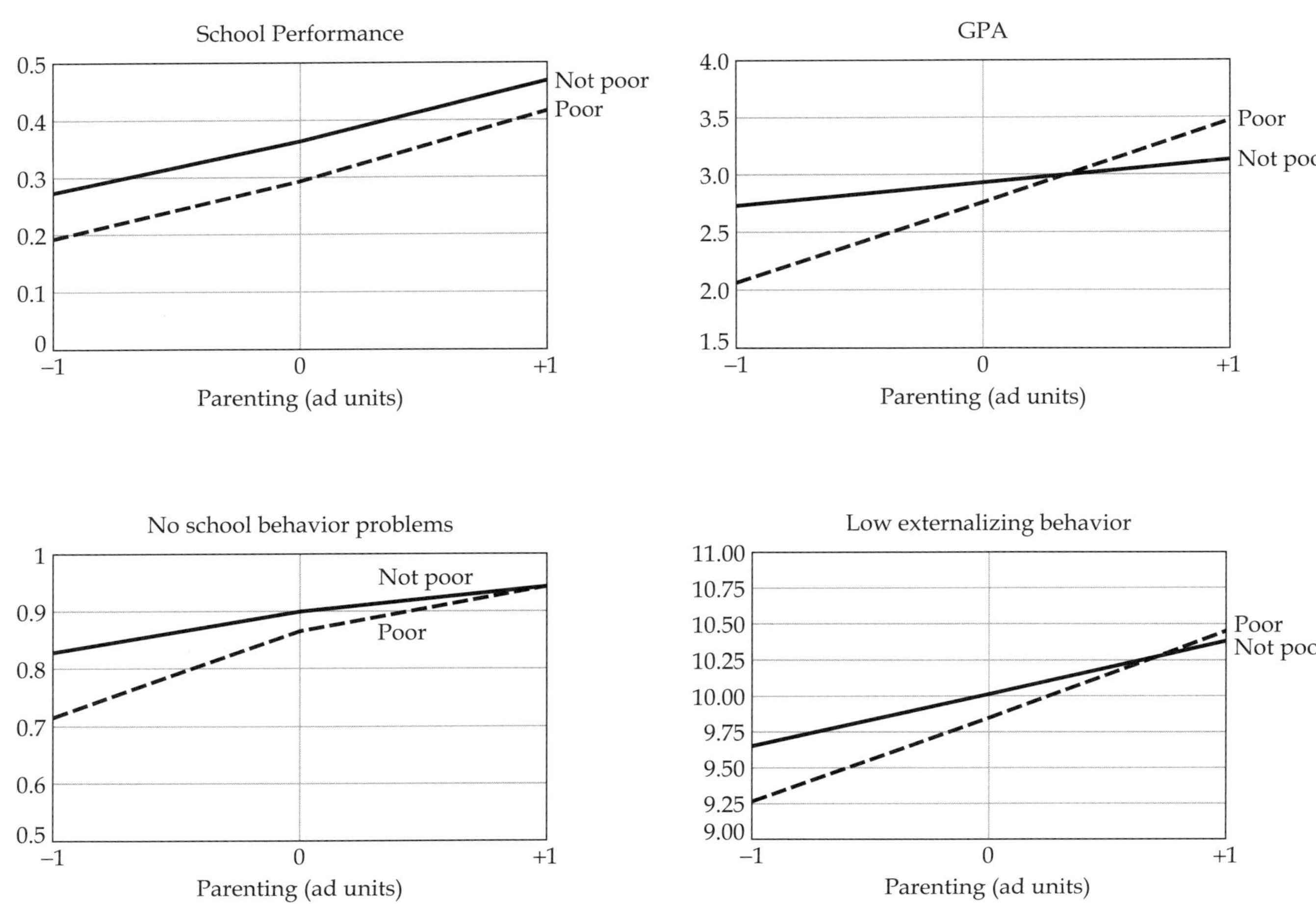

FIGURE 8.1 / *(continued)*

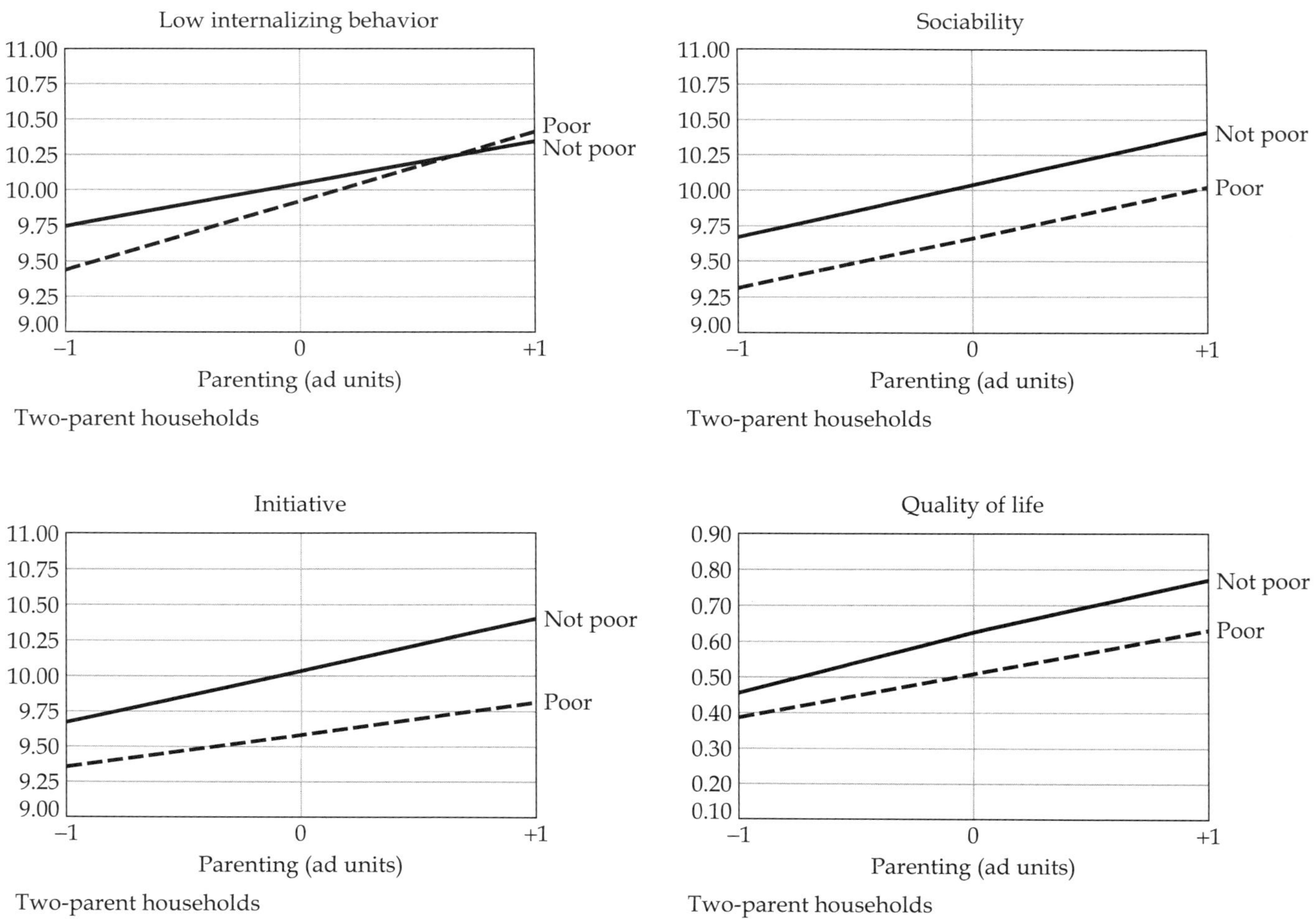

Low internalizing behavior

11.00
10.75
10.50
10.25
10.00
9.75
9.50
9.25
9.00

−1 0 +1

Poor
Not poor

Parenting (ad units)

Two-parent households

Sociability

11.00
10.75
10.50
10.25
10.00
9.75
9.50
9.25
9.00

−1 0 +1

Not poor
Poor

Parenting (ad units)

Two-parent households

Initiative

11.00
10.75
10.50
10.25
10.00
9.75
9.50
9.25
9.00

−1 0 +1

Not poor
Poor

Parenting (ad units)

Two-parent households

Quality of life

0.90
0.80
0.70
0.60
0.50
0.40
0.30
0.20
0.10

−1 0 +1

Not poor
Poor

Parenting (ad units)

Two-parent households

FIGURE 8.1 / *(continued)*

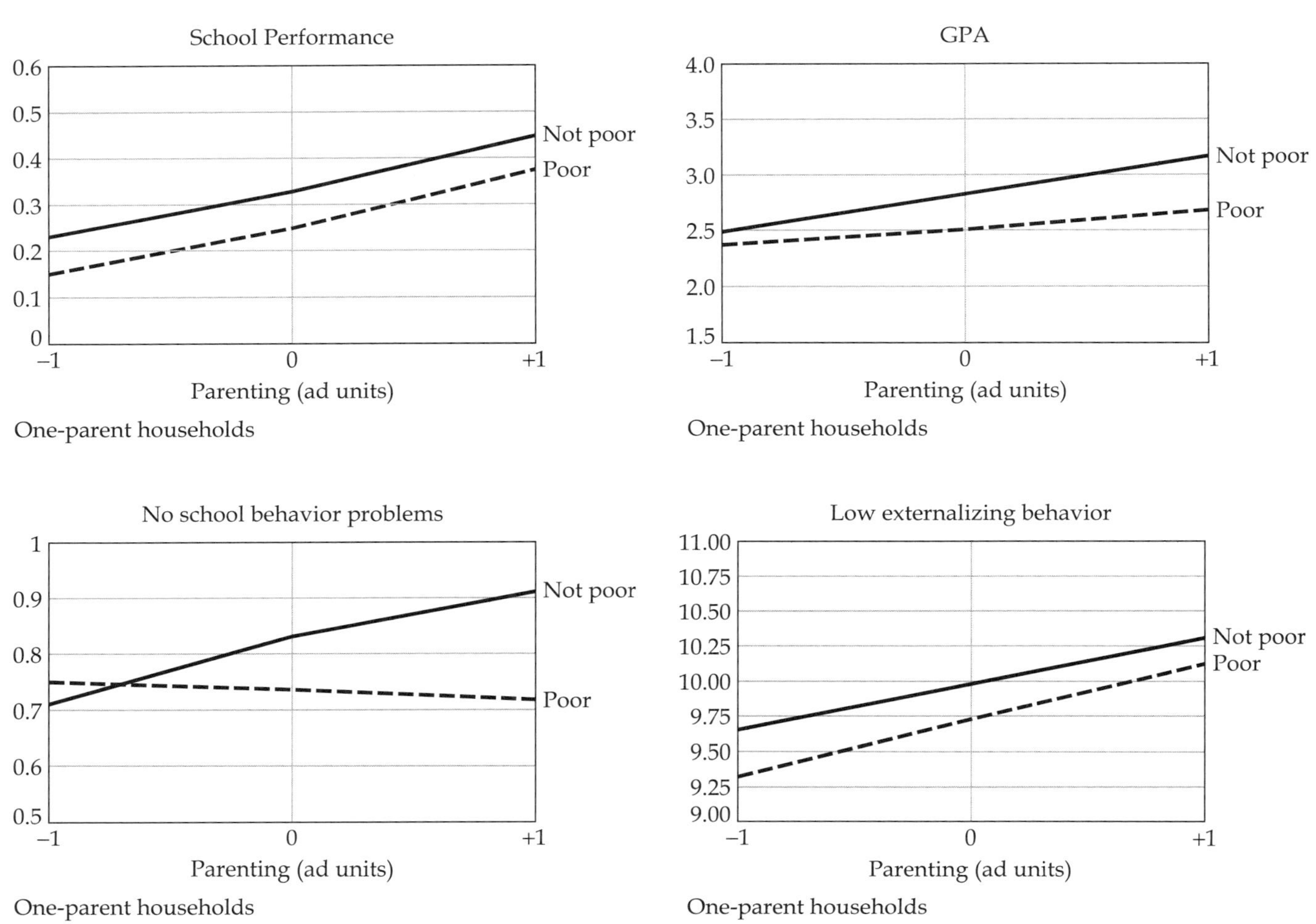

FIGURE 8.1 / *(continued)*

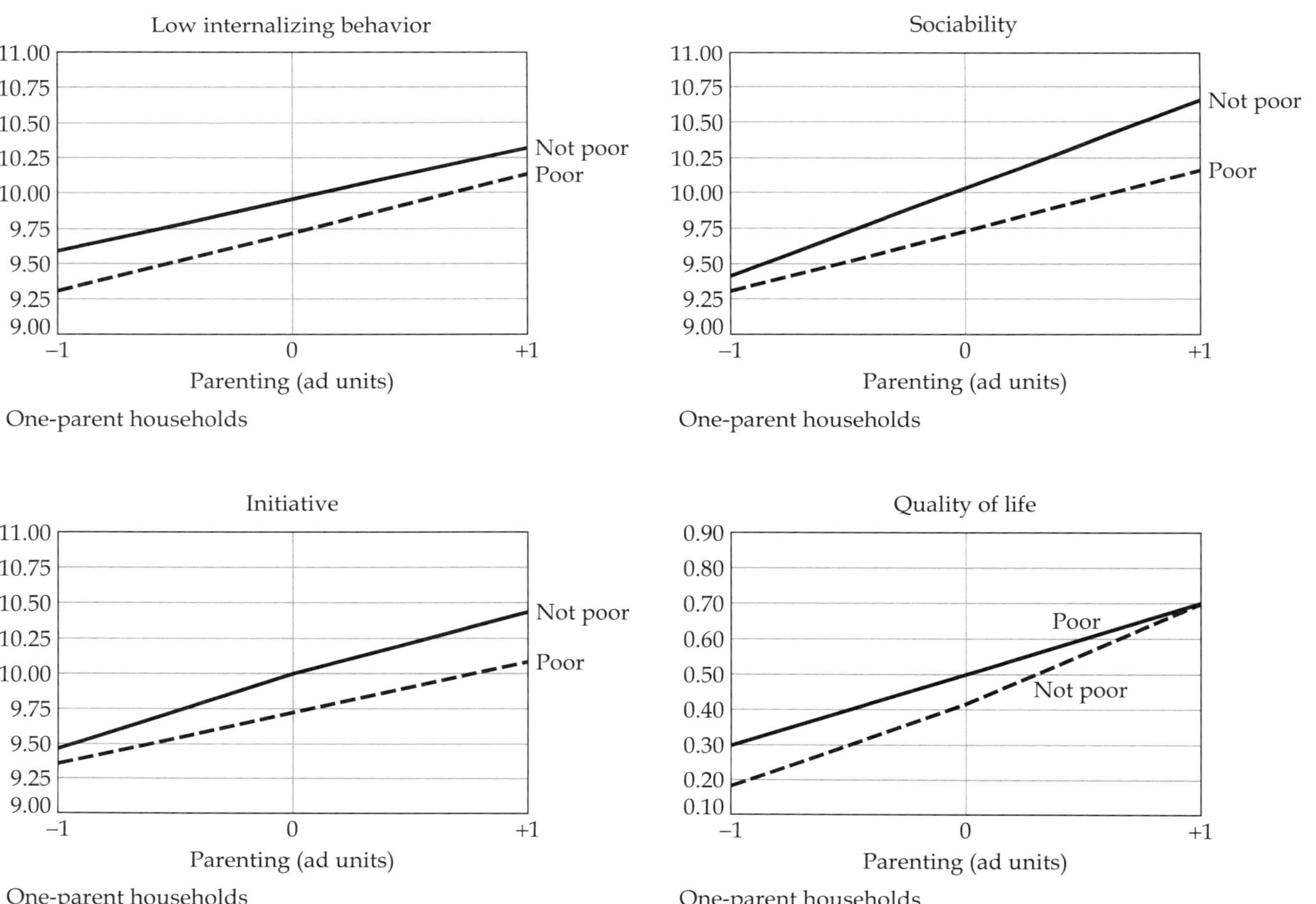

havior problems, externalizing behavior, and internalizing behavior. In these areas, differences in the effects of parenting practices tended to diminish differences in the well-being of poor and nonpoor children as the frequency of good parental practices increased. This tendency is dramatically illustrated by the GPA figure. The points at the far left side of the figure indicate that the well-being of poor children in households with low levels of parenting was more than half a standard deviation lower than that for other children. The center point indicates that this deficit was almost completely eliminated for children exposed to average levels of parenting practices. The points at the far right side indicate that when the values of parenting practices were high, poor children actually exhibited higher GPAs than other children did.

For other indicators of children's well-being, however, we found little evidence that parenting practices have more beneficial effects on poor children than on nonpoor children in two-parent households. In the areas of initiative and quality of life, differences in the effects of parenting practices actually tended to exacerbate differences in the well-being of poor and nonpoor children. Thus, in these areas our results are consistent with the notion that economic deprivation reduces a child's capacity to respond positively to good parental practices.

The results for one-parent households also provide some evidence that parenting practices have less beneficial effects on poor children. In the areas of GPA, school behavior problems, sociability, and initiative, children in poor households did less well than those in nonpoor households as parenting practices improved. For the other areas of children's well-being considered, the effects of parenting practices were either similar for the poor and the nonpoor (internalizing, school performance) or had more beneficial effects on poor children (externalizing behavior, quality of life). Overall, however, the results suggest that economic hardship reduces the benefits of good parenting practices for children in one-parent households.

CONCLUSION

In examining the effects of household economic resources on a wide variety of indicators of children's well-being in both two-parent and one-parent households, we found that income generally increases children's welfare and that household debt is negatively related to a number of well-being indicators for children in one-parent and two-parent households. We also looked at the relationship between economic resources, parenting practices, and children's well-being, asking whether differences in parenting might explain differences in well-being between children in low- and high-income households. We found that household income and debt are only weakly related to effective parenting. Consequently, differences in the levels of parenting do not account for much of the association between economic resources and children's well-being. Two exceptions, however, are that in two-parent households differences in levels of parenting accounted for about

30 percent of the effect of income on externalizing behavior and about 23 percent of the effect of household debt on internalizing behavior.

With respect to interactions, we found that parenting had somewhat different effects for children in poor and nonpoor households. Most notably, supervision and control appear to increase children's well-being in poor households while reducing well-being in nonpoor households, perhaps because the economically deprived children encounter more risks than other children do. Many of the other differences in the effects of parenting practices on child well-being depend on family structure. In two-parent households, parenting practices have more beneficial effects on poor children than on nonpoor children, and praising and hugging as well as high parental aspirations affect the well-being of economically deprived children more strongly. These results suggest that high levels of warmth and support and high expectations may act to buffer children in two-parent families from the negative consequences of economic distress. Conversely, in one-parent households, parenting practices tend to benefit children who are not poor more than those who are. The mother's activities and the parents' aspirations affect the well-being of nonpoor children in one-parent households more strongly, suggesting that residence in a nonintact family and economic deprivation combine to reduce children's capacity to respond positively to good parenting practices.

In sum, differences in the levels of parental practices did not account for the association between income and children's achievement and adjustment. Because our results differ from those of other studies with respect to the effects of income on parenting, we must ask whether these differences might be due to peculiarities in the NSFH data. One reason for the discrepancy is that we did not consider changes in household income. Much of the work finding a relationship between economic deprivation and parenting practices has focused on income loss and unemployment, while our analysis examined the effects of the level of income on parenting practices and children's well-being (Conger et al. 1992; McLoyd et al. 1994). Our measures of economic resources also may influence parenting less than parents' subjective economic well-being or parents' behavioral responses to material hardship. In chapter 10, Conger, Conger, and Elder found that family financial cutbacks and parents' appraisals of material hardship affected adolescent well-being by increasing both the frequency of parents' conflict about financial matters and harsh parenting. These results suggest that perceptions of economic well-being and behavior responses to financial hardship may be more strongly related to parenting practices than household income is.

For two reasons, the NSFH data may be less than ideal for measuring the relationship between income, parenting practices, and children's well-being. First, the income measure refers to income received during the calendar year preceding the survey year, while the measures of parenting and children's well-being refer to practices and behaviors at or near the time of the survey. These differences in time frame may attenuate the observed effects of income on parenting and, to a lesser extent, on children's well-being. The income measure may be a better measure of past than of current economic hardship, and past economic stress may not influence parenting practices strongly (McLeod and Shanahan 1993). That said, however, our measure of current economic stress—debt from bills—was not strongly related to parenting practices. Second, the parenting measures may not be good indicators of parents' behavior. If low-income respondents are more likely than others to be influenced by social desirability when reporting parents' behaviors, the effects of income on parenting will be biased downward. Our findings may also have been different if we had used children's assessments of parenting practices and their own well-being. In addition, our income measures are likely to have low reliability because they were measured at a single point in time. These issues require further scrutiny. Certainly, the first wave of the NSFH provides little evidence that differences in parenting account for the association between low income and low achievement and adjustment among children.

APPENDIX: REPLICATION ANALYSIS

Tables 8.A1–8.A8 contain the coefficients from the models in tables 8.2.

TABLE 8A.1 / Effects of Background Factors and Economic Resources on NSFH Children's School Performance

	Model															
	1		2		3		4		5		6		7		8	
Independent Variable	Coef-ficient	z	Coef-ficient	z	Coef-ficient	z	Coef-ficient	z	Coef-ficient	z	Coef-ficient	z	Coef-ficient	z	Coef-ficient	z
Race/ethnicity																
White																
African American	−.003	−0.02	−.024	−0.20	.056	0.45	.061	0.48	.037	0.29	.039	0.30	.083	0.41	.056	0.44
Mexican American	−.520	−2.81	−.505	−2.83	−.448	−2.41	−.431	−2.31	−.436	−2.33	−.437	−2.33	−.776	−2.84	−.451	−2.43
Other	−.414	−2.15	−.292	−1.53	−.327	−1.69	−.332	−1.71	−.351	−1.81	−.351	−1.81	−.420	−1.32	−.327	−1.69
Parental age	−.006	−0.82	.004	0.52	−.010	−1.21	−.011	−1.30	−.007	−0.98	−.007	−0.98	−.009	−1.13	−.010	−1.23
Child 12–18 in household	−.099	−0.83	−.112	−0.95	−.094	−0.79	−.114	−0.86	−.091	−0.76	−.090	−0.75	−.094	−0.79	−.093	−0.77
Child 7–11 in household																
Child <6 in household	.134	1.30	.227	2.21	.179	1.73	.163	1.45	.177	1.70	.177	1.70	.184	1.77	.176	1.69
Metropolitan area	−.072	−0.67	−.112	−1.05	−.125	−1.15	−.131	−1.20	−.102	−0.94	−.101	−0.93	−.114	−1.05	−.122	−1.13
Region																
West																
Northeast	−.157	−1.03	−.259	−1.73	−.210	−1.37	−.201	−1.32	−.180	−1.18	−.180	−1.18	−.201	−1.32	−.210	−1.37
North Central	−.260	−1.88	−.262	−1.91	−.272	−1.96	−.271	−1.95	−.262	−1.89	−.262	−1.88	−.261	−1.88	−.270	−1.94
South	−.057	−0.42	−.051	−0.38	−.058	−0.43	−.045	−0.34	−.046	−0.34	−.044	−0.32	−.049	−0.36	−.055	−0.41
Parents' education																
Less than high school																
High school	.388	3.04			.305	2.35	.289	2.21	.285	2.15	.285	2.15	.286	2.19	.304	2.34
Some college	.451	3.17			.327	2.23	.312	2.11	.318	2.14	.317	2.13	.309	2.10	.330	2.25
College	1.175	7.01			.922	5.05	.913	4.99	.982	5.50	.981	5.50	.906	4.94	.915	5.02
Child's age	−.061	−2.34	−.068	−3.00	−.057	−2.16	−.057	−2.15	−.057	−2.18	−.057	−2.18	−.056	−2.12	−.056	−2.13
Female child	.554	6.16	.534	6.00	.558	6.20	.554	6.16	.566	6.28	.566	6.28	.560	6.22	.734	4.79
Family structure																
Original two-parent																
Mother-stepfather	−.175	−1.20			−.189	−1.29	−.171	−1.17	−.173	−1.18	−.173	−1.18	−.194	−1.32	−.189	−1.29
Father-stepmother	.050	0.14			.064	0.18	.077	0.22	.079	0.22	.079	0.22	.067	0.19	.069	0.19
Two stepparents	−.232	−0.55			−.162	−0.39	−.172	−0.41	−.176	−0.42	−.178	−0.42	−.152	−0.37	−.162	−0.39

Original cohabitation	.001	0.00			−.008	−0.02	−.039	−0.09	.058	0.13	.061	0.13	−.030	−0.07	−.011	−0.02
Mother-partner cohabitation	−.842	−3.65			−.830	−3.54	−.800	−3.41	−.836	−3.56	−.835	−3.56	−.834	−3.56	−.829	−3.53
Father-partner cohabitation	−.706	−1.24			−.754	−1.32	−.725	−1.27	−.730	−1.27	−.730	−1.27	−.754	−1.32	−.746	−1.31
Two-parent cohabitation	−.288	−0.37			−.191	−0.25	−.241	−0.31	−.230	−0.29	−.231	−0.29	−.204	−0.26	−.200	−0.26
Divorced mother	−.308	−2.49			−.153	−1.17	−.080	−0.57	−.173	−1.33	−.172	−1.32	−.157	−1.20	−.157	−1.20
Never-married mother	−.501	−2.66			−.341	−1.76	−.275	−1.38	−.333	−1.68	−.333	−1.68	−.360	−1.79	−.324	−1.67
Income-to-needs ratio			.167	7.05	.099	3.55							.090	2.93	.130	3.67
Household income ($10,000)							.085*	3.57								
Number of children							−.021	−0.40								
Income-to-needs category																
<0.5																
0.5–1.0											.045	0.20				
1.0–2.0									.152	0.96	.179	0.87				
2.0–3.0									.379	2.28	.406	1.91				
3.0–4.0									.361	1.97	.388	1.72				
4.0+									.574	3.19	.602	2.69				
Income-to-needs * African American													−.016	−0.26		
Income-to-needs * Mexican American													.164	1.65		
Income-to-needs * other													.035	0.34		
Income-to-needs * female															−.062	−1.42
Income missing			−.139	−1.16	.005	0.04	−.010	0.08	.328	1.98	.356	1.68	.002	0.02	.009	0.08
Constant																
1	−4.942		−4.429		−4.804		−4.828		−4.706		−4.677		−4.809		−4.721	
2	−3.318		−2.808		−3.179		−3.213		−3.080		−3.051		−3.184		−3.094	
3	−1.066		−.581		−.922		−.955		−.822		−.793		−.924		−.834	
4	.319		.783		.472		.439		.571		.600		.472		.561	
χ^2	168.73		135.34		181.56		181.89		180.41		180.45		184.70		183.57	
df	24		14		26		27		29		30		29		27	

Source: Authors' calculations based on ordered logit models using data from the NSFH, Wave I, on 1,739 children between the ages of five and eleven years.

TABLE 8A.2 / Effects of Background Factors and Economic Resources on Grade Point Average

	Model															
	1		2		3		4		5		6		7		8	
Independent Variable	Coef- ficient	*t*	Coef- ficient	*t*	Coef- ficient	*t*	Coef- ficient	*t*	Coef- ficient	*t*	Coef- ficient	*t*	Coef- ficient	*t*	Coef- ficient	*t*
Race/ethnicity																
White																
African American	.092	1.73	.085	1.61	.113	2.09	.112	2.08	.109	2.02	.109	2.02	.020	0.23	.115	2.13
Mexican American	.094	1.02	.062	0.68	.118	1.27	.124	1.32	.130	1.39	.127	1.36	.099	0.75	.122	1.31
Other	.121	1.26	.111	0.15	.152	1.57	.151	1.56	.145	1.50	.145	1.51	.162	1.08	.159	1.64
Parental age	.007	2.40	.010	3.33	.007	2.31	.007	2.24	.008	2.54	.008	2.59	.007	2.27	.007	2.32
Child 12–18 in household	−.053	−1.17	−.067	−1.44	−.057	−1.24	−.048	−1.03	−.061	−1.33	−.060	−1.31	−.058	−1.26	−.058	−1.26
Child 7–11 in household																
Child <6 in household	.133	1.98	.184	2.71	.153	2.26	.158	2.12	.152	2.24	.153	2.25	.157	2.31	.157	2.31
Metropolitan area	−.030	−0.67	−.032	−0.70	−.045	−0.99	−.046	−1.01	−.036	−0.80	−.035	−0.78	−.045	−0.98	−.044	−0.98
Region																
West																
Northeast	.012	0.19	−.037	−0.56	.004	0.06	.007	0.11	.020	0.30	.019	0.29	.002	0.04	.005	0.07
North Central	−.132	−2.22	−.154	−2.57	−.137	−2.30	−.134	−2.25	−.129	−2.18	−.130	−2.18	−.140	−2.35	−.136	−2.29
South	.048	0.85	.022	0.38	.047	0.84	.048	0.86	.053	0.95	.053	0.94	.051	0.90	.047	0.82
Parents' education																
Less than high school																
High school	.160	2.97			.143	2.63	.141	2.58	.144	2.64	.145	2.65	.137	2.50	.145	2.66
Some college	.243	4.02			.206	3.29	.206	3.26	.215	3.44	.215	3.44	.202	3.19	.207	3.31
College	.524	7.67			.459	6.17	.459	6.08	.497	6.97	.497	6.97	.457	6.14	.456	6.13
Child's age	−.035	−3.29	−.042	−3.83	−.037	−3.42	−.038	−3.44	−.036	−3.38	−.037	−3.40	−.036	−3.32	−.038	−3.48
Female child	.275	7.29	.264	6.93	.274	7.25	.274	7.25	.277	7.34	.277	7.34	.273	7.21	.340	5.11

Family structure																
Original two-parent																
Mother-stepfather	−.053	−0.88			−.061	−1.00	−.057	−0.94	−.056	−0.92	−.055	−0.90	−.058	−0.95	−.061	−1.01
Father-stepmother	−.153	−1.33			−.171	−1.49	−.169	−1.47	−.154	−1.34	−.152	−1.32	−.165	−1.43	−.182	−1.57
Two stepparents	−.166	−1.10			−.155	−1.03	−.159	−1.05	−.166	−1.10	−.167	−1.10	−.155	−1.03	−.157	−1.04
Original cohabitation	−.421	−1.59			−.391	−1.49	−.381	−1.44	−.405	−1.53	−.403	−1.52	−.400	−1.52	−.391	−1.48
Mother-partner cohabitation	−.359	−2.85			−.354	−2.80	−.348	−2.75	−.357	−2.82	−.355	−2.81	−.347	−2.74	−.351	−2.78
Father-partner cohabitation	.020	0.05			.014	0.04	−.009	−0.03	.028	0.08	.029	0.08	.006	0.02	.004	0.01
Two-parent cohabitation	−.765	−1.68			−.795	−1.75	−.805	−1.76	−.771	−1.69	−.772	−1.69	−.783	−1.72	−.776	−1.70
Divorced mother	−.184	−3.97			−.145	−2.90	−.132	−2.43	−.159	−3.25	−.157	−3.19	−.137	−2.74	−.146	−2.91
Never-married mother	−.095	−0.86			−.058	−0.52	−.046	−0.40	−.055	−0.49	−.050	−0.44	−.029	−0.26	−.058	−0.52
Income-to-needs ratio			.056	6.44	.023	2.23							.019	1.70	.033	2.50
Household income ($10,000)							.019	1.98								
Number of children							−.010	−0.49								
Income-to-needs category																
<0.5																
0.5–1.0											.079	0.77				
1.0–2.0									.164	2.25	.206	2.25				
2.0–3.0									.116	1.52	.160	1.68				
3.0–4.0									.205	2.52	.249	2.51				
4.0+									.148	1.98	.191	2.04				
Income-to-needs * African American													.034	1.42		
Income-to-needs * Mexican American													.003	0.08		
Income-to-needs * other													−.010	−0.19		
Income-to-needs * female															−.019	−1.21
Income missing			−.048	−0.95	−.030	−0.60	−.035	−0.70	.103	1.43	.146	1.60	−.032	−0.63	−.030	−0.60
Constant	2.868	15.15	2.830	16.00	2.848	15.04	2.865	13.59	2.743	14.06	2.696	13.18	2.856	15.04	2.824	14.83
R^2	.102		.073		.103		.104		.106		.106		.106		.105	

Source: Authors' calculations based on OLS models using data from the NSFH, Wave I, on 1,740 children between the ages of twelve and fifteen years.

TABLE 8A.3 / Effects of Background Factors and Economic Resources on No School Behavior Problems

	Model															
	1		2		3		4		5		6		7		8	
Independent Variable	Coefficient	z	Coefficient	z	Coefficient	z	Coefficient	z	Coefficient	z	Coefficient	z	Coefficient	z	Coefficient	z
Race/ethnicity																
White																
African American	−.093	−0.72	−.148	−1.19	−.067	−0.51	−.076	−0.58	−.068	−0.52	−.066	−0.50	.046	0.22	−.067	−0.51
Mexican American	−.016	−0.07	.074	0.36	.016	0.08	−.007	−0.03	.024	0.11	.023	0.10	−.105	−0.34	.013	0.06
Other	.328	1.35	.356	1.48	.369	1.51	.360	1.47	.358	1.47	.363	1.48	.641	1.69	.364	1.49
Parental age	.008	0.99	.024	2.99	.007	0.88	.008	0.99	.008	0.97	.008	1.00	.008	0.92	.007	0.88
Child 12–18 in household	.151	1.29	.122	1.06	.151	1.29	.124	1.02	.146	1.24	.148	1.26	.150	1.28	.151	1.29
Child 7–11 in household																
Child <6 in household	.278	2.00	.383	2.81	.298	2.14	.249	1.71	.301	2.15	.301	2.15	.303	2.17	.297	2.14
Metropolitan area	−.392	−3.22	−.453	−3.74	−.412	−3.36	−.415	−3.37	−.414	−3.37	−.412	−3.35	−.411	−3.34	−.413	−3.37
Region																
West																
Northeast	.190	1.14	.150	0.91	.176	1.05	.173	1.04	.185	1.10	.183	1.09	.176	1.05	.176	1.05
North Central	−.033	−0.22	−.034	−0.23	−.039	−0.26	−.040	−0.27	−.036	−0.24	−.036	−0.24	−.033	−0.22	−.038	−0.26
South	.136	0.93	.150	1.05	.135	0.93	.142	0.98	.132	0.91	.133	0.91	.139	0.95	.136	0.94
Parents' education																
Less than high school																
High school	.126	0.96			.098	0.74	.110	0.82	.099	0.74	.098	0.73	.103	0.78	.095	0.72
Some college	.086	0.59			.038	0.25	.054	0.36	.040	0.26	.037	0.24	.044	0.29	.033	0.22
College	.653	3.42			.553	2.66	.564	2.70	.574	2.87	.573	2.87	.563	2.71	.558	2.68
Child's age	−.071	−4.03	−.087	−4.98	−.073	−4.10	−.072	−4.03	−.073	−4.11	−.073	−4.12	−.074	−4.12	−.073	−4.10
Female child	1.128	10.86	1.094	10.63	1.127	10.84	1.126	10.83	1.129	10.85	1.129	10.84	1.131	10.87	1.008	5.83

Family structure																
Original two-parent																
Mother-stepfather	−.629	−4.17			−.639	−4.22	−.621	−4.10	−.637	−4.21	−.636	−4.20	−.648	−4.27	−.641	−4.23
Father-stepmother	−.152	−0.45			−.177	−0.53	−.158	−0.47	−.168	−0.50	−.166	−0.50	−.198	−0.59	−.165	−0.50
Two stepparents	.015	0.03			.036	0.08	−.050	−0.11	.012	0.02	.014	0.03	.024	0.05	.038	0.08
Original cohabitation	.694	0.92			.700	0.93	.727	0.97	.725	0.96	.729	0.97	.697	0.93	.703	0.94
Mother-partner cohabitation	−.913	−3.70			−.918	−3.68	−.894	−3.57	−.925	−3.70	−.922	−3.69	−.922	−3.69	−.924	−3.70
Father-partner cohabitation	−.999	−1.64			−1.038	−1.70	−1.004	−1.64	−1.011	−1.65	−1.009	−1.64	−1.033	−1.69	−1.054	−1.72
Two-parent cohabitation	−1.265	−1.73			−1.255	−1.71	−1.334	−1.82	−1.259	−1.71	−1.258	−1.71	−1.245	−1.70	−1.268	−1.73
Divorced mother	−.619	−5.11			−.559	−4.29	−.521	−3.67	−.565	−4.43	−.562	−4.39	−.570	−4.36	−.557	−4.28
Never-married mother	−.889	−4.32			−.833	−3.94	−.785	−3.58	−.836	−3.92	−.835	−3.92	−.873	−4.02	−.836	−3.96
Income-to-needs ratio			.103	4.18	.036	1.23							.043	1.33	.023	0.71
Household income ($10,000)							.032	1.23								
Number of children							.047	0.87								
Income-to-needs category																
<0.5																
0.5–1.0											.125	0.54				
1.0–2.0									.093	0.55	.162	0.77				
2.0–3.0									.014	0.08	.084	0.38				
3.0–4.0									.255	1.25	.324	1.36				
4.0+									.238	1.26	.308	1.36				
Income-to-needs * African American													−.047	−0.74		
Income-to-needs * Mexican American													.081	0.65		
Income-to-needs * other													−.139	−0.98		
Income-to-needs * female															.041	0.85
Income missing			−.067	−0.54	.018	0.14	.018	0.14	.141	0.82	.210	0.99	.019	0.15	.016	0.13
Constant	2.042	5.68	1.197	3.89	2.008	5.58	1.855	4.73	1.970	5.23	1.891	4.70	1.973	5.46	2.047	5.64
χ^2	265.97		213.60		267.54		268.19		269.12		269.42		269.51		268.28	
df	24		14		26		27		29		30		29		27	

Source: Authors' calculations based on logit models using data from the NSFH, Wave I, on 3,595 children between the ages of five and eighteen years.

TABLE 8A.4 / Effects of Background Factors and Economic Resources on Low Externalizing Behavior

	Model															
	1		2		3		4		5		6		7		8	
Independent Variable	Coef-ficient	*t*	Coef-ficient	*t*	Coef-ficient	*t*	Coef-ficient	*t*	Coef-ficient	*t*	Coef-ficient	*t*	Coef-ficient	*t*	Coef-ficient	*t*
Race/ethnicity																
White																
African American	.302	6.66	.302	6.85	.320	6.98	.323	7.07	.314	6.87	.312	6.83	.326	4.48	.321	7.00
Mexican American	.236	3.27	.310	4.00	.266	3.67	.298	4.09	.271	3.72	.271	3.72	.302	2.93	.269	3.71
Other	.216	2.78	.270	3.46	.251	3.21	.250	3.20	.240	3.07	.237	3.03	.452	3.67	.255	3.25
Parental age	.013	4.73	.016	6.03	.012	4.31	.011	3.85	.012	4.52	.012	4.47	.012	4.31	.012	4.31
Child 12–18 in household	−.078	−1.95	−.084	−2.09	−.075	−1.86	−.010	−0.24	−.074	−1.86	−.076	−1.89	−.076	−1.91	−.075	−1.88
Child 7–11 in household																
Child <6 in household	−.098	−2.25	−.059	−1.36	−.081	−1.86	−.012	−0.27	−.082	−1.87	−.082	−1.87	−.078	−1.78	−.082	−1.87
Metropolitan area	−.093	−2.40	−.126	−3.21	−.113	−2.86	−.110	−2.78	−.108	−2.75	−.109	−2.78	−.116	−2.93	−.113	−2.86
Region																
West																
Northeast	.104	1.84	.090	1.61	.087	1.53	.096	1.71	.098	1.73	.098	1.74	.081	1.43	.087	1.54
North Central	−.018	−0.35	−.019	−0.38	−.024	−0.47	−.019	−0.37	−.020	−0.40	−.020	−0.40	−.025	−0.49	−.024	−0.46
South	.119	2.41	.132	2.69	.116	2.35	.108	2.19	.117	2.38	.116	2.35	.117	2.37	.116	2.35
Parents' education																
Less than high school																
High school	−.024	−0.53			−.051	−1.08	−.068	−1.44	−.052	−1.10	−.052	−1.09	−.043	−0.91	−.049	−1.05
Some college	−.031	−0.59			−.074	−1.37	−.087	−1.60	−.070	−1.31	−.069	−1.28	−.065	−1.20	−.072	−1.33
College	.110	1.85			.024	0.37	.044	0.67	.051	0.82	.052	0.83	.032	0.49	.022	0.34
Child's age	−.002	−0.37	−.007	−1.26	−.004	−0.61	−.005	−0.92	−.003	−0.55	−.003	−0.52	−.004	−0.61	−.004	−0.61
Female child	.067	2.07	.064	1.96	.068	2.09	.071	2.19	.070	2.14	.070	2.14	.070	2.15	.150	2.69

Family structure																
Original two-parent																
Mother-stepfather	−.165	−3.11			−.175	−3.28	−.183	−3.44	−.169	−3.17	−.170	−3.19	−.178	−3.33	−.175	−3.28
Father-stepmother	−.089	−0.81			−.108	−0.98	−.117	−1.06	−.096	−0.87	−.098	−0.89	−.111	−1.00	−.115	−1.04
Two stepparents	.013	0.09			.032	0.22	.128	0.88	.020	0.14	.020	0.14	.025	0.18	.030	0.21
Original cohabitation	−.266	−1.39			−.266	−1.40	−.279	−1.47	−.249	−1.30	−.251	−1.32	−.268	−1.41	−.270	−1.42
Mother-partner cohabitation	−.093	−0.98			−.109	−1.14	−.120	−1.25	−.113	−1.18	−.114	−1.19	−.104	−1.09	−.107	−1.12
Father-partner cohabitation	−.245	−1.02			−.298	−1.25	−.322	−1.35	−.279	−1.16	−.280	−1.17	−.282	−1.18	−.290	−1.21
Two-parent cohabitation	−.008	−0.02			.008	0.02	.105	0.34	−.001	−0.00	−.001	−0.00	.016	0.05	.017	0.06
Divorced mother	−.213	−5.03			−.158	−3.49	−.188	−3.87	−.167	−3.75	−.170	−3.80	−.159	−3.51	−.159	−3.52
Never-married mother	−.238	−3.02			−.186	−2.33	−.226	−2.75	−.186	−2.29	−.187	−2.30	−.190	−2.32	−.183	−2.29
Income-to-needs ratio			.043	5.49	.032	3.41							.036	3.47	.045	3.81
Household income ($10,000)							.015	1.76								
Number of children							−.098	−5.66								
Income-to-needs category																
<0.5																
0.5–1.0											−.089	−1.07				
1.0–2.0									.046	0.76	−.004	−0.05				
2.0–3.0									.097	1.53	.045	0.58				
3.0–4.0									.164	2.41	.113	1.36				
4.0+									.178	2.77	.126	1.58				
Income-to-needs * African American													.000	0.01		
Income-to-needs * Mexican American													−.015	−0.42		
Income-to-needs * other													−.091	−2.11		
Income-to-needs * female															−.026	−1.81
Income missing			.060	1.37	.067	1.52	.061	1.38	.177	2.89	.126	1.63	.067	1.52	.069	1.56
Constant	−.433	−3.52	−.709	−6.61	−.461	−3.75	−.188	−1.43	−.497	−3.83	−.441	−3.15	−.478	−3.87	−.503	−4.02
R^2	.049		.046		.053		.060		.053		.053		.054		.054	

Source: Authors' calculations based on OLS models using data from the NSFH, Wave I, on 3,595 children between the ages of five and eighteen years.

TABLE 8A.5 / Effects of Background Factors and Economic Resources on Low Internalizing Behavior

	Model															
	1		2		3		4		5		6		7		8	
Independent Variable	Coef-ficient	t	Coef-ficient	t	Coef-ficient	t	Coef-ficient	t	Coef-ficient	t	Coef-ficient	t	Coef-ficient	t	Coef-ficient	t
Race/ethnicity																
White																
African American	.246	5.44	.255	5.77	.263	5.74	.262	5.73	.257	5.63	.257	5.63	.256	3.53	.264	5.77
Mexican American	.192	2.67	.271	3.86	.220	3.04	.236	3.23	.227	3.11	.227	3.11	.326	3.16	.224	3.10
Other	.239	3.09	.292	3.75	.272	3.47	.267	3.42	.261	3.35	.261	3.35	.405	3.29	.276	3.54
Parental age	.013	4.82	.016	6.12	.013	4.42	.012	4.19	.013	4.63	.013	4.63	.012	4.37	.013	4.43
Child 12–18 in household	−.089	−2.22	−.097	−2.43	−.086	−2.14	−.052	−1.24	−.085	−2.12	−.085	−2.12	−.087	−2.18	−.086	−2.16
Child 7–11 in household																
Child <6 in household	−.101	−2.32	−.064	−1.48	−.085	−1.95	−.053	−1.15	−.086	−1.96	−.086	−1.96	−.086	−1.96	−.086	−1.97
Metropolitan area	−.071	−1.82	−.103	−2.62	−.089	−2.26	−.086	−2.19	−.084	−2.13	−.083	−2.13	−.094	−2.37	−.089	−2.25
Region																
West																
Northeast	.065	1.16	.049	0.87	.049	0.87	.056	1.00	.061	1.09	.061	1.09	.044	0.78	.050	0.88
North Central	−.025	−0.50	−.027	−0.59	−.031	−0.61	−.028	−0.55	−.027	−0.53	−.027	−0.53	−.033	−0.65	−.031	−0.60
South	.120	2.44	.131	2.57	.118	2.39	.115	2.33	.120	2.44	.121	2.45	.117	2.37	.117	2.38
Parents' education																
Less than high school																
High school	−.021	−0.45			−.045	−0.95	−.052	−1.10	−.048	−1.03	−.048	−1.03	−.035	−0.74	−.043	−0.92
Some college	.017	0.34			−.021	−0.40	−.024	−0.45	−.020	−0.37	−.020	−0.38	−.011	0.20	−.018	−0.34
College	.065	1.09			.014	0.22	.003	0.05	.012	0.20	.012	0.20	−.007	0.11	.018	0.27
Child's age	−.022	−3.79	−.028	−4.83	−.024	−4.02	−.025	−4.17	−.023	−3.95	−.023	−3.95	−.023	−4.01	−.024	−4.03
Female child	−.016	−0.50	−.020	−0.60	−.016	−0.49	−.015	−0.45	−.013	−0.42	−.013	−0.41	−.015	−0.45	.101	1.82

Family structure																
Original two-parent																
Mother-stepfather	−.200	−3.75			−.208	−3.91	−.210	−3.94	−.201	−3.78	−.201	−3.78	−.209	−3.93	−.209	−3.92
Father-stepmother	−.199	−1.81			−.216	−1.97	−.219	−1.98	−.203	−1.85	−.203	−1.84	−.216	−1.96	−.227	−2.06
Two stepparents	.054	0.37			.072	0.50	.116	0.80	.061	0.42	.061	0.42	.066	0.46	.069	0.48
Original cohabitation	−.169	−0.89			−.169	−0.89	−.171	−0.90	−.153	−0.80	−.153	−0.80	−.170	−0.89	−.175	−0.92
Mother-partner cohabitation	−.175	−1.84			−.190	−1.99	−.193	−2.01	−.192	−2.01	−.192	−2.00	−.184	−1.92	−.188	−1.96
Father-partner cohabitation	−.172	−0.72			−.222	−0.93	−.230	−0.96	−.203	−0.85	−.203	−0.85	−.213	−0.89	−.211	−0.88
Two-parent cohabitation	−.137	−0.44			−.123	−0.40	−.080	−0.26	−.136	−0.43	−.136	−0.43	−.117	−0.38	−.110	−0.36
Divorced mother	−.255	−6.05			−.205	−4.54	−.218	−4.47	−.213	−4.78	−.212	−4.76	−.204	−4.51	−.206	−4.58
Never-married mother	−.213	−2.71			−.166	−2.07	−.183	−2.23	−.161	−1.99	−.161	−1.98	−.163	−1.98	−.161	−2.01
Income-to-needs ratio			.041	5.19	.030	3.14							.033	3.25	.048	4.07
Household income ($10,000)							.016	1.96								
Number of children							−.052	−3.01								
Income-to-needs category																
<0.5																
0.5–1.0											.009	0.11				
1.0–2.0									.039	0.65	.044	0.58				
2.0–3.0									.123	1.96	.129	1.63				
3.0–4.0									.162	2.38	.167	2.01				
4.0+									.158	2.47	.163	2.05				
Income-to-needs * African American													.006	0.26		
Income-to-needs * Mexican American													−.050	−1.43		
Income-to-needs * other													−.059	−1.37		
Income-to-needs * female															−.037	−2.60
Income missing			.055	1.25	.065	1.48	.061	1.38	.172	2.81	.177	2.29	.065	1.48	.068	1.53
Constant	−.144	−1.17	−.415	−3.87	−.169	−1.38	−.026	−0.20	−.213	−1.64	−.219	−1.56	−.180	−1.46	−.229	−1.83
R^2	.048		.042		.051		.052		.051		.051		.052		.053	

Source: Authors' calculations based on OLS models using data from the NSFH, Wave I, on 3,595 children between the ages of five and eighteen years.

TABLE 8A.6 / Effects of Background Factors and Economic Resources on Sociability

	Model															
	1		2		3		4		5		6		7		8	
Independent Variable	Coef-ficient	*t*	Coef-ficient	*t*	Coef-ficient	*t*	Coef-ficient	*t*	Coef-ficient	*t*	Coef-ficient	*t*	Coef-ficient	t	Coef-ficient	*t*
Race/ethnicity																
White																
African American	.260	5.72	.280	6.30	.278	6.04	.281	6.11	.276	6.03	.276	6.03	.287	3.95	.277	6.04
Mexican American	.085	1.18	.169	2.38	.113	1.57	.132	1.80	.135	1.86	.135	1.86	.038	0.37	.113	1.56
Other	.107	1.37	.172	2.19	.140	1.79	.143	1.82	.139	1.79	.139	1.79	.317	2.57	.140	1.78
Parental age	.005	1.85	.010	3.70	.004	1.48	.004	1.26	.004	1.76	.004	1.76	.004	1.54	.004	1.47
Child 12–18 in household	−.036	−0.92	−.051	−1.27	−.034	−0.85	−.010	−0.24	−.036	−0.91	−.036	−0.91	−.035	−0.88	−.034	−0.85
Child 7–11 in household																
Child <6 in household	−.088	−2.01	−.049	−1.11	−.072	−1.64	−.050	−1.08	−.064	−1.46	−.064	−1.46	−.066	−1.49	−.072	−1.64
Metropolitan area	−.057	−1.47	−.086	−2.18	−.076	−1.92	−.078	−1.97	−.070	−1.79	−.070	−1.79	−.075	−1.89	−.076	−1.92
Region																
West																
Northeast	.075	1.32	.075	1.32	.059	1.03	.062	1.09	.075	1.33	.075	1.33	.055	0.97	.058	1.03
North Central	−.033	−0.65	−.025	−0.48	−.039	−0.76	−.037	−0.73	−.032	−0.63	−.032	−0.63	−.038	−0.75	−.039	−0.77
South	−.032	−0.66	−.013	−0.26	−.036	−0.72	−.036	−0.74	−.026	−0.54	−.026	−0.54	−.032	−0.66	−.036	−0.72
Parents' education																
Less than high school																
High school	−.036	−0.78			−.061	−1.29	−.072	−1.51	−.084	−1.77	−.084	−1.77	−.061	−1.28	−.061	−1.30
Some college	−.057	−1.09			−.098	−1.82	−.109	−2.01	−.121	−2.24	−.121	−2.24	−.097	−1.78	−.099	−1.83
College	.134	2.25			.052	0.79	.047	0.71	.058	0.93	.058	0.93	.055	0.84	.052	0.80
Child's age	−.002	−0.45	−.009	−1.54	−.004	−0.69	−.005	−0.83	−.003	−0.59	−.003	−0.59	−.004	−0.65	−.004	−0.67

Female child	.112	3.43	.105	3.18	.113	3.45	.113	3.45	.119	3.63	.119	3.63	.114	3.48	.097	1.73
Family structure																
Original two-parent																
Mother-stepfather	−.262	−4.91			−.271	−5.06	−.270	−5.04	−.260	−4.87	−.260	−4.87	−.274	−5.13	−.271	−5.06
Father-stepmother	−.326	−2.95			−.343	−3.11	−.346	−3.13	−.328	−2.98	−.328	−2.98	−.348	−3.15	−.342	−3.09
Two stepparents	−.021	−0.14			−.003	−0.02	.026	0.18	−.009	−0.06	−.009	−0.06	−.007	−0.05	−.003	−0.02
Original cohabitation	−.131	−0.69			−.130	−0.68	−.122	−0.64	−.112	−0.58	−.112	−0.58	−.134	−0.70	−.129	−0.68
Mother-partner cohabitation	−.248	−2.60			−.260	−2.70	−.255	−2.65	−.258	−2.69	−.258	−2.69	−.259	−2.69	−.260	−2.70
Father-partner cohabitation	−.507	−2.11			−.554	−2.31	−.560	−2.34	−.532	−2.22	−.532	−2.22	−.537	−2.24	−.555	−2.31
Two-parent cohabitation	.423	1.35			.438	1.41	.460	1.48	.409	1.31	.409	1.31	.444	1.43	.436	1.40
Divorced mother	−.200	−4.72			−.147	−3.26	−.135	−2.77	−.136	−3.05	−.136	−3.05	−.150	−3.32	−.147	−3.25
Never-married mother	−.189	−2.40			−.140	−1.74	−.131	−1.58	−.090	−1.11	−.090	−1.11	−.147	−1.79	−.140	−1.75
Income-to-needs ratio			.039	4.90	.031	3.24							.032	3.06	.028	2.38
Household income ($10,000)							.025	2.97								
Number of children							−.039	−2.22								
Income-to-needs category																
<0.5																
0.5–1.0											−.001	−0.02				
1.0–2.0									.177	2.96	.176	2.31				
2.0–3.0									.257	4.06	.256	3.23				
3.0–4.0									.295	4.33	.294	3.54				
4.0+									.267	4.17	.266	3.33				
Income-to-needs * African American													−.003	−0.16		
Income-to-needs * Mexican American													.040	1.13		
Income-to-needs * other													−.082	−1.91		
Income-to-needs * female															.005	0.36
Income missing			.032	0.74	.053	1.20	.046	1.03	.261	4.26	.260	3.37	.053	1.20	.053	1.19
Constant	−.080	−0.65	−.430	−3.98	−.107	−0.87	−.013	−0.10	−.258	−1.98	−.257	−1.83	−.121	−0.98	−.098	−0.78
R^2	.038		.026		.041		.042		.045		.045		.043		.041	

Source: Authors' calculations based on OLS models using data from the NSFH, Wave I, on 3,595 children between the ages of five and eighteen years.

TABLE 8A.7 / Effects of Background Factors and Economic Resources on Initiative

Independent Variable	Model 1 Coefficient	Model 1 t	Model 2 Coefficient	Model 2 t	Model 3 Coefficient	Model 3 t	Model 4 Coefficient	Model 4 t	Model 5 Coefficient	Model 5 t	Model 6 Coefficient	Model 6 t	Model 7 Coefficient	Model 7 t	Model 8 Coefficient	Model 8 t
Race/ethnicity																
White																
African American	.178	3.94	.202	4.57	.197	4.29	.197	4.29	.192	4.21	.195	4.28	.158	2.18	.197	4.30
Mexican American	−.042	−0.58	.043	0.61	−.014	−0.20	−.005	−0.07	.003	0.04	.002	0.02	−.111	−1.07	−.014	−0.19
Other	.061	0.79	.124	1.59	.095	1.21	.093	1.19	.090	1.16	.096	1.24	.203	1.65	.096	1.22
Parental age	.008	3.14	.013	4.85	.008	2.77	.008	2.65	.008	3.12	.009	3.21	.008	2.83	.008	2.77
Child 12–18 in household	−.042	−1.07	−.056	−1.39	−.041	−1.02	−.028	−0.67	−.045	−1.12	−.042	−1.05	−.042	−1.04	−.041	−1.02
Child 7–11 in household																
Child <6 in household	−.119	−2.75	−.086	−1.96	−.104	−2.38	−.096	−2.09	−.097	−2.22	−.098	−2.24	−.097	−2.22	−.104	−2.38
Metropolitan area	.010	0.26	−.018	−0.46	−.007	−0.18	−.008	−0.21	.000	0.01	.002	0.07	−.005	0.13	−.007	−0.18
Region																
West																
Northeast	−.025	−0.45	−.032	−0.56	−.042	−0.74	−.038	−0.67	−.022	−0.40	−.023	−0.42	−.044	−0.78	−.042	−0.74
North Central	−.051	−1.00	−.047	−0.92	−.057	−1.11	−.055	−1.08	−.049	−0.97	−.049	−0.96	−.056	−1.10	−.056	−1.10
South	−.057	−1.16	−.042	−0.85	−.060	−1.22	−.059	−1.20	−.051	−1.03	−.048	−0.98	−.056	−1.14	−.060	−1.22
Parents' education																
Less than high school																
High school	−.045	−0.98			−.070	−1.49	−.075	−1.58	−.090	−1.91	−.091	−1.93	−.073	−1.55	−.070	−1.49
Some college	−.025	−0.48			−.067	−1.25	−.070	−1.29	−.085	−1.58	−.087	−1.63	−.069	−1.27	−.066	−1.23
College	.081	1.35			.002	0.03	.0002	0.004	.012	0.19	.011	0.18	−.001	−0.02	−.003	−0.04
Child's age	−.038	−6.47	−.044	−7.57	−.039	−6.68	−.040	−6.75	−.038	−6.58	−.039	−6.64	−.039	−6.62	−.039	−6.68
Female child	.031	0.95	.025	0.75	.031	0.96	.031	0.95	.037	1.14	.037	1.15	.031	0.96	.054	0.98

Family structure																
Original two-parent																
Mother-stepfather	−.248	−4.65			−.256	−4.80	−.252	−4.73	−.245	−4.60	−.243	−4.57	−.258	−4.83	−.256	−4.80
Father-stepmother	−.319	−2.89			−.336	−3.04	−.334	−3.03	−.321	−2.92	−.316	−2.87	−.336	−3.05	−.338	−3.06
Two stepparents	−.103	−0.71			−.085	−0.59	−.076	−0.52	−.094	−0.65	−.095	−0.66	−.086	−0.60	−.085	−0.59
Original cohabitation	−.121	−0.63			−.118	−0.62	−.108	−0.57	−.106	−0.56	−.102	−0.53	−.126	−0.66	−.120	−0.63
Mother-partner cohabitation	−.297	−3.12			−.306	−3.19	−.299	−3.11	−.306	−3.19	−.303	−3.16	−.305	−3.18	−.305	−3.18
Father-partner cohabitation	−.322	−1.34			−.365	−1.53	−.363	−1.52	−.341	−1.42	−.338	−1.41	−.350	−1.46	−.363	−1.52
Two-parent cohabitation	.086	0.27			.100	0.32	.103	0.33	.069	0.22	.070	0.22	.110	0.35	.103	0.33
Divorced mother	−.204	−4.83			−.152	−3.37	−.140	−2.86	−.146	−3.29	−.141	−3.17	−.153	−3.38	−.153	−3.38
Never-married mother	−.172	−2.20			−.123	−1.54	−.112	−1.36	−.076	−0.94	−.075	−0.93	−.114	−1.39	−.122	−1.53
Income-to-needs ratio			.037	4.66	.031	3.24							.028	2.70	.034	2.90
Household income ($10,000)							.024	2.84								
Number of children							−.022	−1.25								
Income-to-needs category																
<0.5																
0.5–1.0											.188	2.27				
1.0–2.0									.208	3.49	.315	4.15				
2.0–3.0									.241	3.83	.349	4.42				
3.0–4.0									.309	4.54	.417	5.03				
4.0+									.251	3.93	.359	4.51				
Income-to-needs * African American													.014	0.67		
Income-to-needs * Mexican American													.046	1.32		
Income-to-needs * other													−.054	−1.26		
Income-to-needs * female															−.007	−0.51
Income missing			.022	0.50	.043	0.97	.037	0.84	.251	4.11	.358	4.64	.043	0.98	.043	0.98
Constant	.258	2.10	−.067	−0.62	.233	1.89	.282	2.13	.069	0.54	−.048	−0.34	.231	1.87	.221	1.76
R^2	.043		.035		.047		.046		.050		.052		.048		.047	

Source: Authors' calculations based on OLS models using data from the NSFH, Wave I, on 3,595 children between the ages of five and eighteen years.

TABLE 8A.8 / Effects of Background Factors and Economic Resources on Children's Quality of Life

	Model															
	1		2		3		4		5		6		7		8	
Independent Variable	Coef-ficient	z	Coef-ficient	z	Coef-ficient	z	Coef-ficient	z	Coef-ficient	z	Coef-ficient	z	Coef-ficient	z	Coef-ficient	z
Race/ethnicity																
White																
African American	.454	4.69	.521	5.57	.519	5.27	.532	5.39	.510	5.19	.516	5.24	.559	3.59	.520	5.27
Mexican American	−.069	−0.46	.182	1.26	.012	0.08	.065	0.43	.040	0.27	.039	0.25	.071	0.33	.014	0.09
Other	.331	1.99	.465	2.83	.435	2.59	.450	2.67	.412	2.46	.424	2.53	.604	2.31	.438	2.61
Parental age	.031	5.17	.038	6.69	.028	4.69	.027	4.41	.030	4.94	.030	5.03	.028	4.68	.028	4.70
Child 12–18 in household	−.104	−1.24	−.130	−1.56	−.101	−1.20	−.050	−0.56	−.101	−1.19	−.097	−1.14	−.103	−1.22	−.101	−1.20
Child 7–11 in household																
Child <6 in household	.171	1.85	.273	2.99	.223	2.40	.269	2.74	.222	2.38	.222	2.38	.223	2.38	.223	2.39
Metropolitan area	−.094	−1.15	−.206	−2.52	−.149	−1.79	−.162	−1.94	−.144	−1.74	−.140	−1.69	−.153	−1.83	−.149	−1.79
Region																
West																
Northeast	.145	1.23	.132	1.13	.098	0.83	.106	0.89	.130	1.10	.128	1.08	.094	0.79	.098	0.82
North Central	−.151	−1.42	−.127	−1.21	−.171	−1.61	−.167	−1.57	−.159	−1.49	−.157	−1.47	−.172	−1.61	−.171	−1.60
South	.156	1.52	.205	2.03	.150	1.46	.153	1.49	.156	1.51	.161	1.56	.149	1.44	.150	1.46
Parents' education																
Less than high school																
High school	.077	0.80			−.0003	−0.003	.029	−0.29	−.014	−0.14	−.014	−0.14	.008	0.08	.001	0.01
Some college	.002	0.02			−.128	−1.14	−.061	−1.42	−.133	−1.17	−.137	−1.21	−.118	−1.04	−.127	−1.12
College	.050	0.39			−.206	−1.49	−.239	−1.70	−.148	−1.11	−.150	−1.12	−.198	−1.43	−.208	−1.50
Child's age	−.086	−6.93	−.101	−8.14	−.091	−7.23	−.094	−7.41	−.090	−7.18	−.091	−7.23	−.091	−7.23	−.091	−7.23
Female child	.319	4.66	.302	4.44	.321	4.66	.319	4.64	.327	4.75	.327	4.75	.323	4.69	.384	3.28
Family structure																
Original two-parent																
Mother-stepfather	−.584	−5.34			−.612	−5.57	−.605	−5.50	−.596	−5.42	−.592	−5.39	−.615	−5.59	−.612	−5.57
Father-stepmother	−.554	−2.45			−.613	−2.71	−.618	−2.73	−.570	−2.52	−.562	−2.48	−.617	−2.73	−.619	−2.74
Two stepparents	−.553	−1.90			−.500	−1.71	−.470	−1.60	−.541	−1.85	−.547	−1.87	−.505	−1.73	−.501	−1.72

Original cohabitation	−.348	−0.89			−.326	−0.83	−.284	−0.73	−.272	−0.69	−.256	−0.65	−.325	−0.83	−.329	−0.84
Mother-partner cohabitation	−1.004	−5.26			−1.025	−5.32	−1.002	−5.19	−1.038	−5.38	−1.034	−5.35	−1.023	−5.30	−1.024	−5.31
Father-partner cohabitation	−1.164	−2.42			−1.287	−2.66	−1.307	−2.70	−1.239	−2.56	−1.234	−2.55	−1.276	−2.64	−1.282	−2.65
Two-parent cohabitation	−.769	−1.23			−.738	−1.18	−.714	−1.14	−.757	−1.21	−.757	−1.21	−.733	−1.17	−.731	−1.17
Divorced mother	−.782	−8.95			−.627	−6.72	−.561	−5.56	−.643	−6.99	−.636	−6.90	−.630	−6.73	−.628	−6.73
Never-married mother	−.443	−2.70			−.295	−1.76	−.237	−1.37	−.281	−1.65	−.279	−1.64	−.309	−1.79	−.292	−1.74
Income-to-needs ratio			.112	6.60	.096	4.68							.101	4.59	.106	4.18
Household income ($10,000)							.085	4.77								
Number of children							−.086	−2.35								
Income-to-needs category																
<0.5																
0.5–1.0											.318	1.85				
1.0–2.0									.111	0.90	.290	1.85				
2.0–3.0									.323	2.46	.504	3.08				
3.0–4.0									.532	3.69	.713	4.10				
4.0+									.574	4.26	.755	4.54				
Income-to-needs * African American													−.014	−0.28		
Income-to-needs * Mexican American													−.025	0.34		
Income-to-needs * other													−.079	−0.83		
Income-to-needs * female															−.021	−0.67
Income missing			.034	0.38	.093	0.99	.071	0.76	.433	3.40	.612	3.84	.092	0.99	.094	1.01
Constant																
1	−4.864		−4.075		−4.791		−4.982		−4.685		−4.484		−4.775		−4.761	
2	−3.372		−2.587		−3.299		−3.489		−3.192		−2.991		−3.283		−3.268	
3	−.191		.560		−.108		−.295		−.000		.203		−.091		−.077	
χ^2	313.15		249.84		337.16		344.21		339.51		342.96		337.94		337.60	
df		24		14		26		27		29		30		29		27

Source: Authors' calculations based on ordered logit models using data from the NSFH, Wave I, on 3,669 children between the ages of five and eighteen years.

NOTES

1. Approximately half of the cases (446) with missing values on the parenting measures were missing because of nonresponse by the secondary respondent.
2. All of the confirmatory factor analysis models that are the basis of the measures of parenting practices treated each item as ordinal or dichotomous measures of latent variable indicators using Muthén's (1984) methodology.
3. We used household size rather than family size as the basis for calculating poverty thresholds. Thus, we included the income and consumption of nonfamily members (e.g., unmarried partners, grandmothers) in determining the household's poverty status.
4. Because the data are cross-sectional, household income is assessed only at one period of time. It is, therefore, likely that our income measure has low reliability.
5. We estimated the models in tables 8.3 and 8.4 using a variety of specifications of the relationship between income-to-needs ratio and children's well-being, including the use of a dummy variable for poverty status. In no case did the results differ markedly from those reported in the previous section.
6. We reverse coded negative responses for the prediction equations so that high values indicated low levels of negative responses.

Chapter 9

Psychosocial Morbidity Among Poor Children in Ontario

Ellen L. Lipman and David R. Offord

In Canada, one child in five is exposed to poverty. Among children under eighteen years old, 1.4 million were poor in 1993, a poverty rate of 20.8 percent (National Council on Welfare [NCW] 1995). Poverty places children at risk for a wide range of health and psychosocial difficulties.

Research has demonstrated repeatedly that poor children have significantly more psychosocial difficulties than nonpoor children do, including more mental and physical health problems, academic difficulties, and social difficulties (Lipman, Offord, and Boyle 1994; Offord, Boyle, and Jones 1987; Rutter et al. 1975; Berger, Yule, and Rutter 1975). For example, in terms of emotional health, a significant association has been found between low family income (less than $10,000) and one or more psychiatric disorders (Lipman, Offord, and Boyle 1994). Among four- to eleven-year-old children, the odds of a poor child having one or more psychiatric disorders such as an attention deficit hyperactivity disorder, a conduct disorder, or an emotional disorder was more than three times that of a nonpoor child (Lipman, Offord, and Boyle 1994). Similar associations have been demonstrated in the educational and social spheres, including poor school readiness, low skills in math concepts in the early grades, and later difficulties such as failing a grade or use of special education services (Hinshaw 1992; Entwisle and Alexander 1990; Lipman, Offord, and Boyle 1994).

Psychosocial morbidity among poor children is even more important since the mental and physical difficulties that poor children experience do not necessarily resolve as they grow up. Instead, they may become adults with impairments in the physical, emotional, social, and occupational spheres. For example, approximately 40 percent of children with conduct disorder continue to experience serious psychosocial difficulties into adulthood (Offord and Bennett 1994).

Although the association between low income and psychosocial morbidity is well documented, the mechanisms or causal pathways through which economic disadvantage (or low income) influences child psychosocial morbidity are poorly understood. Other background characteristics such as maternal and family characteristics clearly influence both the family's economic situation and the child's adjustment (Lipman, Offord, and Boyle 1994). A broad and appropriate conceptualization of the context of poverty therefore includes not only measures of income but also measures of other important influences such as family structure and parents' education.

In this chapter, we use data from the Ontario Child Health Study (OCHS) and Follow-Up (OCHS-FU) to examine the effect of poverty on children's and adolescents' development (Boyle et al. 1987; Boyle et al. 1991; Offord et al. 1992). We conceptualize the context of poverty through measures that include mother's education, family structure, and measures of family economic status in relation to a national low-income threshold and poverty history (that is, the amount of time spent below the low-income threshold).

Specifically, we examine (1) the association between mother's education and family structure, and children's psychosocial morbidity; (2) the association between mother's education, family structure, and long-term measures of household economic status, and children's psychosocial morbidity; (3) the association between mother's education, family structure and longitudinal poverty history, and children's psychosocial morbidity; and (4) the causal role of the family's economic status on children's psychosocial morbidity. Household economic status refers to measures of income and their relationship to the Statistics Canada low-income cutoff (Statistics Canada 1984). Longitudinal poverty history refers to the timing and duration of poverty for the family.

METHODS

Study Population

The OCHS was a provincewide cross-sectional study whose primary objective was to obtain unbiased, precise estimates of the prevalence of four psychiatric disorders (conduct disorder, hyperactivity, emotional disorder, and somatization) among Ontario children aged four to sixteen years. The survey was carried out in 1983 with follow-up in 1987. All families who had participated in the original OCHS were eligible for the follow-up survey.[1]

The target population included all children born between January 1, 1966, and January 1, 1979, whose usual place of residence was a household in Ontario. Three groups of children were excluded from the survey: those living on Indian reserves, in collective dwellings such as institutions, and in dwellings constructed after June 1, 1981 (Census Day). These groups accounted for only 3.3 percent of the target population. The sampling unit consisted of all household dwellings listed in the 1981 Canadian Census. The sample was selected by stratified, clustered, random sampling, and Statistics Canada carried out the survey. In total, 1,869 families including 3,294 children were surveyed. The interviewers collected information from a parent (usually the mother), from a teacher for children four to eleven years old, and from the adolescents themselves for twelve to sixteen-year-olds. Except for information collected from teachers, all data were collected during a home visit. Participation was high (91.1 percent), and the refusal rate low (3.9 percent).

In the OCHS-FU, families were located in late 1986 and data collected in the spring of 1987. Children and adolescents eight to twenty years old made up the follow-up sample.[2]

Our analyses included children four to twelve years old in 1983 and eight to sixteen years old in 1987. We used only information supplied by the parents.

MEASURES

Psychosocial Outcomes

We chose psychosocial outcomes based on the availability of data in the OCHS and OCHS-FU and on evidence of a relationship with low income from previous work.

In the cognitive/educational realm, we measured two outcomes. School outcome was defined using a four-category variable (both failed and full-time remedial education or placement in a special class at some time during the child's school career; failed only, full-time remedial, or special class placement only; neither failed, nor full-time remedial, nor special class placement). Schoolwork was measured by how well a child has done in school over the last six months on a 5-point scale ranging from not well at all (poor student) to very well (excellent student).

In the emotional/behavioral realm, we defined a psychiatric disorder by the number of symptoms of conduct disorder, hyperactivity, and emotional disorder displayed in the last six months (the sum of three scale variables). Measurement of the three disorders was guided by *Diagnostic and Statistical Manual of Mental Disorders*, third ed.; using items from the Child Behavior Checklist and additional items as needed (American Psychiatric Association 1980; Achenbach and Edelbrock 1981). Conduct disorder was characterized by either physical violence against persons or property or a severe violation of societal norms (for example, stealing, truancy, fire setting). Hyperactivity was characterized by inattention, impulsivity, and motor activity (for example, inability to sit still, restlessness, hyperactivity, impulsiveness or acting without thinking). Emotional disorder was characterized primarily by feelings of anxiety and depression (for example, nervousness, being high strung, or tense, feeling worthless or inferior) (Boyle et al. 1987).

In the physical health realm, we defined chronic health problems as the number of illnesses, sometimes including functional limitations in daily living lasting for more than six months. Questions about illness covered vision, hearing, speech, and a number of medical conditions (for example, asthma, hay fever, heart problems) and the duration for which some of these conditions had occurred.

In the realm of social functioning, we defined social impairment by how well children got along with their teacher, family, and peers, each on a 5-point scale ranging from very well to not well at all as identified by the parent (the sum of the three scales).

Family Variables

Mother's education was defined as less than secondary school education, completion of a secondary school education, or education beyond secondary school.

Family structure was defined, as in Sandefur, McLanahan, and Wojtkiewicz (1992), by a set of dummy variables for the following categories: (1) single-mother head (1983 and 1987) (persistent never married); (2) divorced, widowed, or separated mother head (1983); divorced, widowed, or separated mother head (1987) (persistent divorced, widowed, or separated); (3) single, widowed, divorced, or separated mother head (1983 only) (married mother, 1987), (4) single, widowed, divorced, or separated mother head (1987 only) (married mother, 1983); and (5) persistent married mother (1983, 1987).

Economic Variables

The Statistics Canada low-income cutoff is a national threshold measure of poverty that is based on low income, family size, and urbanization of the area of residence (Statistics Canada 1984). Statistics Canada calculates the percentage of gross income spent by the average Canadian family on food, shelter, and clothing and adds 20 percent. This figure corresponds to a given income level, which is identified as the low-income cutoff. We calculated the poverty threshold for 1983 and 1987. The 1987 measure was based on the follow up 1987 information on income and household size and 1983 information on the size of area of residence (since this variable was collected only in 1983).

In the OCHS and OCHS-FU, families were asked about their income in the year prior to the study (that is, 1982 and 1986, respectively). The Statistics Canada low-income cutoffs for 1982 were $15,732 for a family of three in a large urban center (population of 500,000 or more) and $11,537 for the same family living in a rural area. For a family of four in 1982, the low income cutoffs were $18,129 and $13,336 for a large urban center and a rural area, respectively. For 1986, the Statistics Canada low-income cutoffs for a family of three in a large urban and rural area were $18,799 and $13,785, respectively, and for a family of four, $21,663 and $15,936, respectively. Notably, Statistics Canada defines the size of a family unit without respect to family composition. For example, a family unit of three persons may be two parents and a child or a single parent and two children.

We based total family income for 1983 and 1987 on the year prior to the study (1982 or 1986). Responses were given in income categories. When more precision was required, we collapsed income categories and assigned families an income at the midpoint of the category.

Household economic status was total family income divided by the Statistics Canada low-income cutoffs appropriate for each household to give an income-to-needs ratio. We calculated the ratio by dividing family income by the Statistics Canada low-income cutoff threshold calculated for that family. An income-to-needs ratio of 1 indicates family income at the poverty threshold; less than 1, poor families', and greater than 1, nonpoor families.

We constructed dummy variables for each of the income-to-needs ratios of less than 1, 2–3, and greater than 3. Families with income-to-needs ratios of 1–2 were excluded from the regressions. Measures of long-term economic status were based on the ratio of family income to needs averaged from the 1983 and 1987 waves of data collection.

Duration of poverty is defined by the dummy variables sometimes poor (income-to-needs ratio of less than 1 in 1983 or 1987) and always poor (income-to-needs ratio of less than 1 in 1983 and 1987). Never-poor families were excluded from the regressions.

Timing of poverty was defined by the dummy variables early poor (income-to-needs ratio of less than 1 in 1983 but greater than 1 in 1987), late poor (income-to-needs ratio of less than 1 in 1987 but greater than 1 in 1983), and always poor (income-to-needs ratio of less than 1 in 1983 and 1987, as defined above). Never-poor families were excluded from the regressions.

Other Child and Family Variables

The child's sex was defined as male or female (1983). The child's birth weight was given in kilograms (1983).

No information on race was available for these data. Based on information collected on ethnicity from the Canadian census done closest in time to 1983 and 1987, the population of Ontario in 1981 was 8,534,260: 52.6 percent of British origin, 7.7 percent of French origin, 21.0 percent of European origin, 4.3 percent of Asian or African origin, 1.0 percent of aboriginal origin, 4.2 percent of another single origin, and 9.2 percent of multiple (mixed) origin (Census of Canada 1981). In 1986 the population was 9,001,170, including 32.4 percent of British origin, 5.9 percent of French origin, 20.3 percent of European origin, 5.0 percent of Asian or African origin, 0.6 percent of aboriginal origin, 2.0 percent of another single origin, and 33.8 percent of multiple (mixed) origin (Census of Canada 1986).

Analysis

We calculated means and standard deviations for all independent measures. Our purpose was to examine the effect on psychosocial morbidity of (1) maternal education and family structure (regression 1); (2) maternal education, family structure, and long-term economic measures (regressions 2–5, 8); and (3) maternal education, family structure, and long-term poverty measures (regressions 6, 7). We thus conducted linear regression analyses as specified for each of the psychosocial outcomes that included the following independent variables:

1. maternal education and family structure;
2. average income-to-needs ratio;
3. maternal education, family structure, and average income-to-needs;
4. maternal education, family structure, average total family income, and average number of children;
5. maternal education, family structure, average income-to-needs dummy variables (less than 1, 2–3, greater than 3);
6. maternal education, family structure, sometimes poor, and always poor;
7. maternal education, family structure, early poor, late poor, and always poor; and
8. maternal education, family structure, average income-to-needs ratio, and sex times the average income-to-needs interaction.

In addition, all of the above regressions include sex and birth weight. We excluded the regression analysis that used a variable specifying race since no information on race was available for these data. Sample size and goodness of fit were calculated for each regression.

RESULTS

The frequencies, means, and standard deviations of all independent variables are shown in table 9.1. The sample was almost equally split between boys and girls (50.8 percent and 49.2 percent, respectively). Over half the sample (57.5 percent) had at least completed high school. Most families had not been headed by a female in either 1983 or 1987 (86 percent); 1 percent had been persistently headed by a single mother; 6 percent had been persistently headed by a widowed, separated, or divorced mother; and 8 percent were headed by a female in either 1983 or 1987. We did not calculate persistent separated or divorced mothers (1983 and 1987) because of the small sample size ($n = 5$).

The Full Sample

We first analyzed the frequency of the outcomes school outcome, schoolwork, psychiatric disorder, social impairment, and chronic health problems by category

TABLE 9.1 / Characteristics of Children in the Sample

Variable	*n*	%	Mean	*SD*
Sex				
Male	1,121	50.8	0.51	
Female	1,156	49.2		0.50
Birth weight (kg)				
<2	33	1.5	3.36	
2 < 3	490	22.5		0.55
3 < 4	1,391	63.9		
4+	263	12.1		
Mother's education				
Less than high school	957	42.5	1.88	
Completed high school	607	27.0		0.85
Some or completed community college or university	686	30.5		
Family structure				
Never female head of household, 1983 and 1987	1,567	86.6		
Single female head of household, 1983 and 1987	10	0.6		
Divorced, widowed, or separated, 1983 and 1987	102	5.6	4.71	0.81
Female head, 1983 only	46	2.5		
Female head, 1987 only	85	4.7		
Average income-to-needs ratio			2.75	1.15
Average income ($)			50,455.34	19,617.38
Average number in household				
1	268	15.1	2.46	
2	841	47.3		0.90
3	503	28.3		
4	136	7.7		
5	33	1.8		
Income-to-needs ratio				
<1	83	5.3	0.05	0.22
1 < 2	331	21.0	0.21	0.41
2 < 3	542	34.4	0.34	0.48
>3	619	39.3	0.39	0.49

(Table continued on p. 246.)

TABLE 9.1 / (*continued*)

Variable	*n*	%	Mean	*SD*
Duration of poverty				
Never	1,379	83.2	0.83	0.37
Some of the time	278	16.8	0.17	0.37
All of the time	44	2.0	0.02	0.14
Early but not late	69	3.2	0.03	0.18
Late but not early	83	4.9	0.05	0.22
Child's age[a]				
8–11 years	782	39.9	12.3	
12–16 years	1,176	60.0		2.60

Source: Authors' calculations based on data from the Ontario Child Health and Follow-Up study (OCHS-FU) on 2,277 children.

a. Because of the time of sampling in the OCHS-FU, some children were seven years old ($n = 5$) and seventeen years old ($n = 30$). These children are included in the eight- to eleven-year-old and the twelve- to sixteen-year-old groups, respectively.

(table 9.2). In terms of academic outcomes, 2.4 percent of the sample had both failed a grade and had full-time or remedial education; and 7.3 percent had performed poorly or worse than average during the last six months. Over half the sample had five or fewer symptoms of a psychiatric disorder. About two-thirds of the sample (62.2 percent) had few social difficulties (zero to five). Over 95 percent of the sample had fewer than three chronic health problems.

The strongest correlations among the outcomes (table 9.3) were between psychiatric disorder and social impairment and schoolwork and social impairment. The weakest were between schoolwork and chronic health problems and school outcome and social impairment.

The results of the regression analysis for the outcome variables school outcome, schoolwork, psychiatric disorder, social impairment, and chronic medical problems are summarized in table 9.4. Including only statistically significant independent predictor variables allows us to present complicated data more simply, although actual statistical significance is less of interest than the size and direction of standardized regression coefficients and the sample size. Tables 9.5A–9.5E show the individual regression results for each variable.

As for the outcome variable school outcome (table 9.5A), the economic variables high average income-to-needs ratio, high average income, and high income-to-needs ratios (2–3 and greater than 3) were significantly and inversely related to poor school outcome in all regressions in which they appeared (that is, more economically advantaged children were significantly less likely to have had a poor school outcome). For poverty history variables, being in a family that was poor at least sometimes, particularly early in a child's life, was significantly associated with a poor school outcome. Maternal education was significantly and inversely

TABLE 9.2 / Frequency of Outcomes, by Category

Outcome	*n*	%
School outcome		
Failed and full-time remedial education	41	2.4
Failed only	192	11.0
Full-time remedial only	35	2.0
Neither	1,470	84.6
Schoolwork		
Not well at all	18	1.0
Not too well	110	6.3
Pretty well/average	474	27.3
Quite well/good	527	30.3
Very well/excellent	608	35.0
Psychiatric disorder: number of symptoms		
0–5	905	51.9
6–10	460	26.4
11–15	222	12.8
16–20	97	5.7
21+	58	3.4
Social impairment: number of difficulties in getting along with parents, teachers, and peers		
0–5	1,077	62.2
6–10	632	36.5
11+	23	1.3
Chronic health problems: number of symptoms		
0–2	1,581	95.4
3–4	56	3.3
5+	20	1.2

Source: Authors' calculations based on data from the Ontario Child Health and Follow-Up study (OCHS-FU) on 2,277 children.

related to poor school outcome in all regressions. The predictive power of this variable remained fairly consistent, even with the addition of other family or economic predictors. Family status was not significantly related to poor school performance, but both male sex and low birth weight were significantly associated with poor school outcome in all regressions.

The economic variables high average income-to-needs ratio and high average income were significantly inversely related to poor schoolwork in all regressions

TABLE 9.3 / Correlation Coefficients among Dependent Variables

	School Outcome	Schoolwork	Psychiatric Disorder	Social Impairment	Chronic Health Problems
School outcome		0.26	0.20	0.16	0.18
Schoolwork	0.26		0.33	0.37	0.15
Psychiatric disorder	0.20	0.33		0.58	0.19
Social impairment	0.16	0.37	0.58		0.18
Chronic health problems	0.18	0.15	0.19	0.18	

Source: Authors' calculations based on data from the Ontario Child Health and Follow-Up study (OCHS-FU) on 2,277 children.

in which they appeared (that is, more economically advantaged children were significantly less likely to have done poor schoolwork) (table 9.5B). Being poor early in a child's life was significantly associated with poor schoolwork. Maternal education was significantly and inversely related to poor school work in all regressions. The predictive power of this variable remained fairly consistent, even with the addition of other family or economic predictors. Transition to a female-headed family was also significantly associated with poor schoolwork in all regressions in which it appeared. Male sex was consistently significantly associated with poor schoolwork, but birth weight was not.

None of the economic or poverty history variables was significantly associated with psychiatric disorder (table 9.5C) except high average income-to-needs ratio, which was significantly and inversely related to psychiatric disorder in the regression that excluded maternal education and family status. Poverty early in a child's life closely approached significance for psychiatric disorder ($p < .06$). Maternal education was significantly and inversely associated with psychiatric disorder in all regressions where it appeared and varied little with the presence or absence of economic or poverty history variables. Male sex was significantly associated with psychiatric disorder, except where used as an interaction.

None of the economic or poverty history variables nor maternal education was significantly associated with social impairment (table 9.5D). Only transition to a single-parent family or being in a persistently single female–headed family was consistently and significantly associated with social impairment. Birth weight was a significant predictor of social impairment in one regression and neared significance in all other regressions (all $p < .09$).

None of the economic or poverty history variables, nor maternal education, nor sex was significantly associated with chronic medical problems (table 9.5E). Being in a family that was persistently separated, divorced, or widowed was most consistently related to chronic health problems, as was being in a female-headed family early in life ($p < .05$ in regressions 6 and 7; $p < .07$ in regressions 3, 4, 5, and 8).

Notably, all the adjusted R^2 values are 0.06 or less, signifying that the combination of variables entered into each regression accounted maximally for only 6 percent of the variance in outcome. We obtained the highest adjusted R^2 values for the academic variables, schoolwork (0.05–0.06) and school outcome (0.04–0.06).

Sample by Age and Sex

We also examined the regressions for schoolwork by age and sex (see tables 9.6A and 9.6B and tables 9.6C and 9.6D, respectively). The pattern of significant variables remained similar to that in the overall findings. Being in a female-headed family in 1987 was significantly associated with poor schoolwork only for older (twelve- to sixteen-year-old) children, whereas early poverty was associated with poor schoolwork only for younger (eight- to eleven-year-old) children. Poor schoolwork was significantly associated with being in a female-headed family in 1987 only for girls, whereas early poverty was associated with poor schoolwork only in boys.

As noted, the outcome variable school outcome is a composite variable examining two different types of school difficulties, failing a grade and the need for full-time remedial or special education. In this sample, 11.0 percent had failed a grade only, 2.0 percent required remedial or special education only, and 2.4 percent had both failed a grade and required full-time remedial or special education. As these outcomes may vary with the age of the child, we calculated the frequencies for eight- to eleven-year-olds and twelve- to sixteen-year-olds: 11.3 percent and 14.9 percent respectively for failed grade, and 5.0 percent and 3.8 percent for full-time remedial or special education. We ran separate logistic regressions for each of these outcomes to permit an examination of different associations between the independent family and economic variables and each outcome (results not shown).

The results of the logistic regression for the outcome variable failed a grade show that the same economic variables (average income-to-needs ratio, average income, and income-to-needs ratios of 2–3 and greater than 3) and poverty history variables (sometimes poor, early poor), as well as maternal education, were significantly related to a poor outcome in the same direction as they were to the composite variable. Transition to a female-headed family was not significantly related to failing a grade, whereas it was significantly related to the composite variable. Male sex and low birth weight also significantly predicted poor outcomes.

In the results of the logistic regression for full-time remedial or special education, economic and poverty history variables were significantly related to a poor outcome in the same direction as they were to the composite variable. Being in

(Text continued on p. 279.)

TABLE 9.4 / Predictors of OCHS-FU Children's School Outcome, Schoolwork, Psychiatric Disorders, Social Impairment, and Chronic Health Problems[a]

Independent Variable	Predictor				
	School Outcome	Schoolwork	Psychiatric Disorder	Social Impairment	Chronic Health Problems
Male	*(0.12, 0.19)	*(0.09, 0.19)	*(−0.00, 0.08)	*(0.05)	
Birth weight	*(−0.09, −0.08)	*(−0.04)		*(0.05)	
Mother's education	*(−0.14, −0.11)	*(−0.16, −0.12)	*(−0.10, −0.09)		
Single female head, 1983 and 1987				*(0.06, 0.07)	
Divorced/widowed/separated, 1983 and 1987					*(0.05, 0.06)
Female head, 1983 only					*(0.05)
Female head, 1987 only		*(0.06, 0.09)	*(0.07, 0.10)	*(0.07, 0.09)	
Average income-to-needs ratio	*(−0.15, −0.07)	*(−0.13, −0.07)	*(−0.09, −0.04)		

Average income ($1,000)	*(−0.12)	*(−0.08)			
Income-to-needs ratio					
2–3	*(−0.09)				
>3	*(−0.11)				
Duration of poverty					
Sometimes	*(0.09)				
Always	*(0.07)				
Early	*(0.12)	*(0.07)			
Adjusted R^2	0.04–0.06	0.05–0.06	0.01–0.02	0.00–0.02	0.00
N	1,391–1,595	1,391–1,595	1,406–1,605	1,397–1,593	1,332–1,524

Source: Authors' calculations based on data from the Ontario Child Health and Follow-Up study (OCHS-FU) on 2,277 children.

* Significant at $p < .05$ in at least one of eight regressions completed.

a. Values are ranges of standardized regression coefficients among significant regressions (minimum and maximum). See tables 9.5A–9.5E for complete results.

TABLE 9.5A / Replication Analysis: Predictors of School Outcome for OCHS-FU Children[a]

Independent Variable	Model 1[b]	2[c]	3[c]	4[c]	5[c]	6[d]	7[d]	8[c]
Sex	0.20*	0.20*	0.18*	0.18*	0.18*	0.18*	0.18*	0.28*
	(0.04)	(0.04)	(0.04)	(0.04)	(0.04)	(0.04)	(0.04)	(0.10)
	[0.14]	[0.13]	[0.12]	[0.12]	[0.12]	[0.12]	[0.12]	[0.19]
Birth weight (kg)	−0.10*	−0.12*	−0.11*	−0.11*	−0.11*	−0.12*	−0.12*	−0.11*
	(0.03)	(0.04)	(0.04)	(0.04)	(0.04)	(0.04)	(0.04)	(0.04)
	[−0.08]	[−0.09]	[−0.08]	[−0.08]	[−0.08]	[−0.09]	[−0.09]	[−0.08]
Mother's highest level of education	−0.13*		−0.10*	−0.10*	−0.11*	−0.12*	−0.12*	−0.10*
	(0.02)		(0.03)	(0.03)	(0.03)	(0.02)	(0.02)	(0.03)
	[−0.14]		[−0.12]	[−0.11]	[−0.12]	[−0.13]	[−0.13]	[−0.12]
Single female head of household, 1983 and 1987	0.07		−0.06	−0.12	−0.11	−0.20	−0.13	−0.05
	(0.28)		(0.28)	(0.28)	(0.28)	(0.29)	(0.29)	(0.28)
	[0.01]		[−0.01]	[0.01]	[−0.01]	[−0.02]	[−0.01]	[−0.00]
Divorced, widowed, or separated, 1983 and 1987	0.08		0.03	−0.00	0.01	−0.02	0.01	0.03
	(0.08)		(0.09)	(0.09)	(0.09)	(0.09)	(0.09)	(0.09)
	[0.03]		[0.01]	[−0.00]	[0.00]	[−0.01]	[0.00]	[0.01]
Female head, 1983 only	0.02		−0.05	−0.06	−0.06	−0.09	−0.10	−0.05
	(0.11)		(0.12)	(0.12)	(0.12)	(0.12)	(0.12)	(0.12)
	[0.00]		[−0.01]	[−0.01]	[−0.01]	[−0.02]	[−0.02]	[−0.01]
Female head, 1987 only	0.06		0.01	0.03	0.01	−0.03	0.02	0.01
	(0.08)		(0.10)	(0.10)	(0.10)	(0.10)	(0.10)	(0.10)
	[0.02]		[0.00]	[0.01]	[0.00]	[−0.01]	[0.00]	[0.00]

Average income-to-needs ratio	−0.10*	−0.07*					−0.05
	(0.02)	(0.02)					(0.03)
	[−0.15]	[−0.10]					[−0.07]
Average income ($1,000)			−0.00*				
			(0.00)				
			[−0.12]				
Average number in household			−0.01				
			(0.02)				
			[−0.01]				
Income-to-needs ratio							
<1				0.10			
				(0.10)			
				[0.03]			
2–3				−0.14*			
				(0.05)			
				[−0.09]			
>3				−0.17*			
				(0.06)			
				[−0.11]			
Duration of poverty							
Sometimes					0.21*		
					(0.07)		
					[0.09]		

(Table continued on p. 254.)

TABLE 9.5A / *(continued)*

	Model							
Independent Variable	1[b]	2[c]	3[c]	4[c]	5[c]	6[d]	7[d]	8[c]
Always						0.16 (0.14) [0.03]	0.34* (0.14) [0.07]	
Early							0.40* (0.09) [0.12]	
Late							0.01 (0.10) [0.00]	
Sex × average income-to-needs								−0.03 (0.03) [−0.07]
Constant	1.77	1.89	1.96	2.01	1.90	1.81	0.72	1.92
Adjusted R^2	0.04	0.04	0.05	0.05	0.05	0.05	0.06	0.05
N	1,595	1,471	1,415	1,391	1,415	1,415	1,415	1,415

Source: Authors' calculations based on data from the Ontario Child Health and Follow-Up study (OCHS-FU) on 2,277 children.

* Significant at $p < .05$.

a. Values are unstandardized regression coefficients. Standard errors in parentheses; standardized regression coefficients in brackets.

b. Examines mother's education, family structure, control variables, sex, and birth weight.

c. Examines mother's education, family structure, control variables, and measures of long-term economic status.

d. Examines mother's education, family structure, control variables, and measures of long-term poverty history.

TABLE 9.5B / Replication Analysis: Predictors of Schoolwork for OCHS-FU Children[a]

	Model							
Independent Variable	1[b]	2[c]	3[c]	4[c]	5[c]	6[d]	7[d]	8[c]
Sex	0.37* (0.05) [0.19]	0.35* (0.05) [0.18]	0.33* (0.05) [0.17]	0.33* (0.05) [0.17]	0.33* (0.05) [0.17]	0.33* (0.05) [0.17]	0.33* (0.05) [0.17]	0.18* (0.13) [0.09]
Birth weight (kg)	−0.07 (0.04) [−0.04]	−0.08 (0.05) [−0.04]	−0.07 (0.05) [−0.04]	−0.07 (0.05) [−0.04]	−0.06 (0.05) [−0.04]	−0.07 (0.05) [−0.04]	−0.07 (0.05) [−0.04]	−0.06 (0.05) [−0.04]
Mother's highest level of education	−0.19* (0.03) [−0.16]		−0.15* (0.03) [−0.13]	−0.15* (0.04) [−0.12]	−0.15* (0.03) [−0.13]	−0.17* (0.03) [−0.15]	−0.17* (0.01) [−0.15]	−0.15* (0.03) [−0.13]
Single female head of household, 1983 and 1987	0.31 (0.36) [0.02]		0.22 (0.36) [0.02]	0.18 (0.37) [0.01]	0.24 (0.37) [0.02]	0.24 (0.37) [0.02]	0.30 (0.37) [0.02]	0.19 (0.36) [0.01]
Divorced, widowed, or separated, 1983 and 1987	0.08 (0.10) [0.02]		0.02 (0.11) [0.01]	−0.02 (0.12) [−0.00]	0.03 (0.12) [0.00]	0.06 (0.12) [0.02]	0.08 (0.12) [0.02]	0.02 (0.11) [0.01]
Female head, 1983 only	−0.10 (0.15) [−0.02]		−0.10 (0.16) [−0.02]	−0.11 (0.16) [−0.02]	−0.09 (0.16) [−0.01]	−0.10 (0.16) [−0.02]	−0.11 (0.16) [−0.02]	−0.09 (0.16) [−0.02]
Female head, 1987 only	0.29* (0.11) [0.06]		0.40* (0.13) [0.08]	0.35* (0.14) [0.07]	0.41* (0.13) [0.08]	0.40* (0.13) [0.08]	0.43* (0.13) [0.09]	0.40* (0.13) [0.08]

TABLE 9.5B / *(continued)*

Independent Variable	Model 1[b]	2[c]	3[c]	4[c]	5[c]	6[d]	7[d]	8[c]
Average income-to-needs ratio		−0.11*	−0.06*					−0.08*
		(0.02)	(0.03)					(0.03)
		[−0.13]	[−0.07]					[−0.10]
Average income ($1,000)				−0.00*				
				(0.00)				
				[−0.08]				
Average number in household				0.02				
				(0.03)				
				[0.01]				
Income-to-needs ratio								
<1					0.04			
					(0.13)			
					[0.01]			
2–3					−0.02			
					(0.07)			
					[−0.01]			
>3					−0.13			
					(0.07)			
					[−0.07]			
Duration of poverty								
Sometimes						0.15		
						(0.09)		
						[0.05]		

(Table continued on p. 257.)

Always						−0.16 (0.19) [−0.03]	−0.02 (0.18) [−0.00]	
Early							0.32* (0.12) [0.07]	
Late							−0.02 (0.13) [−0.00]	
Sex × average income-to-needs								0.06 (0.04) [0.09]
Constant	2.46	2.46	2.56	2.56	2.52	2.42	2.42	2.63
Adjusted R^2	0.06	0.05	0.06	0.06	0.06	0.06	0.06	0.06
N	1,595	1,470	1,414	1,391	1,414	1,414	1,414	1,414

Source: Authors' calculations based on data from the Ontario Child Health and Follow-Up study (OCHS-FU) on 2,277 children.

* Significant at $p < .05$.

a. Values are unstandardized regression coefficients. Standard errors in parentheses; standardized regression coefficients in brackets.

b. Examines mother's education, family structure, control variables, sex, and birth weight.

c. Examines mother's education, family structure, control variables, and measures of long-term economic status.

d. Examines mother's education, family structure, control variables, and measures of long-term poverty history.

TABLE 9.5C / Replication Analysis: Predictors of Psychiatric Disorder in OCHS-FU Children[a]

Independent Variable	Model 1[b]	2[c]	3[c]	4[c]	5[c]	6[d]	7[d]	8[c]
Sex	0.91*	0.82*	0.79*	0.83*	0.80*	0.79*	0.79*	−0.05
	(0.30)	(0.31)	(0.31)	(0.31)	(0.31)	(0.31)	(0.31)	(0.80)
	[0.08]	[0.07]	[0.07]	[0.07]	[0.07]	[0.07]	[0.07]	[−0.00]
Birth weight (kg)	−0.10	−0.16	−0.13	−0.17	−0.13	−0.14	−0.13	−0.12
	(0.27)	(0.28)	(0.28)	(0.28)	(0.28)	(0.28)	(0.28)	(0.28)
	[−0.01]	[−0.01]	[−0.01]	[−0.02]	[−0.01]	[−0.01]	[−0.01]	[−0.01]
Mother's highest level of education	−0.73*		−0.69*	−0.66*	−0.68*	−0.67*	−0.67*	−0.69*
	(0.18)		(0.20)	(0.20)	(0.20)	(0.19)	(0.19)	(0.20)
	[−0.10]		[−0.10]	[−0.09]	[−0.10]	[−0.10]	[−0.10]	[−0.10]
Single female head of household, 1983 and 1987	2.07		2.04	1.71	1.72	1.63	1.89	1.92
	(2.25)		(2.22)	(2.24)	(2.27)	(2.28)	(2.29)	(2.23)
	[0.02]		[0.02]	[0.02]	[0.02]	[0.02]	[0.02]	[0.02]
Divorced, widowed, or separated, 1983 and 1987	1.10		1.18	0.96	0.99	0.99	1.08	1.18
	(0.63)		(0.69)	(0.71)	(0.72)	(0.73)	(0.73)	(0.69)
	[0.04]		[0.05]	[0.04]	[0.04]	[0.04]	[0.04]	[0.05]
Female head, 1983 only	1.08		1.38	1.31	1.31	1.21	1.15	1.41
	(0.92)		(0.95)	(0.95)	(0.95)	(0.96)	(0.96)	(0.95)
	[0.03]		[0.04]	[0.04]	[0.04]	[0.03]	[0.03]	[0.04]
Female head, 1987 only	2.84*		2.40*	2.21*	2.37*	2.20*	2.37*	2.40*
	(0.69)		(0.80)	(0.83)	(0.79)	(0.81)	(0.82)	(0.80)
	[0.10]		[0.08]	[0.07]	[0.08]	[0.07]	[0.08]	[0.08]

Average income-to-needs ratio	−0.46*	−0.04					−0.20
	(0.13)	(0.15)					(0.21)
	[−0.09]	[−0.01]					[−0.04]
Average income ($1,000)			−0.01				
			(0.01)				
			[−0.03]				
Average number in household			−0.09				
			(0.18)				
			[−0.01]				
Income-to-needs ratio							
<1				0.09			
				(0.80)			
				[0.00]			
2–3				−0.62			
				(0.43)			
				[−0.05]			
>3				−0.30			
				(0.45)			
				[−0.03]			
Duration of poverty							
Sometimes					0.70		
					(0.57)		
					[0.04]		

(Table continued on p. 260.)

TABLE 9.5C / *(continued)*

	Model							
Independent Variable	1[b]	2[c]	3[c]	4[c]	5[c]	6[d]	7[d]	8[c]
Always						−0.34 (1.12) [−0.01]	0.29 (1.08) [0.01]	
Early							1.43 (0.75) [0.05]	
Late							−0.07 (0.77) [−0.00]	
Sex × average income-to-needs								0.30 (0.27) [0.08]
Constant	7.78	8.06	7.89	8.48	8.13	7.72	7.70	8.28
Adjusted R^2	0.02	0.01	0.02	0.02	0.02	0.02	0.02	0.02
N	1,605	1,483	1,429	1,406	1,429	1,429	1,429	1,429

Source: Authors' calculations based on data from the Ontario Child Health and Follow-Up study (OCHS-FU) on 2,277 children.

* Significant at $p < .05$.

a. Values are unstandardized regression coefficients. Standard errors in parentheses; standardized regression coefficients in brackets.

b. Examines mother's education, family structure, control variables, sex, and birth weight.

c. Examines mother's education, family structure, control variables, and measures of long-term economic status.

d. Examines mother's education, family structure, control variables, and measures of long-term poverty history.

TABLE 9.5D / Replication Analysis: Predictors of Social Impairment in OCHS-FU Children[a]

	Model							
Independent Variable	1[b]	2[c]	3[c]	4[c]	5[c]	6[d]	7[d]	8[c]
Sex	0.21*	0.15	0.14	0.15	0.13	0.14	0.13	−0.34
	(0.10)	(0.11)	(0.11)	(0.11)	(0.11)	(0.11)	(0.11)	(0.28)
	[0.05]	[0.04]	[0.04]	[0.04]	[0.03]	[0.03]	[0.03]	[−0.08]
Birth weight (kg)	0.19*	0.18	0.18	0.17	0.18	0.18	0.18	0.19
	(0.09)	(0.10)	(0.10)	(0.10)	(0.10)	(0.10)	(0.10)	(0.10)
	[0.05]	[0.05]	[0.05]	[0.04]	[0.05]	[0.05]	[0.05]	[0.05]
Mother's highest level of education	−0.07		−0.06	−0.05	−0.05	−0.04	−0.04	−0.06
	(0.06)		(0.07)	(0.07)	(0.07)	(0.07)	(0.07)	(0.07)
	[−0.03]		[−0.03]	[−0.02]	[−0.02]	[−0.02]	[−0.02]	[−0.03]
Single female head of household, 1983 and 1987	2.16*		2.16*	2.14*	1.81*	1.83*	1.95*	2.09*
	(0.77)		(0.77)	(0.78)	(0.79)	(0.79)	(0.80)	(0.77)
	[0.07]		[0.07]	[0.07]	[0.06]	[0.06]	[0.07]	[0.07]
Divorced, widowed, or separated, 1983 and 1987	0.23		0.19	0.14	0.04	0.02	0.06	0.19
	(0.22)		(0.24)	(0.25)	(0.25)	(0.25)	(0.26)	(0.24)
	[0.03]		[0.02]	[0.02]	[0.01]	[0.00]	[0.01]	[0.02]
Female head, 1983 only	0.39		0.55	0.53	0.49	0.48	0.46	0.57
	(0.31)		(0.33)	(0.33)	(0.33)	(0.33)	(0.33)	(0.33)
	[0.03]		[0.04]	[0.04]	[0.04]	[0.04]	[0.04]	[0.05]
Female head, 1987 only	0.70*		0.91*	0.85*	0.91*	0.87*	0.94*	0.91*
	(0.24)		(0.28)	(0.29)	(0.28)	(0.28)	(0.29)	(0.28)
	[0.07]		[0.09]	[0.08]	[0.09]	[0.08]	[0.09]	[0.09]

(Table continued on p. 262.)

TABLE 9.5D / *(continued)*

	Model							
Independent Variable	1[b]	2[c]	3[c]	4[c]	5[c]	6[d]	7[d]	8[c]
Average income-to-needs ratio		−0.08	−0.01					−0.09
		(0.05)	(0.05)					(0.07)
		[−0.04]	[−0.00]					[−0.05]
Average income ($1,000)				−0.00				
				(0.00)				
				[−0.02]				
Average number in household				0.05				
				(0.06)				
				[0.02]				
Income-to-needs ratio								
<1					0.49			
					(0.28)			
					[0.05]			
2–3					−0.10			
					(0.15)			
					[−0.02]			
>3					0.03			
					(0.16)			
					[0.01]			

Duration of poverty								
Sometimes						0.10 (0.20) [0.01]		
Always						0.60 (0.39) [0.05]	0.66 (0.38) [0.05]	
Early							0.43 (0.26) [0.04]	
Late							−0.27 (0.27) [−0.03]	
Sex × average income-to-needs								0.17 (0.09) [0.14]
Constant	4.45	4.66	4.47	4.46	4.49	4.44	4.44	4.69
Adjusted R^2	0.01	0.00	0.01	0.01	0.02	0.01	0.02	0.02
N	1,593	1,474	1,418	1,397	1,418	1,418	1,418	1,418

Source: Authors' calculations based on data from the Ontario Child Health and Follow-Up study (OCHS-FU) on 2,277 children.

* Significant at $p < .05$.

a. Values are unstandardized regression coefficients. Standard errors in parentheses; standardized regression coefficients in brackets.

b. Examines mother's education, family structure, control variables, sex, and birth weight.

c. Examines mother's education, family structure, control variables, and measures of long-term economic status.

d. Examines mother's education, family structure, control variables, and measures of long-term poverty history.

TABLE 9.5E / Replication Analysis: Predictors of Chronic Health Problems in OCHS-FU Children[a]

Independent Variable	Model 1[b]	2[c]	3[c]	4[c]	5[c]	6[d]	7[d]	8[c]
Sex	0.06	0.01	0.03	0.05	0.03	0.03	0.03	0.11
	(0.06)	(0.06)	(0.06)	(0.06)	(0.06)	(0.06)	(0.06)	(0.16)
	[0.03]	[0.01]	[0.02]	[0.02]	[0.01]	[0.02]	[0.02]	[0.05]
Birth weight (kg)	−0.02	−0.05	−0.03	−0.03	−0.03	−0.03	−0.03	−0.03
	(0.05)	(0.06)	(0.06)	(0.06)	(0.06)	(0.06)	(0.06)	(0.06)
	[−0.01]	[−0.02]	[−0.02]	[−0.01]	[−0.02]	[−0.02]	[−0.02]	[−0.02]
Mother's highest level of education	−0.05		−0.04	−0.04	−0.05	−0.04	−0.04	−0.04
	(0.03)		(0.04)	(0.04)	(0.04)	(0.04)	(0.04)	(0.04)
	[−0.04]		[−0.03]	[−0.03]	[−0.03]	[−0.03]	[−0.04]	[−0.04]
Single female head of household, 1983 and 1987	0.04		0.05	−0.05	0.03	0.08	0.07	0.05
	(0.45)		(0.46)	(0.46)	(0.47)	(0.47)	(0.47)	(0.46)
	[0.00]		[0.00]	[−0.00]	[0.00]	[0.00]	[0.00]	[0.00]
Divorced, widowed, or separated, 1983 and 1987	0.29*		0.27*	0.24	0.29*	0.29*	0.29*	0.28*
	(0.12)		(0.13)	(0.14)	(0.14)	(0.14)	(0.14)	(0.13)
	[0.06]		[0.06]	[0.05]	[0.06]	[0.06]	[0.06]	[0.06]
Female head, 1983 only	0.31		0.37	0.35	0.37	0.38*	0.38*	0.37
	(0.18)		(0.19)	(0.19)	(0.19)	(0.19)	(0.19)	(0.19)
	[0.04]		[0.05]	[0.05]	[0.05]	[0.05]	[0.05]	[0.05]
Female head, 1987 only	0.10		0.09	0.08	0.10	0.10	0.10	0.09
	(0.13)		(0.15)	(0.16)	(0.15)	(0.15)	(0.16)	(0.15)
	[0.02]		[0.02]	[0.01]	[0.02]	[0.02]	[0.02]	[0.02]

Average income-to-needs ratio	−0.04	0.01					0.02
	(0.03)	(0.03)					(0.04)
	[−0.04]	[0.01]					[0.02]
Average income ($1,000)			−0.00				
			(0.00)				
			[−0.02]				
Average number in household			−0.05				
			(0.03)				
			[−0.04]				
Income-to-needs ratio							
<1				0.10			
				(0.15)			
				[0.02]			
2–3				0.11			
				(0.08)			
				[0.05]			
>3				0.08			
				(0.09)			
				[0.04]			
Duration of poverty							
Sometimes					−0.03		
					(0.11)		
					[−0.01]		
Always					−0.03	−0.06	
					(0.21)	(0.21)	
					[−0.00]	[−0.01]	

(Table continued on p. 266.)

TABLE 9.5E / *(continued)*

Independent Variable	Model 1[b]	2[c]	3[c]	4[c]	5[c]	6[d]	7[d]	8[c]
Early							−0.05 (0.15) [−0.01]	
Late							−0.02 (0.15) [−0.00]	
Sex × average income-to-needs								−0.03 (0.05) [−0.04]
Constant	0.57	0.72	0.59	0.75	0.53	0.61	0.61	0.55
Adjusted R^2	0.00	−0.00	0.00	0.00	0.00	0.00	0.00	0.00
N	1,524	1,407	1,354	1,332	1,354	1,354	1,354	1,354

Source: Authors' calculations based on data from the Ontario Child Health and Follow-Up study (OCHS-FU) on 2,277 children.

* Significant at $p < .05$.

a. Values are unstandardized regression coefficients. Standard errors in parentheses; standardized regression coefficients in brackets.

b. Examines mother's education, family structure, control variables, sex, and birth weight.

c. Examines mother's education, family structure, control variables, and measures of long-term economic status.

d. Examines mother's education, family structure, control variables, and measures of long-term poverty history.

TABLE 9.6A / Predictors of Schoolwork for OCHS-FU Children Aged Eight to Eleven Years[a]

	Model							
Independent Variable	1[b]	2[c]	3[c]	4[c]	5[c]	6[d]	7[d]	8[c]
Sex	0.40*	0.36*	0.36*	0.36*	0.37*	0.37*	0.37*	0.33
	(0.07)	(0.07)	(0.08)	(0.08)	(0.08)	(0.08)	(0.08)	(0.20)
	[0.21]	[0.19]	[0.19]	[0.19]	[0.19]	[0.19]	[0.19]	[0.18]
Birth weight (kg)	−0.07	−0.07	−0.05	−0.04	−0.05	−0.07	−0.06	−0.05
	(0.07)	(0.07)	(0.07)	(0.07)	(0.07)	(0.07)	(0.07)	(0.07)
	[−0.04]	[−0.04]	[−0.03]	[−0.02]	[−0.03]	[−0.04]	[−0.03]	[−0.03]
Mother's highest level of education	−0.19*		0.14*	−0.13*	−0.15*	−0.16*	−0.16*	−0.14*
	(0.04)		(0.05)	(0.05)	(0.05)	(0.05)	(0.05)	(0.05)
	[−0.17]		[−0.12]	[−0.11]	[−0.13]	[−0.13]	[−0.13]	[−0.12]
Single female head of household, 1983 and 1987	0.31		0.23	0.17	0.21	0.16	0.22	0.23
	(0.41)		(0.42)	(0.43)	(0.43)	(0.44)	(0.44)	(0.42)
	[0.03]		[0.02]	[0.02]	[0.02]	[0.02]	[0.02]	[0.02]
Divorced, widowed, or separated, 1983 and 1987	0.24		0.17	0.12	0.16	0.20	0.22	0.17
	(0.15)		(0.17)	(0.18)	(0.18)	(0.18)	(0.18)	(0.17)
	[0.06]		[0.04]	[0.03]	[0.04]	[0.05]	[0.05]	[0.04]
Female head, 1983 only	−0.10		−0.17	−0.18	−0.16	−0.17	−0.18	−0.16
	(0.21)		(0.22)	(0.23)	(0.23)	(0.23)	(0.23)	(0.22)
	[−0.02]		[−0.03]	[−0.03]	[−0.03]	[−0.03]	[−0.03]	[−0.03]
Female head, 1987 only	0.28		0.31	0.24	0.30	0.24	0.29	0.31
	(0.17)		(0.19)	(0.20)	(0.19)	(0.20)	(0.20)	(0.19)
	[0.06]		[0.06]	[0.05]	[0.07]	[0.05]	[0.06]	[0.06]

(Table continued on p. 268.)

TABLE 9.6A / *(continued)*

Independent Variable	Model							
	1[b]	2[c]	3[c]	4[c]	5[c]	6[d]	7[d]	8[c]
Average income-to-needs ratio		−0.10*	−0.06					0.06
		(0.03)	(0.04)					(0.05)
		[−0.13]	[−0.07]					[−0.07]
Average income ($1,000)				−0.00				
				(0.00)				
				[−0.09]				
Average number in household				0.01				
				(0.05)				
				[0.01]				
Income-to-needs ratio								
<1					0.11			
					(0.20)			
					[0.02]			
2–3					−0.08			
					(0.10)			
					[−0.04]			
>3					−0.08			
					(0.11)			
					[−0.04]			
Duration of poverty								
Sometimes						0.28*		
						(0.14)		
						[0.10]		

Always						0.24 (0.27) [−0.04]	0.02 (0.25) [0.00]	
Early							0.48* (0.18) [0.10]	
Late							0.06 (0.19) [0.02]	
Sex × average income-to-needs								0.01 (0.07) [0.02]
Constant	2.42	2.37	2.44	2.43	2.37	2.33	2.30	2.45
Adjusted R^2	0.07	0.05	0.06	0.06	0.05	0.06	0.06	0.06
N	672	637	611	605	611	611	611	611

Source: Authors' calculations based on data from the Ontario Child Health and Follow-Up study (OCHS-FU) on 2,277 children.

* Significant at $p < .05$.

a. Values are unstandardized regression coefficients. Standard errors in parentheses; standardized regression coefficients in brackets.

b. Examines mother's education, family structure, control variables, sex, and birth weight.

c. Examines mother's education, family structure, control variables, and measures of long-term economic status.

d. Examines mother's education, family structure, control variables, and measures of long-term poverty history.

TABLE 9.6B / Predictors of Schoolwork for OCHS-FU Children Aged Twelve to Sixteen Years[a]

	Model							
Independent Variable	1[b]	2[c]	3[c]	4[c]	5[c]	6[d]	7[d]	8[c]
Sex	0.34* (0.07) [0.17]	0.34* (0.07) [0.17]	0.31* (0.07) [0.15]	0.31* (0.07) [0.16]	0.31* (0.07) [0.16]	0.31* (0.07) [0.15]	0.31* (0.07) [0.15]	0.06 (0.18) [0.03]
Birth weight (kg)	−0.07 (0.06) [−0.04]	−0.08 (0.06) [−0.05]	−0.09 (0.06) [−0.05]	−0.09 (0.06) [−0.05]	−0.08 (0.06) [−0.04]	−0.08 (0.06) [−0.05]	−0.09 (0.06) [−0.05]	−0.08 (0.06) [−0.04]
Mother's highest level of education	−0.19* (0.04) [−0.16]		−0.16* (0.05) [−0.13]	−0.15* (0.05) [−0.13]	−0.16* (0.05) [−0.13]	−0.19* (0.04) [−0.16]	−0.19* (0.04) [−0.16]	−0.16* (0.04) [−0.13]
Single female head of household, 1983 and 1987	0.37 (0.70) [0.02]		0.24 (0.69) [0.01]	0.21 (0.70) [0.01]	0.32 (0.71) [0.02]	0.34 (0.71) [0.02]	0.42 (0.71) [0.02]	0.16 (0.70) [0.01]
Divorced, widowed, or separated, 1983 and 1987	−0.04 (0.14) [−0.01]		−0.10 (0.15) [−0.02]	−0.15 (0.16) [−0.03]	−0.07 (0.16) [−0.02]	−0.03 (0.16) [−0.01]	−0.01 (0.16) [−0.00]	−0.10 (0.15) [−0.02]
Female head, 1983 only	−0.11 (0.21) [−0.02]		−0.04 (0.22) [−0.01]	−0.05 (0.22) [−0.01]	−0.04 (0.22) [0.01]	−0.04 (0.23) [−0.01]	−0.05 (0.23) [−0.01]	−0.04 (0.22) [−0.01]
Female head, 1987 only	0.30* (0.15) [0.06]		0.47* (0.18) [0.09]	0.44* (0.19) [0.08]	0.47* (0.18) [0.09]	0.50* (0.18) [0.10]	0.53* (0.18) [0.10]	0.47* (0.18) [0.09]

	(1)	(2)	(3)	(4)	(5)	(6)	(7)
Average income-to-needs ratio	−0.11* (0.03) [−0.13]	−0.06 (0.03) [−0.07]					−0.11* (0.14) [−0.12]
Average income ($1,000)			−0.00 (0.00) [−0.08]				
Average number in household			0.01 (0.04) [0.01]				
Income-to-needs ratio							
<1				−0.02 (0.18) [−0.00]			
2–3				0.01 (0.10) [0.01]			
>3				−0.19 (0.10) [−0.09]			
Duration of poverty							
Sometimes					0.08 (0.13) [0.03]		
Always					−0.11 (0.26) [−0.02]	−0.05 (0.26) [−0.01]	

(Table continued on p. 272.)

TABLE 9.6B / *(continued)*

Independent Variable	Model							
	1[b]	2[c]	3[c]	4[c]	5[c]	6[d]	7[d]	8[c]
Early							0.22 (0.17) [0.05]	
Late							−0.06 (0.17) [−0.01]	
Sex × average income-to-needs								0.09 (0.06) [0.14]
Constant	2.53	2.54	2.70	2.72	2.57	2.56	2.57	2.80
Adjusted R^2	0.05	0.04	0.06	0.05	0.06	0.05	0.05	0.06
N	919	828	799	782	799	799	799	799

Source: Authors' calculations based on data from the Ontario Child Health and Follow-Up study (OCHS-FU) on 2,277 children.

* Significant at $p < .05$.

a. Values are unstandardized regression coefficients. Standard errors in parentheses; standardized regression coefficients in brackets.

b. Examines mother's education, family structure, control variables, sex, and birth weight.

c. Examines mother's education, family structure, control variables, and measures of long-term economic status.

d. Examines mother's education, family structure, control variables, and measures of long-term poverty history.

TABLE 9.6C / Predictors of Schoolwork for Male OCHS-FU Children[a]

Independent Variable	Model 1[b]	2[c]	3[c]	4[c]	5[c]	6[d]	7[d]
Birth weight (kg)	−0.04 (0.06) [−0.02]	−0.06 (0.06) [−0.04]	−0.05 (0.06) [−0.03]	−0.04 (0.07) [−0.02]	−0.05 (0.07) [−0.03]	−0.05 (0.07) [−0.03]	−0.06 (0.07) [−0.03]
Mother's highest level of education	−0.16* (0.04) [−0.13]		−0.13* (0.05) [−0.11]	−0.11* (0.05) [0.09]	−0.13* (0.05) [−0.11]	−0.14* (0.05) [−0.12]	−0.14* (0.05) [−0.12]
Single female head of household, 1983 and 1987	0.26 (0.71) [0.01]		0.19 (0.71) [0.01]	−0.02 (0.71) [−0.00]	−0.21 (0.72) [−0.01]	0.14 (0.72) [0.01]	0.02 (0.72) [0.00]
Divorced, widowed, or separated, 1983 and 1987	0.02 (0.15) [0.00]		−0.03 (0.16) [−0.01]	−0.15 (0.17) [−0.04]	−0.03 (0.17) [−0.01]	−0.05 (0.17) [−0.01]	−0.04 (0.18) [−0.01]
Female head, 1983 only	−0.17 (0.22) [−0.03]		−0.12 (0.23) [−0.02]	−0.15 (0.23) [−0.02]	−0.10 (0.23) [−0.02]	−0.15 (0.24) [−0.02]	−0.19 (0.24) [−0.03]
Female head, 1987 only	0.11 (0.19) [0.02]		0.25 (0.21) [0.04]	0.23 (0.22) [0.04]	0.25 (0.21) [0.04]	0.21 (0.22) [0.04]	0.29 (0.22) [0.05]
Average income-to-needs ratio		−0.08* (0.03) [−0.09]	−0.04 (0.04) [−0.05]				

(Table continued on p. 274.)

TABLE 9.6C / *(continued)*

Independent Variable	Model						
	1[b]	2[c]	3[c]	4[c]	5[c]	6[d]	7[d]
Average income ($1,000)				−0.01*			
				(0.00)			
				[−0.10]			
Average number in household				−0.07			
				(0.05)			
				[−0.06]			
Income-to-needs ratio							
<1					−0.03		
					(0.18)		
					[−0.01]		
2–3					−0.09		
					(0.10)		
					[−0.04]		
>3					−0.13		
					(0.11)		
					[−0.06]		
Duration of poverty							
Sometimes						0.19	
						(0.14)	
						[0.04]	

Always						0.02 (0.25) [0.00]	−0.15 (0.24) [0.03]
Early							0.36* (0.18) [0.08]
Late							−0.13 (0.19) [−0.03]
Sex × average income-to-needs							
Constant	2.68	2.66	2.76	3.03	2.73	2.67	2.67
Adjusted R^2	0.01	0.01	0.01	0.02	0.01	0.01	0.02
N	818	764	733	718	733	732	733

Source: Authors' calculations based on data from the Ontario Child Health and Follow-Up study (OCHS-FU) on 2,277 children.

* Significant at $p < .05$.

a. Values are unstandardized regression coefficients. Standard errors in parentheses; standardized regression coefficients in brackets.

b. Examines mother's education, family structure, control variables, sex, and birth weight.

c. Examines mother's education, family structure, control variables, and measures of long-term economic status.

d. Examines mother's education, family structure, control variables, and measures of long-term poverty history.

TABLE 9.6D / Predictors of Schoolwork for Female OCHS-FU Children[a]

Independent Variable	Model 1[b]	2[c]	3[c]	4[c]	5[c]	6[d]	7[d]
Birth weight (kg)	−0.11	−0.10	−0.08	−0.08	−0.08	−0.09	−0.09
	(0.06)	(0.07)	(0.07)	(0.07)	(0.07)	(0.07)	(0.07)
	[−0.06]	[−0.05]	[−0.05]	[−0.05]	[−0.04]	[−0.05]	[−0.05]
Mother's highest level of education	−0.23*		−0.17*	−0.18*	−0.18*	−0.21*	−0.21*
	(0.04)		(0.05)	(0.05)	(0.04)	(0.04)	(0.04)
	[−0.21]		[−0.16]	[−0.16]	[0.16]	[−0.18]	[−0.18]
Single female head of household, 1983 and 1987	0.30		0.19	0.31	0.20	0.31	0.40
	(0.41)		(0.42)	(0.42)	(0.43)	(0.43)	(0.44)
	[0.03]		[0.02]	[0.03]	[0.02]	[0.03]	[0.04]
Divorced, widowed, or separated, 1983 and 1987	0.13		0.18	0.10	0.11	0.16	0.19
	(0.14)		(0.16)	(0.16)	(0.16)	(0.17)	(0.17)
	[0.03]		[0.02]	[0.03]	[0.03]	[0.04]	[0.05]
Female head, 1983 only	−0.04		−0.07	−0.05	−0.05	−0.05	−0.04
	(0.20)		(0.21)	(0.21)	(0.21)	(0.21)	(0.21)
	[−0.01]		[−0.01]	[−0.01]	[−0.01]	[−0.01]	[−0.01]
Female head, 1987 only	0.43*		0.52*	0.44*	0.53*	0.54*	0.56*
	(0.14)		(0.17)	(0.17)	(0.17)	(0.17)	(0.17)
	[0.11]		[0.12]	[0.10]	[0.12]	[0.12]	[0.13]
Average income-to-needs ratio		−0.14*	−0.07*				
		(0.03)	(0.03)				
		[−0.18]	[−0.09]				

Average income ($1,000)	−0.00 (0.00) [−0.06]		
Average number in household	0.09 (0.04) [0.09]		
Income-to-needs ratio			
<1		0.17 (0.20) [0.03]	
2–3		0.06 (0.10) [0.03]	
>3		−0.13 (0.10) [−0.07]	
Duration of poverty			
Sometimes			0.17 (0.13) [0.06]

(Table continued on p. 278.)

TABLE 9.6D / *(continued)*

Independent Variable	Model 1[b]	2[c]	3[c]	4[c]	5[c]	6[d]	7[d]
Always						−0.40 (0.29) [−0.06]	−0.26 (0.29) [−0.04]
Early							−0.30 (0.17) [0.07]
Late							0.05 (0.17) [0.01]
Sex × average income-to-needs							
Constant	2.66	2.59	2.69	2.43	2.51	2.56	2.54
Adjusted R^2	0.06	0.06	0.06	0.05	0.06	0.05	0.05
N	777	681	681	673	681	681	681

Source: Authors' calculations based on data from the Ontario Child Health and Follow-Up study (OCHS-FU) on 2,277 children.

* Significant at $p < .05$.

a. Values are unstandardized regression coefficients. Standard errors in parentheses; standardized regression coefficients in brackets.

b. Examines mother's education, family structure, control variables, sex, and birth weight.

c. Examines mother's education, family structure, control variables, and measures of long-term economic status.

d. Examines mother's education, family structure, control variables, and measures of long-term poverty history.

the category always poor also predicted a poor outcome. Maternal education and transition to a female-headed family significantly predicted a poor outcome less consistently than they did for the composite variable; the predictive power of maternal education decreased in the presence of economic variables. Male sex and poor outcome were not significant predictors of poor outcome in the presence of economic variables.

One additional logistic regression for having ever failed a grade focused on children twelve years old and older in 1987. These children, who were eight to eleven years old in 1983, were more likely than the younger children (four to seven years old in 1983) to have ever failed a grade. This regression shows results very similar to that for having ever failed a grade over the full age range. The predictive power associated with being in a persistently female-headed household decreased slightly, and the predictive power of being in a female-headed family in 1983 increased slightly, but all family status variables remained insignificant.

To examine the influence of the independent variable income-to-needs ratio on the outcome variables more carefully, we ran a number of additional linear regressions in which we extended the range of average income-to-needs ratio. The outcome variable schoolwork was used for these regressions since it had the largest explained variance of all outcomes.

First, we extended the range of income-to-needs ratios at the upper end: we divided families with income-to-needs ratios of greater than 3 into those with income-to-needs ratios of 3–4 (22.9 percent of the sample; $n = 367$) and those with an income-to-needs ratio greater than 4 (16.2 percent of the sample; $n = 260$). With the extended income-to-needs ratios in regression 5 (excluding families with an income-to-needs ratio of 1–2), only the highest income-to-needs ratio category came close to significance (inverse relationship, $p < .06$) (results not shown), whereas none did previously. The significance of all other variables remained consistent.

Next, we subdivided the families into finer categories by income-to-needs ratio (less than 0.5, 0.5–1.0, 1.0–1.5, 1.5–2.0, 2.0–2.5, 2.5–3.0, 3.0–3.5, 3.5–4.0, and greater than 4.0). Each sequential category accounted for the following proportion of the sample: 0.7, 4.7, 8.7, 12.3, 19.0, 15.4, 12.5, 10.4, and 16.2 percent (n = 11, 76, 140, 197, 305, 246, 201, 166, and 260, respectively). Using these income-to-needs ratios and income-to-needs ratios 1.0–1.5 and 1.5–2.0 in regression 5, we found that only the highest income-to-needs ratio was inversely significantly related to the outcome variables ($p < .05$) (results not shown). The lowest income-to-needs ratio approached significance ($p < .08$), and the significance of all other variables remained consistent.

DISCUSSION

The economic indicators related to low income and income below the Statistics Canada low-income cutoff significantly predicted academic and psychiatric difficulties. Additionally, being poor sometime in a child's life, particularly early in life, placed a child at risk for academic difficulties. Low levels of maternal education and transition into a female-headed family later in life were significant risk factors for poor academic performance and for emotional and behavioral problems. Living in a family with a female head persistently, or in a family that becomes a female-headed family, predicted social impairment. In addition, boys are significantly more likely than girls to experience academic and behavioral problems.

Psychiatric Difficulties and Low Economic Status

The finding that indicators of low economic status are associated with academic and psychiatric difficulties is consistent with previous work using data from the OCHS and OCHS-FU. Lipman, Offord, and Boyle (1994) found that a consistent threshold of family income less than $10,000 was associated with increased morbidity for all outcomes and was strongly and significantly associated with all outcomes measured. The odds of four- to sixteen-year-old children from families with low income having a psychiatric disorder, poor school performance, and social impairment were 2.43, 3.06, and 3.21 respectively. Increased morbidity among younger children (four- to eleven-year-olds) appeared stronger than among older ones (twelve- to sixteen-year-olds), but no significant age differences were found.

Similarly, Offord, Boyle, and Jones (1987) found that children six to sixteen years old from families who had received public assistance such as welfare as any portion of their income over the last year had a significantly increased rate of one or more psychiatric disorders and poor school performance (relative odds 2.84 and 2.86, respectively). This relationship was particularly strong among young boys (six- to eleven-year-olds) for psychiatric disorder and among young girls for poor school performance (relative odds 4.12 and 5.96, respectively).

Based on our analyses of young (eight- to eleven-year-old) and old (twelve- to sixteen-year-old) children for poor schoolwork only, transition to a female-headed family later in life significantly predicts poor schoolwork for older children (twelve to sixteen years old) only, whereas early poverty significantly predicts poor schoolwork in younger children only. The sensitivity of younger children to morbidity associated with early poverty has been reported previously (Carnegie Corporation of New York 1994).

The study by Munroe Blum, Boyle, and Offord (1988) using cross-sectional OCHS data deserves mention. The authors found that children from single-parent families had a significantly higher rate of emotional and behavioral problems and academic difficulties than did children from non-single-parent families. However, this significant association was eliminated when markers of hardship, such as family income less than $10,000 or the receipt of welfare, were taken into account. In the OCHS data set, cross-sectionally low income appears to be a stronger marker for psychiatric and academic morbidity than single-parent status, although we have shown both to have a strong and significant role for these morbidities using longitudinal data in this chapter. Notably, with these longitudinal data and these variables, the predictive power of maternal education remains quite consistent in regressions with or without low economic status variables. This result clearly indicates the need to use longitudinal data sets to capture the relative influences of various markers of poverty.

In our analyses, indicators of low economic status affected academic performance more powerfully than they did psychiatric disorder. This result is consistent with previous work with OCHS and OCHS-FU data, which demonstrated no significant association between low income (less than $10,000) in 1983 and psychiatric disorder in 1987 (Lipman, Offord, and Boyle 1994). The group of children with a psychiatric disorder in 1987 consisted of those with a disorder in 1983 that persisted to 1987 and those with a new disorder in 1987. Psychiatric disorders arising later in life (for example, in adolescence) are less often associated with adverse family circumstances such as poverty and will therefore mute the relationship between low economic status and psychiatric disorder (Rutter et al. 1976).

Academic Performance and Low Economic Status

Poverty appears to be most detrimental to academic performance when it occurs early in a child's life. The school outcome variable, as a lifetime measure of school performance, inflated the number of children performing poorly in school after 1983 and reported in 1987 because that group included those with poor school performance in 1983. However, the variable schoolwork, measured in 1987 only, was also significantly associated with early poverty. These findings are consistent with Lipman, Offord, and Boyle's (1994) work using the OCHS, which showed significantly increased prevalence rates of poor school performance in 1987 among eight- to sixteen-year-olds who lived in families with incomes less than $10,000 in 1983. But unlike our findings that study found social impairment to be associated with early low income. This difference is likely due to the use of different variables in the models for social impairment. Rutter et al. (1976) have claimed that, among those exposed to poverty, younger children may be at higher risk of psychiatric morbidity than older children, in whom psychopathology is less often associated with adverse family circumstances such as poverty.

The composite outcome variable of school outcome combines two concepts, having ever failed a grade and having ever been in full-time remedial or special education. Work done in the United States suggests that these two outcomes may vary differently with poverty, with grade failure being significantly associated with low economic status (Guo, Brooks-Gunn, and Harris 1995). In contrast, special education is not associated with low economic status and may even be associated with more advantaged families, possibly because they are better advocates for their children. Separate bivariate analysis of these outcomes using the OCHS and OCHS-FU data revealed that markers of low economic status and some poverty history, especially early poverty, significantly predicted both outcomes more consistently than family status and low maternal education markers did. We found no difference in the pattern of significantly predictive variables when we restricted the analysis of those who had failed a grade to older children, who would have had a greater chance of failing a grade in their school career. These results suggest, first, that poor children in Ontario are significantly more likely to fail a grade and receive special education than nonpoor children are and, second, that access to special education programs in Ontario is not restricted to students from more advantaged families; in fact, the poor may be overrepresented in these programs.

The finding that low birth weight is not associated with poor schoolwork seems surprising since low birth weight is commonly associated with physical and developmental disabilities, and affected children may do worse in school; one would therefore expect an inverse relationship between birth weight and poor schoolwork. However, the poor schoolwork variable examined school performance over the last six months. It did not specifically take into account the child's class placement or long-term school record. For example, a child's academic performance over the last six months may be good only in relation to the rest of a special education class. The variable of school outcome, which examined school failure and the need for remedial education, was more likely to detect children with physical or developmental disabilities and had a significant inverse relationship with low birth weight.

Social Impairment

Social impairment was not influenced significantly by economic and poverty history variables but was significantly influenced by family composition. Children who had lived in families persistently headed by a single mother appear to have had the most difficulties in social interactions, followed by children in a family that became female-headed later in life. Issues of self-esteem and psychological distress related to a family breakup and disruption (for example, loss of income, need to move, change of home or school) may influence the social interactions in the latter group, as children of divorce are known to commonly suffer poor adjustment, at home and school, and depression (Wallerstein 1991). For the former group, social relationships may be difficult in school and with peers because of material deficiencies and an associated inability to afford the clothes or toys of their peers or to participate in activities such as sports or other nonskill development activities (for example, Offord, Last, and Barrette 1985).

Chronic Health Problems

The finding that chronic health problems were not significantly associated with economic or poverty history markers contrasts with other work using OCHS data.

Cadman et al. (1986) found higher rates of chronic health problems and functional limitations among four- to sixteen-year-old children of families whose income was below the Statistics Canada low-income cutoff based on cross-sectional OCHS data. However, the population studied in this chapter was relatively healthy: 72.8 percent reported no health problems. The inclusion of the other family status variables in our longitudinal analyses likely accounts for this difference in findings.

The strong and significant relationship between being in a family that is persistently separated, divorced, or widowed and chronic health problems is noteworthy. Possibly the child's illness is related to maternal marital status in that such families have increased divorce or separation rates (for example, pre-1983), although one would anticipate that transition to a single-parent family might also be significantly associated with such problems. Caring for a chronically ill child may make a mother less likely to meet others and therefore to change her marital status. A familial hereditary disease may also influence both paternal death and a child's medical status.

Our work makes clear the importance of examining family status in greater detail than allowed by the classic dichotomy of single-parent versus two-parent family, since different family constellations show significantly different influences on children's morbidity. Transition to a single-mother family seems to be most consistently detrimental to child well-being and development. Certainly the literature in the area of divorce indicates significant difficulties for many children of divorce (Wallerstein 1991).

Why Is Explained Variance So Low?

Another very striking result of our regressions is the small amount of variance for any given outcome variable that is explained by the predictor variables: the maximum was only 6 percent. In contrast, Duncan, Brooks-Gunn, and Klebanov (1994), for example, found that more than one-third of the variance of the developmental outcomes was accounted for by a similar group of family and economic variables.

MATERNAL REPORT The low explained variance may be influenced by the fact that data on all outcome variables were obtained by maternal report only. Mothers may underreport the child's depression or anxiety, which may decrease estimates of psychiatric disorder or social impairment. However, maternal depression is known to be highly prevalent in women of childbearing age and may influence mothers to overestimate their child's difficulties (Weissman 1987; Downey and Coyne 1990). Single mothers have been shown to have significantly higher rates of chronic low-grade depression (Weissman, Leaf, and Bruce 1987).

THE SAMPLE The finding of little relationship between family and economic variables may be a characteristic of this diverse, non-high-risk sample. A higher-risk sample, such as that used by Duncan, Brooks-Gunn, and Klebanov (1994), might show higher levels of association and explained variance. As well, in the OCHS-FU children were eight to sixteen years of age at the time of data collection. The absence of children younger than eight years may have muted the relationship between family and economic deprivation and morbidity, as the youngest children may feel these effects most strongly (Carnegie Corporation 1994). Data loss between 1983 and 1987 was most prevalent among participants with higher levels of psychopathology and more family risk variables such as low income (Boyle et al. 1991). Loss of this subgroup, which would have shown the strongest relationship between family and economic predictors and morbidity, also attenuated the relationship seen between these predictors and outcome. Finally, the degree of disadvantage or morbidity experienced between 1983 and 1987, the two years in which data were collected, is unknown. For example, a family may have had low income in 1983 and 1987 but higher income consistently between these points, so the children from that family would be less likely to experience morbidity associated with low income. In contrast to data sets with more frequent points of data collection, the OCHS may be less sensitive to more chronic cases of disadvantage. This difference again may have muted the association found between family and economic variables and psychosocial morbidity.

MEASUREMENT ISSUES The unreliability of the measures may limit the strength of the association between family and economic variables, and psychosocial morbidity, as may limited variability in the exposure and outcome variables. For example, concerning the latter, the vast majority of families (86 percent), sampled were not single-parent families and the lack of variability in family status may have attenuated to a degree the relationship between family status and morbidity. We defined the outcome variables as continuous variables to allow a linear regression, whereas much of the previous work with the OCHS data set demonstrating a strong and significant relationship between economic variables and morbidity used dichotomous variables (for example, Offord, Boyle, and Jones 1987; Munroe Blum, Boyle, and Offord 1988). Even though one would not expect this contrast to make large differences in the influence of predictor variables, we did further logistic regressions using dichotomous variables to check this possibility. For the dichotomous variables school outcome (presence or absence of failed or full-time remedial education) and chronic health problems (presence or absence of one or more health problems or functional limitations in the last six months), logistic regression results revealed patterns of association (or lack of association) between predictor and outcome variables almost identical to those found with linear regression (data not shown). In addition, we performed a number of linear regressions on the influence of average income-to-needs ratio alone versus the influence of a 1983 income less than $10,000 to examine whether the definition of economic disadvantage influenced the magnitude of the explained variance. We found no significant increases in the explained variances obtained for the outcomes tested (schoolwork, school outcome, psychiatric disorder, and social impairment) (data not shown).

CANADA-U.S. DIFFERENCES The differences between Ontario (or, more broadly, Canada) and the United States may substantively account for the differences in explained variance between the analysis of the Ontario and the U.S. samples. The lower strength of the association between family and economic indicators and psychosocial disadvantage in the OCHS data may truly reflect the fact that Ontario does not have the same degree of psychosocial disadvantage as some of the U.S. populations sampled (for example, Duncan, Brooks, and Klebanov 1994). The average income of the families in the OCHS and OCHS-FU sample was approximately $50,000 ($60,416 U.S.; 1992 dollars). The average income of a family of four in Ontario in 1993 was approximately $65,000 ($78,540 U.S.). The OCHS average income seems quite high but is comparable to the provincial average at the time.

The OCHS and OCHS-FU may also include as poor many families that are near poor, that is, whose incomes are 10–20 percent below the Statistics Canada low-income threshold. This situation may differ from that in U.S. poor populations, in which fewer families are near poor and many have incomes substantially below the poverty threshold.

The social programs in Canada, or the "safety net," may have decreased the effect of predictor variables on psychosocial outcome. If a child in a family in Ontario and one in the United States are equally poor, the Canadian child may experience less morbidity, for example, as a result of the availability of health insurance or of less variation in schools between rich and poor neighborhoods. This is the explanation suggested by the analysis demonstrating that full-time remedial or special education is significantly predicted by low economic status, in contrast to U.S. findings (Guo, Brooks-Gunn, and Harris 1995).

In an attempt to more closely match the poverty levels of the OCHS and OCHS-FU population and the U.S. data, we analyzed the outcome variable schoolwork with the Statistics Canada low-income cutoff set at 0.75 of its value. The results differed from the original regressions only in that the predictive power of the variables that included the Statistics Canada low-income cutoff in their derivation (that is, income-to-needs ratios) increased (results not shown). For example, in regression 2 the beta coefficient for average income-to-needs ratio increased from −0.11 to −0.81, and in regression 7 the beta coefficient for always poor increased from −0.02 to 0.39. All significant and nonsignificant predictor variables remained the same, and the predictive power of maternal education remained unchanged (results not shown). Thus, even if the OCHS and OCHS-FU had focused not on a general population sample but on a higher-risk (that is, lower-income) population that might have more closely approximated a U.S. sample, the general results would not have changed significantly. Again, the Ontario "safety net" of more universal services may allow poor children and nonpoor children to differ less than one would expect in the United States.

Chapter 11, the only other study in this book to examine Canadian data, examines a population from Quebec that can be considered more high risk since it includes younger children (six- to twelve-year-olds) from a more disadvantaged population than the OCHS and OCHS-FU sample. For example, 64.6 percent and

13.9 percent of the families in the Quebec sample were never poor and always poor, versus 83.2 percent and 2.0 percent in the Ontario sample, respectively. This is not surprising given that the poverty rate for families in Quebec has been higher than the national average over at least the last fifteen years, whereas the rate in Ontario has been lower (in 1981, 1986, and 1991, for Quebec 14.1 percent, 14.6 percent, and 15.9 percent, respectively; for Ontario 9.5 percent, 8.5 percent, and 11.3 percent, respectively; the national average was 11.3 percent, 11.8 percent, and 13.0 percent, respectively) (Ross, Shillington, and Lochhead 1994).

Our results highlight the richness of comparative work using data from various provinces, states or countries. As noted by Hofferth (1995b), the need for common models and the knowledge and interpretation of differences in public policy can facilitate such comparisons (for example, Kamerman and Kahn, 1982).

CONCLUSION

In summary, markers of low economic status significantly predicted academic difficulties and, to a lesser extent, psychiatric difficulties. Early poverty also placed a child at risk for academic problems. Low maternal education and transition into a female-headed family later in life were significant risk factors for poor academic performance and emotional and behavioral problems. Living in a persistently female-headed family or living in such a family later in life predicted social impairment. Overall, economic, poverty, and family status variables poorly accounted for child morbidity in our analyses, possibly because of bias in the sample (introduced by data loss and sample selection and age). The nature of the OCHS sample and Canada-U.S. policy differences may also have influenced the relationship. Clearly, thoroughly understanding the relationship between family and economic indicators and child morbidity requires a broad knowledge of the population and context studied.

Ellen Lipman was supported by a New Faculty Research Award from the Ontario Mental Health Foundation. David Offord was supported by a National Health Scientist Award from Health Canada. The authors thank Michael Boyle for his helpful consultation, Rupak Mazumdar for his computer assistance, and Diane Klepey for her word processing assistance.

NOTES

1. See Boyle et al. (1987) for a detailed description of the survey methodology and instrumentation of the OCHS.
2. The sample loss between 1983 and 1987 has been evaluated for four- to twelve-year-olds. In brief, 72.5 percent of the children participating in 1983 took part in the 1987

follow-up. Of the children lost from the analysis, about half lived in households that could not be traced, and about half lived in traced households that either refused to participate or had missing information. Nonparticipants at follow-up, based on 1983 characteristics, had a significantly increased risk for conduct disorder and hyperactivity, low income, and family dysfunction. Sample loss did not affect the evaluation of the outcome of disorder (that is, clinically important sequelae such as the persistence of a disorder) and the risk for disorder (that is, risk factors associated with the onset of a new disorder).

Chapter 10

Family Economic Hardship and Adolescent Adjustment: Mediating and Moderating Processes

Rand D. Conger, Katherine Jewsbury Conger, and Glen H. Elder, Jr.

In this chapter we first consider the influence of economic hardship on the school performance of rural adolescents over a four-year period from seventh to tenth grade, building upon initial analyses from the Infant Health and Development Program (IHDP) (see chapter 1). We replicated the earlier research as closelyas possible using a sample of adolescents who provided information regarding their grade point averages (GPAs). Despite differences in the samples and outcomes, we found substantial similarities between the earlier analyses and our own.

For the second phase of the inquiry we substituted externalizing and internalizing problems for GPA and repeated the first set of analyses. This extension examines negative dimensions of adolescent adjustment and determines whether the results related to cognitive functioning will generalize to other types of adolescent behavior. In the third stage of the study, we elaborated upon the replicative findings by proposing a set of mediating processes through which, we hypothesized, family economic disadvantage would affect school performance during adolescence. In particular, we predicted that economic hardship would create daily strains and conflicts in families that would both directly and indirectly influence the lives of adolescents (see Conger et al. 1994). Moreover, we expected financial conflicts between parents to affect the academic competencies of boys more adversely than those of girls, thus implicating sex as an important moderator of these economic stress processes. We first consider the replication study and then report the findings that extend these basic results.

THE REPLICATION STUDY

In their original analyses and in later extensions of that work, Duncan and Brooks-Gunn (see chapter 1) demonstrated the adverse influence of economic disadvantage on the cognitive development of five-year-old children (see, for example, Duncan, Brooks-Gunn, and Klebanov 1994). Their findings showed that low family income (total income divided by the poverty level for a family of a particular size, the income-to-needs ratio) over a four-year period was associated with significantly reduced IQ scores in a sample of approximately 1,000 five-year-old children living in several locations in the northeastern, southeastern, and southern United States. Income relative to family needs influenced IQ even with controls for the children's sex, ethnicity, birthweight (the sample was composed of low-birth-weight children), the receipt of special services for low-birth-weight children, the mother's education, and family structure (head of household and number of persons in the household).

Several variations in economic status measures did not significantly improve upon the income-to-needs ratio as a predictor of children's IQ. The investigators examined whether (1) income influences were curvilinear, (2) poverty status had a greater impact if it was of longer duration, and (3) the timing of poverty (that is, whether it occurred early or late during the four-year period) increased its impact on children's development. The primary message from all of these analyses was that greater poverty for longer periods of time adversely influences children's cognitive development and that this corrosive effect is most parsimoniously captured through the income-to-needs ratio. That is, adding other poverty measures to the regression equations did not significantly increase the explained variance in the outcome beyond that obtained using the measure of income relative to needs.

In our attempt to replicate these findings, we addressed the issue with a quite different sample, one composed of adolescents rather than preschoolers. Moreover, we had available a different measure of cognitive development as a criterion variable, self-reported GPA, rather than a standardized IQ score. In addition, whereas the families in the Duncan and Brooks-Gunn sample were predominantly African American, single parent, and poor at least some of the time, those in our sample were white, primarily two parent, and on average above the poverty line in terms of family income. Given the differences in the study populations, and especially the lower degree of economic deprivation in our sample, one might expect that the findings would not be the same across studies.

Sample

The sample for the replication regression analyses consisted of 357 youths who were seventh graders at year 1 of the study. In 1992, year 4, the tenth-grade adolescents in the study ranged in age from 14.0 to 17.0 years with a mean age of 15.6 years. The subjects represent a subgroup from a larger study of 451 white, primarily lower-middle- or middle-class, intact families. Only white families were selected because there are too few minority families in rural Iowa, where the study was conducted, to generate meaningful data for them. The retention rate at each wave of data collection was about 95 percent. The overall retention rate from 1989

(N = 451) to 1992 (N = 404) was 90 percent, although the final sample for these analyses included just the 357 families for whom we had complete data across all four years.

At wave 1, each family included two parents, a seventh-grade girl or boy, and a sibling within four years of age. These families are part of a study of economic hardship, family relationships, and psychological well-being. They lived in one of eight adjacent counties in Iowa, a midwestern state, and were selected for study because of the dramatic, adverse changes in the rural economy produced by the crisis in agriculture in the 1980s (Murdock and Leistritz 1988). At the initiation of the study, 34 percent of the families lived on farms, 12 percent lived in rural areas but not on a farm, and 54 percent lived in towns or small cities with a population under 6,500 (under 5,000 in all but one of the towns). Families were interviewed in 1989 for wave 1 of the panel study and again each year through 1992. The median ages of the parents at the initiation of the study were thirty-nine years for fathers and thirty-eight years for mothers. Over the course of the study family size ranged from 3.0 to 13.0 members, with the average being 4.86. Divorce or separation occurred in 7 percent of the families in the sample over the four years of the study. Family income from all sources averaged across four years was $39,262. According to federal poverty guidelines, 21 percent of the families had incomes at or below poverty adjusted for family size at some time during the four years of the study.

Procedures

Families were recruited through all public and private schools in the eight counties. Names and addresses of seventh-grade students and their parents were obtained from all schools in communities of 6,500 or less in the identified counties. All eligible families were sent a letter explaining the project and subsequently contacted by telephone and asked to participate. About 78 percent of the families agreed to be interviewed. Family members were each compensated at a rate of about $10 per hour for time spent in the study.

Every year, two interviews of approximately two hours were conducted at each family's home. During the first session, each of the four family members completed a set of questionnaires about the family's economic circumstances, recent activities, individual characteristics, and the quality of relationships and interactions with other family members, friends, and people in their community. During the second interview, which occurred within two weeks of the first, family members were videotaped as they participated in four structured interaction tasks designed to facilitate family discussion and interaction and intended to provide researchers with information on the social skills, parenting behaviors, and emotional affect demonstrated in the relationships between specific family-member dyads.

After explaining the procedures, completing a practice card with the family, and checking the video-recording equipment for task 1, the interviewer left the room for another part of the house where she or he could not hear the discussion.

Family members were asked to take turns reading out loud each question listed on a series of cards. They then discussed one another's answers and repeated some questions, if necessary, until the interviewer returned. A video camera recorded the family's interactions during their discussions. At the end of task 1, the interviewer returned, stopped the discussion, and described task 2. The remaining three tasks were conducted in a similar fashion.

The observations used in this study were obtained from the first interaction task, in which all four family members discussed general questions about family life, such as household chores, family activities, special events, school performance, and parenting. Trained observers coded the videotapes using the Iowa Family Interaction Rating Scales, a global rating system in which context, frequency, and emotional affect are used to determine how characteristic particular behaviors are for each focal person (Melby et al. 1993). The code includes several dimensions of individual characteristics (for example, humor, escalate negative) and the behaviors each family member directed toward other family members (for example, hostility, warmth, lecturing, moralizing). Each behavior or characteristic has a specific definition, and coders are trained to assign a score ranging from 1 (no evidence of the behavior or not characteristic) to 9 (behavior mainly characteristic based on either high frequency or high intensity of the behavior, or both) for every family member. Observers received two months of training and had to pass extensive written and viewing tests before they could code videotapes. A separate, independent coder also rated each task for the same family. For the 1992 interviews, approximately 25 percent of all tasks were randomly assigned to a second observer so that interobserver reliability coefficients (an intraclass correlation) could be estimated. For additional details regarding the observational rating system see Lorenz and Melby (1994).

Measures

ADOLESCENT'S ACADEMIC PERFORMANCE Academic performance was assessed through self-report of GPA by the tenth-grade adolescent who was the target child in each family. The year 4 GPA was the dependent variable or outcome measure. Each adolescent reported his or her own GPA on a scale of 0–11, where 0 was F or failing and 11 was A. The mean GPA for the sample was 7.82, a B average.

ADOLESCENT'S SEX In the regression analyses, the target child's sex was coded female (0) or male (1). Only those families with complete data across all four waves were used in the regression analyses, so the sample included 193 girls and 164 boys.

PARENT EDUCATION The mother's and father's years of completed education were assessed at year 1 by parent self-report. The means were 13.29 years for mothers and 13.57 years for fathers, which indicated completion of high school plus some college-level education.

MARITAL STATUS All marriages were intact at year 1, a requirement for participation, but some couples separated or divorced during the four years of the study. By year 4, 32 couples of the original 451 had either separated or divorced. For regression purposes, we coded marital status as 1 if the couple had separated or divorced and 0 if the couple remained married during the course of the study.

INCOME-TO-NEEDS RATIO Using poverty guidelines published annually in the *Federal Register* (for example, U.S. Department of Commerce 1989), we calculated the poverty income for each family for each of the four years included in the analyses. The guidelines specify what types of income may be used to determine eligibility for various government needs-based programs. The income-to-needs ratio is computed by a formula that takes family size and economies of scale into account to make possible comparisons across varying income levels and household sizes. We summed the income-to-needs-ratios for each family for each of the four years and then divided by four to create a measure of average income-to-needs.

AVERAGE INCOME We summed all sources of family income eligible for inclusion under the federal poverty guidelines described above and divided by four to create a measure of average total income. The mean average income for the families was $39,262 over the course of the study.

AVERAGE HOUSEHOLD SIZE Because of the criteria for inclusion in the study, the average household size of the families in the sample, 4.86 over four years, was slightly larger than would be expected for national norms (U.S. Department of Commerce 1989).

INCOME-TO-NEEDS GROUPS Using the income-to-needs ratio, we constructed a measure of long-term economic status averaged over the four years of the study and identified different income-to-needs groups to investigate possible curvilinear relationships in the data. An income-to-needs ratio of less than 1, for example, indicates that a family's average income during the four years of the study was below the poverty threshold. Based on this dichotomy, we created five mutually exclusive groups for use in the regression equations: group 1 was below the poverty threshold (with an income-to-needs ratio of less than 1); group 2 had a ratio from 1 to 2; group 3, from 2 to 3; group 4, from 3 to 4, and group 5, greater than 4.

DURATION OF POVERTY Two dummy variables, also based on the income-to-needs ratio, were created to indicate whether the family was poor (1) at some time during the four years of the study or (2) during all four years of the study. Never-poor families were excluded from the regressions.

TIMING OF POVERTY The timing of poverty was measured by three dummy variables: whether the family was poor (1) during the child's early adolescence (ages twelve to fourteen years) but not late ages (fifteen to seventeen years), (2) late but not early, or (3) during all four years. Never-poor families were excluded from these regression equations.

TABLE 10.1 / Characteristics of the Families in the Sample

Variable	Mean	*SD*
Outcome variable		
Target child's self-report of grade point average in tenth grade	7.78	2.19
Family-level background variables		
Target child's sex (male = 1)	0.47	0.50
Mother's years of completed education	13.29	1.65
Father's years of completed education	13.57	2.06
Divorced or separated (yes = 1)	0.07	0.25
Family-level income variables		
Average income to needs ratio	2.83	1.75
Average income ($1,000)	39,986	22,874
Average number in household	4.85	0.95
Income-to-needs ratio		
< 1 = 1	0.04	0.19
1–2 = 1	0.26	0.44
2–3 = 1	0.37	0.48
3–4 = 1	0.20	0.40
> 4 = 1	0.14	0.35
Duration of poverty		
Never	0.79	0.44
Some of the time	0.21	0.44
All of the time	0.01	0.07
Timing of poverty		
Never	0.79	0.44
Early but not late	0.04	0.20
Late but not early	0.14	0.35
Early and late	0.01	0.07

Source: Authors' calculations using data from the Iowa Youth and Families Project, years 1–4, on 357 youths.

Results and Discussion

Table 10.1 shows the means and standard deviations for the variables used in the replication analyses. Several of the measures used in the Duncan and Brooks-Gunn study (chapter 1, this volume) are not relevant to the replication sample (for example, the children's birth weight and ethnicity) and thus do not appear in the table. The data contrast dramatically with the descriptive statistics from the earlier study. For example, the families in the Iowa sample had an average income (income-to-needs) over four years that was 2.83 times greater than the poverty level, compared with a figure of 1.77 for the families in the IHDP. Nevertheless, 21 percent of the Iowa families were poor at least some of the time during the study, still substantially less than the 42 percent of those in the IHDP. Another sharp contrast involves marital status. All of the Iowa families were intact at the beginning of the study, but 7 percent of them had divorced or separated by 1992. In the IHDP sample, at least 65 percent of the families had other than an intact marital situation at some time during the course of the research.

The regression coefficients in table 10.2 show the results for the attempted replication. Consistent with the IHDP analyses, we used only the mother's education in the regressions. In findings that included father's education as well (not shown) the results did not change substantially: that is, none of the coefficients in table 10.2 became statistically significant that were not, and vice versa. Thus, although adding the father's education added explained variance in GPA, we omit it here to maintain greater compatibility with the IHDP analyses. The child's sex and family-level variables alone account for 14 percent of the variance in GPA (column 1) (adjusted $R^2 = .14$). Being a male was negatively related to GPA in the tenth grade, ($b = -.58$, $p < .05$); while the mother's education was positively related to school achievement ($b = .44$, $p < .05$). Moreover, separation or divorce disrupted academic performance ($b = -.34$, $p < .05$). The remaining findings in the table repeat the results of the IHDP analyses. For example, the family's average income-to-needs ratio predicted better cognitive performance after controlling for family and child characteristics ($b = .15$, column 3), as was the case for the IHDP study.

Household size did not influence academic achievement (column 4), although it was related to children's IQ scores in the IHDP study. Net of other family and child characteristics, income-to-needs ratios of 3–4 ($b = .73$) or greater than 4 ($b = .84$) were especially related to academic performance (column 5), whereas being poor some of the time ($b = .78$) was particularly detrimental to school achievement (column 6). Finally, recent poverty had a more detrimental influence on GPA than earlier poverty did (column 7). These results are consistent with those from the IHDP study except that lower income-to-needs and the duration of poverty had more dramatic effects in that sample, likely because of the much larger proportion of children and families who were extremely poor for long periods of time.

We added the interaction term between sex and income-to-needs ratio to determine whether the sex of the child conditioned the influence of economic circumstances on school performance (column 8). As was the case for the IHDP study, this interaction term was not statistically significant. Taken together, the results are quite consistent with those of the earlier study: (1) the income-to-needs ratio was significantly related to cognitive functioning net of other important background characteristics, (2) this ratio was a good summary indicator of economic status in the sense that it captured both the promotive aspects of affluence (column 5) and the detrimental consequences of extreme disadvantage (column 6), and (3) the mother's education had a strong independent influence on cognitive abilities. Contrary to the earlier findings, the sex of the adolescent was significantly and independently associated with GPA, suggesting differential, sex-related socialization histories between the preschool and teenage years. In addition, our results indicate a significant family structure influence on cognitive functioning, also inconsistent with the IHDP findings.

Given the extreme differences between our sample and the IHDP sample (that is, the ages of the children, ethnicity, family composition, geographic location, socioeconomic status, and measure of cognitive ability), the similarity in findings is rather remarkable. The data clearly show that economic advantage facilitated cognitive abilities as manifested by improved school performance whereas economic disadvantage impaired intellectual functioning. The remaining analyses address two possible extensions of these findings. First, we asked whether the basic regression equations estimated thus far would also predict other forms of adolescent adjustment—specifically, internalizing and externalizing problems. Second, we returned to the analysis of GPA to ask how the linkage between family financial status and child cognitive functioning came to exist. Duncan, Brooks-Gunn, and Klebanov (1994) showed that for the IHDP families the influence of higher income relative to needs on IQ was partially explained by the richer learning environment it enabled parents to provide for their young children. In the following extension of the basic findings reviewed thus far, we examine other specific family processes that might play a similar mediational role.

EXTENDING THE BASIC REPLICATION STUDY: ADOLESCENT PROBLEM BEHAVIORS

An obvious question regarding the replication model is whether it is generalizable to other forms of adolescent adjustment. For example, Duncan, Brooks-Gunn, and Klebanov (1994) report that the same basic model used to predict early childhood IQ in the IHDP study also predicts externalizing and internalizing symptoms. That is, indicators of economic status such as the income-to-needs ratio and duration of poverty predict these dimensions of maladjustment with controls for the background factors (for example, the child's sex, family structure, parents' education) examined in both the IHDP and our study. An important limitation of those findings, however, was their reliance on the mother's report of adjustment problems.

As the authors note, mothers' accounts of their child's behavior correlate only modestly with other sources of information (for example, teachers' reports) and are confounded with mothers' own mental health (Duncan, Brooks-Gunn, and Klebanov 1994, 315). That is, mothers depressed by their financial situation may be more likely to perceive their children as being distressed as well. Thus, correlations between family economic status and maternal reports of a child's problems may be a spurious reflection of the association between financial difficulties and mothers' psychological distress. In our study we eliminated this confounding by using the parents' report of family financial circumstances and the adolescents' report of their own externalizing or internalizing symptoms.

If Duncan, Brooks-Gunn, and Klebanov's (1994) finding of a positive relation-

(Text continued on p. 299.)

TABLE 10.2 / Replication Analysis: Effects of Family Composition and Economic Status on Children's Grade Point Average in Tenth Grade[a]

	Model							
Independent variable	1	2	3	4	5	6	7	8
Child variable								
Sex (male = 1)	−0.58*	−0.51*	−0.56*	−0.56*	−0.59*	−0.57*	−0.58*	−0.56*
	(0.21)	(0.23)	(0.21)	(0.21)	(0.21)	(0.21)	(0.21)	(0.21)
	[−0.13]	[−0.12]	[−0.13]	[−0.13]	[−0.14]	[−0.13]	[−0.13]	[−0.13]
Family-Level variables								
Mother's years of completed education at year 1	0.44*		0.40*	0.40*	0.39*	0.44*	0.45*	0.40*
	(0.06)		(0.07)	(0.07)	(0.07)	(0.06)	(0.06)	(0.07)
	[0.33]		[0.31]	[0.31]	[0.30]	[0.34]	[0.34]	[0.31]
Marital status (separated or divorced)	−0.34*		−0.32*	−0.32*	−0.32*	−0.30*	−0.29*	−0.32*
	(0.12)		(0.12)	(0.12)	(0.12)	(0.12)	(0.12)	(0.12)
	[−0.14]		[−0.13]	[−0.13]	[−0.14]	[−0.12]	[−0.12]	[−0.13]
Family economic status								
Average income-to-needs ratio		0.25*	0.15*					0.15*
		(0.06)	(0.06)					(0.06)
		[0.20]	[0.12]					[0.12]

Average income ($1,000)	0.01*		
	(0.01)		
	[0.12]		
Average number in household	−0.03		
	(0.11)		
	[−0.02]		
Income-to-needs ratio[b]			
< 1		−0.83	
		(0.61)	
		[−0.07]	
2–3		0.43	
		(0.27)	
		[0.09]	
3–4		0.73*	
		(0.32)	
		[0.13]	
> 4		0.84*	
		(0.36)	
		[0.13]	
Duration of poverty[c]			
Some of the time			−0.78*
			(0.26)
			[−0.15]
All of the time			−0.02
			(1.43)
			[.001]

(Table continued on p. 298.)

TABLE 10.2 / *(continued)*

Independent variable	Model 1	2	3	4	5	6	7	8
Timing of poverty								
Early but not late							−0.22	
							(0.50)	
							[−0.02]	
Late but not early							−0.94*	
							(0.32)	
							[−0.15]	
All of the time							−0.78	
							(1.41)	
							[−0.03]	
Sex of child by average income-to-needs interaction								0.08
								(0.12)
								[0.03]
Constant	2.99	7.35	3.01	3.17	3.26	3.04	2.86	3.02
Adjusted R^2	0.14	0.05	0.15	0.15	0.16	0.16	0.16	0.15

* $p < .05$, two-tailed. + $p < .10$, two-tailed.

Source: Authors' calculations based on ordinary least squares unstandardized regressions using data on 357 youths from the Iowa Youth and Families Project, years 1–4.

a. Values are unstandardized regression coefficients. Standard errors in parentheses; standardized coefficients in brackets.

b. Children from families with income-to-needs ratios of 1–2 were the omitted group.

c. Children from families that were never poor were the omitted group.

ship between economic status and child behavior problems resulted from a method artifact, then we might expect to find no association between adolescents' problem behaviors and the economic status indicators used in the IHDP study and our own. In addition, results from our own and other earlier research indicate that the relationship between economic status and adolescents' internalizing and externalizing problems is indirect through the actions of parents (Conger et al. 1994; McLoyd et al. 1994). Therefore, we should find no direct relationship between family economic hardship and adolescent maladjustment.

Measures

ADOLESCENT'S INTERNALIZING OF PROBLEMS We assessed this construct with the depressed mood and anxiety subscales from the Symptom Checklist (SCL)-90-R (Derogatis 1983). The depression subscale included twelve items such as feeling lonely, feeling blue, feeling no interest in things, and feeling everything is an effort. The adolescents indicated whether they were not at all (1) to extremely (5) bothered or distressed by each feeling or behavior during the previous week. The depressed mood subscale demonstrated good internal consistency ($a = .91$). The anxiety subscale included ten items assessing feelings such as anxiety, fearfulness, and nervousness answered on the same scale and had good internal consistency ($a = .90$). The two subscales were correlated ($r = .78$) and summed to create an index of internalizing problems.

ADOLESCENT'S EXTERNALIZING OF PROBLEMS We combined adolescents' reports of their own delinquent behaviors, smoking, and alcohol use to create an index of externalizing problem behaviors. The delinquency subscale included twenty-three items that ranged in severity from skipping school and damaging property to theft, drunk driving, and physical violence. The adolescents reported how often—never (0) to six or more times (4)—they engaged in each behavior during the past year. Frequency of alcohol (beer, wine, and hard liquor) use and smoking were reported on a scale from never (0) to three or more times per week (5). The three subscales were standardized and summed to create an overall index of externalizing problem behaviors.

Results and Discussion

We repeated the analyses reported in table 10.2, first with adolescents' externalizing problems as the criterion variable and then with adolescents' internalizing. None of the economic variables was a significant predictor of externalizing problems with the control variables (the adolescent's sex, the parents' education, their marital status, and household size) in the equations. Only one economic variable was a significant predictor of internalizing problems, an income-to-needs ratio of 2–3 ($b = 3.71$, unstandardized regression coefficient). The positive sign for this association suggests that adolescents in the intermediate income range were more likely to be anxious or depressed. However, given the large number of coefficients that were not statistically significant, we interpret this finding as a random result rather than as a substantively meaningful outcome. These nonsignificant results might simply reflect insensitive measures of adjustment problems; however, boys were significantly more likely than girls to exhibit externalizing behaviors, while girls scored higher on internalizing symptoms, consistent with earlier research (Conger et al. 1994).

Several factors might account for the failure to find a significant relationship between behavior problems and the economic status variables. Regarding the method construct hypothesis noted earlier, data reported by Elder, Nguyen, and Caspi (1985) showed that economic deprivation during the 1930s predicted clinical ratings of adjustment problems for adolescent boys and girls only indirectly through parent behaviors that were influenced by deprivation (for example, rejection by the father). This finding is consistent with contemporary research that typically finds only an indirect association between financial hardship and adolescent adjustment problems through disruptions in parenting practices. Contemporary research is also likely to use measures of maladjustment and economic status that are reported by different informants (for example, Conger et al. 1994; McLoyd et al. 1994). Elder, Nguyen, and Caspi (1985), however, also found a direct correlation between economic hardship and adjustment problems, but only when mothers reported adolescent difficulties, consistent with Duncan, Brooks-Gunn, and Klebanov's (1994) findings from the IHDP.

Our results, those from the IHDP, and findings from other studies suggest that the impact of economic hardship on adolescent adjustment problems must be assessed with great care. Depending on the sources of information used, the association between economic status and developmental difficulties may be either direct or indirect through disruptions in child-rearing behaviors. In any case, all of the reported research indicates that economic problems are associated with maladjustment; the only discrepancy in the findings is whether the relationship is independently significant or dependent on parental response to economic stress. Of course, young children, such as those in the IHDP sample, are more likely to be directly affected by hardship conditions than adolescents, who made up our sample. Only future research will be able to address this possibility. In any case, family economic circumstances appear to directly affect the cognitive or academic abilities of either adolescents or young children. In the next section we examine a sequence of mediating processes that might account for this relationship.

EXTENDING THE BASIC REPLICATION STUDY: A MEDIATIONAL MODEL

In a series of earlier reports we proposed that parents' response to economic difficulties provides an important pathway through which economic problems affect children and adolescents (see, for example, Conger et al. 1992, 1993, 1994). Our

FIGURE 10.1 / Conceptual Model of Family-Mediated Influences on Adolescents' Grade Point Average

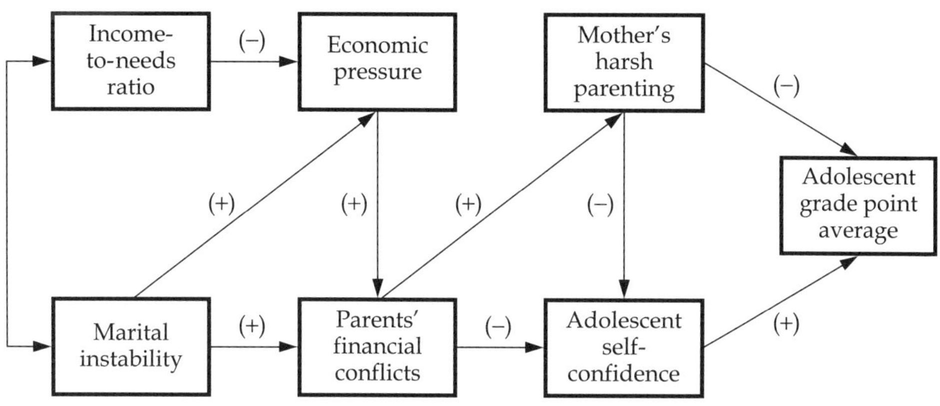

Source: Authors.

basic model proposes that income loss or continuing financial strains are painful for parents and lead to negative emotions that range from depressed mood to feelings of anger and hostility. The model suggests that negative mood, in turn, influences interactions with one's spouse and children, leading to an increased risk for expressions of hostility, reductions in warmth and support, and impairments in marital communication and skillful child rearing. According to the model, these economically linked difficulties in family functioning have adverse consequences for the emotional well-being of parents and children.

Both our own and others' research have provided support for this basic model (for example, Brody et al. 1994; Conger et al. 1994; Dodge, Pettit, and Bates 1994; McLoyd et al. 1994). In the analyses described below we used variation of this basic model to consider family-mediated influences not on the emotional functioning of adolescents but on their school performance. The major themes in the model are dimensions of parental response to economic stress that should impair the self-confidence adolescents need to effectively pursue their school studies and the role of lowered self-confidence in jeopardizing academic achievement.

The conceptual model that guides the following analyses employs the income-to-needs ratio as the basic measure of family economic status (figure 10.1). We include the second exogenous variable, marital instability, in the model because it has an important impact on economic strain, especially when divorce or separation occurs and two households have to be supported on an amount of money similar to that which supported one. This measure is also important because we expect it to have an important influence on later elements in the model.

The model in figure 10.1 proposes that income relative to needs and marital instability will have a direct association with family economic pressure. This variable assesses the degree to which families (1) cannot pay their bills each month,

(2) do not have enough money to meet their most basic needs, and (3) have had to make sometimes drastic cutbacks (for example, giving up health insurance) to live within their available means. In earlier reports, we proposed that these ongoing strains provide the daily experiences through which family members become distressed by economic disadvantage (see, for example, Conger et al. 1992). Obviously, if low income does not create problems in paying bills or meeting material needs, it is unlikely to have any psychological influence on parents or children. Unfortunately, the lack of resources is not so benign.

In fact, we propose that the psychological stresses and strains associated with economic pressure increase the risk for conflicts between parents about their finances. Spouses who are angered and demoralized by their disadvantaged economic situation and who have to negotiate with one another about the use of scarce resources are living in a situation ripe for conflicts about income generation, needed cutbacks, and appropriate expenditures. The model also shows that these conflicts will be exacerbated by marital instability, which in the following analyses ranges from serious thoughts about separation or divorce to the breakup of the marriage. We expect spouses who are unhappy in their marriage to be more likely to have conflicts in general, including those regarding finances. In addition, the termination of the marriage may even increase these disputes as fights over child support, alimony, and the division of property proceed to the level of legal proceedings.

The model indicates that parents' conflicts over finances will lead to increased harsh parenting by the mother (a focus on mothers is consistent with the IHDP). We reason that parents who are already irritable and angry with one another are more likely to respond in a hostile fashion during interactions with their children. This spillover effect from marital conflict to aversive behavior toward children is consistent with earlier findings and with the thesis that the experience of anger and negative emotion in one social context acts as a stimulus for similar feelings and behaviors in related social contexts (Berkowitz 1989; Conger et al. 1992).

The model also shows that parents' conflicts should decrease adolescents' sense of self-confidence (operationalized here as feelings of mastery and self-esteem). This path derives from the argument by Davies and Cummings (1994) that conflicts in marriage disrupt the emotional security of children and adolescents. We expect this disruption to be especially severe when parents fight about money in that children will be threatened by fears not only about the stability of the marriage but also about the economic security of their family. These conditions should reduce children's sense of control or mastery over their environment and, as part of that process, their sense of self-worth or competence. Similarly, the model proposes that harsh maternal behaviors will erode the adolescent's sense of self-worth and control. Mothers' continued disapproval, derogation, and anger should lead children to question their competence and value as family members.

The final two paths in the model, from harsh parenting and adolescent self-confidence to school performance (GPA), derive from two different theoretical notions. One line of previous research has demonstrated that harsh or authoritarian parenting disrupts successful academic performance and increases risk for school failure (Dornbusch et al. 1987; Melby and Conger 1995). We reason that a hostile and unpleasant home environment will fail to support the discipline and effort required to maintain academic performance and will create negative emotional feelings in the adolescent that impede skillful activities in general (Berkowitz 1989). Low self-confidence, on the other hand, will lead the adolescent to question whether the investment of effort will lead to better performance and thus will be associated with the avoidance of activities in pursuit of long-term academic goals (see Mirowsky and Ross 1989 for a discussion of how low self-esteem and lack of a sense of control reduce effort in general).

The following analyses test the empirical adequacy of this mediational model. In addition, we test a recent hypothesis by Cummings, Davies, and Simpson (1994) that conflicts between parents should have a more adverse influence on boys than on girls. They propose that boys are less shielded from conflicts than girls and, as a result, suffer greater impairment when such strife occurs. Consistent with this hypothesis, we test for sex differences in the model and specifically predict that parent financial conflicts will have a more negative influence on boys' than on girls' self-esteem. Elder and Caspi (1988) report that younger boys were more emotionally vulnerable than same-age girls to economic stress; early adolescent girls, however, were more vulnerable than same-age boys. In contrast we focus on boys in the middle adolescent years. We propose that family economic problems will affect boys more negatively than girls of the same age because (1) their relatively higher level of aggressive, externalizing behaviors makes it more likely that they will get embroiled in family conflicts associated with stressful conditions and (2) they are more likely to perceive financially related limitations in their educational and occupational advancement, which will hinder their success at assuming the traditional male roles of earner and household head.

Measures

The sample for the path model analyses (see figure 10.1) consisted of 343 families. Because we included additional measures for the path models, the sample size was slightly reduced from the 357 used for the replication analyses. In addition to the measures used in the earlier analyses from the self-report questionnaires, we used observer ratings from task 1 to assess mothers' harsh, inconsistent behavior toward the target adolescents. Measures used in both the replication analyses and the extension analyses were (1) the outcome or dependent variable, adolescent GPA; (2) the mother's and father's education; and (3) average income-to-needs ratio. Additional measures that may mediate the relationship between these family background variables and adolescent academic performance, measured here as GPA, are described below.

MARITAL INSTABILITY Questions asked each year about problems in the marriage were used to create an index of marital instability over the course of the study. Each parent responded to a set of five questions on whether she or he had considered separation or divorce. Adapted from Booth's (1983) Marital Instability Scale, the questions included items such as whether the parent or spouse had ever seriously suggested the idea of divorce and whether the parent and spouse had talked about consulting an attorney about a divorce. Each positive response was coded 1, and each negative response, 0. Couples who separated or divorced during the four years of the study were coded 1, and all items were summed to create an overall index of marital instability.

MOTHER'S ECONOMIC PRESSURE Three indicators as reported by the mother were used to assess economic pressure. First, three questions assessed whether she felt the family could not make ends meet: whether the family had difficulty paying bills each month (1, no difficulty; 5, a great deal of difficulty), whether there was money left over at the end of the month (1, more than enough money; 4, not enough), and whether family income never caught up with expenses (1, strongly disagree; 5, strongly agree). Items were standardized and summed (α = .91). The material needs indicator consisted of seven items that asked if the mother agreed or disagreed on a five-point scale from strongly agree to strongly disagree that the family had the money necessary for a home, clothing, household items, a car, food, medical care, and recreational activities. The summed scale was internally consistent (α = .87).

The final indicator of the construct, financial cutbacks, consisted of reports on changes the family had made in response to financial difficulties in the past year. The mother reported whether her family had made any of seventeen possible cutbacks in expenditures or assets in the past year, for example, giving up medical insurance, reducing utility costs, and the like (1, yes; 0, no). We standardized and summed these three indicators to create a single indicator of the mother's report of economic pressure at year 4.

PARENTS' CONFLICTS OVER MONEY A single item assessed conflicts over money. The target adolescents reported how often their parents argued with each other about not having enough money (1, never; 5, always).

MOTHER'S HARSH, INCONSISTENT PARENTING Observers' ratings of the mother's behavior toward the adolescent during task 1 were used to assess the mother's parenting. The indicator of harsh, inconsistent parenting is a summative scale based on seven separate, nine-point ratings of the mother's behavior (hostility, contempt, angry-coercion, antisocial, neglecting-distancing, inconsistent, and harsh). The scale was internally consistent (α = .81).

ADOLESCENT SELF-CONFIDENCE The final indicator is a summed scale based on Rosenberg's (1965) measure of self-esteem and Pearlin's measure of control or mastery (Pearlin et al. 1981). Each scale demonstrated good internal consistency (α = .89 for self-esteem; α = .78 mastery). Because the scales were strongly correlated (r = .60), they were combined into a single indicator. A high score reflects a sense of personal worth, control, and self-efficacy.

Results and Discussion

Of the variables included in the mediational model (see figure 10.1), adolescent GPA was significantly related to all of the variables prior to it in the model (table 10.3). For example, income-to-needs ratio and marital instability correlated significantly with GPA. If, as proposed in the model, no direct path exists between either of these exogenous variables and GPA with the intervening variables in the regression equation, we will have good evidence for the hypothesized mediating effects. In general, the pattern of relationships among the observed indicators of the constructs were as expected and suggest that a formal test of the model would be appropriate.

We tested the conceptual model in figure 10.1 using maximum likelihood estimation (the LISREL 7 software package; Joreskog and Sorbom 1989) for the combined sample of tenth-grade boys and girls (figure 10.2). Although not shown in the figure, the mother's and father's education were used as control variables in the analyses.

Consistent with the model, the two exogenous variables (income-to-needs ratio and marital instability) were both significantly related to economic pressure (−.39 and .11, respectively). Also as expected, marital instability was significantly related to parents' financial conflicts. However, there was no direct path from either of the exogenous variables to adolescent GPA with the hypothesized mediating variables in the equation. Thus, even though the zero-order correlations between both of these variables and GPA were statistically significant, those associations appear to be accounted for entirely by the proposed mediational processes.

Economic pressure was positively related to parents' financial conflicts, as hypothesized. Not expected, however, was the direct and significant path from economic pressure to GPA. In earlier tests of this basic model using different behavioral or psychological outcomes, we did not observe this direct path when mediators involving parent emotions and behaviors were included in the analyses (for example, Conger et al. 1994). Apparently, daily stressors involving family finances have a particularly strong direct influence on the school performance of adolescents.

As proposed, financial conflicts reduced the adolescents' self-confidence, but there was no direct path from financial conflicts to the mother's harsh parenting. Again, this result is contrary to earlier findings (for example, Conger et al. 1992, 1993, 1994). In those reports, however, our measures of marital conflicts included disputes in all areas of marriage, not just disagreements related to finances. Apparently, marital conflicts are more likely to spill over into child-rearing behaviors if marital disagreements are more diffuse rather than focused primarily on financial problems. Consistent with the conceptual model, the mother's harsh parenting had a negative affect on adolescent self-confidence, which in turn disrupted school performance. Finally, harsh parenting had a similar adverse impact on academic achievement. The overall fit of the model was quite good, with a nonsignificant chi-square and an adjusted goodness-of-fit index of .963.

In the final step in the analyses, we compared the fit of the model separately

TABLE 10.3 / Descriptive Statistics for Variables Used in Tests of the Mediational Model

Variable	Correlation 1	2	3	4	5	6	Mean	*SD*
1. Income-to-needs ratio averaged across four years	—						2.85	1.77
2. Marital instability averaged across four years	−.06	—					2.25	0.87
3. Economic pressure at year four (mother's report)[a]	−.40**	.13*	—				−0.05	2.66
4. Parents' conflicts over money (adolescent's report)	−.15**	.25**	.34**	—			2.25	0.95
5. Mother's harsh and inconsistent parenting (observer's report)	−.06	.08	.09	.09	—		21.53	8.70
6. Adolescent's report of self-confidence at year 4	−.02	−.12*	−.09	−.22**	−.21**	—	67.02	10.20
7. Adolescent's report of grade point average in tenth grade (year 4)	.20**	−.14*	−.28**	−.15**	−.35**	.27**	7.83	2.16

* $p \leq .05$. ** $p \leq .01$.

Source: Authors' calculations using data from the Iowa Youth and Families Project, years 1–4, on 357 youths.

a. The three indicators of economic pressure have been standardized and summed. See text.

FIGURE 10.2 / Estimation of the Conceptual Model Predicting Adolescents' Grade Point Average from Family Economic Conditions and Interpersonal Relationships[a]

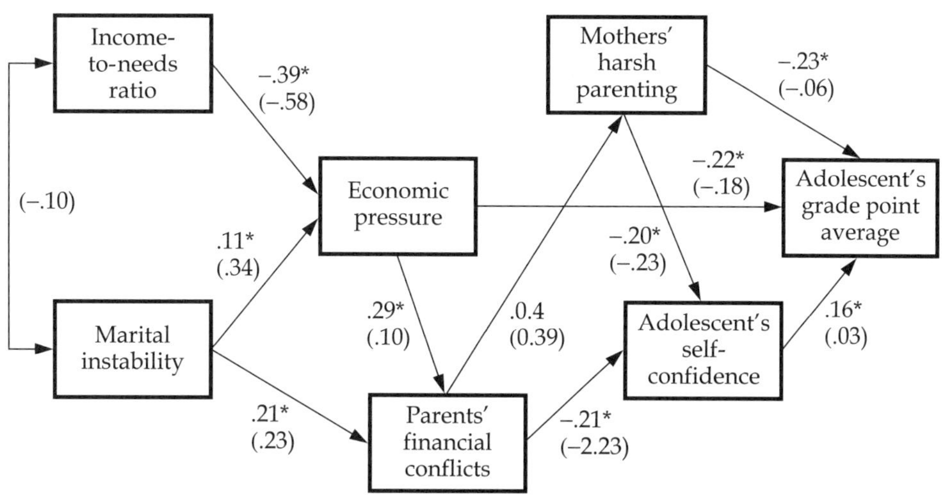

* $p < .05$.

Source: Authors' calculations based on the LISREL software package and data as described in source note to table 10.1.

a. Controls included for mother's and father's education. Values are standardized path coefficients; unstandardized coefficients in parentheses, $\chi^2_{(12)} = 15.50$, $p = .215$; goodness-of-fit index = .990; and adjusted goodness-of-fit index = .963.

for girls and boys using the subgroup procedures available in LISREL. Following the work of Cummings, Davies, and Simpson (1994), we predicted that financial conflicts between parents would threaten boys' psychological adjustment more than girls'. In the analyses, the only significant difference between the findings for boys and those for girls involved the path between parents' conflicts and self-confidence, as shown in figure 10.3. For girls (top panel), the standardized path coefficient (−.09) from conflicts to self-confidence was not statistically significant ($t = -1.18$), even though it is in the expected direction (top panel). For boys, however, the relationship between conflicts and self-confidence (−.37) is quite robust and also is in the expected direction (bottom panel). Allowing the two paths for boys and girls to differ rather than constraining them to be equal in the model, produced a significant chi-square with one degree of freedom (7.41, $p \leq .01$).

GENERAL DISCUSSION

The findings from the analyses reported here are consistent with the notion that family economic problems have an adverse impact on the school performance of teenage girls and boys. The replication findings showed that, net of family

FIGURE 10.3 / Path between Parents' Conflicts over Money and Adolescents' Self-Confidence[a]

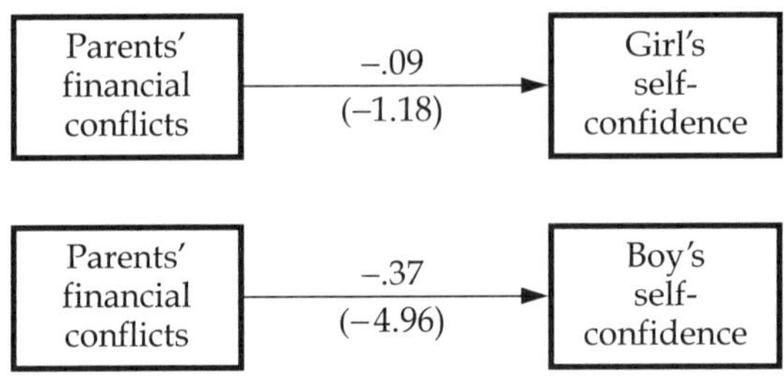

$p < .01$.

Source: Authors' calculations based on the LISREL software package and data as described in source note to table 10.1.

a. Moderated by sex of adolescent. Values are standardized coefficients; t = values in parentheses. $\Delta\chi^2_{(1)} = 7.41$.

background characteristics, several different measures of economic status directly influenced school performance. In the tests of the mediating model, the effects of economic conditions on GPA were largely accounted for by the ongoing economic pressures they created as well as by parents' responses to these pressures. Parents' conflicts over finances were especially detrimental to boys, a predicted sex-related moderating effect.

Our results are all the more distressing because the less advantaged segment of U.S. society appears to be getting relatively poorer as the end of the twentieth century approaches (Duncan 1994). Thus, if current economic trends continue, the processes we depict as disrupting school performance should become more rather than less common. The findings also indicate that such relative disadvantage jeopardizes not only cognitive development during the early childhood years but also academic achievement during adolescence. Quite likely, economically linked impairments in cognitive development early in life make financially disadvantaged adolescents even more vulnerable to academic failures.

Also noteworthy was the special threat that parents' financial conflicts pose for boys. Adolescent males appear to be particularly susceptible to a reduced sense of self-esteem and personal control when parents have disagreements about money. As Cummings, Davies, and Simpson (1994) have noted, boys are probably less shielded from such conflicts than girls are and are more likely to become overtly angry and hostile themselves, increasing the risk that they will become personally caught up in family conflicts. Academic failure by males, especially when combined with a coercive family environment, has been linked to associating with deviant companions and engaging in antisocial activities (Patterson, Reid, and Dishion 1992). In addition, boys at midadolescence may be especially threatened by family economic problems that could limit their opportunities for educational and occupational success and thus their ability to assume the traditional male role of family breadwinner. Therefore, the economic disadvantage of a large portion of U.S. youth has already become especially costly to society and is likely to become more so as economically related developmental problems both impede conventional success and exacerbate emotional and behavioral problems that often require an official response.

Interestingly, the economic status variables used in the IHDP replication analyses did not directly predict adolescent maladjustment in the form of either externalizing behaviors or internalizing symptoms. The discrepancy between our findings and those reported by Duncan, Brooks, and Klebanov (1994) may result at least in part from method variance effects in their analyses that relied on maternal reports for both the financial and adjustment measures. For example, Ge et al. (1994), in reviewing the literature on the association between parents' stressful life events and measures of children's and adolescents' adjustment problems, found that studies using a single informant, either a parent or a child, to report both parents' stress and child maladjustment, usually found a significant association between the two constructs. When different informants assessed parents' stress and developmental outcomes, however, the association between the constructs was not statistically significant in most reports. A similar effect could account for the differences between our findings and those from the IHDP.

Of course, other explanations are possible for the differences between the two studies in their findings on externalizing and internalizing problems. For instance, younger children may simply be more directly vulnerable to economic stress than adolescents are (see Elder and Caspi 1988). More likely, economic influences are primarily indirect when it comes to adjustment problems. That is, earlier findings suggest that only when parents become distressed and overwhelmed by economic difficulties are children and adolescents at risk for developing behavioral problems (for example, Conger et al. 1994; McLoyd et al. 1994). In any case, whether the influence is direct or indirect, the evidence is clear that family economic hardship puts children and adolescents at increased risk for emotional and behavioral problems.

But the largely indirect effect of economic conditions on maladjustment makes the direct effects of family finances on cognitive and academic functioning even more dramatic. Apparently it does not take serious, economically related disruptions in the emotions or behaviors of parents to translate economic hardship into a threat to the successful development of children and adolescents. Even when these mediators are taken into account, as in figure 10.2, economic pressure and academic performance were still directly related. Financial security, independently of parental functioning, appears to influence children's ability to think effectively and perform well in an academic setting. To place children in seriously deprived economic circumstances creates enormous social risks by threatening to reduce the human capital necessary to maintain a globally competitive, modern society.

These findings have several policy implications. The most obvious, of course, involves support for policies that can reduce family poverty and financial deprivation. Transfer payments, job training programs, and other such interventions may be appropriate vehicles for helping families meet their basic economic needs when times are bad. The data also suggest, however, that parents and children need to be educated about the possible adverse consequences of economic difficulties on their own psychological functioning and interpersonal relationships. Even with economic assistance programs in place, a large proportion of families will experience some degree of hardship during some periods of their lives. While they adjust and regroup to accommodate these problems, the data suggest, conflicts may occur, feelings of self-esteem may decline, and academic performance may suffer.

These events and conditions in family life may have long-term negative consequences in their own right even after the restoration of some degree of economic equilibrium. For that reason, programs must be developed to help people deal successfully with the potentially destructive family processes and personal changes that are associated with financial hardship. Spouses can learn communication practices that are more effective than yelling or arguing for dealing with financial negotiations, and children can learn that they are not responsible either for such conflicts or for the economic problems of their families. School-based programs, for example, might assist economically stressed youngsters not only with their studies but also with strategies for dealing more effectively with the difficulties in their home environments. Given the pervasive influence of economic problems on the quality of family life and the development of children, such programs will be a wise investment in the nation's future.

The research reported here was supported by the National Institute of Mental Health (MH43270, MH48165).

Chapter 11

The Influence of Poverty on Children's Classroom Placement and Behavior Problems

Linda Pagani, Bernard Boulerice, and Richard E. Tremblay

The long-term negative effects of poor school achievement and behavior problems have been well documented in both prospective and retrospective longitudinal research. Using data from the birth cohort of the 1958 British National Child Development Study, Power, Manor, and Fox (1991) observed that behavior problems (followed by failure to finish high school) at age sixteen were the best predictors of poor physical and mental health in men and women at age twenty-four. Similar results were obtained in smaller longitudinal studies in Britain, Finland, Sweden, and the United States (for example, Farrington 1994; Rodgers 1990; Pulkkinen 1990; Pulkkinen and Tremblay 1992; Magnusson 1988; Caspi, Elder, and Herbener 1990; Robins 1966).

In most of these studies, family socioeconomic status (SES) was inversely associated with behavior problems and school failure in children. Although it has been established that SES generally is a crude indicator of financial hardship (Huston 1994), one plausible interpretation of these findings is that poverty leads to behavior problems and inferior school performance. Results from two recent studies indicate that family processes could mediate the effects of poverty on social adjustment in adolescents. From a reanalysis of Glueck and Glueck's (1950) retrospective data on the prediction of juvenile delinquency, Sampson and Laub (1994, 538) conclude that "poverty appears to inhibit the capacity of families to achieve informal social control, which in turn increases the likelihood of adolescent delinquency." Similarly, a three-year longitudinal study using direct observations of family interactions suggests that economic pressure and marital conflict may lead to financial conflict and hostility between parents and adolescents, which may lead adolescents to externalize and internalize behavior problems (Conger et al. 1994).

The literature addressing family transition has also increasingly applied mediational models of family processes to explain children's outcomes (Forehand et al.

1990; Peterson and Zill 1986; Webster-Stratton 1990; Wallerstein 1991). Economic deprivation appears to be the best predicted concomitant of divorce, consequently placing a strain on the family's lifestyle, relationships, and opportunities (Kurtz and Derevensky 1994). The lower wages of women and lower educational attainment levels merely exacerbate the economic challenges faced by such families, placing children's development at greater risk. Children often perceive remarriage as a second transition that compounds the emotional stressors of the postdivorce period (Hetherington 1989). Nevertheless, it frequently offers the possibility of financial support from a new spouse. Kurdek and Sinclair (1988) have generally concluded that family structure differences are nonsignificant when controls are provided for SES and family size. What remains to be determined is the degree of developmental risk posed by divorce and remarriage once a more precise measure of income is controlled for in the analyses.

An alternative interpretation of the link between family poverty and children's social adjustment problems is that youths exhibiting behavior problems eventually become parents with limited financial resources and skills to manage the economic challenges of family life (Power, Manor, and Fox 1991). Young adults with adjustment problems are more likely to choose a mate with similar adjustment problems, have marital conflicts, and provide less adequate parenting (Quinton and Rutter 1988; Farrington 1994; Serbin et al. 1991). Last, biological processes related to genetics, and complications in utero and at birth, could lead to difficult temperament in early childhood and later behavior problems (Fox 1989; Kagan, Reznick and Snidman, 1988; Rowe 1994).

To conclusively demonstrate the validity of either one of these hypotheses ideally requires following twins and adoptees, with frequent repeated measures over two generations. Until this major enterprise can be accomplished, the alternatives are to experimentally manipulate the financial resources of families and observe the effects on children or to use a change model approach to causal modeling. Considering social scientists' view that poverty is an important determining factor in children's outcomes, surprisingly few randomized experiments have manipulated income to assess its influence on development (Duncan, Brooks-Gunn, and Klebanov 1994; Salkind and Haskins 1982).

Although not as powerful as randomized experiments, the change model approach represents a useful alternative for studies that have repeated measures of specific variables of interest (Duncan, Brooks-Gunn, and Klebanov 1994; Rodgers 1989). Cherlin et al. (1990) employed this model in examining the relationship between marital disruption and children's adjustment with data from two longitudinal studies, the 1958 British National Child Development Study and the 1976 American National Survey of Children. Children who experienced parental divorce (or separation) within four childhood years were compared with children whose families remained intact. For boys, the apparent effect of parental divorce on general behavior and academic problems at age eleven was drastically reduced by considering behavior, SES, race, achievement, and emotional difficulties that were present four years earlier, before any of the boys had experienced divorce. Although not as sharp once preexisting factors were considered, a reduction in the impact of marital disruption on girls remained discernible. While these results underscore the importance of considering predivorce behavior and SES related factors, they did not consider a measure of income. Tremblay et al. (1992) also used this approach to test the effect of elementary school failure on juvenile delinquency. After having controlled for behavior problems and school achievement in first grade, they found that elementary school failure had no impact on juvenile delinquency at age fourteen in either boys or girls.

More recently Duncan, Brooks-Gunn, and Klebanov (1994) used a change model approach to assess the effect of economic deprivation on IQ and behavioral development between ages three and five. Initially family income was a powerful predictor of IQ at age five and of externalizing and internalizing behavior problems (rated by mothers). Assessments of these same variables at age three were then employed as control variables. The effect of family income at age five remained significant on IQ but not on internalizing and externalizing behavior problems. These results indicate that the effect of family income on children's behavior problems observed at age five could occur before age three. Indeed, substantial stability in behavior problems has been observed from ages two and three to school entry (for example, Bates et al. 1991; Campbell 1995; Cummings, Iannotti, and Zahn-Waxler 1989; White et al. 1990).

Identifying when poverty poses a significant risk to children's development has important implications for economic policies concerning the well-being of children. If poverty has its main effect in the first two or three years of life, economic support of some kind could be limited to pregnant women and mothers of infants from impoverished populations, as opposed to costly provisions to all poor families. Alternatively, if poverty can have long-term negative consequences at any point during a child's development, then all poor adults living with children should receive some form of economic help. These alternatives obviously have different consequences for the formation of social welfare policies.

The elementary school years appear to be a period of development when economic circumstances are critical for later social adjustment. Longitudinal studies from middle childhood to adolescence and adulthood have shown that behavior problems and poor academic achievement during elementary school predict failure to complete high school, serious delinquency problems, early parenthood, unemployment, and physical and mental health problems (Cairns, Cairns, and Neckerman 1989; Huesmann et al. 1984; Farrington 1989; Pulkkinen 1990; Robins 1966; Seidman et al. 1994). Alternatively, behavior and academic problems during the elementary school years could merely reflect the continuation of problems that started during the preschool years (Moffitt 1990; Tremblay et al. 1994; White et al. 1990).

We addressed this problem by studying a population sample of children who were first assessed during their kindergarten year and then annually until grade six. Our aim was to assess the impact of income and family structure on teacher-rated behavior problems (hyperactivity, physical aggression, and anxiety) and school adjustment (classroom placement) at age twelve, after having controlled for the child's sex and behavior problems at age six, and maternal education and age at the birth of the target child. In light of studies indicating great diversity in the patterns of poverty and the differential influence of economic patterns on children's development, we examine the contribution of the duration and timing of poverty to children's risk for disrupted development (Corcoran et al. 1992; Duncan and Rodgers 1988).

METHOD

Subjects and Procedure

In the spring of 1986 and 1987, kindergarten teachers from all French school boards of the eleven administrative regions of the Canadian province of Québec completed behavioral assessments for a random sample of between one and eight target students per kindergarten classroom (N = 6,397) for a longitudinal study on child development. At this first assessment, teachers rated the behavior of 4,494 French-speaking kindergarten children (mean = 6.15 years of age, SD = 0.46). Mothers also answered a series of demographic questions annually pertaining to family income, marital status, and maternal characteristics. This study focuses on the children's behavioral and academic adjustment at age twelve while considering their family income history and family configuration. A total of 2,130 children had complete data from their teacher and their mother at both ages six and twelve (or for age eleven when not available at age twelve). This subsample did not significantly differ from the overall sample in terms of the variables of interest.[1]

We selected the sample for this investigation from the children who were followed from ages six to twelve according to several criteria. First, annual data on family income (measured from ages eight through twelve), family configuration, and maternal characteristics (assessed from ages six through twelve) could not be missing for two consecutive years or more. As such, 257 subjects had to be excluded. Second, behavioral assessments and classroom placement data had to be available for age twelve (or age eleven when missing at age twelve). Another 44 subjects were excluded because data on these dependent measures were incomplete at both ages eleven and twelve. Of the remainder of the children who met the above criteria (N = 1,829, 947 girls and 882 boys), data on fighting (n = 258), hyperactivity (n = 263), anxiety (n = 259) and classroom placement (n = 297) were unavailable at age twelve. The corresponding measures at age eleven were used.[2]

Measures: Dependent Variables

SOCIAL BEHAVIOR QUESTIONNAIRE (SBQ) Completed by teachers from kindergarten through age twelve, this sociobehavioral assessment comprises the main factor items of two instruments with well-established psychometric properties:

the Preschool Behavior Questionnaire (Behar and Stringfield 1974; Fowler and Park 1979; Rutter 1967; Tremblay et al. 1987) and (2) the Prosocial Behavior Questionnaire (Weir and Duveen 1981).

We used three factors from the thirty-eight-item SBQ as dependent measures: fighting, three items ($\alpha = 0.84$); hyperactivity, two items ($\alpha = 0.87$); and anxiety, six items ($\alpha = 0.73$) (see Tremblay et al. 1991). The SBQ also contains a four-item inattentiveness factor ($\alpha = 0.85$). The aforementioned internal consistency coefficients represent an average α from ages six through twelve. The kindergarten assessments have been found to be good predictors of social adjustment in later childhood and adolescence (Dobkin et al. 1995; Haapasalo and Tremblay 1994; Tremblay et al. 1994).

CLASSROOM PLACEMENT Being placed out of an age-appropriate regular classroom (A-ARC) served as an indicator of severe school maladjustment (Tremblay et al. 1991). At age twelve, children should have been in grade six, the last year of elementary school in the province of Québec.

Measures: Independent Variables

POVERTY INDICES We assessed the net family income of the families annually from the child's ages eight to twelve years and assigned them a value by category. The categories (in Canadian dollars) were less than \$5,000; \$5,000–\$9,000; \$10,000–14,900; \$15,000–\$19,900; \$20,000–\$24,900; \$25,000–\$29,900; \$30,000–\$34,900; \$35,000–\$39,900; \$40,000–\$44,900; \$45,000–\$49,900; \$50,000–\$54,900; \$55,000–\$59,900; and more than \$60,000. For statistical purposes, a value of 5 was assigned to the first category and a value of 70 to the last, with the midpoint of the range employed for all other categories.

We then computed the income-to-needs ratio for each year (from the child's ages eight to twelve) by dividing the reported income by an income-to-needs value for that year (determined by Statistics Canada, 1992, and based on family size and composition).[3] A mean income-to-needs ratio was then computed, and subjects were grouped by income-to-needs ratio as follows: less than 1 ($n = 405$, 22 percent); 1–2 ($n = 786$, 43 percent); 2–3 ($n = 465$, 25 percent); and greater than 3 ($n = 173$, 9 percent).

To consider the duration and timing of poverty, we grouped the subjects into five categories (table 11.1): (1) never poor (65 percent), when the income-to-needs ratio was consistently greater than 1 between the child's ages eight and twelve; (2) always poor (14 percent), when the income-to-needs ratio was consistently less than 1 between the child's ages eight and twelve; (3) poor late (5 percent), when poverty status changed only once between the child's ages eight and twelve and the family was categorized as poor (income-to-needs less than 1) at age twelve; (4) poor early (8 percent), when poverty status changed only once between the child's ages eight and twelve and the family was categorized as not poor (income-

TABLE 11.1 / Mother's Education and Age at the Birth of the Target Child, by Duration and Timing of Poverty[a]

Duration and Timing of Poverty	*n*	Mother's Education (years)	Mother's Age at Birth of Target Child (years)
Never poor	1,182	12.51 (2.47)	27.47 (4.05)
Always poor	255	10.47 (2.15)	25.41 (5.36)
Poor early	140	11.28 (2.33)	26.74 (4.59)
Poor late	98	11.38 (2.05)	25.97 (4.15)
Transitory poverty	154	11.14 (2.55)	26.61 (4.70)
Total	1,829	11.96 (2.53)	26.98 (4.41)

Source: Authors' calculations based on data for 1,829 French-speaking children from Québec.

a. Values are means. Standard deviations in parentheses.

to-needs greater than 1) at age twelve; and (5) transitory poverty (8 percent), families with children who experienced two or more changes in the income-to-needs ratio when the child was between eight and twelve years of age.

PARENTAL STATUS This variable served as an index of the marital history and family context for the psychosocial development of the children from ages six to twelve (table 11.2). The children's families were placed in one of six categories: (1) continuous two-parent (that is, intact) families (74 percent); (2) short-term single-parent families (4 percent), in which children had experienced one marital transition (that is, parental divorce) for less than three years; (3) long-term single-parent families (5 percent), in which children had experienced parental divorce for more than three years; (4) short-term remarried families (4 percent), in which children had experienced two marital transitions (that is, parental divorce and subsequent remarriage) in less than three years; (5) long-term remarried families (5 percent), in which children had experienced remarriage for more than three years; and (6) families with multiple marital transitions (8 percent), which had undergone numerous marital transitions that did not correspond to any of the aforementioned groups.

TABLE 11.2 / Family Income and Mother's Characteristics, by Parental Status[a]

Parental Status	*n*	Income-to-Needs Ratio	Mother's Education (Years)	Mother's Age at Birth of Target Child (Years)
Continuous two-parent	1,358	1.87 (0.81)	12.00 (2.50)	27.27 (4.22)
Long-term single-parent	94	1.11 (0.72)	12.28 (2.61)	27.11 (5.26)
Short-term single-parent	77	1.36 (0.77)	11.94 (2.53)	27.13 (5.13)
Long-term remarried	89	1.63 (0.80)	12.27 (2.58)	25.11 (3.21)
Short-term remarried	70	1.32 (0.82)	11.44 (2.80)	24.73 (4.43)
Multiple marital transitions	141	1.31 (0.81)	11.34 (2.50)	26.19 (5.18)
Total	1,829	1.73 (0.84)	11.96 (2.53)	26.98 (4.41)

Source: Authors' calculations based on data for 1,829 French-speaking children from Québec.
a. Values are means. Standard deviations in parentheses.

At age twelve, the custodial arrangements for the five groups of children from families with a history of marital transition(s) were as follows. The majority of children lived with their mothers (94.7 percent) in the long-term single-parent families, with the remainder of the families (5.3 percent) headed by fathers. Of the children in short-term single-parent families, 77.9 percent were in maternal custody, and 22.1 percent resided with their fathers. The majority of children in the long-term remarried families were in the custody of their mothers (83.1 percent), with the remainder (16.9 percent) in paternal custody. Similarly, the majority of children (80 percent) in the short-term remarried families resided with their mothers, with 20 percent living with their fathers. The custodial arrangements were most diverse for the children in the multiple marital transitions category: 47.5 percent were in maternal custody; 10 percent, in paternal custody; 30.5 percent, in shared parenting arrangements; and 12 percent, neither in maternal nor paternal custody.

Data Analyses

To control for SES-related factors that were present prior to the beginning of the longitudinal study, we included in all logistic regressions maternal education and age at the birth of the target child and the sex of the target child. Consistent with the requirements of a change model approach, each logistic regression also controlled for the level of specific behavior problems rated by teachers in kindergarten. Given the strong predictive relationship observed between inattentiveness and academic failure, the analyses addressing grade placement controlled for the kindergarten level of inattention on the SBQ (Tremblay and Zhou 1991). We first present detailed results using a change model approach and then discuss the results using a nonchange model approach.

We employed a hierarchical approach in all four logistic regression analyses, with the above covariates entered in the model first. Next, we tested the main effect of parental status, average income-to-needs ratio, and the duration and timing of poverty separately and simultaneously (permitting the assessment of possible confounding between these dimensions). Last, we tested the interactions between these independent variables and the child's sex while considering the main effects within the model. The never poor category and the continuous two-parent category served as the reference group in the analyses addressing the effects of duration and timing of poverty and parental status, respectively.

Cutoff points for the high and low ends of the SBQ factors had to be selected to dichotomize the data for logistic analyses. The fighting and hyperactivity subscales had highly skewed distributions. Approximately 75.9 percent of the subjects had a score of 0 for the hyperactivity factor, and 79 percent of the subjects had a score of 0 for the fighting subscale. We chose these scores as the low-end cutoff points for both dimensions. Although the distribution for the anxiety subscale was more evenly distributed across the range, the 74th percentile was used as the low-end cutoff point for the anxiety subscale.

RESULTS

Anxiety

We found that the child's sex had no significant effect with respect to main effects and interactions (table 11.3A). When the parental status variable was not entered in the model, the duration and timing of poverty variable had a significant main effect (likelihood-ratio test $\chi^2(4) = 12.00$, $p = .02$), with the always poor and the poor early groups being most at risk for anxiety in comparison with children in the never poor group. However, model 1 showed poor predictive capability.

When parental status was considered in model 4, the duration and timing of poverty variable was no longer significant (likelihood-ratio test $\chi^2(4) = 4.77$, $p = .31$). Parental status had a significant main effect (likelihood-ratio test $\chi^2(5) =$

TABLE 11.3A / Children's Anxiety at Twelve Years of Age (Change Model)[a]

Independent Variable	Model 1	2	3	4
Mother's education	0.96*	0.94**	0.95*	0.94*
Mother's age at child's birth	1.00	1.00	1.00	1.00
Sex[b]	0.96	0.96	0.96	0.97
Anxiety at age 6	1.16**	1.16**	1.16**	1.16**
Parental status[c]		(0.0001)	(0.0001)	(0.0001)
Long-term single > 3		2.60**	2.44**	2.35**
Short-term single ≤ 3		1.93**	1.85*	1.98**
Long-term remarried > 3		2.10**	2.06**	2.07**
Short-term remarried ≤ 3		2.07**	2.02**	2.05**
Multiple marital transitions		1.83**	1.77**	1.78**
Average income-to-needs ratio[d]			(0.25)	
1–2			1.04	
2–3			0.82	
≥ 3			0.72	
Duration and timing of poverty[e]	(0.02)			(0.31)
Always poor	1.61**			1.24
Poor early	1.47*			1.20
Poor late	0.88			0.71
Transitory poverty	1.14			0.98
Sex by parental status[f]		(0.40)	(0.38)	(0.48)
Sex by average income-to-needs ratio[f]			(0.20)	
Sex by duration and timing of poverty[f]	(0.96)			(0.97)
Hosmer-Lemeshow goodness-of-fit (p-value)	0.04	0.73	0.97	0.74

* $p < .05$; ** $p < .01$.

Source: Authors' calculations based on logistic models using data as described in table 11.1.

a. p-values of the likelihood ratio test statistic in parentheses.

b. Males are the reference group.

c. Odds ratios are given with respect to the children in the continuous two-parent group.

d. Odds ratios with respect to the group with an average income-to-needs ratio less than 1.

e. Reference group is the never-poor category.

f. Not included in the model.

FIGURE 11.1 / Effects of Parental Status and of Duration and Timing of Poverty on Children's Anxiety (Change Model).

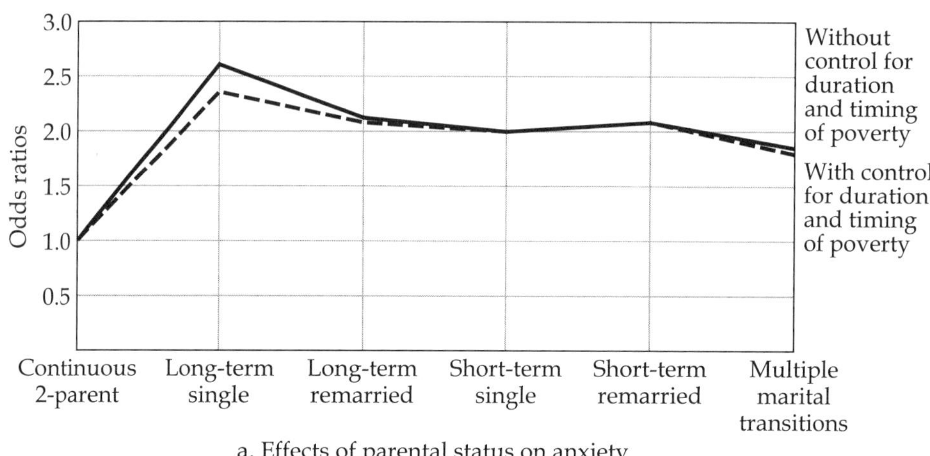

a. Effects of parental status on anxiety

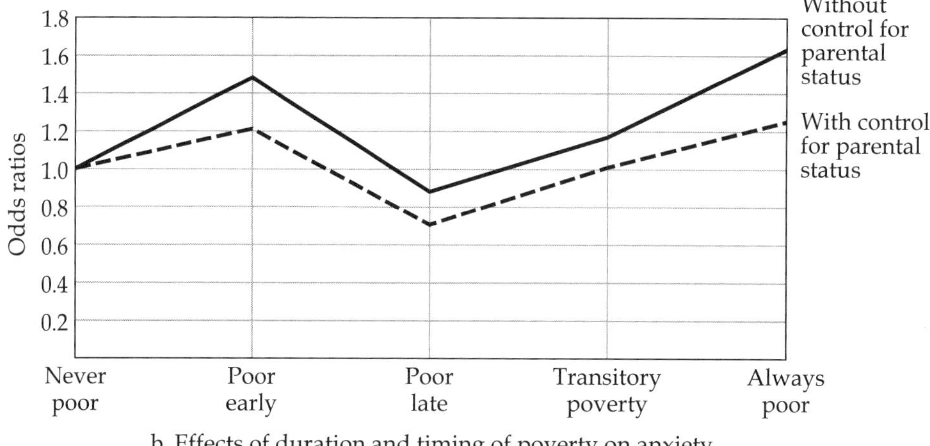

b. Effects of duration and timing of poverty on anxiety

Source: Authors' calculations based on logistic models using data as described in table 11.1.

31.69, $p < .0001$). Children who were not living in an intact family had 1.8 to 2.3 times greater risk of exhibiting anxiousness than their peers from the continuous two-parent group. More specifically, children in the long-term single-parent group were most at risk for anxiety, as reported by teachers. Surprisingly, children from families that experienced numerous marital transitions were least at risk for anxiety.

Figure 11.1A and 11.1B show the effects of parental status on anxiety (with and without controlling for the duration and timing of poverty) and the effects of duration and timing of poverty on anxiety (with and without controlling for parental status), both within the context of a change model. The results when a change model is not used are reported in table 11.3B. Interestingly, the effects of income on anxiety were almost the same in the nonchange and change model, particularly models 1, 3, and 4. Similarly, for parental status, the odds ratios for the multiple marital transitions and remarried groups were comparable, indicating that the effects of parental status on anxiety are specific to changes in parental status and do not depend on anxiety levels at age six. The odds ratios for the short-term single-parent group increased in the change model, whereas the odds ratios for the long-term single-parent group decreased. This difference possibly reflects a strong effect of marital transition when it occurs during early childhood.

Hyperactivity

The odds of girls showing hyperactivity was roughly half that of boys (table 11.4A). More important, the main effect of parental status and its interaction with sex were significant in all the regressions (likelihood-ratio test $\chi^2(5) = 15.19$, $p = .009$ for the main effect, and $\chi^2(5) = 18.39$, $p = .003$ for the interaction). The main effect of the average income-to-needs variable and its interaction with sex did not significantly contribute to the explanation of hyperactivity. In fact, parental status and its interaction with sex were the best predictive model for hyperactivity (goodness of fit, $p = .82$). Interestingly, girls and boys showed opposite trends in risk status according to family configuration. Model 2 suggests that boys living with a remarried parent (that is, the short- and long-term remarried groups) and girls living with a single parent for more than three years (that is, the long-term single parent group) were the most at risk for hyperactivity. Girls living with a single parent for more than three years (that is, the long-term single parent group) showed 3.8 times the risk of hyperactivity of their same-sex peers in the continuous two-parent group. Conversely, girls living in a single-parent home for less than three years were least at risk for hyperactivity (odds ratio of 0.18). In fact, girls in this group showed much lower risk than those in the intact group. Boys living with only one parent for more than three years demonstrated the same odds as those who always lived with both parents.

Figures 11.2A and 11.2B illustrate the effects of parental status on hyperactivity (by sex, without controlling for the duration and timing of poverty) and the effects of duration and timing of poverty on hyperactivity (with and without controlling for parental status), within the context of a change model.

We report the results for a nonchange model in table 11.4B. As for anxiety, using a nonchange rather than a change model did not greatly affect the odds ratios for the duration and timing of poverty variable, nor did it affect the average income-to-needs variable. Parental status significantly explained children's risk for hyperactivity whereas the poverty-related variables did not. For boys, the most

(Text continued on p. 326.)

TABLE 11.3B / Children's Anxiety at Twelve Years of Age (Nonchange Model)[a]

Independent Variable	Model 1	2	3	4
Maternal education	0.90*	0.93**	0.95	0.94*
Mother's age at child's birth	1.00	1.00	1.00	1.00
Sex[b]	0.90	0.90	0.90	0.91
Parental status[c]		(<0.0001)	(<0.0001)	(<0.0001)
Long-term single > 3		2.78**	2.59**	2.51**
Short-term single ≤ 3		1.80*	1.72*	1.84*
Long-term remarried > 3		2.11**	2.06**	2.07**
Short-term remarried ≤ 3		2.01**	1.95**	1.99**
Multiple marital transitions		1.87**	1.80**	1.80**
Average income-to-needs ratio[d]			(0.16)	
1–2			1.03	
2–3			0.80	
≥ 3			0.69	
Duration and timing of poverty[e]	(0.01)			(0.31)
Always poor	1.63**			1.25
Poor early	1.51*			1.23
Poor late	0.90			0.74
Transitory poverty	1.12			0.97
Sex by parental status[f]		(0.35)	(0.32)	(0.44)
Sex by average income-to-needs ratio[f]			(0.12)	
Sex by duration and timing of poverty[f]	(0.99)			(0.99)
Hosmer-Lemeshow goodness-of-fit (p-value)	0.26	0.90	0.90	0.71

* $p < .05$; ** $p < .01$.

Source: Authors' calculations based on logistic models using data as described in table 11.1.

a. p-values of the likelihood ratio test statistic in parentheses.

b. Males are the reference group.

c. Odds ratios are given with respect to the children in the continuous two-parent group.

d. Odds ratios with respect to the group with an average income-to-needs ratio less than 1.

e. Reference group is the never-poor category.

f. Not included in the model.

TABLE 11.4A / Children's Hyperactivity at Twelve Years of Age (Change Model)[a]

	Model			
Independent Variable	1	2	3	4
Maternal education	0.98	0.97	0.96	0.97
Mother's age at child's birth	1.00	1.00	1.00	1.00
Sex	0.44**	0.46**	0.46**	0.46**
Hyperactivity at age 6	1.40**	1.38**	1.39**	1.38**
Parental status		(0.009)	(0.007)	(0.005)
Long-term single > 3		1.01	1.07	1.03
Short-term single ≤ 3		1.76	1.84	1.90
Long-term remarried > 3		1.99*	2.03*	2.03*
Short-term remarried ≤ 3		2.80**	2.91**	2.93**
Multiple marital transitions		1.57	1.64	1.66
Average income-to-needs ratio			(0.44)	
1–2			1.04	
2–3			1.19	
≥ 3			1.44	
Duration and timing of poverty	(0.64)			(0.50)
Always poor	1.14			0.92
Poor early	0.89			0.75
Poor late	0.73			0.66
Transitory poverty	1.02			0.90
Sex by parental status		(0.003)[b]	(0.002)[b]	(0.003)[b]
Long-term single > 3		3.79**	3.90**	3.94**
Short-term single ≤ 3		0.18*	0.18*	0.18*
Long-term remarried > 3		0.48	0.49	0.48
Short-term remarried ≤ 3		0.62	0.61	0.65
Multiple marital transitions		0.75	0.75	0.77
Sex by average income-to-needs ratio[c]			(0.37)	
Sex by duration and timing of poverty[c]	(0.64)			(0.36)
Hosmer-Lemeshow goodness-of-fit (p-value)	0.34	0.82	0.72	0.74

* $p < .05$; ** $p < .01$.

Source: Authors' calculations based on logistic models using data as described in table 11.1.

a. p-values of the likelihood ratio test statistic in parentheses.

b. Interaction is part of the model; corresponding odds ratios indicate effect of parental status for girls. For boys, odds ratios are under parental status variable.

c. Not included in the model.

FIGURE 11.2 / Effects of Parental Status on Hyperactivity and of Duration and Timing of Poverty on Hyperactivity (Change Model).

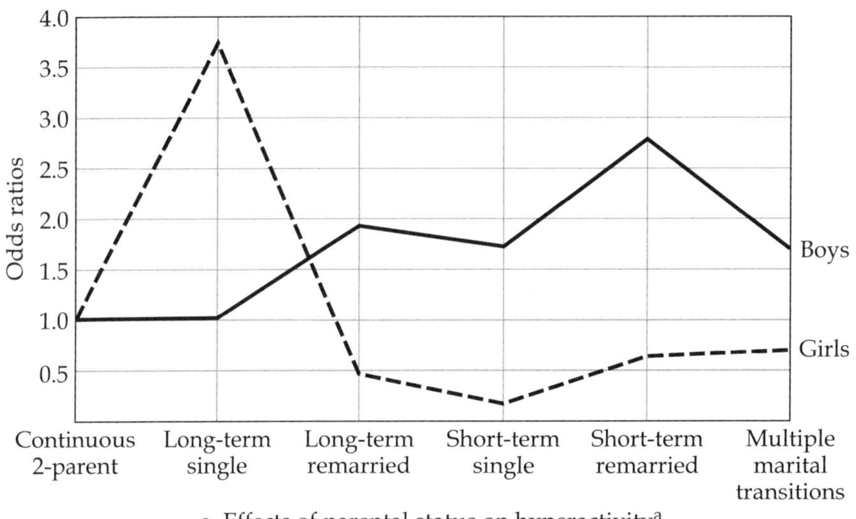

a. Effects of parental status on hyperactivity[a] (without poverty variables)

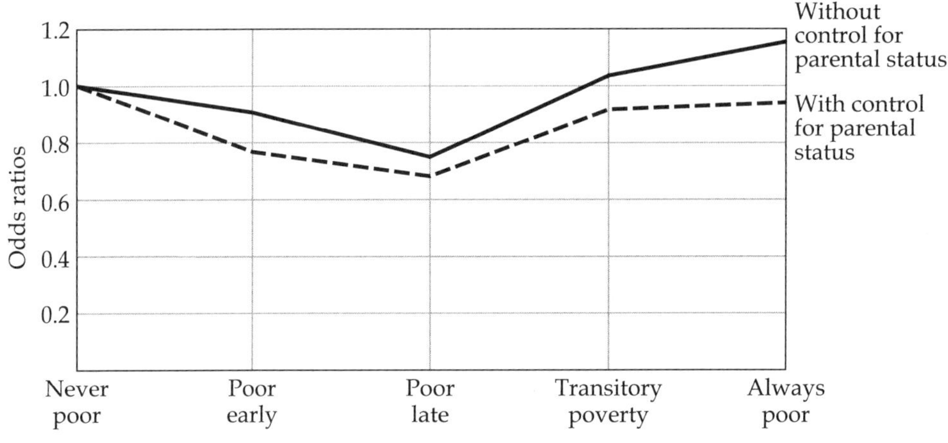

b. Effects of duration and timing of poverty on hyperactivity

Source: Authors' calculations based on logistic models using data as described in table 11.1.
a. Odds ratios with respect to boys in continuous two-parent category.

TABLE 11.4B / Children's Hyperactivity at Twelve Years of Age (Nonchange Model)[a]

Independent Variable	Model 1	2	3	4
Mother's education	0.98	0.97	0.95	0.96
Mother's age at child's birth	1.00	1.00	1.00	1.00
Sex	0.38**	0.39**	0.39**	0.39**
Parental status		(0.002)	(0.002)	(0.001)
Long-term single > 3		1.03	1.10	1.07
Short-term single ≤ 3		1.80	1.87	1.93
Long-term remarried > 3		2.01*	2.05*	2.04*
Short-term remarried ≤ 3		3.12**	3.24**	3.26**
Multiple marital transitions		1.71	1.78*	1.80*
Average income-to-needs ratio			(0.56)	
1–2			1.07	
2–3			1.18	
≥ 3			1.38	
Duration and timing of poverty	(0.71)			(0.60)
Always poor	1.15			0.90
Poor early	0.96			0.78
Poor late	0.77			0.68
Transitory poverty	1.08			0.94
Sex by parental status		(0.001)[b]	(0.001)[b]	(0.001)[b]
Long-term single > 3		4.03**	4.16**	4.18**
Short-term single ≤ 3		0.18*	0.18*	0.18*
Long-term remarried > 3		0.49	0.50	0.49
Short-term remarried ≤ 3		0.56	0.56	0.59
Multiple marital transitions		0.81	0.81	0.83
Sex by average income-to-needs ratio[c]			(0.37)	
Sex by duration and timing of poverty[c]	(0.59)			(0.30)
Hosmer-Lemeshow goodness-of-fit (*p*-value)	0.65	0.94	0.97	0.99

$^{*} p < .05$; $^{**} p < .01$.

Source: Authors' calculations based on logistic models using data as described in table 11.1.

a. *p*-values of the likelihood ratio test statistic in parentheses.

b. Interaction is part of the model; corresponding odds ratios indicate effect of parental status for girls. For boys, odds ratios are under parental status variable.

c. Not included in the model.

important change in odds ratios occurred in the short-term remarried group: they were lower than those in the nonchange model. The odds ratios for girls in the long-term single-parent group were only slightly lower than in the nonchange model.

Fighting

Notably, only eighty-four girls (9 percent) were fighters, according to their teachers. Distributing this small subsample of girls between the parental status and income categories created many cells with fewer than five observations. As a result, the interactions between these variables and sex could have yielded erroneous results. We thus took a conservative approach, performing the analyses for boys only and for boys and girls combined. The two sets of analyses showed the same pattern of odds ratios and *p*-values (table 11.5A).

When tested separately, the main effects of both parental status and duration and timing of poverty were significant (likelihood ratio test $\chi^2(5) = 12.69$, $p = .03$; and likelihood ratio test $\chi^2(4) = 10.09$, $p = .01$, respectively). However, neither of the two variables was significant when both were entered in model 4, controlling for one another ($p = .14$ and $p = .09$, respectively). Nevertheless, the simultaneous entry of both variables was significant (likelihood ratio test $\chi^2(9) = 20.76$, $p = .014$), indicating a strong possibility of confounding between these two variables. Therefore, the most reliable model consisted of both variables, parental status and duration and timing of poverty. Note that children who had recently experienced the divorce or remarriage of their parents were at greater risk for fighting, as reported by teachers (teachers identified children from recently remarried and divorced families as being fighters 2.0 and 1.7 times as often as they did children in the continuous two-parent group, respectively). Children in the always poor group were the most at risk for fighting, while their peers from the poor early group exhibited nearly the same risk as those from the never-poor group.

Figures 11.3A and 11.3B shows the effects of parental status on fighting (with and without controlling for the duration and timing of poverty) and the effects of duration and timing of poverty on fighting (with and without controlling for parental status), within the context of a change model.

The results for the nonchange model approach revealed that the parental status variable was more significant and the duration and timing of poverty was less significant than with the change model (table 11.5B). Parental status was consistently significant in the nonchange model. This result clarifies the confounding observed between duration and timing of poverty and parental status variables in the change model (table 11.5A). Although the change model results revealed that parental status influenced children's fighting already at age six, the fact that parental status was the most reliable predictor of children's fighting in both models 3 and 4 of the nonchange approach suggests that parental status may play a greater role in determining children's risk for physical aggression than poverty does.

TABLE 11.5A / Children's Fighting at Twelve Years of Age (Change Model)[a]

Independent Variable	Model 1	Model 2	Model 3	Model 4
Mother's education	0.96	0.94*	0.97	0.96
Mother's age at child's birth	0.97*	0.97*	0.97*	0.97*
Sex	0.22**	0.23**	0.23**	0.22**
Fighting at age six	1.46**	1.43**	1.44**	1.44**
Parental status		(0.03)	(0.08)	(0.14)
Long-term single > 3		1.19	1.03	1.02
Short-term single ≤ 3		1.91*	1.72*	1.69*
Long-term remarried > 3		0.95	0.91	0.92
Short-term remarried ≤ 3		2.33**	2.09**	1.99**
Multiple marital transitions		1.35	1.23	1.21
Average income-to-needs ratio			(0.12)	
1–2			0.81	
2–3			0.63**	
≥ 3			0.64	
Duration and timing of poverty	(0.01)			(0.09)
Always poor	1.75**			1.62**
Poor early	1.15			1.08
Poor late	1.54			1.32
Transitory poverty	1.60**			1.51
Hosmer-Lemeshow goodness-of-fit (*p*-value)	0.38	0.65	0.52	0.67

* $p < .05$; ** $p < .01$.

Source: Authors' calculations based on logistic models using data as described in table 11.1.

a. *p*-values of the likelihood ratio test statistic in parentheses.

Class Placement

A main effect of the duration and timing of poverty was significant in model 1 (likelihood ratio test $\chi^2(4) = 16.24$, $p = .003$) (table 11.6A). Children in the always poor category ran almost twice the risk of not being in an age-appropriate classroom than did their peers from families with no history of poverty.

Parental status did not contribute significantly to the model (likelihood ratio

FIGURE 11.3 / Effects of Parental Status and of Duration and Timing of Poverty on Children's Fighting (Change Model).

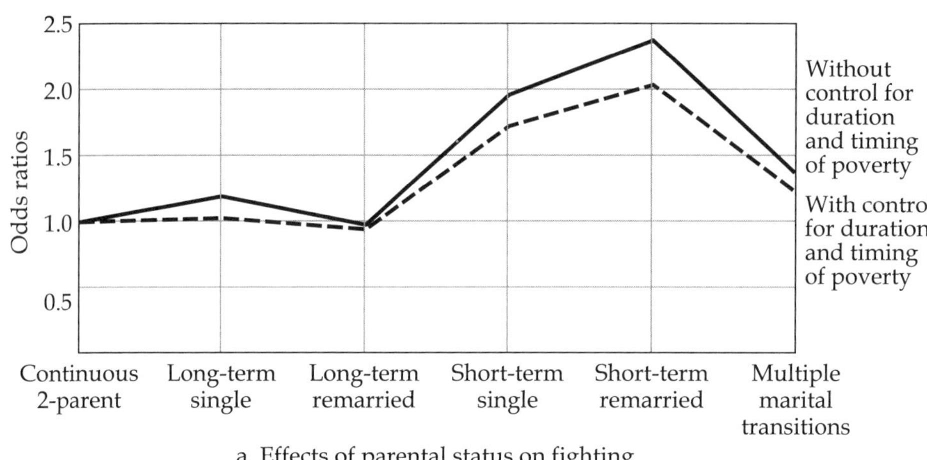

a. Effects of parental status on fighting

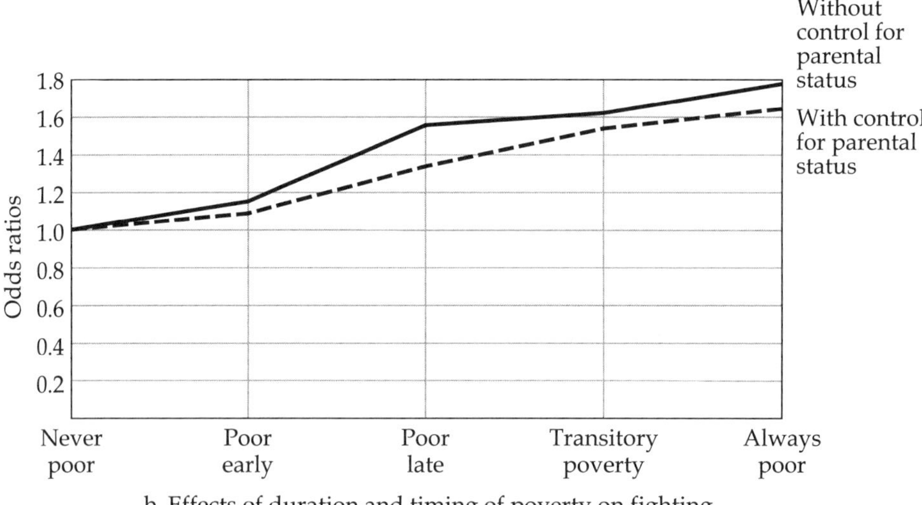

b. Effects of duration and timing of poverty on fighting

Source: Authors' calculations based on logistic models using data as described in table 11.1.

test $\chi^2(5) = 9.66$, $p = .09$), particularly when average income-to-needs (model 3, likelihood ratio test $\chi^2(5) = 4.95$, $p = .42$) or duration and timing of poverty was entered into the model (model 4, likelihood-ratio test $\chi^2(5) = 6.02$, $p = .30$). The duration and timing of poverty remained significant when entered with parental status (likelihood ratio test $\chi^2(4) = 12.60$, $p = .01$). With respect to the average

TABLE 11.5B / Children's Fighting at Twelve Years of Age (Nonchange Model)[a]

Independent Variable	Model 1	2	3	4
Mother's education	0.96	0.94**	0.96	0.96
Mother's age at child's birth	0.96**	0.96*	0.97*	0.97*
Sex	0.19**	0.19**	0.19**	0.18**
Parental status		(0.002)	(0.01)	(0.02)
Long-term single > 3		1.29	1.14	1.12
Short-term single ≤ 3		2.03**	1.85*	1.83*
Long-term remarried > 3		1.08	1.04	1.04
Short-term remarried ≤ 3		2.53**	2.39**	2.28**
Multiple marital transitions		1.62*	1.49	1.46
Average income-to-needs ratio			(0.14)	
1–2			0.84	
2–3			0.65*	
≥ 3			0.66	
Duration and timing of poverty	(0.02)			(0.16)
Always poor	1.72**			1.52*
Poor early	1.31			1.19
Poor late	1.43			1.19
Transitory poverty	1.61*			1.47
Hosmer-Lemeshow goodness-of-fit (p-value)	0.23	0.14	0.64	0.31

* $p < .05$; ** $p < .01$.

Source: Authors' calculations based on logistic models using data as described in table 11.1.

a. p-values of the likelihood ratio test statistic in parentheses.

income-to-needs variable, examination of the odds ratios indicates that the risk of not being in an A-ARC rapidly decreased as the mean income-to-needs ratio increased (likelihood ratio test $\chi^2(3) = 14.89$, $p = .002$). Maternal education consistently had a strong effect on the classroom placement of children, as the risk of not being in an A-ARC decreased by approximately 15 percent (odds = 0.85) for each additional year of schooling. Interactions between sex and parental status, sex and average income to needs, and sex and duration and timing of poverty were consistently not significant.

Figures 11.4A and 11.4B show the effects of parental status on school placement

TABLE 11.6A / Children's Classroom Placement at Twelve Years of Age (Change Model)[a]

Independent Variable	Model 1	2	3	4
Mother's education	0.85**	0.83**	0.87**	0.85**
Mother's age at child's birth	0.97	0.97*	0.97	0.97
Sex	0.76*	0.76*	0.76*	0.75*
Inattention at age six	1.43**	1.43**	1.43**	1.43**
Parental status		(0.09)	(0.42)	(0.30)
Long-term single > 3		1.16	0.90	0.93
Short-term single ≤ 3		1.86*	1.56	1.62
Long-term remarried > 3		1.29	1.20	1.27
Short-term remarried ≤ 3		1.46	1.27	1.27
Multiple marital transitions		1.71*	1.45	1.55
Average income-to-needs ratio			(0.002)	
1–2			0.67*	
2–3			0.47**	
≥ 3			0.39**	
Duration and timing of poverty	(0.003)			(0.01)
Always poor	1.97**			1.85**
Poor early	0.91			0.84
Poor late	1.56			1.38
Transitory poverty	1.35			1.27
Sex by parental status		(0.15)	(0.21)	(0.15)
Sex by average income-to-needs ratio			(0.63)	
Sex by duration and timing of poverty	(0.41)			(0.43)
Hosmer-Lemeshow goodness-of-fit (p-value)	0.14	0.30	0.20	0.06

* $p < .05$; ** $p < .01$.

Source: Authors' calculations based on logistic models using data as described in table 11.1.

a. p-values of the likelihood ratio test statistic in parentheses.

FIGURE 11.4 / Effects of Parental Status and of Duration and Timing of Poverty on School Placement (Change Model).

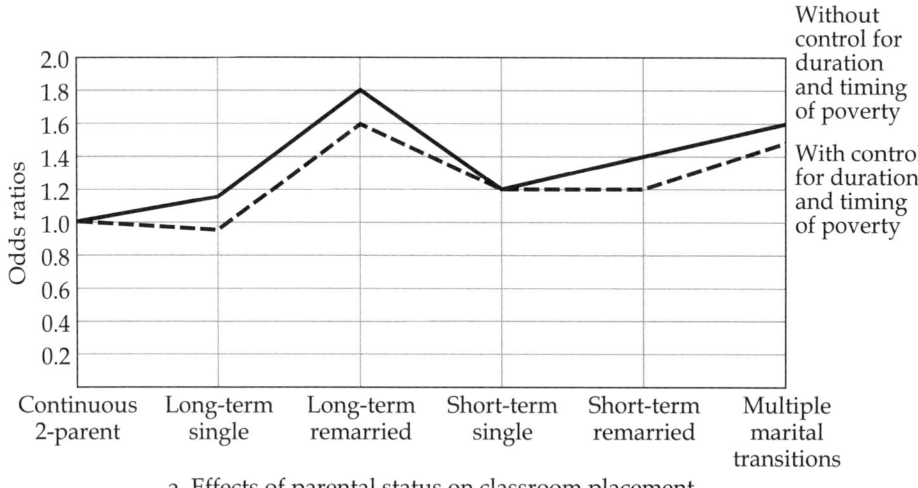

a. Effects of parental status on classroom placement

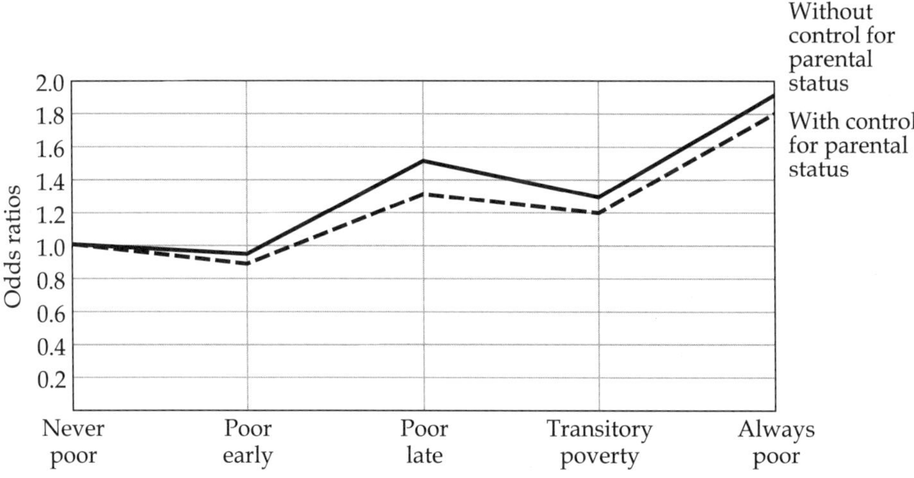

b. Effects of duration and timing of poverty on classroom placement

Source: Authors' calculations based on logistic models using data as described in table 11.1.

(with and without controlling for the duration and timing of poverty) and the effects of duration and timing of poverty on school placement (with and without controlling for parental status), within the context of a change model.

Controlling for the SBQ inattention factor diminished the sex differences observed for classroom placement (table 11.6B). As for the results for the change and nonchange approaches, the effect of parental status was significant in model 2 when we did not control for inattention at age six. However, parental status became nonsignificant in models 3 and 4. The duration and timing of poverty variable was less affected by the addition of inattention as a control variable, especially for model 1, which did not include parental status. This result indicates the primacy of income effects on classroom placement, also suggested by the important decrease in the *p*-value for the parental status variable when we controlled for inattention at age six.

The fact that the measurement of academic failure may have preceded that of income posed a problem in the interpretation of the above results. More specifically, we measured academic placement at age twelve and measured annual income between ages eight and twelve. To clarify the influence of poverty and parental status on this outcome variable, we ran the change model with classroom placement at age eight as a covariate. Adding classroom placement as a control variable resulted in a loss of 18.5 percent of the subjects ($n = 338$), of whom 272 (18.3 percent) were in a regular classroom at age twelve and 66 (19.8 percent) were not in an age-appropriate classroom at age eight. We observed an elevated odds ratio (69.9, $p < .01$) for classroom placement covariate for model 1. Also important is that the effects of parental status diminished greatly (likelihood ratio test $\chi^2(5) = 5.53$, $p = .35$). Although the duration and timing of poverty showed a comparative decrease in predictive strength, it remained significant (likelihood ratio test $\chi^2(4) = 9.78$, $p = .04$). Contrary to the results observed with the change and nonchange models, the children in the transitory poverty category were at significantly greater risk than those in the never-poor category when academic placement at age eight was controlled ($p < .05$). With both the change and the nonchange approach, children in the always poor category showed a significantly greater risk for academic failure than children in the never poor category. These results indicate that most of the academic problems were present prior to age eight, thus preceding the first assessment of income.

DISCUSSION

This study examined the influence of poverty, its temporal characteristics, and family structure on *change* in children's behavioral problems and classroom placement during the last year of elementary school. With controls for a number of income-related variables and corresponding behavior problems in kindergarten, children's family income when they are between ages eight and twelve had a

TABLE 11.6B / Children's Classroom Placement at Twelve Years of Age (Nonchange Model)[a]

Independent Variable	Model 1	Model 2	Model 3	Model 4
Mother's education	0.84**	0.82**	0.85**	0.83**
Mother's age at child's birth	0.97*	0.97*	0.97	0.97
Sex	0.58**	0.58**	0.58**	0.58**
Parental status		(0.02)	(0.24)	(0.17)
Long-term single > 3		1.35	1.06	1.09
Short-term single ≤ 3		1.74	1.47	1.51
Long-term remarried > 3		1.48	1.38	1.45
Short-term remarried ≤ 3		1.51	1.34	1.31
Multiple marital transitions		1.86**	1.59*	1.67
Average income-to-needs ratio			(0.001)	
1–2			0.71*	
2–3			0.48**	
≥ 3			0.40**	
Duration and timing of poverty	(0.002)			(0.03)
Always poor	1.95**			1.77**
Poor early	1.09			0.99
Poor late	1.60			1.41
Transitory poverty	1.25			1.16
Sex by parental status		(0.14)	(0.19)	(0.15)
Sex by average income-to-needs ratio			(0.90)	
Sex by duration and timing of poverty	(0.43)			(0.45)
Hosmer-Lemeshow goodness-of-fit (p-value)	0.47	0.38	0.57	0.48

* $p < .05$; ** $p < .01$.

Source: Authors' calculations based on logistic models using data as described in table 11.1.

a. p-values of the likelihood ratio test statistic in parentheses.

significant impact on classroom placement. However, family income did not influence changes in hyperactive and anxious behavior. Although the change model approach to studying the development of physically aggressive behavior indicated that the effect of income and parental status could not be disentangled, the nonchange model approach indicated that parental status was the more important variable.

Poverty and Academic Failure

In comparison to those classified as never being poor, children whose families' income-to-needs ratio was consistently less than 1 when they were between the ages of eight and twelve were at greatest risk for serious academic failure. That is, children from families that were always poor were more likely to be placed out of an age-appropriate regular classroom at age twelve. The persistent nature of poverty in families falling into this category apparently had a considerable effect on children's academic standing, perhaps influencing their risk for high school attrition and future employment options. Children from families that were classified as poor earlier or later in childhood did not experience difficulties in academic progress in comparison to their classmates from families that were never poor. These results are not unexpected in light of the findings of Duncan, Brooks-Gunn, and Klebanov (1994) in their analyses of data from the Infant Health and Development Program: the duration of poverty mattered for cognitive development, but timing did not influence children's outcomes. Further, Corcoran et al. (1992) noted that, even after controlling for average level of family income, the number of years adolescents lived in poor families was an important predictor of school attainment and early career achievements. Some evidence suggests that duration of poverty may influence mediating factors. Garrett, Ng'andu, and Ferron (1994) observed that the longer children resided in poverty, the lower the quality of their family environment. However, a competing argument maintains that parents' social adjustment and cognitive competence prior to parenthood could explain the relationship between the persistence of poverty and cognitive outcomes (Benson et al. 1993; Serbin et al. 1991). Our results further underscore the importance of considering the duration factor in studies addressing the impact of poverty.

Marital Transition

ACADEMIC FAILURE A family history of marital transition was not a significant predictor of academic outcomes when income characteristics were entered into the model. Although our results indicate that family income has an impact above and beyond that of maternal education and age at the birth of the child, parental IQ and social adjustment would likely serve as more adequate control variables.

BEHAVIORAL DEVELOPMENT A family history of marital transition appeared to have a greater impact on behavioral development than did financial hardship, with the exception of children's fighting. This finding does not support Kurdek and Sinclair's (1988) conclusion that family structure differences are not significant when SES and family size are controlled. Our study found that boys who had experienced remarriage were at greater risk for hyperactivity than their peers from two-parent families that remained intact, regardless of time elapsed since remarriage. Using data from the American National Surveys of Children, Peterson and Zill (1986) found that boys (aged twelve to sixteen) living with a recently remarried parent exhibited the most hyperactive behavior in the academic environment, with controls for family income and maternal education. This finding is inconsistent with recent evidence indicating that boys tend to adjust better to remarriage than girls do (Hetherington 1989; Vuchinich et al. 1991). On the one hand, Anderson, Hetherington, and Clingempeel (1989) obtained evidence suggesting that boys' adjustment to parental remarriage may be most difficult prior to puberty. Perhaps the results were influenced by the fact that the boys in our sample were entering this developmental period. On the other hand, previous studies have not used early childhood behavior as a control measure. Our results clarify the nature of children's risk beyond what kindergarten behavior, maternal education, and the mother's age at the birth of the target child could already explain. Hence, according to these results, boys potentially have some difficulty adjusting to their custodial parent's remarriage.

Girls from families headed by a single parent for more than three years were observed to be at greatest risk for hyperactive behavior in comparison to girls from intact families. These findings are consistent with those of Peterson and Zill (1986), suggesting that boys and girls demonstrate opposing trends in risk for hyperactivity according to family configuration. While Zill (1988) has noted externalizing behavior of this nature in both sexes during the postdivorce period, it was surprising that girls would be at increased risk for hyperactivity over the long term (that is, over three years), especially in light of (1) our results indicating that girls in a single-parent household for less than three years showed less risk for hyperactivity than both their peers who had experienced family transition and their peers living in families that remained intact throughout the study and (2) literature suggesting that girls tend to fare comparatively better than boys in single-parent families and are no different from girls from intact families after the acute postdivorce period has passed (Hetherington 1989). Clearly, our results indicate a timing effect. Mother-daughter relations tend to be closer (with the risk of enmeshment) during the first two years following divorce. Hetherington (1989) suggests that once the acute period has passed, parents are better able to set limits and meet their children's needs. Perhaps the contrast in child-rearing practices between the initial period after divorce (in our study, the first three years) and the later period (after three years) is too sharp for daughters to adjust, creating resentment and resistance toward their mothers' attempts to reestablish their parenting roles. On the other hand, the results may reflect the progressive development of coercive patterns between parent (or teacher) and child (Patterson 1982) that may evolve in the face of stress during the postdivorce period, eventually resulting in a greater risk for hyperactivity in girls over the long term. These explanations are both plausible and complementary.

As we observed for hyperactivity, a family history of marital transition appeared to have a stronger effect on levels of anxiety in children than poverty did. Not only did the model that considered poverty alone have poor predictive capacity, it was no longer significant when parental status was considered. More important, parental status remained significant in the context of this model. The results indicate that children who have experienced any marital transition were at increased risk for anxious behavior in comparison to their elementary school classmates from intact families. Children from families headed by a single parent (for more than three years) exhibited the highest risk for anxiousness. This finding is interesting in that the preponderance of evidence suggests that externalizing behaviors are most common during the postdivorce period, especially among boys (Cherlin et al. 1990; Hetherington 1992), with internalizing behaviors less frequently noted. The absence of an interaction with sex was equally intriguing because internalizing behaviors observed in response to marital conflict and divorce have been found more commonly among girls (Emery and O'Leary 1982). However, thus far studies of the effects of marital transition on children's behavioral outcomes have tended to rely on small samples, not to treat divorced and remarried families as distinct family systems, not to respect the time elapsed since marital transition, and not to apply a change model that examines predivorce versus postdivorce adjustment (Amato and Keith 1991; Guttman 1993). Hence, the results reported here indicate that of family breakup could have relatively long-term effects on anxious behavior in children and that these effects may not be sex specific.

Not surprisingly, according to teacher reports boys were more at risk for physical aggression than girls in the school context. The relationship between fighting and a family history of marital transition and poverty appears somewhat complex because of the substantial amount of confounding between these two variables in the change model results. Nevertheless, when we did not employ a change model approach, parental status had a greater impact on children's risk for fighting than did the income-related variables. A larger sample would be needed to convincingly tease apart the independent effects of each.

According to the change model results, children from a family that was consistently poor when they were ages eight to twelve were more likely to engage in fighting than those from families classified as never poor, once again highlighting the effects of the persistence of poverty. Consistent with our results for hyperactive behavior, children from recently remarried families were more at risk for fighting than their peers from intact families. Timing mattered for divorce as well;

children from recently divorced families were more at risk of being rated as fighters by their elementary school teachers.

CONCLUSION

These results with French-speaking elementary school children in Canada replicate those obtained with preschool children from the Infant Health and Development Program in the United States (Duncan, Brooks-Gunn, and Klebanov 1994). A child's family income appears to significantly affect changes in cognitive performance between ages three and twelve but not changes in internalizing and externalizing behaviors. Because Duncan, Brooks-Gunn, and Klebanov (1994) observed that income affected internalizing and externalizing behavior problems at five years of age without controlling for behavior problems at age three, low income may have affected behavior problems before the children were three years of age. The changes following this developmental period appear to be mainly attributable to a family history of marital disruption or reconstitution and to last for at least a few years. Follow-up of the subjects during adolescence will be needed to assess the longer-term effects.

Because poverty did not play a role in children's risk status for hyperactivity and anxiousness, the long-term effects of divorce (Wallerstein 1991) on these specific behavioral characteristics in children are likely attributable to the psychosocial concomitants of divorce (that is, changes in parent-child relationships, the absence of a parent, interparental conflict, stresses associated with single-parenting), besides the financial hardship experienced by parents during the postdivorce period. Further investigations are needed to understand the sex interactions observed for hyperactivity in our study and the increase in risk for hyperactivity in girls after the three-year mark.

Previous developmental studies addressing economic deprivation have been limited by a number of methodological pitfalls, namely, failing to employ an accurate measure of poverty, frequently relying on measures of SES, generally disregarding the temporal dimension of poverty in developmental research, and taking a casual approach to sampling and measurement (Huston, McLoyd, and Garcia Coll 1994). This lack of methodological rigor increased the probability of a type II error, which may lead to serious consequences when researchers fail to adequately inform policy makers about the outcomes of children in poverty (Huston 1994). While this study represents an improvement in the study of economic deprivation, it is not without limitations (see Blumer 1956, for criticisms of approaches used in social sciences). The lack of detailed information on parents' social and cognitive competence before the birth of the target child and the lack of control for genetic effects do not preclude the hypothesis that parental characteristics that are antecedent to parenthood explain the effects of income and family transition on children's development. Although the mother's education and age at childbirth account for part of the parents' cognitive and social competence before the child's birth, behavioral and cognitive assessments of both parents would allow better control of the presumed effects of these variables. Information on cognitive and social development in siblings would also offer a stronger design, especially if twin and singleton data were available.

The interpretation of the results from the present study is also limited by lack of a multivariate approach to the dependent variables. More specifically, the effect of income on grade placement could apply only to children who were placed out of an A-ARC because of learning deficits, while family breakup could explain the cases of children placed out of an A-ARC because of behavior problems. Similarly, it is not clear whether parental status predicts anxious, hyperactive, and aggressive behavior in one child or does it have differential effects, with some children becoming more anxious and others becoming more hyperactive or aggressive. Although our study used the largest samples available for the elementary school years, with measures repeated annually, it remains somewhat challenged by sample size. Ideally, with a larger sample we could have studied the nature of the interaction between income and parental status categories.

Finally, although family transition was associated with a greater risk for behavior problems, the effects of poverty on serious academic failure appear more serious for two reasons. First, in light of the mainstreaming movement in North American primary and secondary school systems, it takes extreme difficulties to make a child repeat a grade or attend special classes. The effects of divorce, albeit serious, last several years, with two-thirds of children adapting after five years (Hetherington, Stanley-Hagan, and Anderson 1989; Wallerstein 1991). Poverty in this population may be considered transitory, as the custodial parent often remarries within five years, bringing in a new partner and added financial support. The challenges transitory poverty presents to children's development may not be as enduring as the effects of persistent poverty and its associated adverse effects on children's development. Families living in chronic material hardship are an ecologically distinct population. They often reside in unsanitary conditions, in inadequate housing, in areas with environmental toxins, and in violent neighborhoods with poor educational facilities (Huston 1994). Results from the Michigan Panel Study of Income Dynamics suggest that the majority of these children will not escape poverty throughout their childhood, making the intergenerational transmission of poverty more likely (Duncan 1984, 1991). In practical terms, because children living in persistent poverty appear to be at greater risk for serious academic failure, their potential contribution to society remains limited.

This study was supported by Québec's funding agencies: Fonds Formation Chercheurs et Aide Recherche, Fonds de la Recherche en Santé du Québec, Conseil Quebécois de la Recherche Sociale; and Canada's Social Sciences and Humanities Research Council of Canada. The authors thank Hélène Beauchesne and Lucille David for coordinating the data collection, Nathalie Fréchette for assisting with the statistical analyses, Lyse Desmarais-Gervais and Nicole Thériault for creating the data bank, and Minh Trinh for the documentation. The authors also gratefully acknowledge Louise Mâsse for her help in the preliminary planning of this paper, and Claude Gagnon and Frank Vitaro for their contribution to the design and execution of this study.

NOTES

1. Using *t*-tests, we found nonsignificant differences between the selected sample (n = 1,829) and the remaining subjects for whom we had insufficient information on maternal education and maternal age at birth of the target child (n = 2,816). A significant sex difference was observed, with the proportion of boys in the selected sample being 48.2 percent and 51.5 percent in the remaining sample (Pearson $\chi^2 = 4.84$, $df = 1$, $p < .05$). Using Pearson chi-square tests and *t*-tests, we found no significant between-group differences in income distributions at age eight and twelve; family status at ages six and twelve; and anxiety, hyperactivity, and fighting at ages six and twelve. We did note a significant between-group difference for classroom placement at age twelve (18.2 percent versus 21.2 percent were not in A-ARCs). This difference was no longer significant when the log-linear analysis considered the existing sex differences.
2. See note 1 for the analyses used to compare those for whom we had complete and incomplete (imputed) data within the selected sample at ages six, eleven, and twelve. We observed no significant differences.
3. The poverty threshold is based on the low-income measure, a fixed percentage (50 percent) of the adjusted median family income for Canada, where *adjusted* refers to the consideration of family needs (that is, family size and composition) for a given year (Statistics Canada 1992). The poverty thresholds for a family of two adults and two children from 1988 to 1993 were $22,027; $23,837; $24,860; $24,982; $25,511; and $26,084. The poverty thresholds for a family of one adult and two children from 1988 to 1993 were $17,831; $19,297; $20,125; $20,223; $20,652; and $21,115.

Chapter 12

The Role of Family Income and Sources of Income in Adolescent Achievement

H. Elizabeth Peters and Natalie C. Mullis

The concurrent increase in poverty rates and welfare expenditures since the 1970s raises important questions. If children grow up in impoverished homes, how much harder is it for them to succeed than their economically advantaged counterparts? To what extent is the U.S. welfare system acting as a safety net, and to what extent does long-term welfare receipt have negative consequences for children? Many children fall into poverty because their parents divorce or separate or were never married. How does child support receipt affect children's well-being and outcomes?

In this chapter we estimate the effects of family income, long-term poverty, welfare receipt, and child support receipt on two measures of academic outcomes (an achievement test score and completed schooling) for adolescents and labor market outcomes (wages and experience) for adults. To isolate the effects of income we also control for a large number of confounding family background characteristics. We first describe the data that we use from the National Longitudinal Survey of Youth (NLSY). We then report the results of a standard set of regressions that include various measures of family income, poverty status, and family background and present additional regressions that distinguish between various components of income—in particular, child support and welfare. The concluding section summarizes our main findings.

DATA

The National Longitudinal Survey of Labor Market Experience of Youth is an ongoing panel of men and women who were between the ages of fourteen and twenty-two in 1979, the first year of the survey. The initial sample consisted of approximately 12,000 individuals. Interviews have been conducted annually since that time. Blacks, Hispanics, and economically disadvantaged whites were oversampled in the data. Extensive information is available about the respondents' educational attainment, employment behavior, income, fertility, and marital status over time. In addition, the survey collects information about the economic and demographic characteristics of family members currently in the household and asks retrospective questions about other background characteristics relating to the respondent's family of origin.

In the study described here we limited our analysis to the respondents who were fourteen or fifteen by January 1, 1979, and not living on their own or in an institution.[1] Since very few individuals of this age will have left home, this restriction allowed us to obtain measures of parents' income and other family background chracteristics for a representative sample of adolescents. Note that the sample design allowed for the possibility of more than one respondent per household. We randomly chose one respondent per household to yield a sample of 1,908 respondents.[2]

Outcomes

We used two measures each of adolescent academic outcomes and young adult labor market outcomes: (1) the percentile rank on the Armed Forces Qualifying Test (AFQT), (2) schooling completed by 1989, (3) total weeks of labor market experience attained by 1990, and (4) wage rate in 1990. The AFQT is a measure of aptitude that is used by the armed forces to determine enlistment eligibility. The score is derived from several sections of the Armed Services Vocational Aptitude Battery (ASVAB) that measure math and reading skills. As part of a project sponsored by the U.S. Department of Defense to update the norms of the ASVAB, the test was administered in 1980 to 11,914 NLSY respondents, 94 percent of the original sample. The data contain a percentile rank for which the norms are based on individuals who are at least seventeen years old. The respondents in our sample were aged fifteen to sixteen when they took the test, so for this group the measure cannot strictly be interpreted as a percentile rank. With a control for birth cohort, however, it is appropriate to use the score as a rank measure of achievement.

We measured completed schooling as the highest grade completed by May 1, 1989, when the respondents in our sample were aged twenty-four to twenty-five. Labor market outcomes were measured in 1990, during the following survey. Experience was the total number of weeks the respondent had worked in the labor market since age sixteen. The wage rate was the hourly rate of pay on the current or most recent job; we excluded nonworkers from the wage rate analyses. The last three measures were available only for respondents who were interviewed in 1989 or 1990. For comparability across the different outcomes, we restricted our sample to those respondents with data on the AFQT, completed schooling, and labor market experience. Because of attrition from the sample, this restriction reduced our sample size by 215. To test for the possibility of attrition bias, we also ran the AFQT regressions on the larger sample and found that attrition did not affect our basic results. Minor exceptions to this generalization are noted as we report specific results.

Family Income

For respondents who are not living on their own or in an institution, the NLSY contains a measure of total family income as reported by the parents or household head. From that amount we subtracted the income of the respondent. Income is reported for the calendar year prior to the survey. Using the consumer price index (CPI-U), we converted all incomes to real 1992 dollars. Mean family income was the average of incomes reported during the first three surveys (calendar years 1978–80).[3] Based on family size we also calculated the Census Bureau's poverty threshold for each year (that is, the income below which the family would be considered poor). From this number we created both a dichotomous measure of poverty status (above or below the poverty level) and a continuous measure of income-to-needs (the ratio of family income to the poverty level). We averaged these measures over three years to create the variables mean family income-to-needs, below poverty, and family income (1–2, 2–3, etc.) times poverty level. We measured the amount of time the family is below the poverty level with two dichotomous variables, below poverty some (all) years. In addition, in each year the household head was asked if any family member, including the respondent, had received income from a variety of sources, including public assistance or welfare, Supplemental Security Income, and alimony or child support. From this information on the components income, we created dichotomous variables indicating welfare and child support receipt (received welfare (some/all) years, received child support (some/all) years).[4] The amount of income from each source was not available. Note that the data did not allow us to separate alimony from child support receipt, and we did not know which family member was the intended recipient of child support. This problem led to some measurement error in the child support variables. However, the measurement error is likely to be small because very few women received alimony.[5]

Family Background Controls

We included in the regressions variables measuring the educational attainment of the mother and father in 1979 (in years), the number of siblings the respondent had; the birth order of the respondent (firstborn); sex (female), race/ethnicity (black and Hispanic); whether the respondent lived in a rural, suburban, or center-city location in 1979; whether a foreign language was spoken at home during the respondent's childhood; the immigrant status of the respondent and the respondent's parents (first- and second-generation immigrant); the household composition when the respondent was aged fourteen (lived with both biological parents, with the mother only, with the father only, in a stepparent household, or in another household structure); and reading resources.[6]

Table 12.1 reports the sample means separately by race/ethnicity, weighted to population totals. The adolescents in our sample were born during 1963 and 1964—the trailing edge of the baby boom. Only 28 percent were firstborn children, and the average number of siblings was just over three. Note that almost three-quarters of our respondents were still living with both their biological parents when they were aged fourteen. This statistic is in sharp contrast to estimates that half of children born during the last decade will spend some portion of their childhood in a female-headed household as a result of divorce or birth out of wedlock (Haveman and Wolfe 1994, 2). Mean family income was below poverty for 13 percent of the sample, and 37 percent had a family income of more than three times the poverty level.

Blacks and Hispanics were clearly disadvantaged relative to whites in terms of a number of key family background variables that have been shown to affect later outcomes. Their parents had lower levels of education than white parents did, and they were less likely to live with both biological parents at age fourteen; they were more likely to live in a center city, have more siblings, and come from a family with an income below the poverty level.

RESULTS: REPLICATION ANALYSIS

We report the results of our replication regressions for the four outcomes in tables 12.2–12.6.[7] The regressions for work experience are reported separately by sex (tables 12.5 and 12.6).[8] All regressions include a dummy variable for birth year (to control for the age effect on the AFQT and other age-sensitive outcomes) and controls for sex, race, and ethnicity. Column 1 in each table includes only family background variables, and column 2 includes only income (plus birth year, sex, race, and ethnicity). Columns 3–8 include both family background variables and income, with variants on the specification of income.

Family Income

The regressions in columns 3–8 report the results of different income specifications. Model 3 used a continuous measure of mean family income-to-needs. In this model we adjusted for family size differences with the assumptions embedded in the Census Bureau's definition of the poverty threshold. Model 4 relaxed this restriction and included mean family income and mean family size separately. Model 5 allowed for nonlinearities in the effect of mean family income-to-needs by specifying four separate income categories (family income 1.0–2.0 times poverty level was omitted); model 6 expands the number of categories to eight (family

(Text continued on p. 366.)

TABLE 12.1 / Characteristics of Adolescents in the Sample, by Race[a]

Variable	Race/Ethnicity		
	White	Black	Hispanic
AFQT (1980 interview)	46.00 (25.62)	18.55 (16.54)	27.25 (21.69)
Education completed (years as of May 1, 1989)	13.24 (2.25)	12.65 (1.80)	12.29 (2.17)
1990 log hourly wage (1992 dollars)	2.25 (0.66)	2.01 (0.62)	2.13 (0.50)
1990 work experience (years)	6.00 (2.52)	4.86 (2.61)	5.80 (2.65)
Born in 1963[b]	0.53	0.54	0.52
Mother's education (1979 survey)	11.89 (2.36)	11.09 (2.46)	8.39 (3.86)
Missing mother's education (1979 survey)[b]	0.04	0.08	0.08
Father's education (1979 survey)	12.14 (3.16)	10.65 (2.90)	9.16 (4.04)
Missing father's education (1979 survey)[b]	0.07	0.25	0.17
Household composition at age 14[b]			
Biological mother and father	0.78	0.46	0.67
Stepparent	0.08	0.08	0.11
Mother only	0.10	0.39	0.20
Father only	0.02	0.01	0.01
Other	0.01	0.06	0.02
Location of household at 1979 survey[b]			
Rural	0.32	0.26	0.23
Unknown city type	0.20	0.27	0.29
Center city	0.11	0.31	0.29
Standard Metropolitan Statistical Area, non–center city	0.38	0.16	0.19
Female[b]	0.49	0.48	0.50
Reading resources at age 14[c]	2.37 (0.82)	1.71 (1.00)	1.61 (1.07)

Variable	Race/Ethnicity		
	White	Black	Hispanic
Number of siblings (1979 survey)	2.83 (1.87)	4.31 (2.74)	3.89 (2.68)
Firstborn[b]	0.29	0.22	0.30
Foreign language spoken at home during childhood[b]	0.08	0.02	0.88
Second-generation immigrant[b]	0.01	0.004	0.14
First-generation immigrant[b]	0.02	0.01	0.18
Mean family income-to-needs ratio (1978–80)[d]	3.00 (1.62)	1.56 (1.34)	1.81 (1.36)
Mean family income (1,000 1992 dollars)[d]	46.08 (24.40)	25.13 (19.52)	30.43 (20.99)
Mean family size (1979–81 surveys)	4.60 (1.35)	5.44 (2.20)	5.47 (1.90)
Mean family income (1978–80)[d]			
0.0–0.5 times poverty level	0.01	0.17	0.08
0.5–1.0 times poverty level	0.05	0.26	0.24
1.0–1.5 times poverty level	0.10	0.17	0.24
1.5–2.0 times poverty level	0.11	0.12	0.12
2.0–2.5 times poverty level	0.16	0.11	0.09
2.5–3.0 times poverty level	0.14	0.06	0.07
More than three times poverty level	0.43	0.10	0.17
Family income below poverty (1978–80)[b]			
Some years	0.09	0.18	0.20
All years	0.04	0.35	0.25
N	1,077	498	333

Source: Authors' calculations based on data from the National Longitudinal Survey of Youth (NLSY) on respondents born during 1963 and 1964 who were not living on their own or in an institution during the 1979 and 1980 interviews (that is, at ages fourteen to sixteen) and who either had not had a child or been married by that time.

a. Means weighted to population totals. Standard deviations in parentheses.

b. 1 if the respondent has the characteristic; 0 otherwise.

c. Ranges from 0 to 3, indicating whether the respondent's household had none, one, two, or three resources. See text.

d. Excludes respondent's income.

TABLE 12.2 / Replication Analysis: Effect of Background Characteristics and Family Income on Achievement Test Scores[a]

	Model							
Independent Variable	1	2	3	4	5	6	7	8
Constant	0.89	25.17	−1.20	3.42	1.97	0.31	3.54	−3.23
	(0.30)	(19.33)**	(0.41)	(1.08)	(0.65)	(0.10)	(1.17)	(1.06)
Born in 1963	4.16	4.32	4.10	4.10	4.10	4.14	4.06	4.15
	(4.39)**	(4.31)**	(4.38)**	(4.39)**	(4.35)**	(4.40)**	(4.30)**	(4.43)**
Mother's education	1.45		1.25	1.26	1.26	1.26	1.36	1.28
	(6.87)**		(5.92)**	(5.97)**	(5.94)**	(5.95)**	(6.40)**	(6.08)**
Missing mother's education	−9.20		−9.02	−8.90	−9.04	−8.92	−9.06	−9.08
	(4.45)**		(4.40)**	(4.35)**	(4.39)**	(4.34)**	(4.39)**	(4.43)**
Father's education	1.19		1.01	1.01	1.07	1.06	1.13	0.99
	(6.96)**		(5.89)**	(5.80)**	(6.20)**	(6.13)**	(6.60)**	(5.73)**
Missing father's education	−1.50		−1.45	−1.39	−1.35	−1.36	−1.38	−1.64
	(0.99)		(0.97)	(0.93)	(0.90)	(0.90)	(0.92)	(1.10)
Household composition								
Stepparent	−5.44		−4.90	−5.12	−4.91	−4.99	−5.41	−4.75
	(3.20)**		(2.91)**	(3.03)**	(2.90)**	(2.94)**	(3.19)**	(2.82)**
Mother only	−1.11		0.62	0.08	0.52	0.73	0.02	0.40
	(0.89)		(0.49)	(0.06)	(0.41)	(0.56)	(0.02)	(0.32)
Father only	1.19		0.73	−0.04	0.87	0.59	0.51	0.76
	(0.31)		(0.19)	(0.01)	(0.23)	(0.15)	(0.13)	(0.20)
Other	−1.49		−0.47	−1.01	−0.17	−0.11	−0.50	−0.51
	(0.52)		(0.16)	(0.35)	(0.06)	(0.04)	(0.18)	(0.18)

Location of household								
Rural	−0.65		0.52	0.68	0.28	0.32	−0.23	0.57
	(0.53)		(0.42)	(0.55)	(0.23)	(0.26)	(0.19)	(0.46)
Unknown city type	−0.85		−0.22	−0.24	−0.38	−0.36	−0.66	−0.26
	(0.62)		(0.16)	(0.17)	(0.28)	(0.26)	(0.48)	(0.19)
Center city	−2.81		−2.03	−2.04	−2.31	−2.19	−2.63	−1.86
	(1.90)*		(1.38)	(1.39)	(1.57)	(1.49)	(1.78)*	(1.27)
Black	−16.33	−17.54	−15.24	−14.68	−15.20	−15.16	−15.81	−12.50
	(13.06)**	(14.22)**	(12.18)**	(11.59)**	(12.05)**	(11.99)**	(12.58)**	(6.52)**
Hispanic	−3.83	−9.95	−3.78	−3.61	−4.01	−3.90	−3.91	−0.40
	(1.96)**	(7.13)**	(1.96)*	(1.87)*	(2.07)**	(2.01)**	(2.01)**	(0.15)
Female	0.98	1.12	0.81	0.74	0.76	0.84	0.83	2.43
	(1.05)	(1.13)	(0.88)	(0.80)	(0.82)	(0.90)	(0.89)	(1.56)
Reading resources	5.04		4.43	4.32	4.45	4.35	4.66	4.51
	(9.27)**		(8.11)**	(7.88)**	(8.04)**	(7.84)**	(8.45)**	(8.24)**
Number of siblings	−0.62		−0.36	−0.06	−0.36	−0.32	−0.45	−0.41
	(2.77)**		(1.63)	(0.22)	(1.57)	(1.40)	(1.97)**	(1.83)*
Firstborn	1.24		1.79	2.15	1.83	1.77	1.51	1.82
	(1.08)		(1.56)	(1.87)*	(1.58)	(1.54)	(1.31)	(1.59)
Foreign language spoken at home during childhood	0.78		1.10	1.19	1.29	1.34	1.21	1.04
	(0.41)		(0.58)	(0.63)	(0.68)	(0.71)	(0.64)	(0.55)
Second-generation immigrant	4.14		3.88	3.92	3.96	3.83	3.46	4.02
	(1.44)		(1.36)	(1.38)	(1.38)	(1.34)	(1.20)	(1.41)

(Table continued on p. 348.)

TABLE 12.2 / *(continued)*

Independent Variable	Model 1	2	3	4	5	6	7	8
First-generation immigrant	1.50 (0.62)		1.41 (0.59)	1.80 (0.76)	1.56 (0.65)	1.60 (0.67)	1.28 (0.53)	1.52 (0.64)
Family income-to-needs ratio		5.27 (15.98)**	2.27 (6.14)**					3.77 (3.92)**
Family income				0.15 (5.98)**				
Family size				−1.18 (3.52)**				
Family income below poverty level					−2.82 (2.10)**			
Family income								
0.0–0.5 times poverty level						−1.65† (0.78)		
0.5–1.0 times poverty level						−1.23† (0.78)		
1.5–2.0 times poverty level						4.16 (2.30)**		
2.0–3.0 times poverty level					2.20 (1.59)			

2.0–2.5 times poverty level						2.88‡		
						(1.58)		
2.5–3.0 times poverty level						5.34‡		
						(2.73)**		
>3.0 times poverty level					5.75	7.59		
					(3.96)**	(4.60)**		
Family income below poverty								
Some years							−3.93§	
							(2.82)**	
All years							−4.61§	
							(3.23)**	
Mean family income-to-needs ratio								
By black								−1.42
								(1.76)*
By Hispanic								−1.65
								(1.70)*
By female								−0.73
								(1.26)
R^2	0.37	0.27	0.38	0.38	0.38	0.38	0.37	0.38

** p = .05; *p = .10; †not significantly different from one another; ‡not significantly different from one another; §not significantly different from one another.

Source: Authors' calculations based on ordinary least squares (OLS) regressions for sample in table 12.1.

a. Absolute value of t-statistics in parentheses. See text and table 12.1 for description of variables. N = 1,908.

TABLE 12.3 / Replication Analysis: Effect of Background Characteristics and Family Income on Completed Schooling[a]

	Model							
Independent Variable	1	2	3	4	5	6	7	8
Constant	9.24	11.31	9.00	9.31	9.24	9.07	9.52	8.78
	(33.27)**	(95.65)**	(32.66)**	(31.52)**	(32.71)**	(31.30)**	(33.43)**	(30.63)**
Born in 1963	0.06	0.04	0.05	0.05	0.06	0.06	0.05	0.06
	(0.64)	(0.48)	(0.58)	(0.59)	(0.64)	(0.69)	(0.52)	(0.63)
Mother's education	0.14		0.12	0.12	0.12	0.12	0.13	0.12
	(7.02)**		(5.90)**	(5.93)**	(5.95)**	(5.97)**	(6.57)**	(6.04)**
Missing mother's education	−0.53		−0.51	−0.50	−0.50	−0.49	−0.51	−0.51
	(2.07)**		(2.64)**	(2.62)**	(2.61)**	(2.54)**	(2.62)**	(2.67)**
Father's education	0.12		0.10	0.10	0.10	0.10	0.11	0.10
	(7.43)**		(6.16)**	(5.90)**	(6.42)**	(6.35)**	(7.00)**	(6.00)**
Missing father's education	−0.24		−0.24	−0.22	−0.24	−0.24	−0.23	−0.25
	(1.72)*		(1.70)*	(1.60)	(1.69)*	(1.68)*	(1.65)*	(1.78)*
Household composition								
Stepparent	−0.77		−0.71	−0.71	−0.70	−0.71	−0.77	−0.70
	(4.82)**		(4.50)**	(4.49)**	(4.40)**	(4.48)**	(4.80)**	(4.41)**
Mother only	−0.28		−0.08	−0.06	−0.10	−0.07	−0.16	−0.10
	(2.37)**		(0.69)	(0.49)	(0.81)	(0.62)	(1.32)	(0.86)
Father only	−0.41		−0.47	−0.46	−0.42	−0.46	−0.48	−0.47
	(1.14)		(1.31)	(1.29)	(1.18)	(1.28)	(0.36)	(1.32)
Other	−0.41		−0.29	−0.25	−0.28	−0.27	−0.31	−0.29
	(1.51)		(1.09)	(0.93)	(1.04)	(1.00)	(1.13)	(1.08)

Location of household								
Rural	−0.03		0.10	0.13	0.08	0.08	0.01	0.11
	(0.27)		(0.87)	(1.08)	(0.66)	(0.71)	(0.10)	(0.97)
Unknown city type	−0.27		−0.20	−0.19	−0.21	−0.21	−0.25	−0.20
	(2.08)**		(1.55)	(1.48)	(1.68)*	(1.66)*	(1.93)*	(1.56)
Center city	−0.42		−0.33	−0.32	−0.36	−0.34	−0.40	−0.31
	(2.99)**		(2.38)**	(2.35)**	(2.61)**	(2.50)**	(2.89)**	(2.24)**
Black	0.57	0.36	0.69	0.72	0.70	0.70	0.62	0.90
	(4.82)**	(3.12)**	(5.90)**	(6.08)**	(5.89)**	(5.94)**	(5.25)**	(5.00)**
Hispanic	0.11	−0.11	0.12	0.12	0.09	0.10	0.10	0.38
	(0.61)	(0.86)	(0.65)	(0.64)	(0.50)	(0.58)	(0.56)	(1.51)
Female	0.25	0.24	0.23	0.22	0.22	0.23	0.23	0.48
	(2.79)**	(2.58)**	(2.61)**	(2.59)**	(2.58)**	(2.68)**	(2.62)**	(3.30)**
Reading resources	0.41		0.35	0.33	0.35	0.34	0.38	0.35
	(8.12)**		(6.76)**	(6.52)**	(6.74)**	(6.52)**	(7.25)**	(6.88)**
Number of siblings	−0.08		−0.05	−0.04	−0.05	−0.05	−0.06	−0.06
	(3.84)**		(2.48)**	(1.69)*	(2.47)**	(2.24)**	(2.99)**	(2.63)**
Firstborn	0.07		0.13	0.15	0.13	0.12	0.09	0.13
	(0.63)		(1.22)	(1.37)	(1.17)	(1.11)	(0.86)	(1.24)
Foreign language spoken at home during childhood	0.34		0.37	0.38	0.40	0.41	0.38	0.36
	(1.88)*		(2.11)**	(2.14)**	(2.28)**	(2.30)**	(2.14)**	(2.05)**
Second-generation immigrant	1.16		1.13	1.13	1.15	1.14	1.09	1.14
	(4.28)**		(4.23)**	(4.24)**	(4.30)**	(4.24)**	(4.02)**	(4.28)**

(Table continued on p. 352.)

TABLE 12.3 / (*continued*)

Independent Variable	Model 1	2	3	4	5	6	7	8
First-generation immigrant	0.65 (2.88)**		0.64 (2.88)**	0.66 (2.96)**	0.67 (2.98)**	0.67 (2.99)**	0.63 (2.80)**	0.66 (2.94)**
Family income-to-needs ratio		0.53 (17.22)**	0.25 (7.45)**					0.46 (5.13)**
Family income				0.02 (7.60)**				
Family size				−0.08 (2.42)**				
Family income below poverty level					−0.12 (0.97)			
Family income								
0.0–0.5 times poverty level						−0.02† (0.13)		
0.5–1.0 times poverty level						0.06† (0.38)		
1.5–2.0 times poverty level						0.44 (2.61)**		
2.0–3.0 times poverty level					0.42 (3.26)**			

2.0–2.5 times poverty level						0.46		
						(2.70)**		
2.5–3.0 times poverty level						0.81		
						(4.40)**		
>3.0 times poverty level					0.81	1.01		
					(5.96)**	(6.52)**		
Family income below poverty								
Some years							−0.46‡	
							(3.53)**	
All years							−0.45‡	
							(3.38)**	
Mean family income-to-needs ratio								
By black								−0.11
								(1.41)
By Hispanic								−0.12
								(1.38)
By female								−0.12
								(2.14)**
R^2	0.25	0.15	0.28	0.28	0.27	0.28	0.26	0.28

** p = .05; *p = .10; †not significantly different from one another; ‡not significantly different from one another.

Source: Authors' calculations based on ordinary least squares (OLS) regressions for sample in table 12.1.

a. Absolute value of t-statistics in parentheses. See text and table 12.1 for description of variables. N = 1,908.

TABLE 12.4 / Effect of Background Characteristics and Family Income on 1990 Log Hourly Wage[a]

	Model							
Independent Variable	1	2	3	4	5	6	7	8
Constant	1.99	2.11	1.96	1.99	2.04	2.00	2.07	1.95
	(20.58)**	(52.29)**	(20.21)**	(19.10)**	(20.49)**	(19.58)**	(20.91)**	(19.29)**
Born in 1963	0.001	−0.002	0.001	0.001	−0.001	−0.001	−0.001	0.0003
	(0.03)	(0.07)	(0.02)	(0.04)	(0.04)	(0.02)	(0.04)	(0.01)
Mother's education	0.01		0.01	0.01	0.01	0.01	0.01	0.01
	(1.44)		(1.00)	(0.98)	(0.94)	(0.93)	(1.01)	(1.01)
Missing mother's education	−0.12		−0.12	−0.12	−0.12	−0.12	−0.11	−0.12
	(1.69)*		(1.67)*	(1.68)*	(1.69)*	(1.70)*	(1.64)*	(1.68)*
Father's education	0.01		0.01	0.01	0.01	0.01	0.01	0.01
	(2.62)**		(2.16)**	(2.01)**	(2.33)**	(2.29)**	(2.30)**	(2.13)**
Missing father's education	−0.04		−0.04	−0.04	−0.04	−0.03	−0.04	−0.04
	(0.85)		(0.84)	(0.81)	(0.73)	(0.65)	(0.77)	(0.78)
Household composition								
Stepparent	−0.06		−0.06	−0.06	−0.06	−0.06	−0.06	−0.06
	(1.15)		(1.04)	(1.00)	(1.08)	(1.13)	(1.16)	(1.02)
Mother only	−0.02		0.01	0.02	0.01	0.02	0.02	0.005
	(0.41)		(0.15)	(0.33)	(0.25)	(0.40)	(0.38)	(0.12)
Father only	0.06		0.05	0.06	0.04	0.03	0.04	0.05
	(0.52)		(0.44)	(0.47)	(0.34)	(0.26)	(0.30)	(0.40)
Other	−0.15		−0.13	−0.12	−0.12	−0.11	−0.11	−0.13
	(1.53)		(1.33)	(1.21)	(1.21)	(1.13)	(1.13)	(1.32)

Location of household								
Rural	−0.07		−0.06	−0.05	−0.06	−0.06	−0.06	−0.05
	(1.83)*		(1.38)	(1.26)	(1.41)	(1.38)	(1.44)	(1.34)
Unknown city type	−0.03		−0.03	−0.02	−0.03	−0.03	−0.03	−0.03
	(0.76)		(0.61)	(0.55)	(0.64)	(0.64)	(0.69)	(0.60)
Center city	−0.02		−0.01	−0.01	−0.02	−0.01	−0.02	−0.01
	(0.45)		(0.25)	(0.21)	(0.33)	(0.25)	(0.33)	(0.22)
Black	−0.09	−0.12	−0.07	−0.07	−0.07	−0.07	−0.07	−0.09
	(2.20)**	(3.10)**	(1.82)*	(1.72)*	(1.70)*	(1.65)*	(1.72)*	(1.47)
Hispanic	0.01	0.0002	0.01	0.01	0.01	0.01	0.004	0.01
	(0.19)	(0.01)	(0.17)	(0.14)	(0.12)	(0.12)	(0.06)	(0.08)
Female	−0.19	−0.19	−0.20	−0.20	−0.20	−0.20	−0.20	−0.15
	(6.29)**	(6.13)**	(6.37)**	(6.38)**	(6.46)**	(6.42)**	(6.52)**	(2.78)**
Reading resources	0.05		0.04	0.04	0.02	0.04	0.04	0.04
	(3.03)**		(2.55)**	(2.42)**	(2.37)**	(2.21)**	(2.34)**	(2.52)**
Number of siblings	−0.02		−0.02	−0.02	−0.01	−0.01	−0.01	−0.02
	(2.64)**		(2.12)**	(1.76)*	(1.91)*	(1.74)*	(1.84)*	(2.08)**
Firstborn	−0.04		−0.03	−0.02	−0.02	−0.03	−0.03	−0.03
	(1.01)		(0.81)	(0.76)	(0.67)	(0.72)	(0.72)	(0.81)
Foreign language spoken at home during childhood	−0.01		−0.01	−0.004	−0.004	−0.001	0.01	−0.01
	(0.19)		(0.09)	(0.07)	(0.07)	(0.02)	(0.10)	(0.14)
Second-generation immigrant	0.08		0.07	0.07	0.07	0.06	0.05	0.07
	(0.84)		(0.80)	(0.79)	(0.77)	(0.67)	(0.56)	(0.77)

(Table continued on p. 356.)

TABLE 12.4 / *(continued)*

Independent Variable	Model 1	2	3	4	5	6	7	8
First-generation immigrant	0.36 (4.60)**		0.36 (4.59)**	0.36 (4.59)**	0.36 (4.57)**	0.36 (4.60)**	0.35 (4.51)**	0.36 (4.56)**
Family income-to-needs ratio		0.07 (6.57)**	0.03 (2.51)**					0.06 (1.96)**
Family income				0.002 (2.78)**				
Family size				−0.01 (0.58)				
Family income below poverty level					−0.11 (2.35)**			
Family income								
0.0–0.5 times poverty level						−0.10† (1.42)		
0.5–1.0 times poverty level						−0.06† (1.11)		
1.5–2.0 times poverty level						0.10 (1.64)		
2.0–3.0 times poverty level					0.01 (0.19)			

	(1)	(2)	(3)	(4)	(5)	(6)	(7)	(8)
2.0–2.5 times poverty level						0.02‡		
						(0.30)		
2.5–3.0 times poverty level						0.10‡		
						(1.49)		
>3.0 times poverty level					0.04	0.09		
					(0.94)	(1.67)*		
Family income below poverty								
Some years							−0.12§	
							(2.51)**	
All years							−0.15§	
							(3.23)**	
Mean family income-to-needs ratio								
By black								0.01
								(0.36)
By Hispanic								0.003
								(0.92)
By female								−0.02
								(1.15)
R^2	0.10	0.06	0.10	0.10	0.10	0.10	0.10	0.10

** $p = .05$; * $p = .10$; †not significantly different from one another; ‡not significantly different from one another; §not significantly different from one another.

Source: Authors' calculations based on ordinary least squares (OLS) regressions for sample in table 12.1.

a. Absolute value of t-statistics in parentheses. See text and table 12.1 for description of variables. N = 1,908. N = 1,604. Hourly wage converted to 1992 dollars.

TABLE 12.5 / Effect of Background Characteristics and Family Income on Total Years of Work Experience in 1990 (Females)[a]

	Model							
Independent Variable	1	2	3	4	5	6	7	8
Constant	6.28	5.29	6.29	5.97	6.58	6.43	6.92	6.37
	(9.28)**	(10.08)**	(9.29)**	(8.29)**	(9.57)**	(9.35)**	(9.90)**	(9.38)**
Born in 1963	0.52	0.58	0.52	0.52	0.52	0.51	0.49	0.51
	(3.09)**	(3.51)**	(3.09)**	(3.13)**	(3.13)**	(3.11)**	(2.96)**	(3.04)**
Mother's education	−0.03		−0.04	−0.04	−0.06	−0.05	−0.05	−0.04
	(0.84)		(0.99)	(1.02)	(1.45)	(1.41)	(1.36)	(1.09)
Missing mother's education	−0.51		−0.51	−0.51	−0.48	−0.51	−0.50	−0.51
	(1.30)		(1.30)	(1.31)	(1.23)	(1.32)	(1.28)	(1.29)
Father's education	0.04		0.03	0.03	0.03	0.02	0.03	0.03
	(1.18)		(1.04)	(0.95)	(0.96)	(0.83)	(1.04)	(1.08)
Missing father's education	−0.61		−0.62	−0.62	−0.60	−0.61	−0.58	−0.60
	(2.26)**		(2.27)**	(2.26)**	(2.20)**	(2.25)**	(2.14)**	(2.21)**
Household composition								
Stepparent	0.09		0.09	0.12	0.08	0.10	0.08	0.09
	(0.29)		(0.31)	(0.39)	(0.26)	(0.34)	(0.26)	(0.28)
Mother only	−0.46		−0.41	−0.24	−0.26	−0.18	−0.28	−0.41
	(2.15)**		(1.87)*	(1.00)	(1.17)	(0.82)	(1.28)	(1.85)*
Father only	0.30		0.28	0.37	0.22	0.27	0.06	0.32
	(0.34)		(0.32)	(0.42)	(0.25)	(0.30)	(0.07)	(0.36)
Other	−1.05		−1.05	−0.86	−0.95	−0.82	−0.93	−1.04
	(1.90)*		(1.88)*	(1.53)	(1.72)*	(1.48)	(1.68)*	(1.87)*

Location of household								
Rural	−0.05		−0.02	−0.01	0.01	−0.01	−0.02	−0.03
	(0.23)		(0.11)	(0.05)	(0.04)	(0.04)	(0.10)	(0.12)
Unknown city type	0.16		0.18	0.20	0.20	0.19	0.18	0.18
	(0.64)		(0.72)	(0.82)	(0.82)	(0.78)	(0.74)	(0.75)
Center city	−0.12		−0.10	−0.10	−0.09	−0.10	−0.08	−0.12
	(0.47)		(0.40)	(0.37)	(0.36)	(0.39)	(0.33)	(0.45)
Black	−0.92	−1.26	−0.88	−0.93	−0.77	−0.75	−0.81	−1.01
	(4.10)**	(6.07)**	(3.85)**	(4.04)**	(3.41)**	(3.30)**	(3.63)**	(2.90)**
Hispanic	−0.11	−0.27	−0.13	−0.16	−0.14	−0.15	−0.15	−0.69
	(0.31)	(1.16)	(0.35)	(0.45)	(0.39)	(0.42)	(0.42)	(1.42)
Reading resources	0.21		0.19	0.19	0.11	0.08	0.12	0.18
	(2.08)**		(1.84)*	(1.87)*	(1.14)	(0.83)	(1.21)	(1.78)*
Number of siblings	−0.10		−0.09	−0.12	−0.06	−0.05	−0.06	−0.08
	(2.50)**		(2.29)**	(2.77)**	(1.47)	(1.22)	(1.55)	(2.14)**
Firstborn	−0.18		−0.16	−0.19	−0.11	−0.12	−0.11	−0.17
	(0.86)		(0.78)	(0.93)	(0.52)	(0.57)	(0.52)	(0.81)
Foreign language spoken at home during childhood	−0.14		−0.12	−0.12	−0.09	−0.04	−0.10	−0.10
	(0.43)		(0.35)	(0.36)	(0.27)	(0.13)	(0.30)	(0.29)
Second-generation immigrant	−0.08		−0.08	−0.08	−0.12	−0.17	−0.21	−0.11
	(0.15)		(0.16)	(0.16)	(0.23)	(0.33)	(0.40)	(0.22)
First-generation immigrant	0.47		0.47	0.44	0.52	0.45	0.39	0.49
	(1.07)		(1.06)	(0.99)	(1.20)	(1.04)	(0.89)	(1.11)

(Table continued on p. 360.)

TABLE 12.5 / *(continued)*

Independent Variable	Model 1	2	3	4	5	6	7	8
Education	−0.07 (1.63)	−0.04 (0.89)	−0.08 (1.78)*	−0.08 (1.81)*	−0.09 (2.04)**	−0.10 (2.18)**	−0.09 (1.94)*	−0.08 (1.68)*
Family income-to-needs ratio		0.18 (3.16)**	0.07 (1.14)					0.03 (0.48)
Family income				0.01 (1.56)				
Family size				0.08 (1.30)				
Family income below poverty level					−0.50 (2.07)**			
Family income								
0.0–0.5 times poverty level						−0.66† (1.78)*		
0.5–1.0 times poverty level						−0.12† (0.44)		
1.5–2.0 times poverty level						0.70 (2.19)**		
2.0–3.0 times poverty level					0.70 (2.92)**			

	(1)	(2)	(3)	(4)	(5)	(6)	(7)	(8)
2.0–2.5 times poverty level						1.27		
						(4.09)**		
2.5–3.0 times poverty level						0.63		
						(1.87)*		
>3.0 times poverty level					0.49	0.81		
					(1.93)*	(2.84)**		
Family income below poverty								
Some years							−0.35	
							(1.39)	
All years							−1.02	
							(3.97)**	
Mean family income-to-needs ratio								
By black								0.05
								(0.34)
By Hispanic								0.28
								(1.69)*
R^2	0.11	0.08	0.11	0.12	0.13	0.14	0.13	0.12

** $p = .05$; *$p = .10$; †not significantly different from one another.

Source: Authors' calculations based on ordinary least squares (OLS) regressions for sample in table 12.1.

a. Absolute value of t-statistics in parentheses. See text and table 12.1 for description of variables. $N = 919$.

TABLE 12.6 / Effect of Background Characteristics and Family Income on Total Years of Work Experience in 1990 (Males)[a]

Independent Variable	Model 1	2	3	4	5	6	7	8
Constant	11.46	9.89	11.47	11.71	11.64	11.55	11.73	11.50
	(18.78)**	(21.03)**	(18.78)**	(18.22)**	(18.74)**	(18.26)**	(18.79)**	(18.62)**
Born in 1963	0.85	0.78	0.85	0.85	0.85	0.86	0.85	0.83
	(5.34)**	(4.89)**	(5.32)**	(5.32)**	(5.34)**	(5.34)**	(5.33)**	(5.23)**
Mother's education	−0.02		−0.03	−0.02	−0.03	−0.04	−0.03	−0.03
	(0.61)		(0.72)	(0.69)	(0.94)	(1.01)	(0.77)	(0.75)
Missing mother's education	−0.57		−0.58	−0.56	−0.57	−0.58	−0.57	−0.56
	(1.71)*		(1.71)*	(1.68)*	(1.73)*	(1.74)*	(1.71)*	(1.70)*
Father's education	−0.01		−0.02	−0.01	−0.02	−0.02	−0.01	−0.02
	(0.33)		(0.50)	(0.36)	(0.62)	(0.54)	(0.45)	(0.57)
Missing father's education	0.30		0.30	0.29	0.31	0.33	0.30	0.25
	(1.18)		(1.19)	(1.16)	(1.24)	(1.32)	(1.19)	(1.01)
Household composition								
Stepparent	−0.35		−0.33	−0.36	−0.31	−0.28	−0.36	−0.31
	(1.20)		(1.14)	(1.23)	(1.06)	(0.97)	(1.24)	(1.07)
Mother only	−0.84		−0.79	−0.86	−0.70	−0.68	−0.74	−0.79
	(3.87)**		(3.54)**	(3.67)**	(3.11)**	(3.04)**	(3.31)**	(3.54)**
Father only	−0.38		−0.40	−0.49	−0.43	−0.45	−0.44	−0.41
	(0.69)		(0.72)	(0.86)	(0.78)	(0.82)	(0.80)	(0.75)
Other	−0.89		−0.85	−0.94	−0.76	−0.78	−0.78	−0.82
	(1.99)**		(1.88)*	(2.04)**	(1.69)*	(1.72)*	(1.73)*	(1.83)*

Location of household								
Rural	−0.58		−0.54	−0.55	−0.48	−0.47	−0.51	−0.55
	(2.77)**		(2.51)**	(2.56)**	(2.22)**	(2.19)**	(2.42)**	(2.56)**
Unknown city type	−0.19		−0.17	−0.18	−0.15	−0.16	−0.17	−0.19
	(0.82)		(0.76)	(0.80)	(0.66)	(0.68)	(0.76)	(0.81)
Center city	−0.86		−0.83	−0.85	−0.82	−0.83	−0.84	−0.80
	(3.41)**		(3.30)**	(3.35)**	(3.24)**	(3.30)**	(3.33)**	(3.16)**
Black	−0.46	−0.71	−0.43	−0.40	−0.36	−0.35	−0.39	−0.08
	(2.17)**	(3.65)**	(1.98)**	(1.86)**	(1.69)*	(1.61)	(1.82)*	(0.25)
Hispanic	−0.23	−0.01	−0.22	−0.20	−0.23	−0.25	−0.23	−0.53
	(0.72)	(0.06)	(0.67)	(0.62)	(0.71)	(0.77)	(0.70)	(1.16)
Reading resources	−0.14		−0.15	−0.14	−0.17	−0.17	−0.16	−0.15
	(1.47)		(1.57)	(1.56)	(1.84)*	(1.85)*	(1.69)*	(1.66)*
Number of siblings	−0.11		−0.10	−0.08	−0.09	−0.08	−0.09	−0.10
	(2.81)**		(2.56)**	(1.64)	(2.18)**	(2.07)**	(2.35)**	(2.58)**
Firstborn	−0.15		−0.13	−0.11	−0.12	−0.11	−0.12	−0.14
	(0.78)		(0.70)	(0.60)	(0.60)	(0.59)	(0.62)	(0.73)
Foreign language spoken at home during childhood	0.33		0.33	0.34	0.37	0.40	0.37	0.33
	(1.01)		(1.01)	(1.04)	(1.13)	(1.24)	(1.15)	(1.03)
Second-generation immigrant	−0.11		−0.10	−0.11	−0.09	−0.13	−0.15	−0.05
	(0.22)		(0.21)	(0.22)	(0.20)	(0.27)	(0.31)	(0.10)
First-generation immigrant	−0.22		−0.21	−0.19	−0.19	−0.22	−0.22	−0.14
	(0.56)		(0.54)	(0.47)	(0.48)	(0.55)	(0.57)	(0.36)

(Table continued on p. 364.)

TABLE 12.6 / *(continued)*

Independent Variable	Model 1	2	3	4	5	6	7	8
Education	−0.33	−0.35	−0.34	−0.34	−0.35	−0.35	−0.34	−0.34
	(8.18)**	(9.14)**	(8.22)**	(8.20)**	(8.45)**	(8.38)**	(8.36)**	(8.30)**
Family income-to-needs ratio		0.13	0.07					0.10
		(2.32)**	(1.03)					(1.31)
Family income				0.00				
				(0.65)				
Family size				−0.07				
				(1.18)				
Family income below poverty level					−0.23			
					(1.04)			
Family income								
0.0–0.5 times poverty level						−0.50†		
						(1.36)		
0.5–1.0 times poverty level						−0.08†		
						(0.30)		
1.5–2.0 times poverty level						0.13		
						(0.42)		

2.0–3.0 times poverty level					0.32			
					(1.32)			
2.0–2.5 times poverty level						0.53‡		
						(1.67)*		
2.5–3.0 times poverty level						0.20‡		
						(0.59)		
>3.0 times poverty level					0.43	0.49		
					(1.69)*	(1.69)*		
Family income below poverty								
Some years							−0.38§	
							(1.63)	
All years							−0.41§	
							(1.74)*	
Mean family income-to-needs ratio								
By black								−0.21
								(1.56)
By Hispanic								0.19
								(1.10)
R^2	0.15	0.11	0.15	0.15	0.15	0.15	0.15	0.15

** p = .05; *p = .10; †not significantly different from one another; ‡not significantly different from one another; §not significantly different from one another.

Source: Authors' calculations based on ordinary least squares (OLS) regressions for sample in table 12.1.

a. Absolute value of t-statistics in parentheses. See text and table 12.1 for description of variables. N = 989.

income 1.0–1.5 times poverty level was omitted). For most outcomes, using eight categories did not describe the data better than using only four categories did.

The exact nature of the income effect depended on the particular outcome being measured. For education (table 12.3) and AFQT (table 12.2), the income effect was monotonic: higher levels of family income for adolescents were positively associated with better outcomes at all points in the income distribution. Experiencing poverty as an adolescent was negatively associated with the wages of working adults, but incomes above poverty did not have any differential impact on wages (table 12.4). Income did not matter at all for male labor market experience (table 12.6). As the regressions for females' work experience (table 12.5) show, women from poor families had the lowest levels of labor market experience, but women from middle-income backgrounds had higher levels of experience than women from the highest-income backgrounds. Model 7 tested the hypothesis that the length of time in poverty as an adolescent mattered for academic and labor market outcomes. Except for its effect on females' work experience, we cannot reject the hypothesis that being in poverty some years has the same effect as being in poverty all years.[9]

Given our set of family background controls, family income during early adolescence explained very little additional variation in academic and labor market outcomes. Comparing columns 1 and 3, the R^2 (that is, the proportion of the variation in the dependent variable explained by variation in the independent variables) increased from .37 to .38 in the AFQT regressions and from .25 to .28 in the education regressions, and the wage and experience regressions showed no increase in the R^2.[10] Because family income and family background characteristics were highly correlated, we expected that adding income to the regressions in column one would reduce the size of many of the family background characteristics. Similarly, adding family background characteristics to the regressions in column two should reduce the size of the income effect. In fact, the income effects fell to half the size, but the family background effects were reduced by only a little, in general, 5–15 percent. The exceptions were that the inclusion of income had a larger effect on number of siblings in the education and AFQT regressions, and controlling for income in the education regressions made the mother-only effect fall to one-fifth its size and become statistically insignificant.

Family Background

One surprising result was that living in a female-headed household at age fourteen (mother only) did not significantly affect academic outcomes. For the AFQT regressions, the variable mother only was never significant (either statistically or quantitatively), even in the regression that did not control for family income (model 1).[11] As mentioned, the mother-only effect in the schooling regression disappeared completely as soon as we controlled for income. In contrast, living in a stepparent family had large negative effects on both outcomes. Achievement test percentile rankings were about five points lower, and completed schooling was three-quarters of a year lower for those living in stepparent families, even after controlling for income. Other research has found that growing up in a single-parent household has significant negative effects on children's outcomes, but this research combined single-parent with stepparent families (McLanahan and Sandefur 1994).[12] Turning to adult labor market outcomes, the stepparent effect disappeared, but living in a female-headed household at age fourteen reduced subsequent labor market experience. This effect was most likely due to the increased probability that a single-parent household would receive welfare, which, as we document in the next section, reduces adult labor market experience.

Another aspect of family structure is the number of siblings and their birth order. Consistent with other literature, we found some evidence that being a firstborn child increases performance on the AFQT, but the effects were small and only marginally significant (Retherford and Sewell 1991; Zajonc et al. 1991). The variable firstborn had no significant effect on schooling outcomes or labor market outcomes.

Both sociological and economic theories suggest that children born in larger families will have worse outcomes than those in smaller families (Blake 1989; Becker 1991). Blake argues that large families have fewer resources to go around. Becker argues that providing a given level of quality (for example, in education) is more expensive in large families because parents want to give all their children the same level of quality. Similarly, parents who desire a high level of quality will find having additional children more expensive than parents who would choose lower levels. As predicted, we found that the number of siblings was negatively correlated with all outcomes, and the estimates were generally statistically significant. The magnitudes of the sibling effects were not large, in part because the regressions in columns 3–8 already include some measure of family size, either directly (model 4) or indirectly through the poverty threshold adjustment, and family size was highly correlated with the number of siblings. In theory, it is possible that the effect of the number of siblings could differ from that of family size. The latter adjusts income for the consumption needs of more family members, but if children are time intensive, the former would account for competing demands on parents' time as well.

As expected, parents' education had significant and positive effects on adolescents' academic outcomes, increasing the AFQT percentile by more than 1 point and the respondent's schooling by more than a tenth of a year for each year of the mother's education. The effect of the father's education is about 20 percent smaller than that of the mother's. The results suggest that someone whose parents were both college graduates would rank more than 9 percentile points higher on the AFQT than someone whose parents were both high school graduates. The father's education, but not the mother's, also significantly increased adult wage rates. In standard log wage regressions that include the respondents' own education, the coefficient on education usually ranges from 0.07 to 0.10, so the effect of the father's education is about one-tenth the size of the effect of the respondent's education (Ehrenberg and Smith 1994). Note also that neither parent's education had a statistically significant effect on years of labor market experience for males or females.

The negative effect of not reporting the mother's education was quite large: such respondents ranked about 9 percentile points lower on the AFQT, received a half a year less schooling, earned 12 percent lower wages, and had half a year less labor market experience. This variable may be a proxy for a particular kind of family structure—such as, respondents who never knew their mother—and may partly explain the insignificance of living in a father-only household or in other household structures. Four percent of whites and 8 percent of blacks and Hispanics did not report their mother's education. The category missing father's education also had a negative effect on outcomes, but except for its effect on females' work experience, the size of the effect is much smaller and is less precisely measured.

Our results show that a very important family resource is the availability of reading material—access to the library, magazines, or newspapers. For each of these resources available, the respondents' AFQT percentile increased by more than four points, schooling increased by more than one-third of a year, wages increased by 4 percent, and labor market experience for women increased by 0.2 years. We cannot determine from our analysis whether these results were due to a correlation between the availability of reading resources in the household and other unmeasured characteristics of the family that promote educational values, or whether subsidizing libraries in a neighborhood or providing free subscriptions to newspapers or magazines would improve children's outcomes.

Residential location also had significant effects on adolescents' outcomes. In particular living in a center city lowered AFQT percentile rank by more than 2 points, lowered completed schooling by more than one-third of a year, and reduced the labor market experience of males by 0.8 years.[13] Center-city location can be a proxy for a number of negative environmental variables, including exposure to lead paint during infancy, the presence of gangs, high local unemployment rates, lack of successful role models, and a poor social infrastructure (schools, parks, and other neighborhood resources). Note that in the AFQT regressions the estimates for living in a center-city location did not always reach conventional levels of statistical significance. In the AFQT regressions that did not limit the sample to those who were interviewed in 1989, the coefficient on living in a center-city location was much more precisely estimated. This result implies that there was selective sample attrition for center city residents with the worst outcomes.

First-generation immigrants attained more education than natives, and second-generation immigrants attained even more. There is some controversy in the literature over the degree of economic mobility of immigrants and their children and the selective nature of the decision to immigrate in terms of the unobserved skill levels of immigrants. Borjas (1994) argues that the skill level of new immigrants has been declining over time, but that before 1970 it was, on average, somewhat higher than that of natives. Borjas also reports that in the 1970 and 1980 censuses immigrants were more likely than natives to be or become college graduates. This evidence is consistent with our results for completed schooling (table 12.3). But if Borjas is correct, we would find different results for cohorts of more recent immigrants. Surprisingly, respondents living in homes where a foreign language was spoken during childhood also received more education. Because we controlled for Hispanic ethnicity and immigrant status, it is not clear how to interpret this finding.

Racial / Ethnic Differences

With controls for family background and income, blacks ranked fifteen percentile points lower on the AFQT than whites did and earned wages that were 7 percent lower; black women worked 0.9 fewer years in the labor market, and black men worked 0.4 fewer years. Surprisingly, when we controlled for the same set of variables, blacks received two-thirds of a year *more* schooling than whites.[14] Without controls for family background and income, blacks ranked twenty-seven percentile points lower than whites on the AFQT and had wages that were 24 percent lower, so these measurable differences in background accounted for 44 percent of the AFQT gap and 30 percent of the wage gap. Family background and income must have been highly correlated for black respondents, because controlling for only family background, only income, or both made little difference in the AFQT differential. Model eight presents some evidence that the effect of income on the AFQT ranking was smaller for blacks than for whites. One possible explanation for this result is the finding that, holding income constant, blacks have lower levels of wealth than whites (Blau and Graham 1990). Thus, blacks with the same level of income may have command over fewer total economic resources.

For Hispanics, controlling for family background and income reduced the AFQT differential from nineteen percentile points to four percentile points, the educational attainment differential from one year to essentially zero, and the wage gap from 13 percent to zero. Variations in family background were much more important for Hispanics than were variations in income. Controlling only for income still resulted in a large differential in the AFQT ranking, but controlling for only family background produced almost the same result as controlling for both family background and income. Similar to the results for blacks, model eight shows that the effect of income on AFQT scores was smaller for Hispanics than for whites.

COMPONENTS OF INCOME: WELFARE AND CHILD SUPPORT

A common assumption in standard microeconomic models of household expenditures and investments in children is that income from all sources is fungible, that is, all dollars are put into a common pot and, holding relevant variables such as parental time inputs constant, the source of income has no effect on children's outcomes (see, for example, Lazear and Michael 1988; Weiss and Willis 1985). In contrast, an underlying assumption of much of the public debate over welfare reform in the 1990s was based on the idea of a culture of poverty that is in part created and sustained by the welfare system. Proponents of this view claim that welfare receipt has negative psychological consequences that reduce an individual's motivation to develop the skills to achieve independence. This view implies a negative correlation between welfare receipt—especially long-term welfare receipt—and adolescent or adult outcomes that reflects a *causal* link. An alternative interpretation of that negative correlation is that families who receive welfare have other, preexisting characteristics that are associated with lower motivation or less ability to succeed. For example, families with lower assets or social support might be more likely to receive welfare and to complete less schooling, earn lower wages, or gain fewer years of labor market experience. Similarly, family violence might have negative consequences for children, but the resulting interaction with social services might also make the family more likely to apply for welfare. If this interpretation is correct, then there is no causal link between welfare receipt and outcomes.

Policy makers have also focused on a second kind of income relevant to children: child support. The Title IV-D program was set up initially to help welfare recipients establish paternity and child support awards and collect delinquent child support payments.[15] The basic idea was that children from nonintact families should receive financial support from the absent parent and not rely on the government for support. Legislation such as the 1984 Child Support Enforcement Amendments and the 1988 Family Support Act was enacted to establish child support awards for all children with absent parents, improve the adequacy of the awards, and ensure full compliance. Proposals in the mid-1990s included a child support assurance program.

An assessment of the likely consequences of the legislation and proposals must take into account both the role of income in children's well-being and the way children are affected by the source of income. Is it beneficial to children to substitute child support dollars for welfare dollars? When absent parents are forced to pay child support, does the payment have as beneficial an effect on children's outcomes as when parents pay willingly? Do child support payments help maintain a connection between the child and the absent parent that is itself beneficial? To begin to answer these questions, we first address the basic issue of whether all components of income are alike in affecting children's outcomes.

Who Receives Welfare and Child Support?

Based on weighted frequencies of child support and welfare receipt, one-third of families with a mean family income below the poverty threshold received welfare during all the years included in our sample (1978–80), but 34 percent never received welfare during those years. Note that the proportion of poor whites who

TABLE 12.7 / Welfare Receipt, by Income Category and Race/Ethnicity[a]

Welfare Status and Race/Ethnicity[b]	Mean Income[c] Below Poverty	1–2 Times Poverty Level	2–3 Times Poverty Level	>3 Times Poverty Level
Never received welfare				
White	39.5	77.2	91.7	95.7
Black	30.1	71.7	84.4	93.6
Hispanic	33.3	71.1	96.2	91.7
Received welfare some years				
White	28.7	17.2	7.9	4.0
Black	34.1	20.7	11.7	6.4
Hispanic	34.2	19.0	3.8	4.2
Received welfare all years				
White	31.7	5.6	0.8	0.3
Black	35.8	7.6	3.9	0.0
Hispanic	32.4	9.9	0	4.2

Source: Authors' calculations based on data from the National Longitudinal Survey of Youth (NLSY) on respondents born during 1963 and 1964 who were not living on their own or in an institution during the 1979 and 1980 interviews (that is, at ages fourteen to sixteen) and who either had not had a child or been married by that time.

a. Values are weighted frequencies.

b. Of the 1,908 observations in the full sample, 1,077 respondents identified their race/ethnicity as white, 498 as black, and 333 as Hispanic.

c. Family income from calendar year 1978–80. Excludes respondent's income. All incomes converted to 1992 dollars. Within each income category, the frequency distribution by racial group sums to approximately 100 percent.

never received welfare is much higher than the proportion of poor blacks or Hispanics who never received welfare (table 12.7). Less than 10 percent of those with mean family income one to two times the poverty level received welfare all years, but almost 20 percent received welfare some years. For those with mean family income more than three times the poverty level, less than 5 percent reported receiving welfare some years.

Child support receipt varied predictably by family type (table 12.8). Less than 1 percent of respondents who lived with their biological mother and father or their father only received child support in all three years.[16] About 40 percent of white respondents living in mother-only or stepparent families ever received child support during 1978–80, but only 11 to 15 percent of blacks living in those kinds of families ever received child support during the same period. These numbers

TABLE 12.8 / Child Support Receipt, by Respondent's Living Arrangement at Age Fourteen and Race[a]

	Living Arrangement at Age 14[c]				
Child Support Status and Race/Ethnicity[b]	Biological Mother and Father	Mother Only	Father Only	Stepparent Family	Other Family Type
Never received child support					
White	94.4	58.1	77.8	59.4	94.1
Black	94.3	84.7	100.0	88.6	96.8
Hispanic	94.4	84.3	100.0	69.4	87.5
Received child support some years					
White	5.2	19.4	22.2	29.2	0.0
Black	4.8	12.8	0.0	5.7	3.2
Hispanic	4.6	12.9	0.0	19.4	12.5
Received child support all years					
White	0.4	22.5	0.0	11.5	5.9
Black	0.9	2.6	0.0	5.7	0.0
Hispanic	0.9	2.9	0.0	11.1	0.0

Source: Authors' calculations based on data from the National Longitudinal Survey of Youth (NLSY) on respondents born during 1963 and 1964 who were not living on their own or in an institution during the 1979 and 1980 interviews (that is, at ages fourteen to sixteen) and who either had not had a child or been married by that time.

a. Values are weighted frequencies.

b. Of the 1,908 observations in the full sample, 1,077 respondents identified their race/ethnicity as white, 498 as black, and 333 as Hispanic.

c. Family income from calendar year 1978–80. Excludes respondent's income. All incomes converted to 1992 dollars. Within each income category, the frequency distribution by racial group sums to approximately 100 percent.

are generally consistent with national data estimates that 34.6 percent of mothers with children with an absent father received some child support in 1978 and 1981 (U.S. Department of Commerce 1981, 1986).

Does Receipt of Welfare and Child Support during Adolescence Affect Outcomes?

Would two otherwise identical individuals have the same outcomes, if during adolescence one lived in a family that received welfare or child support but the other lived in a family that did not? If, as argued earlier, families who receive welfare or child support also have characteristics that directly affect their children's later outcomes, then welfare or child support receipt is endogenous, and standard ordinary least squares (OLS) estimates are biased.

To account for this endogeneity, we used an econometric technique called two-stage least squares (2SLS). The first stage of the 2SLS estimate consisted of two probit regressions that estimate, respectively, the probability that respondents lived in a household that received welfare or child support when they were growing up. In the second stage we predicted welfare and child support receipt for each respondent based on the two probit regressions in the first stage and used these predictions as exogenous independent variables. We then regressed the five academic and labor market outcome variables on the standard set of income and family background variables along with the predicted welfare and child support receipt.

To identify the effects of receiving welfare and child support, we had to include in the first stage some explanatory variables that are believed to affect the probability of welfare (or child support) receipt but not to directly affect the academic or labor market outcomes measured in the second stage. As identifying instruments in the probit regressions we included (1) the unemployment rate for the respondent's local area of residence in 1979–80, (2) the maximum Aid to Families with Dependent Children guarantee in the respondent's state of residence in 1979–80; (3) a dummy variable indicating whether that state had adopted no-fault divorce at the time respondents stopped living with their biological mother and father, and (4) variables measuring the income levels and prevalence of welfare receipt in the respondent's county of residence in 1979–80. The first-stage results show that respondents living in states with high unemployment rates and more generous welfare benefits were more likely than others to receive welfare (table 12A.1). Child support receipt was more likely for respondents whose state of residence in 1979 had adopted a no-fault divorce law at the time they stopped living with their biological mother and father.[17]

To simplify our presentation of the results of both OLS and 2SLS estimation techniques, we report only the coefficients on welfare and child support (table 12.9).[18] With controls for income, the OLS results indicated that welfare receipt had a consistently negative effect on the outcomes. After 2SLS estimation to account for the possibility of endogeneity, the effect of welfare on AFQT and com-

TABLE 12.9 / Effects of Child Support and Welfare Receipt, Full Sample and by Race/Ethnicity[a]

	Outcome									
Welfare and Child Support Status[b]	AFQT		Completed Schooling		1990 Log Hourly Earnings		1990 Years of Work Experience: Female		1990 Years of Work Experience: Male	
	OLS	2SLS	OLS	2SLS	OLS	2SLS	OLS	2SLS	OLS	2SLS
Full sample										
Received any welfare	−3.90	0.14	−0.44	0.66	−0.06	−0.07	−0.68	−3.11	−0.58	−2.32
	(3.05)**	(0.03)	(3.72)**	(1.46)	(1.40)	(0.45)	(2.91)**	(3.00)**	(2.70)**	(3.23)**
Received any child support	4.15	1.05	−0.16	0.06	−0.04	−0.21	−0.35	−0.91	0.006	−1.32
	(2.18)**	(0.18)	(0.91)	(0.11)	(0.58)	(1.04)	(1.06)	(0.80)	(0.02)	(1.24)
By race/ethnicity[c]										
Received any welfare										
White	−8.48	−6.27	−0.82	−0.19	−0.12	0.09	−0.66	−3.55	−0.64	−2.80
	(4.89)**	(0.94)	(5.08)**	(0.30)	(2.01)**	(0.40)	(2.11)**	(2.18)**	(2.11)**	(2.85)**
Black	−0.03	10.86	−0.35	0.80	−0.05	0.17	−0.75	−1.92	−0.28	−0.79
	(0.01)	(2.20)**	(1.95)*	(1.73)*	(0.74)	(1.05)	(2.12)**	(1.80)*	(0.87)	(1.01)
Hispanic	−0.49	1.66	0.27	1.07	0.04	0.08	−0.63	−3.07	−0.96	−2.91
	(0.20)	(0.32)	(1.19)	(2.18)**	(0.44)	(0.45)	(1.41)	(2.86)**	(2.32)**	(3.31)**
Received any child support										
White	4.22	12.62	−0.02	0.91	−0.10	0.02	−0.39	−0.98	−0.14	−1.10
	(1.83)*	(2.57)**	(0.10)	(1.96)*	(1.22)	(0.15)	(1.00)	(1.15)	(0.32)	(1.17)
Black	4.38	19.68	−0.35	1.08	0.19	0.70	−0.24	−0.18	−0.47	−3.07
	(1.20)	(2.23)**	(1.03)	(1.31)	(1.48)	(2.28)**	(0.40)	(0.15)	(0.71)	(1.29)
Hispanic	3.30	1.64	−0.44	−0.35	−0.11	−0.04	−0.29	1.96	1.08	−0.23
	(0.73)	(0.24)	(1.05)	(0.53)	(0.76)	(0.16)	(0.34)	(1.34)	(1.49)	(0.20)
N	1,908	1,908	1,908	1,908	1,604	1,604	919	919	989	989

** $p = .05$; * $p = .10$.

Source: Authors' calculations of OLS and two-stage least squares (2SLS) analysis based on sample in table 12.1. Regressions also include same background and family income controls as in Tables 12.2–12.6.

a. Absolute value of t-statistics in parentheses. See text and table 12.1 for description of variables.

b. The data do not identify whether child support received by the household is intended for the target child. To minimize measurement error we define child support receipt (yes or no) only when the target child's household structure is mother only or stepparent. For all observations, the child support variable is automatically 0.

c. Of the 1,908 observations in the full sample, 1,077 respondents identified their race/ethnicity as white, 498 as black, and 333 as Hispanic.

pleted schooling disappeared, but its negative effect on the work experience of men and women became even larger. One possible explanation for the latter finding relates to the intergenerational transmission of welfare receipt. If the children of welfare recipients are more likely to receive welfare when they are adults, they will work less as a result. Note that Duncan and Yeung (1994) also find that welfare receipt has negative effects on educational attainment, but Teachman et al. (chapter 13, this volume) find that welfare receipt has no effect net of income.

As for the effects of welfare receipt by race/ethnicity, the OLS results again showed negative and significant effects on all outcomes for whites, but for blacks welfare affected only education and female labor market experience negatively and significantly, and for Hispanics, only male labor market experience (table 12.9, bottom panel). The 2SLS results for whites mirrored those for the full-sample analysis: for AFQT, schooling, and wages, the magnitude of the negative welfare effect decreased, and the coefficients were no longer significantly different from zero; for male and female experience, the magnitude of the negative effect increased and remained significant. Similarly, with 2SLS the effects of welfare receipt remained negative and significant for the labor market experience of Hispanic men and women and black women. However, the 2SLS AFQT and schooling regressions for blacks and Hispanics contrast sharply with those for whites: the welfare effect was positive, and three out of four coefficients were statistically significant.[19] Why might we expect welfare receipt to have a positive effect independent of income? Perhaps families who receive welfare also receive other social services (for example, Medicaid, Head Start) that enhance the well-being of their adolescents. The racial/ethnic differences in the effects of welfare receipt could also be related to stigma. Because welfare receipt is less prevalent among whites than among blacks even with controls for income (see table 12.7 and table 12A.1), white welfare recipients may experience a higher degree of stigma.

Evidence on the consequences of child support receipt for child well-being and access to resources is just beginning to emerge. Del Boca and Flinn (1994) find that child expenditures are a larger proportion of child support income than of other income. Graham, Beller, and Hernandez (1994) and Knox and Bane (1994) find that child support has positive effects on educational outcomes, but these effects are greatly reduced when the endogeneity of child support receipt is accounted for. Baydar and Brooks-Gunn (1994) also find that child support positively affects early childhood achievement, but again the effects may be due to preexisting characteristics of those who are more likely to receive child support.

Receipt of child support has significant and positive effects only for the full-sample OLS AFQT regressions, and that one effect goes away in the 2SLS estimates (table 12.9, top panel). The lack of any significant effect of child support receipt on education is surprising given the literature cited above. By race (bottom panel), child support receipt had positive effects on AFQT ranking (whites and blacks), education (whites only), and wages (blacks only). The 2SLS child support results, however, are a bit unstable, because it is difficult to find appropriate instruments to predict child support receipt during the period covered by this study.

CONCLUSIONS

In this chapter we examined the effects of family background and income on measures of adolescents' academic outcomes (an achievement test score and completed schooling) and adult labor market outcomes (wages and experience). Family income explained a much smaller proportion of the variation in all outcomes than did family background. For most outcomes the income effect was close to linear, so poverty is not a special case: increases in income at all levels of socioeconomic status will improve outcomes. In addition, children who lived in poverty some of the years covered in the study were no worse off than children who lived in poverty all of the years. The number of years of income used in our sample, however, was small (three or fewer), which is likely to limit the generalizability of our results on the effect of duration of poverty. In addition, we measured poverty during adolescence, and chapter one documents that poverty during the earlier formative stages of a child's life may have stronger effects than later poverty does.

Our results show that the components as well as the level of income are important. With controls for the level of income, adolescents living in families that received welfare had worse academic outcomes and less labor market experience. Accounting for possible endogeneity, however, the welfare effect remained negative only for labor market experience. A separate analysis by race/ethnicity yielded quite different results. The consequences of welfare receipt were much less negative for blacks than for whites. In fact, our results show that, accounting for endogeneity, black adolescents living in families that received welfare actually had *higher* achievement test scores and more years of completed education than did similar blacks living in families that did not receive welfare.

Black and white adolescents living in families that received child support had higher achievement test scores, and whites also obtained more education than did those in families with no child support. The receipt of child support had no effect on labor market outcomes. The source of the child support effect is an open question. Future research needs to examine the role of the father and to look at more recent data, in which changes in the legal environment, such as the imposition of child support guidelines and enforcement laws, may have altered absent fathers' incentives to pay child support.

Family structure is an important component of family background. Based on adolescent academic outcomes, children living in stepparent families did worse than those living with both biological parents, but children living in a female-headed household did not. Although the negative consequences of stepparent families have been confirmed in a few other studies (McLanahan and Booth 1988), most studies have combined stepparent families either with two-biological-parent families (Teachman et al., chapter 13) or with single-parent families (McLanahan and Sandefur, 1994) and have not isolated the stepparent effect. Our results do not allow us to identify the reason for the stepparent effect. Future work might explore the possibility that it results from competition for resources from half- or step-siblings. The duration of time spent in a stepparent family might also be important. For adult labor market outcomes, the stepparent effect disappeared, but living in a female-headed household at age fourteen reduced subsequent labor market experience. The female-headed household effect is most likely due to the increased probability of welfare receipt, which, in turn, reduces adult labor market experience.

APPENDIX

Table 12A.1 shows the first-stage results of probit estimation of the effects of the background characteristics and family income of the adolescents in the sample on the receipt of welfare and child support.

TABLE 12A.1 / Probit Estimation of the Effect of Background Characteristics and Family Income on Child Support and Welfare Receipt[a]

Independent Variable	Receive Any Welfare[b]	Receive Any Child Support[c]
Constant	0.24 (0.63)	−1.88 (2.88)**
Born in 1963	−0.02 (0.26)	0.10 (0.79)
Mother's education	−0.02 (1.30)	0.04 (1.61)
Missing mother's education	0.04 (0.26)	0.19 (0.75)
Father's education	−0.03 (2.40)**	0.07 (2.68)**
Missing father's education	0.16 (1.44)	−0.44 (2.97)**
Household composition		
Stepparent	0.31 (2.36)**	—
Mother only	0.70 (7.30)**	—
Father only	0.70 (2.68)**	—

(Table continued on p. 378.)

TABLE 12A.1 / (*continued*)

Independent Variable	Receive Any Welfare[b]	Receive Any Child Support[c]
Other	0.85	—
	(4.11)**	
Location of household		
Rural	−0.05	0.08
	(0.38)	(0.38)
Unknown city type	0.14	−0.06
	(1.17)	(0.36)
Center city	0.29	−0.04
	(2.35)**	(0.22)
Black	0.04	−0.70
	(0.40)	(4.44)**
Hispanic	−0.04	−0.15
	(0.28)	(0.56)
Female	0.003	−0.003
	(0.04)	(0.02)
Reading resources	−0.07	0.15
	(1.62)	(2.12)**
Number of siblings	0.05	−0.04
	(2.69)**	(1.35)
Firstborn	0.08	−0.22
	(0.81)	(1.51)
Foreign language spoken at home during childhood	0.11	−0.11
	(0.72)	(0.43)
Second-generation immigrant	−0.70	0.18
	(2.96)**	(0.46)
First-generation immigrant	−0.74	0.07
	(3.92)**	(0.17)
Mean family income-to-needs ratio	−1.09	−0.05
	(14.03)**	(0.35)

TABLE 12A.1 / (*continued*)

Independent Variable	Receive Any Welfare[b]	Receive Any Child Support[c]
Mean family income-to-needs ratio^2	0.10 (11.20)**	0.02 (0.67)
Unemployment rate in local area	0.005 (2.19)**	0.005 (1.49)
Maximum state AFDC guarantee for a family of three ($1,000)	0.80 (1.83)*	−0.97 (1.33)
Median family income in county ($1,000)	0.08 (1.52)	0.03 (0.36)
Number of AFDC recipients in county (100,000)	−0.02 (0.61)	0.02 (0.45)
Per capita income in county ($1,000)	−0.12 (1.10)	−0.002 (0.01)
No-fault divorce law in state	−0.20 (1.23)	0.34 (1.93)*
Log likelihood	−728.60	−295.59
N	1,908	593

** p = .05; *p = .10.

Source: Authors' calculations based on data from the National Longitudinal Survey of Youth (NLSY) on respondents born during 1963 and 1964 who were not living on their own or in an institution during the 1979 and 1980 interviews (that is, at ages fourteen to sixteen) and who either had not had a child or been married by that time.

a. Absolute value of *t*-statistics in parentheses. See table 12.1 and text for description of variables.

b. Reported during the 1978–81 surveys.

c. The data do not identify whether child support received by the household is intended for the target child. To minimize measurement error we define child support receipt (yes or no) only when the target child's household structure is mother only or stepparent. For all observations, the child support variable is automatically 0.

The research reported in this chapter has been funded in part by the National Institute of Child Health and Human Development Family and Child Well-Being Network, grant HD30944, and by a Summer Undergraduate Research Fellowship awarded to Mullis by the University of Colorado. We thank Lisa Gennetan for excellent research assistance.

NOTES

1. The sample consists of respondents who were born during 1963 or 1964, who were not living on their own or in an institution during the 1979 and 1980 interviews (when they were aged fourteen to sixteen), and who had not been married or had a child by the 1980 interview.
2. The NLSY data included 2,815 respondents born during 1963 or 1964. We eliminated 141 respondents who were either living on their own or in an institution during the 1979 or 1980 interviews, 211 respondents who lived in multiple-respondent households, 332 respondents with no information available on the dependent variables (the Armed Forces Qualifying Test score, education completed in 1989, or weeks of labor market experience attained by 1990), 124 respondents with no information on income available for all three years (1978–80), and 99 respondents with no information available on other independent variables.
3. Of the respondents in our final sample, 5.5 percent were either living on their own, had had a child, or had married by the 1981 survey. For these respondents we used only the income reported during the first two surveys. For respondents with information on income missing for one or two years, we averaged income over the years for which it was reported. For 17 percent of our sample we included only one year of income in the average; for 39 percent, two years; and for 44 percent, three years.
4. Note that we include Supplemental Security Income in welfare.
5. According to the Bureau of the Census, in 1978 less than 10 percent of divorced or separated women received any alimony (U.S. Department of Commerce 1981). Many of these must have received child support as well, so the proportion receiving only alimony was probably even smaller.
6. If information on either parent's education was missing, we assigned the mean value for that variable and included indicators of missing parental education in the regressions. The categories black and Hispanic were defined to be mutually exclusive. We required both parents to have been born outside the United States for the respondent to be classified as a second-generation immigrant. If the respondent was born outside the United States but either parent was born in the United States, the respondent was not classified as a first-generation immigrant. For reading resources, the respondent was asked, "When you were fourteen years old, did any household member (1) have a library card, (2) receive any newspapers, or (3) receive any magazines?" The resulting variable ranged from 0–3, indicating whether the respondent's household had none, one, two, or all three of these resources.
7. We report unweighted regression results. Weighted regressions yielded similar results.

8. For labor market experience, an *F*-test showed that the regression parameters were significantly different for men and women. Similar *F*-tests for the other outcome regressions showed that the regression parameters did not differ significantly by sex.
9. Our panel on family income is fairly short (three years). In addition, for 17 percent of our sample we included only one year of family income in the mean. These problems limit the generalizability of the inferences that we can make about the effects of persistent versus sporadic or occasional poverty.
10. For comparability with some of the other studies in this volume, we ran additional regressions excluding the variables reading resources, number of siblings, firstborn, immigrant status, and foreign language. The additional impact of family income was not much larger in these regressions.
11. The coefficient on the mother-only variable became significant in model 1 when we dropped the reading resources variable but the coefficient fell in magnitude and was not significantly different from zero as soon as we controlled for family income.
12. McLanahan and Sandefur (1994) found that the residential parent's remarriage had no significant effect on an adolescent's risk for high school dropout and teen birth.
13. Twenty-one percent of our sample was coded "unknown," primarily because of multiple county zip codes or because the respondent's Metropolitan Statistical Area has more than one Census Place Designation. We included unknown city type as a separate variable in the regressions.
14. Haveman and Wolfe (1994) and Teachman et al. (Chapter 13, this volume) also find that, with a control for income and family background, blacks received more schooling than whites.
15. Access to IV-D services has more recently been extended to nonwelfare cases, but the primary focus is still to use child support collections to reduce AFDC expenditures. The resources devoted to nonwelfare cases vary considerably across states.
16. We could not identify which household member was the intended recipient of the child support. For example, a respondent who lived with his or her biological mother and father may have lived in a household that received child support intended for a half-sibling.
17. This result is the opposite of what Peters (1986) found. One possible reason for the difference is that our analysis included disruptions that occurred any time between 1963 and 1979, whereas Peters included only divorces that occurred between 1975–78. Because no-fault divorce laws were adopted mostly during the 1970s, our no-fault variable might have captured the length of time since the respondent had lived with both biological parents (if ever). The length of time since disruption is negatively correlated with child support receipt for two reasons. First, child support payments drop off over time. Second, children who are born out of wedlock are less likely to receive child support and, because most of these children never lived with their fathers, the disruption date would be 1963 or 1964, when almost no states had no-fault divorce laws.
18. To capture possible nonlinearities in the income effect in a flexible but parsimonious way, we included mean family income-to-needs and the square of that variable.
19. See Currie (1995) for similar results.

Chapter 13

Poverty During Adolescence and Subsequent Educational Attainment

Jay D. Teachman, Kathleen M. Paasch, Randal D. Day, and Karen P. Carver

The immediate effects of poverty on the living conditions, nutrition and physical and emotional health of children are relatively well documented (Mare 1982; McLeod and Shanahan 1993; McLoyd 1990; Miller and Korenman 1994a, 1994b; Parker, Greer, and Zuckerman 1988). Less evidence is available on the longer-term consequences of poverty for children. This chapter focuses on the potential link between the experience of poverty in adolescence and subsequent educational achievement.

A variety of evidence linking events and circumstances in childhood to outcomes in later life suggests that a childhood lived in poverty may have lasting effects. A substantial body of literature indicates the importance of parental socioeconomic and household characteristics for their offspring's eventual level of education, occupational status, and income (Blau and Duncan 1967; Corcoran et al. 1992; Duncan, Featherman, and Duncan 1972; Featherman and Hauser 1978; Hauser and Daymont 1977; Hauser and Featherman 1977; Jencks et al. 1972, 1979; Jencks, Crouse, and Meuser 1983; Sewell and Hauser 1975; Sewell, Hauser, and Wolfe 1980). We build on this literature by examining the link between poverty experienced during adolescence and several educational outcomes, including high school completion, college attendance, and years of schooling attained. We take a longitudinal perspective, distinguishing between short-term and longer-term poverty. We also consider various measures of poverty as well as the impact of welfare receipt. Finally, we implement controls for a wide range of potentially confounding influences such as race, sex, parental education, family structure and intellectual ability (IQ).

PRIOR LITERATURE

A small body of literature has begun to link children's experience with poverty to later outcomes such as high school completion, years of schooling attained, teenage out-of-wedlock births and income (Duncan and Yeung 1994; Haveman, Wolfe, and Spaulding 1991; Haveman and Wolfe 1994; Corcoran et al. 1992). These studies are themselves based on earlier work seeking to link family income to the socioeconomic attainments of children (Alwin and Thornton 1984; Corcoran and Datcher 1981; Hauser and Daymont 1977; Hill and Duncan 1987; Jencks, Crouse, and Meuser 1983; Kiker and Gordon 1981; Sewell and Hauser 1975). A common feature of this literature is that it uses longitudinal data available from both parents and children in order to measure the relationship between parental economic circumstances and the well-being of children as they move into adulthood.

A key finding from this poverty research is that longer-term poverty is more strongly correlated with subsequent outcomes than is poverty measured at one point in time. Children who spend more time in poverty are less likely to graduate from high school, obtain fewer years of schooling, and earn less. This finding is important because earlier literature tended to use static measures of family social and economic status, although a substantial proportion of American families experience considerable change in their economic fortune from year to year (Duncan 1988). Consequently, static measures fail to adequately capture the long-term economic climate under which many children are raised.

Using a longitudinal database and over-time measures of poverty, we extend the literature on the effects of poverty in three ways. First, we replicate prior studies using a different database. Previous studies of the impact of poverty on long-term outcomes for children have relied almost exclusively upon the Panel Study of Income Dynamics. We make use of the National Longitudinal Surveys (NLS) first conducted between 1966 and 1968. We link social and economic data collected on mature men and women to outcomes measured for their children. Specifically, we consider the effects of poverty on various measures of educational success—high school graduation, college enrollment and years of schooling completed—using a consistent analytical framework.

Second, we examine several measures of poverty. While each measure is longitudinal, each represents a slightly different perspective on poverty. We also consider the effects of a number of control variables, including measures of parents' education, race, sex, welfare receipt, and experience in a single-parent family, on educational success. We include these variables in our analysis using a coding structure for independent variables that is common (within the limits of various databases) to the chapters in this volume, allowing greater comparability of results across chapters.

Third, we extend the analysis plan used in most of the chapters to examine the effects of intellectual ability on each of the educational outcomes. A separate body of literature has linked income and poverty to intellectual ability (Brooks-Gunn, Klebanov, and Duncan 1996; Duncan, Brooks-Gunn, and Klebanov 1994; Kim 1992; Korenman, Miller, and Sjaastad 1994). These studies indicate that poverty, especially poverty experienced over a longer period, decreases mental ability. In light of the substantial body of evidence positively linking mental ability to educational outcomes, implementing a control for ability is an important addition to previously estimated models (Duncan, Featherman, and Duncan 1972; Hauser and Daymont 1977; Sewell, Hauser, and Wolf 1980).

DATA AND METHOD

The data for the study were taken from the NLS of Young Men (aged fourteen to twenty-four in 1966; $N = 5{,}225$), Young Women (aged fourteen to twenty-four in 1968; $N = 5{,}159$), Older Men (aged forty-five to fifty-nine in 1967; $N = 5{,}020$), and Mature Women (aged thirty to forty-four in 1968; $N = 5{,}083$). Each of these age-sex cohorts was designed to be representative of the corresponding civilian noninstitutionalized population of the United States (Center for Human Resource Research 1993). Because some households were common to the sampling universe of each survey, we were able to use variables generated by the NLS to link parents to their children (through information collected in a household roster). Our data files consist of records for children with information about parents appended ($N = 1{,}594$).[1]

Our sample was restricted to adolescents aged fourteen or fifteen in the base survey year so that we could obtain at least four years of information on family income before they were likely to have left home (thus we observed adolescents either from age fourteen through age seventeen or from age fifteen through age eighteen). Note that this group of children reached adolescence during the height of the war on poverty and during a period when divorce rates were relatively low but were beginning to climb rapidly. They also represent a cohort that reached adulthood during the massive economic slowdown and stagnation that characterized the post-1973 U.S. economy. Accordingly, making direct comparisons between this cohort of respondents and both earlier and later cohorts may be hazardous.

For each year between ages fourteen/fifteen and seventeen/eighteen, we coded values for family income and welfare receipt as reported by parents. We also coded values for the living arrangements of the adolescents over this four-year period. Outcome variables—high school graduation, college attendance, and years of schooling obtained—were coded from information in subsequent follow-ups to the Young Men and Young Women surveys. We followed both young men and young women until they were twenty-five years of age.

Measures of Family Income

We measured poverty according to thresholds originally developed in the 1960s and then adjusted annually based on changes in the consumer price index. Our procedure simply compared annual cash income of the family, before taxes, to the official threshold for families of the same size.[2] Based on this comparison, we developed three measures of poverty status. The first counted the number of years between ages fourteen/fifteen and seventeen/eighteen that a child lived in a family with a total income below the poverty level. Two dummy variables measuring duration of poverty status were included in the regressions described below: whether the family was poor all four years and whether the family was poor one to three years. The baseline group consisted of children who never experienced poverty.

This first measure of poverty was crude in that it considered poverty to be an all-or-nothing state. For example, it did not distinguish children who spent four years barely above the poverty line from children who spent four years in affluence. To account for finer gradations in relative poverty, we computed an income-to-needs ratio for each year by dividing the annual cash income of the family by the poverty threshold for a family of the same size and then an average value for the income-to-needs ratio for the four years corresponding to ages fourteen/fifteen to seventeen/eighteen. The values of this variable indicate relative poverty over a four-year period.

Results based on the average income-to-needs ratio assumed that the effect of relative poverty was linear. The third measure allowed for nonlinear effects by categorizing the average income-to-needs ratio into four groups—less than 1.0, 1.0–2.0 times poverty (the baseline), 2.0–3.0 times poverty, and more than 3.0 times poverty. Unequal coefficients for the three dummy variables included in the regressions indicate nonlinear effects.

Measures of Welfare Receipt

We included two measures of welfare receipt in order to clearly distinguish between poverty status and the receipt of unearned income. Previous research has found that parental welfare receipt has negative effects on children's education and earnings (Corcoran et al. 1992; Duncan and Yeung 1994). Because poverty status and welfare receipt are so closely linked, failure to implement this control could risk confounding the impact of relative income with the source of income.

The first measure of welfare receipt was based on a question that ascertained source of income for two of the four years of adolescence covered (ages fourteen and sixteen or ages fifteen and seventeen). The measure was simply the number of years (zero to two) that the adolescent lived in a family that received welfare. The second measure, which indicated the proportion of family income that came from welfare, was an average based on the number of years information was available on both total family income and income received from welfare.

Other Variables

To account for the potential confounding impact of family structure experienced during adolescence, we counted the number of years an adolescent did not live with both parents. A variety of previous research has shown the negative effect of living in a single-parent family on children's educational and economic achievement as well as the greater likelihood that children living in poverty will live in a single-parent family (Astone and McLanahan 1991; McLanahan and Bumpass 1988; McLanahan and Sandefur 1994; Sandefur, McLanahan, and Wojtkiewicz 1992; Garfinkel and McLanahan 1986).

The two dummy variables included in the regressions were based on the number of years lived with one parent—whether the adolescent never spent time between the ages of fourteen/fifteen and seventeen/eighteen living with both parents and whether the adolescent spent one to three years between those ages living with only one parent. The baseline category consisted of adolescents who spent all years between those ages living with both parents. Unfortunately, we were unable to distinguish between children who were living with both natural parents and those living with a stepparent.

The remaining control variables were straightforward and common to most chapters in this volume. They included measures of both the mother's and the father's level of education as well as the race and sex of the adolescent. Parents' education was coded in years of schooling obtained. Race was coded as a dichotomy distinguishing between whites and blacks.

For our extension analyses, we coded ability based on a composite score constructed by the NLS staff. Scores on various aptitude and intelligence tests for adolescents were gathered in a companion survey of high schools. The composite score combined results from tests such as the Otis/Beta/Gamma, the California Test of Mental Maturity, and the Lorge-Thorndike Intelligence Test. While the psychometric properties of this composite score are uncertain, our intent was simply to construct a control for variations in general intellectual ability, not to make statements about IQ in general.[3]

Sample Means

The means and standard deviations (weighted and unweighted values) of the variables used in the regressions are shown in table 13.1. Because the NLS oversampled blacks, weighted data more correctly approximate the population of adolescents in the United States, and we discuss those figures below.

Fifteen percent of the children in the NLS sample experienced poverty during their adolescence. Four percent of the children were in poverty for their entire adolescence.[4] The average income-to-needs ratio was 2.7. Twelve percent of the families had an average income-to-needs ratio less than 1.0, and 22 percent, between 1.0 and 2.0.

Eighty-five percent of the adolescents in the NLS sample graduated from high school, and a little more than one-half attended college of some sort. The average level of schooling attained among children in the NLS was 13.06 years, substantially more than among both mothers (10.87 years) and fathers (10.90 years).

Four percent of the children in the NLS sample lived in a family that received

TABLE 13.1 / Characteristics of Individuals in the Sample

	Unweighted Data		Weighted Data	
Independent Variable	Mean	*SD*	Mean	*SD*
High school graduate	0.78	0.4115	0.85	0.3576
Attended college	0.52	0.4997	0.53	0.5165
Education (years)	12.70	2.6248	13.06	2.4662
Family poor 1–3 years	0.13	0.3349	0.11	0.3070
Family poor at all ages	0.08	0.2649	0.04	0.1941
Information on poverty status missing	0.15	0.3521	0.10	0.2954
Average income-to-needs ratio	2.33	1.5579	2.67	1.5510
Income-to-needs ratio				
Missing	0.11	0.3088	0.11	0.3047
<1	0.21	0.4062	0.12	0.3224
2–3	0.30	0.4602	0.34	0.4715
>3	0.25	0.4351	0.32	0.4634
Intervals respondent's family received welfare (0–2)	0.05	0.2171	0.04	0.2290
Average percentage of family income from welfare	0.01	0.0665	0.01	0.0566
Black	0.32	0.4673	0.14	0.3478
Male	0.57	0.4946	0.49	0.4968
Mother's education (years)	10.36	2.9131	10.87	2.7106
Father's education (years)	10.16	3.8339	10.90	3.6312
One parent absent				
1–3 years	0.09	0.2851	0.08	0.2677
At all ages	0.11	0.3173	0.08	0.2651
IQ of respondent	104.10	9.7259	105.04	9.3084
IQ score missing	0.58	0.4936	0.54	0.4949

Source: Authors' calculations using data from the National Longitudinal Surveys of Young Men (N = 5,225, aged fourteen to twenty-four in 1966), Young Women (N = 5,159, aged fourteen to twenty-four in 1968), Older Men (N = 5,020, aged forty-five to fifty-nine in 1967), and Mature Women (N = 5,083, aged thirty to forty-four in 1968).

welfare in at least one year. (Not shown is the fact that slightly over one-quarter of the families receiving welfare did so for more than one year.) Averaged over all families, welfare accounted for only 1 percent of family income.

Sixteen percent of the children spent some time in a single-parent family; 8 percent spent all four years in a single-parent family.[5] The average IQ was about 105, with a standard deviation of about 9. These values are quite close to those registered for other populations using different testing tools (Sattler 1982). Note, though, that nearly one-half the sample was missing an IQ score.[6]

RESULTS

Effects of Poverty and Control Variables

Without considering welfare receipt, we ran logistic regressions on each of the three outcomes considered: graduation from high school (table 13.2), enrollment in college (table 13.3), and years of schooling completed (table 13.4).[7] Model 1 indicates the bivariate effect of poverty status on the outcome of interest; model 2, the effects of the control variables, not including IQ; model 3, the effects of the control variables, including IQ; model 4, the net effects of poverty status and the control variables, not including IQ; and model 5, the net effects of poverty status and the control variables, including IQ.

We estimated the models on the same sample (less differences due to missing values) with the same specification of variables, with one exception: the models for college attendance were conditioned on high school graduation. Models in columns 1, 2, and 4 represent analyses replicated across chapters 5–17 in this volume. Models 3 and 5 represent the extension of the common analysis structure to include the effect of intellectual ability.

The coefficients from the bivariate models indicate a consistent effect of poverty on the education of children. Children were less likely to graduate from high school, were less likely to attend college, and completed fewer years of schooling if they had spent time living in poverty during their adolescence. Moreover, the effects were substantial. For example, children who had spent one to three years of their adolescence in a family below the poverty line were about 60 percent less likely to graduate from high school than children who had never been poor. Children who had spent four years of their adolescence living in a family below the poverty line were about 75 percent less likely to graduate from high school. The corresponding reductions in the likelihood of attending college were about 40 percent and 60 percent, respectively. On average, children who had spent some or all of their adolescence living in poverty obtained between 1.0 and 1.75 fewer years of schooling than other children.

The effects of the control variables, when they were statistically significant, were generally in the expected direction. Once other variables were taken into

(Text continued on p. 398.)

TABLE 13.2 / Replication Analysis: Effects of Poverty and Controls on High School Graduation, Full Sample[a]

Independent Variable	Model 1[b]	2[b]	3	4[b]	5
Intercept	1.7526**	−0.9435**	−3.5497**	−0.4769	−3.1259**
Family poor 1–3 years	−0.8604			−0.3944	−0.2691
	(0.423)**			(0.674)+	(0.764)
Family poor at all ages	−1.3123			−0.3958	−0.3484
	(0.269)**			(0.673)	(0.706)
Black		−0.3450	−0.1338	−0.2016	−0.0166
		(0.708)+	(0.875)	(0.817)	(0.983)
Male		0.0102	−0.0815	0.0283	−0.0543
		(1.010)	(0.922)	(1.029)	(0.947)
Mother's education (years)		0.2314	0.2072	0.2147	0.1936
		(1.260)**	(1.230)**	(1.239)**	(1.214)**
Father's education (years)		0.0365	0.0291	0.0178	0.0124
		(1.037)	(1.030)	(1.018)	(1.013)
One parent absent 1–3 years		−0.2248	−0.1909	−0.0867	−0.0605
		(0.799)	(0.826)	(0.917)	(0.941)
One parent absent at all ages		−0.4005	−0.3362	−0.3230	−0.2706
		(0.670)	(0.714)	(0.724)	(0.763)
IQ			0.0354		0.0348
			(1.036)**		(1.035)**
Information on poverty status missing	−1.1947			−0.8657	−0.8021
	(0.303)**			(0.421)**	(0.448)**
IQ score missing			−1.1337		−1.1014
			(0.322)**		(0.332)**
N	1,580	1,273	1,273	1,273	1,273
Model chi-square	82.036	127.662	167.603	139.222	176.875
df	3	6	8	9	11

(Table continued on p. 390.)

TABLE 13.2 / *(continued)*

	Model				
Independent Variable	1[b]	2[b]	3	4[b]	5
Intercept	0.0850	−0.9435**	−3.5497**	−1.2818**	−3.6056**
Average income-to-needs ratio	0.6907			0.4387	0.4113
	(1.995)**			(1.551)**	(1.509)**
Black		−0.3450	−0.1338	−0.0704	0.1112
		(0.708)+	(0.875)	(0.932)	(1.118)
Male		0.0102	−0.0815	0.0217	−0.0672
		(1.010)	(0.922)	(1.022)	(0.935)
Mother's education (years)		0.2312	0.2072	0.1980	0.1769
		(1.260)**	(1.230)**	(1.219)**	(1.194)**
Father's education (years)		0.0365	0.0291	0.0063	0.0023
		(1.037)	(1.030)	(1.006)	(1.002)
One parent absent 1–3 years		−0.2248	−0.1909	0.0301	0.0619
		(0.799)	(0.826)	(1.031)	(1.064)
One parent absent at all ages		−0.4005	−0.3362	−0.1887	−0.1358
		(0.670)	(0.714)	(0.828)	(0.873)
IQ			0.0354		0.0326
			(1.036)**		(1.033)**
Income-to-needs ratio missing	−1.1085			−0.9092	−0.9575
	(0.330)**			(0.403)**	(0.384)**
IQ score missing			−1.1337		−1.1137
			(0.322)**		(0.328)**
N	1,580	1,273	1,273	1,273	1,273
Model chi-square	168.354	127.662	167.603	166.729	202.901
df	2	6	8	8	10
Intercept	1.2016**	−0.9435**	−3.5497**	−0.7200+	−3.1315**
Income-to-needs ratio <1	−0.7759			−0.2831	−0.3018
	(0.460)**			(0.753)	(0.740)*

Income-to-needs ratio 2–3	0.6430			0.3374	0.3162
	(1.902)**			(1.401)	(1.372)
Income-to-needs ratio >3	1.5525			1.1559	1.0690
	(4.723)**			(3.177)**	(2.912)**
Black		−0.3450	−0.1338	−0.1311	0.0669
		(0.708)+	(0.875)	(0.877)	(1.069)
Male		0.0102	−0.0815	0.0125	−0.0731
		(1.010)	(0.922)	(1.013)	(0.931)
Mother's education (years)		0.2312	0.2072	0.2058	0.1833
		(1.260)**	(1.230)**	(1.228)**	(1.201)**
Father's education (years)		0.0365	0.0291	0.0106	0.0063
		(1.037)	(1.030)	(1.011)	(1.005)
One parent absent 1–3 years		−0.2248	−0.1909	−0.0049	0.0419
		(0.799)	(0.826)	(0.995)	(1.043)
One parent absent at all ages		−0.4005	−0.3362	−0.2416	−0.1748
		(0.670)	(0.714)	(0.785)	(0.840)
IQ			0.0354		0.0333
			(1.036)**		(1.034)**
Income-to-needs ratio missing	−1.2511			−0.8848	−0.9437
	(0.286)**			(0.413)**	(0.389)**
IQ score missing			−1.1337		−1.1231
			(0.322)**		(0.325)**
N	1,580	1,273	1,273	1,273	1,273
Model chi-square	159.349	127.662	167.603	162.591	199.615
df	4	6	8	10	12

* $p < .05$; ** $p < .01$; + $p < .10$.

Source: Authors' calculations of parameter estimates for logistic regressions using data as described in table 13.1. See text for description of models.

a. Odds ratios in parentheses.

b. Replication analysis.

TABLE 13.3 / Replication Analysis: Effects of Poverty and Controls on College Attendance, High School Graduates[a]

	Model				
Independent Variable	1[b]	2[b]	3	4[b]	5
Intercept	0.2591**	−3.2401**	−6.3939**	−3.2910**	−6.5140**
Family poor 1–3 years	−0.5105			0.1036	0.1968
	(0.600)**			(1.109)	(1.218)
Family poor at all ages	−0.8512			−0.0775	−0.0655
	(0.427)**			(0.925)	(0.937)
Black		−0.3335	0.5202	0.3297	0.5135
		(1.396)+	(1.682)**	(1.391)+	(1.671)**
Male		0.7067	0.6555	0.7065	0.6556
		(2.027)**	(1.926)**	(2.027)**	(1.926)**
Mother's education (years)		0.1237	0.1140	0.1240	0.1146
		(1.132)**	(1.121)**	(1.132)**	(1.121)**
Father's education (years)		0.1475	0.1392	0.1506	0.1442
		(1.159)**	(1.149)**	(1.162)**	(1.155)**
One parent absent 1–3 years		−0.1166	−0.0629	−0.1381	−0.0956
		(0.890)	(0.939)	(0.871)	(0.909)
One parent absent at all ages		0.8829	0.9059	0.9024	0.9168
		(2.418)	(2.474)	(2.466)	(2.501)
IQ			0.0331		0.0334
			(1.034)**		(1.034)**
Information on poverty status missing	−0.5227			0.1525	0.1722
	(0.593)**			(1.165)	(1.188)
IQ score missing			−0.2531		−0.2630
			(0.776)+		(0.769)+
N	1,239	1,049	1,049	1,049	1,049
Model chi-square	23.038	136.052	160.683	136.630	161.825
df	3	6	8	9	11

Intercept	−0.5717**	−3.2401**	−6.3939**	−3.3317**	−6.3898**
Average income-to-needs ratio	0.2636			0.1154	0.0997
	(1.302)**			(1.122)*	(1.105)*
Black		0.3335	0.5202	0.4285	0.5975
		(1.396)+	(1.682)**	(1.535)*	(1.818)**
Male		0.7067	0.6555	0.7136	0.6613
		(2.027)**	(1.926)**	(2.041)**	(1.937)**
Mother's education (years)		0.1237	0.1140	0.1098	0.1020
		(1.132)**	(1.121)**	(1.116)**	(1.107)**
Father's education (years)		0.1475	0.1392	0.1377	0.1307
		(1.159)**	(1.149)**	(1.148)**	(1.140)**
One parent absent 1–3 years		−0.1166	−0.0629	−0.0560	−0.0107
		(0.890)	(0.939)	(0.946)	(0.989)
One parent absent at all ages		0.8892	0.9059	0.9762	0.9836
		(2.418)	(2.474)	(2.654)	(2.674)
IQ			0.0331		0.0322
			(1.034)**		(1.033)**
Income-to-needs ratio missing	0.0118			0.0816	0.0672
	(1.012)			(1.085)	(1.069)
IQ score missing			−0.2531		−0.2463
			(0.776)+		(0.782)+
N	1,239	1,049	1,049	1,049	1,049
Model chi-square	48.885	136.052	160.683	141.435	164.645
df	2	6	8	8	10
Intercept	−0.1120	−3.2401**	−6.3939**	−3.2013**	−6.1943**
Income-to-needs ratio <1	−0.4122			0.0985	0.1010
	(0.662)*			(1.103)	(1.106)
Income-to-needs ratio 2–3	0.0237			−0.2135	−0.1913
	(1.024)			(0.808)	(0.826)

(Table continued on p. 394.)

TABLE 13.3 / (*continued*)

Independent Variable	Model				
	1[b]	2[b]	3	4[b]	5
Income-to-needs ratio >3	0.8372 (2.310)**			0.4502 (1.569)*	0.4119 (1.510)*
Black		0.3335 (1.396)+	0.5202 (1.682)**	0.3560 (1.428)+	0.5281 (1.696)**
Male		0.7067 (2.027)**	0.6555 (1.926)**	0.6944 (2.003)**	0.6476 (1.911)**
Mother's education (years)		0.1237 (1.132)**	0.1140 (1.121)**	0.1159 (1.123)**	0.1075 (1.113)**
Father's education (years)		0.1475 (1.159)**	0.1392 (1.149)**	0.1407 (1.151)**	0.1332 (1.142)**
One parent absent 1–3 years		−0.1166 (0.890)	−0.0629 (0.939)	−0.0800 (0.923)	−0.0263 (0.974)
One parent absent at all ages		0.8829 (2.418)	0.9059 (2.474)	0.9252 (2.522)	0.9411 (2.563)
IQ			0.0331 (1.034)**		0.0313 (1.032)**
Income-to-needs ratio missing	0.1455 (1.157)			0.3545 (1.425)	0.3185 (1.375)
IQ score missing			−0.2531 (0.776)+		0.2361 (0.790)+
N	1,239	1,049	1,049	1,049	1,049
Model chi-square	58.769	136.052	160.683	150.939	172.615
df	4	6	8	10	12

* $p < .05$; ** $p < .01$; + $p < .10$.

Source: Authors' calculations of parameter estimates for logistic regressions using data as described in table 13.1. See text for description of models.

a. Odds ratios in parentheses.

b. Replication analysis.

TABLE 13.4 / Replication Analysis: Effects of Poverty and Controls on Years of Schooling, Full Sample[a]

Independent Variable	Model 1[b]	2[b]	3	4[b]	5
Intercept	13.1944	9.1333	6.4755	9.3942	6.5998
	(0.079)**	(0.306)**	(0.754)**	(0.335)**	(0.766)**
Family poor 1–3 years	−0.9875			−0.0916	0.0585
	(0.195)**			(0.215)	(0.211)
Family poor at all ages	−1.769			−0.4206	−0.3781
	(0.244)**			(0.313)	(0.305)
Black		0.0001	0.2560	0.1032	0.3417
		(0.166)	(0.165)	(0.175)	(0.173)*
Male		0.2952	0.1678	0.3043	0.1803
		(0.132)*	(0.130)	(0.132)*	(0.130)
Mother's education (years)		0.2283	0.1996	0.2163	0.1892
		(0.029)**	(0.029)**	(0.030)**	(0.029)**
Father's education (years)		0.1245	0.1105	0.1165	0.1056
		(0.023)**	(0.022)**	(0.023)**	(0.023)**
One parent absent 1–3 years		−0.3244	−0.2911	−0.2598	−0.2471
		(0.255)	(0.249)	(0.257)	(0.251)
One parent absent at all ages		−0.2149	−0.1665	−0.0863	−0.0410
		(0.560)	(0.547)	(0.569)	(0.555)
IQ			0.0343		0.0349
			(0.007)**		(0.007)**
Information on poverty status missing	−10.585			−0.6021	−0.5376
	(0.185)**			(0.252)*	(0.246)*
IQ score missing			−0.8645		−0.8570
			(0.133)**		(0.133)**
N	1,579	1,272	1,272	1,272	1,270
R^2	0.0705	0.1651	0.2066	0.1634	0.2105

(Table continued on p. 396.)

TABLE 13.4 / *(continued)*

Independent Variable	Model				
	1[b]	2[b]	3	4[b]	5
Intercept	11.5577	9.1333	6.4755	9.0548	6.6039
	(0.114)**	(0.305)**	(0.754)**	(0.304)**	(0.747)**
Average income-to-needs ratio	0.5293			0.2127	0.1858
	(0.040)**			(0.049)**	(0.048)**
Black		0.0002	0.2561	0.1525	0.3770
		(0.166)	(0.165)	(0.169)	(0.167)*
Male		0.2952	0.1678	0.2775	0.1537
		(0.132)*	(0.130)	(0.131)*	(0.168)
Mother's education (years)		0.2283	0.1996	0.2062	0.1815
		(0.029)**	(0.029)**	(0.029)**	(0.029)**
Father's education (years)		0.1245	0.1105	0.1041	0.0934
		(0.023)**	(0.022)**	(0.023)**	(0.022)**
One parent absent 1–3 years		−0.3244	−0.2912	−0.1774	−0.1626
		(0.255)	(0.249)	(0.254)	(0.248)
One parent absent at all ages		−0.2149	−0.1665	−0.1048	−0.0736
		(0.560)	(0.547)	(0.555)	(0.542)
IQ			0.0343		0.0322
			(0.007)**		(0.007)**
Income-to-needs ratio missing	−0.8581			−0.7244	−0.7221
	(0.205)**			(0.230)**	(0.225)**
IQ score missing			−0.8645		−0.8446
			(0.133)**		(0.132)**
N	1,579	1,272	1,272	1,272	1,272
R^2	0.1077	0.165	0.2066	0.1801	0.2174
Intercept	12.5565	9.1333	6.4755	9.4992	7.0711
	(0.127)**	(0.306)**	(0.754)**	(0.326)**	(0.755)**

Income-to-needs ratio <1	−1.1522			−0.4071	−0.4152
	(0.186)**			(0.230)+	(0.225)+
Income-to-needs ratio 2–3	0.3674			−0.0614	−0.0584
	(0.188)+			(0.195)	(0.191)
Income-to-needs ratio >3	1.4909			0.8004	0.6973
	(0.177)**			(0.191)**	(0.188)**
Black		0.0002	0.2561	0.1804	0.4087
		(0.166)	(0.165)	(0.173)	(0.172)*
Male		0.2952	0.1678	0.2630	0.1435
		(0.132)*	(0.130)	(0.130)*	(0.128)
Mother's education (years)		0.2283	0.1996	0.1999	0.1750
		(0.029)**	(0.029)**	(0.029)**	(0.029)**
Father's education (years)		0.1245	0.1105	0.1022	0.0913
		(0.023)**	(0.022)**	(0.023)**	(0.022)**
One parent absent 1–3 years		−0.3244	−0.2911	−0.1353	−0.1153
		(0.255)	(0.249)	(0.255)	(0.249)
One parent absent at all ages		−0.2149	−0.1665	−0.0137	0.0260
		(0.560)	(0.547)	(0.557)	(0.554)
IQ			0.0343		0.0316
			(0.007)**		(0.007)**
Income-to-needs ratio missing	−0.9852			−0.5228	−0.5509
	(0.237)**			(0.256)**	(0.250)*
IQ score missing			−0.8645		−0.8288
			(0.133)**		(0.131)**
N	1,579	1,272	1,272	1,272	1,272
R^2	0.1263	0.1651	0.2066	0.1885	0.2242

* $p < .05$; ** $p < .01$; + $p < .10$.

Source: Authors' calculations of parameter estimates for ordinary least squares regressions using data on the sample described in table 13.1. See text for description of models.

a. Standard errors in parentheses.

b. Replication analysis.

account, blacks were more likely to attend college and obtain more years of schooling than were whites.[8] Males were more likely to attend college than females, but we found no differences in the likelihood of males and females graduating from high school or in their years of schooling. Parents' education (particularly the mother's education) had a positive relationship with each educational outcome.

Experience living in a single-parent family was not associated with any of the educational outcomes (although a negative relationship existed on the bivariate level; results not shown). Given the reasonably strong relationship between family structure and educational outcomes shown in other research, this finding is somewhat surprising (Astone and McLanahan 1991; Sandefur, McLanahan, and Wojtkiewicz 1992).

Why a significant relationship failed to appear is difficult to ascertain. Perhaps we were unable to distinguish between never-disrupted and remarried households. Given that children in stepfamilies are less likely to do as well as children in never-disrupted families, our estimates of impact may have been biased by combining never-disrupted and remarried households (Astone and McLanahan 1991). We were also unable to distinguish between children who had never lived with both parents and children who had lived with both parents before adolescence. If children who had never lived with both parents were the most disadvantaged, our estimates would be further biased.

Our results might have paralleled those shown by Astone and McLanahan (1991) if we had been able to measure the living arrangements of children with greater specificity. However, the cohort of adolescents that we considered may have been different from later cohorts more commonly studied. If families consisting of a child living with one parent are increasingly families with fewer economic and social resources, our results may not be unanticipated.

When poverty status and the controls were entered into the models jointly, the effect of number of years spent below the poverty line was no longer significant in any of the models. A simple dichotomization of poverty status was not linked to variations in children's subsequent education.[9] When the average income-to-needs ratio was considered, however, the effects remained statistically significant for the educational outcomes. Respondents with fewer economic resources were less likely to graduate from high school, were less likely to attend college, and obtained fewer years of schooling. Note, however, that the size of the coefficients was substantially smaller (about 40 percent for high school graduation and 60–65 percent for college attendance and years of schooling). Thus, a substantial proportion of the bivariate effect of the income-to-needs ratio can be attributed to its association with other variables affecting educational outcomes.

Net of the control variables, the discrete version of the income-to-needs ratio indicates a significant nonlinear effect on educational outcomes.[10] This measure of poverty status indicates that children who had spent more time below the poverty line were less likely (about 20 percent) to graduate from high school than respondents just above the poverty line. There was no difference between children whose parents earned on average one to two times poverty income and children whose parents earned two to three times poverty income. However, respondents who had spent more time in affluence were several (almost three) times more likely to graduate from high school than were respondents just above the poverty line.

Conditional on high school graduation, only respondents who had spent more of their adolescence in affluence were more likely to attend college. After graduation from high school, no handicap appeared to be associated with having spent more time below the poverty line. With respect to years of schooling, children raised in affluence once again did better. And the coefficient associated with spending more years below the poverty line was of borderline significance, likely reflecting the fact that these children were less likely to graduate from high school.

Effects of Welfare Receipt

Effects of welfare receipt (tables 13.5–13.7) directly parallel those for poverty and the control variables, with the addition of welfare receipt as a predictor variable. Because the effects of the control variables, less poverty status, did not change, we show results for only three models.

The bivariate results indicate that receipt of welfare was negatively related to high school graduation and years of schooling obtained, but not college attendance. However, the multivariate results indicate that receipt of welfare did not affect any of the educational outcomes. Indeed, welfare receipt was characterized by a universal lack of impact on educational outcomes, net of the other variables in the model. Moreover, adding welfare receipt to the models previously discussed did little to change the pattern of effects discussed above.

We replaced welfare receipt with the percent of family income originating from welfare and reestimated the models (tables 13.8–13.10). The bivariate results indicate that this variable has a moderate effect on years of schooling obtained; a greater proportion of income coming from welfare was negatively related to the amount of schooling obtained. The multivariate results do not indicate that the proportion of income received from welfare affected any of the educational outcomes, however.

Effects of Ability

As for the impact of ability on educational success, we found it to be a consistent correlate of the educational outcomes being considered. Individuals with higher IQs were more likely to graduate from high school, attend college, and obtain more years of schooling. Controlling for IQ did not significantly alter the effects of the other controls, though. Contrary to the expected results, very little of the effect of poverty on educational attainment could be attributed to differences in IQ.

(Text continued on p. 412.)

TABLE 13.5 / Effects of Poverty, Welfare Receipt, and Controls on High School Graduation, Full Sample[a]

Independent Variable	Model 1	Model 2	Model 3
Intercept	1.8790**	−0.4333	−3.0803**
Family poor 1–3 years	−0.9457	−0.3992	−0.2709
	(0.388)**	(0.671)	(0.763)
Family poor at all ages	−1.2855	−0.3635	−0.3007
	(0.277)**	(0.695)	(0.740)
Number of intervals family received welfare (0–2)	−0.4425	−0.1966	−0.2632
	(0.642)*	(0.822)	(0.769)
Black		−0.1877	−0.0022
		(0.829)	(0.998)
Male		0.0385	−0.0458
		(1.039)	(0.955)
Mother's education (years)		0.2114	0.1891
		(1.235)**	(1.208)**
Father's education (years)		0.0169	0.0115
		(1.017)	(1.012)
One parent absent 1–3 years		−0.0989	−0.0759
		(0.906)	(0.927)
One parent absent at all ages		−0.2714	−0.2005
		(0.762)	(0.818)
IQ			0.0350
			(1.036)**
Information on poverty status missing	−1.2558	−0.8704	−0.8011
	(0.285)**	(0.419)**	(0.449)**
IQ score missing			−1.1093
			(0.330)**
N	1,543	1,269	1,269
Model chi-square	101.176	138.605	176.601
df	4	10	12
Intercept	0.1804	−1.2428**	−3.5631**
Average income-to-needs ratio	0.6579	0.4382	0.4087
	(1.931)**	(1.550)**	(1.505)**
Number of intervals family received welfare (0–2)	−0.4052	−0.1385	−0.2190
	(0.667)*	(0.871)	(0.803)
Black		−0.0538	0.1310
		(0.948)	(1.140)
Male		0.0300	−0.0623
		(1.030)	(0.940)
Mother's education (years)		0.1941	0.1711
		(1.214)**	(1.187)**
Father's education (years)		0.0061	0.0020
		(1.006)	(1.002)
One parent absent 1–3 years		0.0102	0.0367
		(1.010)	(1.037)

TABLE 13.5 / (*continued*)

Independent Variable	Model 1	Model 2	Model 3
One parent absent at all ages		−0.1448 (0.865)	−0.0637 (0.938)
IQ			0.0330 (1.034)**
Income-to-needs ratio missing	−0.8737 (0.417)**	−0.9054 (0.404)**	−0.9742 (0.378)**
IQ score missing			−1.1307 (0.323)**
N	1,543	1,269	1,269
Model chi-square	161.026	165.505	202.505
df	3	9	11
Intercept	1.2241**	−0.6870	−3.1001**
Income-to-needs ratio <1	−0.7047 (0.494)**	−0.2626 (0.769)	−0.2719 (0.762)
Income-to-needs ratio 2–3	0.6235 (1.865)**	0.3405 (1.406)	0.3199 (1.377)
Income-to-needs ratio >3	1.5325 (4.630)**	1.1633 (3.200)**	1.0785 (2.940)**
Number of intervals family received welfare (0–2)	−0.4028 (0.668)*	−0.1665 (0.847)	−0.2374 (0.789)
Black		−0.1181 (0.889)	0.0825 (1.086)
Male		0.0210 (1.021)	−0.0661 (0.936)
Mother's education (years)		0.2020 (1.224)**	0.1779 (1.195)**
Father's education (years)		0.0105 (1.011)	0.0061 (1.006)
One parent absent 1–3 years		−0.0291 (0.971)	0.0108 (1.011)
One parent absent at all ages		−0.1939 (0.824)	−0.1047 (0.901)
IQ			0.0336 (1.034)**
Income-to-needs ratio missing	−1.0006 (0.368)**	−0.8801 (0.415)**	−0.9579 (0.384)**
IQ score missing			−1.1399 (0.320)**
N	1,543	1,269	1,269
Model chi-square	151.870	161.369	199.217
df	5	11	13

* $p < .05$; ** $p < .01$.

Source: Authors' calculations of parameter estimates for logistic regressions using data as described in table 13.1. See text for description of models.

a. Odds ratios in parentheses.

TABLE 13.6 / Effects of Poverty, Welfare Receipt, and Controls on College Attendance, High School Graduates[a]

Independent Variable	Model 1	Model 2	Model 3
Intercept	0.2625**	−3.3270**	−6.5423**
Family poor 1–3 years	−0.5093	0.0946	0.1894
	(0.601)**	(1.099)	(1.209)
Family poor at all ages	−0.8255	−0.1969	−0.1828
	(0.438)**	(0.821)	(0.833)
Number of intervals family received welfare (0–2)	−0.0940	0.3668	0.3532
	(0.910)	(1.443)	(1.424)
Black		0.3407	0.5250
		(1.406)	(1.691)**
Male		0.7126	0.6610
		(2.039)**	(1.937)**
Mother's education (years)		0.1244	0.1148
		(1.132)**	(1.122)**
Father's education (years)		0.1530	0.1466
		(1.165)**	(1.158)**
One parent absent 1–3 years		−0.1865	−0.1456
		(0.830)	(0.865)
One parent absent at all ages		0.8559	0.8776
		(2.353)	(2.405)
IQ			0.0334
			(1.034)**
Information on poverty status missing	−0.5152	0.1289	0.1514
	(0.597)**	(1.138)	(1.164)
IQ score missing			−0.2642
			(0.786)
N	1,222	1,046	1,046
Model chi-square	22.258	138.218	163.308
df	4	10	12
Intercept	−0.5628**	−3.4040**	−6.4455**
Average income-to-needs ratio	0.2612	0.1215	0.1055
	(1.299)**	(1.129)*	(1.111)*
Number of intervals family received welfare (0–2)	−0.0696	0.3985	0.3747
	(0.933)	(1.490)	(1.455)
Black		0.4252	0.5948
		(1.530)*	(1.813)**
Male		0.7198	0.6666
		(2.054)**	(1.948)**
Mother's education (years)		0.1116	0.1035
		(1.118)**	(1.109)**
Father's education (years)		0.1400	0.1330
		(1.150)**	(1.142)**
One parent absent 1–3 years		−0.1035	−0.0594
		(0.902)	(0.942)

Independent Variable	Model 1	Model 2	Model 3
One parent absent at all ages		0.9015 (2.463)	0.9165 (2.501)
IQ			0.0321 (1.033)**
Income-to-needs ratio missing	−0.0034 (0.997)	0.0859 (1.090)	0.0638 (1.066)
IQ score missing			−0.2464 (0.782)
N	1,222	1,046	1,046
Model chi-square	48.981	143.273	166.272
df	3	9	11
Intercept	−0.1116	−3.2278**	−6.2072**
Income-to-needs ratio <1	−0.4092 (0.664)*	0.0257 (1.026)	0.0313 (1.032)
Income-to-needs ratio 2–3	0.0234 (1.024)	−0.2127 (0.808)	−0.1903 (0.827)
Income-to-needs ratio >3	0.8368 (2.309)**	0.4518 (1.571)*	0.4134 (1.512)*
Number of intervals family received welfare (0–2)	−.0160 (0.984)	0.3368 (1.400)	0.3187 (1.375)
Black		0.3654 (1.441)	0.5377 (1.712)**
Male		0.7015 (2.017)**	0.6535 (1.922)**
Mother's education (years)		0.1160 (1.123)**	0.1075 (1.113)**
Father's education (years)		0.1425 (1.153)**	0.1349 (1.144)**
One parent absent 1–3 years		−0.1196 (0.887)	−0.0677 (0.935)
One parent absent at all ages		0.8831 (2.418)	0.9034 (2.468)
IQ			0.0312 (1.032)**
Income-to-needs ratio missing	0.1336 (1.143)	0.3485 (1.417)	0.3055 (1.357)
IQ score missing			−0.2370 (0.789)
N	1,222	1,046	1,046
Model chi-square	58.788	152.246	173.774
df	5	11	13

* $p < .05$; ** $p < .01$.

Source: Authors' calculations of parameter estimates for logistic regressions using data as described in table 13.1. See text for description of models.

Note: Odds ratios in parentheses.

a. Odds ratios in parentheses.

TABLE 13.7 / Effects of Poverty, Welfare Receipt, and Controls on Years of Schooling, Full Sample[a]

Independent Variable	Model 1	Model 2	Model 3
Intercept	13.2707	9.4082	6.6077
	(0.080)**	(0.337)**	(0.767)**
Family poor 1–3 years	−1.0308	−0.1030	0.0521
	(0.194)**	(0.216)	(0.212)
Family poor at all ages	−1.7141	−0.4480	−0.3901
	(0.253)**	(0.322)	(0.314)
Number of intervals family received welfare (0–2)	−0.3948	0.0467	−0.0053
	(0.226)+	(0.272)	(0.266)
Black		0.1117	0.3505
		(0.175)	(0.174)*
Male		0.3068	0.1814
		(0.132)*	(0.130)
Mother's education (years)		0.2160	0.1880
		(0.030)**	(0.029)**
Father's education (years)		0.1154	0.1044
		(0.023)**	(0.023)**
One parent absent 1–3 years		−0.2636	−0.2547
		(0.259)	(0.253)
One parent absent at all ages		−0.1019	−0.0433
		(0.574)	(0.560)
IQ			0.0351
			(0.007)**
Information on poverty status missing	−1.6057	−0.6157	−0.5462
	(0.186)**	(0.253)*	(0.247)*
IQ score missing			−0.8603
			(0.134)**
N	1,542	1,268	1,268
R^2	0.0788	0.1615	0.2021
Intercept	11.6402	9.0672	6.6227
	(0.118)**	(0.309)**	(0.750)**
Average income-to-needs ratio	0.5094	0.2154	0.1880
	(0.041)**	(0.049)**	(0.048)**
Number of intervals family received welfare (0–2)	−0.5319	0.0127	−0.0362
	(0.216)*	(0.262)	(0.256)
Black		0.1582	0.3857
		(0.169)	(0.168)*
Male		0.2778	0.1513
		(0.131)*	(0.129)
Mother's education (years)		0.2052	0.1794
		(0.030)**	(0.029)**
Father's education (years)		0.1031	0.0921
		(0.023)**	(0.023)**
One parent absent 1–3 years		−0.1874	−0.1750
		(0.255)	(0.250)

TABLE 13.7 / (*continued*)

Independent Variable	Model 1	Model 2	Model 3
One parent absent at all ages		−0.1149 (0.562)	−0.0672 (0.549)
IQ			0.0324 (0.007)**
Income-to-needs ratio missing	−0.6814 (0.229)**	−0.7378 (0.235)**	−0.7531 (0.229)**
IQ score missing			−0.8544 (0.132)**
N	1,542	1,268	1,268
R^2	0.1091	0.1784	0.2164
Intercept	12.5725 (0.127)**	9.5116 (0.328)**	7.0811 (0.757)**
Income-to-needs ratio <1	−1.0938 (0.189)**	−0.4246 (0.235)	−0.4267 (0.229)
Income-to-needs ratio 2–3	0.3535 (0.187)+	−0.0549 (0.195)	−0.0519 (0.191)
Income-to-needs ratio >3	1.4766 (0.176)**	0.8089 (0.192)**	0.7057 (0.188)**
Number of intervals family received welfare (0–2)	−0.3308 (0.219)	0.0640 (0.266)	0.0223 (0.260)
Black		0.1884 (0.174)	0.4186 (0.173)*
Male		0.2629 (0.131)*	0.1407 (0.129)
Mother's education (years)		0.1992 (0.030)**	0.1734 (0.029)**
Father's education (years)		0.1012 (0.023)**	0.0901 (0.023)**
One parent absent 1–3 years		−0.1424 (0.256)	−0.1256 (0.251)
One parent absent at all ages		−0.0361 (0.562)	0.0158 (0.550)
IQ			0.0318 (0.007)**
Income-to-needs ratio missing	−0.7778 (0.257)**	−0.5404 (0.260)*	−0.5846 (0.254)*
IQ score missing			−0.8375 (0.132)**
N	1,542	1,268	1,268
R^2	0.1262	0.1869	0.2233

* $p < .05$; ** $p < .01$; + $p < .10$.

Source: Authors' calculations of parameter estimates for ordinary least squares regressions using data on the sample described in table 13.1 See text for description of models.

a. Standard errors in parentheses.

TABLE 13.8 / Effects of Poverty, Percentage of Income Received from Welfare, and Controls on High School Graduation, Full Sample[a]

	Model		
Independent Variable	1	2	3
Intercept	1.9774**	−0.4161	3.5590**
Family poor 1–3 years	−1.0572	−0.4409	−0.3193
	(0.347)**	(0.905)	(0.727)
Family poor at all ages	−1.4180	−0.4881	−0.4274
	(0.242)**	(0.614)	(0.652)
Percentage of income received from welfare	−1.4127	−0.0671	−0.4597
	(0.243)	(0.935)	(0.631)
Black		−0.1637	0.0349
		(0.849)	(1.035)
Male		0.0905	0.0160
		(1.095)	(1.016)
Mother's education (years)		0.2012	0.1823
		(1.222)**	(1.200)**
Father's education (years)		0.0290	0.0207
		(1.030)	(1.020)
One parent absent 1–3 years		−0.2079	−0.1765
		(0.812)	(0.838)
One parent absent at all ages		−0.3049	−0.2160
		(0.737)	(0.806)
IQ			0.0400
			(1.041)**
Information on poverty status missing	−1.4485	−0.9646	−0.9062
	(0.235)**	(0.381)**	(0.404)**
IQ score missing			−1.1334
			(0.322)**
N	1,438	1,175	1,175
Model chi-square	108.835	133.553	168.572
df	4	10	12
Intercept	0.1258	−1.2867**	−4.0939**
Average income-to-needs ratio	0.6850	0.4696	0.4366
	(1.984)**	(1.600)**	(1.548)**
Percent of income received from welfare	−1.3463	0.3203	−0.1113
	(0.260)	(1.377)	(0.894)
Black		−0.0362	0.1531
		(0.964)	(1.166)
Male		0.0912	0.0114
		(1.095)	(1.011)
Mother's education (years)		0.1819	0.1636
		(1.199)**	(1.178)**
Father's education (years)		0.0134	0.0069
		(1.013)	(1.007)
One parent absent 1–3 years		−0.0776	−0.0431
		(0.925)	(0.958)

TABLE 13.8 / (*continued*)

Independent Variable	Model 1	2	3
One parent absent at all ages		−0.1987 (0.820)	−0.1021 (0.903)
IQ			0.0374 (1.038)**
Income-to-needs ratio missing	−1.0079 (0.365)**	−1.1501 (0.317)**	−1.0911 (0.336)**
IQ score missing			−1.1090 (0.330)**
N	1,438	1,175	1,175
Model chi-square	155.816	157.670	188.992
df	3	9	11
Intercept	1.2181**	−0.6734	−3.5968**
Income-to-needs ratio <1	−0.7427 (0.476)**	−0.3239 (0.723)	−0.3237 (0.723)
Income-to-needs ratio 2–3	0.6359 (1.889)**	0.3503 (1.419)	0.3290 (1.390)
Income-to-needs ratio >3	1.5799 (4.855)**	1.2195 (3.386)**	1.1332 (3.106)**
Percent of income received from welfare	−1.3837 (0.251)+	0.1947 (1.215)	−0.2031 (0.816)
Black		−0.1019 (0.903)	0.1046 (1.110)
Male		0.0791 (1.082)	0.0060 (1.006)
Mother's education (years)		0.1899 (1.209)**	.1703 (1.186)**
Father's education (years)		0.0184 (1.019)	0.0112 (1.011)
One parent absent 1–3 years		−0.1074 (0.898)	−0.0615 (0.940)
One parent absent at all ages		−0.2303 (0.794)	−0.1291 (0.879)
IQ			0.0382 (1.039)**
Income-to-needs ratio missing	−1.1323 (0.322)**	−1.1178 (0.327)**	−1.0669 (0.344)**
IQ score missing			−1.1230 (0.325)**
N	1,438	1,175	1,175
Model chi-square	147.870	153.807	186.152
df	5	11	13

* $p < .05$; ** $p < .01$; + $p < .10$.

Source: Authors' calculations of parameter estimates for logistic regressions using data as described in table 13.1. See text for description of models.

a. Odds ratios in parentheses.

TABLE 13.9 / Effects of Poverty, Percentage of Income Received from Welfare, and Controls on College Attendance, Full Sample[a]

Independent Variable	Model 1	Model 2	Model 3
Intercept	0.2584**	−3.3292**	−6.6362**
Family poor 1–3 years	−0.5085	0.0999	0.1954
	(0.601)**	(1.105)	(1.216)
Family poor at all ages	−0.8309	−0.2286	−0.2086
	(0.436)**	(0.796)	(0.812)
Percent of income received from welfare	−0.2593	1.3027	1.2327
	(0.772)	(3.679)	(3.430)
Black		0.4349	0.6167
		(1.545)*	(1.853)**
Male		0.6636	0.6170
		(1.942)**	(1.853)**
Mother's education (years)		0.1224	0.1138
		(1.130)**	(1.121)**
Father's education (years)		0.1565	0.1490
		(1.169)**	(1.161)**
One parent absent 1–3 years		−0.2489	−0.2025
		(0.780)	(0.817)
One parent absent at all ages		0.8327	0.8568
		(2.300)	(2.356)
IQ			0.0343
			(1.035)**
Information on poverty status missing	−0.5297	0.1623	0.1965
	(0.589)**	(1.176)	(1.217)
IQ score missing			−0.2782
			(0.757)
N	1,143	971	971
Model chi-square	22.256	127.011	151.371
df	4	10	12
Intercept	−0.5694	−3.3811**	−6.4975**
	(0.566)**		
Average income-to-needs ratio	0.2642	0.1246	0.1094
	(1.302)**	(1.133)*	(1.116)*
Percent of income received from welfare	−0.4102	1.1705	1.0634
	(0.664)	(3.223)	(2.896)
Black		0.5228	0.6923
		(1.687)**	(1.998)**
Male		0.6708	0.6235
		(1.956)**	(1.865)**
Mother's education (years)		0.1090	0.1013
		(1.115)**	(1.107)**
Father's education (years)		0.1416	0.1336
		(1.152)**	(1.143)**
One parent absent 1–3 years		−0.1577	−0.1071
		(0.854)	(0.898)

TABLE 13.9 / (*continued*)

Independent Variable	Model 1	Model 2	Model 3
One parent absent at all ages		0.8740 (2.396)	0.8952 (2.448)
IQ			0.0329 (1.033)**
Income-to-needs ratio missing	−0.2117 (0.809)	−0.0230 (0.977)	0.0176 (1.018)
IQ score missing			−0.2642 (0.768)
N	1,143	971	971
Model chi-square	48.561	131.895	154.210
df	3	9	11
Intercept	−0.1060	−3.1821**	−6.2326**
Income-to-needs ratio <1	−0.4291 (0.651)*	−0.0224 (0.978)	−0.0175 (0.983)
Income-to-needs ratio 2–3	0.0165 (1.017)	−0.2003 (0.818)	−0.1789 (0.836)
Income-to-needs ratio >3	0.8410 (2.319)**	0.4608 (1.585)*	0.4242 (1.528)*
Percent of income received from welfare	−0.2461 (0.782)	0.9602 (2.612)	0.8769 (2.403)
Black		0.4670 (1.595)*	0.6402 (1.897)**
Male		0.6518 (1.919)**	0.6097 (1.840)**
Mother's education (years)		0.1125 (1.119)**	0.1043 (1.110)**
Father's education (years)		0.1434 (1.154)**	0.1350 (1.145)**
One parent absent 1–3 years		−0.1644 (0.848)	−0.1063 (0.899)
One parent absent at all ages		0.8699 (2.387)	0.8956 (2.449)
IQ			0.0320 (1.033)**
Income-to-needs ratio missing	−0.0730 (0.930)	0.2278 (1.256)	0.2465 (1.279)
IQ score missing			−0.2561 (0.774)
N	1,143	971	971
Model chi-square	59.464	140.429	161.343
df	5	11	13

* $p < .05$; ** $p < .01$.

Source: Authors' calculations of parameter estimates for logistic regressions using data as described in table 13.1. See text for description of models.

a. Odds ratios in parentheses.

TABLE 13.10 / Effects of Poverty, Percentage of Income Received from Welfare, and Controls on Years of Schooling, Full Sample[a]

Independent Variable	Model 1	Model 2	Model 3
Intercept	13.3129	9.4496	6.4438
	(0.083)**	(0.350)**	(0.800)**
Family poor 1–3 years	−1.0713	−0.1006	0.0450
	(0.194)**	(0.219)	(0.214)
Family poor at all ages	−1.7328	−0.5006	−0.4444
	(0.257)**	(0.331)	(0.323)
Percent of income received from welfare	−1.9028	0.4894	0.1752
	(1.047)+	(1.393)	(1.360)
Black		0.1418	0.3830
		(0.181)	(0.179)*
Male		0.2748	0.1572
		(0.137)*	(0.135)
Mother's education (years)		0.2061	0.1808
		(0.030)**	(0.030)**
Father's education (years)		0.1257	0.1118
		(0.024)**	(0.024)**
One parent absent 1–3 years		−0.3561	−0.3349
		(0.268)	(0.262)
One parent absent at all ages		−0.1511	−0.0809
		(0.581)	(0.567)
IQ			0.0370
			(0.007)**
Information on poverty status missing	−1.7198	−0.6051	−0.5438
	(0.191)**	(0.273)*	(0.266)*
IQ score missing			−0.8501
			(0.139)**
N	1,437	1,174	1,174
R^2	0.0866	0.1706	0.2125
Intercept	11.6141	9.1240	6.4707
	(0.117)**	(0.316)**	(0.781)**
Average income-to-needs ratio	0.5184	0.2244	0.1964
	(0.041)**	(0.051)**	(0.050)**
Percent of income received from welfare	−2.5624	0.2644	−0.0444
	(0.985)**	(1.318)	(1.290)
Black		0.1847	0.4096
		(0.174)	(0.173)*
Male		0.2589	0.1448
		(0.136)	(0.132)
Mother's education (years)		0.1932	0.1709
		(0.030)**	(0.030)**
Father's education (years)		0.1085	0.0956
		(0.024)**	(0.024)**
One parent absent 1–3 years		−0.2632	−0.2440
		(0.264)	(0.259)

TABLE 13.10 / *(continued)*

Independent Variable	Model 1	Model 2	Model 3
One parent absent at all ages		−0.1383 (0.572)	−0.0825 (0.560)
IQ			0.0340 (0.007)**
Income-to-needs ratio missing	−1.0620 (0.338)**	−1.0473 (0.349)**	−0.9172 (0.342)**
IQ score missing			−0.8155 (0.138)**
N	1,437	1,174	1,174
R^2	0.1164	0.1869	0.2241
Intercept	12.5821 (0.127)**	9.6332 (0.337)**	6.9994 (0.788)**
Income-to-needs ratio <1	−1.1247 (0.188)**	−0.5137 (0.237)*	−0.5080 (0.232)*
Income-to-needs ratio 2–3	0.3349 (0.188)+	−0.0576 (0.197)	−0.0566 (0.193)
Income-to-needs ratio >3	1.4808 (0.178)**	0.8201 (0.196)**	0.7173 (0.192)**
Percent of income received from welfare	−1.8106 (0.989)+	0.5360 (1.329)	0.2567 (1.302)
Black		0.2291 (0.179)	0.4555 (0.178)*
Male		0.2431 (0.135)	0.1336 (0.134)
Mother's education (years)		0.1852 (0.030)**	0.1629 (0.030)**
Father's education (years)		0.1053 (0.024)**	0.0924 (0.023)**
One parent absent 1–3 years		−0.1944 (0.266)	−0.1725 (0.260)
One parent absent at all ages		−0.0464 (0.571)	0.0106 (0.559)
IQ			0.0333 (0.007)**
Income-to-needs ratio missing	−1.1519 (0.355)**	−0.8686 (0.367)*	−0.7684 (0.359)*
IQ score missing			−0.7980 (0.137)**
N	1,437	1,174	1,174
R^2	0.1358	0.1902	0.2247

* $p < .05$; ** $p < .01$; + $p < .10$.

Source: Authors' calculations of parameter estimates for ordinary least squares regressions using data on the sample described in table 13.1 See text for description of models.

a. Standard errors in parentheses.

TABLE 13.11 / Summary of Models Testing Interactions among Race, Sex, and Poverty Status

	High School Graduation[a]		College Attendance[a]		Years of Schooling[b]	
Model and Variables	χ^2	*df*	χ^2	*df*	*F*	*df*
Without welfare						
ALLPOOR/SOMEPOOR	3.9	4	5.2	4	0.88	4, 1257
AVITNR	0.2	2	2.9	2	1.76	2, 1260
ITNRLE1/ITNR23/ITNR3	15.9*	6	8.6	6	1.83	6, 1254
With welfare receipt						
ALLPOOR/SOMEPOOR	1.1	2	0.1	2	0.03	2, 1254
AVITNR	1.3	2	0.0	2	1.29	2, 1255
ITNRLE1/ITNR23/ITNR3	1.4	2	0.0	2	.05	2, 1253
With welfare percentage						
ALLPOOR/SOMEPOOR	0.2	2	0.6	2	0.00	2, 1160
AVITNR	0.3	2	0.7	2	0.00	2, 1161
ITNRLE1/ITNR23/ITNR3	0.3	2	0.7	2	0.00	2, 1158

* $p < .05$; INTRLE1 = income-to-needs ratio < 1.0; INTR23 = income-to-needs ratio 2–3; INTR3 = income-to-needs ratio > 3; ALLPOOR = family poor at all ages; SOMEPOOR = family poor 1–3 years; AVITNR = average income-to-needs ratio.

Source: Authors' calculations based on models in tables 13.2–13.10. See text.

a. χ^2 and *df* values based on the difference between a model not including the terms indicated and one including these terms.

b. *F* and *df* values based on increment to R^2 test comparing a model not including the terms indicated with one including these terms.

Variation by Race and Sex

Because the experience of poverty is likely to vary according to race as a result of factors like neighborhood quality, sources of social support, and experience with the educational system, we tested whether the impact of poverty varied for whites and blacks (Crane 1991; Mayer and Jencks 1989; Mayer 1991c; Wilson 1987). We did the same for sex, because males and females may perceive different paths out of poverty, have different motivations and aspirations, and experience the educational system differently (Sewell, Hauser, and Wolf 1980).

The procedure followed is straightforward. We extended the previous models by including product terms to capture the interaction between the poverty measures and both race and sex separately (two-way interactions: table 13.11, panel 1), between receipt of welfare and both race and sex separately (panel 2), and between percentage of income received from welfare and race and sex separately (panel 3).

The relatively small sample size and the fact that blacks were concentrated at lower incomes meant that we could not test for interactions by race and sex jointly (many of the relevant models would not converge and produced nonsense results when they did).[11] Accordingly, our results may fail to reflect differences in the impact of poverty among specific race-sex groups.

Based on the results in table 13.11, there is little evidence that the effects of poverty or welfare receipt vary according to race and sex. In only one instance was the race-sex interaction significant. And the impact of the categorized version of the income-to-needs ratio on high school graduation appeared to vary according to the race and sex of the respondent.

We hesitate to place much emphasis on this finding, however, because no other significant interactions were present in the data. Moreover, all but one of the coefficient estimates for the interaction terms in this model were insignificant (not shown). With this caveat in mind, we note that an income-to-needs ratio less than 1.0 appeared more detrimental to the chances of graduation from high school for whites than blacks. At an income-to-needs ratio two to three times the poverty level, women were more likely to graduate from high school than were men. At an income-to-needs ratio three or more times the poverty level, men were more likely than women to graduate from high school.

SUMMARY AND DISCUSSION

We have used several longitudinal measures of poverty status to investigate the impact of poverty on educational outcomes for a group of adolescents taken from NLS cohorts sampled during the late 1960s. Our findings indicate that poverty was negatively related to high school graduation, college attendance, and years of schooling obtained. However, much of the observed relationship can be attributed to differences in a number of control variables, such as parental education, family structure, and IQ. After the control variables were taken into account, the number of years spent below the poverty line during adolescence were not related to any of the educational outcomes considered.

A more consistent relationship is the one we observed between the average income-to-needs ratio of young men and women during their adolescence and educational success. This finding suggests that a simple measure of poverty status based on the conventional government definition fails to capture variation in important outcomes. The coarseness of conventional poverty measures has long concerned social scientists investigating the causes and consequences of being poor (Danziger and Weinberg 1994).

When we categorized the average income-to-needs ratio, its effect was apparently nonlinear, with significant effects associated with the lowest and highest categories only. Children coming from the poorest families received less education, while children from the most prosperous families received more. Families in the middle of the income distribution differed little with respect to the educational attainment of their children.

The results also indicate that poverty status has a greater impact on high school graduation than college attendance. Indeed, conditional on high school graduation, only children from the most prosperous families differed in their likelihood of attending college (they were more likely to do so). Thus, poverty affects years of schooling relatively early in the educational process.

That poverty was more closely related to high school graduation than to college attendance is not surprising. Families just above the poverty line, or even those living on incomes two to three times the poverty level, are not significantly more able than families living below the poverty line to afford to send a child to college. Only among families with greater resources does college attendance become economically feasible. This differential was likely heightened in this cohort of adolescents, who reached college-going age at a time when federal financial assistance for college attendance began to shift from grants to loans, increasing out-of-pocket expenses for families (Hauser and Anderson 1991).

Much less likely is that the purchasing ability of income is directly relevant to the completion of high school.[12] Rather, the social and psychological events surrounding poverty are more likely linked to the decreased likelihood of high school graduation. As discussed below, this possibility forms an important arena for future research.

Because college attendance is conditional on graduation from high school, selectivity is also likely to be at work. That is, students from lower-income families who graduate from high school are likely to be more able and more committed to education than are graduates from higher-income families. This variation in commitment may mitigate the impact of poverty on subsequent educational outcomes.

Our results do not indicate that welfare receipt, net of family income and the control variables, is related to the educational outcomes we consider. There was no indication that government transfers negatively affected the subsequent educational attainment of the adolescents in our sample.

This result is not consistent with results reported by other researchers, who note a negative relationship between welfare receipt and the educational attainment of children (Duncan and Yeung 1994; see chapters 12 and 15). The reason for this difference is not immediately clear. However, the cohort of individuals we examined is different from that considered by other researchers. While all of the respondents in our sample were adolescents in the late 1960s, the respondents in prior research either spanned a much broader period of time or corresponded to later cohorts.

As reported by Duncan and Yeung (1994), over time welfare benefits have dropped by almost one-half, and recipients of Aid to Families with Dependent Children increasingly report no other source of income. These trends may indicate that welfare families are becoming more impoverished and more likely to include individuals who are less likely to be successful in the world of work and may have difficulty stimulating the educational attainment of their children. Accordingly, the receipt of welfare may indicate an increasingly negative environment for children's well-being.

The impact of poverty on high school graduation is important to note because of the disadvantaged economic position held by individuals who fail to graduate from high school, particularly the cohort of individuals represented here. They reached adolescence at the end of the post–World War II economic boom and entered the labor force during the long economic stagnation of the 1970s. During that period income differentials increased according to the education obtained (Murnane 1994). Thus, while the incomes of college graduates grew and the incomes of high school graduates declined slowly, those of high school dropouts declined substantially. The economic recovery of the 1980s failed to rectify this disparity, as income inequality according to education grew at an even more rapid pace.

In light of these findings, what might be required of future research? In addition to replicating our analysis with other data bases and for other cohorts, research should pay more attention to the intervening mechanisms linking poverty to high school graduation. As noted, financial considerations are not likely to be directly involved. Rather, social and psychological conditions associated with poverty (other than those directly linked to IQ, one of the controls we implement) are more likely implicated.

A promising line of research has begun to link poverty to the emotional well-being of children (McLeod and Shanahan 1993). Elder et al. (1992) have shown that economic loss is associated with shifts in parenting practices, with negative consequences for the emotional well-being of children. Family stress and the lack of learning resources that are associated with poverty probably dampen the likelihood of high school completion. Subsequent research should document the specific elements of the home environment that reduce educational success. Whether the precursors are particular patterns of parent-child interaction, the availability of educational materials, or some combination of these and other factors is an important element in devising adequate policy interventions.

Examinations of the pattern of forces linked to high school completion should not overlook characteristics that are associated with living in a particular family but not necessarily connected to its internal dynamics. Specifically, characteristics of neighborhoods and schools are likely to influence the educational progress of children (Snow et al. 1991; Wilson 1987). The choices families make concerning neighborhoods and schools affect the social environment within which children interact outside the home. These patterns of social interaction are likely to structure the opportunities and constraints perceived by adolescents as they make decisions about the relevance of continued education (Crane 1991; Mayer 1991c; Mayer and Jencks 1989).

In passing, we note that our finding that IQ has no mediating effect on educational outcomes runs contrary to arguments made by Herrnstein and Murray (1994) about the primary importance of intellectual ability. According to our results, while intellectual ability has a positive impact on educational attainment, it does not mediate the influence of measures of family background. Indeed, our results were virtually unchanged when IQ was included in the model. Explanatory power increased with the inclusion of IQ, but the effects of the other predictor variables remained largely unaffected. In the data we considered, the influence of family background on educational outcomes was not due to variations in the intellectual capacity of children. Families make a difference, and for reasons other than intellectual skill.

Clearly, poverty experienced during adolescence negatively affects the educational attainment of children. The role played by education in determining the economic and occupational success of Americans suggests longer-term consequences. The consequences of dropping out of high school are particularly drastic: over the past two decades, individuals with less than a high school degree have suffered an absolute decline in real income and have dropped farther behind individuals with more education. The increasing economic marginalization of the least educated Americans is a pattern that policy makers can ill afford to ignore. That such marginalization may possess an intergenerational engine is particularly deserving of further scrutiny.

This chapter benefited from support provided by the National Institute of Child Health and Human Development, grant U01 HD31723.

NOTES

1. While both spouses in a married couple might be represented in the NLS, they were not for the majority of the sample we considered. This point is important because otherwise the age distribution of mothers would have been skewed downward, while the age distribution of fathers would have been skewed upward (that is, younger women married to older men). However, given that most adult respondents were not married to an NLS sample member, the age distribution of parents is more representative of the U.S. population.
2. Because not all families reported an income for all four years, and dropping families based on a missing value for even one year of income results in a large reduction in sample size, we included cases with missing values. For the first measure of poverty (number of years below the poverty line), we simply coded another dummy variable, indicating whether at least one year of income data was missing. For the second and third measures of poverty, we computed the average income-to-needs ratio based on the number of years of income data available. If fewer than four years of data were used, we coded a dummy variable indicating so.
3. If no data were reported for IQ, we substituted the mean, as indicated by a missing value dummy variable.
4. The 4 percent figure is likely an underestimate. Because about 15 percent of the sample did not report a value for family income for one or more years, our decision to code the available years of income means that some families placed in the category "poor one to three years" may actually have been poor all four years.
5. Again, this figure is likely an underestimate, given the presence of missing data and our decision to code values of this variable on the number of years for which data were available.

6. Nevertheless, the majority of these cases probably closely approximate a "missing-at-random" situation. By contacting schools, the NLS ascertained test scores for adolescents who had completed the ninth grade as of the first year of the survey. Because the normative age to have completed the ninth grade is fifteen, adolescents followed from ages fourteen to seventeen probably will have no test scores.

7. The regression results presented are based on unweighted data. We ran the regressions using weights and found few differences that would warrant a change in our substantive interpretation of the results. We also found little difference in the results when models were estimated separately by race (the major variable along which oversampling occurred). Accordingly, to preserve the asymptotic properties under which the standard errors of the coefficients are calculated, we elected to use the unweighted regressions.

8. This finding may seem counterintuitive, but it is consistent with other results indicating that blacks obtain more education once other variables are controlled (Haveman and Wolfe 1994).

9. The coefficient for the missing value indicator remained large and statistically significant. Indeed, the missing value indicators for each of the poverty variables were relatively large and significant. If respondents who were poor, who had the poorest social skills, and who were the least literate are those more likely not to report an income, then these results would be expected. To test this possibility, we regressed the missing value indicators on as large a subset of the family background variables as possible for the years in which these values were available. The results consistently indicated that missing values were more concentrated among children whose parents had less education and earned less.

10. Consistent with other chapters in this volume, we divided the families into three categories by income-to-needs ratio. However, to determine whether such a gross categorization hides more substantial nonlinearities in the relationship between educational outcomes and relative income, we created ten categories of approximately equal size and then replicated the analyses reported using the trichotomization. The coefficients for this finer categorization are reported below (coefficients for high school graduation and college attendance are reported as odds ratios):

Income-to-Needs Category 0.0–0.6	High School Graduation Baseline	College Attendance	Years of Schooling
0.6–0.9	1.35	1.11	0.62
0.9–1.3	1.18	1.22	0.63
1.3–1.8	2.65*	1.26	1.03*
1.8–2.2	2.04*	0.68	0.44
2.2–2.3	2.16	1.01	0.62
2.3–2.8	2.83*	0.84	0.91*
2.8–3.6	2.73*	1.64	1.44*
3.6–4.6	3.55*	1.31	1.31*
>4.6	12.30*	1.70	1.33*

* $p < .05$

These coefficients convey much the same information as the trichotomized variable does. That is, the income-to-needs ratio was more closely tied to high school graduation than to college attendance. In addition, the relationship between high school graduation and the income-to-needs ratio was strongest at higher income levels. The one potential "anomaly" rests in the relationship between educational outcomes and an income-to-needs ratio of 0.9–1.3, which appears to be stronger and more positive than would be expected on the basis of a purely linear relationship.

11. We estimated models separately by race and looked for sex interactions within race groups. The results did not suggest an interpretation different from that reported below.
12. One might argue that poverty, by reducing the likelihood that an adolescent will attend college, reduces overall motivation for success in school.

Chapter 14

Childhood Poverty and Adolescent Schooling and Fertility Outcomes: Reduced-Form and Structural Estimates

Robert Haveman, Barbara Wolfe, and Kathryn Wilson

The literature on the determinants of children's attainments has focused on the effects of families' circumstances and choices (for example, parental education, family income, or family structure) and neighborhood characteristics (for example, the percentage of high school dropouts in the neighborhood or of professional workers). The viewpoint of this research, consistent with a variety of models in all of the social sciences, is that children are products of their home, their family and its circumstances, their peers, and their environments, and the effort is to reliably identify the elements or timing of each with the most important effects (see Haveman and Wolfe 1995 for a review). Little attention has been paid to the choices that the children themselves make or the incentives and opportunities affecting these decisions.

In this chapter, we report on a study of the effects of family circumstances and events as determinants of children's attainments as well as the responses of children themselves to the patterns of expected returns—the "payouts"—associated with alternative schooling choices and the choice of whether or not to give birth as an unmarried teen. In both research approaches, we emphasize the importance of growing up in poverty, together with a variety of correlates of growing up poor.

First, we present reduced-form estimates of the determinants of educational attainment and teen nonmarital births (for young women). These estimates, consistent with the approach of much of the previous literature, emphasize the role of parental choices and circumstances. Second, we present estimates from a structural model of the determinants of youths' decisions regarding whether or not to graduate from high school and (for young women) whether or not to give birth out of wedlock as a teenager. In this framework, both expected utilities (incomes) in alternative states of educational attainment (or alternative childbearing states) and family circumstances and events can influence the choices made.

In our analyses of education choices, we study the determinants of whether or not a person graduated high school. In the United States, high school graduation represents the minimum level of attainment necessary for securing entry-level jobs that have career characteristics. For the choice of out-of-wedlock birth, we analyze the determinants of a young unmarried woman's choice to give birth or not between ages fifteen and eighteen.

We first discuss the potential determinants of educational choices and teen fertility, and provide some background information on trends in both. We also characterize the empirical approaches that we pursue. The second section describes our data, followed by our reduced-form estimates of the determinants of the decisions to graduate high school and to give birth out of wedlock as a teen in the third section, and our structural model estimates in the fourth section. As indicated, the structural model estimates reflect the view that educational choices and unmarried teenagers' childbearing choices are rational responses by youths to the economic returns, or payoffs, associated with alternative choices.

DETERMINANTS OF THE ATTAINMENT OF YOUNG ADULTS

Educational Attainment

Education has long been viewed as the primary key to socioeconomic success. Persons with more education have higher wage rates and labor market earnings, obtain larger fringe benefits associated with employment, and are less likely to be unemployed. Hence, inequality in the distribution of earnings reflects variation in the distribution of educational attainments. But the gains from education go beyond the labor market—persons with more education tend to have jobs with more prestige, to have better health, to secure the number of children they desire, to be more efficient consumers, and to raise children who are likely to receive more education than those with less education (Haveman and Wolfe 1984). As a result, high levels of education in the population yield a variety of important social gains, and, as a corollary, dispersion in educational attainments is reflected in larger disparities in comprehensive measures of levels of living. For these reasons, identifying those factors that determine individuals' level of education is of substantial interest.

Over the postwar period, the level of education attained by the average American has increased steadily. In 1950, for example, the average American aged twenty-five years or more had 9.3 years of education; by 1990, this figure had increased to 12.7 years. This increase is reflected in a higher rate of high school completion. In the cohort aged twenty-five to twenty-nine in 1960, nearly 40 percent failed to graduate high school; by 1989, the proportion of high school dropouts in this age cohort had fallen to 14.5 percent.

Throughout the postwar period, the level of education of whites has exceeded that of African Americans; similarly, the proportion of whites in any given age cohort who graduated high school has exceeded that of African Americans. During the 1970s and 1980s, however, the gap between whites' and African Americans' level of education narrowed. By 1989, the median education for African Americans aged twenty-five to twenty-nine was 12.7 years, compared with 12.9 years for the overall population in that age group.

Numerous factors have been cited as contributors to these changing patterns of educational attainment and the economic status that is associated with them. In addition to a wide variety of "background factors" are decisions made by governments, parents, and children themselves. Our analysis builds on work by researchers who have sought to measure the effects of a variety of these determinants of educational success (see, for example, Alwin and Thornton 1984; Krein 1986; Graham, Beller, and Hernandez 1994; Manski et al. 1992; Hill and Duncan 1987; Datcher 1982; Corcoran et al. 1992; Haveman, Wolfe, and Spaulding 1991). Most of these studies analyze information on individual children and their families and emphasize the potential role of parental characteristics and choices. A variety of factors have been found to be consistently related to the schooling attainments of children; the parents' education, the family's income, the number of parents in the child's family, the parents' expectations, and characteristics of the child's school and teacher are among the more important (Haveman and Wolfe 1995).[1]

Teen Out-of-Wedlock Childbearing

As in our study of the determinants of educational choices, in our study of the childbearing decisions of unmarried young women we emphasize in our reduced-form models the parental choices and opportunities and family circumstances that affect the decisions made by teenage women and then attempt to estimate the response of young women to the opportunities and returns associated with alternative childbearing choices.

Implicit in our analysis is that the state of unmarried teen motherhood represents "lack of success." The high correlation between being a teenage unmarried mother and a wide variety of indicators of low achievement (for example, failing to complete high school, being on welfare, being poor, and being out of the labor force) provides the basis for this presumption. That the overwhelming bulk of teenagers' out-of-wedlock births are "unexpected," "unintended," or unplanned (and hence that many are probably unwanted) indicates the likely importance of lack of information in the decisions of young women.[2]

During the postwar period, the average age at which women experience their first birth has drifted up, in part because of the increase in their age at first marriage. Consistent with these trends, the number and rate per 1,000 women of births to teenage women has also decreased. For example, in 1955 the teenage birthrate stood at more than 90; by 1975 it had fallen to 56, and in the early 1980s it hovered in the low 50s. However, from 1986 to 1992 the number of teen births in the United

States increased from 472,000 to 518,000, an increase of nearly 50,000. After reaching a low of 51 in 1986, birthrates to American teens increased steadily and reached 61 in 1992 for both young (ages fifteen to seventeen) and older teenagers. Since then, these rates have declined modestly.

While the majority of the teen births—about two-thirds—are to white teenagers, this proportion has been falling over time. By 1989, although African American women aged fifteen to nineteen composed 15.7 percent of this female age cohort, they accounted for 35 percent of the teen births. Indeed, teen births account for nearly one-quarter of all births to African American women.

Few social issues attract as much attention in the popular press as the high level and rapid increase in the number of births to teenagers who are not married, and the reason for this is not hard to discern. Children born to unmarried teen mothers do not have an even start in life. They are more likely to grow up in a poor and mother-only family, live in a poor or underclass neighborhood, and experience high risks to both their health status and potential school achievement. Those who value equal opportunity as a social goal view the high rate of births to unmarried teens with great apprehension.

Teen mothers, too, appear to be harmed by the experience of giving birth out of wedlock. The probability that these mothers will be receiving welfare benefits within a short period after giving birth is well over one-half. Moreover, a relatively small percentage of teen unmarried mothers finish high school. Lone teen mothers clearly prejudice economic and marriage opportunities that they might otherwise have had and in any case experience a sudden end to their own childhood.

The high level and recent growth in the number of teen nonmarital births also has implications for public policy. Among recipients of Aid to Families with Dependent Children (AFDC) who are less than thirty years old, three-quarters first gave birth as a teenager, in most cases out of wedlock. About $22 billion is paid annually through AFDC, food stamps, and Medicaid to women who are or were teenage mothers. Each family that began with a birth to a teenager has cost the public an average of about $17,000 in some form of support over the following twenty years (see Center for Population Options 1990).[3]

The prevalence of births to unmarried teens (and the subsequent receipt of welfare), particularly among African Americans, is a social phenomenon worthy of understanding. Yet, as is true of many other social developments, the determinants of this phenomenon are complex, and attempts to quantitatively attribute causation lead into murky waters. Again, previous studies of this phenomenon have identified a variety of family and neighborhood factors that influence the choice of teens to give birth while unmarried (Antel 1988; Lundberg and Plotnick 1990; An, Haveman, and Wolfe 1993; Plotnick 1992; Wu and Martinson 1993; see Haveman and Wolfe 1995 for a review). Like the studies of educational attainment, most of these studies rely on detailed survey information on teenage girls to assess the relationship between a variety of potentially causal factors and the probability that these girls will give birth out of wedlock. Our reduced-form estimates include variables that reflect the circumstances and events of the families of teenage girls while they were growing up; in our structural model estimates, we also include measures of the opportunities that are available to teenage girls both if they do and do not give birth out of wedlock.

Empirical Approach

Our approach differs in several ways from prior research on the family-based determinants of educational attainment and teen fertility. First, the models that we estimate reflect our view that children's ultimate attainments are the result of conscious decisions made by society (for example, the community environment in which the child lives), the children's parents, and children themselves. We view both postadolescent children and their parents as rational decision makers who process information on the gains and losses associated with specific options so as to make choices that will maximize their well-being. For example, beyond the minimum number of years of education mandated by the state, we view youths as a part of the process leading to the choice of when to cease school attendance; that decision process determines whether or not they graduate from high school (see Haveman and Wolfe 1994). Decisions made by communities and parents—for example, on the resources devoted to schools attended by the child (a government decision)—also influence choices regarding how much education to seek or whether or not to give birth out of wedlock as a teen. The quality of the schooling provided to young children, for example, is likely to affect their tastes for schooling and their perception of their success in education. Similarly, parents' monitoring of behavior or their expressions of expectations regarding teen out-of-wedlock childbearing are likely to influence the child's ultimate evaluations of the gains and costs of this choice. Additional factors include the influence of parents as role models (suggesting that parents' own behaviors affect the decisions of children).

Second, as we have implied, we leaven an economic perspective with insights from other social sciences—sociology and developmental psychology—on the determinants of children's choices in educational attainment and childbearing. Hence, we introduced into our analysis parental decisions that may have created stress during the child's formative years and may have altered the evaluation of the benefits and costs of additional schooling or teen childbearing.

Finally, as noted, our structural models of the education and childbearing choices explicitly incorporate the returns to the youth associated with the options available. These estimates are more self-conscious about the response of the youth to those options and enable us to account for the direct effect of parental factors on youths' decisions and the indirect way they affect the available opportunities.[4]

DATA

Our analysis is based on a large longitudinal data set constructed from observations of a national stratified sample of families, the Michigan Panel Study of Income Dynamics (PSID). The PSID includes longitudinal information on 6,000 families beginning in 1968. As of 1991, twenty-one years of information were available (1968–88). We selected children aged zero to six years in the beginning year of the survey and followed them for the full twenty-one years. For each child, the data include family status; income and source of income; parental education; neighborhood characteristics; background characteristics such as race, religion, and location; and a variety of children's attainments. By 1988, the children were young adults ranging in age from twenty-one to twenty-seven years. We studied only those individuals who remained in the survey for each year until 1988.[5]

To analyze the influence on children's choices of various family and community decisions and characteristics while the children were young, we transformed the time-varying data elements of either the children or their parents into an age-indexed data set. That is, rather than define the data by year of its occurrence (1968 or 1974, for example), we converted the data so that it is assigned to the child by the child's age (age six or nine, for example). Thus, for two children, one aged two and the other aged six in 1968, we obtained comparable information for each from ages six to eighteen using data from 1972 to 1984 for the first child and data from 1968 to 1980 for the second child. Transforming the data in this way enabled age-specific comparisons of individuals with different birth years and allowed us to analyze whether the timing of particular events—whether an event or circumstance occurs when the child is young or an adolescent—had a differential influence on the ultimate attainments of the child. To compare income and other monetary values over time, we expressed all dollar values from the PSID in 1992 prices using the consumer price index.[6]

To estimate our structural model, we imputed to each observation expected income values in alternative educational attainment states and (for women) in alternative states of out-of-wedlock teen childbearing. These income values were obtained from an older cohort of youths included in the PSID, in particular those aged thirty to thirty-four in 1989.

REDUCED-FORM MODELS OF ATTAINMENT

High School Graduation

Graduation from high school is a dependent variable in our model (table 14.1). Our reduced-form estimates are based on a probit regression run over the 1,705 individuals in our sample; unweighted data are used for estimation. The dependent variable is equal to 1 if the individual had twelve or more years of schooling by 1988 and 0 otherwise. Eighty-four percent of the children in our sample had graduated high school.

These baseline estimates do not provide for the simultaneous determination of high school graduation and other factors; nor do they view the decision of whether to graduate as influenced by the expected economic returns to educational attainment.

TABLE 14.1 / Determinants of High School Graduation, Reduced-Form Model

Independent Variable	Model[a] 1	2	3	Mean	*SD*
Constant	0.7741	0.6593	0.9302	1	0
	9.14	4.65	9.96		
African American	0.1434	0.3226	0.2765	0.45689	0.4983
	1.65	3.40	2.99		
	0.0254	0.0548	0.0478		
Female	0.1597	0.1629	0.1598	0.51202	0.5000
	2.06	2.08	2.05		
	0.0283	0.0277	0.0276		
Mother's education					
High school graduate	0.5466	0.4420	0.4720	0.39003	0.4879
	6.30	4.89	5.33		
	0.0967	0.0751	0.0816		
Some college	1.0299	0.8689	0.8774	0.08094	0.2728
	5.11	4.19	4.26		
	0.1822	0.1475	0.1516		
College graduate	5.1612	4.9743	5.0635	0.04458	0.2064
	0.01	0.01	0.01		
	0.9130	0.8447	0.8750		
Lived with one parent[b]					
Ages 6–8, not 12–15	−0.3658	−0.3487	−0.2293	0.0434	0.2038
	2.04	1.93	1.25		
	−0.0647	−0.0592	−0.0396		
Ages 12–15, not 6–8	−0.2980	−0.2269	−0.1852	0.11437	0.3184
	2.44	1.81	1.47		
	−0.0527	−0.0385	−0.0320		
Ages 6–15	−0.4941	−0.3974	−0.3238	0.23695	0.4253
	5.23	3.85	3.19		
	−0.0874	−0.0675	−0.0560		
Other	−0.3030	−0.2655	−0.1755	0.01877	0.1358
	1.18	1.03	0.68		
	−0.0536	−0.0451	−0.0303		
Average total income (marginal effect of $1,000)		8E-06		39747	26651
		3.35			
		0.0014			

(Table continued on p. 426.)

TABLE 14.1 / (*continued*)

Independent Variable	Model[a] 1	2	3	Mean	*SD*
Average number of siblings		−0.0898 3.60 −0.0153		2.5181	1.6051
Duration of poverty, ages 6–15[c]					
Some of the time			−0.4222 4.43 −0.0730	0.42991	0.4952
Every year, ages 6–15			−0.7116 3.92 −0.1230	0.04633	0.2103
Log-likelihood	675.70	662.83	663.58		

Source: Authors' calculations based on data from the Panel Study of Income Dynamics on 1,705 children aged zero to six years in 1968 and followed until 1988.

a. Values are reduced-form coefficient estimates, *t*-statistics, and marginal effects.

b. Children who never lived with one parent from ages six to fifteen are the omitted category.

c. Children who were never poor from ages six to fifteen are the omitted category.

Model 1 is a multivariate probit estimate in which a basic set of background variables is entered into the analysis (table 14.1). The parsimonious set of explanatory variables in this model are grouped into background variables and variables pertaining to parents' choices and opportunities. Background variables include sex (coded 1 for female and 0 for male) and race (coded 1 for African American and 0 otherwise). Variables representing parents' choices and opportunities are as follows. For the mother's education, one variable is coded 1 if she graduated high school and 0 if she did not; another is coded 1 if she attended some college and 0 if she did not; and another is coded 1 if she graduated college and 0 if she did not. The omitted category is represented by mothers with less than a high school education.

For family structure we enter four variables into model 1: one is coded 1 if the child lived with one parent from age six to age eight but not from age twelve to age fifteen, and 0 otherwise; another is coded 1 if the child lived with one parent from age twelve to age fifteen but not from age six to age eight, and 0 otherwise; another is coded 1 if the child lived with one parent from age six to age eight, from age nine to age eleven, and from age twelve to age fifteen, and 0 otherwise; and another is coded 1 if the child lived with one parent during other age periods. Children who lived with both parents from age six to age fifteen are the omitted category.[7]

Models 2 and 3 present a somewhat richer specification of the determinants of these choices, adding variables related to the income levels and poverty status of the child's family. In model 2 we add variables representing the family's average posttax income and the average number of siblings in the family when the child was aged six to fifteen years. In model 3 we add a variable representing poverty for some of the time that the child was aged six to fifteen and one representing poverty for all of that time. Children who were never poor during that time are the omitted category.[8]

When the broad set of factors in model 1 is taken into account, African American and female children are significantly more likely to graduate high school than their race-sex counterparts. In addition, children who grew up in a single-parent family have a significantly lower probability of graduating than those from intact families, and the impact is greater the longer the age span the child spent with one parent. The mother's educational attainment is significantly related to the child's graduation chances: the higher her level of education, the greater the probability her child graduates.

Most of the basic relationships seen in model 1 are sustained in the extended specifications of models 2 and 3.[9] However, a few of the coefficients become insignificant when we include measures of family economic resources as explanatory variables. For example, two of the variables indicating that the child spent some but not all years living with one parent become statistically insignificant at the 5 percent level when the family income variables are included.

The results for model 2 suggest that family economic resources are significantly associated with the probability of high school graduation. Average total family income has a positive and significant coefficient. Similarly, children who grew up in large families are significantly less likely to graduate than are children with fewer siblings. Including duration of poverty in the specification conveys a somewhat different picture of the role of economic resources. The variables indicating the length of time spent living in poverty suggest a negative and significant association with the probability of graduating; the variable indicating a longer duration in poverty has the larger estimated marginal effect. Children who spent the entire period from age six to age fifteen living in poverty are significantly less likely than other children to graduate high school.

Teen Nonmarital Births

Our second indicator of success (or lack of success) is giving birth as a nonmarried teen (table 14.2). Our reduced-form estimates of the determinants of this outcome follow in the same form as those for high school graduation.[10] The estimates are based on a probit specification run over the 873 female children in our sample. Of them, 125, or 14.3 percent, had given birth out of wedlock as a teen. The results convey much the same story as those for high school graduation. However, many of the variables in the model 1 specification have the opposite sign of their coun-

TABLE 14.2 / Determinants of Teen Out-of-Wedlock Birth, Reduced-Form Model

Independent Variable	Model[a] 1	2	3	Mean	*SD*
Constant	−1.4010	−1.3973	−1.4343	1	0
	10.62	5.74	10.16		
African American	0.5063	0.3209	0.4751	0.48683	0.5001
	3.69	2.14	3.29		
	0.0724	0.0428	0.0679		
Mother's education					
High school graduate	−0.7219	−0.6226	−0.7051	0.37801	0.4852
	5.02	4.15	4.81		
	−0.1032	−0.0830	−0.1008		
Some college	−0.9364	−0.7636	−0.9017	0.08018	0.2717
	2.91	2.30	2.77		
	−0.1339	−0.1018	−0.1288		
College graduate	−4.4357	−4.3888	−4.3912	0.03780	0.1908
	0.02	0.01	0.02		
	−0.6343	−0.5852	−0.6275		
Lived with one parent[b]					
Ages 6–8, not 12–15	0.4140	0.4429	0.3923	0.03436	0.1823
	1.37	1.47	1.29		
	0.0592	0.0591	0.0561		
Ages 12–15, not 6–8	0.8558	0.8094	0.8287	0.12486	0.3308
	5.21	4.75	4.91		
	0.1224	0.1079	0.1184		
Ages 6–15	0.4765	0.4131	0.4446	0.23368	0.4234
	3.43	2.69	3.03		
	0.0681	0.0551	0.0635		
Other	0.2508	0.1078	0.2202	0.02062	0.1422
	0.66	0.27	0.57		
	0.0359	0.0144	0.0315		
Average total income (marginal effect of $1,000)		−7E-06		40410	28376
		1.55			
		−0.0009			
Average number of siblings		0.1094		2.606	1.6470
		3.10			
		0.0146			

TABLE 14.2 / (*continued*)

Independent Variable	Model[a] 1	2	3	Mean	*SD*
Duration of poverty, ages 6–15[c]					
Some of the time			0.0982 0.68 0.0140	0.43757	0.4964
Every year, ages 6–15			0.1248 0.49 0.0178	0.05155	0.2212
Log-likelihood	294.96	288.7	294.71		

Source: Authors' calculations based on data from the Panel Study of Income Dynamics on 1,705 children aged zero to six years in 1968 and followed until 1988.

a. Values are reduced-form coefficient estimates, *t*-statistics, and marginal effects.

b. Children who never lived with one parent from ages six to fifteen are the omitted category.

c. Children who were never poor from ages six to fifteen are the omitted category.

terparts for high school graduation, suggesting that the direction of the association with success is the same for both the education and childbearing outcomes. Two changes are noteworthy. First, while African American children are more likely to graduate from high school than non–African Americans, other things equal, they are more likely to give birth as unmarried teens. Second, living with a single parent while they were ages six to fifteen and during adolescence (ages twelve to fifteen) has a significant and positive association with the probability of giving birth as an unmarried teen, but living with a single parent while young (ages six to eight) is not significantly associated with an increased probability of doing so.

The estimates for models 2 and 3 are quite different from their counterparts for high school graduation. Economic resources (measured by either average total family income or years living in poverty) are statistically significant in the education estimates but are not significant determinants of giving birth as an unmarried teen. While the signs of these economic variables are as expected, in no case are they statistically significant at standard levels.[11]

A STRUCTURAL MODEL OF THE CHOICES TO GRADUATE HIGH SCHOOL AND GIVE BIRTH AS A TEEN

The reduced-form approach used for the estimates in tables 14.1 and 14.2 neglects the fact that children's decisions on graduating high school and giving birth as unmarried teens are likely to reflect the expected income implications of their choices. As a result, our estimates of the determinants of the decisions may attribute to background or family choice and circumstance variables some effects that are properly attributed to the youth's choices in response to the incentives or returns associated with the alternatives.

The model we now describe presumes that youths are rational decision makers who choose from among the available options the one that leaves them better off than any of the others. In our estimation, we use predicted values of incomes associated with various options as an indicator of the well-being associated with that option. This presumption suggests the need for a structural model that reflects decision making in response to the structure of prices or incentives associated with the options. We construct a structural model of the decisions to complete high school or not and to give birth as an unmarried teen or not. We focus our discussion on the model explaining the high school graduation outcome.

The Nature of the Structural Model

In this model, we hypothesize that a youth's decision to graduate high school or not is influenced by the rewards associated with being a high school graduate relative to those of being a dropout. While "rewards" in this context may include a variety of attractive effects—including higher wages, more secure jobs, better health, more attractive work environments—we assume that all of these relevant effects are captured in the expected value of lifetime income if one does graduate relative to that expected if one does not graduate.[12]

Let U^*_{in} equal the utility of individual n conditional upon the selection of option I (graduation or not) within this binary set of education choices; $\boldsymbol{Y}^*_{in}$, a random vector of realized outcomes (income) for individual n, conditional on the selection of alternative I; $\boldsymbol{S}_n$, a vector of exogenous characteristics and past choices of child n; $\boldsymbol{F}_n$, a vector of family characteristics and parental choices made prior to the schooling choice of individual n; and $\boldsymbol{C}_n$, a vector of past economic opportunities including family income and society's choices and opportunities afforded individual n prior to the n's schooling choice.

In the presence of uncertainty regarding the outcome of alternative educational choices, $\boldsymbol{Y}^*_{in}$, the objective of the child is to choose whether to graduate or not in order to maximize expected utility:

$$EU^*_{in} = EU^*(\boldsymbol{Y}^*_{in}, \boldsymbol{S}_n, \boldsymbol{F}_n, \boldsymbol{C}_n), \tag{14.1}$$

subject to lifetime wealth constraints.

The individual chooses I if and only if the expected utility of option I is greater than that of option j for all $I \neq j$.

$$EU^*(\boldsymbol{Y}^*_{in}, \boldsymbol{S}_n, \boldsymbol{F}_n, \boldsymbol{C}_n) > EU^*(\boldsymbol{Y}^*_{jn}, \boldsymbol{S}_n, \boldsymbol{F}_n, \boldsymbol{C}_n), \tag{14.2}$$

for all $I \in \mathrm{V}$, $I \neq j$.[13]

To simplify, we write vector $\mathbf{Z}_n = (\boldsymbol{S}_n, \boldsymbol{F}_n, \boldsymbol{C}_n)$ and assume that the expected indirect utility of alternative I, U_i, can be characterized as

$$U_i = \mathbf{Z}_n\beta_i + E(\boldsymbol{Y}^*|\boldsymbol{Q}, i)\ \beta_2 + e_i. \tag{14.3}$$

The child knows that $\boldsymbol{Y}^*$ depends on the schooling choice made and believes that $\boldsymbol{Y}^*$ depends on the realization of an unobserved random vector $\boldsymbol{Q}$, where $\boldsymbol{Q}$ depends on prior choices of society ($\boldsymbol{C}$), the child's parents ($\boldsymbol{F}$), and the child's own prior choices ($\boldsymbol{S}$).

If $E(\boldsymbol{Y}^*|\boldsymbol{Q}, i)$ denotes the child's expected value of $\boldsymbol{Y}^*$, conditional on $\boldsymbol{Q}$ and the hypothesized choice of I, and e_i denotes the unobserved random component of the utility associated with alternative I, then the child chooses the alternative that maximizes expected utility, $\mathbf{Z}_n\beta_i + E(\boldsymbol{Y}_i^*|\boldsymbol{Q}, i)\beta_2 + e_i$. In other words, the child chooses alternative I:

$$\text{iff}\{\mathbf{Z}_n\beta_1 + [E(\boldsymbol{Y}^*|\boldsymbol{Q}, i) - E(\boldsymbol{Y}^*|\boldsymbol{Q}, j)]\beta_2\} > \text{e}, \tag{14.4}$$

where $\beta_1 = \beta_i - \beta_j$, $e = e_j - e_i$ for all $I \in \boldsymbol{V}$, $I \neq j$.

In fact, the choices made by older children in this model are not random—they would repeat them if faced with the same set of choices and the same information. Therefore, the probability of the individual choosing alternative I is

$$Pr_i = Pr\{e < \mathbf{Z}_n\beta_1 + [E(\boldsymbol{Y}^*|\boldsymbol{Q}, i) - E(\boldsymbol{Y}^*|\boldsymbol{Q}, j)]\beta_2\} \tag{14.5}$$

for all $I \in \boldsymbol{V}$, $I \neq j$.

In modeling the decision of whether or not to complete high school in the context of equation (14.5), we include variables in our model—in addition to the difference in expected income $[E(\boldsymbol{Y}^*|\boldsymbol{Q}, i) - E(\boldsymbol{Y}^*|\boldsymbol{Q}, j)]$—that are similar to those included in our reduced-form estimates. $\boldsymbol{S}$ includes exogenous individual characteristics of the child, such as age, sex, and race; $\boldsymbol{F}$, family structure, parental education, and so on; and $\boldsymbol{C}$, the family's income or years in poverty, which reflect both the work effort of family members (and so can be included in $\boldsymbol{F}$) and public income transfers.[14] A variety of factors influence the child's perception of $\boldsymbol{Y}_i^*$, including the unemployment rate in the area, the early career incomes of high school dropouts and high school graduates in the community, and the availability of financial assistance for postgraduation schooling.

The value of the expected income associated with option I, $\hat{\boldsymbol{Y}}_i^*$, is based on an equation estimated over persons with education I:

$$\boldsymbol{Y}_I^* = \boldsymbol{Q}_i\alpha + v_i, \tag{14.6}$$

where α is the estimated coefficient from a tobit model fit over observations with schooling level I, $\boldsymbol{Q}_i$ is a vector of exogenous predictor variables, and v_i is an error term.[15]

We estimate the variables measuring expected income with and without a high school degree using a second data set constructed from the PSID. We use personal incomes for each year from age nineteen to age twenty-nine of our older cohort from the PSID (a sample of 1,373 individuals in the PSID who were all aged thirty to thirty-four as of 1989—eight to twelve in 1968, the first year of the survey) to generate the income streams expected if they were high school graduates and if not, discounted to age sixteen. We again arrange the data so that they are age—rather than year—specific and convert all income values into 1992 dollars.

Because the children in this sample are older, we are constrained in the intergenerational information we can use as predictor variables—we use only data based on ages twelve to fifteen rather than the longer childhood experiences used in our reduced-form estimates. And, because we wish to use background information to obtain predictions of future income streams that take into account individual differences, we include incomes only to age twenty-nine.

Our procedure implicitly assumes that at age sixteen youths form their expectations of future education-conditioned incomes by observing the realized incomes of persons like themselves who are in their late teens and twenties—hence our use of conditional income terms constructed over individuals aged nineteen to twenty-nine. In this sense, our expected income terms may be superior to estimates of full lifetime education–conditioned incomes. Note that by including incomes during the late teens and early twenties, we capture the opportunity cost of choosing additional schooling beyond high school.

We divide this older cohort into those who have and those who have not graduated from high school. We first fit a reduced-form probit equation to "explain" the selected outcome.[16] Then, for each age over ages nineteen to twenty-nine, we fit an ordinary least squares model separately over the sample of graduates and nongraduates. In each equation, we include the inverse Mills ratio selectivity term (λ) estimated from the first-stage probit equation in order to control for self-selection into either of the schooling outcomes. We use the coefficients from these estimated equations to predict the level of personal income of each individual in our primary sample for each age from nineteen to twenty-nine, if that individual graduate from high school and if that individual does not.

Estimation

THE DECISION TO GRADUATE HIGH SCHOOL The first step in estimating our structural model of the high school graduation decision is to specify and estimate a reduced form probit equation fit over the older sample from the PSID in order to obtain inverse Mills ratio selectivity correction (lambda) variables. In our sample of 1,373 older youths, 1,202 graduated high school, and 171 did not. The variables in the reduced-form probit equation include parental education (dummy variables indicating high school graduation, some college, or college completion for each parent); race, sex, and a race-sex interaction term; family position (firstborn, average number of siblings) and background variables measured over ages twelve to fifteen (years living in each of three regions, years living in an urban area, years the head of household is disabled, years living with one parent, years the mother works, years the family receives AFDC, and the average ratio of family posttax income relative to needs). Also included (and used as identifiers) are the youths' health (two dummy variables indicating if it is fair or poor and if it is excellent), the years the families lives in poverty, whether their mother first gave birth as a teen, and average total income.[17] From this equation, we calculate a λ variable for each person in the older sample.

In the second stage, we run eleven tobit equations (one for each year from age nineteen to age twenty-nine) with personal income as the dependent variable for each of the two education groups—the group of high school graduates and the group that does not complete high school. We include in these equations variables thought likely to be related to income—race (African American is coded as 1), sex (female is coded as 1), a race-sex interaction variable, family position (first-born, average number of siblings while twelve to fifteen years old), parents' education (high school graduation, some college, and college graduation, for each parent), and a variety of background variables, including the number of years spent living with one parent, the number of years the mother works, the number of years the family lives in an urban area, the number of years the head of household is disabled, the average family income relative to needs, the number of years the family receives AFDC, and the number of years the family lives in each region (each measured over ages twelve to fifteen). The last set is included to capture the variation in regional prices and earnings. The appropriate λ variable is also included.[18] (The means and standard deviations of these variables are shown in appendix table 14A.3.) The results of the first- and second-stage estimates are generally as expected and are not reported here.[19]

In the final stage of our structural model, we use the coefficients (except for the coefficient on the λ term) from these two sets of eleven regressions to predict eleven income values (one for each of ages nineteen to twenty-nine) for each youth if that youth graduates from high school and another eleven income values if the youth chooses not to graduate from high school.[20] The education-conditioned income patterns for the full sample are as expected (table 14.3, top panel): the predicted income for those who failed to complete high school is similar to that of high school graduates in the first few years, but the incomes for the nongraduates show slower growth after they reach their early twenties; the predicted income for the high school graduates generally increases over the eleven years and has a steeper slope. At all ages except nineteen years, the predicted income of a graduate exceeded that of a nongraduate. (Note that the predicted incomes with and without a high school degree are for the same individuals in the top panel.) Beginning at age twenty-one, the relative predicted income trajectories suggest substantial gains to high school graduation.

After age twenty-three, assuming high school graduation, predicted incomes of the actual graduates in the sample diverge rapidly from those of the nongraduates (assuming nongraduation, there is no difference) (table 14.3, second and third panels). Perhaps most interestingly, nongraduates have substantially higher expected incomes if they do not graduate than do graduates if they do not graduate.[21]

TABLE 14.3 / Predicted Personal Incomes, If a High School Graduate and If a Nongraduate (1992 $)

	If Graduate		If Nongraduate	
Sample and Age	Mean	*SD*	Mean	*SD*
Full sample (n = 1,705)				
Age 19	5,274	2,011	5,519	3,057
Age 20	7,327	2,676	6,607	3,265
Age 21	9,109	3,057	7,879	3,446
Age 22	10,611	3,256	6,045	4,096
Age 23	12,762	3,743	8,275	5,107
Age 24	13,994	4,402	7,531	4,793
Age 25	15,180	4,646	7,972	5,624
Age 26	16,922	5,496	10,396	6,115
Age 27	18,294	6,053	9,141	4,681
Age 28	19,296	6,225	9,687	5,669
Age 29	20,372	6,901	7,759	5,518
Net present value at age 16	123,056	36,441	72,178	36,528
Actual high school graduates (n = 1,437)				
Age 19	5,276	1,999	5,589	3,098
Age 20	7,270	2,690	6,556	3,302
Age 21	9,026	3,075	7,907	3,504
Age 22	10,496	3,259	5,717	4,041
Age 23	12,757	3,770	8,130	5,138
Age 24	14,088	4,410	7,319	4,781
Age 25	15,296	4,693	7,720	5,599
Age 26	17,017	5,573	10,574	6,238
Age 27	18,464	6,129	9,064	4,708
Age 28	19,432	6,321	9,648	5,707
Age 29	20,546	7,028	7,400	5,418
Net present value at age 16	123,473	36,710	71,209	36,695
Actual high school nongraduates (n = 268)				
Age 19	5,263	2,074	5,141	2,802
Age 20	7,636	2,582	6,882	3,048
Age 21	9,557	2,923	7,733	3,119
Age 22	11,231	3,173	7,804	3,941
Age 23	12,791	3,602	9,052	4,872
Age 24	13,487	4,331	8,671	4,703
Age 25	14,557	4,339	9,323	5,581
Age 26	16,413	5,043	9,440	5,320
Age 27	17,381	5,550	9,556	4,522
Age 28	18,569	5,640	9,898	5,467
Age 29	19,436	6,105	9,682	5,664
Net present value at age 16	120,822	34,955	77,373	35,376

Source: Authors' calculations. See text.

We next calculate the present value of these predicted incomes as of age sixteen (a likely age for deciding whether or not to finish high school), using a discount rate of 3 percent (table 14.3). The expected net present value of the income of average individuals in the sample, if they graduated high school, is $123,056; the average expected present value if they do not graduate is $72,178, a difference of $50,878. Interestingly, the gain from graduating high school for those who in fact do graduate ($52,264) is greater than for those who fail to graduate ($43,449).

For each individual in our primary sample, we include this difference—the "if graduate value" minus "if nongraduate" value, $[E(Y^*|Q, I) - E(Y^*|Q, j)]$—as a variable in our structural model of the decision of whether or not to graduate high school (table 14.4). Our models parallel those in table 14.1 but add the difference in expected incomes (the expected gain from graduating high school) to each specification.

The base model, including only the difference in expected incomes (along with a constant), show the strongest influence of the expected gain. In the more extensive models, the expected gain term remains statistically significant.[22] The coefficient on the income gain variable decreases as the set of nonincome variables is expanded but always suggests that the larger the expected gain from graduating high school, the higher the probability of graduating from high school.

The other variables all have the expected sign and are consistent with the reduced-form results in table 14.1. The race and sex variables again suggest that African Americans are more likely than others in the sample to graduate once a variety of other factors are taken into account. Indeed, the estimated positive marginal effect on the race variable is greater in the structural model (table 14.4) than in the reduced-form model (table 14.1). This suggests that once the difference in expected incomes is taken into account, African Americans are even more likely to graduate than their counterparts of other races. Young adults who had mothers with more education are themselves more likely to receive more education (to graduate), while those who spend more years from ages six to fifteen living with a single parent are less likely to graduate. Growing up in a poor family continues to play a role—those who spend more years growing up in a family with income below the poverty line are less likely to graduate.

An interesting question concerns the differences between the estimates of the effects of the background and family variables in the reduced-form and the structural models: do the coefficients in the reduced-form model provide biased results of the relationships? To answer this question, we conduct a log-likelihood test of whether models in table 14.1 differ significantly from their counterparts in table 14.4. The null hypothesis that the models are the same is rejected at the 10 percent level of significance.

THE DECISION TO GIVE BIRTH AS AN UNMARRIED TEEN We use a similar approach to estimate a structural model of youths' childbearing decisions—in particular, the choice to give birth while unmarried or not. In this case we use only the females in our supplementary data set, divided into two groups: those who give birth as unmarried teens and those who do not. Again we construct estimates of

TABLE 14.4 / Determinants of High School Graduation, Structural Model[a]

Independent Variable	Model			
	Base	1	2	3
Constant	0.4448	0.3845	0.4418	0.5967
	4.70	2.76	2.51	3.97
Predicted earnings differential (marginal effect of $1,000)	1.16E-05	7.3E-06	4.12E-06	6.1E-06
	6.25	3.37	1.80	2.76
	0.0027	0.0013	0.0007	0.0010
Background				
African American		0.2067	0.3348	0.3233
		2.30	3.51	3.42
		0.0360	0.0566	0.0551
Female				
Mother's education		0.1474	0.1547	0.1501
		1.89	1.97	1.91
		0.0257	0.0262	0.0256
High school graduate		0.4809	0.4165	0.4206
		5.41	4.57	4.66
		0.0839	0.0704	0.0717
Some college		1.0404	0.8956	0.8959
		5.10	4.29	4.30
		0.1814	0.1515	0.1527
College graduate		5.2071	5.0278	5.1301
		0.01	0.01	0.01
		0.9082	0.8503	0.8744
Lived with one parent[b]				
Ages 6–8, not 12–15		−0.3381	−0.3304	−0.2137
		1.88	1.83	1.16
		−0.0590	−0.0559	−0.0364
Ages 12–15, not 6–8		−0.2529	−0.2034	−0.1535
		2.05	1.62	1.22
		−0.0441	−0.0344	−0.0262
Ages 6–15		−0.3928	−0.3359	−0.2465
		4.03	3.21	2.38
		−0.0685	−0.0568	−0.0420
Other		−0.3174	−0.2779	−0.1928
		1.23	1.07	0.74
		−0.0554	−0.0470	−0.0329

TABLE 14.4 / (*continued*)

Independent Variable	Model			
	Base	1	2	3
Average total income (marginal effect of $1,000)			7.26E-06 2.94 0.0012	
Siblings (average)			−0.0792 3.11 −0.0134	
Duration of poverty, ages 6–15[c]				
Some of the time				−0.3966 4.14 −0.0676
Always				−0.7044 3.88 −0.1201
Log-likelihood	721.09	671.71	662.57	660.6

Source: Authors' calculations based on data from the Panel Study of Income Dynamics on 1,705 children aged zero to six years in 1968 and followed until 1988.

a. Values are reduced-form coefficient estimates, *t*-statistics, and marginal effects.

b. Children who never lived with one parent from ages six to fifteen are the omitted category.

c. Children who were never poor from ages six to fifteen are the omitted category.

expected income by estimating first a selectivity model (to obtain the λ variable), a set of twenty-two tobit equations with personal income as the dependent variable and including the λ variable. We use the estimated coefficients from these income equations (without the estimate on the λ term) to obtain expected income values for our primary sample under each choice (to give birth as an unmarried teen or not). As before, we calculate the present value of these expected incomes at age sixteen, again using the 3 percent discount rate.

The pattern is not surprising: higher predicted incomes at the earliest age (nineteen) for those giving birth as teens but over time a growing disparity in favor of those not giving birth (table 14.5). Over the entire sample, the net present value is $50,687 if the adolescent gives birth out-of-wedlock as a teen and $96,791 if she does not; the difference is $46,104. Consistent with the pattern for high school graduates, those teens who give birth out-of-wedlock have a higher expected income under that option than do those who do not.

In the probit estimates of our structural models of teen nonmarital births (table 14.6), again the base model includes only the difference in the expected incomes while models 1–3 parallel their counterparts in table 14.2. The results suggest that

TABLE 14.5 / Predicted Personal Incomes If a Teen Gives Birth Out of Wedlock and If a Teen Does Not

	Birth		No Birth	
Sample and Age	Mean	*SD*	Mean	*SD*
Full sample (n = 873)				
Age 19	6,227	2,991	4,439	1,779
Age 20	5,426	2,915	6,110	2,081
Age 21	4,639	2,142	7,461	2,240
Age 22	3,782	3,217	9,080	2,094
Age 23	4,593	3,396	10,659	2,164
Age 24	4,469	4,135	11,189	1,621
Age 25	5,431	4,244	11,789	2,384
Age 26	6,710	2,658	12,817	3,433
Age 27	5,777	4,238	14,104	3,047
Age 28	7,279	3,853	14,615	2,708
Age 29	6,324	5,271	14,927	2,598
Net present value at age 16	50,687	23,387	96,791	16,101
Teens who gave birth (n = 125)				
Age 19	4,237	1,934	3,917	1,727
Age 20	6,161	3,072	5,716	1,475
Age 21	6,090	1,867	8,160	1,845
Age 22	6,151	3,076	9,409	1,469
Age 23	6,850	2,969	10,478	1,426
Age 24	7,583	3,658	11,214	1,293
Age 25	8,459	3,484	11,503	1,422
Age 26	7,983	2,617	12,237	1,728
Age 27	8,486	4,157	13,954	1,810
Age 28	9,780	3,931	14,344	1,684
Age 29	9,709	4,803	15,489	1,986
Net present value at age 16	67,606	20,851	96,126	10,563
Teens who did not give birth (n = 748)				
Age 19	6,560	3,009	4,527	1,774
Age 20	5,303	2,872	6,176	2,160
Age 21	4,397	2,090	7,344	2,280
Age 22	3,386	3,068	9,025	2,176
Age 23	4,216	3,317	10,690	2,263
Age 24	3,948	3,981	11,184	1,670
Age 25	4,925	4,149	11,837	2,507
Age 26	6,497	2,607	12,914	3,632
Age 27	5,325	4,082	14,129	3,208
Age 28	8,861	3,680	14,660	2,842
Age 29	5,758	5,135	14,833	2,676
Net present value at age 16	47,860	22,592	96,903	16,853

Source: Authors' calculations. See text.

TABLE 14.6 / Determinants of Teen Out-of-Wedlock Birth, Structural Model[a]

	Model			
Independent Variable	Base	1	2	3
Constant	−0.4385	−1.1346	−1.3500	−1.1245
	4.61	5.74	5.45	4.80
Predicted earnings differential	1.60E-05	5.12E-06	3.31E-06	5.20E-06
(marginal effect of $1,000)	7.27	1.76	0.90	1.62
	0.00320	0.00071	0.00044	0.00072
Background				
African American		0.3914	0.2770	0.3931
		2.60	1.78	2.58
		0.0542	0.0370	0.0544
Female				
High School		−0.6752	−0.6161	−0.6760
		4.61	4.09	4.57
		−0.0935	−0.0824	−0.0936
Some College		−0.8595	−0.7696	−0.8618
		2.65	2.32	2.65
		−0.1191	−0.1029	−0.1194
College graduate		−4.5480	−4.3750	−4.5552
		0.01	0.01	0.01
		−0.6301	−0.5849	−0.6304
Lived with one parent[b]				
Ages 6–8, not 12–15		0.4512	0.4730	0.4546
		1.49	1.56	1.49
		0.0625	−0.0632	0.0630
Ages 12–15, not 6–8		0.8306	0.8221	0.8333
		5.02	4.82	4.93
		0.1151	0.1099	0.1154
Ages 6–15		0.4271	0.4285	0.4292
		2.96	2.78	2.88
		0.0592	0.0573	0.0594
Other		0.2184	0.1021	0.2201
		0.57	0.26	0.56
		0.0303	0.0136	0.0305
Average total income (marginal			−3.85E-06	
effect of $1,000)			0.71	
			−0.00051	

(*Table continued on p. 440.*)

TABLE 14.6 / (*continued*)

Independent Variable	Model			
	Base	1	2	3
Siblings (average)			0.1094 3.09 0.0146	
Duration of poverty, ages 6–15[c]				
Some of the time				−0.0131 0.08 −0.0018
Always				−0.0114 0.04 −0.0016
Log-likelihood	328.23	293.09	288.04	293.09

Source: Authors' calculations based on data from the Panel Study of Income Dynamics on 1,705 children aged zero to six years in 1968 and followed until 1988.

a. Values are reduced-form coefficient estimates, *t*-statistics, and marginal effects.

b. Children who never lived with one parent from ages six to fifteen are the omitted category.

c. Children who were never poor from ages six to fifteen are the omitted category.

the difference in expected incomes conditional on the decision made do not play a significant role in influencing a young woman's choice of giving birth as a teen or not. Only in the base model is the difference in expected incomes statistically significant at the 5 percent level, and only in model 1 at the 10 percent level. In all other specifications, the expected income difference variable is not significant.[23] Not surprisingly, the results for the variables in the reduced-form model change very little. Log-likelihood tests like those described above indicate that the models in table 14.6 do not differ significantly from their counterparts in table 14.2.

SOME ROBUSTNESS EXERCISES We perform a number of robustness exercises designed to determine the sensitivity of our results to conventions that we adopted in the estimations reported. First, we use the predicted income for each individual for each age from nineteen to twenty-nine to create a present-value term for a longer period of time by forecasting individual income trajectories beyond age twenty-nine. Two forecasts are constructed for each individual, one based on the individual's income growth trend from ages nineteen to twenty-nine and the other on the value of income predicted for age twenty-nine. Our results from substituting either of these estimates of lifetime personal income for the present value from age nineteen through age twenty-nine show little difference from those reported both for education and for childbirth as an unmarried teen.

Second, we test the robustness of the association with income by allowing it to enter the utility function nonlinearly in two alternative specifications. In the first, we use the ratio of incomes in the alternative states, and in the second, the difference of the natural logs of the predicted income terms. The latter allows for diminishing marginal value of income. Both sets of results are very similar to those shown, with higher *t*-statistics for the income terms in the high school graduation model.

Third, we use discount rates of 25 percent and 50 percent in constructing our present value of expected income variables to reflect the possibility that youths make decisions on the basis of what they observe in the short run and do not take into account effects that may not be realized for a number of years. The sign and significance of the income terms in the structural model are quite insensitive to the discount rate used in the education model, although in model 2 of table 14.4 the coefficient on the income term becomes significant at the 5 percent level.[24]

Finally, to explore the possible nonlinear effect of family resources on the education and childbearing outcomes, we reestimate model C of tables 14A.4 and 14.A5 using ten categories of the income-to-needs ratio rather than the four categories shown. We choose categories so as to maintain a roughly equal number of observations in each. The patterns of marginal effects for the high school graduation outcome (figure 14.1) and for giving birth as an unmarried teen (figure 14.2) are fairly monotonic with the exception of the 1.33–1.66 income-to-needs ratio category (which seems to have a disproportionate number of high school dropouts and teen out-of-wedlock births). For the education outcome, the marginal effects (and the statistical significance) are the strongest at very low (below 0.66) and high (above 2.00) income-to-needs ratios; for the childbearing outcome, only high income-to-needs ratios appear to have large and significant effects, with no poverty category showing much of an impact.[25]

CONCLUSION

This study focuses on understanding the determinants of educational attainment and out-of-wedlock teen births and, in particular, on understanding the role of poverty and its family-related correlates. Rather than testing a single hypothesis regarding the determinants of educational and teen fertility outcomes, we introduce a range of background, economic, and family variables into the analysis, including variables consistent with several of the hypotheses that have been the subject of other studies.[26]

When a fairly rich set of determinants is included, both sex and race influenced the probability of graduating high school; other things equal, being African American and female is associated with a higher probability of graduating. The amount of parental time available while growing up (including the presence of two parents in the home) and having fewer siblings is positively related to educational

FIGURE 14.1 / Effect of Income-to-Needs Ratio on High School Graduation[a]

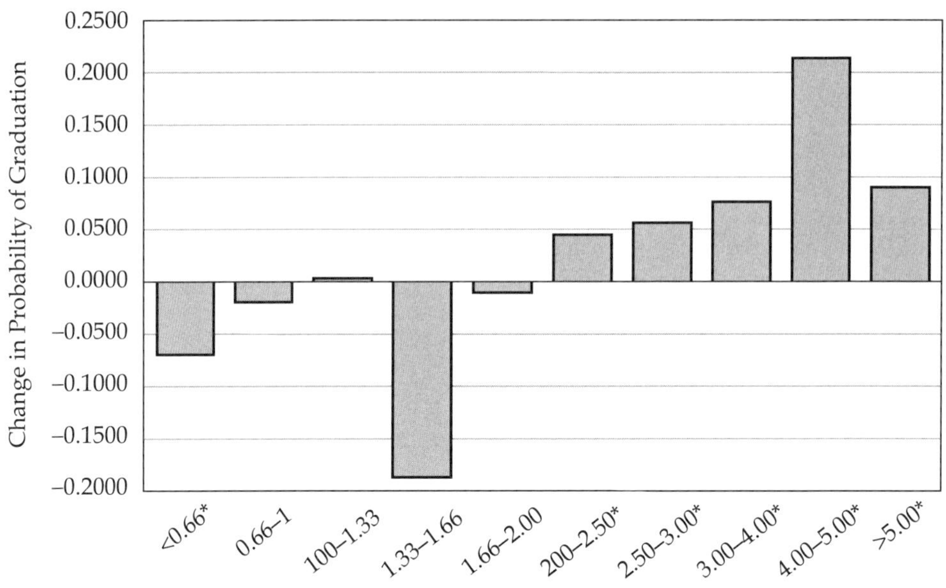

Source: Authors' calculations based on data from the Panel Study of Income Dynamics on 1,705 children aged zero to six years in 1968 and followed until 1988.

a. An asterisk denotes statistically significant difference from reference category. Income-to-needs ratio of 1.00–1.33 is the omitted category.

attainment. Both the educational level of the mother and the economic resources available to the family (proxied by both total family income and the number of years that the family is in poverty) are related to educational success. In particular, the number of years in poverty appears to be an important determinant of the probability of graduating high school. Other things equal, children who grow up in poor families are far less likely than other children to complete high school. When these children also grow up with only a single parent, the probability that they will complete high school is further reduced.

Our estimates that include the expected economic returns associated with alternative choices suggest that if encouraging high school graduation is an important goal, policy makers should support measures that increase the income returns to high school graduation. Such measures, by increasing the net income returns to additional schooling, are likely to reduce the dropout rate. As a result, the number of youths with high school degrees will increase, leaving behind a smaller group of dropouts; this latter group would not gain from the policy. Alternative policies to consider for assisting this residual, dropout population include supplementing

FIGURE 14.2 / Effect of Income-to-Needs Ratio on Teen Birth

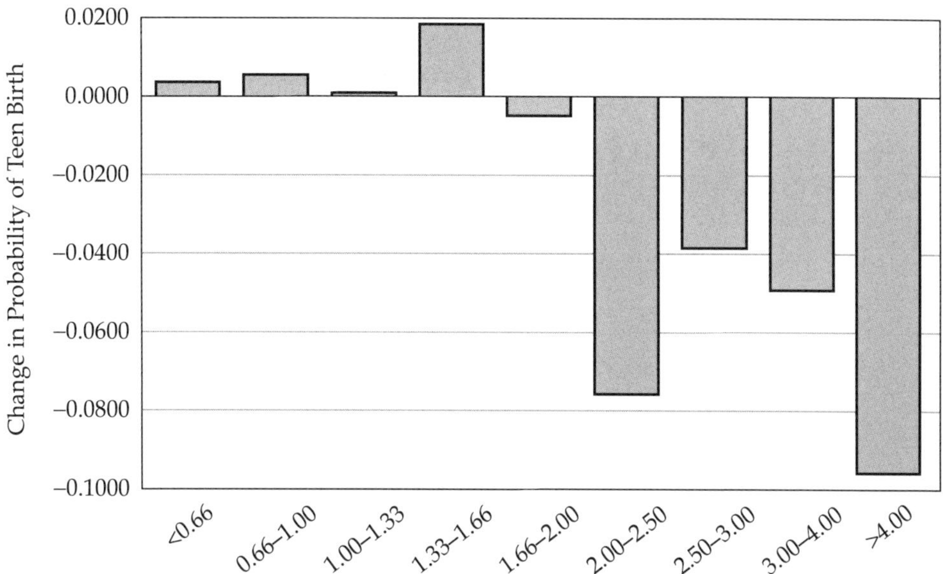

Source: Authors' calculations based on data from the Panel Study of Income Dynamics on 1,705 children aged zero to six years in 1968 and followed until 1988.

their incomes through work-related income transfers, minimum wage increases, or low-wage employment subsidies. While such measures would improve the incomes and economic well-being of these low-skilled workers, they would have the adverse side effect of decreasing the economic incentive to graduate high school.

Our estimates of the determinants of the teen out-of-wedlock birth outcome suggest that parental characteristics (the education of the mother) are important determinants of teens' childbearing choices but that poverty itself is not a significant determinant. However, having income well above the poverty line does appear to reduce teen out-of-wedlock births. A family characteristic frequently associated with poverty—the number of years spent living with a single parent—is also a significant determinant of teenage fertility choices, particularly if a child spends the teenage years from twelve to fifteen living in poverty. The results on expected income do not provide policy makers with any clear direction for income or labor market initiatives to reduce the prevalence of teen out-of-wedlock births. While the sign on the income difference variable suggests that decreasing the economic returns attached to teen nonmarital childbearing tends to reduce such births, the persistent absence of statistical significance of the coefficient on this variable casts doubt on the likely efficacy of such a policy. In the long run, encouraging high school graduation and two-parent families seems to offer more promise for reducing teen out-of-wedlock births.

APPENDIX: SUPPLEMENTAL ANALYSES

Tables 14A.1–14A.5 provide additional estimates of the reduced–form and structural models, as well as summary statistics pertinent to these estimates. Tables 14A.1 and 14A.2 are reduced–form specifications.

TABLE 14A.1 / Replication Analysis: Determinants of High School Graduation, Reduced-Form Model

Independent Variable	Model[a]							
	A	B	C	D	E	F	Mean	*SD*
Constant	0.3165	0.3983	0.5376	0.9336	0.4387	0.4173	1	0
	2.90	3.27	5.46	10.01	3.45	3.19		
Background								
African American	0.1108	0.2732	0.3649	0.2734	0.1127	0.2759	0.45689	0.49828
	1.28	2.96	3.66	2.91	0.65	2.98		
	0.0244	0.0463	0.0580	0.0472	0.0192	0.0466		
Female	0.1376	0.1516	0.1486	0.1550	0.1555	0.1033	0.51202	0.50000
	1.81	1.94	1.89	1.99	1.99	0.72		
	0.0303	0.0257	0.0248	0.0267	0.0264	0.0175		
Parental choices and opportunities								
Mother								
High school graduate		0.4427	0.3901	0.4786	0.4419	0.4403	0.39003	0.48790
		4.92	4.28	5.41	4.91	4.88		
		0.0750	0.0652	0.0826	0.0751	0.0744		
Some college		0.8597	0.7853	0.8853	0.8564	0.8563	0.08094	0.27282
		4.11	3.70	4.29	4.10	4.09		
		0.1457	0.1312	0.1527	0.1456	0.1448		
College graduate		5.0012	5.0084	5.0988	4.9925	5.0008	0.04458	0.20643
		0.01	0.01	0.01	0.01	0.01		
		0.8474	0.8371	0.8797	0.8489	0.8455		

(Table continued on p. 446.)

TABLE 14A.1 / (*continued*)

Independent Variable	Model[a]							
	A	B	C	D	E	F	Mean	*SD*
Lived with one parent[b]								
Ages 6–8, not 12–15		−0.3318	−0.3402	−0.2312	−0.3360	−0.3320	0.04340	0.20382
		1.84	1.87	1.25	1.87	1.85		
		−0.0562	−0.0569	−0.0399	−0.0571	−0.0561		
Ages 12–15, not 6–8		−0.2325	−0.2274	−0.1958	−0.2257	−0.2325	0.11437	0.31835
		1.87	1.83	1.54	1.82	1.87		
		−0.0394	−0.0380	−0.0338	−0.0384	−0.0393		
Ages 6–15		−0.3843	−0.3293	−0.3467	−0.3591	−0.3838	0.23695	0.42534
		3.92	3.24	3.42	3.56	3.91		
		−0.0651	−0.0550	−0.0598	−0.0611	−0.0649		
Other		−0.2940	−0.3037	−0.2066	−0.2919	−0.2923	0.01877	0.13575
		1.13	1.16	0.80	1.13	1.13		
		−0.0498	−0.0508	−0.0357	−0.0496	−0.0494		
Income-to-needs ratio[c]								
Average	0.2797	0.1626			0.1440	0.1522	2.3384	1.7350
	7.87	4.19			3.43	3.27		
	0.0615	0.0276			0.0245	0.0257		
<1			−0.1774				0.18416	0.38773
			1.65					
			−0.0296					
2–3			0.3784				0.21760	0.41273
			3.37					
			0.0632					

>3			0.6927				0.26393	0.44089
			5.09					
			0.1158					
Duration of poverty[d]								
Ages 6–8, not 9–15				−0.4160			0.06628	0.24884
				2.69				
				−0.0718				
Ages 9–15, not 6–8				−0.3831			0.10850	0.31111
				2.92				
				−0.0661				
Ages 6–8 and 9–15				−0.4680			0.30147	0.45903
				4.27				
				−0.0807				
Black by income-to-needs ratio					0.1010		0.65713	0.89089
					1.09			
					0.0172			
Female by income-to-needs ratio						0.0263	1.2035	1.7534
						0.40		
						0.0044		
Log-likelihood	697.42	666.17	657.07	664.96	665.56	666.09		

Source: Authors' calculations based on data from the Panel Study of Income Dynamics on 1,705 children aged zero to six years in 1968 and followed until 1988.

a. Values are reduced-form coefficient estimates, *t*-statistics, and marginal effects.

b. Children who never lived with one parent are the omitted category.

c. Children with family income-to-needs ratios of less than 1 are the omitted category.

d. Children who were never poor are the omitted category.

TABLE 14A.2 / Replication Analysis: Determinants of Teen Out-of-Wedlock Birth: Reduced-Form Model

	Model[a]						
Independent Variable	A	B	C	D	E	Mean	*SD*
Constant	−0.6408	−0.9076	−1.1400	−1.4357	−0.8370	1	0
	3.37	4.21	7.29	10.16	3.15		
Background							
African American	0.4135	0.3319	0.3346	0.4728	0.2113	0.48683	0.50011
	2.93	2.22	2.25	3.25	0.70		
	0.0695	0.0425	0.0447	0.0674	0.0264		
Parental choices and opportunities							
Mother							
High school graduate		−0.6213	−0.6331	−0.7076	−0.6210	0.37801	0.48517
		4.17	4.22	4.84	4.16		
		−0.0795	−0.0845	−0.1008	−0.0777		
Some college		−0.6980	−0.7795	−0.9006	−0.6762	0.08018	0.27173
		2.11	2.35	2.77	2.03		
		−0.0894	−0.1041	−0.1283	−0.0846		
College graduate		−4.3854	−4.4742	−4.4133	−4.3657	0.03780	0.19082
		0.01	0.01	0.02	0.01		
		−0.5615	−0.5973	−0.6288	−0.5465		
Lived with one parent[b]							
Ages 6–8, not 12–15		0.4225	0.4142	0.3754	0.4204	0.03436	0.18227
		1.41	1.37	1.22	1.40		
		0.0541	0.0553	0.0535	0.0526		
Ages 12–15, not 6–8		0.7881	0.8129	0.8521	0.7912	0.12486	0.33075
		4.71	4.84	4.90	4.71		
		0.1009	0.1085	0.1214	0.0990		
Ages 6–15		0.3604	0.3951	0.4449	0.3695	0.23368	0.42341
		2.49	2.69	2.98	2.53		
		0.0461	0.0527	0.0634	0.0463		
Other		0.1854	0.2028	0.2262	0.1897	0.02062	0.14219
		0.47	0.52	0.59	0.48		
		0.0237	0.0271	0.0322	0.0238		

Income-to-needs ratio[c]							
Average	−0.3723	−0.2153			−0.2489	2.3504	1.8191
	5.19	2.73			2.27		
	−0.0626	−0.0276			−0.0312		
<1			0.0059			0.19588	0.39710
			0.04				
			0.0008				
2–3			−0.5057			0.19588	0.39710
			2.64				
			−0.0675				
>3			−0.5378			0.27148	0.44498
			2.36				
			−0.0718				
Duration of poverty[d]							
Ages 6–8, not 9–15				0.1780		0.06529	0.24718
				0.72			
				0.0254			
Ages 9–15, not 6–8				0.0318		0.11798	0.32277
				0.16			
				0.0045			
Ages 6–8 and 9–15				0.1103		0.30584	0.46103
				0.68			
				0.0157			
Black by income-to-needs ratio					0.0689	0.68402	0.88348
					0.46		
					0.0086		
Log-likelihood	311.15	290.71	289.45	294.57	290.60		

Source: Authors' calculations based on data from the Panel Study of Income Dynamics on 1,705 children aged zero to six years in 1968 and followed until 1988.

a. Values are reduced-form coefficient estimates, *t*-statistics, and marginal effects.

b. Children who never lived with one parent were the omitted category.

c. Children with family income-to-needs ratios of less than 1 were the omitted category.

d. Children who were never poor were the omitted category.

TABLE 14A.3 / Means and Standard Deviations of Variables in Income Prediction Equation, Older Youth Sample[a]

	Graduated High School				Gave Birth as a Teen			
	Yes		No		Yes		No	
Variable	Mean	*SD*	Mean	*SD*	Mean	*SD*	Mean	*SD*
Number of siblings	2.8858	1.9548	3.5980	2.2213	3.8223	2.1797	2.8492	1.9133
Firstborn	0.1764	0.3813	0.0819	0.2750	0.0781	0.2694	0.1858	0.3893
Average years lived with one parent	0.2571	0.4128	0.3099	0.4327	0.4629	0.4790	0.2504	0.4102
Average years mother worked	0.5435	0.4290	0.4678	0.4037	0.6074	0.4182	0.5131	0.4242
Average years on Aid to Families with Dependent Children	0.1165	0.2739	0.2091	0.3194	0.2773	0.3715	0.1035	0.2514
Mother's education								
High school graduate+			0.1462	0.3543	0.2500	0.4347		
High school graduate	0.3860	0.4870					0.3429	0.4751
Some college	0.0607	0.2389					0.0676	0.2512
College graduate	0.0524	0.2230					0.0473	0.2125
Father's education								
High school graduate+			0.1170	0.3223	0.0781	0.2694		
High school graduate	0.1947	0.3961					0.2010	0.4011
Some college	0.0724	0.2592					0.0760	0.2652
College graduate	0.1048	0.3065					0.0929	0.2906

African American	0.4567	0.4983	0.5673	0.4969	0.8125	0.3919	0.4392	0.4967
Female	0.5341	0.4990	0.4561	0.4995				
African American by female	0.2621	0.4399	0.2866	0.4535				
Average years lived in Standard Metropolitan Statistical Area	0.7386	0.4194	0.7091	0.4311	0.7676	0.4057	0.7411	0.4134
Average years in family with disabled head	0.1862	0.3453	0.3260	0.4167	0.3340	0.4106	0.2010	0.3570
Average income-to-needs ratio	2.3559	1.8575	1.3212	0.8069	1.2900	0.7626	2.2986	1.7005
Average years in West	0.1387	0.3433	0.0994	0.3001	0.0684	0.2504	0.1402	0.3444
Average years in Northeast	0.1697	0.3736	0.0702	0.2562	0.0898	0.2836	0.1951	0.3942
Average years in South	0.4172	0.4908	0.5629	0.4964	0.5898	0.4918	0.4320	0.4931
Inverse Mills ratio (lambda)	0.1896	0.1789	−1.3331	0.4333	1.1838	0.3868	−0.2560	0.2234
N	1,202		171		128		592	

Source: Authors' calculations based on data from the Panel Study of Income Dynamics on 1,705 children aged zero to six years in 1968 and followed until 1988.

+ additional education after high school (13 years or more).

a. Average years refers to ages twelve to fifteen.

TABLE 14A.4 / Replication Analysis: Determinants of High School Graduation, Structural Model

	Model					
Independent Variable	A	B	C	D	E	F
Constant	0.1291	0.2051	0.3811	0.6083	0.2472	0.2165
	0.95	1.37	2.66	4.05	1.61	1.35
Predicted earnings differential	4.97E-06	4.54E-06	3.25E-06	5.92E-06	4.65E-06	4.49E-06
(marginal effect of $1,000)	2.28	1.98	1.40	2.69	2.02	1.95
	0.0011	0.0008	0.0005	0.0010	0.0008	0.0008
Background						
African American	0.1424	0.2911	0.3593	0.3183	0.1084	0.2922
	1.63	3.13	3.76	3.33	0.63	3.13
	0.0312	0.0491	0.0600	0.0541	0.0184	0.0493
Female	0.1325	0.1448	0.1444	0.1455	0.1492	0.1208
	1.74	1.85	1.83	1.86	1.92	0.84
	0.0291	0.0244	0.0241	0.0248	0.0253	0.0204
Parental choices and opportunities						
Mother						
High school graduate		0.4176	0.3718	0.4293	0.4161	0.4167
		4.61	4.05	4.76	4.58	4.59
		0.0705	0.0621	0.0730	0.0705	0.0703
Some college		0.8941	0.8085	0.9039	0.8918	0.8921
		4.24	3.79	4.33	4.23	4.22
		0.1509	0.1350	0.1538	0.1511	0.1504
College graduate		5.0661	5.0383	5.1733	5.0560	5.0648
		0.01	0.01	0.01	0.01	0.01
		0.8551	0.8411	0.8802	0.8567	0.8540

	(1)	(2)	(3)	(4)	(5)	(6)
Lived with one parent[b]						
Ages 6–8, not 12–15		−0.3164	−0.3263	−0.2153	−0.3214	−0.3165
		1.75	1.79	1.16	1.78	1.76
		−0.0534	−0.0545	−0.0366	−0.0545	0.0534
Ages 12–15, not 6–8		−0.2100	−0.2067	−0.1652	−0.2018	−0.2100
		1.69	1.66	1.29	1.62	1.69
		−0.0354	−0.0345	−0.0281	−0.0342	−0.0354
Ages 6–15		−0.3264	−0.2752	−0.2746	−0.2970	−0.3264
		3.28	2.66	2.67	2.90	3.28
		−0.0551	−0.0459	−0.0467	−0.0503	−0.0550
Other		−0.3041	−0.3106	−0.2243	−0.3021	−0.3032
		1.17	1.19	0.86	1.16	1.17
		−0.0513	−0.0519	−0.0382	−0.0512	−0.0511
Income-to-needs ratio[c]						
Average	0.2478	0.1400			0.1180	0.1350
	6.53	3.41			2.67	2.82
	0.0543	0.0236			0.0200	0.0228
<1			−0.1883			
			1.75			
			−0.0314			
2–3			0.3506			
			3.07			
			0.0585			
>3			0.6328			
			4.40			
			0.1056			

(Table continued on p. 454.)

TABLE 14A.4 / *(continued)*

	Model					
Independent Variable	A	B	C	D	E	F
Duration of poverty[d]						
Ages 6–8, not 9–15				−0.3947		
				2.54		
				−0.0671		
Ages 9–15, not 6–8				−0.3593		
				2.72		
				−0.0611		
Ages 6–8 and 9–15				−0.4427		
				4.03		
				−0.0753		
Black by income-to-needs ratio					0.1151	
					1.24	
					0.0195	
Female by income-to-needs ratio						0.0131
						0.20
						0.0022
Log-likelihood	694.80	665.49	657.11	662.20	664.70	665.47

Source: Authors' calculations based on data from the Panel Study of Income Dynamics on 1,705 children aged zero to six years in 1968 and followed until 1988.

a. Values are reduced-form coefficient estimates, *t*-statistics, and marginal effects.

b. Children who never lived with one parent were the omitted category.

c. Children with family income-to-needs ratios of less than 1 were the omitted category.

d. Children who were never poor were the omitted category.

TABLE 14A.5 / Replication Analysis: Determinants of Teen Out-of-Wedlock Birth, Structural Model[a]

	Model				
Independent Variable	A	B	C	D	E
Constant	−0.6316	−0.9092	−1.1165	−1.1096	−0.8308
	3.23	4.09	5.19	4.70	3.01
Predicted earnings differential (marginal effect of $1,000)	−7.01E-07	1.03E-11	−5.50E-07	−5.57E-06	−2.29E-07
	0.20	0.00	0.15	1.69	0.06
	−1.18E-04	1.31E-09	−7.33E-05	−7.67E-04	−2.86E-05
Background					
African American	0.4076	0.3245	0.3220	0.3916	0.1943
	2.83	2.13	2.10	2.57	0.63
	0.0687	0.0415	0.0429	0.0539	0.0243
Parental choices and opportunities					
Mother					
High school graduate		−0.6226	−0.6328	−0.6789	−0.6219
		4.17	4.22	4.61	4.16
		−0.0797	−0.0843	−0.0935	−0.0778
Some college		−0.6994	−0.7789	−0.8569	−0.6769
		2.12	2.35	2.64	2.03
		−0.0895	−0.1038	−0.1180	−0.0846
College graduate		−4.3873	−4.4722	−4.5881	−4.3669
		0.01	0.01	0.01	0.01
		−0.5615	−0.5960	−0.6320	−0.5461
Lived with one parent[b]					
Ages 6–8, not 12–15		0.4272	0.4216	0.4296	0.4264
		1.42	1.39	1.39	1.42
		0.0547	0.0562	0.0592	0.0533
Ages 12–15, not 6–8		0.7926	0.8160	0.8601	0.7959
		4.74	4.86	4.93	4.75
		0.1014	0.1087	0.1185	0.0995
Ages 6–15		0.3761	0.4087	0.4377	0.3851
		2.58	2.76	2.91	2.62
		0.0481	0.0545	0.0603	0.0482
Other		0.1833	0.2005	0.2282	0.1875
		0.47	0.52	0.59	0.48
		0.0235	0.0267	0.0314	0.0234

(Table continued on p. 456.)

TABLE 14A.5 / *(continued)*

Independent Variable	Model A	Model B	Model C	Model D	Model E
Income-to-needs ratio[c]					
Average	−0.3605	−0.2140			−0.2460
	3.89	2.20			2.05
	−0.0608	−0.0274			−0.0308
<1			−0.0050		
			0.03		
			−0.0007		
2–3			−0.4965		
			2.49		
			−0.0662		
>3			−0.5194		
			2.00		
			−0.0692		
Duration of poverty[d]					
Ages 6–8, not 9–15				0.1274	
				0.51	
				0.0175	
Ages 9–15, not 6–8				−0.0788	
				0.37	
				−0.0108	
Ages 6–8 and 9–15				−0.0333	
				0.18	
				−0.0046	
Black by income-to-needs ratio					−0.0732
					0.49
					−0.0092
Log-likelihood	311.13	290.46	289.17	292.82	290.34

Source: Authors' calculations based on data from the Panel Study of Income Dynamics on 1,705 children aged zero to six years in 1968 and followed until 1988.

a. Values are reduced-form coefficient estimates, *t*-statistics, and marginal effects.

b. Children who never lived with one parent were the omitted category.

c. Children with family income-to-needs ratios of less than 1 were the omitted category.

d. Children who were never poor were the omitted category.

NOTES

1. There is a rather extensive literature on school-based determinants as well. See, for example, Hanushek (1986), who reviews the school production function literature, and Mayer (1991), who reviews the role of student body composition. For a related study, see chapter 16.
2. According to the Alan Guttmacher Institute (1992), seven in ten births to teens are from unplanned pregnancies.
3. Although the implications of the unmarried teen birthrate that we have noted seem consistent with both casual observation and common sense, it is not necessarily the birth of a child to an unmarried teen that is responsible for the observed patterns of poverty, failure to complete high school, and welfare recipiency. Girls who give birth out of wedlock could have these poor outcomes even if they had not given birth; maybe they have family backgrounds or personal characteristics that foster low attainments. To an unmarried teen, giving birth may be but another manifestation of this poor outlook for future success.

   A number of researchers have suggested this position (Luker 1991; Nathanson 1991); moreover, a recent study comparing sisters (hence controlling for family background) who become mothers at different ages found only negligible differences between teen and nonteen mothers in a wide variety of outcomes (see Geronimous and Korenman 1992). For a variety of reasons, however, the results from this study do not appear robust, and a recent critique of this study (and a reanalysis of its model) concludes that "the effects of teenage childbearing do not disappear, nor, indeed, are they particularly small" (Hoffman, Foster, and Furstenberg 1993, p. 2).
4. Few studies have attempted to model the effect of opportunity or income differences associated with different choices on the ultimate decisions that are made; an important exception is Duncan and Hoffman (1990).
5. In 1968, there were 3,120 children aged zero to six years in the PSID. During the subsequent twenty-one years, 1,370 children were lost from the sample for one reason or another. With the exception of race, those lost to attrition do not appear to differ from the remaining sample.
6. In a few cases, observations that could not be used were excluded from the analysis. For the full sample, these included those persons with two or more contiguous years of data missing. We retained observations with only one (contiguous) year of data missing and filled in the missing data by averaging the data for the two years contiguous to the year of missing data. For the first and last years of the sample, averaging the contiguous years was not possible. In this case, we assigned the contiguous year's value adjusted if appropriate using other information that was reported.
7. For the variables describing family structure, we assigned a value of 1 if the event or circumstance occurred or existed in at least one year during that age interval, and 0 otherwise.
8. Additional specifications are shown in appendix table 14A.1, in which the models include alternative measures of family income.
9. It has been suggested that the underlying process determining educational attainment may differ for African Americans and non–African Americans, and the significant coef-

ficient on the race variables indicated that race was playing an important role in the determination of educational attainment. We tested for structural differences in the slope coefficients of models equivalent to those for model 2 run separately over the African American and non–African American subsamples. We used a test of omitted variables in which the variables omitted in the full-sample specification were the independent variables interacted with race (see Engle 1984, 776–826). The test indicated that the null hypothesis of no structural difference could not be rejected at a 10 percent significance level. The results of this model are available from the authors.

10. Table 14A.2 provides additional specifications.

11. In a few of the additional specifications reported in table 14A.2, the coefficients on the economic resources variables were statistically significant. For example, in the simplest model not including parental education and living with a single parent, the coefficient on the economic resources variable was statistically significant. Furthermore, when income was specified relative to the poverty line (the ratio of income to needs), it was statistically significant, in the expected negative direction. These estimates suggest that although living in poverty does not significantly increase the probability that a teen will give birth out of wedlock, living in a family with income above the poverty line is associated with a reduction in the probability of a teen nonmarital birth. However, given the lack of a significant coefficient on the family income variable in model 2 of table 14.2, the ratio of income to needs may be reflecting family size effects rather than economic resources.

12. Alternatively, we could describe this framework in more strictly economic terms by noting that the model rests on the standard assumption of utility maximization where individuals face the choice of whether or not to graduate high school. The income flows associated with each option determine the well-being (utility) expected in each option.

13. $E(\cdot)$ denotes the child's subjective expected value of utility conditional on information available before making the choice.

14. C might also include additional factors measuring the community's choices, such as the proportion of youths who are high school dropouts or the proportion of workers in successful occupations in the neighborhood in which the child grew up.

15. We estimated a similar model of the determinants of teens' choices to give birth out of wedlock. In this case, the coefficients were estimated from a tobit model fit over teens in the sample who did or did not give birth as unmarried teenagers.

16. Manski (1987) estimates a two-stage model very similar to ours in analyzing the determinants of the choice to become a teacher or not. See also Lee (1979).

17. In the model of teen out-of-wedlock childbearing, we also included state-level data on teen births and abortions as identifiers.

18. In fact, one λ term is used for each individual in these income equations since we ran the income regressions over those who were in the matched subsample (high school graduates in the income equations for high school graduates, etc.).

19. The estimated first-stage probit that produced the selection correction variable for the second-stage income regressions and the income regressions themselves are available from the authors. In the income regressions, having a parent who attended college had a negative and significant coefficient in the estimates for younger ages, but the coeffi-

cient became positive and significant in estimates for older ages. This pattern may reflect the fact that children of college graduates have a higher probability of attending college and hence are likely to have lower earnings in the college-attending years. For the sample that did not graduate, having a father who graduated from high school had a negative and often significant coefficient for all ages. The variables black and female had negative and very significant coefficients, while black*female has a positive and significant coefficient. The coefficient on the income-to-needs ratio was generally insignificant, while years spent in a Standard Metropolitan Statistical Area had a positive sign and sometimes a significant coefficient. Relative to the omitted dummy variable north central, region of residence was not significant for the sample that did not graduate, but living in the West was positive and significant for high school graduates. The λ term was negative and significant in about three-fourths of the income regressions for the high school group and in one-half of the income regressions for the nongraduates.

20. In using the coefficients to predict income for the individuals in our sample at each age if a graduate and if not a graduate, we did not use the λ term—that is, we made an unconditional prediction. To avoid reducing or increasing the expected income by omitting this term, we added the mean expected value of the λ times its coefficient to the constant term in predicting income for each age and for both schooling options.

21. These predictions can be interpreted as the impact of providing a high school degree to all persons in our sample. If nongraduates were simulated as graduating, they would increase their income substantially. Their incomes in early years would be greater than those of actual graduates, but they would face a lower rate of growth. This interpretation, however, requires the heroic assumption that the income-generating process would not be affected by a sudden increase in the proportion of persons graduating high school.

22. The only exception to this is in a supplementary equation, reported in table 14A.4, which includes a set of dummy variables indicating that the person grew up living in a family whose income was below the poverty line, between one and two times the poverty line, and three or more times the poverty line.

23. This general conclusion also holds for the additional estimated models shown in table 14A.5, where only for model D is the estimate significant at the 10 percent level.

24. For the unmarried teen birth outcome, using the present value of income variables constructed with the higher discount rates also produced only small changes in the results. Only in model 1 of table 14.6 is the change noteworthy; there the coefficient on the income term changed from significant at the 10 percent level to insignificant. If youths are indeed myopic in making such childbearing choices, the income terms constructed using the higher discount rates should have been more closely related to the childbearing outcome; in fact, there was a weaker relationship. The *t*-statistics on the coefficient of the income term tended to be inversely related to the value of the discount rate. Little should be made of this, however; with a 25 or a 50 percent discount rate, the resulting present value of the income variable was heavily influenced by two or three years of predicted incomes and hence was measured with less precision than the present-value variable that weights more equally the predicted values from all eleven years. This loss of precision may account for the reduction in the significance levels of the coefficients on the income terms constructed using the high discount rates.

25. We ran a series of log-likelihood tests for joint significance to determine if the effects of groups of income-to-needs categories were jointly significant. For the education outcome, the two categories of below-unity ratios were jointly significant at the 5 percent level, as were the set of categories for income-to-needs greater than 1.33. Because the two categories between 1.33 and 2.00 were not jointly significant, family resources apparently need to be well above the poverty line before their effect on the education outcome is significant. For the teen out-of-wedlock birth outcome, none of the substantial number of log-likelihood tests to measure joint significance was statistically significant. A recategorization of income-to-needs ratios into six rather than ten categories yielded a joint log-likelihood test that income-to-needs ratios in excess of 2.00 were statistically significant at a 10 percent level.
26. A word of caution: while our estimates included a rich specification of the parental choice and opportunity factors influencing children's decisions, we were unable to measure a variety of other factors that may, in their own right, significantly influence these decisions: the quality and socioeconomic and racial composition of the children's schools, the attitudes and expectations of the children's parents, the effort with which they monitor their children's activities, and the children's inherent mental powers and physical characteristics. For postsecondary schooling, the financial aid available and the performance of the child in secondary school are likely to be important factors, yet we cannot measure them. These considerations must remain unobserved variables, given the information available in our data set.

Chapter 15

Race, Sex, and the Intergenerational Transmission of Poverty

Mary Corcoran and Terry Adams

The study described in this chapter estimates the extent to which income poverty persists across generations and tests four alternative explanations for this persistence. That is, we ask, "How much and why are poor children destined to remain poor as adults?"

Considerable research, beginning with Sewell and Hauser's (1975) pioneering study, has documented an association between fathers' incomes and sons' earnings. Sewell and Hauser found that parental income predicted sons' earnings even with schooling and test scores controlled. When other analysts replicated Sewell and Hauser's analyses using other data sets, they obtained similar results (Hauser and Daymont 1977; Jencks et al. 1979; Kiker and Condon 1981; Solon 1992; Corcoran et al. 1992; Zimmerman 1992).

The above research demonstrates that parental income predicts sons' earnings but is less informative about intergenerational poverty. One limitation is the populations examined. None of the studies cited above looked at women's intergenerational income mobility, and several used samples of mostly white, employed men. As Winship (1992) notes, many of the poor are nonwhite, female and jobless, and few status attainment studies look directly at parental poverty either as a predictor or as an outcome variable, instead focusing on fathers' and sons' occupational statuses, labor incomes, or hourly wages.[1] Considerable intergenerational income mobility may exist even as many children from extremely poor families are permanently stuck in poverty. The new structural/environmental theories of poverty pose a third challenge to the status attainment research. Wilson (1987, 1991a, 1991b, 1993) argues that underclass neighborhoods and depressed labor markets trap poor inner-city children in intergenerational poverty. Few status attainment studies have included environmental and economic variables in their analyses, in large part because of a lack of data. The "welfare culture" and "welfare incentive" models pose a fourth challenge. According to these models, parents' receipt of welfare and perverse welfare incentives promote intergenerational poverty and dependency (Mead 1986, 1992; Murray 1984). Testing such models requires measures of parental welfare receipt and of state welfare benefits.

We extend past research on intergenerational income mobility in three ways. First, we directly estimate the effects of parental poverty on children's chances of experiencing poverty in their late twenties and early thirties. Second, we estimate models separately for black men, white men, white women, and black women. Since poverty, not earned income, is our outcome measure, our analyses include both working and nonworking men and women. Third, we include measures of parental poverty, parental welfare use, neighborhood underclass characteristics, labor market conditions, and state welfare benefits so that we can directly test predictions of the welfare culture models and of Wilson's (1987) structural/environmental model.

We start by outlining the four sets of explanations of intergenerational poverty: the economic resources models, the noneconomic resources models, the welfare trap models, and Wilson's environmental/structural model. Then we describe our data set, sample, and variables. The third section reports the results of two sets of analyses: a set of replication analyses common to all chapters in this volume and a series of analyses that test the four explanations of intergenerational poverty. We conclude by evaluating each of these four explanations in light of our results.

MODELS OF INTERGENERATIONAL POVERTY

The first and simplest model maintains parents' lack of economic resources hinders children's human capital development and abilities to find steady, well-paying jobs. According to Becker (1981), families allocate resources between current consumption and investments in children's human capital. Poor parents will need most of their resources for economic survival and will have little time, money, and energy left over to invest in children's human capital.

Parental poverty could affect children's economic attainments in other ways. Poor parents may be less able to afford housing in "good" neighborhoods (i.e., safe neighborhoods with high-quality schools and good role models) and may be less connected to job networks than are nonpoor parents (Loury, 1981; Coleman, 1990). Loury (1981), Massey (1991), and Wilson (1987, 1991a, 1991b, 1993) contend that access to "good" neighborhoods (and hence the ability to increase children's social capital) is even more restricted for poor, minority parents because of "tastes," historical housing discrimination, and current housing discrimination.

If parents' lack of economic resources causes intergenerational poverty, then the solution is easy: provide more resources and enable poor families to gain access to "good" neighborhoods through programs such as the Earned Income Tax Credit, the refundable child tax credit, and housing vouchers.

The second explanation of intergenerational poverty is that parents' noneconomic resources, correlated with their poverty, account for both parents' poverty and children's poverty as adults. One possible resource is parents' schooling. Poor parents have less schooling, on average, than do nonpoor parents, and schooling may affect parents' abilities to encourage and help their children to get an education. A second possibility is family structure. The breakup of a marriage (or the parents' failure to marry) increases the chances that a child will be poor during childhood, may lead to psychological distress, may reduce parental supervision, and may limit the child's role models for marriage and work. The distress, lack of supervision, and lack of role models could in turn lead children to be poor as adults. Herrnstein and Murray's (1994) argument that cross-generational, genetically based differences in IQ fuel intergenerational inequality is another "noneconomic resources" model. In this model, low IQs cause parental poverty, poor children genetically inherit their parents' low IQs, and these children's low IQs cause the children in the next generation to be poor.

If intergenerational poverty were caused by parents' noneconomic resources, then those resources must be identified in order to develop an appropriate policy solution. This answer is easy to propose but difficult to implement. Research can rule out certain possibilities but is unlikely to identify and control all the possible noneconomic disadvantages parents may have (that is, unmeasured values, health conditions, abilities) that are correlated with parental poverty and that constrain children's abilities to escape poverty as adults.

Mead (1986, 1992) argues that intergenerational poverty is fueled not by a lack of parental economic and noneconomic resources but by the government welfare system. According to Mead, when individuals rely heavily on welfare, the stigma associated with being on welfare disappears, and welfare recipients develop self-defeating work attitudes and poor work ethics and pass them on to their children. Girls raised in welfare-dependent homes will be likely to drop out of high school, give birth as teens, become poor, and go on welfare themselves. Boys raised in welfare-dependent homes will be likely to grow up to father children out of wedlock, drop out of high school, hang out, engage in crime and avoid regular work. Mead's "welfare culture" story assumes that welfare receipt changes parents' and children's values, attitudes, and behaviors so that they eventually become "trapped" in poverty and dependency because of these deviant values and dysfunctional behaviors. Time limits on welfare would be a good solution here since welfare itself is the culprit.

Murray (1984) and Anderson (1978) also claim that government welfare policies trap parents and children into poverty and dependency but frame the issue as one of incentives. Murray argues that welfare offers both parents and children a viable alternative to work and marriage by reducing the benefit of low-wage work relative to no work. States differ in the levels of Aid to Families with Dependent Children, (AFDC), so incentives for going on welfare versus working or getting married vary across states. Since children are likely to remain in the same states in which they were raised, they are likely to face the same set of welfare incentives as adults that their parents faced when the children were growing up. This theory suggests that, to get unbiased estimates of the effects of parental poverty and parental welfare receipt, analysts need to control the welfare incentives children face when they become adults. One way to do so is to include measures of the state AFDC benefit levels children would receive in their adult years.

The fourth set of models, the "structural/environmental" models, emphasize that labor market conditions, demographic changes, racial discrimination, and historical and current patterns of racial segregation all play a strong role in shaping intergenerational poverty (Wilson 1987, 1991a, 1991b, 1993; Massey 1991). Wilson's "social isolation" or "underclass" model is the most prominent and influential of these models. Wilson claims that the loss of well-paid manufacturing jobs from the inner city and the outmigration of middle-class blacks from urban, poor areas together reduce the chances for the remaining residents of the poor area and their children to escape poverty.

Wilson's model runs as follows. First, the shift of manufacturing employment from the cities to the suburbs means that the number of jobs compatible with ghetto residents' skills has dropped. At the same time, the migration of middle-class blacks out of the inner city leaves poor inner-city residents behind, resulting in a concentration of poverty in inner-city neighborhoods, weakening many important socialization institutions (that is, churches, political machines, community organizations), reducing job-finding networks in inner cities, and reducing the number of working role models for children.

While Wilson identifies four key environmental conditions—high rates of male unemployment in local labor markets, high rates of joblessness in inner-city ghettos, highly concentrated poverty, and low proportions of middle-class neighbors—he emphasizes that lack of available jobs is the most important of the four. According to Wilson, it accounts both for the high rates of welfare use by parents in inner-city neighborhoods and for the diminished economic mobility of children living there. Wilson's model implies that time limits on AFDC need to be accompanied by programs that will improve job opportunities for ghetto residents.

Wilson's reasoning suggests that, in addition to structural/environmental forces, socialization by parents and neighbors inhibits inner-city children's chances of escaping poverty as adults. In particular, Wilson emphasizes that working parents and employed neighbors provide children with role models for work and that middle-class neighbors are important both as socializing agents and as sources of "social control." Wilson's model implies that both macroeconomic policies to provide jobs and social service policies to fight the effects of social isolation are necessary and suggests that limiting welfare will be counterproductive unless job opportunities are opened up for ghetto residents.

Mead's welfare culture and Wilson's structural/environmental models can both be interpreted as "contagion" models (Jencks and Mayer 1990; Crane 1991). Both suggest that at some point families on welfare, poor communities, or both become isolated from mainstream values and become trapped in poverty. To the extent this is true, parents' receipt of welfare and neighborhood poverty will have little or no effect on children's economic mobility until some crucial threshold is passed. Tests of Mead's and Wilson's models should thus include nonlinear specifications of parental welfare and neighborhood poverty.

The four models identify six factors that potentially affect the intergenerational transmission of poverty: parents' economic resources; parents' noneconomic resources such as schooling and family structure; parents' welfare receipt; the welfare incentives facing children as adults; the labor market opportunities facing children as adults; and underclass neighborhood characteristics such as a high poverty rate, the absence of middle-class residents, and the presence of few employed men. Note that these models are not necessarily mutually exclusive; all six factors could be important determinants of children's economic mobility.

DATA SET, SAMPLE, AND VARIABLES

We explored intergenerational poverty using the Panel Study of Income Dynamics (PSID), a national longitudinal survey of about 5,000 families followed annually since 1968. Our sample consisted of 565 black men, 773 white men, 735 black women, and 825 white women aged twenty-five to thirty-five years in 1988. In 1968 these respondents were aged five to fifteen years and were children in PSID families. To be included in the sample, respondents had to be observed in at least three years as children and to have been a head or wife in their own household in at least one year after age twenty-four years.[2]

We examined three outcomes: whether income was sufficient—the extent to which children's family incomes as adults exceeded their needs; whether children were ever poor when they become adults; and whether children were persistently poor as adults. Family income included income from all sources plus the value of food stamps received. The family needs measure was the census poverty line. Income sufficiency was the natural log of the ratio of family income to family needs averaged over all the years a respondent was observed as an adult. We defined individuals as ever being poor if their family needs exceeded their adult family incomes in at least one year and as persistently poor if their adult family incomes were less than their family needs in at least half the years they were observed as adults. Outcomes were measured over all the years an individual was observed after age twenty-four years. Thus, we had from one to eleven years of outcome data for each individual in the sample, depending on that person's age when last observed in the sample. Because outcomes were measured at different ages and in different years for individuals, we included age and year controls in all analyses to control for business-cycle and life-cycle effects.

These outcome measures were related to a set of family, community, labor market, and state welfare benefits measures (table 15.1). The family economic resource variables included measures of parents' income, parents' income-to-needs, and time spent in poverty as a child. We included both linear and nonlinear specifications for parental income to needs. The family noneconomic resource measures included the mother's schooling, the head of household's annual work hours, the percentage of years the child lived with a disabled head of household, and two family structure measures: whether the child ever lived in a female-headed household and the percentage of years the child lived in a female-headed household.[3]

TABLE 15.1 / Characteristics of the Individuals in the Sample, by Sex and Race[a]

Measure	Men		Women	
	Black	White	Black	White
Family income measures				
Average family income-to-needs ratio	1.6	3.4	1.7	3.4
	(1.1)	(2.1)	(1.2)	(2.0)
Average family income ($1,000)	24.4	44.9	24.7	45.1
	(14.2)	(25.0)	(14.8)	(25.1)
Average number of children	4.4	3.1	4.2	3.3
	(2.2)	(1.6)	(2.1)	(1.6)
Income-to-needs ratio				
<1.0	0.33	0.03	0.33	0.03
1.0–2.0	0.42	0.19	0.33	0.19
2.0–3.0	0.13	0.26	0.18	0.28
>3.0	0.13	0.52	0.16	0.50
<0.5	0.06	0	0.04	0
0.5–1.0	0.27	0.03	0.29	0.03
1.0–1.5	0.29	0.08	0.25	0.08
1.5–2.0	0.13	0.12	0.08	0.11
2.0–2.5	0.07	0.14	0.12	0.15
2.5–3.0	0.06	0.12	0.06	0.13
3.0–4.0	0.07	0.25	0.10	0.22
4.0–5.0	0.04	0.12	0.04	0.12
>5.0	0.01	0.15	0.01	0.16
Duration of poverty				
Never poor	0.35	0.86	0.39	0.87
Poor 1–50% of years	0.24	0.10	0.21	0.09
Poor 50%+ of years	0.41	0.05	0.40	0.04
Other family measures				
Mother's years of schooling	9.7	11.8	9.7	11.6
	(2.8)	(2.6)	(3.1)	(2.9)
Ever lived in female-headed household	0.40	0.15	0.44	0.17
% years lived in female-headed household	32	9	31	9
	(42)	(23)	(40)	(25)
% years lived with disabled head	21	10	24	10
	(35)	(26)	(36)	(25)
Mean hours worked by head	1,523	2,148	1,450	2,192
	(987)	(710)	(913)	(707)

Measure	Men		Women	
	Black	White	Black	White
Parental welfare receipt				
Ratio of average welfare income to family income				
0	0.40	0.78	0.27	0.74
.01–.50	0.42		0.57	
≥.50	0.18		0.16	
.01–.15		0.18		0.22
>.15		0.04		0.04
Childhood neighborhood measures				
% poor >30%	0.37	0.07	0.37	0.05
% with annual incomes >$15,000	11	24	12	24
Male unemployment rate	6.3	3.8	6.1	4.0
	(4.7)	(2.4)	(4.5)	(2.5)
Labor market variables				
Male unemployment rate	6.3	6.6		
	(0.2)	(2.6)		
Female unemployment rate			6.6	6.8
			(2.2)	(1.8)
State welfare				
Mean state Aid to Families with Dependent Children and food stamp benefit ($100/month)	599	643	649	591
	(122)	(121)	(121)	(130)
Intervening variables				
Years of schooling	12.6	13.4	12.5	13.3
	(1.9)	(2.3)	(1.8)	(2.3)
Gave birth as teen			0.40	0.19
Dependent variables				
Average family income-to-needs ratio	3.0	4.1	2.4	4.3
	(2.2)	(2.1)	(1.7)	(2.2)
Ever poor	0.29	0.11	0.40	0.11
Poor at least 50% of years	0.18	0.03	0.24	0.03
N	565	773	735	825

Source: Authors' calculations using data from the Panel Study of Income Dynamics (PSID) on respondents aged five to fifteen in 1968 and twenty-five to thirty-five in 1988, observed in at least three years as children, and described as head or wife in a household in at least one year after age twenty-four.

a. Values are weighted means. Standard deviations in parentheses.

Parents' welfare receipt was the proportion of family income during the years observed as a child that came from welfare. Welfare income was the sum of income from AFDC, other welfare, Supplemental Security Income, and food stamps. Since the "welfare trap" models are really about dependency on welfare, we split the welfare variable into two dummies: one representing moderate levels of receipt and the other, high levels. Because patterns of receipt vary enormously by race, we used different breakpoints for blacks and whites. For blacks, moderate welfare receipt was defined as receiving 1–50 percent of income from welfare, and high welfare receipt, as receiving more than 50 percent. For whites, moderate welfare receipt was defined as receiving 1–15 percent of income from welfare, and high receipt, as receiving more than 15 percent. We averaged these family variables over all the years a child was observed in the PSID between ages five and fifteen years. (Parents' income and welfare receipt were reported for the previous years, so they were measured when the child was between ages four and sixteen years). We obtained between three and thirteen years of family data for each child, depending on that child's age in 1968. If a child was five in 1968, the family measures were averaged over a thirteen-year period, ages four to sixteen years. If a child was fifteen in 1968, the family measures were averaged over a three-year period, ages fourteen to sixteen years.

We included three neighborhood measures: whether the poverty rate exceeded 30 percent, the percentage of families with incomes greater than $15,000 in 1970 ($30,000 in 1980), and the male unemployment rate.[4] Neighborhood measures, like family measures, were averaged over all the years a child was observed at home. We included two measures of labor market demand, the male unemployment rate and the female unemployment rate facing the child during adulthood, averaged over all the years a child is observed after age twenty-four years.[5] To control for welfare incentives, we also measured the average value of the combined AFDC and food stamp guarantee for a family of three for the states respondents lived in after age twenty-four years.

MEANS ON PREDICTOR AND OUTCOME VARIABLES

Black and white children differed considerably in their access to material resources during childhood (see table 15.1). White children's families reported almost twice as much income as did black children's parents. Half of all white children were raised in families whose income was more than three times the poverty line (income-to-needs ratio > 3.0); only 13 percent of black children were raised in such families. About 5 percent of black children grew up in families whose income averaged less than half the poverty line (income-to-needs ratio < 0.5); no white children were raised in severely poor families. Almost two out of three black children were poor for at least one year during the period observed as a child, and 40 percent of black children were poor for more than half of the time observed as a child. Only one of seven white children was ever poor during the period observed as a child, and less than one in twenty was poor for more than half of the time observed as a child.

These differences in black and white parents' economic resources were paralleled by differences in welfare receipt. Over 60 percent of black children grew up in households that received welfare at some point, and about 17 percent grew up in households that depended on welfare for more than half their income. In contrast, one in four white children lived in a household that ever received welfare, and 4 percent of white children lived in households that relied on welfare for more than 15 percent of their income.

Black children were disadvantaged relative to white children in terms of family noneconomic and neighborhood resources as well. Black mothers averaged two fewer years of schooling than did white mothers. Black children were two and a half times more likely than white children to live in a female-headed household, twice as likely to live with a disabled head of household, five to seven times more likely to live in a neighborhood where 30 percent or more of the residents were poor, and only half as likely to live in a neighborhood with affluent residents.

Black children's relative economic disadvantages extended into adulthood, especially for young black women. Young blacks were three to four times more likely to be poor and six to eight times more likely to be persistently poor than were young whites. Blacks' income-to-needs ratios were 1.1 to 1.9 points lower than were whites'.

ANALYSIS

The analysis had two phases. We began by calculating transitions between childhood and adult poverty and by estimating adult income status, before and after controlling family noneconomic advantages. Each outcome was estimated as a function of five income specifications, and one specification was chosen for the remaining analyses. We used ordinary least squares (OLS) to estimate models predicting the natural log of adult income-to-needs and logistic regressions to estimate models predicting poverty status. All models were run separately on all children, black sons, white sons, black daughters, and white daughters. We did not predict persistent adult poverty for whites because so few whites (less than 3 percent) are persistently poor as adults. At the end of phase 1, we selected an income specification to use for the remaining analyses.

In the second phase we tested the four models of intergenerational poverty by regressing adult income-to-needs ratio and adult poverty status on the preferred parental income specification, parents' welfare receipt, parents' noneconomic advantages, advantages of the child's neighborhood, the unemployment rate faced as an adult, and the state welfare benefits faced as an adult. Models were run separately for black sons, white sons, black daughters, and white daughters.

We investigated three routes by which parental poverty and parental welfare receipt might have inhibited boys' and girls' economic mobility. First, we added

TABLE 15.2 / Transitions from Childhood to Early Adulthood Poverty, by Race (percent)[a]

Race and Poverty Status during Childhood[b]	Early Adult Outcome: Never Poor	Poor 1–50% of years	Poor 51–100% of years
Black			
Never poor	73.8	17.9	8.3
Poor 1–50% of years	63.3	17.0	19.8
Poor 51–100% of years	53.7	19.9	26.4
White			
Never poor	89.8	9.0	1.2
Poor 1–50% of years	77.9	18.6	3.7
Poor 51–100% of years	75.9	14.3	9.8

Source: See table 15.1. Based on data from the PSID on adults aged twenty-seven to thirty-five years in 1988 and seven to fifteen years in 1968. They were observed three to thirteen years as children before age seventeen years and three to eleven years as adults after age twenty-four years.

a. All percentages are weighted.

b. Percent years poor = 100 × (number of years poor as a child)/(number of years observed as a child).

controls for schooling to regressions and to logistic regressions to see if childhood poverty and childhood welfare receipt reduced children's economic prospects as adults primarily because poor children acquired less schooling. For daughters, we also added a control for teen birth to see if poor girls and girls raised on welfare remain poor as adults because they are more likely to give birth as teenagers. Finally, since men's family incomes are largely a function of their adult labor income, we estimate models predicting men's annual earnings, annual work hours, and hourly wages as a function of parental poverty, parents' welfare receipt, parents' noneconomic advantages, neighborhood characteristics, labor market characteristics, and state welfare incentives.

Phase 1:

POVERTY TRANSITIONS Our PSID sample showed considerable mobility out of childhood poverty: three-quarters of white poor children and over half of black poor children escaped poverty in early adulthood (table 15.2). Despite this mobility, children in poor families were much more likely to be poor in early adulthood than were children raised in nonpoor families. Black children raised in poor families were 35–60 percent more likely to be poor and 2.5 times more likely to be persistently poor in early adulthood than were black children raised in nonpoor families. White children raised in poor families were 2.0 times more likely to be poor and 3.0–8.0 times more likely to be persistently poor than were white children raised in nonpoor families.

COMPARING MODELS OF PARENTS' INCOME The persistence of income disadvantage remained when we looked at parents' income and parents' poverty in a multivariate context. A large and significant association persisted between children's and parents' income-to-needs ratios (table 15.3, model 1). A 1-point increase in the ratio of parental income to needs during childhood increased children's adult income-to-needs ratios by 10 percent.[6] When we added controls for the mother's schooling, the head-of-household's work hours, and family structure, the coefficient on the parental income-to-needs measure dropped by almost 40 percent (from 0.106 to 0.066) but still remained large and significant (model 3). Background noneconomic advantages correlated with parental income-to-needs ratio explained some but by no means all of the intergenerational association between parents' and children's income-to-needs ratios.

We then replaced the parents' income-to-needs measure by variables measuring parental income and average number of children (table 15.3, model 4). Not surprisingly, both affected children's income-to-needs ratios as adults; higher parental incomes raised adult income to needs, while larger family sizes lowered adult income to needs.

We also tested whether the effects of the parents' income-to-needs ratio on children's adult income-to-needs were nonlinear by breaking up the parental income-to-needs measure into four dummies: poor (less than 1); low income (1–2); moderate income (2–3); and average to high income (greater than 3) (table 15.3, models 5 and 6). The regressions are identical, the only difference being which income-to-needs dummy was omitted.

The effects of parents' income were clearly nonlinear. Children raised in poor or low-income families had much lower income-to-needs ratios as adults than did children raised in moderate-income families, while children from families with average to high incomes were only slightly better off as adults than were children from moderate income families.

We explored the nonlinear relationship between parental income-to-needs ratios and those of their adult children further by breaking up the parental income-to-needs measure into eight dummies: less than 0.5; 0.5–1.0; 1.0–1.5; 1.5–2.0; 2.0–2.5; 2.5–3.0; 3.0–4.0; 4.0–5.0; greater than 5.0 (table 15.3, model 7; figure 15.1). Increases in parental income-to-needs ratios in the range 0.5–2.0 had large effects on children's adult income-to-needs ratios.

The parental income status measures examined in models 1–7 were all based on parents' average income status. We examined the effects of *time* spent in poverty on children's adult income sufficiency in model 8. The effects were strong: children who were poor 50 percent or more of the time they were observed as children had 36 percent lower income-to-needs ratios in early adulthood than did nonpoor children, while children who lived in poor families for 1–50 percent of their childhood had 20 percent lower income-to-needs ratios as adults.[7]

TABLE 15.3 / Childhood Predictors of Adults' Log Total Family Income-to-Needs Ratio under Alternative Family Income Specifications, Full Sample[a]

	Model									
Independent Variable	1	2	3	4	5	6	7	8	9	10
Family income variables										
Average family income-to-needs	0.106*		0.066*						0.052*	0.058*
	(0.010)		(0.011)						(0.021)	(0.014)
Average family income ($10,000)				0.046*						
				(0.009)						
Average number of children				−0.054*						
				(0.009)						
Income-to-needs ratio										
<1.0					−0.230*	−0.446*				
					(0.047)	(0.060)				
1.0–2.0						−0.215*				
						(0.046)				
2.0–3.0					0.215*					
					(0.046)					
>3.0					0.324*	0.108*				
					(0.051)	(0.046)				
<0.5							−0.728*			
							(0.132)			
0.5–1.0							−0.495*			
							(0.075)			
1.0–1.5							−0.342*			
							(0.068)			
1.5–2.0							−0.181*			
							(0.066)			
2.0–2.5							−0.066			
							(0.067)			
2.5–3.0							—			
3.0–4.0							0.072			
							(0.066)			
4.0–5.0							0.036			
							(0.081)			
>5.0							0.136			
							(0.077)			

Family poor 1–50% of years								−0.210*		
								(0.048)		
Family poor 50%+ of years								−0.439*		
								(0.052)		
Black by average income-to-needs									0.202*	
									(0.033)	
Female by average income-to-needs										0.017
										(0.017)
Child variables										
Female	0.058†	0.063*	0.062*	0.067*	0.060*	0.060*	0.059†	0.058†	0.058†	0.021
	(0.031)	(0.031)	(0.031)	(0.031)	(0.031)	(0.031)	(0.031)	(0.031)	(0.031)	(0.052)
Black	−0.517*	−0.527*	−0.452*	−0.409*	−0.367*	−0.367*	−0.344*	−0.390*	−0.778*	−0.451*
	(0.037)	(0.036)	(0.038)	(0.038)	(0.040)	(0.040)	(0.040)	(0.039)	(0.065)	(0.038)
Family variables										
Mother's years of schooling		0.042*	0.029*	0.028*	0.023*	0.023*	0.019*	0.027*	0.025*	0.029*
		(0.006)	(0.006)	(0.006)	(0.006)	(0.006)	(0.006)	(0.006)	(0.006)	(0.006)
Ever lived in a female-headed household		−0.161*	−0.147*	−0.130†	−0.144†	−0.144†	−0.142*	−0.139†	−0.148*	−0.148*
		(0.075)	(0.075)	(0.074)	(0.074)	(0.074)	(0.074)	(0.075)	(0.074)	(0.074)
% of years in female-headed household		0.001	0.001	0.001	0.001	0.001	0.001	0.001	0.001	0.001
		(0.001)	(0.001)	(0.001)	(0.001)	(0.001)	(0.001)	(0.001)	(0.001)	(0.001)
% of years head was disabled		0.000	0.000	0.000	0.001	0.001	0.001	0.001	0.000	0.000
		(0.001)	(0.001)	(0.001)	(0.001)	(0.001)	(0.001)	(0.001)	(0.001)	(0.001)
Head's average work hours (1,000/year)		0.122*	0.100*	0.098*	0.074*	0.074*	0.066*	0.084*	0.085*	0.100*
		(0.026)	(0.026)	(0.026)	(0.026)	(0.026)	(0.026)	(0.026)	(0.026)	(0.026)
Adjusted R^2	0.192	0.198	0.208	0.215	0.218	0.218	0.229	0.218	0.217	0.208

* $p < .05$; † $p < .10$.

Source: Authors' calculations of ordinary least squares (OLS) estimates using data from the PSID on 2,898 children aged five to fifteen in 1968 and twenty-five to thirty-five in 1988.

a. Standard errors in parentheses.

FIGURE 15.1 / Log Adult Family Income-to-Needs Ratios by Childhood Family Income-to-Needs Ratio, Full Sample

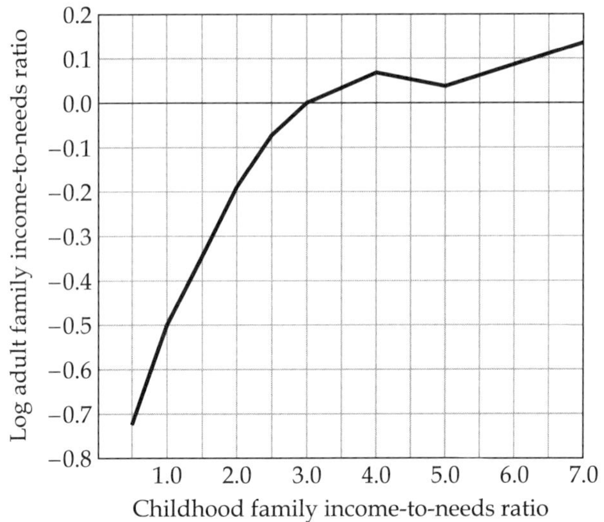

Source: Authors' calculations. The graph plots the coefficients on the family income-to-needs dummies in table 15.3, column 7.

We investigate race and sex differences in the effects of parents' income status on children's adult income-to-needs ratios by adding race and sex dummies to all models in table 15.3, by estimating race and sex interactions with parental income-to-needs in models 9 and 10, and by rerunning the first eight models separately for black sons, (table 15.4), white sons (table 15.5), black daughters (table 15.6) and white daughters (table 15.7).[8] Three clear patterns emerged: black children had much lower income-to-needs ratios as adults than did whites, even with controls for parental income and family background. Females had slightly higher adult income-to-needs ratios as adults than did men, perhaps because women married older men.

The effects of parental income also appeared to differ significantly by race. In the regressions that measured parental income status in dollars or with the continuous income-to-needs measure, an increase in parental income (or income-to-needs ratio) had a substantially larger effect on blacks' adult income-to-needs ratios than on whites' (table 15.3, model 9, and tables 15.4–15.7, models 3–4). But once we allowed for nonlinear income effects, these observed differences disappeared entirely for men and became smaller for women (compare tables 15.4–15.7, models 5–8, and figures 15.2–15.5). Parental income effects appeared larger for blacks when linear income specifications were used because blacks were concentrated at the low end of the income distribution.[9]

Note that we estimated much larger associations between poverty during childhood and sufficient income in adulthood and between poverty during childhood and poverty during adulthood than Hauser and Sweeney did (chapter 17). We suspect that the samples used and that differences in the definition of "poor" explain the apparent differences in results.

Hauser and Sweeney analyzed a sample of mostly white high school seniors in Wisconsin in 1958. Thus, their sample was an earlier cohort, had few African Americans, and omitted high school dropouts. Solon (1992) has shown that the correlation between fathers' and sons' economic statuses was about one-third higher in a sample of male high school graduates and high school dropouts than in a sample of male high school graduates. Duncan and Rogers (1991) have shown that African American children constitute over 90 percent of long-term poor children.

Another difference between our analyses and those in chapter 17 is that we categorized a smaller proportion of white children as being in long-term poverty than Hauser and Sweeney did. In our PSID sample, less than 3 percent of white children grew up in homes where the household income-to-needs ratio averaged less than 1 and about 20 percent, in households where the household income-to-needs ratio averaged 1–2. About 23 percent of the high school seniors in the Hauser and Sweeney sample lived in households where the income-to-needs ratio averaged less than 1. The white children whom we defined as poor were likely in more severe economic distress relative to the average white child than were the children Hauser and Sweeney defined as poor.

This distinction is important since the size of the association between childhood income-to-needs ratio and white sons' adult income-to-needs ratio dropped sharply in the PSID sample once the childhood income-to-needs ratio exceeded 1 (see tables 15.5, models 6 and 7, and figure 15.3). Indeed, we estimated that children raised in low-income (income-to-needs ratio = 1–2) families had income-to-needs ratios as adults that were about 13 percent lower than were those of children raised in moderate income families (income-to-needs ratio of 2–3). This figure is much closer to the numbers reported by Hauser and Sweeney.

The other background measures yielded few surprises. Maternal education was associated with higher income-to-needs ratios in early adulthood. Having ever lived in a female-headed household was associated with a less sufficient adult income, but the effects were weaker the more time spent in a female-headed household. Being raised in a household where the head works regularly raised adult income-to-needs ratios for all groups except white sons. The effects of parental work hours on black sons' adult income-to-needs ratios were strikingly large.

Growing up in poor families clearly reduced children's adult income sufficiency. We now pose a different question: how big is the intergenerational transmission of poverty? To answer, we estimated the adults' poverty status using logistic regressions as a function of the seven alternative models of parental income (tables 15.8–15.12). We looked at two poverty outcomes: whether those in our sample were ever poor and whether they were persistently poor (that is, poor in 50 percent or more of the years observed since age twenty-four). Because fewer

(Text continued on p. 484.)

TABLE 15.4 / Childhood Predictors of Adults' Log Total Family Income-to-Needs Ratio under Alternative Family Income Specifications, Black Sons[a]

	Model							
Independent Variable	1	2	3	4	5	6	7	8
Family income variables								
Average family income-to-needs	0.380*		0.256*					
	(0.068)		(0.078)					
Average family income ($10,000)				0.082				
				(0.054)				
Average number of children				−0.075*				
				(0.026)				
Income-to-needs ratio[b]								
<1.0					−0.148	−0.493*		
					(0.114)	(0.187)		
1.0–2.0						−0.345*		
						(0.173)		
2.0–3.0					0.345*			
					(0.173)			
>3.0					0.457†	0.112		
					(0.263)	(0.290)		
<0.5							−0.647†	
							(0.346)	
0.5–1.0							−0.563*	
							(0.269)	
1.0–1.5							−0.484†	
							(0.262)	
1.5–2.0							−0.274	
							(0.273)	

	(1)	(2)	(3)	(4)	(5)	(6)	(7)	(8)
2.0–2.5							−0.096	
							(0.309)	
>3.0							0.065	
							(0.345)	
Family poor 1–50% of years								−0.239†
								(0.143)
Family poor 50%+ of years								−0.476*
								(0.137)
Family variables								
Mother's years of schooling		0.027	0.009	0.022	0.013	0.013	0.007	0.011
		(0.018)	(0.018)	(0.018)	(0.018)	(0.018)	(0.019)	(0.018)
Ever lived in a female-headed household		−0.142	−0.093	−0.094	−0.104	−0.104	−0.106	−0.086
		(0.235)	(0.233)	(0.234)	(0.235)	(0.235)	(0.245)	(0.236)
% years in female-headed household		0.003	0.002	0.002	0.002	0.002	0.002	0.002
		(0.002)	(0.002)	(0.002)	(0.002)	(0.002)	(0.003)	(0.002)
% years head was disabled		0.002	0.002	0.002	0.002	0.002	0.003	0.002
		(0.002)	(0.002)	(0.002)	(0.002)	(0.002)	(0.002)	(0.002)
Head's average work hours (1,000/year)		0.352*	0.273*	0.304*	0.291*	0.291*	0.234*	0.287*
		(0.080)	(0.083)	(0.083)	(0.082)	(0.082)	(0.085)	(0.081)
Adjusted R^2	0.151	0.155	0.170	0.168	0.164	0.164	0.163	0.171

* $p < .05$; † $p < .10$.

Source: Authors' calculations of OLS estimates using data from the PSID on 565 black sons aged five to fifteen in 1968 and twenty-five to thirty-five in 1988.

a. Standard errors in parentheses.

b. Children from families with income-to-needs ratios of 2.5–3.0 were the omitted category.

TABLE 15.5 / Childhood Predictors of Adults' Log Total Family Income-to-Needs Ratio under Alternative Family Income Specifications, White Sons[a]

Independent Variable	Model 1	2	3	4	5	6	7	8
Family income variables								
Average family income-to-needs	0.073*		0.039*					
	(0.013)		(0.014)					
Average family income ($10,000)				0.032*				
				(0.012)				
Average number of children				−0.030†				
				(0.016)				
Income-to-needs ratio[b]								
<1.0					−0.518*	−0.659*		
					(0.141)	(0.146)		
1.0–2.0						−0.141†		
						(0.073)		
2.0–3.0					0.141*			
					(0.073)			
>3.0					0.259*	0.118†		
					(0.073)	(0.061)		
<0.1							−0.727*	
							(0.158)	
1.0–1.5							−0.283*	
							(0.117)	
1.5–2.0							−0.140	
							(0.100)	
2.0–2.5							−0.086	
							(0.094)	
3.0–4.0							0.112	
							(0.088)	

	(1)	(2)	(3)	(4)	(5)	(6)	(7)	(8)
4.0–5.0							−0.010	
							(0.106)	
>5.0							0.069	
							(0.100)	
Family poor 1–50% of years								−0.242*
								(0.088)
Family poor 50%+ of years								−0.601*
								(0.121)
Family variables								
Mother's years of schooling		0.055*	0.044*	0.041*	0.033*	0.033*	0.029*	0.036*
		(0.009)	(0.010)	(0.010)	(0.010)	(0.010)	(0.011)	(0.010)
Ever lived in a female-headed household		−0.166	−0.160	−0.156	−0.167	−0.167	−0.174	−0.174
		(0.138)	(0.137)	(0.137)	(0.136)	(0.136)	(0.135)	(0.135)
% years in female-headed household		0.002	0.002	0.002	0.002	0.002	0.002	0.002
		(0.002)	(0.002)	(0.002)	(0.002)	(0.002)	(0.002)	(0.002)
% years head was disabled		−0.002*	−0.002*	−0.002*	−0.002*	−0.002*	−0.001	−0.002*
		(0.001)	(0.001)	(0.001)	(0.001)	(0.001)	(0.001)	(0.001)
Head's average work hours (1,000/year)		−0.008	−0.022	−0.022	−0.050	−0.050	−0.053	−0.044
		(0.042)	(0.042)	(0.042)	(0.042)	(0.042)	(0.042)	(0.042)
Adjusted R^2	0.052	0.074	0.082	0.085	0.107	0.107	0.107	0.104

* $p < .05$; † $p < .10$.

Source: Authors' calculations of OLS estimates using data from the PSID on 773 white sons aged five to fifteen years in 1968 and twenty-five to thirty-five years in 1988.

a. Standard errors in parentheses.

b. Children from families with income-to-needs ratios of 2.5–3.0 were the omitted category.

TABLE 15.6 / Childhood Predictors of Adults' Log Total Family Income-to-Needs Ratio under Alternative Family Income Specifications, Black Daughters[a]

	Model							
Independent Variable	1	2	3	4	5	6	7	8
Family income variables								
Average family income-to-needs	0.268*		0.216*					
	(0.042)		(0.049)					
Average family income ($10,000)				0.104*				
				(0.038)				
Average number of children				−0.080*				
				(0.017)				
Income-to-needs ratio[b]								
<1.0					−0.164*	−0.429*		
					(0.076)	(0.110)		
1.0–2.0						−0.266*		
						(0.099)		
2.0–3.0					0.266*			
					(0.099)			
>3.0					0.400*	0.134		
					(0.173)	(0.182)		
0.5							−0.882*	
							(0.227)	
0.5–1.0							−0.418*	
							(0.160)	
1.0–1.5							−0.321*	
							(0.156)	
1.5–2.0							−0.240	
							(0.164)	
2.5–3.0							−0.035	
							(0.175)	

>3.0							0.113	
							(0.222)	
Family poor 1–50% of years								−0.152†
								(0.091)
Family poor 50%+ of years								−0.341*
								(0.091)
Family variables								
Mother's years of schooling		0.039*	0.021†	0.025*	0.023†	0.023†	0.023	0.024†
		(0.012)	(0.012)	(0.012)	(0.012)	(0.012)	(0.013)	(0.013)
Ever lived in a female-headed household		−0.202	−0.162	−0.130	−0.169	−0.169	−0.166	−0.178
		(0.145)	(0.143)	(0.142)	(0.143)	(0.143)	(0.143)	(0.144)
% years in female-headed household		0.001	0.001	0	0.001	0.001	0.001	0.001
		(0.002)	(0.002)	(0.002)	(0.002)	(0.002)	(0.002)	(0.002)
% years head was disabled		0.001	0.001	0.001	0.001	0.001	0.001	0.001
		(0.001)	(0.001)	(0.001)	(0.001)	(0.001)	(0.001)	(0.001)
Head's average work hours (1,000/year)		0.115*	0.064	0.067	0.072	0.072	0.061	0.076
		(0.052)	(0.052)	(0.052)	(0.052)	(0.052)	(0.052)	(0.052)
Adjusted R^2	0.068	0.040	0.071	0.084	0.068	0.068	0.074	0.063

* $p < .05$; † $p < .10$.

Source: Authors' calculations of OLS estimates using data from the PSID on 735 black daughters aged five to fifteen in 1968 and twenty-five to thirty-five in 1988.

a. Standard errors in parentheses.

b. Children from families with income-to-needs ratios of 2.5–3.0 were the omitted category.

TABLE 15.7 / Childhood Predictors of Adults' Log Total Family Income-to-Needs Ratio under Alternative Family Income Specifications, White Daughters[a]

Independent Variable	Equation 1	2	3	4	5	6	7	8
Family income variables								
Average family income-to-needs	0.091*		0.064*					
	(0.011)		(0.012)					
Average family income ($10,000)				0.049*				
				(0.010)				
Average number of children				−0.023†				
				(0.012)				
Income-to-needs ratio[b]								
<1.0					−0.254*	−0.341*		
					(0.112)	(0.117)		
1.0–2.0						−0.087		
						(0.059)		
2.0–3.0					0.087			
					(0.059)			
>3.0					0.270*	0.183*		
					(0.061)	(0.049)		
<1.0							−0.337*	
							(0.124)	
1.0–1.5							−0.072	
							(0.093)	
1.5–2.0							−0.141†	
							(0.078)	
2.0–2.5							−0.042	
							(0.074)	
2.5–3.0							—	

3.0–4.0							0.077	
							(0.071)	
4.0–5.0							0.196*	
							(0.083)	
>5.0							0.267*	
							(0.079)	
Family poor 1–50% of years								−0.107
								(0.072)
Family poor 50%+ of years								−0.294*
								(0.099)
Family variables								
Mother's years of schooling		0.043*	0.025*	0.025*	0.024*	0.024*	0.020*	0.036*
		(0.007)	(0.008)	(0.008)	(0.008)	(0.008)	(0.008)	(0.008)
Ever lived in a female-headed household		−0.181†	−0.188†	−0.168†	−0.188†	−0.188†	−0.177†	−0.157
		(0.101)	(0.099)	(0.099)	(0.099)	(0.099)	(0.099)	(0.101)
% years in female-headed household		0.002	0.003†	0.003†	0.003†	0.003†	0.003†	0.002
		(0.002)	(0.002)	(0.002)	(0.002)	(0.002)	(0.002)	(0.002)
% years head was disabled		0.0	0.0	0.0	0.0	0.0	0.0	0.0
		(0.001)	(0.001)	(0.001)	(0.001)	(0.001)	(0.001)	(0.001)
Head's average work hours (1,000/year)		0.100*	0.076*	0.077*	0.056	0.056	0.057	0.087*
		(0.036)	(0.035)	(0.035)	(0.036)	(0.036)	(0.036)	(0.036)
Adjusted R^2	0.081	0.071	0.100	0.101	0.102	0.102	0.104	0.080

* $p < .05$; † $p < .10$.

Source: Authors' calculations of OLS estimates using data from the PSID on 825 white daughters aged five to fifteen years in 1968 and twenty-five to thirty-five in 1988.

a. Standard errors in parentheses.

b. Children from families with income-to-needs ratios of 2.5–3.0 were the omitted category.

FIGURE 15.2 / Log Adult Family Income-to-Needs Ratios by Childhood Family Income-to-Needs Ratio, Black Sons

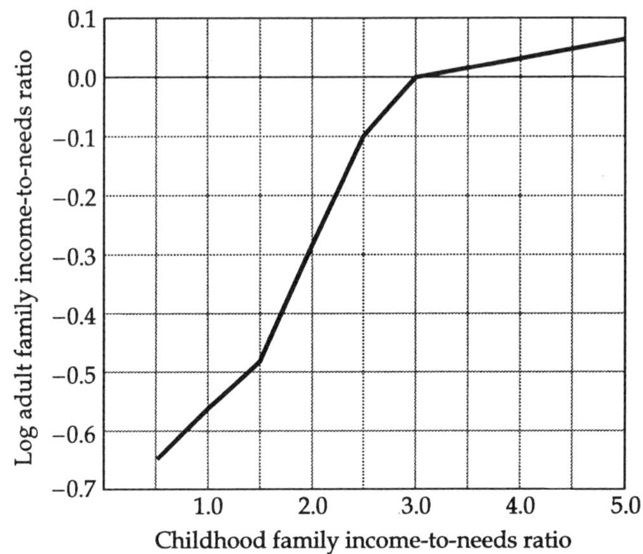

Source: Authors' calculations. The graph plots the coefficients on the family income-to-needs dummies in table 15.4, column 7.

than 3 percent of whites were persistently poor as adults, we estimated equations for persistent poverty only for black men and black women (tables 15.9B and 15.11B).

The pattern of results was similar to that for the first set of parental income models. Parental income status had strong, nonlinear effects on black males', white males', and black females' chances of ever experiencing poverty in early adulthood (see tables 15.8, 15.9A, 15.10, and 15.11A, models 6 and 7). Children who grew up in poor families (income-to-needs ratio less than 1) were much more likely to be poor at some point during their late twenties and early thirties than were children who grew up in moderate-income families (income-to-needs ratio, 2–3). The differences between the poverty outcomes of poor and nonpoor children were even larger for black children (see tables 15.9B and 15.11B, models 6 and 7).

Race and sex differences also figured in the probability of being poor. Blacks were much more likely to be poor than were nonblacks, and women were somewhat more likely to be poor than were men. This sex difference was probably due to the low incomes of female-headed families.

To sum up, for all race-sex groups except white women, the income-to-needs ratios of the children's families had strong, nonlinear relationships to the children's income-to-needs ratios as adults and to their chances of escaping poverty

FIGURE 15.3 / Log Adult Family Income-to-Needs by Childhood Family Income-to-Needs Ratio, White Sons

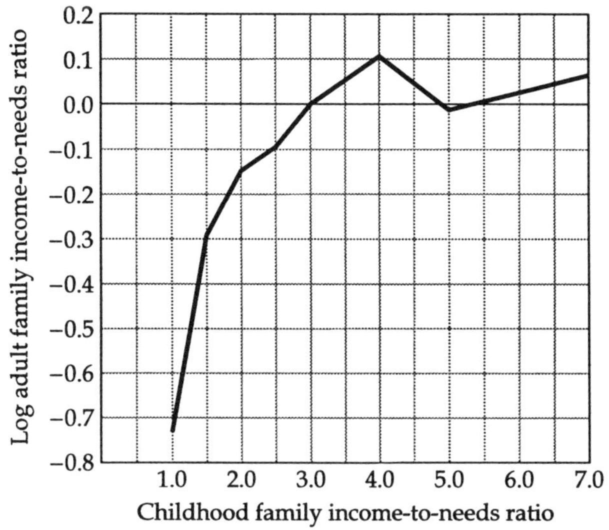

Source: Authors' calculations. The graph plots the coefficients on the family income-to-needs dummies in table 15.5, column 7.

as adults. The pattern and size of the nonlinear income effects were remarkably similar for black men, black women, and white men. Blacks fared less well than whites did, even when parental economic and noneconomic resources were controlled. In the remainder of our analyses we specified parental income and status using four income-to-needs categories: less than 1.0, 1.0–2.0, 2.0–3.0, and greater than 3.0. We did not examine more income-to-needs categories because no whites in our sample had income-to-needs ratios less than 0.5 and few blacks in our sample had income-to-needs ratios greater than 4.0.

Phase 2: Testing the Four Models of Intergenerational Poverty

In this phase of the analysis, we explore the four explanations of intergenerational poverty by reporting our estimates of the outcome variables as a function of parents' economic resources (measured by three income-to-needs dummies), parents' noneconomic resources, parents' welfare receipt, neighborhood characteristics, labor market unemployment rates in the children's labor market area when they became adults, and the average state AFDC–food stamp monthly benefit facing the children when they became adults. We looked at two outcome measures: the log of the income-to-needs ratio (table 15.13) and poverty status as adults (table

FIGURE 15.4 / Log Adult Family Income-to-Needs Ratios by Childhood Family Income-to-Needs Ratio, Black Daughters

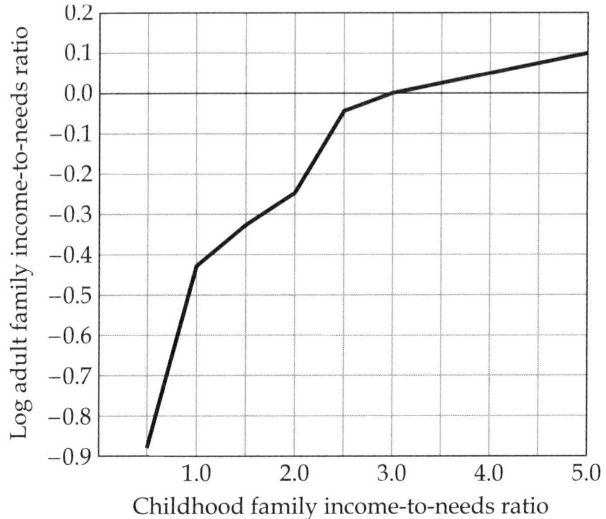

Source: Authors' calculations. The graph plots the coefficients on the family income-to-needs dummies in table 15.6, column 7.

15.14). We measured adults' poverty status as ever having been poor for whites and as poor 50 percent or more of the time for blacks.

Our results for black men, white men, and black women strongly support the idea that parental poverty matters both for children's income sufficiency and for poverty status when they reach adulthood. Children raised in poor households (income-to-needs ratio less than 1) had dramatically lower income-to-needs ratios and were much more likely to be poor in their late twenties and early thirties than were children raised in moderate-income households (income-to-needs ratio, 2–3). These effects were remarkably similar for black men, white men, and black women. The results also suggest that while poverty hurts, affluence helps very little. Children raised in average- to high-income families (income-to-needs ratio greater than 3) did not have significantly higher income-to-needs ratios and were not significantly less likely to be poor than were children raised in moderate-income families (income-to-needs ratio, 2–3).

Parents' noneconomic resources also mattered for children's adult economic status, but their effects were smaller and not always significant. Maternal education raised adult income-to-needs ratios and reduced the probability of poverty in adulthood for all race-sex groups, but its effects were significant only in the income-to-needs regressions. Being raised in a household where the head worked more hours raised adult income-to-needs ratios and lowered the probability that

FIGURE 15.5 / Log Adult Family Income-to-Needs Ratio by Childhood Family Income-to-Needs Ratio, White Daughters

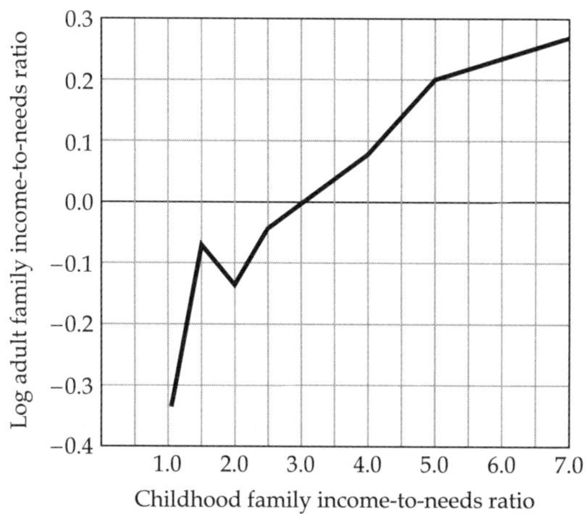

Source: Authors' calculations. The graph plots the coefficients on the family income-to-needs dummies in table 15.7, column 7.

black men and black women would be persistently poor, but the effects were only marginally significant.

THE WELFARE CULTURE We tested Mead's (1986, 1992) welfare culture model by including two welfare dummies that measured how much of the parents' income came from government transfer programs. Since parental welfare receipt patterns vary greatly by race, we constructed different dummies for blacks and whites.[10] A white family was defined as a heavy welfare user when 15 percent or more of the family income came from welfare. Approximately 4 percent of whites in the sample fit this definition. A black family was defined as a heavy welfare user when 50 percent or more of the income came from welfare. About 17 percent of black children were raised in such families.

The results provide mixed support for the welfare culture model. Adult income-to-needs ratios were dramatically lower for black men and for white women raised in families that depended heavily on welfare. Black men whose parents received 50 percent or more of their income from welfare had about 39 percent lower income-to-needs ratios as adults than did black men raised in families that never received welfare. White women raised in families that received 15 percent or more of their income from welfare had about 32 percent lower income-to-needs ratios as adults than did white women raised in families that received no income from welfare.[11] The chances of being poor in early adulthood were also much

(Text continued on p. 506.)

TABLE 15.8 / Childhood Predictors of Any Adult Poverty under Alternative Family Income Specifications, Full Sample[a]

	Model								
Independent Variable	1	2	3	4	5	6	7	8	9
Family income variables									
Average family income-to-needs	−0.300* (0.049)		−0.124* (0.052)					−0.080 (0.054)	−0.086 (0.064)
Average family income ($1,000)				−0.010* (0.001)					
Average number of children				0.068* (0.026)					
Income-to-needs ratio									
<1.0					0.187 (0.124)	0.606* (0.177)			
1.0–2.0					—	0.418* (0.150)			
2.0–3.0					−0.418* (0.150)	—			
>3.0					−0.511* (0.179)	−0.093 (0.183)			
Family poor 1–50% of years							0.404* (0.142)		
Family poor 50%+ of years							0.528* (0.145)		

Black by average income-to-needs ratio								−0.198†	
								(0.104)	
Female by average income-to-needs ratio									−0.072
									(0.076)
Child variables									
Sex: Female	0.227*	0.214*	0.215*	0.207*	0.219*	0.219*	0.219*	0.220*	0.344*
	(0.095)	(0.097)	(0.097)	(0.097)	(0.097)	(0.097)	(0.097)	(0.097)	(0.167)
Race: Black	1.182*	1.282*	1.147*	1.079*	1.064*	1.064*	1.100*	1.477*	1.147*
	(0.117)	(0.108)	(0.120)	(0.120)	(0.122)	(0.122)	(0.119)	(0.209)	(0.120)
Family variables									
Mother's years of schooling		−0.084*	−0.067*	−0.064*	−0.061*	−0.061*	−0.064*	−0.066*	−0.067*
		(0.017)	(0.018)	(0.108)	(0.018)	(0.018)	(0.018)	(0.018)	(0.018)
Ever lived in a female-headed household		0.485*	0.463*	0.431*	0.448*	0.448*	0.419†	0.464*	0.465*
		(0.217)	(0.218)	(0.218)	(0.218)	(0.218)	(0.220)	(0.218)	(0.218)
% years in female-headed household		−0.004	−0.004	−0.003	−0.003	−0.003	−0.003	−0.004	−0.004
		(0.003)	(0.003)	(0.003)	(0.003)	(0.003)	(0.003)	(0.003)	(0.003)
% years head was disabled		0.003†	0.003	0.003	0.002	0.002	0.002	0.003	0.003
		(0.002)	(0.002)	(0.002)	(0.002)	(0.002)	(0.002)	(0.002)	(0.002)
Head's average work hours (1,000/year)		−0.230*	−0.190*	−0.180*	−0.160*	−0.160*	−0.170*	−0.180*	−0.190*
		(0.076)	(0.077)	(0.078)	(0.078)	(0.078)	(0.078)	(0.078)	(0.078)

* $p < .05$; † $p < .10$.

Source: Authors' calculations of logistic regressions based on the sample in table 15.3.

a. Standard errors in parentheses.

TABLE 15.9A / Childhood Predictors of Any Adult Poverty under Alternative Family Income Specifications, Black Sons[a]

Independent Variable	Model 1	2	3	4	5	6	7
Family income variables							
Average family income-to-needs	−0.598*		−0.292†				
	(0.152)		(0.171)				
Average family income ($1,000)				−0.010			
				(0.011)			
Average number of children				0.044			
				(0.049)			
Income-to-needs ratio							
<1.0					0.083	0.880*	
					(0.123)	(0.419)	
1.0–2.0					—	0.797*	
						(0.403)	
2.0–3.0					−0.797*	—	
					(0.403)		
>3.0					−0.341	0.457*	
					(0.602)	(0.089)	

Family poor 1–50% of years						0.204
						(0.288)
Family poor 50%+ of years						0.331
						(0.269)
Family variables						
Mother's years of schooling	−0.067*	−0.051	−0.058	−0.058	−0.058	−0.058
	(0.034)	(0.035)	(0.036)	(0.035)	(0.035)	(0.035)
Ever lived in a female-headed household	0.490	0.456	0.450	0.442	0.422	0.445
	(0.451)	(0.452)	(0.452)	(0.455)	(0.455)	(0.457)
% years in female-headed household	−0.008	−0.008	−0.008	−0.008	−0.008	−0.008
	(0.006)	(0.006)	(0.006)	(0.006)	(0.006)	(0.006)
% years head was disabled	−0.001	−0.001	−0.001	−0.001	−0.001	−0.001
	(0.003)	(0.003)	(0.003)	(0.003)	(0.003)	(0.003)
Head's average work hours (1,000/year)	−0.620*	−0.550*	−0.570*	−0.570*	−0.570*	−0.580*
	(0.156)	(0.161)	(0.161)	(0.161)	(0.161)	(0.159)

* $p < .05$; † $p < .10$.

Source: Authors' calculations of logistic regressions based on the sample in table 15.4.

a. Standard errors in parentheses.

TABLE 15.9B / Childhood Predictors of Being Poor 50 Percent or More of Time since Age Twenty-Four under Alternative Family Income Specifications, Black Sons[a]

Independent Variable	Model 1	2	3	4	5	6	7
Family income variables							
Average family income-to-needs	−0.847*		−0.620*				
	(0.211)		(0.232)				
Average family income ($1,000)				−0.206			
				(0.015)			
Average number of children				0.112†			
				(0.058)			
Income-to-needs ratio							
<1.0					0.253	1.309*	
					(0.246)	(0.572)	
1.0–2.0					—	1.056*	
						(0.556)	
2.0–3.0					−1.056*	—	
					(0.556)		
>3.0					−1.370	−0.314	
					(1.057)	(1.163)	

Family poor 1–50% of years						0.465
						(0.369)
Family poor 50%+ of years						0.846*
						(0.352)
Family variables						
Mother's years of schooling	−0.044	−0.015	−0.032	−0.021	−0.021	−0.023
	(0.040)	(0.042)	(0.042)	(0.041)	(0.041)	(0.042)
Ever lived in a female-headed household	0.234	0.180	0.165	0.170	0.170	0.159
	(0.509)	(0.516)	(0.516)	(0.515)	(0.515)	(0.519)
% years in female-headed household	−0.006	−0.006	−0.005	−0.006	−0.006	−0.006
	(0.006)	(0.006)	(0.006)	(0.006)	(0.006)	(0.007)
% years head was disabled	−0.004	−0.004	−0.004	−0.004	−0.004	−0.004
	(0.004)	(0.004)	(0.004)	(0.004)	(0.004)	(0.004)
Head's average work hours (1,000/year)	−0.700*	−0.570*	−0.610*	−0.590*	−0.590*	−0.590*
	(0.183)	(0.188)	(0.189)	(0.187)	(0.187)	(0.187)

* $p < .05$; † $p < .10$.

Source: Authors' calculations of logistic regressions based on the sample in table 15.4.

a. Standard errors in parentheses.

TABLE 15.10 / Childhood Predictors of Any Adult Poverty under Alternative Family Income Specifications, White Sons[a]

Independent Variable	Model 1	2	3	4	5	6	7
Family income variables							
Average family income-to-needs	−0.182*		−0.062				
	(0.078)		(0.083)				
Average family income ($1,000)				0.0			
				(0.000)			
Average number of children				0.057			
				(0.073)			
Income-to-needs ratio							
<1.0					0.826	1.324*	
					(0.534)	(0.579)	
1.0–2.0						0.498	
					—	(0.336)	
2.0–3.0					−0.498		
					(0.336)	—	
>3.0					−0.656†	−0.158	
					(0.339)	(0.324)	

Family poor 1–50% of years						0.797*
						(0.375)
Family poor 50%+ of years						1.119*
						(0.477)
Family variables						
Mother's years of schooling	−0.156*	−0.142*	−0.130*	−0.100*	−0.100*	−0.101*
	(0.041)	(0.045)	(0.046)	(0.046)	(0.046)	(0.046)
Ever lived in a female-headed household	0.161	0.150	0.142	0.154	0.154	0.139
	(0.668)	(0.669)	(0.668)	(0.673)	(0.673)	(0.675)
% years in female-headed household	−0.007	−0.007	−0.007	−0.008	−0.008	−0.007
	(0.011)	(0.011)	(0.011)	(0.011)	(0.011)	(0.011)
% years head was disabled	0.010*	0.010*	0.009*	0.008*	0.008*	0.008*
	(0.004)	(0.004)	(0.004)	(0.004)	(0.004)	(0.004)
Head's average work hours (1,000/year)	0.184	0.201	0.204	0.267	0.267	0.256
	(0.179)	(0.180)	(0.179)	(0.182)	(0.182)	(0.180)

* $p < .05$; † $p < .10$.

Source: Authors' calculations of logistic regressions based on the sample in table 15.5.

a. Standard errors in parentheses.

TABLE 15.11A / Childhood Predictors of Any Adult Poverty under Alternative Family Income Specifications, Black Daughters[a]

Independent Variable	Model 1	2	3	4	5	6	7
Family income variables							
Average family income-to-needs	−0.461*		−0.269*				
	(0.113)		(0.131)				
Average family income ($1,000)				−0.010			
				(0.010)			
Average number of children				0.130*			
				(0.043)			
Income-to-needs ratio							
<1.0					0.100	0.543†	
					(0.187)	(0.284)	
1.0–2.0					—	0.443†	
						(0.261)	
2.0–3.0					−0.443†	—	
					(0.261)		
>3.0					−0.882†	−0.439	
					(0.524)	(0.552)	

Family poor 1–50% of years						0.262
						(0.232)
Family poor 50%+ of years						0.490*
						(0.227)
Family variables						
Mother's years of schooling	−0.079*	−0.060†	−0.063*	−0.061*	−0.061*	−0.059†
	(0.030)	(0.031)	(0.031)	(0.031)	(0.031)	(0.031)
Ever lived in a female-headed household	0.538	0.501	0.449	0.492	0.492	0.498
	(0.357)	(0.359)	(0.361)	(0.359)	(0.359)	(0.360)
% years in female-headed household	−0.002	−0.002	−0.002	−0.002	−0.002	−0.002
	(0.004)	(0.004)	(0.004)	(0.004)	(0.004)	(0.004)
% years head was disabled	0.001	0.001	0.001	0.001	0.001	0.001
	(0.003)	(0.003)	(0.003)	(0.003)	(0.003)	(0.003)
Head's average work hours (1,000/year)	−0.190	−0.130	−0.130	−0.140	−0.140	−0.140
	(0.125)	(0.129)	(0.131)	(0.128)	(0.128)	(0.129)

* $p < .05$; † $p < .10$.

Source: Authors' calculations of logistic regressions based on the sample in table 15.6.

a. Standard errors in parentheses.

TABLE 15.11B / Childhood Predictors of Being Poor 50 Percent or More of Time since Age Twenty-Four under Alternative Family Income Specifications, Black Daughters[a]

Independent Variable	Model						
	1	2	3	4	5	6	7
Family income variables							
Average family income-to-needs	−0.636*		−0.565*				
	(0.142)		(0.168)				
Average family income ($1,000)				−0.010			
				(0.012)			
Average number of children				0.226*			
				(0.049)			
Income-to-needs ratio							
<1.0					0.336	0.859*	
					(0.207)	(0.335)	
1.0–2.0					—	0.523†	
						(0.312)	
2.0–3.0					−0.523	—	
					(0.312)		
>3.0					−1.324†	−0.801	
					(0.762)	(0.792)	

	(1)	(2)	(3)	(4)	(5)	(6)
Family poor 1–50% of years						0.357
						(0.273)
Family poor 50%+ of years						0.742*
						(0.269)
Family variables						
Mother's years of schooling	−0.064†	−0.028	−0.043	−0.032	−0.032	−0.032
	(0.033)	(0.035)	(0.035)	(0.035)	(0.035)	(0.035)
Ever lived in a female-headed household	0.461	0.408	0.317	0.396	0.396	0.419
	(0.382)	(0.385)	(0.392)	(0.386)	(0.386)	(0.387)
% years in female-headed household	−0.002	−0.002	0.001	−0.001	−0.001	−0.002
	(0.005)	(0.005)	(0.005)	(0.005)	(0.005)	(0.005)
% years head was disabled	−0.003	−0.004	−0.004	−0.004	−0.004	−0.004
	(0.003)	(0.003)	(0.003)	(0.003)	(0.003)	(0.003)
Head's average work hours (1,000/year)	−0.310*	−0.190	−0.240	−0.230	−0.230	−0.230
	(0.139)	(0.143)	(0.148)	(0.142)	(0.142)	(0.143)

* $p < .05$; † $p < .10$.

Source: Authors' calculations of logistic regressions based on the sample in table 15.6.

a. Standard errors in parentheses.

TABLE 15.12 / Childhood Predictors of Any Adult Poverty under Alternative Family Income Specifications, White Daughters[a]

Independent Variable	Model 1	2	3	4	5	6	7
Family income variables							
Average family income-to-needs	−0.233*		−0.108				
	(0.079)		(0.088)				
Average family income ($1,000)				−0.010†			
				(0.007)			
Average number of children				−0.003			
				(0.068)			
Income-to-needs ratio							
<1.0					0.394	0.518	
					(0.470)	(0.516)	
1.0–2.0					—	0.124	
						(0.317)	
2.0–3.0					−0.124	—	
					(0.317)		
>3.0					−0.310	−0.180	
					(0.338)	(0.294)	

Family poor 1–50% of years						0.704*
						(0.332)
Family poor 50%+ of years						0.096
						(0.484)
Family variables						
Mother's years of schooling	−0.075*	−0.051	−0.039	−0.052	−0.052	−0.049
	(0.038)	(0.042)	(0.042)	(0.043)	(0.043)	(0.041)
Ever lived in a female-headed household	1.090*	1.093*	1.088*	1.099*	1.099*	0.983*
	(0.474)	(0.475)	(0.476)	(0.475)	(0.475)	(0.482)
% years in female-headed household	−0.010	−0.011	−0.012	−0.011	−0.011	−0.010
	(0.007)	(0.007)	(0.007)	(0.007)	(0.007)	(0.007)
% years head was disabled	0.006	0.006	0.005	0.005	0.005	0.004
	(0.004)	(0.004)	(0.004)	(0.004)	(0.004)	(0.004)
Head's average work hours (1,000/year)	−0.150	−0.110	−0.090	−0.090	−0.090	−0.140
	(0.185)	(0.187)	(0.186)	(0.193)	(0.193)	(0.187)

* $p < .05$; † $p < .10$.

Source: Authors' calculations of logistic regressions based on the sample in table 15.7.

a. Standard errors in parentheses.

TABLE 15.13 / Effects of Family, Neighborhood, and Labor Market Factors in Childhood on Adults' Log Family Income-to-Needs Ratio[a]

Independent Variable	Model 1 Black Men	Model 2 White Men	Model 3 Black Women	Model 4 White Women
Family variables				
Average family income-to-needs				
<1	−0.498*	−0.587*	−0.432*	−0.046
	(0.210)	(0.165)	(0.123)	(0.127)
1–2	−0.319†	−0.103	−0.254*	0.007
	(0.178)	(0.077)	(0.103)	(0.060)
2–3	—	—	—	—
>3	0.145	0.081	0.029	0.119*
	(0.292)	(0.064)	(0.184)	(0.050)
Ratio of welfare income to family income (W/Y)				
0 < W/Y < 0.15		0.019		−0.107*
		(0.070)		(0.054)
>0.15		0.036		−0.392*
		(0.148)		(0.113)
0 < W/Y < 0.50	−0.223*		−0.084	
	(0.131)		(0.090)	
>0.50	−0.492*		−0.050	
	(0.218)		(0.150)	
Mother's years of schooling	0.013	0.022*	0.028*	0.016*
	(0.019)	(0.011)	(0.013)	(0.008)
Ever lived in a female-headed household	−0.069	−0.150	−0.126	−0.102
	(0.243)	(0.136)	(0.145)	(0.097)

% years in female-headed household	0.003	0.001	0.001	0.002
	(0.003)	(0.002)	(0.002)	(0.001)
% years head was disabled	0.003	0.001	0.001	0.001
	(0.002)	(0.002)	(0.002)	(0.001)
Head's average work hours (1,000/year)	0.171†	−0.036	0.098†	0.044
	(0.093)	(0.044)	(0.060)	(0.037)
Neighborhood variables				
Poverty rate > 30%	0.167	−0.329*	0.125	0.012
	(0.131)	(0.098)	(0.081)	(0.078)
% with incomes > $15,000	0.002	0.005†	0.006	0.002
	(0.009)	(0.002)	(0.006)	(0.002)
Male unemployment rate	−0.003	0.016	0.001	−0.014†
	(0.015)	(0.012)	(0.009)	(0.009)
Labor market variables				
Male unemployment rate	−0.081*	−0.009		
	(0.026)	(0.010)		
Female unemployment rate			−0.041*	−0.018†
			(0.019)	(0.010)
Mean state AFDC–food stamp benefit ($100/month)	0.086	−0.010	0.072†	0.022
	(0.061)	(0.026)	(0.041)	(0.020)
R^2	0.267	0.178	0.152	0.214

* $p < .05$; † $p < .10$.

Source: Authors' calculations of regressions based on sample in table 15.1.

a. Standard errors in parentheses.

TABLE 15.14 / Effects of Family, Neighborhood, and Labor Market Factors in Childhood on Adult Poverty[a]

	Whether Poor		Whether Poor 50% or More of Years	
Independent Variable	1 White Men	2 White Women	3 Black Men	4 Black Women
Family variables				
Average family income-to-needs				
<1	1.418*	−0.494	1.837*	1.052*
	(0.683)	(0.620)	(0.657)	(0.383)
1–2	0.305	−0.338	1.309*	0.592†
	(0.372)	(0.360)	(0.594)	(0.332)
2–3	—	—	—	—
>3	−0.095	−0.017	0.469	−0.606
	(0.345)	(0.314)	(1.204)	(0.819)
Ratio of welfare income to family income (W/Y)				
0 < W/Y < 0.15	0.189	0.641*		
	(0.343)	(0.319)		
>0.15	−0.251	1.807*		
	(0.708)	(0.572)		
0 < W/Y < 0.50			0.210	0.038
			(0.340)	(0.283)
>0.50			0.701	−0.341
			(0.502)	(0.435)
Mother's years of schooling	−0.083	−0.032	−0.049	−0.055
	(0.051)	(0.047)	(0.045)	(0.037)

Ever lived in a female-headed household	0.091	0.856†	0.147	0.424
	(0.706)	(0.510)	(0.565)	(0.414)
% years in female-headed household	−0.004	−0.009	−0.008	−0.002
	(0.011)	(0.007)	(0.007)	(0.005)
% years head was disabled	0.009*	0.003	−0.004	−0.005
	(0.004)	(0.004)	(0.004)	(0.003)
Head's average work hours (1,000/year)	0.279	0.117	−0.260	−0.370*
	(0.200)	(0.212)	(0.218)	(0.174)
Neighborhood variables				
Poverty rate > 30%	0.863*	−0.098	−0.380	−0.269
	(0.408)	(0.422)	(0.316)	(0.244)
% with incomes > $15,000	−0.021	−0.013	0.004	−0.002
	(0.014)	(0.012)	(0.024)	(0.028)
Male unemployment rate	−0.105	0.032	0.011	−0.002
	(0.064)	(0.050)	(0.036)	(0.028)
Labor market variables				
Male unemployment rate	0.083		0.236*	
	(0.052)		(0.062)	
Female unemployment rate		0.134*		0.124*
		(0.058)		(0.059)
Mean state AFDC–food stamp benefit ($100/month)	0.126	−0.203*	−0.231	−0.264*
	(0.133)	(0.138)	(0.150)	(0.127)

* $p < .05$; † $p < .10$.

Source: Authors' calculations of regressions based on sample in table 15.1.

a. Standard errors in parentheses.

higher for white women and for black men whose parents reported high rates of welfare receipt, but these effects were significant only for white women. Parental welfare receipt never had large or significant negative effects on white men's and black women's economic outcomes.

One potential problem with these findings of strong parental welfare effects for black men and white women is that the coefficients on the parental welfare measures may pick up effects of unobserved parental attributes that increase parental welfare receipt and decrease parenting effectiveness. To the extent this occurs, the welfare coefficients will be negatively biased. We explored this possibility by substituting a predicted measure of parental welfare income for the measure of observed parental welfare income in the equation predicting log (income-to-needs ratio).[12] We identified the predicted measure of parental welfare income using: a measure of the average AFDC-Food Stamp guarantee facing the mother during the years the child was observed living at home, a measure of the ratio of employed men to women in the neighborhood in which the family resided during the years the child lived at home, a measure of the labor market male and female unemployment rates the child's parents faced when the child lived at home, and a measure of the mean wage of wage and salaried workers in the labor market at the time the child lived at home. Several of these measures strongly and significantly predicted black mothers' welfare use, but none of these measures strongly predicted white mothers' welfare use. Given this, we discuss only the results for blacks.

If the coefficients on observed parental income were negatively biased, then the coefficients on parental welfare income should have become less negative when the predicted measure of parental welfare income was used. This happened only in the regression predicting black men's log (income-to-needs). In the black women's regression, results were opposite those observed for black men: the coefficients on parental welfare income measures became *more* negative and almost significant when a predicted measure was substituted for the observed measure. These results for blacks are puzzling. It is implausible that unmeasured parental attributes correlated with parental welfare affected black children in ways that lowered black sons' adult income-to-needs ratios and raised black daughters' adult income-to-needs ratios. For the remainder of the analyses, we used the observed measures of parents' welfare income.

THE INCENTIVE ARGUMENT We explored Murray's (1984) incentive argument by including in our models measures of the state AFDC–food stamp benefit facing children during their adult years. Living in a state with high welfare benefits was associated with greater income sufficiency and was significantly associated with less poverty for both black and white women, and state welfare benefits were always insignificant for white and black men. These results provide little support for the incentive model. In models in which we controlled for the state welfare benefits facing the child's mother, the variables had insignificant coefficients, and controlling them had no effects on the size of the parental welfare coefficients.

LABOR MARKETS AND NEIGHBORHOODS We included measures of labor market unemployment in our models to test Wilson's (1987, 1991a, 1991b, 1993) predictions about the effects of a lack of job opportunities on economic mobility and measures of the three neighborhood conditions emphasized by Wilson (the neighborhood poverty rate, the percentage of neighbors who are affluent [incomes over $15,000], and the percentage of men in the neighborhood who are unemployed) to test Wilson's predictions about the effect of neighbors on children's socialization.

Our results strongly confirm that a lack of job opportunities keeps young blacks mired in poverty. Young blacks living near labor markets with high rates of unemployment had lower income-to-needs ratios and were more likely to be persistently poor than young blacks living in labor markets with low unemployment rates (see tables 15.13 and 15.14). These effects are large for black women and very large for black men. A 1-point increase in the unemployment rate lowered black women's expected income-to-needs ratios by 4 percent and black men's by a striking 7.8 percent.[13]

The neighborhood results were less consistent with Wilson's predictions. Neighborhood poverty never predicted economic outcomes for either black men or black women. This was true when we excluded all neighborhood variables but poverty rate, used a continuous neighborhood poverty measure, and experimented with different poverty rate breakpoints. The presence of affluent neighbors had small, positive associations with income-to-needs ratio and small negative associations with adult poverty status for blacks but was never significant.

The only group for whom the neighborhood variables mattered was white men. White men raised in communities with poverty rates of over 30 percent had much lower income-to-needs ratios and were much more likely to be poor than white men raised in less poor communities. White men raised in communities with high proportions of affluent neighbors had slightly high income-to-needs ratios as adults (marginally significant) and slightly lower chances of being poor as adults (not significant). Brooks-Gunn et al. (1993) found similarly that the presence of affluent neighbors positively affected whites' (but not blacks') schooling outcomes.

Why does growing up poor reduce the economic prospects of white men, black men, and black women and growing up in a family that depends heavily on welfare reduce the economic prospects of black men and white women? One possibility, suggested by Becker (1981), is that poor parents have less available income to allocate to investments in children's human capital or schooling then do nonpoor parents. Mead (1986, 1992) argues that children raised in welfare-dependent homes are likely to drop out of high school and to become teen parents. We added measures of schooling to our models predicting young men's and women's income-to-needs and poverty status to see if parents' income and welfare receipt influenced children's adult attainments by affecting their schooling (tables 15.15 and 15.16). We also added controls for ever giving birth as a teen to the women's regressions to see if poverty and welfare effects were mediated by teen births.

Parental poverty and parental welfare did not reduce children's income-to-

(Text continued on p. 511.)

TABLE 15.15 / Effects of Parents' Poverty Status and Parents' Welfare Receipt on Children's Log Family Income-to-Needs, Controlling Schooling and Teen Births, by Race and Sex[a]

	Model[b]					
	1	2	3	4	5	6
Independent Variable	Black Men	White Men	Black Women	Black Women	White Women	White Women
Family variables						
Average family income-to-needs ratio						
<1	−0.413*	−0.526*	−0.302*	−0.294*	−0.016	−0.021
	(0.208)	(0.165)	(0.116)	(0.116)	(0.119)	(0.117)
1–2	−0.387*	−0.074	−0.167*	−0.160†	0.040	0.045
	(0.172)	(0.077)	(0.096)	(0.096)	(0.057)	(0.056)
2–3	—	—	—	—	—	—
>3	−0.046	0.056	−0.081	−0.096	0.057	0.050
	(0.284)	(0.065)	(0.172)	(0.171)	(0.047)	(0.040)
Ratio of welfare income to family income (W/Y)						
0< W/Y < 0.15		0.045			−0.040	−0.036
		(0.070)			(0.051)	(0.050)
>0.15		0.055			−0.255*	−0.246*
		(0.147)			(0.107)	(0.105)
0 < W/Y < 0.50	−0.170		−0.085	−0.086		
	(0.127)		(0.084)	(0.084)		

>0.50	−0.346†		−0.017	−0.013		
	(0.211)		(0.140)	(0.140)		
Child's schooling						
< 12 years	—	—	—	—	—	—
12 years	0.531*	0.225*	0.469*	0.443*	0.522*	0.417*
	(0.118)	(0.081)	(0.079)	(0.079)	(0.065)	(0.066)
13–15 years	0.829*	0.271*	0.741*	0.690*	0.632*	0.494*
	(0.148)	(0.094)	(0.090)	(0.093)	(0.072)	(0.075)
16+ years	1.073*	0.346*	1.158*	1.085*	0.801*	0.644*
	(0.208)	(0.097)	(0.131)	(0.135)	(0.081)	(0.084)
Ever had a teen birth				−0.133*		−0.300*
				(0.065)		(0.050)
R^2	0.318	0.192	0.265	0.269	0.306	0.336

* $p < .05$; † $p < .10$.

Source: Authors' calculations of regressions based on sample in table 15.1.

a. Standard errors in parentheses.

b. All regressions control for mother's schooling; ever lived in a female-headed household; percentage of years lived in a female-headed household; percentage of years head was disabled; neighborhood poverty rate (percent); percentage of neighbors with incomes greater than $15,000; percentage of men in the neighborhood who are unemployed; unemployment rate in adult labor market; and mean state AFDC–food stamp benefits.

TABLE 15.16 / Effects of Parents' Poverty and Parents' Welfare Receipt on Children's Poverty Status, Controlling Schooling and Teen Births, by Race and Sex[a]

	Whether Poor[b]			Whether Poor 50% or More of Years[b]		
	White Men	White Women		Black Men	Black Women	
Independent Variable	1	2	3	4	5	6
Family variables						
Average family income-to-needs ratio[c]						
Y/N < 1	1.403*	−0.590	−0.561	1.643*	0.895*	0.856*
	(0.686)	(0.638)	(0.646)	(0.671)	(0.411)	(0.413)
Y/N = 1–2	0.298	−0.452	−0.450	1.423*	0.492	0.476
	(0.374)	(0.367)	(0.368)	(0.606)	(0.353)	(0.356)
Y/N >3	0.181	0.236	0.263	−0.041	−0.287	−0.225
	(0.344)	(0.328)	(0.330)	(1.227)	(0.850)	(0.863)
Ratio of welfare income to family income (W/Y)						
0 < W/Y < 0.15	0.181	0.521	0.514			
	(0.344)	(0.327)	(0.329)			
>0.15	−0.250	1.553*	1.526*			
	(0.708)	(0.599)	(0.607)			
0 < W/Y < 0.50				0.138	0.007	0.050
				(0.352)	(0.299)	(0.303)
>0.50				0.575	−0.667	−0.634
				(0.526)	(0.475)	(0.478)
Child's years of schooling	−0.015	−0.367*	−0.316*	−0.426*	−0.576*	−0.535*
	(0.066)	(0.077)	(0.079)	(0.081)	(0.075)	(0.077)
Ever had a teen birth			0.596*			0.450*
			(0.281)			(0.212)

* $p < .05$.

Source: Authors' calculations of regressions based on sample in table 15.1.

a. Standard errors in parentheses.

b. All regressions control for mother's schooling; ever lived in a female-headed household; percentage of years lived in a female-headed household; percentage of years head was disabled; neighborhood poverty rate (percent); percentage of neighbors with incomes greater than $15,000; percentage of men in the neighborhood who are unemployed; unemployment rate in adult labor market; and mean state AFDC–food stamp benefits.

c. Children from families with income-to-needs ratios of 2–3 were the omitted group.

needs ratios and decrease their chances of escaping poverty as adults *primarily* by reducing children's schooling. As expected, schooling was a very good predictor of an individual's income-to-needs ratio and adult poverty status. But controlling schooling only modestly reduced the estimated coefficients on the parental poverty and parental welfare measures. This result is not surprising given that earlier researchers have reported that low parental income has only modest effects on schooling (Duncan 1994; Duncan and Yeung 1994). Most of the impact of parental poverty and welfare is independent of schooling.

Nor does it appear that girls raised in poor or welfare-dependent homes remain poor as adults because they have babies as teenagers. Giving birth as a teen powerfully reduced girls' expected income-to-needs ratios and increased their chances of being poor as adults, but controlling teen births only slightly reduced the estimated effects of parental poverty, parental welfare use, or both on girls' adult economic outcomes.

Men's labor incomes are a major component of their income-to-needs ratios. Since labor incomes are the product of hourly wages and work hours, parental poverty and parental welfare can affect men's annual earnings by influencing either their labor supply or their hourly wages. The estimated effects of parents' poverty and parents' welfare receipt on the log of men's annual earnings, as expected, were similar to those estimated in the regression predicting the log of men's income-to-needs ratios (table 15.17).

We then decomposed each background measure's estimated effect in the log of annual earnings into its effect on log hourly wages and on log work hours. Since annual earnings are the product of hourly wages and work hours, the sum of coefficients for any background variable in the log wages and log hours regression will equal the coefficient in the log earnings regression. Parental poverty affected men's annual incomes by reducing both their hourly wages and their work hours. Thus growing up poor reduced the men's ability to obtain well-paid, steady, full-time work. The same pattern held for the effects of parents' welfare receipt on black men's labor incomes. Black men raised in welfare-dependent families earned less per hour and worked fewer hours per year than did black men raised in families that never received welfare.

CONCLUSION

These results provide some support for all the models described earlier but most strongly support the economic resources model. For white men, black men, and black women, having grown up poor was associated with dramatically lower income-to-needs ratios and dramatically higher chances of being poor, even when we controlled for parents' welfare receipt, a wide range of parental noneconomic resources, neighborhood advantages, and welfare incentives. Researchers looking at other economic outcomes using the PSID report similar results (Corcoran et al. 1992; Corcoran and Adams 1993, forthcoming).

TABLE 15.17 / Effects of Parents' Poverty, Welfare Receipt on Log Labor Income, Log Hourly Wage, and Log Work Hours, Black and White Men[a]

	Black Men			White Men		
Independent Variable	1 Log Labor Income	2 Log Hourly Wages	3 Log Work Hours	4 Log Labor Income	5 Log Hourly Wages	6 Log Work Hours
Family variables						
Average family income-to-needs ratio[b]						
<1	−.584*	−0.211†	−0.373*	−0.493*	−0.257*	−0.236*
	(0.187)	(0.116)	(0.115)	(0.184)	(0.113)	(0.119)
1–2	−0.300*	−0.143	−0.156†	−0.078	−0.063	0.015
	(0.155)	(0.096)	(0.095)	(0.085)	(0.053)	(0.055)
>3	0.023	0.143	−0.119	0.069	0.095*	−0.025
	(0.25)	(0.157)	(0.155)	(0.071)	(0.044)	(0.046)
Ratio of welfare income to family income (W/Y)						
0 < W/Y < 0.15				0.053	0.028	0.026
				(0.078)	(0.048)	(0.050)
>0.15				−0.023	−0.060	0.037
				(0.165)	(0.102)	(0.106)
0 < W/Y < 0.50	−0.092	−0.079	−0.013			
	(0.114)	(0.071)	(0.070)			
>0.50	−0.464*	−0.203†	−0.260*			
	(0.188)	(0.117)	(0.115)			
Mother's years of schooling	0.016	0.017†	−0.001	0.008	0.013†	−0.005
	(0.016)	(0.010)	(0.010)	(0.012)	(0.007)	(0.008)
Ever lived in a female-headed household	−0.286	−0.162	−0.123	−0.363*	−0.181*	−0.181†
	(0.211)	(0.132)	(0.130)	(0.151)	(0.093)	(0.097)

% years in female-headed household	0.004	0.002	0.002	0.006*	0.002	0.004*
	(0.008)	(0.002)	(0.002)	(0.002)	(0.001)	(0.002)
% years head was disabled	0	0	0	−0.002*	−0.002*	0
	(0.002)	(0.001)	(0.001)	(0.001)	(0.001)	(0.001)
Head's average work hours (1,000/year)	0.019	0.031	−0.013	−0.041	−0.075*	0.034
	(0.081)	(0.050)	(0.049)	(0.049)	(0.030)	(0.032)
Neighborhood variables						
Poverty rate > 30%	0.145	0.045	0.100	−0.409*	−0.289*	−0.120†
	(0.114)	(0.070)	(0.070)	(0.109)	(0.067)	(0.071)
Percent with incomes > $15,000	0.008	0.004	0.004	0.005†	0.003†	0.002
	(0.008)	(0.005)	(0.005)	(0.003)	(0.002)	(0.002)
Male unemployment rate	−0.016	−0.007	−0.008	0.014	0.025*	−0.011
	(0.013)	(0.008)	(0.008)	(0.014)	(0.008)	(0.009)
Labor market variables						
Male unemployment rate	−0.060*	−0.017	−0.043*	−0.011	−0.005	−0.006
	(0.023)	(0.014)	(0.014)	(0.012)	(0.007)	(0.007)
Mean state AFDC–food stamp benefit ($100/month)	−0.007	0.038	−0.045	−0.028	−0.001	−0.028
	(0.052)	(0.033)	(0.032)	(0.029)	(0.018)	(0.018)
R^2	0.200	0.156	0.227	0.146	0.212	0.096

* $p < .05$; † $p < .10$.

Source: Authors' calculations of regressions based on sample in table 15.1.

a. Standard errors in parentheses.

b. All regressions control for mother's schooling; ever lived in a female-headed household; percentage of years lived in a female-headed household; percentage of years head was disabled; neighborhood poverty rate (percent); percentage of neighbors with incomes greater than $15,000; percentage of men in the neighborhood who are unemployed; unemployment rate in adult labor market; and mean state AFDC–food stamp benefits.

While we know that growing up poor reduces children's economic mobility, these analyses tell us little about why. Past research has documented that poor children acquire less schooling and that poor girls are more likely to become teenage mothers (Sewell and Hauser 1975; Hill and Duncan 1987; Haveman, Wolfe, and Spaulding 1991; Haveman and Wolfe 1994; Brooks-Gunn et al. 1993; Duncan 1994; Hill and Sandfort 1994; Duncan and Hoffman 1990). In our results schooling and teen parenthood powerfully predicted children's income sufficiency and poverty as adults. But controlling schooling and teen births only slightly reduced the effects of parental poverty on children's adult income sufficiency and poverty. Growing up poor did not affect children's economic mobility *primarily* by increasing their chances of dropping out of high school or of becoming a teen parent. Our results suggest, rather, parental poverty affects men's incomes by reducing men's abilities to earn a good wage and acquire steady work but provide few clues as to how these processes operate.

The evidence for Mead's (1986, 1992) welfare culture model is mixed. Heavy parental use of welfare is significantly associated with lower adult income to needs for black sons and with lower adult income to needs and with a higher chance of becoming poor as an adult for white daughters. The parental welfare variables in our study were never significant for either white sons or black daughters. In these data, state welfare benefits (that is, incentives) did not lower income-to-needs ratios or increase the incidence of poverty, providing little or no support for Murray's (1984) and Anderson's (1978) arguments that perverse welfare incentives lead to poverty.

The noneconomic parental resources we examined—family structure, mother's schooling, and parents' work hours—had mostly weak and often insignificant effects on children's economic mobility. In comparison, parental poverty and parental welfare were much more important precursors of children's economic fortunes. However, this result does not argue for dismissing the noneconomic resources model since our analyses certainly did not exhaust the list of potential background advantages that affect children's mobility and that are correlated with parental poverty and welfare dependence.

Our analyses support Wilson's (1987, 1991a, 1991b, 1993) contention that structural economic conditions shape and constrain poor black children's chances of escaping poverty as adults. Young black men's and young black women's adult income sufficiency and adult poverty were strongly tied to the unemployment rates in their adult labor market areas. On the other hand, we found little evidence that *neighborhoods* matter for black children in the way predicted by Wilson (1987, 1991a, 1991b, 1993). Despite this, we do not think our results argue against Wilson's model. Our analyses measured neighborhood by the census tract (probably not the most appropriate measure) and used aggregate measures of neighborhood residents' characteristics as proxies for very complex neighborhood processes such as peer group pressure, school resources, and community norms. As Furstenberg and Hughes (1994) point out, such data do not provide a realistic or appropriate test of the neighborhood models proposed by Wilson and others.

Our most discouraging finding is the persistent importance of race. Black children were five times more likely to be poor and eight times more likely to be persistently poor during childhood than white children were. Other researchers report similar differences (Duncan and Rodgers 1991, Ashworth, Hill, and Walker 1992). Because black children were more likely to be poor, and because poverty was a major determinant of adult income sufficiency and adult poverty, black children had much lower income-to-needs ratios and much higher rates of poverty as adults than white children did.

APPENDIX

Table 15A.1 shows the results of estimating parental income using a tobit procedure and two-stage least squares.

TABLE 15A.1 / Effects of Parents' Welfare Receipt and Predicted Parents' Welfare Receipt on Adults' Income-to-Needs Ratios, Black Men and Women[a]

Welfare Measure ($1,000/year)	Black Men	Black Women
Welfare income	−0.037*	0.007
	(0.019)	(0.013)
Predicted welfare income[b]	0.014	−0.119
	(0.087)	(0.071)

* $p < .05$.

Source: Authors' calculations. Predicted welfare income per year was estimated using two-stage least squares. Predictor variables included all the predictor variables (other than parental welfare) listed in table 15.13, plus the mean AFDC–food stamp benefit facing the parents during the years the child lived at home, the ratio of employed men to women in the neighborhood during the years the child lived at home, the male and female unemployment rates, and the mean earnings of wage and salary workers in the labor market area serving the community in which the child's parents resided.

a. Standard errors in parentheses.

b. Both regressions include all predictor variables (other than parental welfare) listed in table 15.13.

This research was funded by the assistant secretary for planning and evaluation of the U.S. Department of Health and Human Services by the Rockefeller Foundation and by the vice president for research at the University of Michigan. We are grateful to John Bound, Charles Brown, Sheldon Danziger, Greg J. Duncan, Jeanne Brooks-Gunn, Irv Garfinkel, Martha Hill, and Jodi Sandfort for advice and comments and to Marguerite Grabarek, James Kunz, and Scott Allard for valuable research assistance. Most of all, we thank Wendy Niemi for her patient and accurate manuscript preparation.

NOTES

1. Several studies do log parental income measures, which allows for nonlinear income effects.
2. All respondents who met these criteria were included in our sample even if they dropped out of the sample before 1988 or left the sample and returned at some point between 1968 and 1988. Respondents were also eliminated if they had data missing on any of the independent variables.
3. Head was defined as the husband in two-parent households and the woman in female-headed households.
4. We experimented with a wide variety of break-even points for the poverty rate measure: 30 percent, 40 percent, and 50 percent. Neighborhood measures were constructed by taking addresses at which the respondent resided during childhood and matching them to a 1970 or 1980 geocode. The geocode used was the smallest geographic unit available for that address. For most cases, this was the census tract or Enumeration district; in some cases the Minor Civil Division was used.
5. Labor market measures were constructed by taking addresses at which the respondent resided after age twenty-four years and matching those addresses to a 1980 labor market area (LMA), defined as follows: if a person lived in a census metropolitan statistical area (CMSA), then that CMSA was defined as that person's LMA. If a person lived in a primary metropolitan statistical area (PMSA) or in a standard statistical metropolitan area (SMSA) but not in a CMSA, then that PMSA or SMSA was assigned as that person's LMA. For people living in nonmetropolitan areas, the definition of LMA depended on the extent to which workers who lived in a county worked outside the county. If 20 percent or more of workers living in a county commuted to work outside that county, then the state economic area (SEA) that included that county was defined as the LMA; otherwise the county was defined as the LMA. SEAs are the nonmetropolitan analog to metropolitan statistical areas (MSAs) designed by the U.S. Department of Agriculture.
6. We get this by taking antilog (.106).
7. We get these percentages by taking antilog −.439 and antilog −.215.
8. The income-to-needs categories examined in model 7 of tables 15.4–15.7 differ for blacks and whites because no whites were severely poor (income-to-needs ratio less than 0.5) and few blacks had income-to-needs greater than 4.0.
9. We used dummy variables to control for the nonlinear effects of parental income-to-needs ratios. We could also have logged the parental income-to-needs measure.
10. We experimented with a variety of specifications for the parental welfare measures. First, we included a continuous measure of the proportion of income derived from welfare. This was insignificant for white men and black women; negative, sizable, and not significant for black men; and negative and significant for white women. We then experimented with a variety of breakpoints in dummy variables specifications of the welfare measure. For black men, the specifications 1–50 percent and 50 percent or more best captured the nonlinear effects of parental welfare. For white women, the specification that best captured welfare effects was 1–15 percent and 15 percent or more.

11. We get these percentages by taking antilog (−.492), and antilog (−.392).
12. We estimated parental welfare income using a two-stage least square procedure (2SLS). The patterns of results were quite similar; the 2SLS results are reported in table 15A.1. We report results only for blacks, since the instrumenting variables were not strong predictors of white mothers' welfare income.
13. We got these percentages by taking the antilogs of −.041 and −.081.

Chapter 16

The Effects of Parents' Income, Wealth and Attitudes on Children's Completed Schooling and Self-Esteem

William Axinn, Greg J. Duncan, and Arland Thornton

Early work on the intergenerational transmission of socioeconomic status relied on cross-sectional surveys and retrospectively reported measures of parental characteristics such as completed schooling and occupation. Prospective data, gathered from parents while children are young and later when the children reach adulthood, provide opportunities to link richer measures of family characteristics, in particular family income, to adult attainments. Most studies based on data that include reliable measures of parental income find that it is a significant correlate of children's eventual economic success as adults (see Corcoran, Gordon, Laren, Solon 1992; Haveman and Wolfe 1995 for recent reviews of this literature).

Why income matters is a crucial issue for both theory and public policy. One obvious possibility is that income itself has no impact on children's attainments but instead absorbs the explanatory power of other, unmeasured characteristics of high- and low-income parents that are the real causes of their children's success. Characteristics that may be important include family conflict (see chapter 10), learning experiences (see chapter 7), mental ability (see chapters 13 and 17), and parenting styles (see chapter 3). Although statistical approaches can help solve the problem of unmeasured variables, they typically rely on strong and untestable assumptions. A more credible approach to explaining why family income matters is to study data in which typically unmeasured parental characteristics are explicitly measured and included in the analysis.

Our chapter is based on longitudinal data gathered on a cohort of children born in the Detroit, Michigan, area in 1961. The sample frame included only births to white mothers, constraining us to conduct an analysis of a group of children who are ethnically and economically more homogeneous and advantaged than the general population. However, interviews conducted with the parents shortly after the children were born and periodically throughout their childhood yielded a number of interesting measures of parental experience and characteristics not found even in extensive, prospective studies of children's well-being.

Our analysis began with a basic model in which parents' income predicts completed schooling and children's self-esteem as young adults. We then examined the extent to which such factors as parental education and family structure and composition can explain the effects of income.

Next, we exploited several special aspects of our data to extend our basic model to other dimensions of parental economic status, which influenced children's well-being. Our first extension assessed whether parental assets added to the explanatory power of a model based on parental income alone. Although income and wealth had a positive correlation, the association was far from perfect. Evidence that greater parental financial wealth imparts advantages to children in outcomes like completed schooling and self-esteem would support the importance of the role played by the economic dimension of childhood.

Our second extension assessed the importance for children's attainments of having parents whose consumption orientations appear to be toward themselves rather than toward their children. Parents who consume more and save less or, when they do consume, purchase things for their own use rather than for the sake of their children can be expected to have children with less human capital and lower self-esteem.

A third extension focused on more subjective reports of parents' orientation toward their children, including whether the parents reported wanting the given child, reported expectations that their children would go to college, and reported aspirations for their children. In this case we tested whether subjectively reported orientations of the parents toward children when those children are very young influenced the well-being of the children in young adulthood.

BACKGROUND

Our interest is in two early-adult outcomes—completed schooling and self-esteem. The literature on the determinants of completed schooling is multidisciplinary and voluminous, but the number of studies of completed schooling that investigate the effects of parental income is much smaller. Although some intergenerational studies have explored the impact of parental education and parenting behavior on children's self-esteem, few have investigated the impact of parents' income levels from early in children's lives.

Income may influence children's well-being in multiple ways. One mechanism focuses on total parental income without differentiating among its sources, as a crucial factor giving children the resources for schooling and other dimensions of well-being. The income of parents can also be viewed as a reflection of underlying family values and processes. For example, the labor income of the father or mother may convey information about the role model provided by that parent. The receipt of welfare income may reflect the extent to which a household has adopted the counterproductive norms and values sometimes believed to be associated with a "welfare culture" (Wilson 1980, 1981, 1987; see chapter 17).

One of the first and most prominent attempts to incorporate parental income in a model of socioeconomic attainment was that of Sewell and Hauser (1975), who based their estimates on a cohort of male high school seniors in Wisconsin. Their parental income measures, which came from state tax records, showed that the taxable income of parents had highly significant effects on the education and earnings of their sons at about age twenty-five years. A replication study using the same general model with data from the Wisconsin sample, Project Talent and Explorations in Equality of Opportunity, also found significant effects of parental income on completed schooling (Jencks, Crouse, and Meuser 1983).

Alwin and Thornton (1984) analyzed the data set used in this chapter to relate various parental measures, including income and assets, to a set of educational outcomes. They tested the effects of a measure combining income and assets, gathered in early and late childhood, on the amount of schooling completed at age eighteen and on whether the child was in a college preparatory program in high school, finding that the early-childhood measure of the income-asset variable had significant effects.

Haveman, Wolfe, and Spaulding (1991) also tested for the importance of the timing of income levels, using Panel Study of Income Dynamics (PSID) data. They found that the combination of poverty and welfare use between ages twelve and fifteen was a significant predictor of high-school dropout status, whereas a combination of poverty and welfare use at earlier periods in childhood was not.

Hill and Duncan (1987) related family income and other background measures to the completed schooling of individuals in the PSID. They found highly significant but substantively small effects, with a 10 percent increase in income associated with a less than 1 percent increase in completed schooling.

Haveman and Wolfe (1995) comprehensively reviewed studies from the 1980s and 1990s of high school graduation and total years of completed schooling. Regarding the role of income, they concluded,

> With but one exception (Datcher, 1982), the family income variable is positively associated with educational attainment of the child, and the variable is statistically significant in more than half of all cases where a positive relationship is estimated. Simulated changes in family economic resources, however, are associated with small changes in educational attainments. The range of elasticities is wide—about .02 to .20. (p. 16)

In addition to educational attainment, our analyses examine another central component of children's well-being: self-esteem, or internalized sense of worth. Self-esteem is generally conceptualized as the central evaluative component of the self and reflects the extent to which individuals believe they are worthwhile and merit respect (Wylie 1979; Rosenberg 1979, 1989; Coopersmith 1967). Consequently, children who have internalized self-respect, a sense of personal worth, and positive evaluations of themselves have higher levels of well-being than those who view themselves as inadequate, unworthy, or seriously deficient as people. Self-esteem is also related to other dimensions of children's well-being, including their success in school and the work force (Bachman and O'Malley 1977; Wilson and Portes 1975). While children's self-esteem is probably partly determined by their experiences in school and work, there are also reasons to expect that self-esteem is a determining force in subsequent achievement (Bachman and O'Malley 1977; Wylie 1979; Yogev and Ilan 1987).

As the central evaluative component of a person's self-concept, self-esteem is conceptualized as an individual attribute (Wylie 1979; Rosenberg 1979; Coopersmith 1967). Nevertheless, scholars increasingly recognize that the interaction of individuals with the social institutions in which they are embedded creates and molds self-esteem. Consequently, a significant number of people and institutions, including families, schools, churches, and peer groups, affect individuals' self-esteem (Bachman and O'Malley 1977; Gecas and Schwalbe 1986; Rosenberg and Kaplan 1982; Bachman 1982). Of all the institutions influencing internalized beliefs of self-worth, however, the family is recognized as the most powerful (Gecas and Schwalbe 1986; Bachman 1982; Gecas and Seff 1990). The research literature is also beginning to suggest that the emotional and supportive quality of the parental home rather than its structure or composition most strongly influences a child's sense of self-worth (Demo and Acock 1988; Raschke 1987). The quality of relationships between mothers and fathers and between parents and children has been shown to be associated with children's self-esteem (Bachman 1982; Demo and Acock 1988; Raschke 1987; Demo, Small, and Savin-Williams 1987).

Parents' economic resources can influence self-esteem in several ways. Parents' income brings both parents and children social status and respect that can translate into individual self-esteem. Income can also enhance children's self-esteem by providing them with the goods and services that satisfy individual aspirations.

Low income and other economic hardships may reduce children's self-esteem by reducing the emotional or supportive qualities of the parents' home. The pressure that limited economic resources can place on marital relationships can, in turn, translate into negative parent-child relations and lower levels of self-esteem. For example, lower income has been found to increase levels of parental conflict over money, with particularly detrimental consequences for sons (see chapter 10). The hypothesis is also consistent with recent research suggesting that economic stress has negative consequences for children's self-esteem. Whitbeck et al. (1991) found that family economic hardship, as reported by parents, affected self-esteem indirectly "by decreasing parental support and involvement" (1991, p. 353). They found, however, that reported economic hardship had only weak direct effects on children's self-esteem, which appears consistent with the work of other researchers, who have found parental behavior toward children to be an important determinant of children's self-esteem (Gecas and Schwalbe 1986; Demo, Small, and Savin-Williams 1987).

DATA

The data for these analyses come from a twenty-three-year, seven-wave longitudinal study of mothers and their children. The original probability sample was drawn to represent approximately equal numbers of white mothers who had given birth in 1961 to a first, second, or fourth child in the Detroit metropolitan area (Wayne, Oakland, and McComb counties). The mothers were interviewed in person in the winter of 1962 and by telephone in the fall of 1962, 1963, 1966, 1977, 1980, and 1985. The children born in 1961 were interviewed in person in 1980 and 1985, at eighteen and twenty-three years of age. Response rates for all waves of this survey have been high: 92 percent of the mothers selected for the original survey participated. Eighty-two percent of the original families continued to participate in the study twenty-three years later, through the 1985 wave. We had complete longitudinal information from 867 families.

Measures of Children's Well-Being

We focused on two distinct but interrelated aspects of children's well-being: their educational attainment and their self-esteem. We used measures of self-esteem taken from the children at age twenty-three. Our measure of educational attainment was the young person's educational attainment, in years, by age twenty-three. We treated both self-esteem and years of educational attainment as interval-level variables in our analyses (see table 16.1 for means and standard deviations). We used ordinary least squares regression to estimate our models.

Self-Esteem Scale

Our measure of self-esteem consisted of an average of the responses to seven questions answered with always true, almost always true, often true, sometimes true, seldom true, or never true. We coded these response categories from 1 to 6 so that higher numbers indicate higher levels of self-esteem. The correlations of these items ranged from .168 to .648, with a mean correlation of .394 and a standard deviation of .138. The items, based on the measures of self-esteem designed by Rosenberg (1965, 1979, 1989), are listed below:

1. I take a positive attitude toward myself.
2. I feel I do not have much to be proud of.
3. I am able to do things as well as most other people.
4. I feel that I can't do anything right.
5. As a person, I do a good job these days.
6. I feel that I have a number of good qualities.
7. I feel that I'm a person of worth, at least on an equal level with others.

TABLE 16.1 / Characteristics of the Families in the Sample

Variable	Mean	SD
Outcome variables		
Self-esteem (1985)	4.960	0.627
Schooling completed (1985, years)	13.644	2.005
Control variables		
Child female	0.502	0.500
Mother's education (1962, years)	12.195	1.858
Father's education (1962, years)	12.435	2.496
Mother's premarital pregnancy status	0.184	0.388
Mother's age at marriage (years)	20.351	3.049
Mother continuously married (1962–77)	0.761	0.427
Mother widowed (1962–77)[a]	0.040	0.197
Mother divorced and remarried (1962–77)	0.089	0.285
Mother divorced and not remarried (1962–77)	0.110	0.313
Household size (1962)	4.450	1.337
Family income variables		
Average income (1961–62, 1,000 $1992)	34.766	14.566
Average income-to-needs ratio (1961, 1962, 1965, 1976, 1979)	3.121	1.373
Average income (1961, 1962, 1965, 1976, 1979) (1,000 $1992)[a]	49.947	19.804
Average number in household (1962, 1963, 1966, 1977, 1980)	4.795	1.082
Average income-to-needs ratio (1961, 1962, 1965, 1976, 1979)		
< 2	0.138	0.345
2–3	0.394	0.489
3–4	0.256	0.436
> 4	0.213	0.410
Low income (1961, 1962, 1965, 1976, 1979)[b]		
Never	0.383	0.486
At least one year but not all years	0.593	0.492
All years	0.024	0.156
Early (1961, 1962, 1965) but not late (1976, 1979)	0.132	0.339
Late (1976, 1979) but not early (1961, 1962, 1965)	0.005	0.068
Equity and assets variables		
Home equity		
None in 1962 and 1966	0.105	0.307
None in 1962, some in 1966	0.277	0.448
Some in 1962, none in 1966	0.024	0.154

(Table continued on p. 524.)

TABLE 16.1 / *(continued)*

Variable	Mean	*SD*
Equity and assets variables		
Home equity		
Some in 1962 and in 1966 (low average)[c]	0.373	0.484
Some in 1962 and 1966 (high average)[d]	0.220	0.415
Liquid assets		
None in 1962 and 1966	0.076	0.266
None in 1962, some in 1966	0.075	0.264
Some in 1962, none in 1966	0.145	0.353
Some in 1962 and in 1966	0.703	0.457
Average number of cars (1962, 1966)	1.519	0.540
Aspirations for children variables		
Put money aside for child's college in 1962	0.434	0.496
Children should go to college[e]	2.799	0.461
Expects children will go to college[f]	0.523	0.500
Sum of aspirations for child[g]	9.517	1.807
Child wanted by both parents	0.835	0.372

Source: Authors' calculations using data on 867 families from the Intergenerational Panel Study of Mothers and Children.

a. Allows up to two missing data values.

b. Income-to-needs ratio <2.

c. Equity lower than average for households with some equity in both 1962 and 1966.

d. Equity higher than average for households with some equity in both 1962 and 1966.

e. Feels very strongly (1), feels fairly strongly (2), or does not feel strongly (3).

f. 1 if it is expected that all children will go to college and 0 otherwise.

g. Sum of items ranked very important (3), desirable (2), and unimportant (1). These items include desire for child to participate in scouting or other clubs, receiving an allowance by high school, and having their own bedroom by junior high school.

Family Income and Poverty

Our measures of family income came from interviews with mothers and spanned the children's entire lifetimes. At each interview mothers were asked to estimate their total family income from all sources during the preceding year. Thus from the 1962 interview we had a measure of the family's total income in 1961, the year the children in our study were born. In 1962, 1963 and 1966, respondents were asked to estimate their family income within specified categories, which resulted in extremely low levels of missing data on income.[1] We converted the categorical responses into a continuous measure by assigning $20,000 to the top category ($15,000 and above) and the midpoint values to each of the other categories. In 1977 and 1980, respondents were asked to estimate their family income in dollars (rounded to the nearest $1,000). All of these income measures were inflated to 1992 dollars.

Using the official U.S. poverty thresholds as our definition of family "needs," we calculated income-to-needs ratios for each income observation for each family. By definition, an income-to-needs ratio of 1.0 indicates that a family's income is equal to the poverty threshold. However, because respondents in this sample had somewhat higher-than-average income levels, we defined an income-to-needs ratio of 2.0 as the "low-income" threshold.

Our measures of long-term economic status were based on the family income-to-needs ratios averaged over the five time points in the study, when the children were ages zero, one, four, fourteen, and seventeen years. We compared early and late income by contrasting income-to-needs averaged over the first three measures to income-to-needs averaged over the later two measures with three dummy variables: (1) whether the family had a low income early (at zero, one, and four years of age) but not late (at ages fourteen and seventeen), (2) whether the family had low income late but not early, and (3) whether the family had low income all the time. Families who never had low income were the excluded group in regressions using these dummy variables.

We measured the duration of low-income status with two dummy variables: (1) whether the family was low income some but not all of the time (that is, whether the family's income-to-needs ratio was less than 2.0 in one, two, three, or four but not all five of the reports); and (2) whether the family was low income all of the time (that is, the family's income-to-needs ratio was less than 2.0 in all five reports). Families that were never low income were the excluded group in the regressions, so coefficients on these two low-income measures indicated differences between children growing up in the two kinds of low-income families and children raised in families that were never low income.

Wealth

In addition to income, our measure of the family's economic situation included home equity and liquid assets. We measured the level of and change in home equity (that is, the value of the home minus the mortgage) from 1962 to 1966 with a set of dummy variables. Those who held no equity in either year, with renters included, constituted the omitted category in our regressions. The other categories were no equity in 1962 and some in 1966 (no-yes), some in 1962 and none in 1966 (yes-no), some equity in both 1962 and 1966 with the average equity in the two years being low, and some equity in both 1962 and 1966 with the average equity in the two years being high. High average equity was defined as equity higher than the mean ($221,023 in 1992 dollars[2]) for those households with some equity in both 1962 and 1966. In contrast, low average equity is defined as equity lower than the mean for those households with some equity in both 1962 and 1966.

We also constructed dummy variables to measure the level of and change in liquid assets from 1962 to 1966. Liquid assets included money in savings accounts in banks, credit unions, or savings and loan associations. Families with no assets in either year were the reference category. The other categories were holding no liquid assets in 1962 and some in 1966 (no-yes), some in 1962 and none in 1966 (yes-no), and some in 1962 and some in 1966 (yes-yes).

We measured ownership of consumer durables by averaging the number of cars owned by the family in 1962 and 1966, including cars leased or owned by a company and trucks not primarily for business. Unlike other asset measures, the number of cars owned by a family might reflect a consumption orientation that is focused more on parents than on children. If so, the number of cars may have a negative effect on children's outcomes.[3]

Parental Aspirations

We used data from the 1962 interviews with the mothers to construct a series of variables measuring the parents' feelings about their children's college attendance and their behavior in preparing for their children's education. We measured these variables in 1962, before the children had reached age one year and early enough in their lives to ensure that parents did not base their responses on their children's early school performance. The belief that children should go to college was a measure of the strength of mothers' feelings about their children's college attendance in 1962. We coded it 3 if the mothers felt very strongly that their children should go to college, 2 if they felt fairly strongly, and 1 if they did not feel strongly at all. The second measure of mothers' attitudes toward their children's college attendance was whether they expected their children to go to college, coded 1 if mothers expected all of their children to go to college and 0 otherwise.[4] The final college measure was behavioral. Whether the parents were putting money aside for college was coded 1 if the parents reported doing so for all or some of their children as of 1962 and 0 otherwise.

Other Subjective Evaluations from Mothers

In 1962 the mothers were asked about their aspirations for other aspects of their children's lives: their desire for their children to attend private summer camp, take private music, dance, or sports lessons, participate in scouting or other clubs, receive an allowance by high school, and have their own bedroom by junior high school. They ranked all items as very important (3), desirable (2), or unimportant (1). We summed the mothers' responses to these questions to form a single variable measuring aspirations for the child.

Finally, in 1962 mothers were asked if, before they became pregnant, they and their husbands had wanted the child born in 1961. We used responses to these questions to create a measure of being a wanted child coding it 1 if both parents wanted the child and 0 otherwise. For example, if the wife wanted the child but the husband was indifferent, the variable was coded 0.[5]

Parents' Marital Dissolution

Our measures of parents' marital dissolutions were based on marital history data gathered from the mothers across the first fifteen years of the children's lives. We used four dummy variables. The first was coded 1 if the mother experienced widowhood between 1962 and 1977; the second was coded 1 if the mother had divorced and remarried during that period; and the third was coded 1 if the mother had divorced but had not remarried by 1977. Mothers who remained married to the child's father over the entire period were the reference group for these comparisons.

Other Family Characteristics

Several dimensions of the parents' background should be taken into account in modeling the influence of parents' characteristics on children's life courses, including how old the mother was at her marriage and whether she had a premarital pregnancy (Hogan and Kitagawa 1985; Thornton 1991; Thornton and Camburn 1987). Our measure of premarital pregnancy status, which came from a comparison of birth and marriage records, was a dummy variable coded 1 if the mother was pregnant before her first marriage (Pratt 1965). We coded the mother's age at first marriage in years and entered it into the analyses as an interval-level variable. We also included measures of the mother's and father's 1962 educational attainment, each measured in years of schooling. A number of studies have demonstrated the influence of parents' education on children's life courses (Hogan 1978; Marini 1978; Waite and Spitze 1981). These variables were also entered in equations as interval-level variables.

The means and standard deviations of these variables for the sample reveal the relatively advantaged nature of the families (table 16.1). Despite having children in the early 1960s, both mothers and fathers averaged more than twelve years of schooling.[6] Nearly one in five of the mothers was pregnant at the time of marriage, which occurred, on average, when mothers were about twenty years old. More than three-quarters of the marriages remained intact throughout childhood and adolescence.

The family incomes of the sample children averaged nearly $50,000 (in 1992 dollars). Family sizes were smaller than average owing to the equal sampling of first-, second-, and fourth-parity births, so the average ratio of income to the poverty-level "needs" threshold was 3.1. As mentioned, so few families had incomes below the official poverty line that we used twice the poverty line as our cutoff for low-income status. Only 14 percent of the sample had incomes that averaged below the cutoff, but more than half had incomes below the cutoff on at least one of the five occasions on which income was measured. Instead of distinguishing between the effects of persistent and transitory incomes below the official poverty line, we were forced to draw the line at twice the poverty line (roughly $28,000 for a family of four in 1994). As a result, we will speak of persistent and transitory "low-income" status rather than persistent and transitory "poverty" status.

BASIC ANALYSIS

Completed Schooling

Our basic analysis used years of schooling completed by age twenty-three as the dependent variable (table 16.2). The coefficients for model 1 show highly significant effects of the parents' schooling, the mother's age at marriage and family structure. Additional years of fathers' and mothers' schooling were associated with an additional one-quarter and one-sixth year of schooling for children, respectively. Compared with children living in intact families, children in families in which a divorce occurred completed significantly less schooling—nearly one year less in the case of divorces with no remarriage and about one-half year less in the case of a divorce followed by a remarriage.

The income coefficients for model 2 show that average family income was an important correlate of completed schooling before adjustments for the effects of the other parental variables. When we added the other parental variables (model 3), the explanatory power of family income decreased by about half, leaving a coefficient suggesting that an income increase equal to the poverty threshold would add roughly one-quarter of a year to completed schooling. Interestingly, adjustments for family income had relatively little effect on the estimated effects of the other measures, including family structure (model 3).

The coefficients for model 4 show that both income and family size mattered for completed schooling, while model 5 revealed something of a threshold effect of income at roughly three times the poverty line. Children raised in families with incomes above this level averaged between three-quarters and one year more schooling than did children in families with incomes below this level. Differences of a similar magnitude showed up in a comparison of children raised in persistently low-income families with those raised in families in which income was always at least twice the poverty threshold (model 6). Children from families with some spells of low income but not persistent low income finished fewer years of education than did children from families that never had a low income, but they finished fewer years of education than children from families with persistent low income.

Low income for parents early (but not late) in their children's lives had a significant negative effect on the children's educational attainment, although this effect was much smaller than the effect of persistent low income (model 7). The negative effect of low income early was statistically significant whereas the negative effect of low income late was not. This result is consistent with previous research using these data, which also found that parents' economic situations had a stronger influence early in children's lives than late in their lives (Alwin and Thornton 1984). However, we interpret these results with caution since such a small fraction of the families actually had a low income late but not early (see table 16.1).

Finally, the results for model 8 indicated that the effect of family income did not differ for males and females in the sample.

In light of the importance of economic factors and the large out-of-pocket costs associated with college attendance for many students, we replicated the basic analysis (table 16.2) on a dichotomous dependent variable that equaled 1 if the child completed college and 0 otherwise. Although family income and parental schooling significantly predicted college completion, the various asset measures proved to be important for the continuous measure of completed schooling in general did not come close to conventional levels of statistical significance for either males or females. An exception was that females reared in families with reported liquid assets at both ages one and five were more likely to complete college than otherwise similar females reared in families without such assets. This result notwithstanding, economic resources appear to play a much larger role in promoting children's education than merely financing college costs.

Self-Esteem at Age Twenty-Three

The structure of the relationship between the parental variables and self-esteem was quite different from that between parental influences and completed schooling (table 16.3). The father's but not the mother's schooling was a significant predictor of the children's self-esteem as adults, a result that held within both the male and the female subsamples. This finding is consistent with the results of previous research, which has also demonstrated that parents' education strongly affects children's self-esteem but that the effects of the father's education are stronger (Bachman and O'Malley 1977, 1979; Demo, Small, and Savin-Williams 1987). Bachman and O'Malley (1977) also show that children's academic abilities and performance are important intervening mechanisms linking parents education to children's self-esteem.

Family structure during childhood had no significant effect on children's self-esteem. Family income was a significant predictor of self-esteem before but not after controls for the father's schooling and other aspects of the parental family. In fact, in the presence of controls for the father's schooling, none of the income variables had significant associations with self-esteem. These results are quite sim-

(Text continued on p. 534.)

TABLE 16.2 / Effects of Children's Family Income on Years of Schooling Completed by 1985[a]

Independent Variable	Model 1	2	3	4	5	6	7	8
Control variables								
Child female	0.27*	0.28*	0.28**	0.26***	0.28**	0.26*	0.26*	0.41
	(2.27)	(2.17)	(2.36)	(2.25)	(2.43)	(2.17)	(2.20)	(1.37)
Mother's education (1962)	0.17***		0.12**	0.13***	0.12***	0.15***	0.17***	0.12***
	(4.25)		(3.07)	(3.20)	(3.20)	(3.75)	(4.22)	(3.07)
Father's education (1962)	0.26***		0.22***	0.22***	0.21***	0.23***	0.25***	0.22***
	(9.24)		(7.33)	(7.47)	(7.10)	(7.72)	(8.66)	(7.34)
Mother's premarital pregnancy status	−0.09		−0.06	−0.04	−0.02	−0.05	−0.07	−0.06
	(0.57)		(0.40)	(0.23)	(0.10)	(0.32)	(0.44)	(0.39)
Mother's age at marriage	0.06**		0.06**	0.06**	0.06**	0.06**	0.06**	0.06**
	(2.82)		(2.84)	(2.67)	(2.76)	(2.60)	(2.80)	(2.83)
Mother's marital status[b]								
Widowed (1962–77)	−0.05		0.03	−0.002	−0.03	−0.09	−0.04	0.02
	(0.16)		(0.08)	(0.01)	(0.10)	(0.29)	(0.13)	(0.07)
Divorced and remarried (1962–77)	−0.55**		−0.62**	−0.73***	−0.66***	−0.58**	−0.58**	−0.62**
	(2.55)		(2.89)	(3.37)	(3.12)	(2.69)	(2.67)	(2.88)
Divorced and not remarried (1962–77)	−0.91***		−0.77***	−0.93***	−0.74***	−0.83***	−0.91***	−0.77***
	(4.75)		(3.97)	(4.64)	(3.86)	(4.30)	(4.66)	(3.97)
Family income variables								
Average income-to-needs ratio (1961, 1962, 1965, 1976, 1979)		0.54***	0.25***					0.27***
		(11.67)	(4.93)					(4.05)
Average income (1,000 of 1992$)				0.01***				
				(3.76)				
Average number in household (1962, 1963, 1966, 1977, 1980)				0.28***				
				(4.89)				

	(1)	(2)	(3)	(4)	(5)	(6)	(7)	(8)
Average income-to-needs ratio (1961, 1962, 1965, 1976, 1979)[c]								
< 2					−0.28			
					(1.51)			
3–4					0.77***			
					(5.15)			
> 4					0.85***			
					(4.96)			
Duration of low income[d]								
At least one year but not all years						−0.50***		
						(3.66)		
All years						−0.99**		
						(2.46)		
Timing of low average income[e]								
Early (1961, 1962, 1965)							−0.56***	
							(4.15)	
Late (1976, 1979)							−0.36	
							(1.50)	
Early and late							−0.65*	
							(1.66)	
Female by average income-to-needs ratio								−0.04
								(0.48)
Constant	7.17	11.77	7.47	8.93	8.05	8.25	7.41	7.41
Adjusted R^2	0.248	0.139	0.268	0.276	0.286	0.260	0.251	0.267
N	864	861	861	861	864	864	864	861

* $p < .05$; ** $p < .01$; *** $p < .001$.

Source: Authors' calculations using data on 867 families from the Intergenerational Panel Study of Mothers and Children.

a. *t*-ratios in parentheses.

b. Families in which the mother was continuously married were the omitted group.

c. Families with income-to-needs ratios of 2–3 were the omitted group.

d. Families that were never low income were the omitted group.

e. Families that were never low income were the omitted group.

TABLE 16.3 / Effects of Children's Family Income on Self-Esteem in 1985[a]

	Model							
Independent Variable	1	2	3	4	5	6	7	8
Control variables								
Child female	−0.20***	−0.20***	−0.20***	−0.20***	−0.20***	−0.21***	−0.21***	−0.39***
	(4.83)	(4.71)	(4.85)	(4.85)	(4.80)	(4.90)	(4.89)	(3.63)
Mother's education (1962)	−0.01		−0.01	−0.01	−0.01	−0.01	−0.01	−0.01
	(0.57)		(0.61)	(0.63)	(0.72)	(0.62)	(0.68)	(0.62)
Father's education (1962)	0.04***		0.04***	0.04***	0.04***	0.04***	0.04***	0.04***
	(4.12)		(3.69)	(3.59)	(3.82)	(3.95)	(4.08)	(3.68)
Mother's premarital pregnancy status	0.01		0.02	0.02	0.01	0.01	0.01	0.02
	(0.24)		(0.32)	(0.32)	(0.25)	(0.25)	(0.21)	(0.28)
Mother's age at marriage	0.002		0.002	0.002	0.002	0.003	0.002	0.002
	(0.24)		(0.20)	(0.21)	(0.24)	(0.33)	(0.33)	(0.24)
Mother's marital status[b]								
Widowed (1962–77)	−0.17		−0.17	−0.17	−0.17	−0.17	−0.16	−0.17
	(1.63)		(1.60)	(1.58)	(1.61)	(1.55)	(1.50)	(1.57)
Divorced and remarried (1962–77)	0.04		0.04	0.04	0.04	0.04	0.04	0.04
	(0.53)		(0.52)	(0.32)	(0.51)	(0.50)	(0.53)	(0.49)
Divorced and not remarried (1962–77)	−0.09		−0.09	−0.09	−0.09	−0.08	−0.07	−0.09
	(1.29)		(1.35)	(1.26)	(1.27)	(1.23)	(1.06)	(1.36)
Family income variables								
Average income-to-needs ratio (1961, 1962, 1965, 1976, 1979)		0.04**	0.01					−0.02
		(2.74)	(0.63)					(0.73)
Average income (1,000 of 1992$)				0.001				
				(0.74)				
Average number in household (1962, 1963, 1966, 1977, 1980)				−0.005				
				(0.24)				

Average income-to-needs ratio (1961, 1962, 1965, 1976, 1979)[c]								
<2					0.05			
					(0.68)			
3–4					0.01			
					(0.18)			
>4					0.06			
					(0.93)			
Duration of low income[d]								
At least one year but not all years						0.02		
						(0.38)		
All years						−0.16		
						(1.11)		
Timing of low average income[e]								
Early (1961, 1962, 1965)							−0.04	
							(0.85)	
Late (1976, 1979)							0.04	
							(0.46)	
Early and late							−0.17	
							(1.20)	
Female by average income-to-needs ratio								0.06*
								(1.87)
Constant	4.621	4.924	4.628	4.651	4.640	4.611	4.622	4.718
Adjusted R^2	0.045	0.032	0.045	0.044	0.043	0.044	0.044	0.048
N	858	855	855	855	858	858	858	855

* $p < .05$; ** $p < .01$; *** $p < .001$.

Source: Authors' calculations using data on 867 families from the Intergenerational Panel Study of Mothers and Children.

a. t-ratios in parentheses.

b. Families in which the mother was continuously married were the omitted group.

c. Families with income-to-needs ratios of 2–3 were the omitted group.

d. Families that were never low income were the omitted group.

e. Families that were never low income were the omitted group.

ilar to those of Hauser and Sweeney (see chapter 17), who found that income measures failed to influence measures of depression.

While the young women in this sample achieved higher levels of educational attainment than the young men, the opposite was true for self-esteem. Educational attainment may be an important predictor of self-esteem (Bachman and O'Malley 1977), but other factors in our society combine to produce significantly lower levels of self-esteem for young women than for young men by age twenty-three. However, we found some indication that female children benefited more than male children from increments to parental income (table 16.3, model 8). Female children possibly benefit more from secure economic environments than do male children, who tend to have higher self-esteem. Perhaps the sources of male self-esteem are independent of the economic environment in the parents' home, but having a home characterized by higher levels of income helps female children to overcome some of the sex-based differences in self-esteem.

EXTENSIONS

Our longitudinal data were particularly rich in measures of the parents' wealth, their consumption orientations, and their expectations, gathered when the children were very young. The preschool timing of the measurements is particularly important for the expectations measures, since the parents' reports were not affected by feedback received from teachers and school administrators on the promise and performance of their children.

We used these data to focus on several questions. First, to what extent does parents' wealth early in childhood influence children's later attainments and self-esteem? Evidence that the parents' wealth predicted the children's outcomes would support an economic interpretation of parents' effects on children. Second, do the orientations of parents toward their own consumption versus their children's affect children's well-being in adulthood? And third, do subjective reports of whether children were wanted or of what parents' aspirations toward their children are matter for how children turn out?

Completed Schooling

We first related the various measures of parents' wealth, their orientation toward consumption, their desire to have the child, and their aspirations for the child to the child's completed schooling in a series of regression analyses. Finding that the results changed little from simpler to more complete sets of regressors, we settled on two regression models (table 16.4). Clearly, the parents' income, liquid assets, and house equity all significantly predicted children's completed schooling. Each variable had a positive effect on school achievement net of other variables in the model.[7]

Somewhat surprisingly, the more subjective measures of parents' orientation toward investments in their children did not prove to be significant predictors of completed schooling; nor did they mediate the effects of the parental measures examined earlier. Reports of beliefs that their children should go to college or of expectations that their children will go to college approached but did not attain conventional levels of statistical significance.

We found few differences in the completed schooling models when we estimated them separately for males and females. Parental income and schooling levels had remarkably similar coefficients in models fit separately to the two sex groups. There was some indication that the asset measures mattered more for females than males, although the differences were not statistically significant. Among the subjective indicators, maternal beliefs that children should go to college proved significant ($t = 2.2$) for males but not females. All of the other subjective measures were insignificant for both subgroups.

All in all, what appears to matter most for children's completed schooling are the available economic resources, the number of children among whom those resources must be shared, and the quality of the parental inputs, as measured by their completed schooling.

Self-Esteem at Age Twenty-Three

As in our previous analyses, measures of income, home equity, and assets failed to exert a significant influence on children's self-esteem once sex and parents' education were taken into account. The most intriguing exception was the significant positive effect of parents' putting money aside (at age one) for their children's college education on children's self-esteem at age twenty-three (table 16.4, columns 3 and 4).[8] Putting money aside for children's college education did not influence children's educational attainment (columns 1 and 2), so the impact of this financial decision cannot be explained by the children's educational attainments. This result is consistent with the conclusion that parents' decision to save for college early in their children's lives represents an aspect of the home with a long-term impact on children's self-esteem that is independent of children's actual college attendance. Previous research demonstrating that parents' support for their children and involvement in their children's lives have important positive effects on their children's self-esteem may help explain the consequences of saving for college (Gecas and Schwalbe 1986; Robertson and Simon 1989; Whitbeck et al. 1991). Parents' decisions to save for their children's college education while their children are still in infancy probably reflect the parents' inclination to support their children and be involved in their lives. If this is true, our results are quite consistent with the previous research that shows the positive effects of these inclinations on children's self-esteem (Robertson and Simons 1989; Whitbeck et al. 1991).[9]

Some important sex differences came to light in our models of children's self-

TABLE 16.4 / Effects of Children's Family Assets and Equity on Years of Schooling Completed and Self-Esteem in 1985[a]

Independent Variable	Years of Schooling Completed by 1985		Self-Esteem in 1985	
	Model 1	Model 2	Model 1	Model 2
Control variables				
Average income (in 1961–62, 1,000 1992$)	0.01*	0.01*	−0.0003	0.0002
	(2.30)	(2.25)	(0.15)	(0.08)
Child female	0.26*	0.25*	−0.19***	−0.17***
	(2.13)	(2.06)	(4.34)	(4.10)
Mother's education (1962)	0.11**	0.11**	−0.01	−0.01
	(2.81)	(2.59)	(0.82)	(0.65)
Father's education (1962)	0.22***	0.22***	0.04***	0.04***
	(7.15)	(7.36)	(3.89)	(3.60)
Mother's premarital pregnancy status	−0.03	−0.02	−0.02	−0.01
	(0.15)	(0.11)	(0.34)	(0.13)
Mother's age at marriage	0.06**	0.06**	0.0001	0.00004
	(2.82)	(2.72)	(0.02)	(0.01)
Household size (1962)	−0.17***	−0.17***	−0.01	−0.01
	(3.19)	(3.15)	(0.74)	(0.61)
Equity and assets				
Home equity[b]				
None in 1962; some in 1966	0.16	0.16	0.03	0.02
	(0.70)	(0.73)	(0.38)	(0.31)
Some in 1962; none in 1966	−0.25	−0.21	0.18	0.17
	(0.58)	(0.47)	(1.17)	(1.01)
Some in 1962; some in 1966 (high average)	0.44*	0.44*	−0.02	−0.03
	(1.67)	(1.68)	(0.20)	(0.33)
Some in 1962; some in 1966 (low average)	0.19	0.21	−0.05	−0.07
	(0.82)	(0.93)	(0.63)	(0.87)

Assets[c]				
None in 1962; some in 1966	0.32	0.28	−0.15	−0.16
	(1.01)	(0.88)	(1.37)	(1.42)
Some in 1962; none in 1966	0.22	0.22	0.11	0.10
	(0.78)	(0.78)	(1.15)	(1.05)
Some in 1962; some in 1966	0.43*	0.44*	0.09	0.08
	(1.77)	(1.82)	(1.04)	(0.99)
Average number of cars (1962, 1966)	0.02	0.02	−0.06	−0.07
	(0.13)	(0.11)	(1.11)	(1.19)
Aspirations for children				
Put money aside for child's college in 1962	−0.06	−0.06	0.10*	0.10**
	(0.47)	(0.45)	(2.20)	(2.34)
Children should go to college	0.21		−0.04	
	(1.55)		(0.81)	
Expects children will go to college		0.21		−0.03
		(1.63)		(0.67)
Sum of aspirations for child	−0.01	−0.01	0.005	0.003
	(0.40)	(0.23)	(0.38)	(0.27)
Child wanted by both parents	−0.05	−0.03	0.08	0.09
	(0.25)	(0.15)	(1.16)	(1.41)
Constant	7.508	8.009	4.750	4.655
Adjusted R^2	0.239	0.241	0.055	0.052
N	815	825	809	819

* $p < .05$; ** $p < .01$; *** $p < .001$.

Source: Authors' calculations using data on 867 families from the Intergenerational Panel Study of Mothers and Children.

a. t-ratios in parentheses.

b. Families with no home equity in both 1962 and 1966 were the omitted group.

c. Families with no liquid assets in both 1962 and 1966 were the omitted group.

esteem. While liquid assets appeared to have no significant impact on children's self-esteem (table 16.4), this result was actually the product of averaging the strong positive effects of liquid assets on male children's self-esteem with the negative effects of liquid assets on female children's self-esteem. Parents' income had a significantly greater positive effect on females' self-esteem (see table 16.3), but parents' liquid assets improved males' self-esteem and reduced females'. The reasons for this sex difference, or the differential effects of income and liquid assets, are far from obvious. However, both the strong effects of sex on self-esteem and these important sex differences in the impact of parental financial resources suggest that the processes of self-esteem formation may be quite different for young women than for young men. Researchers who examine the impact of parental economic resources on self-esteem thus have the imperative to consider men and women separately.

DISCUSSION

Our investigation of completed schooling and self-esteem revealed important differences in their intergenerational determinants. Like most studies of completed schooling, and despite our relatively homogeneous sample, we found that differences in parental family background accounted for a substantial share of the variance in completed schooling. In contrast, parents' income, assets, and marital experiences accounted for relatively little of the variance in children's self-esteem at age twenty-three.

The economic resources of the parental family appear to be important determinants of completed schooling. Even with controls for parental schooling, children raised in families with income persistently below twice the poverty line completed about one year less schooling, on average, than did children with parental family incomes that were always above this threshold.

To extend our basic analysis of completed schooling, we focused on a set of measures unique to our data set, all gathered in early childhood. A decided advantage of the timing of these parental measures is that they were all gathered prior to the point of entry into school and thus prior to the point before possible contamination by outside opinion on the children's abilities. The analysis reinforced the evidence suggesting that economic resources play a key role in completing school. Parents who reported higher incomes and greater net equity in their homes and who persistently reported liquid assets had children with significantly more years of completed schooling. Children growing up in families with more children and thus more people among whom to apportion income and assets completed less schooling. More than merely providing money to finance college tuition, parents' economic resources appeared to matter at all levels of schooling.

In contrast, subjective reports of parents' aspirations for their children failed to account for many significant differences in how much schooling their children completed. The one exception was that mothers who reported that they felt their children *should* go to college had a significant positive effect on their sons' educational attainment, an effect that was not significant for daughters. Thus parents' aspirations and expectations for their children early in their lives appear to have less impact on levels of completed schooling than do other dimensions of the parents' home, such as education, income, assets, and family size.

In sharp contrast, parents' economic resources appear to have relatively little influence on their children's self-esteem in early adulthood. Instead, in our sample parents' decisions to save money, early in their children's lives, for their children's eventual college enrollment increased their children's self-esteem at age twenty-three. Since the same saving behavior did not influence actual educational attainment, these decisions likely reflect high levels of parental support and involvement in their children's lives, which may be the link to children's self-esteem. Whatever the case, these saving decisions early in infancy appear to have remarkably long-term effects on children, increasing their self-esteem well into early adulthood.

Some economic factors indeed appear to influence self-esteem, but the nature of these effects depends on the children's sex. Parents' income had a significantly more positive influence on daughters' self-esteem than on sons' in our study, while parents' liquid assets had significantly more positive consequences for sons' self-esteem than for daughters'. The contrasting directions of these sex differences are not easy to explain. However, they suggest that the processes linking parental financial resources to children's early adult self-esteem are highly dependent on the children's sex.

Overall, our results provide evidence that future work on both the long-term effect of subjective aspects of the parents' home on educational attainment and on the effect of parents' income and wealth on self-esteem will need to address sex-specific causal processes. Given our results, stronger models of the long-term impact of the parental family on children's self-esteem will likely focus on subjective aspects of the parents' home, such as conflict between parents, parent-child relationships, parents' support for children, and parents' involvement in their children's lives. While parents' income and wealth significantly increased children's educational attainment, we did not find evidence of any significant relationship between the economic attributes of the parents' home and children's self-esteem as adults.

The research summarized in this chapter was funded by the National Institute for Child Health and Development's Family and Child Well-Being Research Network, whose generosity is greatly appreciated. We also thank Jennifer Barber, Gail Johnston, and Stephanie Bohon for their assistance with the analyses reported here and Cassie Johnstonbaugh for help preparing the manuscript.

NOTES

1. For example, no data on income were missing from our measure of 1961 income. Tests for the effects of missing data revealed that controls for missing data on income did not alter the results presented in tables 16.2–16.4.

2. This figure was the mean equity (inflated to 1992 dollars) for the 490 families who had some equity in both 1962 and 1966. The mean equity for all families in the sample was only $149,769 (average of 1962 and 1966 inflated to 1992 dollars).

3. Note that these wealth measures were positively correlated with each other and with our income measures. However, the correlations ranged from only .15 to .35.

4. This measure had a positive correlation of .20 with our measure of average income. The other aspiration measures have smaller correlations with income.

5. Correlations among these subjective evaluation measures and our income measures were trivially small.

6. Mothers' and fathers' educations had a positive correlation of .51 and were positively correlated with our income measures in the range of .30–.50.

7. However, in *F*-tests for the significance of adding the set of dummy variables measuring household equity and that dummy variables measuring liquid assets, each failed to significantly improve the overall model fit.

8. This effect was somewhat (but not significantly) stronger for female children than for male children.

9. Being an unwanted child had a significant negative effect on young people's adult self-esteem when the other economic factors in table 16.4 were excluded from the model.

Chapter 17

Does Poverty in Adolescence Affect the Life Chances of High School Graduates?

Robert M. Hauser and Megan M. Sweeney

For more than thirty-five years, the Wisconsin Longitudinal Study (WLS) has followed a cohort of more than 10,000 men and women who graduated from high school in 1957. The sample was followed up in 1964, 1975, and, most recently, in 1992–93. The WLS is best known for having developed a social psychological model that accounts for the effects of social background and mental ability on postsecondary schooling and occupational careers (Sewell and Hauser 1992a, 1992b). In 1991–94, a cross-disciplinary team of researchers again followed up the WLS sample at ages fifty-three and fifty-four, and a broad array of measurements of socioeconomic, familial, and health outcomes that cover much of the life course are now available (Hauser et al. 1992; Hauser et al. 1994). In this chapter, we report on the estimation of the effects of poverty during adolescence on several social, economic, and health outcomes.

THE WISCONSIN LONGITUDINAL STUDY

The WLS cohort of men and women, born mainly in 1939, precedes by about a decade the bulk of the baby-boom generation that continues to tax social institutions and resources at each stage of life. The WLS is the first of the large, longitudinal studies of American adolescents, and it thus provides the first large-scale opportunity to study the life course from late adolescence through the mid-fifties in the context of a complete record of ability, aspiration, and achievement.[1]

The WLS is based upon a simple one-third random sample of graduates of public and private Wisconsin high schools in the class of 1957. The sample is broadly representative of middle-aged, white American men and women who have completed at least a high school education. Among American women and men aged fifty to fifty-four in 1990 and 1991, approximately 66 percent are whites of non-Hispanic background who have completed at least twelve years of schooling (Kominski and Adams 1992). The members of the sample are mainly of German, English, Irish, Scandinavian, Polish, or Czech ancestry. Some strata of American society are not represented in the WLS. For example, everyone in the primary sample graduated from high school. Sewell and Hauser (1975) estimated that about 75 percent of Wisconsin youth graduated from high schools in the late 1950s, but 7 percent of the WLS siblings did not. Minorities are not well represented; only a handful of African American, Hispanic, or Asian persons are in the sample. About 19 percent of the WLS sample is of farm origin, consistent with national estimates of persons of farm origin in cohorts born in the late 1930s. In 1964, in 1975, and again in 1992, 70 percent of the sample lived in Wisconsin, and 30 percent lived elsewhere in the United States or abroad.

Despite these limitations, the WLS provides a long-term look at the development of the life course from adolescence to midlife in a cohort of men and women who resemble a large segment of the U.S. population. The sample is large, sample retention is very high (compare Jencks et al. 1979, 6–7; Center for Human Resource Research 1992), and measurements are of high (and often of known) quality. In the 1975 survey, approximately 9,140 of the original respondents were interviewed, and in the 1992–93 survey, approximately 8,500. By that time, about 575 of the original 10,317 members of the sample had died. The WLS has fared well in comparisons of findings with national studies of comparable populations (Sewell and Hauser 1975; Jencks, Crouse, and Mueser 1983; Corcoran et al. 1992).[2]

Many previous studies using WLS data have measured the influence of economic origins on social and economic outcomes. Early, cross-tabular analyses of educational aspirations represented socioeconomic background with a factor-weighted composite of mother's education, father's education, father's occupational status, and parents' income. In later analyses of education, occupational status, and earnings, these four variables were disaggregated (Hauser 1972; Sewell and Hauser 1975; Sewell, Hauser, and Wolf 1980). Some of this work with disaggregated measures of social and economic background investigated whether economic, educational, or occupational origins had distinctive effects on post–high school outcomes. In general, each dimension of social standing affected all outcomes, directly or indirectly, and those effects were essentially the same across several adolescent outcomes (Hauser, Tsai, and Sewell 1983). However, economic, educational, and occupational origins also had some specific effects. Parents' schooling had a larger-than-expected effect on sons' and daughters' schooling; parents' occupational status had a persistent effect on sons' and daughters' occupational status; and parents' income had a persistent effect on sons' and daughters' earnings (Sewell and Hauser 1975; Hauser, Sewell, and Warren 1994).

No previous study based on the WLS has focused specifically on the consequences of adolescent poverty. For obvious reasons, one would not expect to find extremely high rates of adolescent poverty in the WLS, and the definition of the sample appears to limit the likely consequences of impoverished origins. All members of the sample are high school graduates, very few are minorities, and the state of Wisconsin, if not uniformly affluent, has historically had relatively low rates of poverty and of income inequality.[3] Another factor in measuring the influence of poverty in this Wisconsin cohort is the prevalence of farm origins. It is no higher than the contemporary national rate, but the production of income in kind was very likely higher in the late 1950s than now, and a measure based on cash income may overstate the incidence of adolescent poverty in the WLS. Thus, we have carried out some analyses for the population of nonfarm origin, as defined by father's occupation in 1957, as well as in the full WLS sample.[4]

DATA

Measures of Socioeconomic Background

If the WLS has substantial limitations for the present purpose, it also has some advantages. Economic origins and several other social background characteristics have been measured well. While we have attempted to produce the standard set of estimates of the effects of adolescent poverty, we have also estimated those same effects using an expanded vector of social background characteristics of men and women (table 17.1).[5] Family structure was not ascertained in the early rounds of the study but was measured retrospectively in the 1975 or 1992 survey. Ninety percent of the sample reported living in an intact family most of the time up to the senior year of high school, and half the female household heads were widows. Thus, the sources of family dissolution in the Wisconsin sample were far different from those prevailing in younger cohorts.

We obtained virtually complete data on parental schooling by combining reports from the 1957, 1975, and 1992 surveys. Paternal and maternal occupations were ascertained in those surveys and, for this analysis, we mapped them into the Stevens-Featherman socioeconomic index of occupational status for men (MSEI2). MSEI2 is a weighted average of occupation-specific education and income among male jobholders in the 1970 census, in which the weights were chosen to predict ratings of occupational prestige during the 1960s (Stevens and Featherman 1981). The MSEI2 index ranges from 11 to 89. About two-thirds of the respondents' mothers did not work for pay when they were seniors in high school. We assigned the mean of the mother's occupational status to cases in which the mother did not work for pay, and we introduced a dummy variable for a mother not working for pay. Thus, the coefficients of the dummy variable contrasted people whose mothers did not work for pay to people with an average working mother. We also introduced a dummy variable for fathers with farm occupations; the coefficients of that variable contrasted people whose fathers farmed with people whose fathers had the same score as farmers (22.2) on the MSEI2. The number of siblings was ascertained in the 1975 or 1992 surveys, and the population of the town containing the respondent's high school was grouped (roughly) into eight categories by log of size in 1960.

(Text continued on p. 548.)

Table 17.1 / Sources and Descriptions of Variables Used in the Analysis of Adolescent Poverty and the Life Course

Variable[a]	Source	Description	All Respondents			Men			Women		
			Mean	*SD*	*N*	Mean	*SD*	*N*	Mean	*SD*	*N*
Social and economic background variables											
Sex	1957 survey	Coded 1 if female; 0 otherwise	0.52	0.50	9,611	0.00	0.00	4,570	1.00	0.00	5,041
Intact family	1993, 1975 surveys[b]	Coded 1 if intact; 0 otherwise	0.90	0.30	9,611	0.90	0.30	4,570	0.89	0.31	5,041
Mother head of household, widowed	—	Coded 1 if mother head, widowed; 0 otherwise	0.03	0.16	9,611	0.02	0.16	4,570	0.03	0.16	5,041
Mother head of household, other reason	—	Coded 1 if mother head, other reason; 0 otherwise	0.03	0.17	9,611	0.03	0.16	4,570	0.03	0.18	5,041
Father head of household, any reason	—	Coded 1 if father head, other reason; 0 otherwise	0.02	0.13	9,611	0.02	0.13	4,570	0.02	0.13	5,041
Other head of household	—	Coded 1 if other person head; 0 otherwise	0.03	0.17	9,611	0.03	0.17	4,570	0.03	0.17	5,041
Mother's education	1993, 1975, 1957 surveys[b]	Years of school completed	10.47	2.80	9,611	10.62	2.78	4,570	10.33	2.81	5,041
Father's education	1993, 1975, 1957 surveys[b]	Years of school completed	9.77	3.37	9,611	9.82	3.41	4,570	9.72	3.33	5,041
Mother's job status	1993, 1975 surveys[b]	MSE12 score of 1957 occupation	29.89	9.34	3,508	29.98	9.40	1,615	29.81	9.29	1,893
Mother's occupational-specific education	1993, 1975 surveys;[b] 1970 Census data	Median years of education for occupation	11.86	0.97	3,508	11.87	0.97	1,615	11.85	0.97	1,893
Mother's occupational-specific earnings	1993, 1975 surveys;[b] 1970 Census data	Mean earnings for occupation, 1992 $ (10,000)	1.50	0.29	3,508	1.50	0.29	1,615	1.50	0.30	1,893
Father's job status	1993, 1975 surveys[b]	MSEI2 score of 1957 occupation	32.25	16.53	9,611	32.43	16.82	4,570	32.08	16.27	5,041

Father's occupational-specific education	1993, 1975 surveys;[b] 1970 Census data	Median years of education for occupation	11.88	1.57	9,611	11.90	1.60	4,570	11.86	1.54	5,041
Father's occupational-specific earnings	1993, 1975 surveys;[b] 1970 Census data	Mean earnings for occupation, 1992 $ (10,000)	3.11	1.12	9,611	3.12	1.14	4,570	3.11	1.11	5,041
No job reported for mother in 1957	1993, 1975 surveys[b]	Coded 1 if no job reported; 0 otherwise	0.64	0.48	9,611	0.65	0.48	4,570	0.62	0.48	5,041
Farm background	Wisconsin tax records	Coded 1 if father was a farmer; 0 otherwise	0.20	0.40	9,611	0.20	0.40	4,570	0.20	0.40	5,041
Number of siblings	1993, 1975 surveys[b]	Living in 1975 (excludes respondent)	2.97	2.27	9,611	2.92	2.23	4,570	3.01	2.30	5,041
Size of place of origin	1957 survey	Scored 2–9 based on size of place, with 9 being largest	5.03	2.27	9,611	4.93	2.23	4,570	5.12	2.31	5,041
Average parental income	Wisconsin tax records	1992 $ (10,000)	2.82	2.55	9,611	2.84	2.62	4,570	2.81	2.49	5,041
Income-to-needs ratio	Tax records; 1975, 1993 surveys[b]	Parent's 1957 income (1992 $) divided by needs as defined by 1992 poverty thresholds	1.99	1.88	9,611	2.00	1.85	4,570	1.98	1.91	5.041
<1	—	Coded if <1; 0 otherwise	0.22	0.42	9,611	0.22	0.41	4,570	0.23	0.42	5,041
1–2	—	Coded 1 if 1–2; 0 otherwise	0.41	0.49	9,611	0.41	0.49	4,570	0.42	0.49	5,041
2–3	—	Coded 1 if 2–3; 0 otherwise	0.24	0.43	9,611	0.25	0.43	4,570	0.23	0.42	5,041
3+	—	Coded 1 if 3+; 0 otherwise	0.13	0.33	9,611	0.13	0.33	4,570	0.13	0.33	5,041
Social psychological variables											
Mental ability	Wisconsin Testing Service	Normalized score on Henmon-Nelson test taken in 11th grade	100.89	14.70	9,611	101.11	15.04	4,570	100.68	14.38	5,041
Rank in high school class	School records	Ranked and normalized report of average grades in high school	100.83	14.36	9,611	97.55	14.14	4,570	103.80	13.91	5,041

(Table continued on p. 546.)

Table 17.1 / (*continued*)

Variable[a]	Source	Description	All Respondents			Men			Women		
			Mean	*SD*	*N*	Mean	*SD*	*N*	Mean	*SD*	*N*
Academic program	1957 survey	Coded 1 if completed University of Wisconsin entrance requirements; 0 otherwise	0.59	0.49	9,611	0.65	0.48	4,570	0.53	0.50	5,041
Parents' encouragement	1957 survey	Coded 1 if reported parental encouragement to attend college; 0 otherwise	0.52	0.50	9,611	0.59	0.49	4,570	0.46	0.50	5,041
Teachers' encouragement	1957 survey	Coded 1 if reported teachers' encouragement to attend college; 0 otherwise	0.43	0.49	9,611	0.45	0.50	4,570	0.40	0.49	5,041
Friends' college plans	1957 survey	Coded 1 if most friends planned to attend college; 0 otherwise	0.39	0.49	9,611	0.37	0.48	4,570	0.41	0.49	5,041
Educational aspiration	1957 survey	Coded 1 if planned to attend college; 0 otherwise	0.44	0.50	9,611	0.41	0.49	4,570	0.46	0.50	5,041
Occupational aspiration	1957 survey	Duncan SEI score	49.58	21.52	9,611	48.73	26.42	4,570	50.87	15.75	5,041
Educational attainment by 1975 (years)											
12	1975, 1993 surveys[b]	Coded 1 if 12 years; 0 otherwise	0.63	0.48	9,611	0.56	0.50	4,570	0.70	0.46	5,041
13–15	—	Coded 1 if 13–15 years; 0 otherwise	0.13	0.34	9,611	0.14	0.35	4,570	0.12	0.33	5,041
16+	—	Coded 1 if 16+ years; 0 otherwise	0.23	0.42	9,611	0.29	0.45	4,570	0.17	0.38	5,041

Outcome variables											
1a: Some post–high school education	1975, 1993 surveys[b]	Coded 1 if 13+ years; 0 otherwise	0.36	0.48	9,549	0.44	0.50	4,547	0.30	0.46	5,002
1b: 16+ years of education (given some post–high school education)	1975, 1993 surveys[b]	Coded 1 if 13+ years; 0 otherwise	0.63	0.48	3,474	0.67	0.47	1,979	0.58	0.49	1,495
2: Status of first occupation	1975, 1993 surveys[b]	MSEI2 score	37.36	19.83	8,970	36.63	23.30	4,320	38.04	15.91	4,650
3: Status of 1992 occupation	1993 survey	MSEI2 score	44.20	20.00	7,181	45.30	21.56	3,675	43.05	18.15	3,506
4: Log of 1992 base hourly wage	1993 survey	Current dollars (plus $.50 start value)	2.64	0.71	6,739	2.92	0.71	3,478	2.33	0.58	3,261
5: Below poverty threshold in 1992	1975, 1993 surveys[b]	Coded 1 if respondent and spouse's total 1992 income is less than needs as defined by 1992 poverty thresholds	0.02	0.15	5,824	0.01	0.12	3,051	0.03	0.17	2,773
6: Fair or poor health	1993 survey	Coded 1 if yes; 0 otherwise	0.13	0.34	6,793	0.12	0.33	3,152	0.13	0.34	3,641
7: High depression in 1992	1993 survey	Coded 1 if top 20% on CES-D depression scale; 0 otherwise	0.21	0.41	6,820	0.19	0.39	3,168	0.23	0.42	3,652
8: Death by 1992	1975, 1993 surveys	Covers survivors to 1975 or later; coded 1 if death occurred, 0 otherwise	0.04	0.19	9,611	0.04	0.20	4,570	0.03	0.17	5,041

Source: Authors' calculations using data from the Wisconsin Longitudinal Study (WLS).

a. In a small number of cases, missing data on regressions were filled with means, and dummy variables for missing data were added to regression models.

b. In most cases, missing data on those not responding to the 1975 survey were filled in during the 1993 interview.

Parents' income was the adjusted gross income reported on federal tax forms for the years 1957–60, the years during which respondents were most likely to have attended postsecondary school. It was ascertained from Wisconsin state income tax files, which include copies of the federal tax forms. Unfortunately, the original, year-by-year measures have been lost, and we now have data on income only in the first year for which it was available along with an average for all available years. In this analysis, we used only the average income, inflated from 1958 to 1992 dollars using the consumer price index. We constructed income-to-needs ratios using the intact family measure, the number of siblings (including the respondent) aged eighteen or less in 1957, and the official 1992 poverty thresholds (U.S. Department of Commerce 1993). Despite the selection of the sample by schooling, more than one-fifth of the sample came from families in which the income-to-needs ratio was less than 1.0, and only in 13 percent of the sample was it larger than 3.0.

Two factors probably contributed to the seemingly high incidence of poverty in the Wisconsin sample. First, the data pertain to the beginning of the current era of poverty measurement. In 1959, for example, 22.4 percent of all persons in the United States were poor by the official definition. Among related children under eighteen, 26.5 percent were poor in 1960. Second, poverty rates differ sharply between the nonfarm and farm populations. Nationally in 1960, in the nonfarm population 19.6 percent were poor, and in the farm population 51.3 percent were poor (Danziger and Weinberg 1994, 26, 37). These estimates are similar to the poverty rates defined by average income in the Wisconsin sample: 14.4 percent among nonfarm youths and 53.9 percent among farm youths. Third, one could reasonably argue that, before 1960, the current official poverty standard may have been too high relative to more recent periods, thus leading to an overestimate of the share of Wisconsin graduates in poverty (Citro and Michael 1995, 34–35).

Measures of Adolescent Achievement and Aspiration

In addition to considering social background variables, in part of the analysis we went beyond the estimation of reduced-form equations to introduce a set of social psychological variables measured during the high school years. In other analyses, these variables have explained much of the influence of social background characteristics on postsecondary schooling and attainment (Sewell 1971; Sewell, Hauser, and Wolf 1980; Hauser, Tsai, and Sewell 1983). Mental ability was measured using the Henmon-Nelson test, which was administered to all high school juniors in Wisconsin. The test scores were obtained from the Wisconsin State Testing Service, a unit of the University of Wisconsin, which helped to administer and evaluate the tests and then archived the records. Scores were converted to percentiles among Wisconsin students on whom the test had been normed, and the percentiles were then transformed into the standard metric of IQ. High school rank was obtained from the records of each high school, expressed as a percentile, and transformed into the IQ metric. In the original 1957 survey, students were asked to report the number of courses completed in several academic fields. These responses were compared with the entrance requirements of the University of Wisconsin in 1957. Students who had completed those requirements were classified as having taken an academic program.

The 1957 survey included three measures of social influence on college attendance: parents' encouragement to attend college, teachers' encouragement to attend college, and friends' college plans. We coded educational aspirations as high if the respondent planned to enter a four-year college or university in the fall of 1957. Occupational aspirations were ascertained in response to a question about the kind of job that the respondents "eventually hoped to enter." We coded these into broad occupational groups and then mapped them into Duncan's (1961) socioeconomic index (SEI) for occupations.[6]

Indicators of the Life Course

We examined the effects of sex, poverty, and social background on nine selected outcomes in the Wisconsin data, ranging in content from education to mental health and covering the life course from high school graduation to the early fifties. We estimated logistic regression equations for dichotomous outcomes and linear regressions for continuously measured outcomes.

In the case of education, we first analyzed the transition from high school graduation to the completion of any further academic schooling. Then, among persons with any further schooling, we analyzed the transition to college graduation. We looked at two measures of occupational standing, each indexed by MSEI2: first full-time civilian occupation held after the respondent left school for the last time and occupation in 1992. We also analyzed base hourly wage rates in 1992–93. Using the combined earnings of the respondent and his or her spouse in 1992–93, along with data on family composition, we constructed and analyzed poverty at midlife. Both the earning and poverty measures were problematic: cases where zero earnings were reported were eliminated from the analysis if positive earnings were indicated by other characteristics of the 1992 job. We believe that many of the "zero" earners were actually refusals rather than nonearners. For example, based on their other social and economic characteristics, zero earners did not appear to be substantially worse off than earners in other respects. However, we may have eliminated some impoverished individuals and families from the analysis. For the analysis of poverty in 1992 we also eliminated retired respondents and spouses. Although the small number of very early retirees often reported low earnings, they were also very likely to have been raised in high-income families.

We also looked at selected measures of health and health-related behavior in the 1992–93 survey. Those analyses were based on roughly 80 percent of telephone respondents who also completed a mail survey on health and personality.

We looked at reports of fair or poor health and at persons in the highest fifth on a standard measure of depression, the Center for Epidemiological Studies Depression scale (CES-D) (Radloff 1977).[7] Finally, we analyzed mortality in the WLS sample. Because our full sample was limited to those responding to either the 1975 or the 1992–93 surveys, this measure reflected mortality occurring after age thirty-six.

MODEL SPECIFICATIONS

We estimated six standard models and their variants for each of the outcomes observed in the WLS (table 17.2). Lowercase roman numerals describe standard models and letters denote our extensions of the standard models. Model *i* includes only sex, plus a minimal specification of socioeconomic status (mother's educational attainment and family structure). Model *ii* includes sex and the income-to-needs ratio but excludes the other background measures. In model *iii* we combined the variables in models *i* and *ii*; that is, it includes sex, income-to-needs ratio, mother's education, and family structure. In model *iv* we substituted number of siblings and average parental income for the income-to-needs ratio in model *iii*, and in model *v* we substituted dummy variables for income-to-needs ratios less than 1.0, from 2.0 to 2.9, and 3.0 or higher for the linear specification in model *iii*; thus, the reference category consisted of families with an income-to-needs ratio between 1.0 and 1.9. Model *ix* added the interaction between sex and income-to-needs ratio to the specification of model *iii*. Our interest lies primarily in the coefficients of income-to-needs ratio, parents' income, and their interactions—the replication analysis common to chapters 5–17 of this volume—and we present the full set of coefficients and standard errors from these equations in tables 17A.1–17A.9.

We estimated five variants of model *iii*. In model *iii-HN*, we added the score on the Henmon-Nelson test of mental ability to the minimal specification of social background. This tells us how much of the effects of social background, in this specification, are explained by its correlation with mental ability, as measured during the junior year of high school. In model *iiia*, we added an extended set of social and economic background characteristics: father's educational attainment, mother's occupational status, father's occupational status, farm background, number of siblings, and size of place of origin.[8] We believe that model *iiia* provides a more complete specification of measured social background than model *iii* does. Thus, we want to see how the effects of the income-to-needs ratio and of parents' average income changed when these variables were added to the model. In model *iiia-HN*, we added the score on the Henmon-Nelson test of mental ability to the extended specification of social background. This tells us the degree to which the effects of the larger vector of social background characteristics are explained by their correlation with mental ability.

In model *iiiaf*, we retained the full specification of social and economic back-

TABLE 17.2 / Models Used in the Analysis of Adolescent Poverty and the Life Course[a]

Model	Independent Variables
i	Sex, socioeconomic status 1[b]
ii	Sex, income-to-needs ratio
iib	Sex, average parental income, number of siblings
iic	Sex, income-to-needs ratio <1, income-to-needs ratio 2–3, income-to-needs ratio 3+
iii	Sex, socioeconomic status 1, income-to-needs ratio
iii-HN	Model iii plus Henmon-Nelson mental ability score
iiia	Model iii plus socioeconomic status 2[c]
iiia-HN	Model iiia plus Henmon-Nelson mental ability score
iiiaf	Model iiia plus all social psychological variables[d]
iiiafe	Model iiiaf plus educational attainment
iv	Sex, socioeconomic status 1, average parental income, number of siblings
iva	Model iv plus socioeconomic status 2
ivaf	Model iva plus all social psychological variables
ivafe	Model ivaf plus educational attainment
v	Sex, socioeconomic status 1, income-to-needs ratio <1, income-to-needs ratio 2–3, income-to-needs ratio 3+
va	Model v plus socioeconomic status 2
vaf	Model va plus all social psychological variables
vafe	Model vaf plus educational attainment
ix	Sex, socioeconomic status 1, income-to-needs ratio, sex by income-to-needs ratio
ixa	Sex, socioeconomic status 1, socioeconomic status 2, income-to-needs ratio, sex by income-to-needs ratio, sex by socioeconomic status 1, sex by socioeconomic status 2

Source: Models to be estimated using data from the Wisconsin Longitudinal Study (WLS).

a. All models also contain dummy variables for missing data.

b. Mother's education, family structure (intact family, mother headed–widowed, mother headed–other reason, father headed–any reason, other head). In a few models, family structure was collapsed into the categories "intact family" and "nonintact family."

c. Father's education, father's occupational status in 1957, mother's occupational status in 1957, dummy variable indicating mother not working in 1957, farm background, number of siblings, 1957 population of high school town.

d. Mental ability, rank in high school class, academic program, parents' encouragement, teachers' encouragement, friends' plans, college plans, and occupational aspiration.

ground, plus mental ability, and added the remaining social psychological variables: the respondent's rank in high school class, academic program, parents' encouragement to attend college, teachers' encouragement to attend college, friends' college plans, educational plans, and occupational aspirations. One might think of mental ability as predetermined, along with the other social background variables, or as a consequence of them; the other variables, we believe, are consequences of social background and ability. With the addition of those variables, we took model *iiiaf* to represent a set of social, economic, and psychological conditions in late adolescence. To the extent that adolescent poverty affects life chances in model *iiiaf*, we argue that its influence persists beyond the completion of secondary school. In model *iiiafe*, we added indicators of postsecondary educational attainment to model *iiiaf*. Thus, to the extent that adolescent poverty affects life chances in model *iiiafe*, we argue that its influence persists beyond entry into adulthood.

We estimated similar sets of models that replaced the income-to-needs ratio with average parental income and number of siblings. In this respect, model *iib* corresponds to model *ii*, model *iv* to model *iii*, model *iva* to model *iiia*, model *ivaf* to model *iiiaf*, and model *ivafe* to model *iiiafe*. We also estimated models in which the income-to-needs ratio was expressed with a series of dummy variables rather than in a single linear term. In model *iic*, the only regressors are the income-to-needs dummies and sex. In model *v*, we added mother's education and family structure to model *iic*. In models *va*, *vaf*, and *vafe*, we added our extended vector of social background variables, the social psychological variables, and educational attainment.

In brief, we wished to know (1) whether adolescent poverty appears to affect life chances merely because it correlates with other family and social background characteristics, (2) whether adolescent poverty appears to affect life chances merely because it correlates with mental ability, (3) whether the effects of adolescent poverty are linear, and (4) whether the effects of adolescent poverty last only through their influence on late adolescent development and opportunity or have a longer-lasting, direct influence on the life course.

We also investigated whether the effects of adolescent poverty and of other social and economic background characteristics differed by sex. Model *ix* added the interaction between sex and the income-to-needs ratio to model *iii*, and model *ixa* added the extended vector of social and economic background variables and the interaction between sex and each of those variables.

Statistical Inference

Because we estimated a great many models containing a large number of variables in a rather large sample, we expected to find many nominally significant effects merely by chance and many that are substantively trivial. To discipline our analysis and discussion, we did not rely upon the usual .05 or .01 significance levels but flagged coefficients for which there was either "strong" or "very strong" evidence, as indicated by the Bayesian information criterion (BIC) developed by Raftery (1995).[9] By strong evidence we mean a posterior probability of 95–99 in favor of the alternative hypothesis ($6 < \text{BIC} < 10$), and by very strong evidence we mean a posterior probability greater than 99 in favor of the alternative hypothesis ($\text{BIC} > 10$). These are stringent criteria. For example, in a logistic regression carried out in the full WLS sample ($N = 9{,}611$), the ratio of a coefficient to its standard error had to be 3.89 to provide strong evidence and 4.38 or larger to provide very strong evidence. In the logistic regression of college graduation, where $N = 3{,}474$, the corresponding t-ratios were 3.76 and 4.26.

FINDINGS

The correlations among the nine outcome variables except those between death by 1992 and outcomes measured only in the 1992–93 surveys all had the expected signs, but none was larger than 0.66 (table 17.3). That is, we found no reason to suppose, a priori, that adolescent poverty needed to have similar relationships with the outcomes. Socioeconomic variables, except poverty status in 1992, were more highly intercorrelated than are the other, more heterogenous set of outcomes.

Effects of Poverty in Adolescence

Table 17.4 summarizes the effects of income-to-needs ratio on the nine outcome variables under a variety of model specifications. The estimates from model *ii* showed strong or very strong evidence that poverty in adolescence was associated with lowered educational, occupational, and economic chances (table 17.4). However, it had no relationship with poverty in 1992. Nor was there strong evidence that poverty in adolescence was associated with any of the recent social or health-related outcome measures: fair or poor health, depression, or mortality. When mother's education and family structure were controlled (model *iii*), the regressions of education, occupational status, and wage rate on income-to-needs were reduced by about 20 percent. In all cases but one (college graduation), the evidence remained very strong. However, when we introduced the extended set of social background characteristics (model *iiia*), the remaining effects of income-to-needs were substantially less. Between model *ii* and model *iiia*, the previously strong coefficients decreased by about 65 percent; between model *iii* and model *iiia*, by about 55 percent. In model *iiia*, the evidence remained very strong only that poverty during adolescence affected completion of some postsecondary education and the status of the first job, and it remained strong that poverty affected base hourly wage in 1992. Thus, model *iii* did not fully control the socioeconomic char-

TABLE 17.3 / Correlations among Outcome Variables

Variable	1a	1b	2	3	4	5	6	7	8
1a: Some post–high school education	1.00								
1b: 16+ years of education (given some post–high school education)		1.00							
2: Status of first occupation	0.66	0.61	1.00						
3: Status of 1992 occupation	0.52	0.40	0.59	1.00					
4: Log of 1992 base hourly wage	0.33	0.20	0.28	0.39	1.00				
5: Below poverty threshold in 1992	−0.03	−0.02	−0.03	−0.05	−0.14	1.00			
6: Fair or poor health	−0.07	−0.07	−0.08	−0.07	−0.07	0.08	1.00		
7: High depression in 1992	−0.08	−0.04	−0.06	−0.09	−0.09	0.07	0.21	1.00	
8: Death by 1992	−0.01	−0.03	−0.00						1.00

Source: Authors' calculations using data from the Wisconsin Longitudinal Study (WLS).

TABLE 17.4 / Effect of Income-to-Needs Ratio under Various Model Specifications[a]

	Dependent Variable								
Model	1a	1b	2	3	4	5	6	7	8
ii	0.413**	0.074*	1.906**	1.622**	0.042**	0.009	−0.035	−0.043	−0.022
	(0.020)	(0.018)	(0.110)	(0.125)	(0.004)	(0.051)	(0.022)	(0.019)	(0.033)
iii	0.336**	0.053	1.482**	1.252**	0.033**	−0.003	−0.021	−0.022	−0.010
	(0.020)	(0.017)	(0.110)	(0.125)	(0.004)	(0.054)	(0.022)	(0.018)	(0.032)
iii-HN	0.309**	0.045	1.141**	0.932**	0.026**	0.014	−0.013	−0.012	−0.010
	(0.021)	(0.017)	(0.102)	(0.117)	(0.004)	(0.051)	(0.021)	(0.018)	(0.033)
iiia	0.149**	0.036	0.518**	0.426	0.017*	−0.009	−0.003	−0.030	−0.045
	(0.020)	(0.018)	(0.115)	(0.132)	(0.004)	(0.060)	(0.022)	(0.020)	(0.041)
iiia-Ed/Earn	0.157**	0.040	0.555**	0.434	0.014	0.011	−0.002	−0.026	−0.050
	(0.020)	(0.018)	(0.117)	(0.134)	(0.005)	(0.060)	(0.022)	(0.020)	(0.041)
iiia-Ed	0.162**	0.036	0.564**	0.465	0.018*	−0.018	−0.003	−0.030	−0.038
	(0.020)	(0.018)	(0.114)	(0.131)	(0.004)	(0.062)	(0.022)	(0.020)	(0.040)
iiia-HN	0.153**	0.038	0.441*	0.364	0.015	−0.005	−0.001	−0.027	−0.045
	(0.021)	(0.019)	(0.108)	(0.124)	(0.004)	(0.060)	(0.022)	(0.020)	(0.041)
iiiaf	0.081*	0.040	0.146	0.115	0.011	−0.001	0.006	−0.022	−0.051
	(0.020)	(0.019)	(0.097)	(0.117)	(0.004)	(0.060)	(0.021)	(0.020)	(0.041)
iiiafe	n/a	n/a	−0.185	−0.065	0.008	−0.000	0.008	−0.021	−0.045
			(0.077)	(0.111)	(0.004)	(0.060)	(0.021)	(0.020)	(0.041)

* Strong evidence; ** very strong evidence.

Source: Authors' calculations using data from the Wisconsin Longitudinal Study (WLS).

a. Variables defined in table 17.1. Models described in table 17.2. Standard errors in parentheses.

acteristics of the family of orientation. The failure to control other relevant background characteristics led to a substantial overstatement of the effects of adolescent poverty on the life course of the Wisconsin graduates. Ultimately, a one-unit change in the income-to-needs ratio led to a 16 percent increase in the odds of completing any postsecondary schooling, a 0.5 point increase in the status of the first occupation, and a 2 percent increase in base hourly wage, but it had little influence on other indicators of the life chances of the Wisconsin graduates.

The best-selling treatise by Herrnstein and Murray (1994) emphasizes the importance of ability relative to socioeconomic background in the attainments of young adults. Thus, we examined the effects of poverty during adolescence when measured mental ability is included in the analysis. Adding mental ability to the minimal specification of social background (model *iii-HN*) weakened the evidence that adolescent poverty affected socioeconomic outcomes. For example, the effect of poverty on continuation to postsecondary schooling fell by about 8 percent, and the effects on the occupational status of the first job, in 1975, and in 1992 by 15–25 percent. All the same, and contrary to some of the arguments of Herrnstein and Murray, there remained very strong evidence that the income-to-needs ratio affected socioeconomic achievement. Therefore, we again added mental ability to the model (model *iiia-HN*), but this time to the specification that also included an expanded vector of social background characteristics. Here, while the influence of the income-to-needs ratio was weaker to begin with, the incremental importance of ability in accounting for that influence was also much less. However, once ability was controlled, the effects of adolescent poverty on base hourly wage no longer met our criterion of strong evidence. It is interesting to compare the effects of adding ability to model *iii* to those of adding the expanded set of socioeconomic background variables to model *iii*; the correlation between poverty and mental ability was less important in explaining the association between adolescent poverty and life chances than was the correlation between poverty and other aspects of social and economic background.

Our measures of ability, as well as of poverty and social background, pertain to late adolescence. Thus, our findings are not inconsistent with the report in chapter 7 that early childhood poverty delays cognitive development. However, before reaching strong conclusions about the effect of economic deprivation *per se*, we think it important to assess its effects in the context of a full array of social background effects, such as those we introduced in model *iiia*.

One friendly critic has suggested that the additional socioeconomic background variables, especially mother's and father's occupational status, are simply proxies for income. If so, the reduced effects of adolescent poverty in our extended specification would not be surprising, nor would they suggest a lesser role for family economic standing in life chances. We disagree with this interpretation of our findings. First, our expanded specification includes several variables other than occupational status: father's education, size of the child's place of origin, farm background, and number of siblings. Second, a four-year average of adjusted gross income from income tax records is unlikely to be dominated by less proximate measures of family income. If that were the case, then we should be inclined to distrust other, survey-based estimates of the effects of family or household income. Third, as a test of the source of the effects of occupational status, we assembled data on the typical educational and income levels of detailed occupations from the 1970 Census of Population (U.S. Department of Commerce 1973). In model *iiia-Ed/Earn,* we substituted mean occupation earnings and median education for the MSEI2 of the mother's and father's occupations with very little effect on the coefficients of the income-to-needs ratio. In model *iiia-Ed,* we dropped mean earnings from the specification, again with very little difference in the coefficients of the income-to-needs ratio. Thus, the typical economic level of occupations had very little to do with the reduction of income-to-needs effects in the expanded specification of social background.

Thus far, we have considered only relevant correlates of adolescent poverty that are predetermined with respect to the life course by adolescence. In model *iiiaf,* we added the full vector of adolescent social and psychological variables (including mental ability) and asked whether they mediated the effects of adolescent poverty. The short answer is that they did: in no case was there very strong evidence, and only for completion of any postsecondary education was there strong evidence, that income-to-needs ratio affected postsecondary outcomes once the social background and social psychological variables were controlled. Even at the usual 0.05 probability level, only three significant coefficients remained, those pertaining to post–high school education and base hourly wage in 1992. This is not to say that income-to-needs ratio had no effects, but rather that the effects that appear in model *iiia* were largely mediated by other adolescent outcomes.

The introduction of ability to the analysis (in models *iii-HN* and *iiia-HN*) differs in important ways from the introduction of the full vector of social psychological variables in model *iiiaf.* When the specification of social background was weak, ability appeared to account for a much larger share of the effect of social background on social and economic outcomes than when the specification of social background was strong. Moreover, although the influence of poverty on the life course appears to be determined in large part by way of late adolescent development, that proposition holds only when one enlarges the definition of development to comprise a much larger set of achievements, aspirations, and social circumstances.

Finally, we introduced educational attainment in model *iiiafe,* and no strong effects of income-to-needs ratio remained. There remained only a nominally significant effect of poverty on the 1992 wage rate and an anomalous negative effect of poverty on the status of first jobs; none of the remaining five effects is even nominally significant. That is, the effects of adolescent poverty were exhausted by way of their direct and indirect influence on academic performance, social support, aspiration, and postsecondary schooling. A good start in early adulthood made deprived economic origins irrelevant to later life chances.

The models for the effects of average parental income on the nine outcome measures parallel those for income-to-needs ratio, except that we dropped the income/needs ratio from the equations and replaced it by number of siblings and parents' average income (table 17.5). The findings were essentially the same as those for income-to-needs ratio: adolescent poverty was strongly associated with education, occupational status, and wages but not with other outcomes. With the exception of obtaining sixteen or more years of education (given some postsecondary schooling), the evidence of these associations remained very strong when mother's education and family structure were controlled. However, the evidence was substantially weaker when the extended set of social background factors was controlled. The remaining, very strong evidence of effects on postsecondary education and the early career was largely explained by the social psychological variables.

The effects of the dummy-variable representation of income-to-needs ratio on each outcome variable were close to linear when they were significant (table 17.6). For example, we contrasted the fit of models *iii* and *v* in tables 17A.1–17A.9, thus comparing the linear and nonlinear specifications of the income-to-needs ratio when sex, maternal schooling, and family structure were controlled. Only the contrast for any postsecondary schooling showed substantial improvement in fit in the nonlinear specification. Thus, effects of the income-to-needs dummy variables mainly reinforced our earlier findings and provided illustrative contrasts between youths whose families were above and those whose families were below the poverty line.

Because so large a share of the families in the Wisconsin sample fell below the official poverty line, we also ran models *v* and *va* with a more detailed breakdown of income-to-needs ratios below the poverty threshold (table 17.7). We might have expected to find that falling into the lowest tenth or lowest twentieth of the family income distribution had substantial effects even if being in the bottom fifth did not. However, the results did not show any substantial or reliable gradations in the effects of adolescent poverty below the 20th percentile. Our inclination is not to conclude that adolescent poverty or extreme poverty is inconsequential in the general population. Again, we remind readers that all of the members of the Wisconsin sample had completed high school and thus had surpassed one of the most important obstacles created by childhood poverty.

Effects of Sex and Social Background

We then examined the effects of sex and mother's schooling on the outcome variables (table 17.8), along with those of income-to-needs ratio (reported in table 17.4, model *iii*). With this specification of social background, the effects both of sex and of mother's education appeared to be more persistent across the life course than those of adolescent poverty. For example, there was very strong evidence that women were more likely than men to fall below the poverty line in 1992, but the effects of the income-to-needs ratio did not meet our standard of strong evidence. Women were also more likely than men to be depressed, while the respondents

(Text continued on p. 564.)

TABLE 17.5 / Effect of Average Parents' Income under Various Model Specifications[a]

	Dependent Variable								
Model	1a	1b	2	3	4	5	6	7	8
iib	0.288**	0.054*	1.209**	1.068**	0.029**	−0.001	−0.030	−0.038	−0.022
	(0.015)	(0.013)	(0.080)	(0.091)	(0.003)	(0.040)	(0.017)	(0.015)	(0.026)
iv	0.226**	0.038	0.928**	0.826**	0.023**	−0.011	−0.020	−0.022	−0.010
	(0.016)	(0.013)	(0.080)	(0.091)	(0.003)	(0.043)	(0.017)	(0.014)	(0.025)
iva	0.114**	0.028	0.386**	0.331	0.012	−0.016	−0.003	−0.024	−0.037
	(0.015)	(0.013)	(0.083)	(0.095)	(0.003)	(0.047)	(0.016)	(0.015)	(0.031)
ivaf	0.048	0.025	0.070	0.064	0.007	−0.007	0.005	−0.016	−0.042
	(0.015)	(0.014)	(0.070)	(0.084)	(0.003)	(0.046)	(0.015)	(0.015)	(0.031)
ivafe	n/a	n/a	−0.134	−0.039	0.005	−0.007	0.006	−0.016	−0.039
			(0.056)	(0.080)	(0.003)	(0.046)	(0.015)	(0.015)	(0.031)

* Strong evidence; ** very strong evidence.

Source: Authors' calculations using data from the Wisconsin Longitudinal Study (WLS).

a. Variables defined in table 17.1. Models described in table 17.2. Standard errors in parentheses.

TABLE 17.6 / Effect of Income-to-Needs Dummy Variables under Various Model Specifications[a]

Model and Income-to-Needs Ratio[b]	Dependent Variable								
	1a	1b	2	3	4	5	6	7	8
iic									
<1	−0.411**	−0.059	−3.771**	−3.814**	−0.109**	0.083	0.173	0.104	−0.036
	(0.064)	(0.112)	(0.547)	(0.621)	(0.021)	(0.245)	(0.095)	(0.080)	(0.145)
2–3	0.421**	−0.018	3.412**	3.025**	0.085*	−0.052	0.024	0.089	−0.194
	(0.055)	(0.089)	(0.529)	(0.597)	(0.020)	(0.231)	(0.093)	(0.076)	(0.145)
3+	1.396**	0.373	10.210**	8.530**	0.245**	−0.047	−0.212	−0.172	−0.114
	(0.071)	(0.100)	(0.667)	(0.753)	(0.025)	(0.309)	(0.125)	(0.101)	(0.179)
v									
<1	−0.303**	−0.023	−2.899**	−3.014**	−0.090*	0.124	0.153	0.065	−0.069
	(0.066)	(0.113)	(0.536)	(0.615)	(0.021)	(0.248)	(0.095)	(0.081)	(0.146)
2–3	0.385**	−0.055	3.026**	2.740**	0.080*	−0.057	0.038	0.104	−0.184
	(0.057)	(0.090)	(0.517)	(0.589)	(0.020)	(0.232)	(0.094)	(0.076)	(0.146)
3+	1.206**	0.261	8.185**	6.761**	0.205**	−0.123	−0.153	−0.084	−0.063
	(0.074)	(0.102)	(0.660)	(0.751)	(0.026)	(0.314)	(0.126)	(0.102)	(0.181)
va									
<1	−0.103	−0.041	−0.902	−0.775	−0.047	0.144	0.163	0.106	0.031
	(0.071)	(0.119)	(0.556)	(0.644)	(0.022)	(0.265)	(0.102)	(0.086)	(0.155)
2–3	0.164	−0.061	0.808	0.893	0.052	−0.078	0.044	0.066	−0.275
	(0.062)	(0.094)	(0.522)	(0.601)	(0.021)	(0.241)	(0.097)	(0.079)	(0.150)
3+	0.690**	0.146	2.928*	2.611	0.136**	−0.207	−0.069	−0.107	−0.239
	(0.082)	(0.112)	(0.693)	(0.796)	(0.027)	(0.336)	(0.135)	(0.109)	(0.195)

vaf									
<1	0.114	0.063	0.083	0.077	−0.028	0.148	0.139	0.085	0.027
	(0.093)	(0.129)	(0.468)	(0.569)	(0.021)	(0.266)	(0.103)	(0.087)	(0.155)
2–3	0.202	−0.018	0.458	0.357	0.043	−0.058	0.054	0.079	−0.286
	(0.082)	(0.102)	(0.440)	(0.532)	(0.020)	(0.243)	(0.098)	(0.080)	(0.151)
3+	0.602**	0.208	1.102	1.075	0.109*	−0.204	−0.024	−0.083	−0.270
	(0.108)	(0.121)	(0.586)	(0.707)	(0.026)	(0.338)	(0.136)	(0.111)	(0.197)
vafe									
<1			−0.271	−0.145	−0.032	0.150	0.140	0.085	0.036
			(0.373)	(0.539)	(0.021)	(0.266)	(0.103)	(0.087)	(0.155)
2–3			0.093	0.170	0.041	−0.059	0.054	0.079	−0.281
			(0.350)	(0.504)	(0.020)	(0.243)	(0.098)	(0.080)	(0.151)
3+			−1.264	−0.325	0.090	−0.197	−0.009	−0.081	−0.233
			(0.468)	(0.671)	(0.026)	(0.339)	(0.136)	(0.111)	(0.197)

* Strong evidence; ** very strong evidence.

Source: Authors' calculations using data from the Wisconsin Longitudinal Study (WLS).

a. Variables defined in table 17.1. Models described in table 17.2. Standard errors in parentheses.

b. Families with income-to-needs ratios of 1–2 were the omitted category.

TABLE 17.7 / Effect of Detailed Income-to-Needs Dummy Variables under Various Model Specifications[a]

Model and Rank in Income Distribution[b]	Dependent Variable								
	1a	1b	2	3	4	5	6	7	8
v									
Lowest 5%	−0.340	−0.363	−3.029	−2.695	−0.063	−0.615	−0.144	−0.021	0.173
	(0.120)	(0.206)	(0.948)	(1.107)	(0.037)	(0.603)	(0.186)	(0.148)	(0.233)
Lowest 5–10%	−0.335	0.419	−2.609	−2.287	−0.134	0.173	0.215	0.055	−0.072
	(0.120)	(0.221)	(0.933)	(1.078)	(0.037)	(0.415)	(0.161)	(0.140)	(0.257)
Lowest 10–15%	−0.207	0.024	−2.962	−3.163	−0.097	0.581	0.246	0.132	−0.329
	(0.116)	(0.200)	(0.946)	(1.058)	(0.036)	(0.359)	(0.158)	(0.137)	(0.286)
Lowest 15–22%	−0.325	−0.106	−2.976	−3.631*	−0.071	0.035	0.216	0.078	−0.096
	(0.102)	(0.176)	(0.816)	(0.933)	(0.032)	(0.390)	(0.141)	(0.122)	(0.226)
Income-to-needs ratio 2–3	0.385**	−0.056	3.026**	2.740**	0.080*	−0.057	0.038	0.104	−0.184
	(0.057)	(0.090)	(0.517)	(0.589)	(0.020)	(0.232)	(0.094)	(0.076)	(0.146)
Income-to-needs ratio 3+	1.206**	0.261	8.184**	6.758**	0.205**	−0.123	−0.153	−0.083	−0.064
	(0.074)	(0.102)	(0.660)	(0.751)	(0.026)	(0.314)	(0.126)	(0.102)	(0.181)
va									
Lowest 5%	−0.143	−0.387	−1.087	−0.554	−0.026	−0.592	−0.126	0.016	0.227
	(0.125)	(0.209)	(0.939)	(1.108)	(0.038)	(0.609)	(0.189)	(0.151)	(0.239)
Lowest 5–10%	−0.114	0.383	−0.422	0.347	−0.084	0.221	0.239	0.108	0.054
	(0.125)	(0.226)	(0.937)	(1.097)	(0.038)	(0.433)	(0.168)	(0.145)	(0.265)
Lowest 10–15%	0.008	−0.004	−0.750	−0.695	−0.052	0.595	0.255	0.183	−0.203
	(0.121)	(0.205)	(0.944)	(1.067)	(0.037)	(0.373)	(0.164)	(0.141)	(0.292)
Lowest 15–22%	−0.145	−0.088	−1.197	−1.687	−0.033	0.061	0.221	0.110	−0.002
	(0.106)	(0.180)	(0.810)	(0.934)	(0.032)	(0.398)	(0.145)	(0.125)	(0.231)
Income-to-needs ratio 2–3	0.164	−0.062	0.803	0.877	0.052	−0.079	0.044	0.065	−0.275
	(0.062)	(0.094)	(0.522)	(0.601)	(0.021)	(0.241)	(0.097)	(0.079)	(0.150)
Income-to-needs ratio 3+	0.690**	0.144	2.922*	2.591	0.136**	−0.207	−0.070	−0.107	−0.239
	(0.082)	(0.112)	(0.693)	(0.797)	(0.027)	(0.336)	(0.135)	(0.110)	(0.195)

* Strong evidence; ** very strong evidence.

Source: Authors' calculations using data from the Wisconsin Longitudinal Study (WLS).

a. Variables defined in table 17.1. Models described in table 17.2. Standard errors in parentheses.

b. Families with income-to-needs ratios of 1–2 were the omitted category.

TABLE 17.8 / Effects of Sex, Mother's Education, and Income-to-Needs Ratio under Models iii and ix[a]

	Dependent Variable								
Model and Variable[b]	1a	1b	2	3	4	5	6	7	8
iii									
Sex	−0.609**	−0.430**	2.002**	−1.933*	−0.583**	0.803*	0.081	0.267**	−0.321
	(0.046)	(0.072)	(0.403)	(0.459)	(0.016)	(0.191)	(0.073)	(0.061)	(0.111)
Mother's education	0.199**	0.070**	1.491**	1.286**	0.031**	0.048	−0.043	−0.063**	−0.026
	(0.009)	(0.013)	(0.074)	(0.083)	(0.003)	(0.033)	(0.013)	(0.011)	(0.020)
Income-to-needs ratio	0.336**	0.053	1.482**	1.252**	0.033**	−0.003	−0.021	−0.022	−0.010
	(0.020)	(0.017)	(0.110)	(0.125)	(0.004)	(0.054)	(0.022)	(0.018)	(0.032)
ix									
Sex	−0.894**	−0.333	2.980**	−1.257	−0.540**	0.872	0.013	0.364*	−0.351
	(0.090)	(0.111)	(0.585)	(0.668)	(0.023)	(0.286)	(0.112)	(0.091)	(0.165)
Mother's education	0.198**	0.070**	1.494**	1.290**	0.032**	0.048	−0.043	−0.062**	−0.026
	(0.009)	(0.013)	(0.073)	(0.083)	(0.003)	(0.033)	(0.013)	(0.011)	(0.020)
Income-to-needs ratio	0.410**	0.038	1.244**	1.088**	0.023*	−0.017	−0.007	−0.047	−0.002
(females)	(0.029)	(0.020)	(0.151)	(0.171)	(0.006)	(0.070)	(0.027)	(0.026)	(0.045)
Income-to-needs ratio	0.262**	0.079	1.740**	1.430**	0.045**	0.018	−0.042	0.004	−0.018
(males)	(0.027)	(0.029)	(0.156)	(0.179)	(0.006)	(0.080)	(0.036)	(0.024)	(0.046)
Income-to-needs ratio	0.148	−0.041	−0.496	−0.342	−0.022	−0.034	0.035	−0.050	0.016
by sex	(0.040)	(0.035)	(0.215)	(0.245)	(0.008)	(0.106)	(0.045)	(0.036)	(0.063)

* Strong evidence; ** very strong evidence.

Source: Authors' calculations using data from the Wisconsin Longitudinal Study (WLS).

a. Variables defined in table 17.1. Models described in table 17.2. Standard errors in parentheses.

b. Family structure variables are included in the models, but their effects are not presented.

whose mothers had higher levels of education had lower chances of depression. Adolescent poverty did not affect either poverty or depression in 1992.

The lower panel of table 17.8 shows sex-related differences in the effects of income-to-needs ratio on the outcome variables. None of these interactions met our standard of strong evidence, but the income-to-needs ratio had nominally significant interaction effects on the completion of any postsecondary schooling, early occupational status, and base hourly wage. Women were more likely to complete some postsecondary schooling, but they entered the labor force in lower status jobs and earned lower wages in 1992. In most cases, the income-to-needs ratio affected the same socioeconomic outcomes among men and among women.[10]

We then investigated the effects and sex interactions of each variable in our expanded definition of social and economic background (table 17.9). In the first panel, the line for income-to-needs ratio is the same as that in table 17.4. We found no strong evidence that the effects of any of the background variables except sex extended beyond the socioeconomic outcomes, aside from a negative association between mother's education and depression. At the same time, the evidence that mother's education, father's education, father's occupational status, number of siblings, and size of place of origin affected education, occupational status, and wages was generally as strong as or stronger than it was for the income-to-needs ratio. Again, we do not claim that adolescent poverty had no effects, but its effects are a small share of the overall influence of disadvantaged or advantaged social background.

We next extracted the main effect of sex and its interaction effects with each of the other social background variables from equations that also included the main effects of the background variables and of family structure (table 17.9, panel 2). Briefly, very few sex interactions met our evidentiary criteria. The estimates showed very strong evidence for an interaction effect of sex with income-to-needs ratio only for obtaining any postsecondary schooling. There were few other noteworthy interaction effects. Women with farm backgrounds were more likely than men with farm backgrounds to obtain any postsecondary schooling, and they were also advantaged in occupational status. Presumably, these effects reflect the greater likelihood that farm boys themselves entered farming. In addition, there was strong evidence that mother's education had a larger effect on the postsecondary schooling of daughters than of sons and that size of the place of origin had a stronger effect on the secondary schooling of sons than of daughters. We also found strong evidence that father's occupational status had a larger effect on the status of the first jobs of sons than on those of daughters.

Social Psychological Factors in Attainment

We have shown that many of the effects of adolescent poverty are exhausted through their influence on late adolescent development and opportunity; that is, poverty had no lagged effects later in the life course of the Wisconsin graduates.[11]

Here we look more closely at early adult outcomes and at the longer-term effects of the social and psychological variables. Our analysis is guided by the causal scheme in figure 17.1, developed by Sewell and his colleagues (Sewell, Haller, and Portes 1969; Sewell, Haller, and Ohlendorf 1970; Sewell 1971; Sewell, Hauser, and Wolf 1980; Hauser, Tsai, and Sewell 1983). The model posits a recursive causal process leading from social background to postschooling outcomes through school performance, social influences, educational and occupational aspirations, and postsecondary schooling. While the figure shows all possible recursive causal paths, theoretical presentations of the model emphasize the importance of a limited set of paths, leading from background to performance, from performance to social influences, from performance and social influences to aspirations, and from aspirations to schooling and postsecondary outcomes (Hauser, Tsai, and Sewell 1983). In other words, the main paths in the model form a modified causal chain in which the social psychological variables—labeled as the block of intermediate variables in the figure—explain the influence of social background on schooling and later attainment.

We estimated coefficients of sex and the intermediate variables in reduced-form equations for educational attainment in the model of figure 17.1 (table 17.10). Because schooling mediated much of the influence of the intermediate variables on adult outcomes, we show coefficients only for the logistic regressions of any postsecondary schooling and of college graduation. Selected effects of the extended specification of social background have already been presented (table 17.9).

The intermediate variables did not explain the effects of sex on either measure of postsecondary schooling, nor did they account for the effects of mental ability or class rank on college completion. However, social influences and aspirations did account for much of the effect of mental ability, high school rank, and academic program on whether a graduate completed any postsecondary schooling. The effect of mental ability declined from 0.025 to 0.017 as social influences and aspirations were added to the model, while the effect of rank in high school class declined from 0.044 to 0.022. The effect of completing an academic program declined from 1.245 to 0.526 as the intermediate variables were controlled. However, we found very strong evidence that all three measures of school performance affect postsecondary schooling, net of the social influences and aspirations. In the case of college completion, we found only nominal evidence that completion of an academic program affects college graduation among persons with some postsecondary schooling, and much of that effect is mediated by social influences and aspirations.

The evidence is strong that social influences and aspirations affect the completion of some postsecondary schooling but have only nominally significant effects on college completion. About half of the effects of the social influences on postsecondary schooling are mediated by educational and occupational aspirations.

We estimated the effects of sex and the intermediate variables on postschooling outcomes based on model *iiiaf* (table 17.11); thus the models are equivalent to those for schooling outcomes in column 3 of table 17.10. The contrast between

TABLE 17.9 / Effects of Sex, Social Background, and Income-to-Needs Ratio under Models iiia and ixa[a]

Model and Variable[b]	Dependent Variable								
	1a	1b	2	3	4	5	6	7	8
iiia									
Sex	−0.670**	−0.463**	1.945**	−1.987**	−0.587**	0.796*	0.086	0.265**	−0.328
	(0.048)	(0.073)	(0.390)	(0.449)	(0.015)	(0.191)	(0.073)	(0.061)	(0.111)
Mother's education	0.099**	0.024	0.584**	0.602**	0.019**	0.063	−0.021	−0.052*	−0.026
	(0.010)	(0.015)	(0.083)	(0.096)	(0.003)	(0.039)	(0.015)	(0.013)	(0.024)
Father's education	0.098**	0.063**	0.739**	0.510**	0.008	−0.008	−0.035	−0.017	−0.010
	(0.009)	(0.013)	(0.075)	(0.086)	(0.003)	(0.034)	(0.014)	(0.012)	(0.021)
Father's job status	0.021**	0.003	0.169**	0.130**	0.003*	−0.001	−0.006	0.000	0.009
	(0.002)	(0.002)	(0.015)	(0.017)	(0.001)	(0.007)	(0.003)	(0.002)	(0.004)
Mother's job status	0.015**	0.002	0.110**	0.067	0.001	−0.004	0.003	−0.007	−0.011
	(0.003)	(0.004)	(0.022)	(0.025)	(0.001)	(0.011)	(0.004)	(0.004)	(0.007)
Mother not working	−0.024	−0.067	−0.771	−0.936	−0.014	0.428	0.075	−0.068	−0.140
	(0.051)	(0.080)	(0.420)	(0.484)	(0.017)	(0.208)	(0.079)	(0.064)	(0.117)
Number of siblings	−0.090**	−0.023	−0.669**	−0.361	−0.000	−0.008	−0.017	−0.012	0.011
	(0.012)	(0.020)	(0.091)	(0.106)	(0.004)	(0.043)	(0.017)	(0.014)	(0.026)
Farm background	0.116	0.267	−0.654	−2.688*	−0.061	0.211	−0.021	−0.032	−0.266
	(0.071)	(0.120)	(0.550)	(0.630)	(0.022)	(0.258)	(0.100)	(0.085)	(0.171)
Size of place	0.053**	−0.019	0.453**	0.503**	0.021**	0.064	−0.002	0.022	0.011
	(0.012)	(0.017)	(0.096)	(0.111)	(0.004)	(0.045)	(0.018)	(0.015)	(0.027)
Income-to-needs ratio	0.149**	0.036	0.518**	0.426	0.017	−0.009	−0.003	−0.030	−0.045
	(0.020)	(0.018)	(0.115)	(0.132)	(0.004)	(0.060)	(0.022)	(0.020)	(0.041)

ixa									
Sex	−1.815**	−1.343	4.318	−4.103	−0.428**	2.391	−0.068	1.161	−0.304
	(0.307)	(0.438)	(2.275)	(2.640)	(0.090)	(1.191)	(0.436)	(0.358)	(0.692)
Sex by mother's education	0.086*	0.039	0.296	0.263	0.003	−0.087	−0.014	−0.021	0.012
	(0.021)	(0.031)	(0.166)	(0.192)	(0.007)	(0.083)	(0.031)	(0.026)	(0.048)
Sex by father's education	0.002	0.002	−0.405	−0.256	−0.003	0.016	0.010	−0.013	0.029
	(0.018)	(0.026)	(0.148)	(0.172)	(0.006)	(0.071)	(0.028)	(0.023)	(0.042)
Sex by father's job status	0.003	−0.008	−0.121*	−0.044	−0.003	−0.008	0.001	−0.006	−0.009
	(0.004)	(0.005)	(0.029)	(0.034)	(0.001)	(0.014)	(0.006)	(0.005)	(0.008)
Sex by mother's job status	0.001	0.011	0.034	0.062	0.001	0.004	−0.003	−0.003	0.003
	(0.005)	(0.008)	(0.045)	(0.051)	(0.002)	(0.023)	(0.009)	(0.007)	(0.014)
Sex by mother not working	0.216	0.137	1.457	0.175	−0.037	0.702	−0.279	−0.039	−0.200
	(0.104)	(0.162)	(0.836)	(0.966)	(0.033)	(0.431)	(0.160)	(0.131)	(0.172)
Sex by number of siblings	−0.026	−0.011	0.146	0.085	−0.006	−0.022	0.034	−0.044	0.070
	(0.025)	(0.041)	(0.181)	(0.211)	(0.007)	(0.090)	(0.035)	(0.029)	(0.052)
Sex by farm background	0.718**	0.128	5.758**	5.050*	0.087	−1.357	−0.327	−0.036	−0.162
	(0.143)	(0.240)	(1.091)	(1.257)	(0.043)	(0.536)	(0.201)	(0.173)	(0.345)
Sex by size of place	−0.094*	0.066	−0.399	−0.050	−0.013	−0.098	0.089	−0.003	0.014
	(0.024)	(0.035)	(0.191)	(0.222)	(0.008)	(0.095)	(0.037)	(0.030)	(0.053)
Sex by income-to-needs ratio	0.183**	−0.029	0.419	0.115	−0.008	−0.055	−0.006	−0.042	0.055
	(0.040)	(0.038)	(0.228)	(0.263)	(0.009)	(0.114)	(0.044)	(0.041)	(0.080)

* Strong evidence; ** very strong evidence.

Source: Authors' calculations using data from the Wisconsin Longitudinal Study (WLS).

a. Variables defined in table 17.1. Models described in table 17.2. Standard errors in parentheses.

b. Many variables included in the models not shown. Refer to tables 17.1 and 17.2 for variable definitions and model specifications.

FIGURE 17.1 / A Social Psychological Model of Attainment

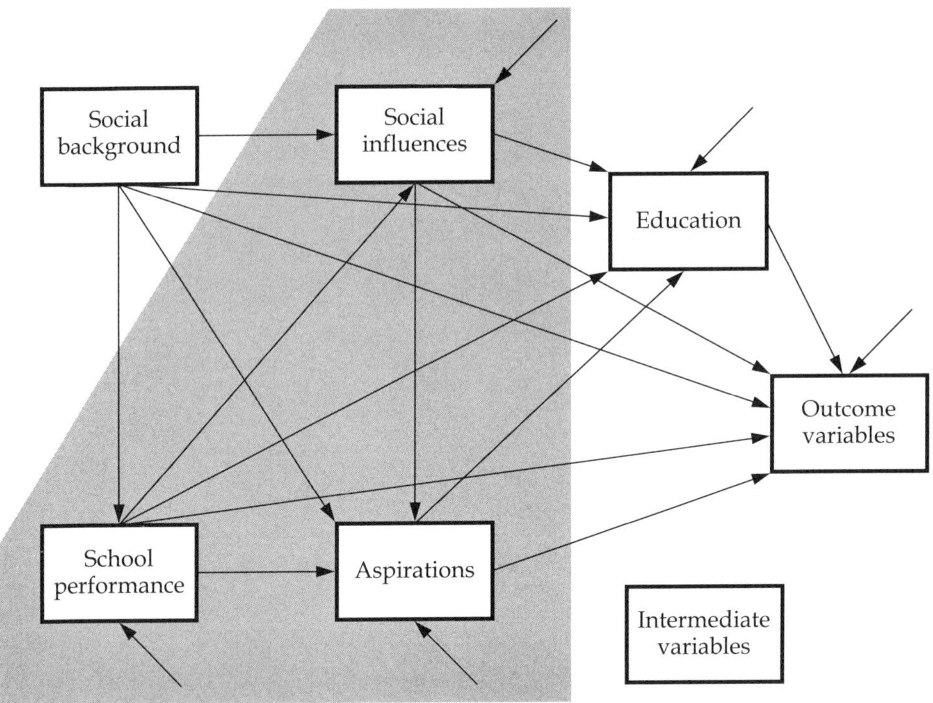

Source: Based on authors' interpretation of Sewell, Haller, and Fortes (1969); Sewell, Haller, and Ohlendorf (1970); Sewell (1971); Sewell, Hauser, and Wolf (1980); Hauser, Tsai, and Sewell (1983).

those coefficients and the corresponding coefficients based on model *iiiafe* (table 17.12), which includes postsecondary schooling, shows the extent to which effects of the social psychological variables were mediated by educational attainment.

Whether or not schooling was controlled, mental ability, rank in high school class, and following an academic program continued to affect some adult socioeconomic outcomes, but none of them affected poverty, physical or mental health, or mortality. Much of the influence of mental ability on early and midlife occupational status was mediated by schooling, but schooling accounted for more of the early than the later effect of ability on job status. Also striking is that the effect of mental ability on occupational status increased from the first job to the 1992 job, while that of rank in high school class declined; these observations held with or without controlling the length of schooling, and they suggest that the Henmon-Nelson test reflects some abilities that are both important and somewhat different from the behaviors rewarded in the school setting. Perhaps occupational standing

TABLE 17.10 / Effects of Sex and Social Psychological Variables on Educational Attainment: Reduced-Form Equations of Model iiiaf[a]

Variable[b]	Any Post–High School Education			16+ Years of Education		
	1	2	3	1	2	3
Sex	−1.017**	−0.925**	−1.195**	−0.856**	−0.881**	−0.928**
	(0.059)	(0.064)	(0.072)	(0.084)	(0.086)	(0.089)
Mental ability	0.025**	0.019**	0.017**	0.021**	0.020**	0.020**
	(0.002)	(0.003)	(0.003)	(0.003)	(0.003)	(0.004)
Rank in high school class	0.044**	0.032**	0.022**	0.048**	0.045**	0.042**
	(0.003)	(0.003)	(0.003)	(0.004)	(0.004)	(0.004)
Academic program	1.245**	0.756**	0.526**	0.256	0.156	0.105
	(0.063)	(0.070)	(0.075)	(0.114)	(0.117)	(0.120)
Parents' encouragement		1.390**	0.765**		0.096	−0.077
		(0.069)	(0.078)		(0.122)	(0.127)
Teachers' encouragement		0.554**	0.263		0.234	0.185
		(0.063)	(0.070)		(0.088)	(0.089)
Friends' college plans		0.961**	0.567**		0.342	0.267
		(0.063)	(0.070)		(0.092)	(0.094)
Educational aspiration			1.353**			0.464
			(0.079)			(0.125)
Occupational aspiration			0.028**			0.005
			(0.002)			(0.002)

* Strong evidence; ** very strong evidence.

Source: Authors' calculations using data from the Wisconsin Longitudinal Study (WLS).

a. Variables defined in table 17.1. Models described in table 17.2. Standard errors in parentheses.

b. Many variables included in the models not shown. Refer to tables 17.1 and 17.2 for variable definitions and model specifications.

TABLE 17.11 / Effects of Sex and Social Psychological Variables under Model iiiaf[a]

	Dependent Variable						
Variable[b]	2	3	4	5	6	7	8
Sex	0.003	−2.989**	−0.608**	0.892**	0.135	0.288**	−0.212
	(0.355)	(0.428)	(0.016)	(0.206)	(0.080)	(0.066)	(0.120)
Mental ability	0.117**	0.191**	0.006**	−0.018	−0.000	−0.008	0.006
	(0.015)	(0.018)	(0.001)	(0.008)	(0.003)	(0.003)	(0.005)
Rank in high school class	0.230**	0.133**	0.001	−0.008	−0.009	−0.007	−0.017
	(0.016)	(0.019)	(0.001)	(0.008)	(0.004)	(0.003)	(0.005)
Academic program	0.292	1.983*	−0.015	−0.168	−0.041	−0.024	0.243
	(0.400)	(0.493)	(0.018)	(0.225)	(0.088)	(0.073)	(0.137)
Parents' encouragement	1.629	2.035	0.039	−0.185	−0.174	−0.199	0.066
	(0.442)	(0.537)	(0.020)	(0.256)	(0.098)	(0.081)	(0.148)
Teachers' encouragement	2.023**	2.651**	0.030	0.033	0.001	−0.099	−0.199
	(0.403)	(0.486)	(0.018)	(0.228)	(0.090)	(0.074)	(0.136)
Friends' college plans	3.069**	2.648**	0.066	0.012	−0.138	−0.155	0.062
	(0.415)	(0.501)	(0.019)	(0.238)	(0.093)	(0.077)	(0.138)
Educational aspiration	3.776**	3.364**	0.085*	−0.012	−0.033	0.048	0.222
	(0.473)	(0.577)	(0.022)	(0.265)	(0.105)	(0.087)	(0.158)
Occupational aspiration	0.224**	0.145**	0.002**	−0.003	−0.002	0.001	−0.002
	(0.010)	(0.012)	(0.000)	(0.006)	(0.002)	(0.002)	(0.003)

* Strong evidence; ** very strong evidence.

Source: Authors' calculations using data from the Wisconsin Longitudinal Study (WLS).

a. Variables defined in table 17.1. Models described in table 17.2. Standard errors in parentheses.

b. Many variables included in the models not shown. Refer to tables 17.1 and 17.2 for variable definitions and model specifications.

early in the career is more affected by signals of school performance, while other influences of ability on job performance take longer to appear. However, this interpretation is complicated by the effects of following an academic program, which affected occupational standing at midlife but not early in the career. One might argue, as in the case of ability, that taking an academic program reflects specific forms of achievement rather than an honorific distinction. That argument appears consistent with our construction of the program measure, which was based upon the courses taken in high school rather than the student's report of having been in a college preparatory program.

Schooling did not mediate the modest effect of ability on the wage rate in 1992; whether or not schooling was controlled, a 1-point difference in Henmon-Nelson IQ test score led to a 0.6 percent difference in the wage rate. Again, mental ability did not affect poverty in 1992, before or after schooling was controlled, nor did it affect our measures of health or mortality.

Among the social influences (parents' encouragement, teachers' encouragement, and friends' college plans), the evidence was very strong that teachers' encouragements and friends' plans affected occupational standing early in the career and at midlife but that these effects were largely mediated by postsecondary schooling. One exception is that teachers' encouragement continued to affect occupational status at midlife. However, parents' encouragement did not affect any of the adult outcomes once aspirations were entered into the model, and neither teachers' encouragement nor friends' plans had lagged effects on wage rates, poverty, or the health outcomes.

As in the case of the social influences, we found strong evidence that educational and occupational aspirations affected occupational status both early in the career and at midlife. Much of the influence of educational aspirations was mediated by postsecondary schooling; indeed, educational aspiration had an anomalous negative effect on early occupational status in model *iiiafe*. However, the evidence was very strong that occupational aspirations had a persistent effect on occupational status at midlife even after schooling entered the model. Educational and occupational aspirations also affected the wage rate in 1992, but these effects no longer met our criterion of strong evidence once schooling entered the model. Neither educational nor occupational aspirations affected poverty at midlife; nor did they affect our other indicators of health and well-being.

Comparisons of the coefficients of sex in tables 17.9, 17.11, and 17.12, show whether the intermediate variables or schooling accounted for sex-related differences in adult outcomes. On the whole, they did not: controlling the intermediate variables and postsecondary schooling made little difference in the significant effects of sex on wage rates, adult poverty, and depression.

The effects of the respondents' sex on occupational status were more complex. When social background alone was controlled, there was strong evidence that women obtained first jobs with higher status than men did but that this advantage was reversed by midlife (table 17.9). After the intermediate variables were controlled, men's and women's first jobs did not differ in status, and in 1992 the jobs of women remained significantly lower in status than those of men (table 17.11).

TABLE 17.12 / Effects of Sex and Social Psychological Variables under Model iiiafe[a]

	Dependent Variable						
Variable[b]	2	3	4	5	6	7	8
Sex	4.757**	−0.248	−0.569**	0.874*	0.097	0.284*	−0.278
	(0.290)	(0.416)	(0.016)	(0.211)	(0.083)	(0.068)	(0.124)
Mental ability	0.048*	0.155**	0.006**	−0.017	0.000	−0.008	0.007
	(0.012)	(0.017)	(0.001)	(0.008)	(0.003)	(0.003)	(0.005)
Rank in high school class	0.113**	0.059	0.000	−0.008	−0.008	−0.007	−0.016
	(0.012)	(0.018)	(0.001)	(0.008)	(0.004)	(0.003)	(0.005)
Academic program	−0.504	1.486	−0.022	−0.165	−0.042	−0.024	0.255
	(0.319)	(0.469)	(0.018)	(0.225)	(0.088)	(0.073)	(0.137)
Parents' encouragement	0.082	1.089	0.026	−0.183	−0.170	−0.199	0.089
	(0.355)	(0.512)	(0.020)	(0.256)	(0.098)	(0.082)	(0.148)
Teachers' encouragement	0.789	1.957*	0.020	0.039	0.008	−0.098	−0.180
	(0.321)	(0.461)	(0.018)	(0.228)	(0.090)	(0.074)	(0.136)

Friends' college plans	0.573	1.187	0.045	0.018	−0.122	−0.153	0.095
	(0.332)	(0.477)	(0.019)	(0.239)	(0.094)	(0.077)	(0.138)
Educational aspiration	−1.808**	0.083	0.039	0.009	0.001	0.050	0.295
	(0.389)	(0.563)	(0.022)	(0.274)	(0.108)	(0.090)	(0.160)
Occupational aspiration	0.113**	0.082**	0.002	−0.002	−0.001	0.002	−0.000
	(0.008)	(0.012)	(0.000)	(0.006)	(0.002)	(0.002)	(0.003)
13–15 years of education	8.556**	5.156**	0.069	0.001	0.066	0.011	−0.169
	(0.470)	(0.650)	(0.025)	(0.323)	(0.126)	(0.106)	(0.184)
16+ years of education	32.126**	17.681**	0.250**	−0.127	−0.257	−0.023	−0.449
	(0.458)	(0.628)	(0.024)	(0.331)	(0.131)	(0.105)	(0.192)

* Strong evidence; ** very strong evidence.

Source: Authors' calculations using data from the Wisconsin Longitudinal Study (WLS).

a. Variables defined in table 17.1. Models described in table 17.2. Standard errors in parentheses.

b. Many variables included in the models not shown. Refer to tables 17.1 and 17.2 for variable definitions and model specifications.

However, net of schooling, the status of women's first jobs was substantially higher than that of men, and there was no longer any significant difference in the status of their jobs in 1992 (table 17.12). These findings consistently show a deterioration of women's occupational standing relative to men throughout the life course; in each model, the sex-related differential in 1992 occupations was less favorable to women than that in first occupations. Women initially tended to enter white-collar jobs and thus were at an advantage relative to men. Women's superior academic achievement in high school explains this advantage to some degree, and the advantage appears even larger in light of women's lower levels of postsecondary schooling, but it eventually withers away as men's careers progress.

Educational attainment had substantial effects on adult socioeconomic outcomes among the Wisconsin graduates (table 17.12). Completion of some postsecondary schooling led to an increase of 9 points on the SEI of the first job and of 5 points on the SEI of the job at midlife. Completion of college increased the status of the first job by 32 points and the status of the 1992 job by 18 points. Postsecondary schooling also affected wages at midlife. When all other variables in the model were controlled, completion of some postsecondary schooling increased the wage rate in 1992 by 7 percent, and completion of college increased it by almost 30 percent. However, schooling had little or no effect on the other outcome variables, which helps to account for the meager influence of background and intermediate variables on those outcomes.

DISCUSSION

We have examined the effects of poverty on the life chances of a cohort of Wisconsin high school graduates in the context of the larger array of social circumstances of their adolescence. If one ignores the full array of educational, occupational, and family circumstances, it is easy to overstate the importance of economic deprivation for adults' life chances. With a wider set of circumstances taken into account, the effects of adolescent poverty appear to be limited to educational and occupational chances and to be exhausted through their influence on late adolescent development and opportunity. That is, there is scant evidence that the direct effects of poverty last beyond entry into adulthood. To be sure, similar observations hold for other social conditions, such as parents' schooling and occupational standing, but there is no evidence that the effects of income or poverty loom larger over the life course than do those of other circumstances of upbringing.

We do not claim that the validity of our specific findings extends beyond the kind of population represented by the WLS, that is, high school graduates, almost all of European stock, raised in the Midwest in the years following World War II. Thus, we do not argue that our findings contradict those in chapter 15, which are based on a heterogeneous population of non–high school graduates.

At the same time, we believe that our findings should be cautionary, at least on methodological grounds, to anyone who might be tempted to focus on economic circumstances alone as determinants of life chances. We cannot think of any reason to discount our finding that maternal education and family structure cannot stand alone as controls for social background against which one can freely extrapolate estimates of the influence of economic standing. In fact, we know that the reliability of our income measurements—obtained as an average of adjusted gross income from tax records over a four-year period—is higher than that of the other measured background variables used in our analysis (Hauser, Tsai, and Sewell 1983, 38). Thus, we believe that efforts to estimate the influence of economic circumstance should be based upon an equally rich specification of noneconomic conditions of origin.

Again, we do not claim that adolescent poverty has no lasting effects. In our sample, adolescent poverty affected schooling and occupational chances, primarily by way of its effects on late adolescent development. In that way, it had indirect effects throughout the life course. Thus, our findings support the widespread belief that the developmental pathways leading from childhood to achievement and aspiration in late adolescence ought to be the main targets of policy intervention. At the same time, the large influence of other social background characteristics suggests that policies affecting income alone are unlikely to compensate fully for social disadvantage.

Nor are noneconomic circumstances of origin either immutable or insensitive to public policy. For example, as shown by the growth of academic achievement and school retention in the U.S. black population over the past twenty years, rising levels of maternal education and reduced incidence of childbearing substantially improve life chances (Hauser 1993a; Hauser 1993b; Grissmer et al. 1994). In our opinion, the social sciences have suffered from a preoccupation with current measures of income or poverty. To some degree we think this focus is program driven. In the evaluation of social, economic, and health programs, researchers have followed administrators and relied upon narrow, temporally specific economic measures of eligibility or outcome. This focus is also perhaps a consequence of the diffusion of economic thinking beyond the disciplinary boundary of economics and may reflect broader social and political trends. Whatever its sources, a narrow focus on economic resources may not be scientifically valid. We believe that overly economistic thinking may have diverted researchers from other major sources, dimensions, and consequences of social inequality.

APPENDIX: REPLICATION ANALYSIS

Tables 17A.1–17A.9 contain regression coefficients for the effects of individual and family variables on all nine outcome variables: (1a) some post–high school education, (1b) sixteen or more years of post–high school education, (2) status of first occupation, (3) status of 1992 occupation, (4) log of 1992 base hourly wage, (5) below the poverty threshold in 1992, (6) fair or poor health, (7) depression in 1992, and (8) death by 1992.

TABLE 17A.1 / Replication Analysis: Effect of Social and Economic Background on Receiving Any Post–High School Education[a]

Independent Variable	Model					
	i	ii	iii	iv	v	ix
Female	−0.580**	−0.624**	−0.609**	−0.613**	−0.610**	−0.894**
	(0.045)	(0.045)	(0.046)	(0.046)	(0.046)	(0.090)
Family-level background variables[b]						
Mother's education (years)	0.229**		0.199**	0.183**	0.202**	0.198**
	(0.009)		(0.009)	(0.009)	(0.009)	(0.009)
Mother head of household, widowed	0.143		0.203	0.371	0.230	0.203
	(0.145)		(0.146)	(0.147)	(0.147)	(0.146)
Mother head of household, other reason	−0.272		−0.242	−0.139	−0.218	−0.244
	(0.137)		(0.139)	(0.140)	(0.139)	(0.139)
Father head of household, any reason	0.004		0.093	0.114	0.086	0.100
	(0.183)		(0.184)	(0.187)	(0.186)	(0.185)
Other head of household	−0.598*		−0.562	−0.547	−0.561	−0.564
	(0.150)		(0.154)	(0.154)	(0.153)	(0.154)
Number of siblings				−0.137**		
				(0.012)		
Family economic status						
Income-to-needs ratio		0.413**	0.336**			0.262**
		(0.020)	(0.020)			(0.027)
Average parental income (10,000 $1992)				0.226**		
				(0.016)		

Income-to-needs ratio[c]						
<1					−0.303**	
					(0.066)	
2–3					0.385**	
					(0.057)	
3+					1.206**	
					(0.074)	
Sex by income-to-needs ratio						0.148
						(0.040)
Constant	−2.686	−1.066	−3.022	−2.455	−2.599	−2.880
−2 Log likelihood	11480.32	11694.35	11090.43	10971.39	11072.61	11076.55
df	7	3	9	11	11	10

* Strong evidence; ** very strong evidence.

Source: Authors' estimations of logistic regression coefficients using data on 9,549 men and women from the Wisconsin Longitudinal Study.

a. Standard errors in parentheses. Models also include dummy variables for missing data.

b. Intact families were the omitted group.

c. Families with income-to-needs ratios of 1–2 were the omitted group.

TABLE 17A.2 / Replication Analysis: Effect of Social and Economic Background on Receiving Sixteen or More Years of Education, Given Some Post–High School Education

	Model					
Independent Variable	i	ii	iii	iv	v	ix
Female	−0.417**	−0.414**	−0.430**	−0.431**	−0.429**	−0.333**
	(0.072)	(0.071)	(0.072)	(0.072)	(0.072)	(0.111)
Family-level background variables[b]						
Mother's education (years)	0.079**		0.070**	0.067**	0.071**	0.070**
	(0.013)		(0.013)	(0.013)	(0.013)	(0.013)
Mother head of household, widowed	0.210		0.241	0.270	0.258	0.248
	(0.229)		(0.230)	(0.231)	(0.231)	(0.230)
Mother head of household, other reason	−0.609		−0.582	−0.568	−0.575	−0.579
	(0.218)		(0.219)	(0.220)	(0.219)	(0.219)
Father head of household, any reason	0.065		0.089	0.108	0.081	0.091
	(0.294)		(0.294)	(0.295)	(0.295)	(0.294)
Other head of household	−0.522		−0.506	−0.484	−0.505	−0.498
	(0.250)		(0.251)	(0.252)	(0.251)	(0.251)
Number of siblings				−0.030		
				(0.019)		
Family economic status						
Income-to-needs ratio		0.074*	0.053			0.079
		(0.018)	(0.017)			(0.029)
Average parental income (10,000 $1992)				0.038		
				(0.013)		

Income-to-needs ratio[c]						
<1					−0.023 (0.113)	
2–3					−0.055 (0.090)	
3+					0.261 (0.102)	
Sex by income-to-needs ratio						−0.041 (0.035)
Constant	−0.148	0.542	−0.185	−0.074	−0.108	−0.241
−2 Log likelihood	4482.86	4516.13	4472.27	4468.09	4472.56	4470.91
df	7	3	9	11	11	10

* Strong evidence; ** very strong evidence.

Source: Authors' estimations of logistic regression coefficients using data on 3,474 men and women from the Wisconsin Longitudinal Study.

a. Standard errors in parentheses. Models also include dummy variables for missing data.

b. Intact families were the omitted group.

c. Families with income-to-needs ratios of 1–2 were the omitted group.

TABLE 17A.3 / Replication Analysis: Effect of Social and Economic Background on Status of First Job[a]

Independent Variable	Model					
	i	ii	iii	iv	v	ix
Female	1.998**	1.504	2.002**	2.079**	2.038**	2.980**
	(0.407)	(0.412)	(0.403)	(0.400)	(0.401)	(0.585)
Family-level background variables[b]						
Mother's education (years)	1.676**		1.491**	1.347**	1.434**	1.494**
	(0.073)		(0.074)	(0.074)	(0.073)	(0.073)
Mother head of household, widowed	1.607		1.970	2.782	2.390	1.973
	(1.293)		(1.297)	(1.281)	(1.283)	(1.286)
Mother head of household, other reason	−5.441**		−5.174**	−4.806*	−4.882*	−5.171**
	(1.186)		(1.182)	(1.176)	(1.177)	(1.181)
Father head of household, any reason	−0.014		0.508	0.712	0.676	0.482
	(1.598)		(1.584)	(1.574)	(1.577)	(1.584)
Other head of household	3.259		−3.119	−2.880	−2.605	−3.113
	(1.217)		(1.212)	(1.205)	(1.207)	(1.212)
Number of siblings				−1.072**		
				(0.089)		
Family economic status						
Income-to-needs ratio		1.906**	1.482**			1.740**
		(0.110)	(0.110)			(0.156)
Average parental income (10,000 $1992)				0.928**		
				(0.080)		

Income-to-needs ratio[c]						
<1					−2.899**	
					(0.536)	
2–3					3.026**	
					(0.517)	
3+					8.185**	
					(0.660)	
Sex by income-to-needs ratio						−0.496
						(0.215)
Constant	19.225	32.877	18.190	23.082	20.613	17.647
Adjusted R^2	0.062	0.033	0.081	0.093	0.089	0.082

* Strong evidence; ** very strong evidence.

Source: Authors' estimations of ordinary least squares (OLS) regression coefficients using data on 8,970 men and women from the Wisconsin Longitudinal Study.

a. Standard errors in parentheses. Models also include dummy variables for missing data.

b. Intact families were the omitted group.

c. Families with income-to-needs ratios of 1–2 were the omitted group.

TABLE 17A.4 / Replication Analysis: Effect of Social and Economic Background on Status of Job Held in 1992[a]

	Model					
Independent Variable	i	ii	iii	iv	v	ix
Female	−1.902*	−2.239**	−1.933*	−1.888*	−1.861*	−1.257
	(0.462)	(0.466)	(0.459)	(0.457)	(0.457)	(0.668)
Family-level background variables[b]						
Mother's education (years)	1.443**		1.286**	1.175**	1.221**	1.290**
	(0.082)		(0.083)	(0.084)	(0.083)	(0.083)
Mother head of household, widowed	1.210		1.402	2.131	1.823	1.414
	(1.385)		(1.385)	(1.383)	(1.381)	(1.385)
Mother head of household, other reason	−1.837		−1.610	−1.335	−1.217	−1.620
	(1.517)		(1.514)	(1.510)	(1.509)	(1.514)
Father head of household, any reason	−0.746		−0.311	−0.112	−0.201	−0.315
	(1.848)		(1.837)	(1.830)	(1.829)	(1.836)
Other head of household	−3.352		−3.158	−3.071	−2.760	−3.174
	(1.410)		(1.407)	(1.402)	(1.402)	(1.407)
Number of siblings				−0.760**		
				(0.103)		
Family economic status						
Income-to-needs ratio		1.622**	1.252**			1.430**
		(0.125)	(0.125)			(0.179)
Average parental income (10,000 $1992)				0.826**		
				(0.091)		

Income-to-needs ratio[c]						
<1					−3.014**	
					(0.615)	
2–3					2.740**	
					(0.589)	
3+					6.761**	
					(0.751)	
Sex by income-to-needs ratio						−0.342
						(0.245)
Constant	30.167	42.060	29.276	32.792	31.584	28.887
Adjusted R^2	0.047	0.026	0.060	0.067	0.068	0.060

* Strong evidence; ** very strong evidence.

Source: Authors' estimations of OLS regression coefficients using data on 7,181 men and women from the Wisconsin Longitudinal Study.

a. Standard errors in parentheses. Models also include dummy variables for missing data.

b. Intact families were the omitted group.

c. Families with income-to-needs ratios of 1–2 were the omitted group.

TABLE 17A.5 / Replication Analysis: Effect of Social and Economic Background on Log of 1992 Hourly Earnings[a]

	Model					
Independent Variable	i	ii	iii	iv	v	ix
Female	−0.583**	−0.590**	−0.583**	−0.582**	−0.581**	−0.540**
	(0.016)	(0.016)	(0.016)	(0.016)	(0.015)	(0.023)
Family-level background variables[b]						
Mother's education (years)	0.035**		0.031**	0.030**	0.029**	0.032**
	(0.003)		(0.003)	(0.003)	(0.003)	(0.003)
Mother head of household, widowed	0.048		0.046	0.061	0.060	0.047
	(0.047)		(0.047)	(0.047)	(0.047)	(0.047)
Mother head of household, other reason	0.058		0.057	0.066	0.070	0.057
	(0.052)		(0.052)	(0.052)	(0.052)	(0.052)
Father head of household, any reason	0.126		0.135	0.137	0.140	0.134
	(0.062)		(0.062)	(0.062)	(0.062)	(0.062)
Other head of household	−0.113		−0.113	−0.114	−0.101	−0.114
	(0.048)		(0.048)	(0.048)	(0.047)	(0.048)
Number of siblings				−0.011		
				(0.003)		
Family economic status						
Income-to-needs ratio		0.042**	0.033**			0.045**
		(0.004)	(0.004)			(0.006)
Average parental income (10,000 $1992)				0.023**		
				(0.003)		

Income-to-needs ratio[c]						
<1					−0.090*	
					(0.021)	
2–3					0.080*	
					(0.020)	
3+					0.205**	
					(0.026)	
Sex by income-to-needs ratio						−0.022
						(0.008)
Constant	2.549	2.837	2.521	2.571	2.587	2.496
Adjusted R^2	0.194	0.184	0.202	0.203	0.209	0.202

* Strong evidence; ** very strong evidence.

Source: Authors' estimations of OLS regression coefficients using data on 6,739 men and women from the Wisconsin Longitudinal Study.

a. Standard errors in parentheses. Models also include dummy variables for missing data.

b. Intact families were the omitted group.

c. Families with income-to-needs ratios of 1–2 were the omitted group.

TABLE 17A.6 / Replication Analysis: Effect of Social and Economic Background on Being in Poverty in 1992[a]

	Model					
Independent Variable	i	ii	iii	iv	v	ix
Female	0.794*	0.781*	0.803*	0.803*	0.803*	0.872
	(0.190)	(0.190)	(0.191)	(0.191)	(0.191)	(0.286)
Family-level background variables[b]						
Mother's education (years)	0.049		0.048	0.050	0.053	0.048
	(0.032)		(0.033)	(0.034)	(0.033)	(0.033)
Mother head of household, widowed	0.327		0.170	0.162	0.158	0.171
	(0.466)		(0.471)	(0.472)	(0.472)	(0.471)
Mother head of household, other reason	−0.418		−0.534	−0.541	−0.541	−0.534
	(0.720)		(0.722)	(0.723)	(0.722)	(0.722)
Father head of household, any reason	0.872		0.804	0.799	0.796	0.803
	(0.492)		(0.491)	(0.491)	(0.491)	(0.491)
Other head of household	−0.574		−0.699	−0.702	−0.709	−0.700
	(0.723)		(0.725)	(0.725)	(0.725)	(0.725)
Number of siblings				0.003		
				(0.041)		
Family economic status						
Income-to-needs ratio		0.009	−0.003			0.018
		(0.051)	(0.054)			(0.080)
Average parental income (10,000 $1992)				−0.011		
				(0.043)		

Income-to-needs ratio[c]						
<1					0.124 (0.248)	
2–3					−0.057 (0.232)	
3+					−0.123 (0.314)	
Sex by income-to-needs ratio						−0.034 (0.106)
Constant	−4.813	−4.363	−4.880	−4.883	−4.943	−4.928
−2 Log likelihood	1187.92	1191.90	1182.16	1182.09	1181.50	1182.06
df	7	3	9	10	11	10

* Strong evidence; ** very strong evidence.

Source: Authors' estimations of logistic regression coefficients using data on 5,824 men and women in the Wisconsin Longitudinal Study.

a. Standard errors in parentheses. Models also include dummy variables for missing data.

b. Intact families were the omitted group.

c. Families with income-to-needs ratios of 1–2 were the omitted group.

TABLE 17A.7 / Replication Analysis: Effect of Social and Economic Background on Having Fair or Poor Health[a]

	Model					
Independent Variable	i	ii	iii	iv	v	ix
Female	0.080	0.091	0.081	0.081	0.082	0.013
	(0.073)	(0.073)	(0.073)	(0.073)	(0.073)	(0.112)
Family-level background variables[b]						
Mother's education (years)	−0.046		−0.043	−0.043	−0.040	−0.043
	(0.013)		(0.013)	(0.013)	(0.013)	(0.013)
Mother head of household, widowed	−0.366		−0.372	−0.383	−0.394	−0.372
	(0.258)		(0.259)	(0.260)	(0.259)	(0.259)
Mother head of household, other reason	0.134		0.128	0.119	0.112	0.127
	(0.220)		(0.221)	(0.221)	(0.221)	(0.221)
Father head of household, any reason	0.304		0.296	0.295	0.294	0.297
	(0.258)		(0.259)	(0.259)	(0.259)	(0.259)
Other head of household	0.134		0.129	0.128	0.120	0.128
	(0.216)		(0.218)	(0.218)	(0.218)	(0.218)
Number of siblings				−0.006		
				(0.016)		
Family economic status						
Income-to-needs ratio		−0.035	−0.021			−0.042
		(0.022)	(0.022)			(0.036)
Average parental income (10,000 $1992)				−0.020		
				(0.017)		

Income-to-needs ratio[c]						
<1					0.153 (0.094)	
2–3					0.038 (0.094)	
3+					−0.153 (0.126)	
Sex by income-to-needs ratio						0.035 (0.045)
Constant	−1.477	−1.884	−1.463	−1.429	−1.570	−1.421
−2 Log likelihood	5226.46	5240.90	5225.47	5224.62	5220.71	5224.83
df	7	3	9	11	11	10

* Strong evidence; ** very strong evidence.

Source: Authors' estimations of logistic regression coefficients using data on 6,793 men and women from the Wisconsin Longitudinal Study.

a. Standard errors in parentheses. Models also include dummy variables for missing data.

b. Intact families were the omitted group.

c. Families with income-to-needs ratios of 1–2 were the omitted group.

TABLE 17A.8 / Replication Analysis: Effect of Social and Economic Background on Being Depressed[a]

	Model					
Independent Variable	i	ii	iii	iv	v	ix
Female	0.266**	0.279**	0.267**	0.268**	0.270**	0.364*
	(0.061)	(0.060)	(0.061)	(0.061)	(0.061)	(0.091)
Family-level background variables[b]						
Mother's education (years)	−0.065**		−0.063**	−0.064**	−0.063**	−0.062**
	(0.011)		(0.011)	(0.011)	(0.011)	(0.011)
Mother head of household, widowed	0.037		−0.014	−0.023	−0.022	−0.014
	(0.183)		(0.184)	(0.184)	(0.184)	(0.184)
Mother head of household, other reason	−0.102		−0.152	−0.163	−0.160	−0.151
	(0.197)		(0.198)	(0.198)	(0.198)	(0.198)
Father head of household, any reason	0.310		0.282	0.283	0.290	0.280
	(0.219)		(0.220)	(0.220)	(0.220)	(0.220)
Other head of household	−0.078		−0.134	−0.134	−0.129	−0.135
	(0.190)		(0.191)	(0.191)	(0.191)	(0.191)
Number of siblings				−0.012		
				(0.014)		
Family economic status						
Income-to-needs ratio		−0.043	−0.022			0.004
		(0.019)	(0.018)			(0.024)
Average parental income (10,000 $1992)				−0.022		
				(0.014)		

Income-to-needs ratio[c]						
<1					0.065	
					(0.081)	
2–3					0.104	
					(0.076)	
3+					−0.084	
					(0.102)	
Sex by income-to-needs ratio						−0.050
						(0.036)
Constant	−0.799	−1.421	−0.806	−0.742	−0.878	−0.863
−2 Log likelihood	6949.74	6979.63	6942.54	6940.39	6940.36	6940.53
df	7	3	9	11	11	10

* Strong evidence; ** very strong evidence.

Source: Authors' estimations of logistic regression coefficients using data on 6,820 men and women from the Wisconsin Longitudinal Study.

a. Standard errors in parentheses. Models also include dummy variables for missing data.

b. Intact families were the omitted group.

c. Families with income-to-needs ratios of 1–2 were the omitted group.

TABLE 17A.9 / Replication Analysis: Effect of Social and Economic Background on Death by 1992[a]

	Model					
Independent Variable	i	ii	iii	iv	v	ix
Female	−0.320	−0.308	−0.321	−0.321	−0.323	−0.351
	(0.111)	(0.110)	(0.111)	(0.111)	(0.111)	(0.165)
Family-level background variables[b]						
Mother's education (years)	−0.027		−0.026	−0.025	−0.026	−0.026
	(0.020)		(0.020)	(0.020)	(0.020)	(0.020)
Intact family	−0.402		−0.422	−0.419	−0.423	−0.422
	(0.159)		(0.162)	(0.163)	(0.162)	(0.162)
Number of siblings				0.000		
				(0.025)		
Family economic status						
Income-to-needs ratio		−0.022	−0.010			−0.018
		(0.033)	(0.032)			(0.046)
Average parental income (10,000 $1992)				−0.010		
				(0.025)		

Income-to-needs ratio						
<1					−0.069	
					(0.146)	
2–3					−0.184	
					(0.146)	
3+					−0.063	
					(0.181)	
Sex by income-to-needs ratio						0.016
						(0.063)
Constant	−2.504	−3.094	−2.461	−2.461	−2.411	−2.446
−2 Log likelihood	2951.01	2958.21	2950.34	2950.22	2948.81	2950.28
df	4	3	6	8	8	7

* Strong evidence; ** very strong evidence.

Source: Authors' estimations of logistic regression coefficients using data on 9,611 men and women from the Wisconsin Longitudinal Study.

a. Standard errors in parentheses. Data could not support more detailed family structure categorization for predicting death by 1992. Models also include dummy variables for missing data.

b. Families with income-to-needs ratios of 1–2 were the omitted group.

Support for this research was provided by the National Institute on Aging (AG-9775), the National Science Foundation, the Vilas Estate Trust, the Graduate School of the University of Wisconsin–Madison, and the Center for Demography and Ecology at the University of Wisconsin–Madison. The Center receives core support for research and training from the National Institute of Child Health and Human Development. The opinions expressed herein are those of the authors.

NOTES

1. Other important and influential longer-term studies of the life course in the United States also exist. Despite the careful and insightful work of many investigators, these studies are based on small, local, or highly selected samples (Oden 1968; Elder 1974; Clausen 1993). The Terman study is based on 1,500 California children who were first nominated by teachers and then scored extremely high on mental tests. By 1982, Clausen's follow-up of the combined Berkeley Growth Study, Berkeley Guidance Study, and Oakland Growth Study covered 283 of 528 individuals, aged fifty-three to sixty-two, who had been recruited as children and 358 for whom some data were available at age eighteen (Clausen 1993, 37). Moreover, the lives of the members of both the Terman and Berkeley-Oakland samples have been affected by their participation in the studies (for example, by group activities or academic or psychological counseling).
2. Solon's (1989) critique of intergenerational income correlations in the WLS evolved from the correct observation that the sample is limited to high school graduates to a characterization of the sample as "peculiarly homogenous" (Solon 1992, 395). However, Corcoran et al. (1992) used WLS findings as a standard of plausibility in their analysis of children in the Panel Study of Income Dynamics.
3. To be sure, the state has more and less affluent areas. Several northern counties and American Indian communities, now joined by much of Milwaukee, have long been economically depressed.
4. Our findings in the nonfarm sample were so similar to those in the total sample that we have not reported them separately.
5. Our analysis was limited to 9,611 individuals responding to either the 1975 or 1992–93 surveys and subsamples defined by the availability of data on specific outcomes.
6. The Duncan SEI is similar in construction to MSEI2, but it is based on characteristics of male jobholders in the 1950 census. It is not strictly comparable to the MSEI2.
7. Although the results are not reported here, we also examined several other social and psychological outcome measures. The effects of adolescents' income-to-needs ratios on the status of the job they held in 1975 and their earnings in 1974 were explained by controls for social background and had little influence on poverty in 1974. Also, we observed weak associations between income-to-needs ratio and marital success, having ever smoked, and positive well-being.
8. Whenever the mother's occupational status was entered, we also added a dummy variable for nonworking mothers.

9. For those who wish to apply other criteria of significance, we have in all cases reported coefficients and standard errors.
10. These estimates are not from a single equation. For convenience, we estimated each equation twice, altering the coding of sex to obtain separate estimates of the slopes for men and women as well as estimating the interaction effects.
11. Similar observations (not presented here) held for the effects of other social background characteristics.

Chapter 18

Income Effects Across the Life Span: Integration and Interpretation

Greg J. Duncan and Jeanne Brooks-Gunn

The goal of this volume has been to forge a consensus on how and how much childhood poverty affects the life chances of children by using longitudinal data from the developmental studies in chapters 5–17. To this end, the authors of those chapters performed a replication analysis: they included the same set of measures—family income, maternal schooling, and family structure—in a regression model predicting child outcomes. The limited measures in these replication models provide a "black-box" estimate of the role of family income, adjusted statistically for the fact that low-income families are more likely to have a single parent and less educated parents but not for the factors that might explain the income effects themselves. To varying degrees, the authors also accounted for these income effects and gauged whether they represent truly causal influences. Some outcomes, such as IQ at age two and motor development between birth and age three, were measured very early in a child's life. Others, such as career attainment and mortality, were measured as late as the sixth decade of life. In all cases the data sets contained reliable measures of the income of the individuals' parents at least once during childhood.

We summarize these replication analyses in tables 18.1 and 18.2. The results for ability and achievement measures are displayed in table 18.1; table 18.2 summarizes the findings on behavior, physical health, and mental health. Each table is organized by the childhood stage over which parents' income was measured and by the estimated size of the effect of parents' income on the given outcome. Since year-to-year variability of family income imparts considerable imprecision to short-run measurement of income, we restrict our summary view to studies containing at least three distinct measurements of income during childhood.[1]

We distinguish three rough sizes of income effect. In a large effect all of the income coefficients from the various income-based models were significant at the .05 level or below, and the effect sizes were arguably large.[2] In a small/moderate effect most of the income coefficients were significant at the .05 level, but the effect sizes were not consistently large. No effect means that few if any of the income coefficients from the various income-based models were statistically significant. The results suggest that family income has at times large but rather selective effects on children's attainments. A comparison of the data in tables 18.1 and 18.2 highlights the importance of the *type* of outcome considered:

- Family income has large effects on some measures of the children's ability and achievement, but not on the behavior, mental health, or physical health measures represented by the developmental studies in chapters 5, 7, 11, 14, 16, and 17.

Roughly half of the measures of ability and achievement listed in table 18.1 had large associations with family income; in contrast, none of the measures of behavior, mental health, and physical health listed in table 18.2 had what we deem large effects.

A look across the columns of table 18.1 reveals the importance of the childhood stage in which income is measured:

- Family economic conditions in early and middle childhood appear to be far more important for shaping ability and achievement than they do during adolescence.

None of the achievement studies with exclusively adolescence-based income measures found large effects (table 18.1). In contrast, all of the studies of ability that measured income during early childhood found large income effects.[3]

For the large effects found, the pattern of income effects is important. Since meeting basic needs is of critical importance, income increases for low-income families—such as those associated with movements out of poverty—might be expected to have more powerful effects on children's development than income increases for middle-class or affluent families. This issue was difficult to evaluate since some of the studies used data from relatively advantaged samples of children, but studies that were able to test for thresholds often found them. Overall, our results suggest that:

- Increasing the incomes of children below or near the poverty line seems to have a bigger impact on ability and attainment than increasing the incomes of children in middle-class and affluent families.

This conclusion applies to almost all of the analyses of ability and achievement measures that found large income effects.

Since virtually all of the replication analyses included measures of maternal schooling and family structure, they provide valuable information on the comparative power of income, parental schooling, and family structure to account for differences in the child outcomes. Here the results are very clear:

- Family income is usually a stronger predictor of ability and achievement outcomes than are measures of parental schooling or family structure.

For example, Smith, Brooks-Gunn, and Klebanov used ten separate measures of cognitive ability in two samples; income was a highly significant predictor in

TABLE 18.1 / Summary Analysis: Effects of Family Income on Children's Performance on Measures of Ability and Achievement[a]

Stage in Which Income Was Measured	Size of Effect[b]		
	Large	Small or Moderate	None
Early childhood	Bayley IQ score (2)[c] PPVT-R score (3)[c] Stanford-Binet score (3)[c] PPVT score (3–4)[d] PPVT-R score (5)[c] PIAT Math score (5–6)[d] PIAT Reading score (5–6)[d]		
Early and middle childhood	PIAT Math score (7–8)[d] PIAT Reading score (7–8)[d]	Completed schooling (23)[e]	
Middle childhood		Behind in grade for age (6–12)[f]	
Middle childhood and adolescence	Family income (25–35)[g] Men's labor income (25–35)[g] Men's hourly earnings (25–35)[g] Men's work hours (25–35)[g]	Odds of completing high school[h]	
Adolescence		AFQT score (16–18)[i] Completed schooling[i] Odds of attending college[k] Status of first job[k] Job status (52)[k] Earnings (52)[k] Hourly earnings (26–27)[i]	Self-reported grades (14–17)[l] Odds of high school graduation[j] Odds of attending college[j] Completed schooling[j] Odds of family poverty (52)[k]

Source: Regression-based analyses in chapters 5, 7, and 10–17 that control for mother's education, family structure, and other demographic measures. Studies using fewer than three measurements of income (chapters 6, 8, and 9) were omitted.

a. Numbers in parentheses are ages at which the outcome was measured.

b. Large: all income coefficients from income-based models were significant at the .05 level or below; the effect size was almost always one-third of a standard deviation or larger. Small to moderate: most income coefficients from income-based models were significant at the .05 level or below; the effect size was consistently less than one-third of a standard deviation. None: few or no income coefficients from income-based models were significant at the .05 level.

c. Smith, Brooks-Gunn, and Klebanov (chapter 7). Data from the Infant Health and Development Program. PPVT: Peabody Picture Vocabulary Test; PPVT-R: Peabody Picture Vocabulary Test-Revised; PIAT: Peabody Individual Achievement Test.

d. Smith, Brooks-Gunn, and Klebanov (chapter 7). Data from the National Longitudinal Survey of Youth (NLSY). See note c for abbreviations.

e. Axinn, Duncan, and Thornton (chapter 16). Data from the Detroit Longitudinal Study of Mothers and Children. Income measured five times from birth to age seventeen years.

f. Pagani, Boulerice, and Tremblay (chapter 11). Data from the Quebec Longitudinal Studies of Behavior.

g. Corcoran and Adams (chapter 15). Data from the Panel Study of Income Dynamics (PSID). Income measured as early as age three and as late as age sixteen years but mostly during adolescence.

h. Haveman, Wolfe, and Wilson (chapter 14). Data from the PSID. Income measured between ages six and eighteen years.

i. Peters and Mullis (chapter 12). Data from the NLSY.

j. Teachman, Paasch, Day, and Carver (chapter 13). Data from the National Longitudinal Surveys of Young Men and Women.

k. Hauser and Sweeney (chapter 17). Data from the Wisconsin Longitudinal Survey.

l. Conger, Conger, and Elder (chapter 10). Data from the Iowa Youth and Family Project.

TABLE 18.2 / Summary Analysis: Effects of Family Income on Children's Behavior and Physical and Mental Health

Stage in Which Income Was Measured	Size of Effect[b]		
	Large	Small or Moderate	None
Early childhood			Motor and social development (0–3)[c]
Early and middle childhood		Stunting (5–8)[d]	Wasting (5–8)[d] Obesity (5–8)[d] Self-esteem (23)[e]
Middle childhood		Fighting (12)[f]	Anxiety (12)[f] Hyperactivity (12)[f]
Middle childhood and adolescence			Odds of out-of-wedlock childbearing[g]
Adolescence			Bad health (52)[h] Depression (52)[h] Mortality (by 52)[h]

Source: See table 18.1.

a. Numbers in parentheses are ages at which the outcome was measured.

b. Large: all income coefficients from income-based models were significant at the .05 level or below; the effect size was almost always one-third of a standard deviation or larger. Small to moderate: most income coefficients from income-based models were significant at the .05 level or below; the effect size was consistently less than one-third of a standard deviation. None: few or no income coefficients from income-based models were significant at the .05 level.

c. Smith, Brooks-Gunn, and Klebanov (chapter 7). Data from the NLSY.

d. Korenman and Miller (chapter 5). Data from the NLSY Mother-Child File.

e. Axinn, Duncan, and Thornton (chapter 16). Data from the Detroit Longitudinal Study of Mothers and Children. Income measured five times from birth to age seventeen years.

f. Pagani, Boulerice, and Tremblay (chapter 11). Data from the Quebec Longitudinal Studies of Behavior.

g. Haveman, Wolfe, and Wilson (chapter 14). Data from the PSID. Income measured between ages six and eighteen years.

h. Hauser and Sweeney (chapter 17). Data from the Wisconsin Longitudinal Survey.

all ten of their models. In the same models, the coefficient on mother's schooling was statistically significant in only three of ten cases, and the coefficients on family structure were significant only once. And neither H. Elizabeth Peters and Natalie Mullis (chapter 12) nor Corcoran and Adams found that maternal schooling significantly predicted the six labor-market outcomes they modeled. On the other hand, Robert Haveman, Barbara Wolfe, and Kathryn Wilson (chapter 14), Peters and Mullis, and Jay D. Teachman, Kathleen M. Paasch, Randal D. Day, and Karen

P. Carver (chapter 13) found that mothers' schooling had statistically significant and quantitatively large effects on school outcomes.

Similar to McLanahan and Sandefur (1994), we found the effects of family structure to be small and, on most of the ability and achievement measures, nonsignificant. For example, the effects of family structure on early ability measures decreased by one-half to three-quarters when an income-to-needs measure was added to the equations (for example, in chapter 7). Interestingly, family structure tended to be a somewhat more important determinant of behavior problems and mental health than other outcomes were, but the effects of family structure were quantitatively large in only a few cases, for example, school behavior problems in Thomas L. Hanson, Sara McLanahan, and Elizabeth Thomson's analysis (chapter 8); anxiety in Linda Pagani, Bernard Boulerice, and Richard Tremblay's analysis (chapter 11); and out-of-wedlock childbearing in Haveman, Wolfe, and Wilson's analysis.

All in all, a safe conclusion is that most of the replication studies found parental income to be a stronger correlate of children's ability and achievement than were maternal schooling and family structure. For behavior and health, however, none of the measures emerged as consistently powerful.

Each chapter's research team followed the replication analysis with more comprehensive causal analysis that took advantage of the strengths of the particular data set used. Some of the extensions were very helpful in explaining the reasons for the effect of income. The extensions pursued in other chapters tested whether the income effects observed in our replication analyses were indeed consistent with a causal interpretation. We treat each of these topics in turn.

WHY INCOME MATTERS

Some of the analyses shed considerable light on how income affects the life chances of children. Most revealing are results in chapter 7, which show that the quality of the home environment—its opportunities for learning, the warmth of mother-child interactions, and the physical condition of the home—accounts for a substantial portion of the powerful effects of family income on cognitive outcomes. Consistent across the two data sets is the finding that differences in the home environments of higher- and lower-income children accounted for one-third of the effects of income on the cognitive development of preschool children and between one-quarter and one-third of the effects of income on elementary-school children. Thus,

- For the cognitive development of preschoolers, income appears to matter because it is associated with the provision of a richer learning environment for children.

Whether the effect is due to the purchase of more stimulating experiences (for example, educational toys, books, travel to concerts and festivals outside the neighborhood) or to the use of such materials is not clear (and it is difficult to tease apart these two possibilities with the measures of home environment used). However, the importance of money in enabling parents to purchase better learning environments for their children is reinforced by the National Institute for Child Health and Human Development Child Care Research Network's data on early child care (chapter 6), which showed that family income was a significant determinant of the quality of nearly all of the child care environments observed, including center-based child care.

The home environment is less important for cognitive development as children enter school, as one might expect in light of the increasing importance of the school and neighborhood environments in children's lives as they leave the preschool period. Although we would have liked to track the comparative power of the home and school environments in accounting for differences in the academic progress of children, we discovered no data set that combined a high-quality measurement of the school environment with a comparably high-quality longitudinal measurement of the parental family.

Rand D. Conger, Kathy J. Conger, and Glen Elder's study (chapter 10) also provides important clues on the effects of income on children's lives. In their models, low income produces economic pressures that can lead to conflict between parents over financial matters, which in turn affects the harshness of the mother's parenting and the adolescent's self-confidence and achievement. They found support for a number of the links in their models. Not surprisingly, a family's income level was a powerful predictor of the economic pressure reported by family members. That pressure had both direct and indirect effects on the adolescents' achievement. Parental financial conflicts were found to be particularly detrimental to boys' self-confidence and achievements.

Conger and Elder (1994) have suggested that a variety of income measures—not just the income-to-needs ratio but income loss, the ratio of debts to assets, and unstable work—are associated with family economic pressure. Perceived economic pressure, in turn, is associated with a depressed mood in parents, which itself feeds marital conflict. Both a depressed and irritable mood and marital conflict influence parenting behavior. The parents' interactions with the child are thought to be the most proximal mediator of income and perceived financial pressure (Conger et al. 1992, 1993, 1994). A low income (or a fluctuating income) sets off a series of family events—perceived economic pressure, a low or labile mood in parents, marital conflict, and unresponsive parenting. However, the Family Stress Model, as termed by the authors, was based on primarily two-parent families, which is reflected in the importance they place on marital conflict. Future research needs to explore whether (1) conflict is as central to the model as predicted, (2) family conflict other than marital conflict might be important (for example, in multigenerational families), and (3) other parental characteristics besides mood and conflict influence parenting. McLoyd (1990) has developed a similar model linking low income to negative outcomes for black children and believes that low income may influence children by paths other than parenting (McLoyd et al. 1994).

Most of the data sets represented in this volume do not measure perceptions of financial pressure or hardship, parents' mood and psychological functioning, or marital or family conflict. Consequently, we cannot test whether these family-level processes mediate the effects of income, but chapter 10 provides an example of this line of work.

THE ENIGMA OF THE SCHOOL YEARS

The pattern of income effects we found—large in early childhood, much smaller during the school years, and, at least in the analysis in chapter 15, large again in the adult years—raises many intriguing questions. First, why do the powerful relationships between income and the ability and achievement measures that existed in the preschool years weaken later, so that parents' income plays less of a role in explaining differences in either achievement test scores or completed schooling? Part of the answer may lie in measurement problems associated with the restriction of the analyses in chapters 12 and 13 and in Robert Hauser and Megan Sweeney's analysis (chapter 17) to measures of parents' income only during their children's adolescence. If, as the studies in the other chapters indicate, economic conditions during early and middle childhood are indeed most important, then these studies may provide a misleading picture of the size of the income effects.

Since the issue of the timing of income effects is so important, we conducted additional analyses of data covering the entire period of childhood from the Panel Study of Income Dynamics (PSID).[4] Although the analyses in chapters 14 and 15 also used data from the PSID, neither took advantage of the fact that the PSID yields economic information on children during their entire childhood—specifically, on 1,323 children born between 1967 and 1973 and observed for the entire period between birth and ages twenty to twenty-five years. These data enable us to test for the relative importance of income in both early and middle childhood and adolescence in explaining an important outcome—completed schooling. As in our replication studies, we included control variables for race, sex, the schooling completed by the mother, family structure, and the age of the mother at the birth of the child.[5]

To test for the limitations of measuring parents' income only during adolescence, we estimated two completed-schooling models, the first of which included the demographic control variables as well as parental-family income and income-to-needs ratio averaged over the years between ages eleven and fifteen (table 18.3). By limiting the measurement period to adolescence, we used in this regression the kind of information available in the studies in chapters 12, 13, and 17. (The chapter 14 analysis averaged income between the ages of six and eighteen for all of the children in the sample, while that in chapter 15 used data from as early as age three but mostly from adolescence.) The second version of the model substituted for the adolescence-based income measure the parents' income averaged over the entire period of childhood—from birth to age fifteen.

The results in the first two columns of table 18.3 show clearly that the adoles-

TABLE 18.3 / Effects of the Ages over Which Parents' Income Is Measured on Children's Completed Schooling[a]

	Parental Income Averaged over Ages				
Income Measure[b]	11–15	0–15	0–5	6–10	11–15
Average income ($10,000)	0.06*	0.11*	0.14*	−0.02	0.04
	(0.01)	(0.02)	(0.04)	(0.03)	(0.02)
Adjusted R^2	0.162	0.164		0.169	
Average income-to-needs ratio	0.10*	0.17*	0.22*	0.02	0.01
	(0.01)	(0.02)	(0.04)	(0.05)	(0.03)
Adjusted R^2	0.146	0.160		0.169	

* Coefficient is at least twice its standard error.

Source: Authors' calculations based on data on 1,323 individuals in the Panel Study of Income Dynamics born between 1967 and 1973 and observed between birth and at least age twenty.

a. Standard errors in parentheses. All regressions include controls for mother's schooling, family structure, race, sex, and the age of the mother at the birth of the child.

b. Income inflated to 1992 price levels using the consumer price index (CPI-UX1).

cence-based income measure is a much weaker predictor of completed schooling than is the whole-childhood measure. For both income measures, the coefficient on income from ages eleven to fifteen is barely half the size of the coefficient on parents' income from birth to age fifteen.

To test further for the importance of the timing of the income effects, we estimated completed-schooling models in which we entered the control variables as well as three income measures: (1) average parental income between birth and age five; (2) average income between ages six and ten; and (3) average income between ages eleven and fifteen. The results are quite remarkable (table 18.3): the *only* stage for which parents' income significantly predicted completed schooling is early childhood—parents' income between ages zero and five years. Thus the only reason that parents' income during adolescence or middle childhood predicts completed schooling is apparently that income during those periods is correlated with income in early childhood.

Although we found that parents' income had stronger effects when measured early in a child's life, note that in no case were the effects on schooling as large as they were on early ability and achievement. For example, the impact of an increase of 1.0 on the income-to-needs measures—the equivalent of going from an income just at the poverty line to an income twice the poverty line—was associated with an increase in completed schooling of 0.2 years, roughly one-eighth of the 1.6-year standard deviation for the completed schooling variable. Thus, the question of why parents' income becomes less important as children move through their school years still remains.

A second puzzle is the reemergence of the power of parents' income in accounting for the differences in the adult earnings and family income of children who are in their late twenties and early thirties (chapter 15). Why did parents' income become important again after more than a decade in which the children's achievement became increasingly independent of their family's economic position? Perhaps labor markets are far less compensatory than schools. Indeed, the patterns of income effects—large in early childhood, small during the school years, and large again during the adult years—may suggest that of the major institutions in people's lives—the parental family, schools, and the labor market—only the schools play an important compensatory role.

Some of the details from the analyses in this volume help explain why parents' income matters for adult outcomes. One important—and surprising—result from chapter 15 is that years of completed schooling failed to account for many of the links between parents' income and success in the labor market. Although this result is consistent with those of the studies showing weak links between parents' income and completed schooling, it raises the important question of how the advantages of parents' economic position are transmitted to the next generation.

One possibility is that the increased cognitive development associated with higher income in early childhood carries through the school years and imparts advantages in the labor market. Although there is abundant evidence that the achievement test scores of adolescents are important predictors of future success in the labor market (Neal and Johnson 1995), it is not at all clear to what extent differences in cognitive ability account for the impact of parents' schooling, even after adjustments for differences in years of completed schooling.

The data used by Hauser and Sweeney contained a Henman-Nelson test score from the eleventh grade, while those used by Teachman et al. contained a composite score from a series of aptitude tests administered in adolescence. In their models of the prestige of adult occupations and hourly earnings, Hauser and Sweeney found that adding test scores to the models in the replication analysis accounted for roughly one-fourth of the effect of parents' income, suggesting a rather limited role for cognitive ability in accounting for the income effects. Confirming this result, Teachman et al. found that adding their test score hardly changed the estimated effect of parents' income on completed schooling.

Perhaps the intervening paths that link parents' income and outcomes lie elsewhere. Hauser and Sweeney also included in their models an unusually complete set of social-psychological measures, including parents' aspirations, encouragement from teachers and parents, and friends' college plans. These measures accounted for the bulk of the effect of parents' income on occupational attainment but less than half of the effect of income on adult earnings. On the other hand, the parental aspiration measures of William Axinn, Greg J. Duncan, and Arland Thornton (chapter 16), which were measured much earlier in childhood, were not important mediators.

Other paths are consistent with a more spurious role for family income itself. Suppose, for example, that higher-paid working-class parents are able to secure high-paying working-class jobs for their children. Since this process works independently of schooling, it would show up in the models in chapter 15 in the form of an effect of parents' income that is independent of the child's own completed schooling. In this case parents' income plays no causal role; rather, income is a proxy measure of occupation. None of our studies tested this hypothesis directly. However, Hauser and Sweeney did find that adding measures of parents' occupational prestige accounted for more of the association between parents' income and outcomes when those outcomes were the children's own occupational attainments than when the outcome is, for example, hourly earnings.

ARE INCOME EFFECTS CAUSAL?

Our replication regressions include parents' income and a modest set of socioeconomic and demographic control variables. As such, they show the associations between parents' income and various outcomes, after the regression techniques adjust statistically for measured socioeconomic and demographic differences between high- and low-income families.

A persistent concern with these kinds of analyses is that the estimated effect of income might be spurious, caused by the mutual association that parents' income and the outcomes share with some unmeasured "true" causal factor. Suppose, for example, that the mental health of parents was the key ingredient in children's success and that we failed to include measures of parents' mental health in our models. Since positive mental health in parents is likely to both make parents more successful in the labor market and lead to fewer problems with their children, the absence of adjustments in our replication studies for differences in parents' mental health may lead us to seriously overstate the role income plays in causing children's success.

Mayer (forthcoming) provides a set of tests for omitted-variable bias. For example, she estimates regressions that are similar to our replication models but adds a measure of parents' income *after* the occurrence of the outcome. Her argument is that the future income cannot have caused the prior outcome, so that it serves as an adjustment for unmeasured characteristics of the parents. The addition of future income almost always produces a large reduction in the estimated effect of prior parental income, leading her to conclude that much of the estimated effect of income from replication models is spurious. However, parents' income during the child's high school years is highly correlated with income in the young-adult years, making it difficult to estimate the effects of income change.

A second example is Mayer's estimation of models that include only those components of parents' income that are fairly independent of the actions of the family. Her argument is that the level of income components such as welfare and earnings (as well as the level of the outcomes under study) may reflect the effects of important, unmeasured characteristics. If components such as asset income are less affected by these unmeasured characteristics, their coefficients ought to provide a better gauge of the "true" effects of income. Following this procedure, Mayer finds small and often insignificant coefficients on these income components. However, whether asset income is less influenced by unmeasured characteristics remains unclear.

As Mayer herself points out, these procedures are not without problems. If families anticipate future income changes and adjust their consumption accordingly, and the adjustments benefit or hurt children, then future income does indeed play a causal role. And the likely measurement error in the values imparted to income sources such as dividends and interest will bias their coefficients downward (as will the fact that interest and dividends are relatively meaningless measures of the effects of income on almost all of the families at or below the poverty line). These problems notwithstanding, Mayer performs the valuable service of highlighting problems of causal analysis that all intergenerational studies should address.

A number of the chapters in this volume address the issue of causality. For example, the replication analysis in chapter 16 drew on a longitudinal sample of relatively advantaged children to relate children's completed schooling to parents' income measured at five points during childhood, including very early childhood. Their extension took advantage of their study's detailed measures of economic status—in particular the net worth of the parental family—and measures of the parents' plans and aspirations for their children when their child was born. Studies of the effect of parents' background on achievement typically omit both sets of measures. For the authors, the extension analysis reinforced the replication analysis by showing that the expanded set of economic measures was more important than income alone while the aspiration measures were not significant predictors of completed schooling.

The extension analysis of Haveman, Wolfe, and Wilson, which involved estimating structural models of high school graduation and out-of-wedlock childbearing, produced virtually identical estimates for the (modest) impact of parents' income on schooling. The estimates of the effect of parents' income on out-of-wedlock childbearing were statistically insignificant in both the replication and the structural models. Pagani, Boulerice, and Tremblay extended their replication analysis by estimating models of *changes* in outcome between ages six and twelve. In effect these models tested whether differences in children's average level of family income during middle childhood accounted for differential changes in academic and mental health outcomes between the beginning and the end of middle childhood. This change-based analysis did little to alter the conclusion of the level-based replication analysis.

Hauser and Sweeney present more convincing evidence on the limitations of the income effect. Their data included many additional measures of family background, including the occupational prestige of the father's and mother's jobs. Adding these measures, along with education, to the replication model reduced the estimated effect of parents' income by close to one-half in the adult earnings equation and by two-thirds in the adult occupational prestige equation (see chapter 7 for a discussion of maternal education). Further analysis showed that this drop was not merely the result of the measures of parental occupational prestige being a slightly transformed variant of a measure of parent income.

As Sanders Korenman and Jane Miller argue (chapter 5), one of the most appealing techniques for handling unobserved parental characteristics is to compare individuals in the same family. Models that relate differences in outcomes between, say, siblings to differences in the family income histories of those siblings are arguably free from the confounding influence of persistent parental characteristics, both measured and unmeasured. Korenman and Miller illustrate this technique by comparing stunting and wasting of cousins—children of the sister pairs found in the National Longitudinal Survey of Youth data set.

POLICY IMPLICATIONS

Income transfer programs are but one weapon in an arsenal of possible programs that might improve the life chances of children. We ignore for the moment the dramatic changes in the U.S. safety net that will be caused by the Personal Responsibility and Work Opportunity Reconciliation Act of 1996 and assume a world in which the government has the resources and the will to consider what combination of programs makes the most sense for poor children's development.

Taken together, the studies in this volume suggest that programs that raise the incomes of poor families will enhance the cognitive development of children and may improve their chances of success in the labor market during adulthood. Most important appears to be the elimination of deep and persistent poverty during a child's early years. Transfers to nonpoor families or to families with older children may be justifiable on other grounds but do not appear as effective in enhancing children's ability or achievement during their school years.

Since the 1960s, the Aid to Families with Dependent Children (AFDC) program has served as the major cash assistance program directed at low-income families with children. A combination of categorical restriction of benefits to single-parent families in some states and the low participation rates of two-parent families in other states has led the AFDC program to concentrate its benefits on lone-mother families. Benefit levels vary widely from one state to the next and fell by more than one-third over the twenty-year period leading to the mid-1990s. By itself the AFDC program has not been particularly effective in giving low-income families with children adequate levels of financial assistance.

The food stamp program has been somewhat more successful. Although food stamps themselves can only be used to purchase food, they enable low-income families to use their cash income to buy things that they otherwise would not be able to afford. Participation in the program among persistently low-income families is high. And there is substantial evidence that the growth of the food stamp program during the 1970s and 1980s dramatically reduced the number of children living in families with persistently very low income (Duncan and Rodgers 1991).

Cash or near-cash programs are hardly a cure-all, however. In no case did the evidence here suggest that income transfers alone would produce a dramatic improvement in the physical health, mental health, or in behavioral development of children. Important here are targeted programs, such as those that provide nutrition supplements and education (for example, Women, Infants, and Children), medical care (for example, Medicaid), early childhood education (for example, Head Start), and housing (for example, section 8 vouchers).

The 1996 welfare reforms change the structure of cash income support programs for families with children. The AFDC program has been replaced by block grants to states, which, in the late 1990s will reduce the total amount of federal support for programs covered by the block grants. States have wide latitude to design replacement programs, even to deny benefits to qualifying families if program funding is not sufficient. (Programs such as AFDC are currently accorded "entitlement" status by the federal government, which means that all qualifying families are by law entitled to program benefits; replacement programs may drop their entitlement status.)

It is far too early to tell how these changes will affect children's family incomes, if they are enacted. Much will depend on how states use their newfound freedom to design replacement programs and on the economic fortunes of the nation and individual regions. The elimination of entitlement status for income support programs will almost certainly lead states hit hard by an economic downturn to deny benefits to qualifying families.

From the point of view of children, the most important aspects of the new legislation are various provisions that render families ineligible to receive benefits. Incorporated into the federal legislation are provisions that limit the duration of cash assistance to five years. Pavetti (1994) estimates that roughly one-third of new welfare cases and three-quarters of existing cases will remain on the rolls for as long as five years. The number of families affected by the time limits will amount to nearly two million within ten years of the imposition of the five-year limits. Although states can waive the limit in certain restrictive cases, the bulk of the two million families reaching the limit will likely see their benefits fall to zero. Some of these families will find employment, although very few are likely to have family incomes that are higher than they were when they relied on welfare (Blank 1994; Burtless 1994). Most worrisome in terms of our results are families that will run up against the time limits and suffer large drops in their incomes.

Another cause for concern is the extent to which states will adopt policies that place categorical restrictions on who receives aid. Most states are likely to adopt "family caps" that do not increase the benefits paid to women who have additional children while receiving public assistance. This policy will lower the per capita incomes of recipient families, but not dramatically. The consequences of provisions that deny cash assistance to children born to underage, unmarried women or to various immigrant groups are more worrisome because, again, the incomes of a subset of affected families will fall dramatically. Indeed, the case-specific consequences of these categorical provisions will likely be more severe than those of the five-year limit, since most of the categorical provisions deny benefits to families with very young children; most families affected by the five-year limit will tend to have older children. Not only do young children appear most vulnerable to the consequences of deep poverty, but mothers with very young children are least able to support themselves by working in the labor market.

All in all, the welfare-reform legislation passed in 1996 is likely to have a much bigger impact on the distribution of income than on children's average level of economic well-being. Even if the expected increases in the number of poor children materialize, the number of children living in low-income families may not increase that much (estimates of the expected increases in the number of poor children vary greatly). However, the disparities in family income among poor children almost certainly will. These disparities are likely to be much greater than they have been since the beginning of the food stamp program in the early 1970s. If occurring early in childhood, the additional episodes of deep poverty produced by these disparities are likely to harm the ability and achievement of our nation's children.

NOTES

1. This restriction eliminated from the summary tables the cross-sectional studies in chapters 6 and 8 as well as the two-year longitudinal study in chapter 9.
2. We considered income effects to be large if the changes in the dependent variable associated with (1) an additional $10,000 of income, (2) an increase in family income from below the poverty line to between the poverty line and twice the poverty line (that is, income-to-needs ratio from less than 1.0 to between 1.0 and 2.0), and (3) a change from persistent poverty to no poverty amounted to at least one-third of a standard deviation for most of the dependent variables used in a particular analysis. These results came from the three replication regressions that included each of these income-related measures as well as maternal schooling, family structure, and other demographic control variables.
3. Although the results are not included in the summary table because of the limited number of income measurements, chapter 9 produced evidence that is not inconsistent with these patterns. Specifically, the earlier measurement of income was a much more powerful predictor of achievement than the later measurement of income, and no income measure was very predictive of the mental health outcomes.
4. Jean Yeung kindly provided assistance with these analyses.
5. Our family structure measure took the form of a series of dummy variables measuring whether the child ever spent time in (1) an intact, two-biological-parent family, (2) a mother-only family, (3) a mother-grandmother family, (4) a mother-stepfather family, or (5) some other, more complicated family structure. For the "whole childhood" analysis these variables are measures between birth and age fifteen. For the eleven to fifteen-year analysis, these variables are measured between ages eleven and fifteen. Our analyses of family income also included the number of siblings of the child whose completed schooling is being analyzed. (The income-to-needs analysis did not include an explicit measure of siblings since family size is already incorporated into the denominator of the income-to-needs measure.)

References

Abbott-Shim, M., and A. Sibley. 1987. *Assessment Profile for Early Childhood Education Programs.* Atlanta, Ga.: Quality Assist.

Achenbach, T. M., and C. D. Edelbrock. 1981. "Behavioral Problems and Competencies by Parents of Normal and Disturbed Children Aged Four through Sixteen." *Monograph of Social Research and Child Development* 46(1): 1–78.

Adler, N. E., T. Boyce, M. A. Chesney, S. Folkman, and S. L. Syme. 1993. "Socioeconomic Inequalities in Health: No Easy Solution." *Journal of the American Medical Association* 269: 3140–45.

Alan Guttmacher Institutes. 1992. *Facts in Brief: Teenage Sexual and Reproductive Behavior.* New York: Alan Guttmacher Institute.

Allen, L. H. 1990. "Functional Indicators and Outcomes of Undernutrition." *Journal of Nutrition* 120(8): 924–32.

Alwin, D., and A. Thornton. 1984. "Family Origins and the Schooling Process: Early versus Late Influence of Parental Characteristics." *American Sociological Review* 49(6): 784–802.

Amato, P. R. 1993. "Children's Adjustment to Divorce: Theories, Hypotheses, and Empirical Support." *Journal of Marriage and the Family* 5(1) Feb.

Amato, P. R., and B. Keith. 1991. "Parental Divorce and the Well-Being of Children: A Meta-Analysis." *Psychological Bulletin* 110(1): 26–46.

Amato, P. R., and S. J. Rezac. 1994. "Contact with Nonresident Parents, Interparental Conflict, and Children's Behavior." *Journal of Family Issues* 15: 191–228.

American Psychiatric Association. 1980. *Diagnostic and Statistical Manual of Mental Disorders.* 3rd ed. Washington, D.C.: American Psychiatric Press.

An, C. B., R. Haveman, and B. Wolfe. 1993. "Teen Out-of-Wedlock Births and Welfare Receipt: The Role of Childhood Events and Economic Circumstances." *Review of Economics and Statistics* 75(May): 195–208.

Anderson, E. R., E. M. Hetherington, and W. G. Clingempeel. 1989. "Transformations in Family Relations at Puberty: Effects on Family Context." *Journal of Early Adolescence* 9(3): 310–34.

Anderson, M. 1978. *Welfare: The Political Economy of Welfare Reform.* Institution Press.

Angoff, W. H. 1988. "The Nature-Nurture Debate, Aptitudes, and Group Differences." *American Psychologist* 43(9): 713–20.

Angrist, J. D., and V. Lavy. 1994. "Teenage Childbearing, Childhood Disabilities and Progress in School." Hebrew University. Unpublished paper.

Antel, J. 1988. "Mother's Welfare Dependency Effects on Daughter's Early Fertility and Fertility Out-of-Wedlock." University of Houston. Unpublished paper.

Ashworth, K., M. Hill, and R. Walker. 1994. "Patterns of Childhood Poverty: New Challenges for Policy." *Journal of Policy Analysis and Management* 13(4): 658–80.

Astone, N., and S. McLanahan. 1991. "Family Structure and High School Completion: The Role of Parental Practices." *American Sociological Review* 56(3): 309–20.

Bachman, J. G. 1982. "Family Relationships and Self-Esteem." In *Social Psychology of the Self Concept* edited by M. Rosenberg and H. B. Kaplan. Arlington Heights, Ill.: Harlan Davidson.

Bachman, J. G., and P. M. O'Malley. 1977. "Self-Esteem in Young Men: A Longitudinal Analysis of the Impact of Educational and Occupational Attainment." *Journal of Personality and Social Psychology* 35(6): 365–80.

Baker, P. C., C. K. Keck, F. L. Mott, and S. V. Quinlan. 1993. "NLSY Child Handbook: A Guide to the 1986–1990 National Longitudinal Survey of Youth Child Data." Rev. ed. Columbus, Ohio: Ohio State University, Center for Human Resource Research.

Baker, P., and F. Mott. 1989. "NLSY Handbook 1989: A Guide and Resource Document for the National Longitudinal Survey of Youth 1986 Child Data." Columbus, Ohio: Ohio State University, Center for Human Resource Research.

Bane, M. J., and D. Ellwood. 1986. "Slipping Into and Out of Poverty: the Dynamics of Spells." *Journal of Human Resources* 21: 1–23.

Bates, J. E., K. Bayles, D. S. Bennett, B. Ridge, and M. M. Brown. 1991. "Origins of Externalizing Behavior Problems at 8 Years of Age." In *The Development and Treatment of Childhood Aggression,* edited by D. J. Pepler and K. H. Rubin. Hillsdale, N.J.: Lawrence Erlbaum.

Baumrind, D. 1966. "Effects of Authoritative Parental Control on Child Behavior." *Child Development* 37(4): 887–907.

Baydar, N., and J. Brooks-Gunn. 1991. "Effects of Maternal Employment and Child Care Arrangements in Infancy on Preschoolers' Cognitive and Behavioral Outcomes: Evidence from the Children of the National Longitudinal Study of Youth." *Developmental Psychology* 27(6): 932–45.

———. 1994. "The Dynamics of Child Support and Its Consequences For Children." In *Child Support and Child Well-being,* edited by I. Garfinkel, S. McLanahan, and P. Robins. Washington, D.C.: Urban Institute Press.

Baydar, N., J. Brooks-Gunn, F. F. Furstenberg, Jr. 1993. "Early Warning signs of Functional Illiteracy: Predictors in Childhood and Adolescence." *Child Development* 64(3): 815–29.

Bayley, N. 1969. *Manual for the Bayley Scales of Infant Development.* San Antonio, Tex.: Psychological Corp.

Becerra, R. M., and I. Chi. 1992. "Child Care Preferences among Low-Income Minority Families." *International Social Work* 35: 35–47.

Becker, G. S. 1981. *A Treatise on the Family.* Cambridge, Mass.: Harvard University Press.

Becker, G. S. 1991. *A Treatise on the Family.* 2nd. ed. Cambridge, Mass.: Harvard University Press.

Becker, G., and N. Tomes. 1986. "Human Capital and the Rise and Fall of Families." *Journal of Labor Economics* 4(2): S1–S139.

Behar, L. B., and S. Stringfield. 1974. "A Behavior Rating Scale for the Preschool Child." *Developmental Psychology* 10(5): 601–10.

Beller, A. A., and J. T. Graham. 1991. "The Effect of Child Support Enforcement on Child Support Payments." *Population Research and Policy Review* 10(2): 91–116.

Benson, J. B., S. S. Cherny, M. M. Haith, and D. W. Fulker. 1993. "Rapid Assessment of Infant Predictors of Adult IQ: Midtwin-Midparent Analyses." *Developmental Psychology* 29(3): 434–47.

Berger, M., W. Yule, and M. Rutter. 1975. "Attainment and Adjustment in Two Geographical Areas. II. The Prevalence of Specific Reading Retardation." *British Journal of Psychiatry* 126: 510–19.

Berkowitz, L. 1989. "Frustration-Aggression Hypothesis: Examination and Reformulation." *Psychological Bulletin* 106(1): 59–73.

Betson, D. 1990. *Alternative Estimates of the Cost of Child Care from the 1980–1986 Consumer Expenditure Survey.* Washington: U.S. Government Printing Office for U.S. Department of Health and Human Services.

Blake, J. 1989. *Family Size and Achievement,* Berkeley, Calif.: University of California Press.

Blank, R. 1994. "Outlook for the U.S. Labor Market and Prospects for Low-Wage Entry Jobs." Paper presented at the Urban Institute conference on Self-Sufficiency and the Low-Wage Labor Market: A Reality Check for Welfare Reform.

Blau, F. D., and J. W. Graham. 1990. "Black-White Differences in Wealth and Asset Composition." *Quarterly Journal of Economics* 105(2): 321–39.

Blau, P., and O. Duncan. 1967. *The American Occupational Structure.* New York: John Wiley and Sons.

Bloom, B. S. 1961. *Stability and Change in Human Characteristics.* New York: John Wiley and Sons.

Blumer, H. 1956. "Sociological Analysis and the Variable." *American Sociological Review* 22(2): 683–90.

Bolger, K. E., C. J. Patterson, W. W. Thompson, and J. B. Kupersmidt. 1995. "Psychosocial Adjustment among Children Experiencing Persistent and Intermittent Family Hardship." *Child Development* 66: 1107–29.

Bollen, K. A. 1989. *Structural Equations with Latent Variables.* New York: John Wiley and Sons.

Booth, A., and J. Dunn. 1994. *Stepfamilies: Who Benefits? Who Does not?* Hillsdale, N.J.: Lawrence Erlbaum.

Booth, A., D. Johnson, and J. N. Edwards. 1983. "Measuring Marital Stability." *Journal of Marriage and the Family* 38(2): 387–94.

Borjas, G. J. 1994. "The Economics of Immigration." *Journal of Economic Literature* 32(4): 1667–1717.

Bornstein, M., and M. Sigman. 1986. "Continuity in Mental Development from Infancy." *Child Development* 57: 251–74.

Bound, J., D. A. Jaeger, and R. M. Baker. 1995. "Problems with Instrumental Variables

Estimation When the Correlation between the Instrument and Endogenous Explanatory Variable Is Weak." *Journal of the American Statistical Association* 90(June): 443–50.

Boyle, M. H., D. R. Offord, H. G. Hoffman, G. P. Catlin, J. W. Byles, P. S. Links, N. I. Rae-Grant, and P. Szatmari. 1987. "Ontario Child Health Study: I. Methodology." *Archives of General Psychiatry* 44: 826–31.

Boyle, M. H., D. R. Offord, Y. A. Racine, and G. P. Caitlin. 1991. "Ontario Child Health Study Follow-up: Evaluation of Sample Loss." *Journal of the American Academy of Child and Adolescent Psychiatry* 30(3): 449–56.

Bradley, R. H., B. M. Caldwell, and S. L. Rock. 1988. "Home Environment and School Performance: A Ten-Year Follow-up and Examination of Three Models of Environmental Action." *Child Development* 59: 852–67.

Bradley, R. H., B. M. Caldwell, S. L. Rock, C. T. Ramey, K. E. Barnard, C. Gray, M. A. Hammond, S. Mitchell, A. W. Gottfried, L. Siegel, and D. L. Johnson. 1989. "Home Environment and Cognitive Development in the First Three Years of Life: A Collaborative Study Involving Six Sites and Three Ethnic Groups in North America." *Developmental Psychology* 25: 217–35.

Bradley, R. H., L. Whiteside, D. L. Mundfrom, P. H. Casey, K. J., Kelleher, and S. K. Pope. 1994. "Early Indications of Resilience and Their Relation to Experiences in the Home Environment of Low Birthweight, Premature Children Living in Poverty." *Child Development* 65: 346–60.

Brayfield, A., S. G. Deich, and S. Hofferth. 1993. *Caring for Children in Low-Income Families: A Substudy of the National Child Care Survey, 1990.* Washington, D.C.: Urban Institute Press.

Brody, G. H., Z. Stoneman, D. Flor, C. McCrary, L. Hastings, O. Conyers. 1994. "Financial Resources, Parent Psychological Functioning, Parent Co-Caregiving, and Early Adolescent Competence in Rural Two-Parent African-American Families." *Child Development* 65(2): 590–605.

Bronfenbrenner, U. 1979. *The Ecology of Human Development: Experiments by Nature and Design.* Cambridge, Mass.: Harvard University Press.

———. 1989. "Ecological Systems Theory." *Annals of Child Development* 6: 187–249.

Brooks-Gunn, J. 1995. "Children and Families in Communities: Risk and Intervention in the Bronfenbrenner Tradition." In *Examining Lives in Context: Perspective on the Ecology of Human Development*, edited by P. Moen, G. H. Elder, and K. Lusher. Washington, D.C.: American Psychological Association Press.

———. 1995. "Transitions in and out of Welfare: Effects on Children." Paper presented to the meeting of the Society for Research in Child Development. Indianapolis, Ind. (March 30, 1995).

Brooks-Gunn, J., B. Brown, G. Duncan, and K. A. Moore. 1995. "Child Development in the Context of Family and Community Resources: An Agenda for National Data Collection." In *Integrating Federal Statistics on Children: Report of a Workshop.* Washington, D.C.: National Academy Press.

Brooks-Gunn, J., J. Denner, and P. K. Klebanov. 1995. "Families and Neighborhoods as Contexts for Education." In *Changing Populations, Changing schools: Ninety-fourth Yearbook of the National Society for the Study of Education,* edited by E. Flaxman and A. H. Passow. Part 2. Chicago: National Society for the Study of Education.

Brooks-Gunn, J., and G. Duncan. Forthcoming. "Growing Up Poor: Consequences for Children and Youth." *Future of Children.*

Brooks-Gunn, J., G. J. Duncan, and L. Aber, eds. Forthcoming. *Neighborhood Poverty: Context and Consequences for Children.* New York: Russell Sage Foundation.

Brooks-Gunn, J., G. J. Duncan, P. K. Klebanov, and N. Sealand. 1993. "Do Neighborhoods Influence Child and Adolescent Development?" *American Journal of Sociology* 99(2): 353–95.

Brooks-Gunn, J., G. Guo, and F. F. Furstenberg, Jr. 1993. "Who Drops Out of and Who Continues Beyond High School? A 20-Year Study of Black Youth." *Journal of Research in Adolescence* 3(37): 271–94.

Brooks-Gunn, J., and R. Hearn. 1982. "Early Intervention and Developmental Dysfunction: Implications for Pediatrics." In *Advances in Pediatrics.* New York: Yearbook Publishers.

Brooks-Gunn, J., P. K. Klebanov, and G. Duncan. 1996. "Ethnic Differences in Children's Intelligence Test Scores: Role of Economic Deprivation, Home Environment, and Maternal Characteristics." *Child Development* 67(2): 396–408.

Brooks-Gunn, J., P. K. Klebanov, and F. Liaw. 1995. "The Learning, Physical, and Emotional Environment of the Home in the Context of Poverty: The Infant Health and Development Program." *Children and Youth Services Review* 17: 1–2.

Brooks-Gunn, J., P. K. Klebanov, F. Liaw, and D. Spiker. 1993. "Enhancing the Development of Low Birthweight, Premature Infants: Changes in Cognition and Behavior over the First Three Years." *Child Development* 63: 736–53.

Brooks-Gunn, J., F. Liaw, and P. K. Klebanov. 1992. "Effects of Early Intervention on Low Birthweight Preterm Infants: What Aspects of Cognitive Functioning Are Enhanced?" *Journal of Pediatrics* 120: 350–59. (Abbreviated version published in *The Infant Health and Development Program for Low Birthweight Premature Infants,* edited by R. T. Gross and D. Spiker. Stanford, Calif.: Stanford University Press.)

Brooks-Gunn, J., C. McCarton, et al. 1994. "Early Intervention in Low Birth Weight, Premature Infants: Results Through Age Five Years from the Infant Health Development Program." *Journal of the American Medical Association* 272(16): 1257–62.

Brooks-Gunn, J., M. C. McCormick, C. McCarton, and P. K. Klebanov. Forthcoming. *Young Children's Health Care Use: Effects of Family and Neighborhood Poverty.* Burlington, Vt.: Pediatrics.

Brooks-Gunnn, J., E. Phelps, and G. H. Elder. 1991. "Studying Lives Through Time: Secondary Data Analyses in Developmental Psychology." *Developmental Psychology* 27(6): 889–910.

Brooks-Gunn, J., and E. O. Reiter. 1990. "The Role of Pubertal Processes in the Early Adolescent Transition." In *At the Threshold: The Developing Adolescent,* edited by S. Feldman and G. Elliott. Cambridge, Mass.: Harvard University Press.

Brooks-Gunn, J., and M. Weinraub. 1983. "Origins of Infant Intelligence Testing." In *Origins of Intelligence,* edited by M. Lewis. 2d ed. New York: Plenum Press.

Browning, M. 1992. "Children and Household Economic Behavior." *Journal of Economic Literature* 30(3): 1434–75.

Bumpass, L. 1984. "Children and Marital Distruption: A Replication and Update," *Demography* 21: 71-82.

Bumpass, L., and K. Raley. 1984. "Trends in the Duration of Single-Parent Families." NSFH Working Paper 58, University of Wisconsin-Madison.

Burtless, G. 1994. "The Employment Prospects of Welfare Recipients." Paper presented at the Urban Institute conference on Self-Sufficiency and the Low-Wage Labor Market: A Reality Check for Welfare Reform (1994).

Cadman, D., M. H. Boyle, D. R. Offord, P. Szatmari, N. I. Rae-Grant, J. Crawford, and J. Byles. 1986. "Chronic Illness and Functional Limitation in Ontario Children: Findings of the Ontario Child Health Study." *Canadian Medical Association Journal* 135: 761–67.

Cairns, R. B., and B. D. Cairns. 1986. "The Developmental Interactional View of Social Behavior: Four Issues of Adolescent Aggression." In *Development of Antisocial Behavior,* edited by D. Olweus, J. Black, and M. Radke-Yarrow. New York: Academic Press.

Cairns, R. B., B. D. Cairns, and J. Neckerman. 1989. "Early School Dropout: Configurations and Determinants." *Child Development* 60(2): 1437–52.

Caldwell, B., and R. H. Bradley. 1984. "Home Observation for Measurement of the Environment." Little Rock, Ark.: University of Arkansas, Center for Research on Teaching and Learning.

Campbell, S. B. 1995. "Behavior Problems in Preschool Children: A Review of Recent Research." *Journal of Child Psychology and Psychiatry* 36(1): 113–49.

Carnegie Corporation of New York. 1994. *Starting Points: Meeting the Needs of our Youngest Children.* New York: Carnegie Corp.

Caspi, A., G. H. Elder, and E. S. Herbener. 1990. "Childhood Personality and the Prediction of Life-Course Patterns." In *Straight and Devious Pathways from Childhood to Adulthood,* edited by L. N. Robins and M. Rutter. New York: Cambridge University Press.

Cattan, P. 1991. "Child Care Problems: An Obstacle to Work." *Monthly Labor Review* October: 3–9.

Caughy, M. O. B., J. A. DiPietro, and D. M. Strobino. 1994. "Day-Care Participation as a Protective Factor in the Cognitive Development of Low-Income Children." *Child Development* 65: 457–71.

Center for Human Resource Research. 1992. NLS Update: *The National Longitudinal Studies of Labor Market Experience,* l. Columbus, Ohio: Ohio State University.

———. 1993. *NLS User's Guide, 1993.* Columbus, Ohio: Ohio State University.

Center for Population Options. 1990. "Teenage Pregnancy and Too-Early Childbearing: Public Costs, Personal Consequences." Washington, D.C.: Center for Population Options.

Chase-Lansdale, P. L., and J. Brooks-Gunn. 1995. *Escape from Poverty: What Makes a Difference for Children?* New York: Cambridge University Press.

Chase-Lansdale, L., R. Gordon, J. Brooks-Gunn, and P. K. Klebanov. Forthcoming. "Neighborhood and Family Influences on the Intellectual and Behavioral Competence of Preschool and Early School-Age Children." In *Neighborhood Poverty: Context and Consequences for Children,* edited by J. Brooks-Gunn, G. Duncan, and L. Aber. New York: Russell Sage Foundation.

Chase-Lansdale, P. L., F. L. Mott, J. Brooks-Gunn, and D. H. Phillips. 1991. "Children of the National Longitudinal Survey of Youth: A Unique Research Opportunity." *Developmental Psychology* 27(6): 918–31.

Cherlin, A. J. 1992. *Marriage, Divorce, Remarriage.* Cambridge, Mass.: Harvard University Press.

Cherlin, A. J., and F. Furstenberg, Jr. 1986. *The New American Grandparent. A Place in the Family, A Life Apart.* New York: Basic Books.

Cherlin, A. J., and F. F. Furstenberg, Jr. 1991. *Divided Families.* Cambridge, Mass.: Harvard University Press.

Cherlin, A. J., F. F. Furstenberg, Jr., P. L. Chase-Lansdale, K. E. Kiernan, P. K. Robins, D. Ruane Morrison, and J. O. Teitler. 1990. "Longitudinal Studies of Effects of Divorce on Children in Great Britain and the United States." *Science* 252(5011): 1386–89.

Children's Defense Fund. 1994. *Wasting America's Future: The Children's Defense Fund Report on the Costs of Child Poverty.* Boston, Mass.: Beacon Press.

Chugani, H., M. E. Phelps, and J. C. Mazziota. 1987. "Positron Emission Tomography Study of Human Brain Functional Development." *Annals of Neurology* 22(4): 495.

Citro, C. F., and R. T. Michael. eds. 1995. *Measuring Poverty: A New Approach.* Washington, D.C.: National Academy Press.

Clarke-Stewart, K. A., and G. Fein. 1983. Early Childhood Program. In *Handbook of Child Psychology,* edited by M. M. Haith and J. J. Compos. New York: John Wiley and Sons.

Clarke-Stewart, K. A., C. P. Gruber, and L. M. Fitzgerald. 1994. *Children at Home and in Daycare.* Hillsdale, N.J.: Lawrence Erlbaum.

Clausen, J. A. 1993. *American Lives: Looking Back at the Children of the Great Depression.* New York: Free Press.

Coleman, J. S. 1990. *Foundations of Social Theory.* Cambridge, Mass.: Belknap Press.

Collins, N., and S. Hofferth. 1996. "Child Care and Employment Turnover." Paper presented at the annual meeting of the Population Association of American. New Orleans, La. (May 11, 1996).

Conger, R. D., K. J. Conger, G. H. Elder, Jr., F. O. Lorenz, R. L. Simons, and L. B. Whitbeck. 1992. "A Family Process Model of Economic Hardship and Adjustment of Early Adolescent Boys." *Child Development* 63(2): 526–41.

———. 1993. "Family Economic Stress and Adjustment of Early Adolescent Girls." *Developmental Psychology* 29(2): 206–19.

Conger, R., and G. Elder. 1994. *Families in Troubled Times: Adapting to Change in Rural America.* Hawthorne, N.Y.: Aldine de Gruyter.

Conger, R. D., G. H. Elder, Jr., F. O. Lorenz, K. J. Conger, R. L. Simons, L. B. Whitbeck, J. Huck, and J. N. Melby. 1990. "Linking Economic Hardship and Marital Quality and Instability." *Journal of Marriage and the Family* 52(3): 643–56.

Conger, R. D., X. Ge, G. H. Elder, Jr., F. O. Lorenz, and R. L. Simons. 1994. "Economic

Stress, Coercive Family Process, and Developmental Problems of Adolescents." *Child Development* 65(2): 541–61.

Connell, J. P., M. B. Spencer, and J. L. Aber. 1994. "Educational Risk and Resilience in African American Youth: Context, Self, Action, and Outcomes in School." *Child Development* 65(2): 493–506.

Coopersmith, S. 1967. *The Antecedents of Self-Esteem.* San Francisco, Calif.: W. H. Freeman.

Corcoran, M. 1992. "Background, Earnings and the American Dream." *Contemporary Sociology* 21(5): 603–09.

Corcoran, M., and T. Adams. Forthcoming. "Family and Neighborhood Welfare Dependency and Sons' Labor Supply." *Journal of Family and Economic Issues.*

———. 1993. "Race, Poverty, Welfare and Neighborhood Influences on Men's Economic Outcomes." Ann Arbor, Mich.: University of Michigan, Institute for Social Research.

Corcoran, M., and L. Datcher. 1981. "Intergenerational Status Transmission and the Process of Individual Attainment." In *Five Thousand American Families—Patterns of Economic Progress,* edited by M. Hill, D. Hill, and J. Morgan. Ann Arbor, Mich.: University of Michigan, Institute for Social Research, Survey Research Center.

Corcoran, M., R. Gordon, D. Laren, and G. Solon. 1992. "The Association Between Men's Economic Status and Their Family and Community Origins." *Journal of Human Resources* 27(4): 575–601.

Crane, J. 1991. "The Epidemic Theory of Ghettos and Neighborhood Effects on Dropping Out and Teenage Childbearing." *American Journal of Sociology* 96(5): 1226–59.

Cruise, M. O. 1973. "A Longitudinal Study of the Growth of Low Birth Weight Infants: I. Velocity and Distance Growth, Birth to Three Years." *Pediatrics* 51(4): 620–28.

Culkin, M., J. R. Morris, and S. W. Helburn. 1991. "Quality and the True Cost of Child Care." *Journal of Social Issues* 47: 71–86.

Cummings, E. M., P. T. Davies, and K. S. Simpson. 1994. "Marital Conflict, Gender, and Children's Appraisals and Coping Efficacy as Mediators of Child Adjustment." *Journal of Family Psychology* 8(2): 141–49.

Cummings, E. M., R. J. Iannotti, and C. Zahn-Waxler. 1989. "Aggression between Peers in Early Childhood: Individual Continuity and Developmental Change." *Child Development* 60(4): 887–95.

Cunningham, P. J., and B. A. Hahn. 1994. "The Changing American Family: Implications for Chidren's Health Insurance Coverage and the Use of Ambulatory Care Services." *The Futures of Children* 4(3): 24–42.

Currie, J. M. 1995. *Welfare and the Well-Being of Children.* Chur, Switzerland: Harwood Academic Publishers.

Currie, J., and D. Thomas. 1993a. "Does Head Start Make a Difference?" NBER Working Paper 4406. Cambridge, Mass.: National Bureau of Economic Research.

———. 1993b. "Measurement of Height and Weight in the NLSY." Yale University. Unpublished paper.

———. 1995. "Does Head Start Make a Difference?" *American Economic Review* 85(3): 341–64.

Danziger, S. H., and D. H. Weinberg. 1994. "The Historical Record: Trends in Family Income, Inequality, and Poverty." In *Confronting Poverty: Prescriptions for Change,* edited by S. H. Danziger, G. D. Sandefur, and D. H. Weinberg. Cambridge, Mass.: Harvard University Press.

Datcher, L. 1982. "Effects of Community and Family Background on Achievement." *Review of Economics and Statistics* 64(1): 32–41.

Davies, P. T., and E. M. Cummings. 1994. "Marital Conflict and Child Adjustment: An Emotional Security Hypothesis." *Psychological Bulletin* 116(3): 387–411.

Del Boca, D. and C. J. Flinn. 1994. "Expenditure Decisions of Divorced Mothers and Income Composition." *Journal of Human Resources* 29(3): 742–61.

Demo, D. H., and A. C. Acock. 1988. "The Impact of Divorce on Children." *Journal of Marriage and the Family* 50(3): 619–48.

Demo, D. H., S. A. Small, and R. C. Savin-Williams. 1987. "Family Relations and the Self-Esteem of Adolescents and their Parents." *Journal of Marriage and the Family* 49(4): 705–15.

Derogatis, L. R. 1983. *SCL-90-R Administration, Scoring, and Procedures Manual - II.* Towson, Md.: Clinical Psychometric Research.

Dobkin, P. L., R. E. Tremblay, L. C. Mâsse, and F. Vitaro. 1995. "Individual and Peer Characteristics in Predicting Boys' Early Onset of Substance Abuse: A Seven Year Longitudinal Study." *Child Development* 66(4): 1198–14.

Dodge, K. A., G. S. Pettit, and J. E. Bates. 1994. "Socialization Mediators of the Relation between Socioeconomic Status and Child Conduct Problems." *Child Development* 65(2): 649–65.

Dornbusch, S. M., P. L. Ritter, P. H. Leiderman, D. F. Roberts, and M. J. Fraleigh. 1987. "The Relation of Parenting Style to Adolescent School Performance." *Child Development* 58(5): 1244–57.

Downey, G., and J. C. Coyne. 1990. "Children of Depressed Parents: An Integrative Review." *Psychological Bulletin* 108(1): 50–76.

Duncan, G. J. 1988. "Volatility of Family Income over the Life Course." In *Life-Span Development and Behavior,* edited by P. Baltes, D. Featherman, and R. Lerner. Hillsdale, N.J.: Lawrence Erlbaum.

———. 1984. "Years of Poverty, Years of Plenty." Ann Arbor, Mich.: University of Michigan, Institute for Social Research.

———. 1991. "The Economic Environment of Childhood." In *Children in Poverty: Child Development and Public Policy,* edited by A. C. Huston. New York: Cambridge University Press.

———. 1994a. "Families and Neighbors as Sources of Disadvantage in the Schooling Decisions of White and Black Adolescents." Ann Arbor, Mich.: University of Michigan, Survey Research Center.

———. 1994a. "Income Dynamics and Health." Ann Arbor, Mich.: University of Michigan, Institute for Social Research.

Duncan, G. J., J. Brooks-Gunn, and P. Klebanov. 1994. "Economic Deprivation and Early-Childhood Development." *Child Development* 62(2): 296–318.

Duncan, G. J., M. S. Hill, and S. D. Hoffman. 1988. "Welfare Dependence within and across Generations." *Science,* 239(1): 467–71.

Duncan, G. J., and S. F. Hoffman. 1990. "Welfare Benefits, Economic Opportunities and the Incidence of Out-of-Wedlock Births among Black Teenage Girls." *Demography* 27(4): 519–35.

Duncan, G. J., and W. Rodgers. 1988. "Longitudinal Aspects of Childhood Poverty." *Journal of Marriage and the Family* 50(4): 538–50.

———. 1991. "Has Children's Poverty Become More Persistent?" *American Sociological Review* 56(August): 538–50.

Duncan, G. J., T. Smeeding, and W. Rodgers. 1992. "Why Is the Middle Class Shrinking?" Ann Arbor, Mich.: University of Michigan, Institute for Social Research, Survey Research Center.

Duncan, G. J., and W. J. Yeung. 1994. "Extent and Consequences of Welfare Dependence Among America's Children." University of Michigan, Survey Research Center. Unpublished paper.

Duncan, G. J., J. Yeung, J. Brooks-Gunn, and J. Smith. Forthcoming. "Does Poverty Affect the Life Chances of Children?" *American Sociological Review.*

Duncan, O. D. 1961. "A Socioeconomic Index for all Occupations." In *Occupations and Social Status,* edited by A. J. Reiss, Jr. New York: Free Press.

Duncan, O., D. Featherman, and B. Duncan. 1972. *Socioeconomic Background and Achievement.* New York: Seminar.

Dunn, L. M., and L. M. Dunn. 1981. *Peabody Picture Vocabulary Test—Revised.* Circle Pines, Minn.: American Guidance Services.

Dunn, L. M., and F. Markwardt, Jr. 1970. *Peabody Individual Achievement Test Manual.* Circle Pines, Minn.: American Guidance Services.

Early Child Care Research Network. 1994. "Child Care and Child Development: The NICHD Study of Early Child Care." In *Developmental Follow-up: Concepts, Domains and Methods,* edited by S. L. Friedman and H. C. Haywood. San Diego, Calif.: Academic Press.

Eccles, J. S., S. Lord, and C. M. Buchanan. 1996. "School Transitions in Early Adolescence: What Are We Doing to Our Young People?" In *Transitions through Adolescence: Interpersonal Domains and Context,* edited by J. A. Graber, J. Brooks-Gunn, and A. C. Petersen. Mahwah, N.J.: Erlbaum.

Eccles, J., C. Midgley, C. M. Buchanan, A. Wigfield, D. Reuman, and D. MacIver. 1993. "Development during Adolescence: The Impact of Stage/Environment Fit." *American Psychologist* 48: 90–101.

Egbuonu, L., and B. Starfield. 1982. "Child health and Social Status." *Pediatrics* 69: 550–57.

Egeland, B. R. and M. Zaslow. 1995. "The Effects of the New Chance Program on Mother-Child Interactions." Paper presented at the Society for Research in Child Development. Indianapolis, Ind. (March 30, 1995).

Eggebeen, D. J., and D. T. Lichter. 1991. "Race, Family Structure, and Changing Poverty." *American Sociological Review* 56(6): 801–17.

Ehrenberg, R. G., and R. S. Smith. 1994. *Modern Labor Economics.* 5th ed. New York: HarperCollins Publishers.

Elder, G. H., Jr. 1974. *Children of the Great Depression: Social Change in Life Experience.* Chicago: University of Chicago Press.

Elder, G. H., Jr., and A. Caspi. 1988. "Economic Stress in Lives: Developmental Perspectives." *Journal of Social Issues,* 44(4): 25–45.

Elder, G. H., Jr., R. D. Conger, E. M. Foster, and M. Ardelt. 1992. "Families under Economic Pressure." *Journal of Family Issues* 13(1): 5–37.

Elder, G. H., Jr., J. K. Liker, and C. E. Cross. 1984. "Parent-Child Behavior in the Great Depression: Life Course and Intergenerational Influences." In *Life-Span Development and Behavior,* vol. 6, edited by P. B. Baltes and O. G. Brim, Jr. New York: Academic Press.

Elder, G. H., Jr., T. V. Nguyen, and A. Caspi. 1985. "Linking Family Hardship to Children's Lives." *Child Development* 56(3): 361–75.

Ellwood, D. T. 1988. *Poor Support: Poverty in the America Family.* New York: Academic Press.

Elo, I. T., and S. H. Preston. 1992. "Effects of Early-Life Conditions on Adult Mortality: A Review." *Population Index* 58(2): 186–212.

Emery, R. E., and D. K. O'Leary. 1982. "Children's Perception of Marital Discord and Behavior Problems of Boys and Girls." *Journal of Abnormal Child Psychology* 12(1): 411–20.

Engle, R. 1984. "Wald, Likelihood Ratio, and LaGrange Multiplier Tests in Econometrics." In *Handbook of Econometrics,* edited by Z. Griliches and M. Intrilligator. Amsterdam: North Holland.

Entwisle, D. R., and K. L. Alexander. 1990. "Beginning School Math Competence: Minority and Majority Comparisons." *Child Development* 61: 454–71.

Espenshade, T. J. 1984. *Investing in Children: New Estimates of Parental Expenditures.* Washington, D.C.: Urban Institute Press.

Expert Committee on Family Budget Revisions. 1980. *New American Family Budget Standards.* Madison, Wisc.: University of Wisconsin, Institute for Research on Poverty.

Farrington, D. P. 1989. "Later Adult Life Outcomes of Offenders and Non-Offenders." In *Children at Risk: Assessment, Longitudinal Research and Intervention,* edited by M. Brambring, F. Loesel, and H. Skowronek. Berlin: de Gruyter.

———. 1994. "Childhood, Adolescent, and Adult Features of Violent Males." In *Aggressive Behavior: Current Perspectives,* edited by L. R. Huesmann. New York: Plenum Press.

Featherman, D., and R. Hauser. 1978. *Opportunity and Change.* New York: Academic Press.

Fitzgerald, H. E., B. M. Lester, and B. S. Zuckerman. 1995. *Children of Poverty: Research, Health, and Policy Issues.* New York: Garland Press.

Flanagan, C. A., and J. S. Eccles. 1993. "Changes in Parents' Work Status and Adolescents' Adjustment at School." *Child Development* 64: 246–57.

Forehand, R., A. Thomas McCombs, M. Wierson, G. Brody, and R. Fauber. 1990. "Role of Maternal Functioning and Parenting Skills in Adolescent Functioning Following Parental Divorce." *Journal of Abnormal Psychology* 99(3): 278–83.

Fowler, P. O., and R. M. Park. 1979. "Factor Structure on the Preschool Behavior Questionnaire in a Normal Population." *Psychological Reports* 45(2): 599–606.

Fox, N. A. 1989. "Psychophysiological Correlates of Emotional Reactivity during the First Year of Life. *Developmental Psychology* 25(3): 364–72.

Fronstin, P., and D. Wissoker. 1994. "The Effects of the Availability of Low-Cost Child Care on the Labor Supply of Low-Income Women." Paper presented to the annual meeting of the Population Association of America. Miami, Fla. (May 5–7).

Fuchs, V. F. 1965. "Towards a Theory of Poverty." In *The Concept of Poverty.* Washington, D.C.: Chamber of Commerce of the United States.

Furstenberg, F. F., J. Brooks-Gunn, and S. P. Morgan. 1987. *Adolescent Mothers and Their Children in Later Life.* New York: Cambridge University Press.

Furstenberg, F., and M. E. Hughes. 1994. "The Influence of Neighborhoods on Children's Development: A Theoretical Perspective and a Research Agenda." University of Pennsylvania. Unpublished paper.

Furstenberg, F., S. P. Morgan, and P. Allison. 1987. "Parental Participation and Children's Well-being." *American Sociological Review:* 695–701.

Galbraith, J. K. 1958. *The Affluent Society.* Boston: Houghton Mifflin.

Galinsky, E., C. Howes, S. Kontos, and M. Shinn. 1994. *The Study of Children in Family Child Care and Relative Care.* New York: Families and Work Institute.

Garcia-Coll, C., G. Lamberty, R. Jenkins, H. P. McAdoo, K. Crnic, B. H. Wasik, and H. Vazquez Garcia. Forthcoming. "An Integrative Model for the Study of Developmental Competencies in Minority Children." *Child Development* 67(5): 1891–1914.

Garfinkel, I., and S. McLanahan. 1986. *Single Mothers and Their Children: A New American Dilemma.* Washington, D.C.: Urban Institute Press.

Garfinkel, I., S. McLanahan, and P. Robins. 1994. *Child Support Reform and Child Well-Being.* Washington, D.C.: Urban Institute Press.

Garmezy, N., and M. Rutter. 1983. *Stress, Coping and Development in Children.* New York: McGraw-Hill.

Garrett, P., S. Lubeck, and D. Wenk, 1991. "Childbirth and Maternal Employment: Data from a National Longitudinal Survey." In *Parental Leave and Child Care: Setting a Research and Policy Agenda,* edited by J. S. Hyde and M. J. Essex. Philadelphia: Temple University Press.

Garrett, P., N. Ng'andu, and J. Ferron. 1994. "Poverty Experiences of Young Children and the Quality of Their Home Environments." *Child Development* 65(2): 331–45.

Gayle, H. D., M. J. Dibley, J. Marks, and F. L. Trowbridge. 1987. "Malnutrition in the First Two Years of Life: The Contribution of Low Birth Weight to Population Estimates in the United States." *American Journal of Diseases of Children* 141(May): 531–34.

Ge, X., R. D. Conger, F. O. Lorenz, and R. L. Simons. 1994. "Parents' Stressful Life Events and Adolescent Depressed Mood." *Journal of Health and Social Behavior* 35(7): 28–44.

Gecas, V., and M. L. Schwalbe. 1986. "Parental Behavior and Adolescent Self-Esteem." *Journal of Marriage and the Family* 48(1): 37–46.

Gecas, V., and M. A. Seff. 1990. "Families and Adolescents: A Review of the 1980s." *Journal of Marriage and the Family* 52(4): 941–958.

Geronimous, A., and S. Korenman. 1992. "The Socioeconomic Consequences of Teen Childbearing Reconsidered." *Quarterly Journal of Economics* 107(November): 1187–1214.

Glueck, S., and E. Glueck. 1950. *Unraveling Juvenile Delinquency.* New York: Commonwealth Fund.

Gottfried, A., ed. 1984. *Home Environment and Early Cognitive Development.* Orlando, Fla.: Academic Press.

Gottschalk, P. and S. Mayer. 1995. "Trends in Home Production and Changes in Inequality." Unpublished paper.

Gould, J. B., and S. LeRoy. 1988. "Socioeconomic Status and Low Birth Weight: A Racial Comparison." *Pediatrics* 82(6): 896–904.

Graber, J. A., and J. Brooks-Gunn. 1996. "Transitions and Turning Points: Navigating the Passage from Childhood through Adolescence." *Developmental Psychology* 32(4): 768–76.

Graham, J. W., A. H. Beller, and P. M. Hernandez. 1994. "The Effect of Child Support on Educational Attainment." *Child Support and Child Well-Being,* edited by I. Garfinkel, S. McLanahan, and P. Robins. Washington, D.C.: Urban Institute Press.

Grissmer, D. W., S. N. Kirby, M. Berends, and S. Williamson. 1994. *Student Achievement and the Changing American Family.* Washington: RAND Institute on Education and Training.

Guo, G., J. Brooks-Gunn, and K. M. Harris. Forthcoming. "Parental Labor Force Attachment and Grade Retention among Urban Black Children." *Sociology of Education.*

Guo, G., J. Brooks-Gunn, I. Wallace, C. Bauer, F. Bennett, J. Bernbaum, R. Broyles, P. Casey, M. McCormick, D. Scott, J. Tyson, J. Tonascia, and C. Meinert. 1997. "Results at Eight Years of Intervention for Low Birthweight Premature Infants: The Infant Health and Development Program." *Journal of the American Medical Association.* 227(2): 126–32.

Guttman, J. 1993. *Divorce in Psycho-social Perspective: Theory and Research.* Hillsdale, N.J.: Lawrence Erlbaum.

Haapasalo, J., and R. E. Tremblay. 1994. "Physically Aggressive Boys from Age 6 to 12: Family Background, Parenting Behavior, and Prediction of Delinquency." *Journal of Consulting and Clinical Psychology* 62(5): 1–9.

Hamill, P. V., F. E. Johnston, and S. Lemeshow. 1972. "Height and Weight of Children: Socioeconomic Status, United States." *Vital and Health Statistics,* ser. 11, no. 119. DHEW Publication (HSM) 75–1601. Washington: U. S. Government Printing Office for the National Center for Health Statistics.

Hanson, T., S. McLanahan, and E. Thomson. 1996. "Double Jeopardy: Parental Conflict and Stepfamily Outcomes for Children." *Journal of Marriage and the Family* 58(1): 141–54.

Hanushek, E. 1986. "The Economics of Schooling: Production and Efficiency in Public Schools." *Journal of Economic Literature* 24(3): 1141–77.

Harter, S. 1990. "Self and Identity Development." In *At the Threshold: The Developing Adolescent,* edited by S. S. Feldman and G. R. Elliott, Cambridge, Mass.: Harvard University Press.

Hauser, R. M. 1972. "Disaggregating a Social-Psychological Model of Educational Attainment." *Social Science Research* 1(2): 159–88.

———. 1993a. "The Decline in College Entry among African Americans: Findings in Search of Explanations." In *Prejudice, Politics, and the American Dilemma,* edited by P. Sniderman, P. Tetlock, and E. Carmines. Stanford, Calif.: Stanford University Press.

———. 1993b. "Trends in College Entry among Blacks, Hispanics, and Whites." In *Studies of Supply and Demand in Higher Education,* edited by C. Clotfelter and M. Rothschild. Chicago: University of Chicago Press.

Hauser, R., and D. Anderson. 1991. "Post–High School Plans and Aspirations of Black and White High School Seniors: 1976–1986." *Sociology of Education* 64(4): 263–77.

Hauser, R., and T. Daymont. 1977. "Schooling, Ability and Earnings: Cross-sectional Findings 8 to 14 Years after High School Graduation." *Sociology of Education* 50(3): 182–206.

Hauser, R., and D. Featherman. 1977. *The Process of Stratification.* New York: Academic Press.

Hauser, R. M., D. Carr, T. Hauser, M. Krecker, D. Kuo, J. Presti, D. Shinberg, M. Sweeney, T. Thompson-Colon, and S. N. Uhrig. 1994. "The Class of 1957 after Thirty-Five Years: Overview and Preliminary Findings." CDE Working Paper 93–17. Madison, Wisc.: University of Wisconsin, Center for Demography and Ecology.

Hauser, R. M., W. H. Sewell, J. A. Logan, T. S. Hauser, C. Ryff, A. Caspi, and M. M. MacDonald. 1992. "The Wisconsin Longitudinal Study: Adults as Parents and Children at Age 50." *IASSIST Quarterly* 16(2): 23–38.

Hauser, R. M., W. H. Sewell, and J. R. Warren. 1994. "Education, Occupation, and Earnings in the Long Run: Men and Women from Adolescence to Midlife." Paper presented to the meetings of the American Sociological Association. Los Angeles, Calif. (Aug 5–9, 1994).

Hauser, R. M., S.-L. Tsai, and W. H. Sewell. 1983. "A Model of Stratification with Response Error in Social and Psychological Variables." *Sociology of Education* 56(January): 20–46.

Haveman, R. and B. Wolfe. 1984. "Schooling and Economic Well-Being: The Role of Non-Market Effects." *Journal of Human Resources* 19(3): 377–407.

———. 1994. *Succeeding Generations: On the Effects of Investments in Children.* New York: Russell Sage Foundation.

———. 1995. "The Determinants of Children's Attainments: A Review of Methods and Findings." *Journal of Economic Literature* 33(4): 1829–78.

Haveman, R., B. Wolfe, and J. Spaulding. 1991. "Childhood Events and Circumstances Influencing High School Completion." *Demography* 28(1): 133–57.

———. 1991. "Childhood Events and Circumstances Influencing High School Completion." *Demography* 28(1): 133–57.

Hayes, C. D., J. L. Palmer, and M. J. Zaslow, eds. 1990. *Who Cares for America's Children? Child Care Policy for the 1990's.* Washington, D.C.: National Academy Press.

Helburn, S., ed. 1995. "Cost, Quality, and Child Outcomes in Child Care Centers." Technical Report. Denver, Colo.: University of Colorado, Economics Department.

Hernandez, D. J. 1993. *America's Children: Resources from Family, Government, and the Economy.* New York: Russell Sage Foundation.

Herrnstein, R. J., and C. Murray. 1994. *The Bell Curve: Intelligence and Class Structure in American Life.* New York: Free Press.

Herzog, E., and C. E. Sudia. 1973. "Children in Fatherless Families." In *Review of Child Development Research,* edited by B. Caldwell and H. N. Riccinth. Vol. 3. Chicago: University of Chicago Press.

Hetherington, E. M. 1989. "Coping with Family Transition: Winners, Losers, and Survivors." *Child Development* 60(1): 1–14.

———. 1992. "Coping with Marital Transitions: A Family Systems Perspective." *Monographs of the Society for Research in Child Development* 57(2–3): 1–14.

Hetherington, E. M., K. A. Camara, and D. L. Featherman. 1983. "Achievements and Intellectual Functioning of Children in One Parent Housholds." In *Achievement and Achievement Motives,* edited by J. T. Spence. San Francisco, Calif.: W. H. Freeman.

Hetherington, E. M. and W. G. Clingenspeel. 1993. *Coping With Marital Transitions: A Family Systems Perspective, Monographs of the Society for Research in Child Development.* Chicago: Chicago University Press.

Hetherington, E. M., M. Cox, and R. Cox. 1978. "The Aftermath of Divorce." In *Mother-Child, Father-Child Relations,* edited by Joseph Stevens and Marilyn Mathews. Washington, D.C.: National Association for the Education of Young Children Press.

Hetherington, E. M., M. Stanley-Hagan, and E. R. Anderson. 1989. "Marital Transitions: A Child's Perspective." *American Psychologist* 44(2): 303–12.

Hill, M., and G. J. Duncan. 1987. "Parental Family Income and the Socioeconomic Attainment of Children." *Social Science Research* 16(1): 39–73.

Hill, M. S., and J. R. Sandfort. 1994. "Effects of Childhood Poverty on Productivity Later in Life: Implications for Public Policy." Ann Arbor: University of Michigan, Survey Research Center.

Hinshaw, S. P. 1992. "Externalizing Behaviour Problems and Academic Underachievement in Childhood and Adolescence: Causal Relationships and Underlying Mechanisms." *Psychological Bulletin,* 111(1): 127–55.

Hofferth, S. L. 1995a. "Caring for Children at the Poverty Line." *Children and Youth Services Review* 17: 61–90.

———. 1995b. "Poverty and Late Childhood." Discussion presented to the National Institute of Child Health and Human Development Research Network on Child and Family Well-Being, Conference on Growing Up Poor: Consequences for Youth. Washington, D.C. (February 2–3, 1995).

Hofferth, S. L., A. Brayfield, S. Deich, and P. Holcomb. 1991. *National Child Care Survey, 1990.* Washington, D.C.: Urban Institute Press.

Hofferth, S. L., and D. A. Phillips. 1991. "Child Care Policy Research." *Journal of Social Issues* 47: 1–13.

Hoffman, S., M. Foster, and F. Furstenberg. 1993. "Reevaluating the Costs of Teenage Childbearing." *Demography* 30 (February): 1–13.

Hogan, D. P. 1978. "The Effects of Demographic Factors, Family Background, and Early Job Achievement on Age at Marriage." *Demography* 15(2): 161–75.

Hogan, D. P., and E. M. Kitagawa. 1985. "The Impact of Social Status, Family Structure, and Neighborhood on the Fertility of Black Adolescents." *American Journal of Sociology* 90(4): 825–55.

Howes, C. 1990. "Can the Age of Entry into Child Care and the Quality of Care Predict Adjustment in Kindergarten?" *Developmental Psychology* 26: 293–303.

Howes, C., and M. Olenick. 1986. "Family and Child Influences on Toddlers' Compliance." *Child Development* 26: 292–303.

Howes, C., and P. Stewart. 1987. "Child's Play with Adults, Toys, and Peers: An Examination of Family and Child Care Influences." *Developmental Psychology* 23: 423–30.

Huber, P. J. 1967. "The Behavior of Maximum Likelihood Estimates under Nonstandard Conditions." In *Proceedings of the Fifth Berkeley Symposium in Mathematical Statistics and Probability,* edited by J. Neyman. Berkeley, Calif.: University of California Press.

Huesmann, L. R., L. D. Eron, M. M. Lefkowitz, and L. O. Walder. 1984. "Stability of Aggression over Time and Generations." *Developmental Psychology* 20(6): 1120–34.

Hunt, J. M. 1961a. *Environment and Experience.* New York: Roland Press.

———. 1961b. *Intelligence and Experience.* New York: John Wiley and Sons.

Huston, A. C., ed. 1991. *Children in Poverty: Child Development and Public Policy.* New York: Cambridge University Press.

———. 1994. "Children in Poverty: Designing Research to Affect Policy." *Social Policy Report* 8(2): 1–12.

Huston, A. C., V. C. McLoyd, and C. Garcia Coll. 1994. "Children and Poverty: Issues in Contemporary Research" *Child Development* 65(2): 275–82.

Infant Health and Development Program. 1990. "Enhancing the Outcomes of Low-Birth-Weight, Premature Infants." *Journal of the American Medical Association* 263(22): 3035–42.

Institute of Medicine. 1985. *Preventing Low Birthweight.* Washington, D.C.: National Academy Press.

Jacobson, P. H. 1950. *American Marriage and Divorce.* New York: Rinehart.

Jencks, C., S. Bartlett, M. Corcoran, J. Crouse, D. Eaglesfield, G. Jackson, K. McClelland, P. Mueser, M. Olneck, J. Schwartz, S. Ward, and J. Williams. 1979. *Who Gets Ahead? The Determinants of Economic Success in America.* New York: Basic Books.

Jencks, C., J. Crouse, and P. Meuser. 1983. "The Wisconsin Model of Status Attainment: A National Replication with Improved Measures of Ability and Aspiration." *Sociology of Education* 56(1): 3–19.

Jencks, C., and S. E. Mayer. 1990. "The Social Consequences of Growing Up in a Poor Neighborhood." In *Inner-City Poverty in the United States,* edited by L. L. Geary. Washington, D.C.: National Academy Press.

———. 1996. "Do Official Poverty Rates Provide Useful Information about Trends in Children's Economic Welfare?" Working Paper 94–14. Evanston, Ill.: Northwestern University Center for Urban Affairs and Poverty Research.

Jencks, C., and P. E. Peterson, eds. 1991. *The Urban Underclass.* Washington, D.C.: Brookings Institution.

Jencks, C., M. Smith, H. Acland, M. J. Bane, D. Cohen, H. Gintis, B. Heyns, and S. Michelson. 1972. *Inequality: A Reassessment of Family and Schooling in America.* New York: Basic Books.

Jones, D. Y., M. C. Nesheim, and J. P. Habicht. 1985. "Influences in Child Growth Associated with Poverty in the 1970's: An Examination of HANESI and HANESII, Cross-sectional US National Surveys." *American Journal of Clinical Nutrition* 42(4):714–24.

Joreskog, K. G., and D. Sorbom. 1989. *LISREL 7: User's Reference Guide.* Mooresville, Ind. Scientific Software.

Kagan, J., J. S. Reznick, and N. Snidman. 1988. "Biological Bases of Childhood Shyness." *Science* 240(4849): 167–71.

Kamerman, S. B., and A. J. Kahn. 1982. "Income Transfers, Work and the Economic Well-being of Families with Children: A Comparative Study." *International Social Security Review* 3: 345–82.

Kiker, B. F., and C. M. Condon. 1981. "The Influence of Socioeconomic Background on the Earnings of Young Men." *Journal of Human Resources* 16(1): 94–105.

Kim, K. 1992. "The Effects of Poverty on Children's Academic Performance." Ph.D diss., Univeristy of Texas at Dallas.

Kisker, E., and M. Silverberg. 1991. "Child Care Utilization by Disadvantaged Teenage Mothers." *Journal of Social Issues* 47: 159–78.

Klebanov, P. K., J. Brooks-Gunn, L. Chase-Lansdale, and R. Gordon. Forthcoming. "The Intersection of the Neighborhood and Home Environment and Its Influence on Young Children." In *Neighborhood Poverty: Context and Consequences for Development,* edited by J. Brooks-Gunn, G. Duncan, and J. L. Aber. New York: Russell Sage Foundation.

Klebanov, P. K., J. Brooks-Gunn, and G. J. Duncan. 1994. "Does Neighborhood and Family Affect Mothers' Parenting, Mental Health, and Social Support?" *Journal of Marriage and the Family* 56(2): 441–55.

Klebanov, P. K., J. Brooks-Gunn, and M. C. McCormick. 1994a. "School Achievement and Failure in Very Low Birth Weight Children." *Journal of Developmental and Behavioral Pediatrics* 15(4): 248–56.

———. 1994b. "Classroom Behavior of Very Low Birth Weight Elementary School Children." *Pediatrics* 94(5): 700–08.

Kleinman, J., and S. Kessel. 1987. "Racial Differences in Low Birthweight Trends and Risk Factors." *New England Journal of Medicine* 317: 749–53.

Klerman, L. V. 1991. "The Health of Poor Children: Problems and Programs." In *Children and Poverty: Child Development and Public Policy,* edited by A. C. Huston. New York: Cambridge University Press.

Knox, V. W., and M. J. Bane. 1994. "Child Support and Schooling." In *Child Support and Child Well-being,* edited by I. Garfinkel, S. McLanahan, and P. Robins. Washington, D.C.: Urban Institute Press.

Kochanek, K. D., and B. L. Hudson. 1995. "Advance Report of Final Mortality Statistics, 1992." Monthly Vital Statistics Report 43 (6, suppl.). Hyattsville, Md.: U.S. Department of Health and Human Services, Centers for Disease Control, National Center for Heatlh Statistics.

Kolb, B. 1989. "Brain Development, Plasticity, and Behavior." *American Psychologist* 44(9): 1203–12.

Kominski, R., and A. Adams. 1992. "Educational Attainment in the United States: March 1991 and 1990." *Current Population Reports,* series P20, no. 462. Washington: U.S. Government Printing Office for U.S. Bureau of the Census.

Korenman, S., J. E. Miller, and J. E. Sjaastad. 1995. "Long-Term Poverty and Child Development: Evidence from the NLSY." *Children and Youth Services Review* 17(1–2): 127–55.

Krein, S. F. 1986. "Growing Up in a Single-Parent Family: The Effect on Education and Earnings of Young Men." *Family Relations* 35 (January): 161–68.

Kurdek, L. A., and R. J. Sinclair. 1988. "Adjustment of Young Adolescents in Two-Parent Nuclear, Stepfather, and Mother Custody Families." *Journal of Consulting and Clinical Psychology* 56(1): 91–96.

Kurtz, L., and J. L. Derevensky. 1994. "Family Configuration and Maternal Employment: Effects on Family Environment and Children's Outcomes." In *Economics of Divorce,* edited by C. Everett. New York: Haworth Press.

Layzer, J. I., B. D. Goodson, and M. Moss. 1993. *Final Report.* Vol. 1, *Life in Preschool.* Cambridge, Mass.: Abt Associates.

Lazear, E. P., and R. T. Michael. 1988. *Allocation of Income within the Household.* Chicago: University of Chicago Press.

Lee, L. F. 1979. "Identification and Estimation in Binary Choice Models with Limited (Censored) Dependent Variables." *Econometrica* 47(4): 977–96.

Lee, V., J. Brooks-Gunn, E. Schnur, and F. R. Liaw. 1990. "Are Head Start Effects Sustained? A Longitudinal Follow-up Comparison of Disadvantaged Children Attending Head Start, No Preschool, and Other Preschool Programs." *Child Development* 61: 112–33.

Leibowitz, A., J. A. Klerman, and L. J. Waite. 1992. "Employment of New Mothers and Child Care Choice: Differences by Children's Age." *Journal of Human Resources* 27: 112–33.

Lempers, J. D., D. Clark-Lempers, and R. L Simons. 1989. "Economic Hardship, Parenting, and Distress in Adolescence." *Child Development* 60(1): 25–39.

Lerner, R. M. 1987. "Early Adolescent Transitions: The Lore and the Laws of Adolescence." Report No. 15. Philadelphia, Pa.: Scholarly Report Series Center for the Study of Child and Adolescent Development.

Lerner, R. and T. Foch. 1987. *Biological-Psychosocial Interactions in Early Adolescence.* Hillsdale, New Jersey: Lawrence Erlbaum.

Lewis, M. 1983. Editor *Origins of Intelligence: Infancy and Early Childhood.* New York: Plenum Press.

Liaw, F., and J. Brooks-Gunn. 1994. "Cumulative Familial Risks and Low-Birthweight Children's Cognitive and Behavioral Development." *Journal of Clinical Child Psychology* 23(4): 360–72.

Liker, J. K., and G. H. Elder. 1983. "Economic Hardship and Marital Relations in the 1930s." *American Sociological Review* 48(3): 343–59.

Lipman, E. L., D. Offord, and M. H. Boyle. 1994. "Economic Disadvantage and Child Psychosocial Morbidity." *Canadian Medical Association Journal* 151: 431–37.

Loeber, R., and M. Stouthamer-Loeber. 1986. "Family Factors as Correlates and Predictors of Juvenile Conduct Problems and Delinquency." In *Crime and Justice: An Annual Review of Research,* edited by M. Tonry and N. Morris. Vol. 7. Chicago: University of Chicago Press.

Long, S. K., and S. J. Clark. 1995. "Child Care Prices: A Profile of Six Communities." Prepared for the U.S. Department of Health and Human Services. Washington, D.C.: Urban Institute.

Lorenz, F. O., and J. N. Melby. 1994. "Analyzing Family Stress and Adaptation: Methods of Study." In *Families in Troubled Times: Adapting to Change in Rural America,* edited by R. D. Conger and G. H. Elder, Jr. Hawthorne, N.Y.: Aldine.

Loury, G. 1981. "Intergenerational Transfers and the Distribution of Earnings." *Econometrica* 49(4): 843–67.

Luker, K. 1991. "Dubious Conceptions: The Controversy over Teen Pregnancy." *The American Prospect* 5(Spring): 73–83.

Lundberg, S., and R. Plotnick. 1990. "Effects of State Welfare, Abortion and Family Planning Policies on Premarital Childbearing among White Adolescents." *Family Planning Perspectives* 22(6): 246–51.

Maccoby, E. E., and J. A. Martin. 1983. "Socialization in the Context of the Family: Parent-Child Interaction." In *Handbook of Child Psychology,* edited by E. M. Hetherington. Vol. 4. New York: John Wiley and Sons.

Maccoby, E. E., and R. H. Mnookin. 1992. *Dividing the Child: Social and Legal Dilemmas of Custody.* Cambridge, Mass.: Harvard University Press.

Magnusson, D. 1988. *Individual Development from an Interactional Perspective: A Longitudinal Study.* Hillsdale, N.J.: Lawrence Erlbaum.

Manski, C. 1987. "Academic Ability, Earnings and the Decision to Become a Teacher: Evidence from the National Longitudinal Study of the High School Class of 1972." In *Public Sector Payrolls,* edited by D. Wise. Chicago: University of Chicago Press.

Manski, C., G. Sandefur, S. McLanahan, and D. Powers. 1992. "Alternative Estimates of the Effect of Family Structure during Adolescence on High School Graduation." *Journal of the American Statistical Association* 87(417): 25–37.

Mare, R. 1982. "Socioeconomic Effects on Child Mortality in the United States." *American Journal of Public Health* 72(61): 539–547.

Marini, M. M. 1978. "The Transition to Adulthood: Sex Differences in Educational Attainment and Age at Marriage." *American Sociological Review* 43(4): 483–507.

Marini, M. M., and B. Singer. 1988. "Causality in the Social Sciences." In *Sociological Methodology 1988,* edited by C. Clogg. Washington, D.C.: American Sociological Association.

Martell, M., F. Falkner, L. B. Bertolini, J. L. Diaz, F. Nieto, S. M. Tenzer, and R. Belitzky. 1978. "Early Postnatal Growth Evaluation in Full-Term, Preterm and Small-for-Dates Infants." *Early Human Development* 11(4): 313–23.

Martorell, R., and J. P. Habicht. 1986. "Growth in Early Childhood in Developing Countries." In *Human Growth: A Comprehensive Treatise,* edited by F. Falkner and J. M. Tanner. New York: Plenum Press.

Martorell, R., and T. J. Ho. 1984. "Malnutrition, Morbidity, and Mortality." *Population and Development Review. Child Survival: Strategies for Research* 10(suppl.): 49–68.

Massey, D. S. 1991. "American Apartheid: Segregation and the Making of the American Underclass." *American Journal of Sociology* 96(1): 329–57.

Mayer, S. E. 1991. "How Much Does a High School's Racial and Socioeconomic Mix Affect Graduation and Teenage Fertility Rates?" In *The Urban Underclass,* edited by C. Jencks and P. Peterson. Washington, D.C.: Brookings Institution.

———. 1991. "The Effect of Schools' Racial and Socioeconomic Mix on High School Students: Chances of Dropping Out." University of Chicago. Unpublished paper.

———. 1992. "Are There Economic Barriers to Visiting the Doctor?" Working paper no. 92–6. University of Chicago, Harris School of Public Policy Studies.

———. 1997. *What Money Can't Buy: Family Income and Children's Life Chances.* Cambridge, Mass.: Harvard University Press.

Mayer, S. E., and C. Jencks. 1989. "Growing Up in Poor Neighborhoods: How Much Does it Matter?" *Science* 243: 1441–45.

———. 1989. "Poverty and the Distribution of Material Hardship." *Journal of Human Resources* 24(1): 88–114.

———. 1993. "Recent Trends in Economic Inequality in the United States: Income versus Expenditure versus Material Well-Being." In *Poverty and Prosperity in America at the Close of the Twentieth Century,* edited by D. Papadimitriou and E. Wolfe. London: Macmillan.

McCall, R. B. 1983. "A Conceptual Approach to Early Mental Development." In *Origins of Intelligence: Infancy and Early Childhood,* edited by M. Lewis. 2nd ed. New York: Plenum Press.

McCarton, C., J. Brooks-Gunn, I. Wallace, C. Bauer, F. Bennett, J. Bernbaum, R. Broyles, P. Casey, M. McCormick, D. Scott, J. Tyson, J. Tonascia, and C. Meiner. 1997. "Results at Eight Years of Intervention for Low Birthweight Premature Infants: The Infant Health Development Program." *Journal of the American Medical Association* 227(2): 126–32.

McCormick, M. C. 1989. "Long-Term Follow-up of Infants Discharged from Neonatal Intensive Care Units." *Journal of the American Medical Association* 261: 1767–72.

McCormick, M. C., and J. Brooks-Gunn. 1989. "Health Care for Children and Adolescents." In *Handbook of Medical Sociology,* edited by H. Freeman and S. Levine. Englewood Cliffs, N.J.: Prentice Hall.

McCormick, M. C., J. Brooks-Gunn, S. Shapiro, A. A. Benasich, G. Black, and R. T. Gross. 1991. "Health Care Use among Young Children in Day-Care: Results Seen in a Randomized Trial of Early Intervention." *Journal of the American Medical Association* 265: 2212–17. (Abbreviated version published in *The Infant Health and Development Program for Low Birth Weight Premature Infants,* edited by R. T. Gross and D. Spiker. Stanford, Calif.: Stanford University Press.)

McCormick, M. C., J. Brooks-Gunn, K. Workman-Daniels, J. Turner, and G. Peckham, 1992. "The Health and Development Status of Very Low Birth Weight Children at School Age." *Journal of American Medical Association* 267(16): 2204–08.

McDonald, M. A., M. Sigman, M. P. Espinosa, and C. G. Neumann. 1994. "Impact of a Temporary Food Shortage on Children and Their Mothers." *Child Development* 65(2): 404–15.

McEwen, B. S. 1992. "Hormones and Brain Development." Address to the American Health Foundation. Washington, D.C. (April, 1992).

McEwen, B. S., and E. Stellar. 1993. "Stress and the Individual: Mechanisms Leading to Disease." *Archives of Internal Medicine* 153: 2093–2101.

McGauhey, P. J., and B. Starfield. 1993. "Child Health and the Social Environment of White and Black Children." *Social Science Medicine* 36(7): 867–74.

McLanahan, S. 1985. "Family Structure and the Reproduction of Poverty." *American Journal of Sociology* 90: 873–901.

McLanahan, S., and K. Booth. 1988. "Mother-Only Families: Problems, Reproductions, and Politics." Discussion Paper 855–87. Madison, Wisc.: University of Wisconsin, Institute for Research on Poverty.

McLanahan, S., and L. Bumpass. 1988. "Intergenerational Consequences of Marital Disruption." *American Journal of Sociology* 94(1): 130–52.

McLanahan, S. and G. D. Sandefur. 1994. *Growing Up with a Single Parent: What Hurts, What Helps?* Cambridge, Mass. Harvard University Press.

McLeod, J., and M. Shanahan. 1993. "Poverty, Parenting and Children's Mental Health." *American Sociological Review* 58(3): 351–66.

McLoyd, V. C. 1990. "The Impact of Economic Hardship on Black Families and Children: Psychological Distress, Parenting and Socioemotional Development." *Child Development* 61(2): 311–46.

McLoyd, V. 1990. "The Impact of Economic Hardship on Black Families and Development." *Child Development* 65: 562–89.

McLoyd, V. C., T. E. Jayaratne, R. Ceballo, and J. Borquez. 1994. "Unemployment and Work Interruption among African American Single Mothers: Effect on Parenting and Adolescent Socioemotional Functioning." *Child Development* 65(2): 562–89.

McNeil, John. 1992. "Workers with Low Earnings: 1964–1990." *Current Population Reports*, ser. p. 60, no. 170. Washington: U.S. Government Printing Office.

Mead, L. 1986. *Beyond Entitlement: The Non Working Poor in America.* New York: Basic Books.

———. 1992. *The New Politics of Poverty: The Non-Working Poor in America.* New York: Basic Books.

Melby, J. N., and R. D. Conger. 1995. "Parental Behaviors and Adolescent Academic Performance: A Longitudinal Analysis." *Journal of Research on Adolescence* 6(1): 113–37.

Melby, J., R. Conger, M. Rueter, L. Lucy, D. Repinski, K. Ahrens, D. Black, D. Brown, S. Huck, L. Mutchler, S. Rogers, J. Ross, and T. Staros. 1993. "The Iowa Family Interaction Rating Scales." 4th ed. Iowa State University, Center for Family Research in Rural Mental Health. Unpublished paper.

Meyers, M. K. 1993. "Child Care in JOBS Employment and Training Program: What Difference Does Quality Make?" *Journal of Marriage and the Family* 55: 767–83.

Meyers, M. K., and K. Van Leuwen. 1992. "Child Care Preferences and Choices: Are AFDC Recipients Unique? " *Social Work Research and Abstracts* 28: 28–34.

Michael, R. T. 1994. "Money Illusion: The Importance of Household Time Use in Social Policy Making." University of Chicago, Unpublished manuscript.

Miller, C. A., A. Fine, and S. Adams-Taylor. 1989. *Monitoring Children's Health: Key Indicators.* 2d ed. Washington, D.C.: American Public Health Association.

Miller, J. E., and S. Korenman. 1993. "Poverty, Nutritional Status, Growth and Cognitive Development of Children in the United States." Office of Population Research Working Paper 93–5. Princeton, N.J.: Princeton University.

———. 1994a. "Poverty and Children's Nutritional Status in the United States." *American Journal of Epidemiology* 140(3): 233–43.

———. 1994b. "Poverty Dynamics and Child Well-Being in the United States." Unpublished paper.

Mirowsky, J., and C. E. Ross. 1989. *Social Causes of Psychological Distress.* New York: Aldine.

Moen, P., G. H. Elder, and K. Luscher. eds. 1995. *Examining Lives in Context: Perspective on the Ecology of Human Development.* Washington, D.C.: American Psychological Association Press.

Moffitt, T. E. 1990. "Juvenile Delinquency and Attention Deficit Disorder: Developmental Trajectories from Age Three to Age Fifteen." *Child Development* 61(3): 893–910.

Monheit, A. C., and P. F. Cunningham. 1992. "Children without Health Insurance." *The Futures of Children* 2(2): 154–70.

Moore, K. A., M. J. Coiro, C. S. Blumenthal, and S. M. Miller. 1995. "Home Environments and the Developmental Status of Children in AFDC Families." Paper presented to the biennial meeting of the Society for Research in Child Development. Indianapolis, Ind. (April 1, 1995).

Mosley, J., and E. Thomason. 1994. "Fathering Behavior and Child Outcomes: The Role of Race and Poverty." In *Fatherhood,* edited by W. Marsiglio. Newbury, Calif.: Sage.

Munroe Blum, H., M. H. Boyle, and D. R. Offord. 1988. "Single Parent Families: Child Psychiatric Disorder and School Performance." *Journal of the American Academy of Child and Adolescent Psychiatry* 27(2): 214–19.

Murdock, S. H., and F. L. Leistritz. 1988. *The Farm Financial Crisis: Socioeconomic Dimensions and Implications for Producers and Rural Areas.* Boulder, Colo.: Westview Press.

Murnane, R. 1994. "Education and the Education of the Next Generation." In *Confronting Poverty: Prescriptions for Change,* edited by S. Danziger, G. Sandefur, and D. Weinberg. Cambridge, Mass.: Harvard University Press.

Murray, C. 1984. *Losing Ground: American Social Policy 1950–1980.* New York: Basic Books.

Muthén, B. O. 1984. "A General Structural Equation Model with Dichotomous, Ordered Categorical, and Continuous Latent Variable Indicators." *Psychometrika* 49(1): 115–32.

Nathanson, C. A. 1991. *Dangerous Passage: The Social Control of Women's Adolescence.* Philadelphia: Temple University Press.

National Center for Children in Poverty. 1995. "Young Children in Poverty: A Statistical Update." New York: Columbia University, School of Public Health.

National Council on Welfare. 1995. *Poverty Profile 1993.* Ottawa: Ministry of Supply and Services Canada.

Neal, D., and W. Johnson. 1996. "The Role of Premarket Factors in Black-White Wage Differences." *Journal of Political Economy* 104(5).

NICHD Early Child Care Research Network. 1966. "Characteristics of Infant Care: Factors Contributing to Positive Caregiving." *Early Childhood Research Quarterly* 11: 269–306.

———. Forthcoming. "Child Care Experiences During the First Year of Life." *Merrill-Palmer Quarterly.*

Nolen-Hoeksema, S. 1994. "An Interactive Model for the Emergence of Gender Differences in Depression in Adolescence." *Journal of Research on Adolescence* 4(4): 519–34.

Oden, M. H. 1968. "The Fulfillment of Promise: 40-Year Follow-Up of the Terman Gifted Group." *Genetic Psychology Monographs* 77: 3–93.

Offord, D. R., and K. Bennett. 1994. "Conduct Disorder: Long-term Outcomes and Intervention Effectiveness." *Journal of the American Academy of Child and Adolescent Psychiatry* 33(8): 1069–78.

Offord, D. R., M. H. Boyle, and B. R. Jones. 1987. "Psychiatric Disorder and Poor School Performance among Welfare Children in Ontario." *Canadian Journal of Psychiatry* 32(7): 518–25.

Offord, D. R., M. H. Boyle, Y. A. Racine, J. E. Fleming, D. T. Cadman, H. Munroe Blum, C. Byrne, P. S. Links, E. L. Lipman, H. L. MacMillan, N. I. Rae-Grant, M. N. Sanford, P. Szatmari, H. Thomas, and C. A. Woodward. 1992. "Outcome, Prognosis, and Risk in a Longitudinal Follow-up Study." *Journal of the American Academy of Child and Adolescent Psychiatry* 31(5): 916–23.

Offord, D. R., J. M. Last and P. A. Barrette. 1985. "A Comparison of the School Performance, Emotional Adjustment and Skill Development of Poor and Middle-Class Children." *Canadian Journal of Public Health* 76(May / June): 174–78.

Ogbu, J. 1981. "Origins of Human Competence: A Cultural-Ecological Perspective." *Child Development* 52: 413–29.

Oppenheimer, V. K. 1970. *The Female Labor Force in the United States.* Population Monograph Series of the Institute of International Studies, no. 5. Berkeley, Calif.: University of California Press.

———. 1982. *Work and the Family.* New York: Academic Press.

Owen, G., K. M. Kram, P. J. Garry, et al. 1974. "A Study of Nutritional Status of Preschool Children in the United States, 1968–70." *Pediatrics* 53(suppl., pt. 2): 597–646.

Paikoff, R., and J. Brooks-Gunn. 1991. "Do Parent-Child Relationships Change during Puberty?" *Psychological Bulletin* 110(1): 47–66.

Parker, S., S. Greer, and B. Zuckerman. 1988. "Double Jeopardy: The Impact of Poverty on Early Child Development." *Pediatric Clinics of North America* 35(6): 1227–40.

Patterson, C. J. 1992. "Psychosocial Adjustment among Children Experiencing Persistent and Intermittent Family Economic Stress." IRP Working Paper 986–92. Madison, Wisc.: University of Wisconsin Institute for Research on Poverty.

Patterson, G. R. 1982. *A Social Learning Approach to Family Intervention.* Vol. 3, *Coercive Family Process.* Eugene, Ore.: Castalia.

Patterson, G. R., J. G. Reid, and T. J. Dishion. 1992. *Antisocial Boys.* Eugene, Ore.: Castalia.

Pavetti, L. 1994. *Policies to Time-Limit AFDC Benefits: What Can We Learn from Welfare Dynamics?* Mimeo. Washington, D.C.: The Urban Institute.

Pearlin, L. I., M. A. Lieberman, E. G. Meneghan, and J. T. Mullan. 1981. "The Stress Process." *Journal of Health and Social Behavior* 22(3): 337–56.

Peters, H. E. 1986. "Marriage and Divorce: Informational Constraints and Private Contracting." *American Economic Review* 76(3): 437–54.

Peterson, J. L., and N. Zill. 1986. "Marital Disruption, Parent-Child Relationships, and Behavior Problems in Children." *Journal of Marriage and the Family* 48(2): 295–307.

Peterson, K. E., and L. C. Chen. 1990. "Defining Undernutrition for Public Health Purposes in the United States." *Journal of Nutrition* 120(8): 933–42.

Phillips, D., ed. 1995. *Child Care for Low-Income Families: Summary of Two Workshops.* Washington, D.C.: National Academy Press.

Phillips, D., and A. Bridgman, eds. 1995. *New Findings on Children, Families, and Economic Self-Sufficiency.* Washington, D.C.: National Academy Press.

Phillips, D., K. McCartney, and S. Scarr. 1987. "Child Care Quality and Children's Social Development." *Developmental Psychology* 23: 537–43.

Phillips, D., M. Voran, E. Kisker, C. Howes, and M. Whitebook. 1994. "Child Care for Children in Poverty: Opportunity or Inequity?" *Child Development* 65: 472–92.

Plotnick, R. 1992. "The Effects of Attitudes on Teenage Premarital Pregnancy and Its Resolution." *American Sociological Review* 57(6): 800–11.

Pollitt, E. 1988. "Developmental Impact of Nutrition on Pregnancy, Infancy, and Childhood: Public Health Issues in the United States." In *International Review of Research in Mental Retardation.* Vol. 15, edited by N. W. Bray. New York: Academic Press.

Power, C., O. Manor, and J. Fox. 1991. *Health and Class: The Early Years.* London: Chapman and Hall.

Pratt, W. 1965. "A Study of Marriage Involving Premarital Pregnancies." Phd. diss., University of Michigan.

Pulkkinen, L. 1990. "Adult Life-Styles and Their Precursors in the Social Behaviour of Children and Adolescents." *European Journal of Personality* 4(3): 237–51.

Pulkkinen, L., and R. E. Tremblay. 1992. "Patterns of Boys' Social Adjustment in Two Cultures and at Different Ages: A Longitudinal Perspective." *International Journal of Behavioral Development* 15(4): 527–53.

Quinton, D., and M. Rutter. 1988. *Parenting Breakdown: The Making and Breaking of Intergenerational Links.* Aldershot, England: Avebury.

Radloff, L. 1977. "The CES-D Scale: A Self-Report Depression Scale for Research in the General Population." *Applied Psychological Measurement* 1(3): 385–401.

Raftery, A. E. 1995. "Bayesian Model Selection in Social Research." In *Sociological Methodology 1995,* edited by P. V. Marsden. Cambridge: Basil Blackwell.

Rainwater, L. 1974. *What Money Buys: Inequality and the Social Meanings of Income.* New York: Basic Books.

Raschke, H. J. 1987. "Chapter 22: Divorce." In *Handbook on Marriage and the Family,* edited by M. B. Sussman and S. K. Steinmetz. New York: Plenum Press.

Retherford, R. D., and W. Sewell. 1991. "Birth Order and Intelligence: Further Tests of the Confluence Model." *American Sociological Review* 56(2): 141–58.

Robertson, J. F., and R. L. Simons. 1989. "Family Factors, Self-Esteem, and Adolescent Depression." *Journal of Marriage and the Family* 51(February): 125–38.

Robins, L. N. 1966. *Deviant Children Grown Up.* Baltimore: Williams and Wilkins.

Rodgers, B. 1990. "Behavior and Personality in Childhood as Predictors of Adult Psychiatric Disorder." *Journal of Child Psychology and Psychiatry* 31(3): 393–414.

Rodgers, W. L. 1989. "Comparisons of Alternative Approaches to the Estimation of Simple Causal Models from Panel Data." In *Panel Surveys,* edited by D. Kasprzyk, G. Duncan, G. Kalton, and M. P. Singh. New York: John Wiley and Sons.

Rosenberg, M. 1965. *Society and the Adolescent Self-Image.* Princeton, N.J.: Princeton University Press.

———. 1979. *Conceiving of Self.* New York: Basic Books.

———. 1989. "Self-Concept Research: A Historical Overview." *Social Forces* 68(1): 34–44.

Rosenberg, M. and H. B. Kaplan, eds. 1982. *Social Psychology of the Self Concept.* Arlington Heights, Ill.: Harlan Davidson.

Ross, D. P., E. R. Shillington, and C. Lochhead. 1994. *The Fact Book on Canadian Poverty—1994.* Ottawa: Canadian Council on Social Development.

Rowe, D. C. 1994. *The Limits of Family Influence: Genes, Experience, and Behavior.* New York: Guilford Press.

Ruggles, P. 1990. *Drawing the Line: Alternative Poverty Measures and Their Implications for Public Policy.* Washington, D.C.: Urban Institute Press.

Rutter, M. 1967. "Children's Behaviour Questionnaire for Completion by Teachers: Preliminary Findings." *Journal of Child Psychology and Psychiatry* 8(1): 1–11.

———. 1990. "Psychosocial Resilience and Protective Mechanisms." In *Risk and Protective Factors in the Development of Psychopathology,* edited by J. Rolf, A. S. Masten, D. Cicchetti, K. H. Nuechterlein, and S. Weintraub. New York: Cambridge University Press.

———. 1994. "Continuities, Transitions and Turning Points in Development." In *Development through Life: A Handbook for Clinicians,* edited by M. Rutter and D. F. Hay. Oxford: Blackwell Scientific Publications.

Rutter, M., A. Cox, C. Tupling, M. Berger, and W. Yule. 1975. "Attainment and Adjustment in Two Geographical Areas. I. Prevalence of Psychiatric Disorder." *British Journal of Psychiatry* 126: 493–509.

Rutter, M., P. Graham, O. F. D. Chadwick, and W. Yule. 1976. "Adolescent Turmoil: Fact or Fiction?" *Journal of Child Psychology and Psychiatry* 17: 35–56.

Salkind, N. J., and R. Haskins. 1982. "Negative Income Tax: The Impact on Low-Income Families." *Journal of Family Issues* 3(2): 165–80.

Saluter, A. 1986. "Marital Status and Living Arrangements" *Current Population Reports,* series P20, no. 410. Washington: U.S. Government Printing Office for U.S. Bureau of the Census.

Sameroff, A. J., and M. J. Chandler. 1975. "Reproductive Risk and the Continuum of Care-Taking Casualty." In *Review of Child Development Research,* edited by F. D. Horowitz, M. Hetherington, S. Scarr-Salapatek, and G. Siegel. Vol 4. Chicago: University of Chicago Press.

Sameroff, A. J., R. Seifer, A. Baldwin, and C. Baldwin. 1993. "Stability of Intelligence from Preschool to Adolescence: The Influence of Social and Family Risk Factors." *Child Development* 64: 80–97.

Sampson, R. J., and J. H. Laub. 1994. "Urban Poverty and the Family Context of Delinquency: A New Look at Structure and Process in a Classic Study." *Child Development* 65(2): 523–40.

Sandefur, G. D, S. McLanahan, and R. A. Wojtkiewicz. 1992. "The Effects of Parental Marital Status during Adolescence on High School Graduation." *Social Forces* 71(1): 103–21.

Sattler, J. M. 1982. *Assessment of Children's Intelligence and Special Abilities.* Boston: Allyn and Bacon.

Scarr, S., and K. McCartney. 1983. "How People Make Their Own Environments: A Theory of Genotype – > Environment Effects." *Child Development* 54: 424–35.

Seidman, E., A. LaRue, J. L. Aber, C. Mitchell, and J. Feinmann. 1994. "The Impact of School Transitions on the Self-System and Perceived Social Context of Poor Urban Youth." *Child Development* 65(2): 507–22.

Seltzer, J. A. 1994. "Consequences of Marital Dissolution for Children." *Annual Review of Sociology* 20: 235–266.

Serbin, L. A., P. L. Peters, V. J. McAffer, and A. E. Shwartzman. 1991. "Childhood Aggression and Withdrawal as Predictors of Adolescent Pregnancy, Early Parenthood, and Environmental Risk for the Next Generation." *Canadian Journal of Behavioral Science* 23(3): 318–31.

Sewell, W. H. 1971. "Inequality of Opportunity for Higher Education." *American Sociological Review* 36(October): 793–809.

Sewell, W. H., A. O. Haller, and G. W. Ohlendorf. 1970. "The Educational and Early Occupational Status Attainment Process: Replication and Revision." *American Sociological Review* 35(December): 1014–27.

Sewell, W. H., A. O. Haller, and A. Portes. 1969. "The Educational and Early Occupational Attainment Process." *American Sociological Review* 34(1): 82–92.

Sewell, W. H., and R. M. Hauser. 1975. *Education, Occupation, and Earnings: Achievement in the Early Career.* New York: Academic Press.

———. 1992a. "The Influence of the American Occupational Structure on the Wisconsin Model." *Contemporary Sociology* 21(5): 598–603.

———. 1992b. "A Review of the Wisconsin Longitudinal Study of Social and Psychological Factors in Aspirations and Achievements, 1963–1993." CDE Working Paper 92–01. Madison, Wisc.: University of Wisconsin, Center for Demography and Ecology.

Sewell, W. H., R. M. Hauser, and W. C. Wolf. 1980. "Sex, Schooling and Occupational Status." *American Journal of Sociology* 86(November): 551–83.

Siegel, G. L., and L. A. Loman. 1991. *Child Care and AFDC Recipients in Illinois: Patterns, Problems and Needs.* St. Louis, Mo.: Institute of Applied Research.

Smeeding, T., and L. Rainwater. 1995. "Cross-National Trends in Income Poverty and Dependence: The Evidence for Young Adults in the Eighties." In *Poverty, Inequality, and the Future of Social Policy,* edited by K. McFate. New York: Russell Sage Foundation.

Smith, J. R., J. Brooks-Gunn, K. Lee, and P. K. Klebanov. 1996. "Employment and Welfare: Complementary Strategies for Low-Income Women?" Paper presented at the National Academy of Sciences Workshop on Welfare and Child Development. Washington, D.C.: (April 11, 1996).

Smith, S. 1995. "Two-Generation Programs: A New Intervention Strategy and Directions for Future Research." In *Escape from Poverty: What Makes a Difference for Children?,* edited by P. L. Chase-Lansdale and J. Brooks-Gunn. New York: Cambridge University Press.

Snow, C. E. 1986. "Conversations with Children." In *Language Acquisition: Studies in First Language Development,* edited by P. Fletcher and M. Garman. New York: Cambridge University Press.

Snow, C., W. Barnes, J. Chandler, I. Goodman, and L. Hemphill. 1991. *Unfulfilled Expectations: Home and School Influences on Literacy.* Cambridge, Mass.: Harvard University Press.

Solon, G. 1989. "Biases in the Estimation of Intergenerational Earnings Correlations." *Review of Economics and Statistics* 71(1): 172–74.

———. 1992. "Intergenerational Income Mobility in the United States." *American Economic Review* 82(3): 393–408.

Sonenstein, F. L., and D. A. Wolf. 1991. "Satisfaction with Child Care: Perspectives of Welfare Mothers." *Journal of Social Issues* 47: 15–32.

———. 1991. "Satisfaction with Child Care: Perspectives on Welfare Mothers." *Journal of Social Issues* 47(2): 15–31.

Sorensen, E. 1995. "The Benefits of Increased Child Support Enforcement." In *Welfare Reform: An Analysis of Issues,* edited by I. Sawhill. Washington, D.C.: Urban Institute Press.

Sroufe, L. A. 1979. "The Conference of Individual Development: Early Care, Attachment and Subsequent Issues." *American Psychologist* 34(10): 834–42.

Stack, C. 1974. *All Our Kin: Strategies for Survival in a Black Community,* New York: Harper & Row.

Starfield, B., S. Shapiro, J. Weiss, K. Y. Liang, K. Ra, D. Paige, and X. Wang. 1991. "Race, Family Income, and Low Birth Weight." *American Journal of Epidemiology* 134(10): 1167–74.

Stata Corporation. 1993. *Stata Reference Manual: Release 3.1.* College Station, Tex.: Stata Corp.

Statistics Canada. 1981. *1981 Census of Population.* Nation Series 92–911. Ottawa: Statistics Canada.

———. 1984. "A Note on the Measurement of Poverty in Canada." *Canadian Statistics Review* (June): vi–xiii.

———-. 1986. *1986 Census of Population: Population and Dwelling Characteristics.* Nation Series 93–109. Ottawa: Statistics Canada.

———. 1992. *Income Distributions by Size in Canada.* Ottawa: Statistics Canada.

Stevens, G., and D. L. Featherman. 1981. "A Revised Socioeconomic Index of Occupational Status." *Social Science Research* 10(4): 364–95.

Sugland, B. W., M. J. Zaslow, J. R. Smith, J. Brooks-Gunn, K. A. Moore, C. Blumenthal, T. Griffin, and R. Bradley. 1995. "The Early Childhood HOME Inventory and HOME-Short Form in Differing Sociocultural Groups: Are There Differences in Underlying Structure, Internal Consistency of Subscales, and Patterns of Prediction?" *Journal of Family Issues* 16: 632–63.

Sullivan, K. M., and J. Gorstein. 1990. *ANTHRO: Software for Calculating Pediatric Anthropometry, Version 1.01.* Washington: U.S. Government Printing Office for the U.S. Public Health Service and the U.S. Centers for Disease Control. Geneva: World Health Organization.

Sweet, J. A., L. Bumpass, and V. Call. 1988. "The Design and Content of the National Survey of Families and Households." NSFH Working Paper I. Madison, Wisc.: University of Wisconsin, Center for Demography and Ecology.

Tanner, J. M. 1986. "Growth as a Target Seeking Function: Catch-up and Catch-down Growth in Man." In *Human Growth: A Comprehensive Treatise.* 2nd ed., edited by F. Falkner and J. M. Tanner. New York: Plenum Press.

Teachman, J. D. 1992. "Intergenerational Resource Transfers across Disrupted Households: Absent Fathers' Contributions to the Well-Being of Their Children." In *The Changing American Family,* edited by S. J. South and S. E. Tolnay. Boulder, Colo.: Westview Press.

Terman, L. M., and M. A. Merrill. 1973. *Stanford-Binet Intelligence Scale: Manual for the Fourth Revision, Form L-M.* Boston: Houghton Mifflin.

Thomson, E., T. L. Hanson, and S. S. McLanahan. 1994. "Family Structure and Child Well-Being: Economic Resources vs. Parental Behaviors." *Social Forces* 73(1): 222–42.

Thornton, A. 1991. "Influence of the Marital History of Parents on the Marital and Cohabitational Experiences of Children." *American Journal of Sociology* 96(4): 868–94.

Thornton, A., and D. Camburn. 1987. "The Influence of the Family on Premarital Sexual Attitudes and Behavior." *Demography* 24(3): 323–40.

Tremblay, R. E., L. Desmarais-Gervais, C. Gagnon, and P. Charlebois. 1987. "The Preschool Behavior Questionnaire: Stability of Its Factor Structure between Cultures, Sexes, Ages and Socioeconomic Classes." *International Journal of Behavioral Development* 10(4): 467–84.

Tremblay, R. E., R. Loeber, C. Gagnon, P. Charlebois, S. Larivée, and M. LeBlanc. 1991. "Disruptive Boys with Stable and Unstable High Fighting Behavior Patterns during Junior Elementary School." *Journal of Abnormal Child Psychology* 19(3): 285–300.

Tremblay, R. E., B. Mâsse, D. Perron, M. LeBlanc, A. E. Schwartzman, and J. E. Ledingham. 1992. "Early Disruptive Behavior, Poor School Achievement, Delinquent Behavior and Delinquent Personality: Longitudinal Analyses." *Journal of Consulting and Clinical Psychology* 60(1): 64–72.

Tremblay, R. E., R. O. Pihl, F. Vitaro, and P. L. Dobkin. 1994. "Predicting Early Onset of

Male Antisocial Behavior from Preschool Behavior." *Archives of General Psychiatry* 51: 732–38.

Tremblay, R. E., and R. M. Zhou. 1991. "Le dépistage des difficultés d'adaptation sociale chez les garcons de milieux socioéconomiques faibles: De la maternelle à la fin de l'école primaire." Montréal: Université de Montréal, Groupe de Recherche sur l'Inadaptation Psychosociale chez l'Enfant.

Trowbridge, F. L. 1983. "Prevalence of Growth Stunting and Obesity: Pediatric Nutrition Surveillance System." *Morbidity and Mortality Weekly Report Surveillance Summaries* 32(4SS): 23SS–26SS. Washington: U.S. Government Printing Office for U.S. Centers for Disease Control.

U.S. Bureau of the Census. 1995. "Income, Poverty, and the Valuation of Noncash Benefits: 1993." *Current Population Reports,* ser. P60, no. 188. Washington: U.S. Government Printing Office.

———. 1996. "Poverty in the United States: 1995." *Current Population Survey,* no. P60–194. Washington: U.S. Government Printing Office.

U.S. Department of Commerce. U.S. Bureau of the Census. 1973. *Occupational Characteristics.* Washington: U.S. Government Printing Office.

———. 1981. "Child Support and Alimony: 1978." *Current Population Reports,* series P23, no. 112. Washington: U.S. Government Printing Office.

———. 1986. "Child Support and Alimony: 1983." *Current Population Reports,* series P23, no. 148. Washington: U.S. Government Printing Office.

———. 1989. "Money Income and Poverty Status in the United States: 1988." *Current Population Reports,* series P60, no. 166. Washington: U.S. Government Printing Office.

———. 1993a. *Measuring the Effect of Benefits and Taxes on Income and Poverty: 1992.* Washington: U.S. Government Printing Office.

———. 1993b. "Poverty in the United States." *Current Population Reports,* series P60, no. 185. Washington: U.S. Government Printing Office.

———. 1993c. *Statistical Abstract of the United States.* Washington: U.S. Government Printing Office.

U.S. Department of Health and Human Services. Administration for Children and Families. 1995. *ACYF Child Care Program Serving Children and Families: Fact Sheet.* Washington: U.S. Government Printing Office.

———. U.S. Centers for Disease Control. 1987. "Nutritional Status of Minority Children—United States 1986." *Morbidity and Mortality Weekly Report* 36(23): 366–69. Washington: U.S. Government Printing Office.

———. National Center for Health Statistics. 1991. "Advance Report of Final Divorce Statistics 1988." *Monthly Vital Statistics Report* 39 (12, suppl. 2). Hyattsville, Md.: U.S. Department of Health and Human Services, U.S. Centers for Disease Control, National Center for Health Statistics.

———. National Center for Health Statistics. 1993. *Monthly Vital Statistics Report.* Hyattsville, Md.: U.S. Department of Health and Human Services, U.S. Centers for Disease Control, National Center for Health Statistics.

U.S. Department of Health, Education, and Welfare. 1972. *Ten-State Nutrition Survey, 1968–*

1970. III: Clinical, Anthropometry, Dental. DHEW Publication (HSM) 72–8131. Washington: U.S. Government Printing Office.

U.S. Congress. Joint Economic Committee. 1989. *Alternative Measures of Poverty.* Washington: U.S. Government Printing Office.

U.S. Congress. U.S. General Accounting Office. 1994. *Child Care: Child Care Subsidies Increase Likelihood That Low-Income Mothers Will Work.* Report to the House of Representatives, Congressional Caucus for Women's Issues. Washington: U.S. Government Printing Office.

Vandell, D. L., and M. A. Corasaniti. 1990. "Variations in Early Child Care: Do They Predict Subsequent Social, Emotional, and Cognitive Differences?" *Early Childhood Research Quarterly* 5: 555–72.

Ventura, S. J. 1995. "Births to Unmarried Mothers: United States, 1980–1992." NCHS Series 21, no. 53. U.S. Department of Health and Human Services. Washington: U.S. Government Printing Office.

Volling, D., and J. Belsky. 1993. "Maternal Employment: Parent, Infant, and Contextual Characteristics Related to Maternal Employment Decisions in the First Year of Infancy." *Family Relations* 42: 4–12.

Vuchinich, S., E. M. Hetherington, R. A. Vuchinich, and W. G. Clingempeel. 1991. "Parent-Child Interaction and Gender Differences in Early Adolescents' Adaptation to Stepfamilies." *Developmental Psychology* 27(4): 618–26.

Wachs, L., and G. Gruen. 1982. *Early Experience and Human Development.* New York: Plenum Press.

Wachs, T. D. 1991. "Environmental Considerations in Studies with Nonextreme Groups." In *Conceptualizations and Measurement of Organism-Environment Interaction,* edited by T. D. Wachs and R. Plomin. Washington, D.C.: American Psychological Association Press.

Waite, L. J., A. Leibowitz, and C. Witsberger. 1991. "What Parents Pay for: Child Care Characteristics, Quality, and Costs." *Journal of Social Issues* 47: 33–48.

Waite, L. J., and G. D. Spitze. 1981. "Young Women's Transition to Marriage." *Demography* 18(4): 681–94.

Wallerstein, J. S. 1991. "The Long-Term Effects of Divorce on Children: A Review." *Journal of the American Academy of Child and Adolescent Psychiatry* 30(3): 349–60.

Wallerstein, J., and J. B. Kelly. 1980. *Surviving the Breakup: How Children and Parents Cope with Divorce.* New York: Basic Books.

Waterlow, J. C., R. Buzina, W. Keller, J. M. Lane, M. Z. Nichman, and J. M. Tanner. 1977. "The Presentation and Use of Height and Weight Data Comparing the Nutritional Status of Groups of Children under Ten Years Old." *Bulletin of the World Health Organization* 55(4): 489–98.

Webster-Stratton, C. 1990. "Long-Term Follow-up of Families with Young Conduct Problem Children: From Preschool to Grade School." *Journal of Clinical Child Psychology* 19(2): 144–49.

Wechsler, D. 1989. *Wechsler Preschool and Primary Scale of intelligence.* San Antonio, Tex. Psychological Corp.

Weir, K., and G. Duveen. 1981. "Further Development and Validation of the Prosocial Behaviour Questionnaire for Use by Teachers." *Journal of Child Psychology and Psychiatry* 22(4): 357–74.

Weiss, Y., and R. J. Willis. 1985. "Children as Collective Goods in Divorce Settlements." *Journal of Labor Economics* 3(3): 268–92.

Weissman, M. 1987. "Advances in Psychiatric Epidemiology: Rates and Risks for Major Depression." *American Journal of Public Health* 77(4): 445–51.

Weissman, M. M., P. J. Leaf, and M. L. Bruce. 1987. "Single Parent Women: A Community Study." *Social Psychiatry* 22: 29–36.

Werner, E. E., and R. S. Smith. 1982. *Vulnerable But Invincible: A Longitudinal Study of Resilient Children and Youth.* New York: McGraw-Hill.

Whitbeck, L. B., R. L. Simons, R. D. Conger, F. O. Lorenz, S. Huck, and G. H. Elder, Jr. 1991. "Family Economic Hardship, Parental Support, Adolescent Self-Esteem." *Social Psychology Quarterly* 54(4): 353–63.

White, J. L., T. E. Moffitt, F. Earls, L. Robins, and P. A. Silva. 1990. "How Early Can We Tell? Predictors of Childhood Conduct Disorder and Adolescent Delinquency." *Criminology* 28(4): 507–33.

Wilson, J. B., D. T. Ellwood, and J. Brooks-Gunn. 1995. "Welfare to Work through the Eyes of Children: The Impact on Parenting of Movement from AFDC to Employment." In *Escape from Poverty: What Makes a Difference for Children?,* edited by P. L. Chase-Lansdale and J. Brooks-Gunn. New York: Cambridge University Press.

Wilson, K. L., and A. Portes. 1975. "The Educational Attainment Process: Results from a National Sample." *American Journal of Sociology* 81(2): 343–63.

Wilson, W. J. 1980. *The Declining Significance of Race: Blacks and Changing American Institutions.* 2d ed. Chicago: University of Chicago Press.

———. 1981. "The Black Community in the 1980's: Questions of Race, Class and Public Policy." *Annals of the American Academy of Political and Social Science* 454: 26–41.

———. 1987. *The Truly Disadvantaged: The Inner City, the Underclass, and Public Policy.* Chicago: University of Chicago Press.

———. 1991a. "Studying Inner-City Social Dislocations: The Challenge of Public Agenda Research." *American Sociological Review* 56: 1–14.

———. 1991b. "Public Policy Research and 'The Truly Disadvantaged.' " In *The Urban Underclass,* edited by C. Jencks and P. E. Peterson. Washington: Brookings Institution.

———. 1993. *The New Urban Poverty and the Problem of Race. The Tanner Lecture.* Ann Arbor, Mich.: University of Michigan.

Winship, C. 1992. "Race, Poverty, and the American Occupational Structure." *Contemporary Sociology* 21(5): 639–43.

Wolfe, B. 1991. "Treating Children Fairly." *Society* 28:6(194): 23–28.

"Workers with Low Earnings: 1964 to 1990." *Current Population Reports,* ser. P60, no. 178. Washington: U.S. Government Printing Office for U.S. Bureau of the Census. U.S. Department of Commerce.

World Health Organization Working Group. 1986. "Use and Interpretation of Anthropometric Indicators of Nutritional Status." *Bulletin of the World Health Organization* 64(6): 929–41.

Wu, L., and B. Martinson. 1993. "Family Structure and the Risk of a Premarital Birth." *American Sociological Review* 58(2): 210–32.

Wylie, R. C. 1979. *The Self-Concept: Theory and Research on Selected Topics.* Lincoln, Neb.: University of Nebraska Press.

Yogev, A., and Y. Ilan. 1987. "Does Self-Esteem Affect Educational Aspirations?: The Case of the Ethnic Enclave." *Urban Education* 22(2): 182–202.

Zajonc, R., B. G. Marcus, M. Berbaum, J. Bargh, and R. Moreland. 1991. "One Justified Criticism Plus Three Flawed Analyses Equal Two Unwarranted Conclusions: A Reply to Retherford and Sewell." *American Sociological Review* 56(2): 159–65.

Zaslow, M. J., K. A. Moore, D. R. Morrison, and M. J. Coiro. 1995. "The Family Support Act and Children: Potential Pathways of Influence." *Children and Youth Services Review* 17(1/2): 231–50.

Zigler, E. 1979. "Project Head Start: Success or Failure?" In *Project Head Start: Legacy of the War on Poverty,* edited by E. Zigler and J. Valentine. New York: Free Press.

Zill, N. 1988. "Behavior, Achievement, and Health Problems among Children in Stepfamilies." In *Impact of Divorce, Single Parenting, and Step Parenting on Children,* edited by E. M. Hetherington and J. D. Arasteh. Hillsdale, N.J.: Lawrence Erlbaum.

Zill, N., K. A. Moore, E. W. Smith, T. Stief, and M. J. Coiro. 1991. *Circumstances and Development of Children in Welfare Families: A Profile Based on National Survey Data.* Washington, D.C.: Child Trends.

Zimmerman, D. J. 1992. "Regression toward Mediocrity in Economic Stature." *American Economic Review* 92(3): 409–29.

Name Index

Subject Index

Boldface numbers refer to figures and tables.